Ebel

THEOLOGY
OF THE OLD TESTAMENT

By

DR. PAUL HEINISCH
UNIVERSITY OF NIJMEGEN

ENGLISH EDITION by REV. WILLIAM HEIDT

THE LITURGICAL PRESS
St. John's Abbey
COLLEGEVILLE, MINNESOTA

4

Dr. Paul Heinisch's *Theologie des Alten Testamentes* was published in 1940 as the first supplementary volume to the "Bonn Bible." Nine years later he subjected his work to a thorough revision. Two new chapters were added, one omitted; changes appeared on practically every page, and the bibliography was brought up to date. Due to post-war conditions in Europe this revision has not as yet been published in German; nevertheless Dr. Heinisch kindly consented to its use as the text for the present translation.

Imprimi potest: ✠ ALCUIN DEUTSCH, O.S.B.
Abbot

Nihil obstat: PASCHAL BOTZ, O.S.B., S.T.D.
Censor Librorum

Imprimatur: ✠ JOS. F. BUSCH
Bishop of St. Cloud

January 19, 1950

Table of Contents

7

SECTION 2. THE ATTRIBUTES OF GOD

SECTION 3. PREPARATION FOR THE MYSTERY OF THE MOST HOLY TRINITY

PART II

CREATION

SECTION 1. THE SPIRIT WORLD

PART III

HUMAN ACTS

SECTION 1. MORALITY

SECTION 3. MAN AND GOD'S COMMANDMENTS

PART IV

LIFE AFTER DEATH

PART V

REDEMPTION

SECTION 1. JUDGMENT

THEOLOGY OF THE OLD TESTAMENT

§ 1. INTRODUCTION

Israel was a small nation. It was not her privilege to develop into a mighty state like that of the Babylonians, the Assyrians, the Persians, the Greeks under Alexander the Great or the Romans; she was not destined to produce a specific culture as were the Indians, the Sumerians, the Egyptians, the Hittites, the Greeks. In science, art, jurisprudence Israel was unimportant; she discovered no new continents, and only very late in history did her citizens become merchants, spurred on by the Arameans and later by the Greeks. But Israel did possess a RELIGION which lifted her far above all other peoples of antiquity, and when her national independence came to a definitive end, her religion, perfected and deepened in Christianity, marched in triumph over the whole world.

The religion of Israel claimed to rest upon special divine revelation. It was God Himself who raised up men to teach the people His nature and His wishes, "From the time when your fathers left the land of Egypt until this very day I sent you all my servants, the prophets, early and late."[1] Ever since the days of Moses Israel enjoyed a unique guidance in matters of religion, and this alone explains why monotheism was proclaimed in Israel and why in the course of time even the masses accepted monotheism, while neighboring nations, which far surpassed her in military might or in intellectual or political accomplishments, remained polytheistic.

Sacred Scripture recounts how, alongside the doctrine propounded by the great religious teachers, violently conflicting views prevailed among the masses. The orthodox teachers insisted upon the worship of Yahweh alone, upon moral living; they condemned idolatry and superstition. At the same time we find Yahweh honored under the form of a bull, polytheism, necromancy, magic, child sacrifice, religious prostitution; and there were periods during which the majority of the people, even kings and priests, fostered such practices. Nevertheless it is not numbers which decides the truth and worth of a religion. We must restrict the content of OT religion to the tenets advanced by men divinely illumined, viz., Moses and the prophets, the psalmists, the wisdom teachers and the OT historians. The religion they propounded may also be called prophetic religion (but not in the sense that it was first proclaimed by the literary prophets), or genuine or revealed religion.

The beliefs condemned as erroneous by the orthodox religious leaders form the content of what may be called "folk-religion" in the sense that frequently a much larger circle followed the false rather than the true. This folk-religion had its root and deepest cause in the spiritual sloth of the masses; people at

1. Jer. 7:25; collateral reading for each chapter is given after §54.

large are not wont to lift themselves up to the level advocated by their religious guides. Revealed religion made impositions upon one's lower nature, it demanded high moral standards, self-mastery, avoidance of sin, true repentance; the masses satisfied themselves with external acts, with sacrifices, purifications and fastings. In these superficial observances and in the desire to yield to earthly pleasures the Israelites were strengthened by the example of the Canaanites, who believed that Baal should be thanked for the fertility of the land and the increase in flocks.[2] Contact with neighboring nations as well as dependence upon the mighty empires of Assyria and Babylon opened the door to Mesopotamian gods, while the hope of regaining independence with Egyptian aid moved the Israelites to favor Nilotic divinities. Individuals too did their share in preventing the Israelites from embracing prophetic religion; thus in his later years Solomon, influenced by his pagan wives, honored pagan gods, with unsalutary effects upon the people. When the kingdom broke apart after his death, Jeroboam I introduced the worship of Yahweh under the form of a bull in the major temples at Bethel and Dan in order to satisfy popular demand for a visible representation of Yahweh and to prevent the people from making pilgrimages to the temple at Jerusalem.[3] This act drew Yahweh into the sphere of the profane and effaced the distinction between him and idols. Achab's marriage to the Tyrian princess Jezabel and Joram's marriage with Athalia, the daughter of Achab and Jezabel, introduced Baal of Tyre (Melkart) and furthered the decline of Yahwistic religion in the North as well as in the South.[4] Folk-religion often sank to very low levels; it fostered immorality, it implied apostasy from Yahweh[5] and infidelity to the God of the covenant.[6] It received a fatal blow during and after the Babylonian exile. Prophetic religion triumphed, it had prepared the way for the religion Christ and the apostles were to proclaim.

Because of its divine origin revealed religion always remained essentially the same, yet in the course of centuries it underwent development. Already the Fathers of the Church noted this aspect of Israel's religion.[7] In the course of time new revelations were made, witness the sketching of the Messiah picture. In God's plan certain natural factors also aided this process. The people became acquainted with foreign nations, and were forced to take clearer and more definite positions. Events like the settlement in Canaan, the oppressions by neighboring nations, the dependence upon mightier empires left impressions upon religious life. The destruction of the northern kingdom, the loss of political independence, the exile of thousands, the cessation of regular sacrificial cult made the Israelites reflect upon God's ways, upon sin and retribution. In the diaspora the Jews came into contact with Greek philosophy. Thus under divine guidance new ideas entered to wrestle with older truths, as for instance in the case of the doctrine on retribution in afterlife.

A "History of the Religion of Israel" would show how the people responded

2. Os. 2:7.
3. 3 Kgs. 12:28.
4. 3 Kgs. 16:31f; 4 Kgs. 8:18, 27; 11:1f.

5. Is. 1:2.
6. Deut. 32:20.
7. Cf. Gregory of Nazianzen, Orat. theol. V 25.26 (Migne

36:160f); Cyril of Alexandria, Glaphyr. in Genesim IV 3 (Migne 69:188).

to the directives of their religious teachers, how environment and cultural progress affected the development of spiritual ideas; it would describe religious conditions, recount the ups and downs in the moral life of the people, note defections from Yahweh, growing immorality, persecutions, and indicate the distinctive character of each successive historical period. On the other hand a "Theology of the OT" should present in a systematic manner what those leaders who were raised up by God and the writers whom God inspired required as to faith and morals. A theology can present more clearly than a history what is fundamental and accordingly permanent, what is merely transitional, and what preparation NT revelation had had in the Old. OT theology points out what religious ideas and moral requirements were defended by enlightened souls, what the masses *should* have accepted, while a "History of the Religion of Israel" shows what the religious and moral conditions among the people actually were. The relationship between a theology of the OT and a history of Israel's religion may in various respects be compared to the relationship between dogmatic theology and the history of dogmas. Dogmatic theology has as its purpose to propound the Church's teaching, to extract this teaching from the sources; history of dogmas has as its purpose to survey the battle of the Church's doctrine against conflicting opinions, to trace deviations, to indicate clearly the errors which in the course of centuries threatened to obscure the Church's teaching. But just as dogmatic theology cannot disregard the heresies, although it does not treat them *ex professo,* so also a systematic presentation of the theology of the OT must take into consideration the development of doctrine; if a doctrine suffered no modification it may show this by placing pertinent texts from various historical periods alongside one another.

Sources for OT theology are the canonical books of the OT. In them the sacred writers under divine inspiration clearly expressed the truths and laws which God gave to the Israelites. The apocrypha of the OT and rabbinic literature contain, inasmuch as they go beyond the OT, the religious ideas of post-exilic Jewry, and are taken into consideration only to the extent in which they shed light upon certain tenets appearing in later OT books. To discuss the religions of all those nations with which Israel made contact remains the task of a general history of religions. A systematic comparison with Israel's religion would go beyond the scope of a theology, but since these various religions do aid us to understand better the unique character of revealed religion, reference will be made to them on the more important points.

PART I

GOD

SECTION 1. THE NATURE OF GOD

§ 2. DIVINE REVELATION: THE SOURCE OF OT RELIGION

1. PRE-MOSAIC REVELATION. a) *Primitive revelation.* "At various times and in different ways in ages past God spoke to men."[1] God did not reveal Himself for the first time upon Horeb. He was already well known to the Israelites when He said to Moses, "I am the God of your fathers, the God of Abraham, the God of Isaac, and the God of Jacob,"[2] and commissioned him, "Speak to the elders of Israel: Yahweh, the God of your fathers, has appeared to me, the God of Abraham, Isaac and Jacob."[3] The opening pages of Sacred Scripture tell how God walked with Adam and Eve and manifested His will to them. After they had sinned He awakened in them the hope of regaining His love.[4] He warned Cain against sin[5] and when mankind had abandoned the way of justice, confided to Noe His decision to destroy the world by means of a mighty flood. After the deluge He enabled Noe to foresee how Sem's posterity would never wholly lose the knowledge of God, and how through them the descendants of Japhet and Cham would be blessed.[6]

Primitive history as contained in the Bible as well as the religious consciousness of Israel regarded the knowledge of one God and the obligation to worship Him, to obey Him and to lead a moral life as an inheritance stemming from most ancient times. Polytheism or lower forms of religion were not viewed as contemporaneous with the beginning of the human race but as defection from the true God. The reason for this defection was placed in man's evil will, above all in pride.[7] Thousands of years, of course, passed before tradition took written form. During these millenia it suffered many modifications. The details however are not important, the religious ideas which elevated mankind and led them to God are important. If Israel's religion rested upon revelation, we cannot but conclude that Israel's religious leaders had a true conception of primitive religion and did not paint a false picture; for this matter concerns the education of the people on most vital religious truths. No one who regards the OT as the anteroom to the New and the prophets as Christ's heralds can disregard the religious content of Biblical primitive history.

On the basis of material gathered by profane science no convincing proof

1. Heb. 1:1.　　　　4. Gen. 3:14-15.　　　　6. Gen. 9:26-27.
2. Ex. 3:6.　　　　　5. Gen. 4:5.　　　　　　7. Gen. 3:5; 11:4.
3. Ex. 3:16.

can be advanced to show that the picture drawn in the Bible of primitive religion corresponds to reality in all points, but science does make it probable. From artefacts, dwellings and drawings of the stone age, pre-history shows how primitive men were in no way links between beast and man. Their intelligence was not inferior to that of present day human beings. Concerning religion archeology gives us little information apart from the fact that primitive men believed in a continuation of life after death. Nor is ethnology able to bolster claims regarding primitive monotheism. Just as the character of primitive culture and primitive language cannot be determined by science at the present time, so too the nature of primitive religion remains a mystery. It is interesting to note that the religious beliefs of primitive peoples whose cultures are on a level which we might imagine as similar to that of primitive man are superior to the beliefs held by the cultured nations of pre-Christian times. Primitive people believe in a single higher being who is eternal and almighty, just and merciful, who requires a moral life, who punishes sin and rewards virtue; they honor this being with prayer and sacrifice, and very many of these peoples, if not the majority, hold that God Himself educated the first human beings, gave them moral and social laws and ordained their cult.

By reason primitive men were able to arrive at the knowledge of a being superior to themselves, a being who created and conferred those things necessary for life. They drew the self-evident conclusion that such a being must be honored by prayer and sacrifice. For this no special revelation would have been necessary. But facts show how most men when left to themselves do not arrive at the knowledge of one God or become very clear upon matters of a religious nature. God aided the people of Israel in a most extraordinary manner by revealing Himself to the patriarchs and to Moses, and later by repeatedly raising up prophets. Should He not also have taught men religion in primitive times? Primitive peoples say He did, and thereby confirm what the Bible tells about God's relationship to men at the dawn of the human race.

b) *The patriarchs.* The call of Abraham introduced a new phase in the history of revelation. When man had abandoned God in spite of the deluge, God first ordained that He be known and honored by one family and then by the descendants of this family. Abraham's call took place at Haran in Mesopotamia,[8] but he already was under special divine guidance, though unaware of it, when he left Ur in Chaldea with his father Thare.[9] His relatives were polytheists,[10] given to stellar worship, in particular to the cult of Sin, the moon-god, who was highly venerated at Ur and at Haran. Abraham's call wrought a fundamental change in his religious outlook and in his private life. True, it would be difficult to imagine that he had been till then a polytheist because the knowledge of the true God had never been wholly lost among Sem's children.[11] Abraham had the concept of one God though perhaps quite obscurely; by his call and later revelations and trials this concept was purified and deepened.

8. Gen. 12:4.   9. Gen. 15:7.   10. Jos. 24:2.   11. Gen. 9:26.

God's choice of Abraham was an unmerited favor, a favor extended not merely to him as an individual; his faith should some day become the inheritance of all peoples.[12]

God demanded great sacrifices from Abraham. He had to leave relatives who, far from aiding him in spiritual matters, would be, at least for his children, a spiritual danger. He had to abandon home and country where protection was assured him; he had to journey to a foreign land alone, trusting in God's guidance. God promised that a great nation would descend from him,[13] but how long did he have to wait for his first child, Ismael.[14] He loved Ismael but was forced to drive him away.[15] Through miraculous intervention Isaac was born, whom he was ordered to sacrifice with his own hand.[16] The patriarch was being taught to place God's will above all human feelings and considerations. Abraham's virtue consisted in his obedience to all God's wishes, even when they went counter to personal inclinations and desires. His justice consisted in subjecting himself to God's will,[17] and this made him worthy of new graces and revelations. It was a thorny path upon which God led the man destined to be the teacher and model for posterity unto distant generations.

The religion of the patriarchs rested upon revelation. It was not a nature religion, not polytheism, but monotheism since God could speak only as one God. The patriarchs were equipped to deliver to their descendants genuine religious truths, and accordingly they themselves had to possess a genuine insight into God and God's holy will.[18] For this reason Abraham is called "prophet."[19] The patriarchs worshipped God under the name El.[20] God's relation to them as to Noe[21] rested upon a "covenant" which guaranteed protection and imposed duties.[22] Circumcision served as the external sign of the covenant for Abraham and his descendants.[23] Circumcision was practiced by various peoples (not however among the Babylonians, Assyrians, Canaanites and Philistines), but for the Israelites it had a religious significance from the very beginning: it indicated that Israel belonged to Yahweh as a covenanted people and reminded them of the duties they had assumed. These implications gave rise to the expressions, "circumcision of the heart," and "circumcision of the ear."[24] Circumcision distinguished Israel from her neighbors and therefore great importance was attached to it, particularly during the exile and in postexilic times. By birth one belonged to the Chosen People but only through circumcision did the individual begin to share in the rights to which birth entitled him and assume the duties imposed by membership in a covenanted people. Aliens became members of the Chosen People through circumcision, a privilege from which the Ammonites and Moabites were excluded.[25]

The demands which God imposed by reason of the covenant relationship are tersely summarized in the admonition to Abraham, "Walk before me and be

12. Gen. 12:3.
13. Gen. 12:2.
14. Gen. 15:3.
15. Gen. 21:9f.
16. Gen. 22.
17. Gen. 15:6.
18. Gen. 18:19.
19. Gen. 20:7.
20. §5:2.
21. Gen. 6:18; 9:9.
22. Gen. 15:7; 17:1f.
23. Gen. 17:9-14; 34:14-15; Ex. 4:24-26; Jos. 5:2-9.
24. Lev. 26:41; Deut. 10:16; 30:6; Jer. 4:4; 6:10; Ez. 44:7.
25. Cf. Gal. 5:3; Deut. 23:4.

perfect."[26] One's whole life must be dominated by the desire to fulfill God's will. God was honored by prayer and sacrifice, two natural expressions of religious spirit.

As reward for faithfully observing His commands God promised the patriarchs earthly blessings, good reputation, riches, countless descendants and the land of Canaan.[27] They received assurance that their children would remain in communion with God.[28] Abraham's religion was destined to embrace a much larger circle than a single family or a small people; through the patriarchs the knowledge of the one true God should be transmitted and given to the entire world.[29] All nations upon the earth would some day share in the spiritual blessings they possessed. From the tribe of Juda, as Jacob foretold upon his deathbed, One would arise and bring salvation to all the world.[30]

In the patriarchal account the unique character of pre-Mosaic religion together with its divergencies from current religious ideas is truthfully given. The description of the customs and morals reflects the period perfectly. The patriarchs appear as men of flesh and blood, with prerogatives and defects, and sins are not glossed over. They are not idealized. God revealed Himself to them but they worked no miracles like Moses and the prophets.

2. MOSES. a) *The prophet.* The descendants of the patriarchs had become a people in Egypt. Here they were oppressed by Pharaoh, and there was real danger that they would apathetically submit to their lot with no further thought to the divine promises made to their fathers or to their task of preserving monotheism. At this juncture God called Moses to lead the people out of Egypt into the land promised to the patriarchs. The rise of Moses marks one of the most important events in the religious history of mankind.

Because of Pharaoh's decree against Hebrew babes, Moses, soon after birth, was hid along the Nile. There he was found by one of Pharaoh's daughters and adopted into the royal household. The name Moses[31] (linked with *mašah,* to draw) is Egyptian and means *child;* usually a divine name was prefixed, e.g., Thutmose, Ahmose, Amenmeses. At court Moses would be taught the Egyptian pantheon, at home his parents would instruct him about the God of his fathers; and later when he sought refuge with the Midianites he was brought into contact with the religion of an Arabian tribe. Then came the moment when, as later with the prophets Amos, Isaias, Jeremias, Ezechiel, he was seized so powerfully by the spirit of God that in spite of initial resistance due to his humility, he put himself wholly at God's service. And he persevered against every obstacle. Moses, the greatest of the prophets,[32] was more intimate with God than any of his successors;[33] his face beamed with the reflection of divine majesty when he descended from Sinai and when he spoke with Yahweh in the tent.[34]

Israel, as descended from the family of Jacob, had been God's people before

26. Gen. 17:1; 18:19.
27. Gen. 12:2; 15:7; 18:18; 22:17; 26:4; 27:27-29; 28:13-14; 48:15-16.
28. Gen. 18:14; 22:18; 26:4.
29. Gen. 12:3; 18:18; 22:18; 26:4.
30. Gen. 49:10-12; §50:2.
31. Ex. 2:10.
32. Num. 12:6-8; Deut. 18:15-18; 34:10; Os. 12:14.
33. Ex. 33:18f.
34. Ex. 34:29f.

the time of Moses,[35] but God sought to initiate a more intimate relationship, to make a covenant with her. Moses, Israel's religious leader, should act as mediator in the ratification of this covenant. As the covenant with Abraham did not involve Abraham only, so this covenant with Israel did not involve Israel only but was destined to promote the divine plan for universal salvation; at some future date the covenant should include the Gentiles too.[36] God promised to protect the people and to give them the land of Canaan; the people were to worship Him alone and obey His commands. Israel was not forced to accept these obligations; to make her conscious of what acceptance implied, God revealed Himself in lightning and thunder. This was the most momentous event in the history of the Chosen People until the hour when Pilate let the nation choose between Jesus and Barabbas. God did not need Israel. He was free to reject her,[37] and already in the wilderness many did experience His wrath. Only two of those who left Egypt were permitted to enter Canaan.[38] On one occasion in the desert God intended to destroy the entire nation and make Moses the father of a new people who would listen to His voice.[39] And only after He had dealt patiently with Israel for more than a thousand years, and after He had repeatedly forgiven her sins and her covenant infidelities, and after the wicked vine-dressers had refused Him the fruit of His vineyard and slew His Son whom He had sent, did He turn Himself definitely away from Israel.[40]

Through Moses God entered into a covenant with Israel as a whole, not merely with individuals or separate tribes. In this way a spirit of national consciousness, of unity and solidarity was anchored deeply in religion. The simplest resolution of the covenant relation is given in the words, "You shall be to me a people and I will be God to you[41]. . . . You shall be holy, for I am holy, I, Yahweh, your God."[42] Before the covenant was ratified God outlined their duties and rights, "If you are willing to listen to my voice and heed my covenant, you shall be my very own from among all nations; you shall be to me a kingdom of priests, a holy nation."[43] Yahweh's relation to Israel rested upon an act at a specific historical moment, it was not due to nature nor was it from the beginning. Yahweh could just as well have selected another people. Israel's religion was the religion of a people, and yet it was not just another national religion. The expression "Yahweh, the God of Israel," differs in meaning from the expressions, "Chemosh, the god of Moab," or "Marduk, the god of Babylon," even apart from the fact that Yahweh suffered no other god alongside Himself.

After Yahweh had entered into the covenant with Israel, Israel enjoyed a peculiar position among the nations of the world, "I have separated you from the nations that you may belong to me."[44] This unique relationship is referred to in Balaam's blessing upon Israel, "a people that lives apart and does not

35. Os. 2:17; 11:1; Ez. 16:6.
36. Is. 19:19-25.
37. Num. 14:12; Ex. 32:10.
38. Ex. 32:26-29; Num. 17:6f; 25:1f.
39. Ex. 32:10; Num. 14:12.

40. Matth. 21:33.
41. Ex. 6:7; Lev. 26:12; Deut. 29:12; Jer. 7:23; 11:4; 24:7; Ez. 11:20; 14:11; Zach. 8:8.

42. Lev. 19:2; 11:44; 20:26; 21:8; Num. 15:40; Deut. 14:2.
43. Ex. 19:5-6.
44. Lev. 20:26.

regard herself as one of the nations."[45] From these she should distinguish herself through high moral standards, and to safeguard herself against assimilation with native inhabitants, she was not allowed to make treaties with them.[46] She was ordered to execute *ḥerem* upon them, i.e., utterly destroy them.[47] Israel felt herself as Yahweh's chosen people and viewed her relation to Yahweh as that of a child to its father, a shepherd to his flock, a spouse to her lover.[48]

b) *Mosaic Law.* The Law found in the Pentateuch is presented as God's will directly manifested to Moses and the people. Nevertheless in many points its directives were not wholly new. Primitive and patriarchal history record how God, before the ratification of the covenant upon Sinai, made demands identical to those incorporated in the Mosaic corpus. The second section of the decalog, viz., to honor parents, to respect human life, marriage, property, another's good name, is natural moral law, without which the family and human society could not exist. These injunctions are preceded by the command to honor God, upon whom man is dependent, by prayer and sacrifice. These obligations were known to the Babylonians and Egyptians.[49] Nations upon a very low cultural plane have similar moral principles. The precepts given to youths in Central Australia may be summarized in the following four points: obedience toward parents and older persons, keeping the marriage laws, love of truth, regard for life and for the property of fellow tribesmen.[50] The primitive peoples of America, Australia, Asia and Africa honor God by prayer, sacrifice and first fruits, inasmuch as they offer part of flock and field. Rites at the time of adolescence serve as an opportunity to impress boys and girls to revere parents and older people, and to keep marriage holy. Marriage is monogamous, and with some tribes indissoluble, particularly if there are children. Adultery is severely punished, often by death; polygamy has its origin in levirate practices and in the sterility of the first wife. Girls are encouraged to preserve virginity, illegitimate children are looked upon with disfavor. Collective debauchery is unknown. Property is respected, theft punished. Murder is considered a very serious crime.[51]

The precepts of the decalog were insufficient to regulate the civil and moral life of individuals and of large communities. They needed further development and application, and Moses had to provide fixed norms to govern judicial procedure. And when the Israelites became residents in Canaan it was important for national life that the people feel independent in matters of right and wrong, rather than simply adopt Canaanite law and custom. It is one thing to adopt practices from new surroundings and introduce them into an already existent code, quite another to accept *in globo* the legal procedures of a new environment. The latter would have involved great danger to Israelitic religious life. In Egypt the Israelites saw how the gods were worshipped with rich and elaborate cere-

45. Num. 23:9.
46. Ex. 23:23-33; 34:11-16; Lev. 26:1; Num. 33:50-56; Deut. 7:1-5; 12:2-3; 20:10-18.
47. §32:1e.
48. §16:4.
49. Cf. the incantation Šurpu (AOT 324), the Book of the Dead (AOT 9f) Roeder 274f.
50. N. Söderblom, Das Werden des Gottesglaubens² Leipzig 1926, 121.
51. W. Schmidt, Der Ursprung der Gottesidee VI 1935, 369-508.

monial, and the Canaanites had high places upon which to offer sacrifice. Moses had to provide his people with a ritual that offered sufficient food to the imagination, insisting at the same time upon complete self-dedication to God and sanctity of life. And he had to watch lest superstitious practices slip in and debase the rites in Yahweh's honor.

Centuries before the time of Moses there existed extensive collections of laws in the ancient Orient, e.g., the Code of Hammurabi (18th cent.), Old Assyrian Law (c. 1600), Hittite Law (c. 1500), while smaller collections of Sumerian Law are much older. From these various collections one may cite parallels to the Mosaic Law, and one may cite divergencies. The Code of Hammurabi stands closest to the Mosaic. Through observance Abraham was familiar with Babylonian law before he left the land of the two rivers, even though Hammurabi's code may have received its present formulation first after his departure. Jacob too dwelt in Mesopotamia, and Canaan was culturally and politically dependent upon the East, so that the Babylonian form of ancient Oriental law left traces there. The family of Jacob retained their tribal norms of conduct in Egypt. As time passed they fashioned a system of laws toward which Moses had high respect. Moreover Moses was familiar with the jurisprudence of the Midianites, a people advanced in culture and related to the Hebrews, and this too had fruitful results. His method was to adopt ancient usages and align them with revealed religion. This was true particularly of the ordinances on purifications and foods. We may cite as a specific example the directive not to gather every kernel at harvest time but to let a small portion of grain remain.[52] This seems to have been a very ancient custom reflecting the idea that field spirits must not be driven away. In the Mosaic Law this practice is given a charitable slant: the poor must not go away empty at harvest time. Whatever was adopted from profane sources or reflected ancient pagan usages was first permeated with the spirit of Yahwistic religion, was purified, ennobled and orientated to the high purpose of making Israel a "kingdom of priests, a holy nation."

From the strictly technical or juridical viewpoint the Mosaic Law was inferior to other ancient oriental codes, from an ethical and religious viewpoint it was far superior. Its religious precepts safeguarded the Israelites from falling into polytheism, its moral laws guided them to live according to God's will. Self-control was enjoined, the specifications concerning cult provided a worthy worship of God, the penal code made the Israelites conscious of what disobedience to God really implied. And its ritual typified the new covenant which God would some day make with all mankind.

The Law which Moses proclaimed at Sinai, during the desert journey and upon the plains of Moab before the crossing of the Jordan, always remained fundamental. But a legal code is not an immutable monument, it serves practical living, and life continually presents new problems. Israel was not destined

52. Lev. 19:9; Deut. 24:19-22.

to remain in the desert, but to settle in Canaan and become agricultural. Moses did not neglect this aspect; he enacted legislation on farming and established feasts of an agrarian nature. No lawgiver however can know beforehand the political and cultural modifications which in the course of centuries create entirely new problems in the life of a people. And what purpose would there have been for Moses to have left laws which in the decades or centuries immediately following would have had no point, which could not have been understood and respected? For these reasons legitimate leaders had the task to apply Mosaic Law to changed circumstances and to legislate for new needs. This occurred already under Josue[53] and Samuel.[54] The introductory formula, "Yahweh said to Moses," (which also introduces more recent laws), is a sign that people were conscious of the harmony between the new precepts and those Moses had enjoined, and that subsequent laws were promulgated according to his spirit. And since the priests had a leading part in the development of law and jurisprudence,[55] its religious character was preserved. When a new regulation supplanted an old one, the old was not formally declared null and void, because in antiquity every law was regarded as holy since it had proceeded from God. Therefore a precept which no longer was binding was not expunged from the books; it was allowed to remain alongside the new statute, but the lawyers were not to invoke laws no longer binding. In a similar way Draco's laws were not formally abolished by Solon. In Hammurabi's code older and more recent laws are found, and the Hittite code expressly states which laws are old and which new.

The Law, which was publicly read on the feast of Tabernacles every seventh year,[56] served to unite the Jews, whether in Palestine or in the diaspora, and aided them to see how they differed from other peoples. All were obligated to observe the Law, king and people, priest and prophet. More important than single precepts was the spirit, one's inner thoughts could be sinful too.[57] On this account the prophets did not insist as much upon external details as upon an upright mind.

The Law was continually extended to cover new contingencies, even during postexilic times, and made itself felt in every concern of life. Yet it contained no impossible precepts, for it came from God. That His commands were not too burdensome is stated in Deut. 30:11-14. Nor would the joy of the just in the Law have been possible if it had been an unbearable yoke. The good man meditated upon the Law day and night.[58] The Law enlivens, rejoices the heart, enlightens the eyes, is sweeter than honey and the honeycomb.[59] The glory of the Law is the theme of the longest psalm, Ps. 119. In the Law the Israelite saw an advantage over those peoples to whom God did not manifest His will so clearly or in a similar manner.[60] It was a light enkindled for Israel's benefit.[61] As late as Jesus Sirach we read, "Nothing is sweeter than observing

53. Jos. 24:25.
54. 1 Sam. 10:25.
55. §3:1.
56. Deut. 31:10-13; Neh. 8:18.

57. Gen. 4:6-7; Ex. 20:17; 1 Sam. 24:6.
58. Ps. 1:2.

59. Ps. 19:9-11.
60. Deut. 4:8; Ps. 147:19-20.
61. Is. 2:5; Prov. 6:23.

the Lord's commandments."[62] Certainly the Law demanded renunciation and mastery over passion, but its purpose was to educate men how to serve God in joy.[63] Even Qoheleth wants his readers to enjoy life.[64] Josephus[65] and Philo[66] still glory in the Law. The Law became a burden[67] through the efforts of the scribes and the zeal of the Pharisees, who gave religion a strong juristic slant. In devotion to the letter they forgot the spirit and promulgated an infinite number of rules, those "traditions of the ancients" which they enjoined alongside and even above the precepts contained in the Pentateuch.

c) *Motivation for observing God's law.* Incentives to heed God's wishes arose from x) the thought of divine omnipotence, since "no one is able to withstand the might of his arm;"[68] y) God's omniscience since "his eyes behold those who fear him, and he knows every act of man;"[69] z) a sense of gratitude.[70] The foremost incentive however is man's ambition to succeed. This motive was stressed by the lawmakers, the prophets and the wisdom teachers, who promised good fortune as reward for compliance with the Law and threatened punishment for any violation. They assured an obedient people abundant crops, increase in flocks, growth in population, triumph over enemies, peace, disappearance of predatory animals. Punishment consisted in pestilence and famine, crop failure, attack by hostile armies, devastation of the countryside, increase of wild animals, exile.[71] For observing the Law individuals would be rewarded with health, long life, popularity, riches, numerous children, successful progeny, while the godless would be plagued by disease, early death, shame and misfortune upon themselves and upon their children.[72]

Of course there was danger that some would remain faithful to God only through fear of sanctions. But to round out his training the Israelite was taught that health and sickness, riches and poverty had only a relative value,[73] that death is a punishment only for the wicked,[74] that suffering may also come to the upright,[75] that childlessness is not a misfortune, much less a punishment for the virtuous, nor numerous children a blessing for the wicked.[76] Moreover there were inner joys which the virtuous man finds in the possession of his God.[77] In Ps. 73:26 the just man feels detached from all earthly goods and intimately united with God. The sapiential writers do not fail to remind us of judgment, death, eternity.[78] And finally during the centuries immediately preceding Christ we find mention of reward and punishment in afterlife.[79]

In a theology of the OT specific laws are treated only in so far as they had bearing upon religious life; legal detail, historical development and the ceremonial of religious service are subject matter for biblical archeology.

62. Sir. 23:27.
63. Ps. 100:2; Prov. 10:28; 17:22; Sir. 1:12.
64. Qoh. 9:7-9; 11:8-9.
65. C. Ap. I 42; II 277.
66. Vita Mosis II 4 14 f.
67. Acts 15:10.
68. Wis. 11:21.
69. Sir. 15:19; Wis. 1:7, 10.

70. Deut. 5:15; 8:1-10; Am. 2:10.
71. Ex. 23:22-33; Lev. 26; Deut. 7:12-24; 11:26-28; 28:1-68; on the threats of the prophets, cf. §45:1-2.
72. Cf. 38:3.
73. §29:5, 7.
74. § 42:2.
75. §40.

76. Wis. 3:13-14; 4:1-3; §30:1a.
77. Pss. 16:2; 17:15; 31:20; 34:9; 36:8; 84:3.
78. Prov. 3:32-33; 10:24; 11:7, 10, 20-21; Sir. 2:3; 14:12; Qoh. 2:25; 8:8, 17; 11:9; 12:13.
79. §42:5.

3. THE PROPHETS. a) *Mission and vocation.* The word *nabi*⁾, speaker, desig-nates the prophets as heralds of the divine will manifested to them through a special illumination.[80] The prophet was "Yahweh's mouth."[81] The Greek term προφήτης means speaker, herald, specifically, one who heralds revealed truths. Not without reason the word points to a manifestation of future events. Com-mon to all the prophets was the task of preventing the Israelites from relapsing into paganism. They gave this their best efforts in the face of Israel's inclina-tion to worship false gods, in the face of the example of neighboring nations and the influences of empires dominating over them. They were reformers who did not announce a new concept of God or new ethical norms, but strove against apostasy from Mosaic religion and reminded the Israelites of the duties they had accepted when making the covenant upon Sinai. "After the fashion of a whore has the land abandoned its God."[82] Building upon foundations which Moses had laid they developed some of his ideas, while constantly insisting that mere exterior actions did not suffice before God; above all they enriched the picture of the coming Redeemer and His universal kingdom with many new touches.

The prophets did not perform their missions out of personal inclinations, or merely from a desire to further God's honor. They became prophets because God called them, "I am no prophet, nor the son of a prophet, but *Yahweh* took me away from the flock, and *Yahweh* said to me: Go, prophesy (*hinnabe*⁾) to my people Israel."[83] Amos here avows that he did not become a prophet upon his own decision, as did the (false) prophets who arose at his time, nor was he a member of some prophetic circle—he was called immediately by God. God intervened in the life of the true prophets in very extraordinary ways, they were absolutely convinced that from the moment of their call they stood in a unique relation to God and had received a special mission. This action of grace was so powerful that they were not able to escape. "The Lion has roared; who shall not be afraid? Adonai Yahweh has spoken, who shall refuse to become a prophet?[84] . . . . The hand of Yahweh has overpowered me."[85] We easily recall the scene which changed Saul into Paul.[86] Yet never was a human will forced in any way; fully conscious the prophets freely chose the office proffered and recognized the great responsibility it imposed. God so to speak fought with Moses before he was ready to become His representative.[87] Jeremias objected that he was still too young for so exalted an office.[88]

Pagan soothsayers and the professional (false) prophets in Israel—including even the companions of the companies of the prophets at the time of Samuel—loved to place themselves in ecstatic states which resulted in a peculiar heighten-ing of psychical or physical powers. This can be induced through natural means, e.g., through narcotics, beverages, foods, through inhaling fumes, im-moderate fasting, lack of sleep, or through inflicting wounds upon self, music,

80. Cf. Ex. 7:1.   83. Am. 7:14.   86. Acts 9.
81. Cf. Ex. 4:10; Jer. 15:19.   84. Am. 3:8.   87. Ex. 3:4.
82. Os. 1:2.   85. Is. 8:11; Jer. 20:7.   88. Jer. 1:6.

dance. The true prophets fell into an ecstatic condition without wishing or procuring it, wholly through God's intervention. What God allowed them to see while in this state they proclaimed in their own words. Each prophet's speeches have a distinctive personal character, even when the message came in a vision. They would speak only when Yahweh moved them. Elias journeyed to Horeb to commune with God when for a long time he had received no enlightenment from on High.[89] Jeremias had to let the Jews who came for information and advice wait ten days before Yahweh instructed him, yet circumstances seemed to demand speedy action.[90]

To accredit the prophets as His messengers God granted many of them the power to work miracles or to foretell future events. The miracles rested upon God's omnipotence, the prophecies upon His omniscience. Miracles were more frequent during times when faith was at low ebb, as in the days of Egyptian servitude, when the Israelites had little spirit and trust, or in the days of Elias and Eliseus, when there was danger that Israel would desert Yahweh completely and serve Baal of Tyre. Of the literary prophets but one miracle is recorded: the retrogression of the shadow upon the sun dial (or upon the steps) at Ezechias' palace at the command of Isaias.[91] It seems that prophecies at that period had taken the place of miracles. The prophecies of judgment should have effected Israel's repentance, the prophecies of deliverance and salvation were designed to strengthen the pious in difficult times and keep them from straying from God; the prophecies against foreign nations assured the Israelites that Yahweh ruled the world, and bolstered their hope in the future. Some prophecies came to pass almost immediately and thus served to prove a prophet's divine mission.

b) *Prophets and soothsayers.* There always are individuals who claim the ability to gaze into the future—so too among the Babylonians, Egyptians, Greeks, Romans. Ancient soothsayers observed the motions of the heavens, the position of the stars, the passage of clouds, manifestations in the realm of nature, the flight of birds, the behavior of beasts, the entrails of sacrificed animals. They developed a very definite technique, and composed literature akin to present day dream books. Nor are soothsayers lacking in the twentieth century, e.g., teacup prophets, palm readers, card wizards, dream interpreters, astrologists, fortune tellers, etc. These individuals sought and seek to tell the future through natural means, they regard their work as an art (the ancients regarded it as a science) which can be learnt. A father educated his son to help him in his often very profitable "vocation," and later the son would take it over himself. Soothsayers were employed by the rulers, and all obtained good returns from the practice. In Israel the true prophet received his information about future events through direct divine revelation, not when he wished or because he wished, but when God deigned to confer the favor. He received no benefit from his message, indeed frequently his pay was insults and suffering. The soothsayer restricted himself to earthly needs, condemned no moral abuses, was unconcerned

89. 3 Kgs. 19.   90. Jer. 42:7.   91. 4 Kgs. 20:9-11.

about the religious education or edification of those who consulted him, even confirmed them in superstition. The genuine prophet sought to bolster belief in the one true God by foretelling the future and by urging repentance. No soothsayer ever dared to herald destruction upon king and people as punishment for sin as did Israel's prophets; no soothsayer followed up such prophecy by painting a glorious future when judgment had passed.

c) *The literary prophets.* The stories which tell the activities of the older prophets may have been edited by their disciples. After the middle of the eighth century the prophets themselves wrote their messages and made arrangements to preserve them in writing. This serves as basis for the distinction between the "literary prophets" and their forerunners. The art of writing had then become widespread, and the prophets utilized the opportunity to affect a larger circle by committing their sermons to writing; those who had heard them speak could later read and meditate upon their words, while others who had not been personally present could also be reached. Speeches were committed to writing in whole or in part and circulated so to speak in pamphlet form. Later these were collected into a single volume by the prophet himself or by his disciples. At this point the prophet could develop certain topics at greater length than he did at first, or could cut the matter. Certain things may also have been added which he did not actually say, but were now intended for public or private reading, and thus the prophet became a writer. Such supplementing is found particularly in parts of Jeremias, Ezechiel, and Is. 40-66. In contrast to the earlier prophets the literary prophets heralded the fall of the kingdom and the exile as punishment for sin. Yet they also kept their eyes upon a more distant future; the exile should not mark the end of the people but their amendment and restoration.

d) *The prophets and politics.* Since the prophets pursued the noble end of strengthening those who were faithful to Yahweh and of leading sinners back to God, they could not remain aloof from the political events in national life which had an important bearing upon religion. They made their power felt in political affairs when there was occasion to advance the cause of Yahwistic religion or to stave off a decline. They would tumble dynasties which endangered the interests of religion because they esteemed faith in God and moral uprightness higher than court favor or political advantage. In the interest of religion they strove for influence in diplomatic circles, appeared before kings and ministers to defend their position in political crises. First it was the problem of the relation of the two kingdoms one to the other, then of all Israel to the Arameans. When the world powers of Assyria and Babylon were fighting their way to the Mediterranean, the prophets recognized that soon the small kingdoms in Syria-Palestine would fall under foreign influence, and Egypt would not be able to block enemy advance. The prophets counselled submission as God's will under the circumstances, and advised the people to rest content with their spiritual mission. Had the leaders listened, the two kingdoms would not, it is true, have remained independent politically; they would have become tributary as did the Phoenician city states, but the people would have retained their inheritance. The prophets were regarded as traitors and treated as such although they proposed the right course of action. The false prophets and the politicians brought the kingdom and people to destruction.

e) *False prophets.* In performing their vocation the prophets had to take positions against king and people, against nobles and priests, and against false prophets who likewise claimed to have been divinely called. The latter however had made themselves God's messengers and propounded such notions as pleased king and people. Most of the false prophets consciously deluded the people for the sake of money, viewing their office as good business.[92] They spoke of covenant rights but not of covenant duties; they confirmed the people in the illusion that they possessed God's unqualified love and were certain of divine protection against all enemies; they did not oppose rebellion against the great empires but prophesied triumph and victory;[93] they did not exhort others to keep the commandments or live piously. Willingly many Israelites listened; they wished to be deceived until Yahweh would hold judgment and catastrophe would come.

f) *The burden of the prophetic office.* The vocation to the office of prophet was a great grace, but also entailed a chain of sacrifices. They had to forego certain permissible pleasures, only seldom were they listened to, often they reaped humiliation and persecution, and some even lost liberty or life itself.[94] The greatest cross which God laid upon them was the duty to proclaim the destruction of their own nation, a nation they loved so fervently. They had to preach and yet recognize they were accomplishing nothing, and because of their activity the guilt of the people would be greater and the punishment more terrible.[95] No other nation ever produced such men!

§3. OFFICIALS AND SPIRITUAL LIFE IN ISRAEL

1. THE PRIESTS. In patriarchal times the head of the family acted as family priest, i.e., he offered sacrifice. Upon Sinai Yahweh appointed Aaron and his family priests, not because they had merited it, but as an act of pure grace. Thereafter priesthood in Israel was hereditary, only descendants of Aaron had a right to this office; nevertheless it remained a gift from Yahweh.[1] And this the priests should not have forgotten. While the prophets were Yahweh's extraordinary instruments, each one called in an hour of grace, the priests owed their status to descent from Aaron. As the prophets, so too the priests had the task to maintain faith in God among the people, to deepen it, and to lead sinners back to God. But this difference existed in their relation to the people: the

92. Mich. 3:3-7.   93. Mich. 3:5-11.   94. §1:5-6.   95. §46:4.
1. Num. 18:7.

prophet was primarily a preacher; he was to teach religious truths, to censure sins, to declaim against idolatry, image worship, false estimation of sacrifice, violations of love of neighbor; his was to proclaim the future, while priests were engaged primarily in the work of offering sacrifices. Deut. 33:8-11 assigns to priests the task of instructing others in the Law and of consulting the Urim and Tummim. Since this oracle gave only an affirmative or negative reply, more involved questions were referred to the priests for information and counsel. No instance of recourse to the Urim and Tummim however is recorded after the time of David, and after the exile it no longer existed.[2] Numerous passages testify to the priests' duty of instructing the people in the Law,[3] to them the Law had been entrusted.[4] Because of their legal knowledge they were to act as judges in courts of appeal not only in questions of cult but also in moral cases.[5] Study of the Law in their role as teachers and judges gave them opportunity to develop it further and apply it to changed conditions and new problems. They did not restrict their interests to questions of cult.

Before the ratification of the covenant upon Sinai Yahweh admonished the Israelites, "You shall be to me a kingdom of priests, a holy nation."[6] These words served to remind the priests that by virtue of their office they were obligated to live morally pure lives and edify the people by good example. These words should have been in their minds as they offered sacrifice, particularly atonement sacrifices.[7] The duty of being holy was brought home to priests by the precepts forbidding them to discharge any sacred function when subject to some physical defect,[8] Levitical defilement,[9] or other legal impediment.[10]

The Levitical priesthood rendered a great service by preventing the erection of images in the temple at Jerusalem. Smaller sanctuaries too had priests who performed the divine services in a worthy manner, barred Canaanite practices, images of Yahweh, excesses at peace-offerings, religious prostitution. The priests and Levites who left the northern kingdom to live in Juda after Jeroboam I had erected a bull colossus representing Yahweh in the temples at Bethel and Dan were permeated with the genuine spirit of Mosaic religion.[11] Priests had substantial roles in the reforms under Ezechias and Josias. Queen Athalia, who attempted to introduce the cult of Tyre's Baal, was overthrown by the high priest Joiada.[12] Joiada's son Zacharias openly exhorted the people to return to Yahweh, and suffered a martyr's death for defending the things of God.[13] Undoubtedly there were many priests who neglected their duties. Aaron had shown himself unworthy of his high dignity when he erected the golden bull.[14] The sons of Heli were an occasion of grave scandal to the people.[15] The sins of priests, of whom it is true a large number were not descended from Aaron, gave rise to the religious and moral conditions which Amos and Osee condemned.

2. Esdr. 2:63; Neh. 7:65.
3. Lev. 10:11; 15:31; Deut. 17:9; 2 Chr. 17:7-19; 35:3; Os. 4:6; Mich. 3:11; Jer. 18:18; Ez. 21:26; 44:23; Agg. 2:11-13; Mal. 2:6.
4. Deut. 17:18.
5. Deut. 17:8f; 19:17f; 1 Chr. 23:4; 26:4; 2 Chr. 19:8-11.
6. Ex. 19:6.
7. Lev. 21:6.
8. Lev. 21:16-24.
9. Lev. 22:19.
10. Lev. 10:8-11; 21:1-15.
11. 3 Kgs. 12:31; 2 Chr. 11:13f.
12. 4 Kgs. 11:4f.
13. 2 Chr. 24:20-22.
14. Ex. 32:1f.
15. 1 Sam. 2:12f.

Josaphat had to remind the priests of their duty of instructing the people.[16]
Isaias' picture of priestly life is anything but edifying, "Priest and (false)
prophet reel from intoxicants, they stagger as they arbitrate"[17]—not even while
acting in their official capacity were they sober! Jeremias had bitter opponents
among the priests, some even sought his life.[18] Ezechiel accused the priests of
placing themselves above the Law.[19]

The exile afforded both priests and people a fine opportunity for self-exami-
nation. When the edict of Cyrus granted liberty many souls inspired with a
holy enthusiasm prepared to return home and reinaugurate the sacred cult.
During the exile the priests had studied the Law seriously, now they explained
it to the people. But as with the masses so with the priests, their religious zeal
was not lasting, and in Is. 66:21 we read how Yahweh decided to choose priests
from the Gentile world. Malachias prophesied that Yahweh would destroy the
Aaronic priesthood.[20]

As the priests through evil example lost the respect of the people and limited
their work in increasing degree to that of cult, their spiritual leadership over
the people slowly slipped away into the hands of wisdom teachers and scribes.
At the time of Jesus the higher priests were wholly concerned with ceremony
and had no understanding of true piety; this is shown by the conduct of the
buyers and sellers in the temple.[21] The authors of the apocrypha too complained
bitterly about the godlessness and infidelity of the priests.[22] There were not
lacking however pious and worthy priests in the last period of the old covenant,
e.g., the high priest Simon II and his son Simon III, whose appearances at
the altar deeply impressed the people,[23] and in whose heavenly intercession the
Jews at the time of the Maccabean struggles put their trust.[24] Mention might
also be made of Mattathias and his sons, Zachary, the father of John the Baptist,
and Simeon. The fact that many priests accepted the message of the apostles[25]
prevents us from condemning the whole priesthood as unworthy.

2. THE PSALMISTS. Zealous to make sacred cult as solemn as possible David
ordered the Levites to accompany the rites with music and song.[26] He placed
his talents as a poet in the service of God by composing songs to be sung by
the Levites or in common by the people; in these songs the individual could
express his immolation of self to God. These songs filled his heart with joy
and trust in God; these songs inspired him with strength in time of need, comforted him in misfortune, misery and persecution, imbued him with trust in
God's mercy as he recalled his sins, and taught him to bear patiently the visita-
tions sent from heaven. Thus the psalms had an elevating religious influence
upon the masses.

A great portion of the psalter is due to David, and later psalmists regarded
him as their model. When the exiles gathered together on the Sabbath or on

16. 2 Chr. 17:7-9.
17. Is. 28:7.
18. Jer. 1:18; 20:1-3; 26:1-19.
19. Ez. 22:20; 44:6-14.
20. Mal. 1:10-11; §49:6g.

21. Matth. 21:12; Jn. 2:14;
      Pss. Sol. 2:11; 4:1f; 8:7.
22. Test. Levi. 17.
23. Sir. 45:6-17; 50:1-21.

24. 2 Mach. 15:12-14.
25. Acts 6:7.
26. 1 Chr. 6:16-32; 15:16-22;
      23:3-26.

feasts they sang the religious hymns which they had learnt in Palestine. The psalter afforded them countless ready-made texts with which to voice their sorrow over past transgressions, their hope for forgiveness, their faith in God's might and power, justice and love. Prompted by deeply spiritual emotion one or the other more pious Israelite would compose new songs in praise of God's greatness or to petition His help. Apart from Ps. 137, Pss. 74, 79, 106 date from the exile, and certain other ones as Ps. 89 may come from the same period. The time after the exile was a second spring for the composition of psalms. To the Persian period undoubtedly belong those poems which point back to the exile, e.g., Pss. 85, 126, or describe the reconstruction of Jerusalem, e.g., Ps. 147, or express the hope that Yahweh will inaugurate His universal kingdom, e.g., Pss. 96, 98. The more ancient psalms kept their place alongside the more recent compositions in the public chant at divine worship. Some psalms are directed against a false evaluation of sacrifice and thus move into the orbit of thought proper to the prophets, e.g., Pss. 40:7; 50; 51:18-19; 69:32; §33:7d. The prophets espoused the cause of the poor; certain psalms view the poor and the pious, poverty and piety as practically identical. In the psalms the good Israelite expressed his joy as he approached and beheld the face of God, yet only in Pss. 15; 24:3-6 is the observance of the moral law insisted upon as a prerequisite for this blessing. The expectations of the prophets who foretold the conversion of the Gentiles were re-echoed in those psalms which challenge the pagans to praise Yahweh, e.g., Pss. 117; 150:6, or to behold in Him their king, e.g., Pss. 47:2f; 68:32-33; 98:4; 99; 102:16, or promise them citizenship in Jerusalem, e.g., Ps. 87:4. These psalms show that at a time when the Jews began to isolate themselves from their environment the spirit of universalism was not limited to a few enlightened souls but found a prominent place even at common worship. The propagation of this spirit at the religious celebrations in the synagogues must have deeply impressed the Gentiles who attended Jewish services in the diaspora; it was designed to dispose their hearts for further revelation.[27]

3. WISDOM TEACHERS. David became the master and model for later psalmists, while Solomon, illustrious for his wisdom,[28] laid the foundation for proverb literature.[29] Prov. 10:1-22:16 is accredited to him, and likewise the collection edited by the men of Ezechias,[30] though there may be later additions. The collections in Prov. 22:17-24:22 and 24:23-34 may contain pre-exilic material. After the exile the wisdom teachers had an important task to fulfill since there arose few prophets and the priests gradually restricted their work to cult and interpretation of the Law.

The goal striven after by the sages was to make their disciples persevere in holiness. They stressed the fear of God, "The fear of Yahweh is the beginning of wisdom and the crown of wisdom."[31] Wisdom, piety, morality were almost

27. §48.
28. 3 Kgs. 5:9f; 10:1, 7, 23.
29. Prov. 10:1; 25:1.
30. Prov. 25-29.
31. Cf. Prov. 1:7; 9:10; Job 28:28; Sir. 1:14, 20; Ps. 111:10.

identical terms to the older and to the more recent proverb composers; knowledge which pays no heed to the moral law is equated with foolishness. The sages demanded obedience toward parents, respect for the sanctity of marriage, honesty, temperance, charity toward the poor, widows, and orphans. They supplied their pupils with prudent norms in profane affairs, warned against laziness, going security for others, advised how to rear children and how inferiors are to be treated, how to act toward superiors, what attitude to take toward the feminine sex. All wisdom, including prudence in worldly affairs, comes from God.[32] The psalms give expression to a deeply religious spirit; they edify and console, while proverb literature is calm and sober instruction. It was not the object of the sages to lead a chosen few to the heights of sanctity and perfection, but to make as many as possible lead virtuous lives in the communities where they lived. Since they had the masses in mind, the sages did not emphasize the inner peace of heart which a pious life produces, but the earthly benefits consequent upon observance of sound doctrine. In line with the theology of the time they regarded misfortune as punishment for sin and awaited retribution in this life. All except the authors of the Books of Job and Wisdom felt satisfied with this solution.

Wisdom literature is not a specifically Israelitic contribution. Since the year 2600 B.C. there had existed in Egypt collections of proverbs; and the Israelites considered the "sons of the East" and the Edomites distinguished for wisdom.[33] Solomon entered into discussions with the Queen of Saba.[34] Some of the proverbs of Amen-em-ope appear at least in substance in Prov. 22:17-23:11[35] and maxims by Achikar, a high official at the court of the Assyrian Kings Sennacherib and Esarhaddon, have parallels in Hebrew literature.[36] The collections, Prov. 30:1-14 and 31:1-9 are ascribed to Ishmaelitic authors, and the author of the Book of Job puts the most difficult of problems, why the just man suffers, in the mouth of Arabs. Yet in spite of all implications with foreign wisdom teachers Israelitic sages remained thoroughly independent. They felt themselves members of God's Chosen People and were conscious of having a concept of God far more elevated than that had by non-Jewish writers. They were ready to learn from strangers, yet re-worked all material drawn upon for the benefit of their pupils. They took for granted the demands of Yahwistic religion and at least in the older period seldom spoke of the Law. They gave little attention to cult prescriptions, warned against over-rating sacrifices, as the prophets too had done.[37] Because of contact with foreign wisdom teachers they stressed the universal elements in religion, and on this account they have been called Israel's humanists.

The wisdom teachers maintained their position far into the Hellenistic era. A beautiful fruit of their discourses is the Book of Jesus Sirach (c. 180 B.C.), which the author calls a house of doctrine and a chair of teaching.[38] To this

---

32. 3 Kgs. 3:9-12; Prov. 2:6;   34. 3 Kgs. 10:2.   37. Prov. 15:8; 21:3, 27; Sir.
    Sir. 38:6.   35. AOT 33-46.   34:18-20; Qoh. 4:17.
33. Cf. Bar. 3:23; 3 Kgs. 5:10;   36. AOT 454-462.   38. Sir. 51:23, 29.
    Jer. 49:7; Abd. 8.

period the Book of Qoheleth too belongs. Further works stemming from wisdom circles are the Canticle of Canticles, the didactic stories of Tobias, Judith and Esther, parts of the Book of Daniel, a series of doctrinal psalms and Bar. 3:9-4:4. Between 88 and 30 B.C. the Book of Wisdom was composed in the Greek diaspora. Its purpose was to confirm the Jewish reader in traditional religion, and to show the Greek reader the foolishness of idolatry and the excellence of Israel's revealed religion.

In postexilic times certain schools of wisdom teachers speculated deeply about the nature of divine wisdom.[39]

4. KINGSHIP AND RELIGION IN ISRAEL. Kingship became a necessity in Israel at the time of the Philistine oppression. Till then "judges" arose in critical times to maintain national independence. Such judges gained adherents only from one, two or three tribes, and when their task was accomplished, returned to private life. In the course of time it became necessary to unite all or at least most of the tribes under a single leader, one who would also guide the people during times of peace. The nation as a whole wished to have a king after the fashion of other nations, but only after long and serious reflection and after he had become certain that Yahweh had acceded to popular demand did Samuel concede a king in the person of Saul.

It was late in Israel's history when kingship became a reality. Yahweh had long made the covenant with Israel, and Moses had promulgated the Law which governed the details of daily life. These facts prevented kingship from attaining the significance it possessed in other ancient oriental nations. The king was bound by the Law. The priesthood had been conferred upon the family of Aaron and cult was already regulated in all important points. The king could make no significant changes without violating God's holy will. It was not the king who consulted Yahweh, but the priests through the Urim and Tummim. In spite of these limitations, the king was God's representative. And this position imposed the duty to help Yahwistic religion triumph among the people. The struggle against foreign enemies—when the kingdom was inaugurated it was the Philistines—was included in his office. When the honor of Yahweh was at stake the king had the right and the duty to intervene, even in religious affairs. The king should "rule in the fear of God" as Yahweh informed David.[40] David prescribed how the ark of the covenant should be brought to Jerusalem,[41] made preparations for the construction of the temple,[42] and took pains to have the divine services solemnly performed. Solomon issued detailed instructions concerning the sacred vessels and the construction of the temple and removed the aged Abiathar from the office of high priest in favor of Sadoc. Achaz ordered a new holocaust altar modelled after the one he had seen in Damascus.[43] Asa, Josaphat and Joas initiated reforms, Ezechias and later Josias centralized cult, because the purity of Yahwistic service suffered grave damage from the high

39. §19.
40. 2 Sam. 23:3.
41. 2 Sam. 6.
42. 2 Sam. 7.
43. 4 Kgs. 16:16f.

places throughout the land.[44] During the older period the kings claimed the right to offer sacrifice because the heads of the tribes had had this privilege. Some kings acted from motives of piety, others from political sagacity, believing they rose in popular esteem if they ascended the altar before the eyes of the people. Saul sacrificed,[45] David sacrificed at the transfer of the ark[46] and after the plague,[47] Solomon sacrificed at Gibeon,[48] before the ark,[49] on the last day of the dedication of the temple,[50] and regularly on the three principal feasts; at times he even offered incense.[51] Jeroboam sacrificed,[52] Achaz, who served strange gods, personally dedicated a new altar with sacrifice.[53] No king however received the title "priest."

Of singular importance was the relationship between king and prophet in Israel. Samuel did not surrender his influence in religious affairs after he had anointed Saul. He described in writing the nature of the new kingdom and laid it before Yahweh, i.e., in the sanctuary at Mispa.[54] In the prophet's eyes Saul's triumphs could easily become a source of spiritual disedification. When the king erred and began to act independently, Samuel announced his rejection[55] and anointed David.[56] Solomon owed his throne to the intervention of the prophet Nathan, Jeroboam became king through the prophet Ahias. Thereafter a king was considered legitimate only if he had been called by a prophet or belonged to a dynasty inaugurated by a prophet. If a king violated the requirements of Yahwistic religion, if he gave bad example, if he would not heed the words of Yahweh's prophets, he was failing in his duty as theocratic ruler; outside nations were of no permanent assistance since he stood in opposition to those people in whom spiritual power was a living reality. For a while he might succeed in oppressing Yahweh's faithful adherents, he might persecute the prophets, but in the end his reign would turn into a calamity for all his subjects.

Neither in the northern nor in the southern kingdom did the kings worthily accomplish their mission in religious matters. Certain isolated kings were pious, strove for the advancement of spiritual life and heeded prophetic advice, yet they won no lasting results. The next king would relapse into the wicked ways of his grandfather. Because of this the kings were unable to fulfill Israel's political mission, could not preserve order and harmony among their subjects or maintain independence from outside powers. The net result was that kingship brought about its own and the nation's destruction. The prophets who foresaw this eventuality addressed harsh words against the kings.[57] They spoke of the "demolished house of David"[58] and of the stump of Jesse.[59] Nevertheless no prophet favored abolition of kingship as such, and in the picture they sketched of the future the Messiah appears as a king who rules in the name of Yahweh, equipped with all the gifts of His holy spirit.[60]

44. 2 Chr. 29-31; 4 Kgs. 22-23.
45. 1 Sam. 13:9-14; 15:13-26.
46. 2 Sam. 6:13, 17.
47. 2 Sam. 24:15.
48. 3 Kgs. 3:4.
49. 3 Kgs. 3:15.

50. 3 Kgs. 8:62-64.
51. 3 Kgs. 9:25.
52. 3 Kgs. 12:32.
53. 4 Kgs. 16:12-13.
54. 1 Sam. 10:25.
55. 1 Sam. 15:22f.

56. 1 Sam. 16:13.
57. Os. 7:3-5; 9:15; 13:10-11.
58. Am. 9:11.
59. Is. 11:1.
60. Is. 9:1-6.

§4. BELIEF IN GOD'S EXISTENCE

1. BELIEF IN GOD. The word, *yada⟩*, to know (God), does not signify a knowledge of God acquired through discursive reasoning, but rather an interior experience of God, feeling His love or His anger. Knowledge of God and moral uprightness cannot be separated from one another, "To know you is perfect justice, and to know your justice and your power is the root of immortality."[1]

In this sense also are to be understood those passages which seem to deny God's existence. No Oriental in ancient times denied the existence of beings sovereign over earth and men. The Israelites were no exception; there were no theoretical atheists among them, although, of course, many lived as if God made no moral demands and could call no one to account. The sons of Heli "were children . . . not knowing Yahweh,"[2] i.e., they did not bother about God or about performing His commands. Yahweh grieved, "The guardians of the law knew me not."[3] Any one who practices idolatry "knows nothing about Yahweh."[4] Faithless Israel "denied Yahweh and said: "He isn't; no misfortune shall come upon us."[5] With these words they did not intend to deny Yahweh's existence, rather to assert the superior might of the gods of Babylon and Canaan.[6] The words of the psalmist, "The fool says in his heart: There is no God,"[7] refer to such as do not bother about God, who violate His commandments in the thought that He will not punish them. Further examples betraying the same spirit would be, "Yahweh does not see it, the God of Jacob will keep nought of it in mind[8] . . . . Yahweh does not see us, Yahweh has left the land!"[9] However there were some apostate Jews and pagans at a late date who did deny the existence of a personal God, who rejected the doctrine of the immortality of the soul and became genuine atheists or materialists by abandoning every vestige of belief in a higher Being.[10]

2. PROOFS FOR GOD'S EXISTENCE. Since the Israelites and all their neighbors believed in the existence of higher beings, the authors of the OT had no occasion to bring forward proofs for Yahweh's existence. The question: Is there a *God?* is discussed in the OT for the first time by the author of the Book of Wisdom in the last century before Christ; this was after the Jews in the Egyptian diaspora had come into contact with Hellenistic freethinkers. Before that time the question had been: Is there but *one* God? and the sacred writer in reply would inveigh against polytheism. Arguments were frequently drawn from nature. Man need but consider the order, the greatness and grandeur of the universe to make him think of and praise God, "The heavens show forth the glory of God, and the firmament declares the work of his hands."[11] Such reflection however was not made from an apologetical viewpoint, rather the psalmist sought to express his joy in having so mighty and so gracious a God. Likewise the description of the earth's physical structure, the phenomena in the skies

1. Wis. 15:3.
2. 1 Sam. 2:12.
3. Jer. 2:8.
4. Os. 5:4.
5. Jer. 5:12.
6. Cf. Jer. 12:4; 44:17-19.

7. Pss. 14:1; 10:4.
8. Ps. 94:7.
9. Ez. 8:12; 9:9; cf. Pss. 10:11; 73:11; Soph. 1:12.
10. Wis. 2:1f.

11. Ps. 19:2; cf. Pss. 8; 29; 33; 65; 96; 135; 136; Canticle of the three young men in the fiery furnace, Dan. 3; and especially Ps. 104.

and in the animal kingdom[12] should bring into light God's power, wisdom, and goodness. Jeremias points out that only the true God created the world, sends lightning and rain, not the pagan gods who are helpless.[13] Meditation upon the greatness of creation and upon natural phenomena should strengthen the Israelites in their faith and safeguard them from apostasy into polytheism.

Further, the sacred writers frequently recall the history of the Chosen People to show that Israel's God is mightier than the gods of other nations. Already in Ex. 12:12 we find Yahweh executing "judgment over all the gods of Egypt" by smiting the first-born of the Egyptians, evidently demonstrating their power-lessness. Deut. 4:35-39 recalls some of the many signs of love by which God had protected His people and concludes, "These things were shown to you in order that you might know that Yahweh is (the true) God; there is no other beside him." Ps. 105 scans the history of Israel from patriarchal times to the entry into Canaan for proofs of God's fidelity. The deliverance of Israel from the Babylonian exile will proclaim the might of Israel's God and the nothingness of pagan deities.[14] In greatest detail does the author of the Book of Wisdom treat the wonderful providence of God since the beginning of mankind, with particular stress upon Israel's history down to the deliverance from Egypt.[15] It was his purpose to bolster the faith of his suffering and afflicted kinsfolk, and to move the Gentile reader to honor this God. One observation which was never made by OT writers may well be mentioned: faith in the one true God *was preserved* by a people so prone to idolatry—this in itself constitutes a proof for monotheistic guidance.

The prophets utilized past prophecies to show Yahweh's sovereignty. After the kingdom and the temple had been destroyed, many lost faith and imagined that the gods to whom the Arameans accredited the victory were mightier than Yahweh.[16] Thereupon Ezechiel stressed the fact that Yahweh had foretold both the defeat and the exile, and its accomplishment manifested Yahweh's might and justice in that He punished His people, as also His omniscience in that He had foretold it.[17] Similarly Is. 40-55 makes use of prophecies as proofs for Yahweh's absolute sovereignty. The prophet summons the gods to court; with Yahweh present they are to tell whether they had foretold anything which had come to pass, or whether they could proclaim future events. Their silence makes clear their ignorance of the future. But Yahweh through Isaias did foretell the rise of Cyrus and his significance for the people languishing in exile; of this the gods knew nothing.[18] Therefore Israel must conclude that Yahweh is the one true God.[19]

Lastly the prophets took up the cudgel against representations of the gods, ridiculing them in order to undermine polytheistic beliefs. This type of polemic was resorted to most often when the deportation to Babylon was imminent, and while the Jews were held captive in Mesopotamia. The prophets then had to

12. Job 38:41.
13. Jer. 10:11-15; 14:22.
14. Is. 41:21-29; 42:8-9, 13-17; 46:1.
15. Wis. 10-12; 16-19.
16. Cf. Jer. 44:17-19.
17. Ez. 6:10, 14; 7:9, 27 *et alibi.*
18. Is. 41:21-29.
19. Is. 43:8-12; cf. Is. 44:7; 45:21; 46:9, 10; 48:5.

counteract the dangers to monotheistic belief occasioned by the glorious feasts
and processions held in honor of pagan gods. "What good is an idol which a
(mere) whittler has whittled?"[20] Jeremias points out that idol-images have
been made by human hands, that they must be fastened to prevent toppling
over, that they are unable to speak and walk.[21] The exiles should reflect: what
aid can be given by an idol made by a smith who in making it became tired, or
what help can come from an image carved from a tree which itself needed rain
to grow and whose wood is burnt to give warmth, to bake bread and to cook
meat.[22] Still more sarcastic is the letter of Jeremias.[23] The story of the fraud
perpetrated by the priests of Baal [24] serves the same purpose, likewise the account of the three young men saved from the fiery furnace after they had refused
to adore a golden idol.[25]

The author of the Book of Wisdom is very earnest in his efforts against
image worship. He saw his contemporaries placed in dangers similar to those
which confronted the Jews during the Babylonian exile; moreover he wished
to shake the trust of his pagan neighbors in their gods.[26] With ardent zeal he
inveighed against the polytheism of the Gentile masses, against the pantheism
of the Stoics which, although denying personal existence to the gods, considered
them symbols of physical forces and of celestial bodies, against the skepticism
of the new academy which did not wish to decide whether there be gods, and
proclaimed emphatically that man is capable of knowing God through his own
powers of reason. He argued from effect to cause, from visible creation to a
creator independent of it, "Fools by nature are all who are weighed down by
ignorance of God, who through the means of visible things are unable to know
him who is, or through meditating upon the work fail to recognize the workman."[27] Any one satisfied with honoring natural phenomena and heavenly bodies
acts unreasonably. His error is culpable, for to investigate the universe and its
laws is more difficult and requires more labor than to reason from finite perish-
able things to an infinite creator.[28] The conclusion is clear and certain: the
creator may be seen in His omnipotence and splendor through the greatness and
the beauty of His creatures.[29] The road one must travel to attain the knowledge
of the true God through reflection does have its difficulties. The hagiographer
concedes that those who will not rise above the consideration of earthly things,
preferring to bury themselves in pantheism and polytheism (the text is to be
explained thus), are not as blameworthy as idol worshippers.[30] Knowledge
of God is a grace which will be given to any person who sincerely seeks God,[31]
for God will go to meet him in his efforts for higher wisdom.[32]

3. IMPERFECT CHARACTER OF OUR KNOWLEDGE OF GOD. Even though God
assists us to enable us to know Him, the fullness of that knowledge will vary from
person to person. Our first parents before the fall had a more profound knowledge of God than afterwards, more profound too than their descendants. The

20. Hab. 2:18.
21. Jer. 10:3-5, 9-10, 14-15.
22. Is. 44:1-17; cf. 46:6-7;
    40:21.
23. Bar. 6.
24. Dan. 14:1-21.
25. Dan. 3; cf. Pss. 115:5-8;
    135:15-18.
26. Wis. 13:10-15:17.
27. Wis. 13:1.
28. Wis. 13:8-9.
29. Wis. 13:5; cf. Rom. 1:20.
30. Wis. 13:6, 10.
31. Jer. 29:13; Prov. 8:17.
32. Wis. 1:2; 6:12-16; 7:23.

Israelites had a more accurate knowledge of God than even such eminent Gentile philosophers as Plato. The prophets possessed a deeper insight into things divine than the people.[33] And since they heralded new truths to the Israelites, later generations had a more comprehensive knowledge of God and His ways than their forefathers. Through meditation upon religious truths and a virtuous life man approaches more closely to God. Nevertheless there is always a limit to man's knowledge of God. This is due to the imperfections inherent in human nature on the one hand and to God's incomprehensibility on the other.[34] That man cannot fathom the deep mysteries of God is a thought found throughout the pages of Holy Writ. "There is no searching out of his wisdom[35] . . . his greatness is unfathomable."[36] He is "the Almighty whom we cannot comprehend."[37] Job is justly rebuked, "Can you fathom the depths of God, or can you measure up to the perfection of the Almighty? It is higher than heaven, what can you do? deeper than Sheol, what can you know? Its sphere is longer than the earth, and broader than the sea."[38] Job acknowledged that even natural phenomena, which are but a weak manifestation of God's greatness, are incomprehensible to man—how much more inscrutable must be His inmost nature![39]

Even an individual to whom God appears as, for instance, Abraham,[40] or a prophet,[41] is not thereby enabled to obtain perfect knowledge of God. Moses was the greatest of OT prophets. Yahweh spoke to him quite differently than to the later prophets, i.e., "face to face, as a man is wont to speak to his friend[42] . . . mouth to mouth;"[43] and he was permitted to "see the figure of Yahweh."[44] How these expressions are to be understood may be gathered from the account in Ex. 33:18-23; 34:5-10. To the request, "Show me your glory," Moses received the answer, "You can not behold my face; for man shall not see me and live . . . you shall see my back parts, but my face you are not able to behold." Moses longed most ardently to penetrate deeper into the mystery of the Godhead and Yahweh complied with his desire; more than any other person was he granted to know God. But the cleft between God and man, even the most saintly, is unbridgeable. Moses saw the Lord in a vision, but could only see "his back parts," i.e., only a weak reflection, only a last beam of His glory, only a fleeting glance in passing. Our knowledge of God in the light of the New Testament is still "through a glass in a dark manner,"[45] for He "inhabits light inaccessible; no man has seen him and no man is able to see him."[46] A more perfect knowledge of God than is possible in this life is promised by the author of the Book of Wisdom as reward for the just in eternity.[47]

4. HYPOTHESES REGARDING THE SOURCE OF OT MONOTHEISM. Scholars who will not admit divine revelation seek to explain OT belief in God in terms of evolution. They would have OT monotheism be the resultant from lower stages,

33. Am. 3:7.
34. §9:1.
35. Is. 40:28.
36. Ps. 145:3.
37. Job 37:23.
38. Job 11:7-9.

39. Job 26:8-14; cf. Is. 45:15; Ps. 139:6; Qoh. 3:11; Sir. 43:28, 31; Jud. 8:14.
40. Gen. 18:1f.
41. Is. 6; Ez. 1; Dan. 7:9.
42. Ex. 33:11.

43. Cf. Deut. 34:10.
44. Num. 12:7-8.
45. 1 Cor. 13:12.
46. 1 Tim. 6:16.
47. §43:5.

or from polytheism, or regard it as a peculiar instinct of the Semites, or as borrowed from neighboring nations.

a) *The Wellhausen school* maintains that pre-Mosaic religion in Israel had been polydemonism in the form of totemism, animism, ancestor worship, fetishism. Recent investigations in the countries of the ancient Orient however have demonstrated that the religions of the Near East, as far as can now be ascertained, did not sink to such levels; they were polytheistic in character (star worship, personification of natural forces) and tapered off in a monarchial system. Rather than evolution there was retrogression, because the number of gods gradually increased. Furthermore, prehistory testifies that primitive man was in no way intellectually inferior to his descendants, and that at least in the realm of art he was quite superior. Ethnology too refutes the theory of religious evolution, for the concepts of the so-called primitive peoples are purer than those of their neighbors already engaged in agriculture and cattle raising. Therefore we need but give scant attention to those passages which have been cited as containing traces of the above-mentioned "isms."

Totemism refers to a form of religion in which families and tribes trace their descent from some species of animal or plant, and therefore those concerned consider themselves related to that animal or plant and regard that animal or plant as inviolable. That the ancient Israelites had such notions has been deduced from the fact that names of animals occur as names of persons, e.g., Lea (wild cow), Rachel (mother sheep), Debbora (bee), Caleb (dog), Nun (fish), Jona (dove), and that various laws proscribe certain animals as unclean. Such names however occur everywhere, among ourselves, among the highest officials of King Josias,[48] among the first Christians[49] where they were very numerous. Animals like doves and sheep would not have been eaten had they been regarded as sacred. Furthermore, these Biblical names designated individual persons, not tribes or families. The distinction between clean and unclean animals is due either to natural likes and dislikes, or to some relationship with the gods of the underworld or demons into which certain foods had been brought in pre-Mosaic times. People shunned these foods because they were considered execrable, not because they were regarded as holy.[50] In totemism plants have a role, but there were no plants whose use was prohibited in Israel. Totemists do not (usually) marry persons who have the same totem (exogamy), while the Hebrew patriarchs preferred wives from among relatives, e.g., Abraham and Sara, Isaac and Rebecca, Jacob and Lea and Rachel, Esau and Maheleth.[51] Honor was accorded the bronze serpent which Moses erected in the desert[52] only at a very late date, and that as a relic.[53]

Animism and ancestor worship entails the belief that the spirit of a deceased person has an influence upon the living and their fate, and that the spirit of an ancestor clings to a descendant. The notions which the Israelites had about the soul's stay in Sheol precluded veneration of the dead; never was a sacrifice

48. ZatW 56, 1938, 129.   50. Cf. §23: 1d; 30:6.   52. Num. 21:9.
49. Mnemosyne III 2, 1935,   51. Gen. 28:9.   53. 4 Kgs. 18:4.
    276.

offered to the patriarchs. Invoking the dead implied no cultus of them, nourishment laid out for them was no sacrifice.[54] Belief in spirits that could harm is not peculiar to the Semites; even today it has not ceased altogether (e.g., fear of ghosts, of passing a cemetery at night). No one regards such fear as the forerunner of Christianity, why then of OT religion!

Fetishism renders homage to an object considered to be the dwelling place of a spirit, e.g., a stone, a tree, a spring. The stones which the patriarchs set up *(Maṣṣebah)* were meant to recall important events in their lives, particularly theophanies—an example would be the *Maṣṣebah* which Jacob erected after his dream of the ladder reaching to heaven.[55] The drink offering which Jacob poured out upon the *Maṣṣebah* was directed to God who had revealed Himself there;[56] accordingly the stone served as a primitive altar.

b) *Polytheism.* According to A. Alt, *Elim* or "local numina" were worshipped in ancient Canaan. Abraham, Isaac and Jacob adored and served such nameless divinities, known simply by the tribesmen as the "god of Abraham" or the "god of Isaac" or the "god of Jacob." In the course of time these divinities were amalgamated with Yahweh whom Moses proclaimed as the Covenant-God, thus making Him the God of the whole community. The single tribes however retained the gods of their respective ancestors together with others held in special esteem. This hypothesis does not take into consideration that the Biblical writers know of only ONE God; it fails to explain how it came about that the Israelites bridged the gap from polytheism to monotheism while throughout the remaining world the number of gods was constantly increasing.

c) *Israel's monotheism* was not the result of a peculiar Semitic racial genius. The Babylonian and Assyrian pantheons were well stocked with deities. Likewise the Canaanites, Moabites, Edomites, Phoenicians and Ugaritians worshipped many gods. If these nations possessed that peculiar Semitic instinct toward monotheism, they should, at least after their contact with Israel and Israel's religion, have quickly become converted to monotheism.

Israel could not have received monotheism from neighboring nations simply because those nations did not have it themselves.[57]

§ 5. THE NAMES OF GOD

1. INADEQUACY OF THE DIVINE NAMES. Since God far transcends all human comprehension, He can, strictly speaking, have no name—He is "Nameless," "Unutterable," as the Fathers of the Church have declared. The divine names then are but attempts to express certain facets of God's being; they teach us what concepts Israel had regarding God. The nature of God is shown in the name Yahweh, while the other names point out various divine attributes. The most ancient names are *ʾel, ʾelohim, ʾeloah, ʾadon, ʾel ʿelyon* (the Most High God), *ʾel šadday* (the All Powerful God). God revealed the name Yahweh to Moses, but older appellations continued in use. In later centuries we find the names

54. §42:1, 2.   55. Gen. 28:18.   56. Gen. 35:14.   57. Cf. §7:5.

Yahweh of Hosts, God of Hosts, the Holy One. In exilic and postexilic times arose the titles God of Heaven and the Heavenly One.

2. THE WORD EL[1] was used to designate God among all Semitic peoples except the Ethiopians. The Babylonian form is *ilu,* the Arabian *ilah.* In the Ugaritic texts from Ras Shamra (which carry us back to the 18th century B.C.), El is the usual word for God, though it also indicates a specific individual, the highest and most ancient god whom the Canaanites worshipped. An inscription from Sefire, south of Aleppo, (dated to the 9th century from the style of writing) tells of El as a god in his own right.[2] The etymology of the word is uncertain. The most satisfying derivation is that from *ʾalah,* to be strong, hence, the "strong One"; compare the phrase *yeš leʾel yadi,* i.e., it is in the power of my hand,[3] as also the expression, "The mighty One of Jacob."[4] Another derivation links it with the word *ʾul,* to be strong, or with Arabic *ill,* binding power. These various derivations agree in that the name El gives expression to God's incomparable power.[5] Others align it with the preposition *ʾel,* towards; hence, the aim of one's striving, or the one who sets the course—meanings which again point to God's power. Since El was a common term for God, we find it used to designate strange gods;[6] the plural form *ʾelim* is used of the true God[7] as well as of false gods.[8] When used of the true God the article ordinarily occurs,[9] or some modifiers are attached, e.g., *ʾel ʿolam,* the eternal God,[10] *ʾel ḥay,* the living God,[11] *ʾel raḥum,* God of mercy,[12] *ʾel roʾi,* the God who sees (who reveals Himself and is concerned over the afflicted),[13] *ʾel beth-ʾel,* the God of Bethel (who manifested Himself at Bethel).[14]

3. ELOHIM. The etymology of this word too is controverted. Most scholars regard it as the plural of *ʾel* (alongside *ʾelim*) and consequently it would have the meaning of force, might, power. Some authors derive it from *ʾalah,* to be timid, shy; the implication would be that we ought fear in the presence of higher beings. The plural indicates an intensification of the root idea.[15] In the tablets from Tell el-Amarna and Boghazkoi the plural *ilani* frequently designates a specific god, and at times the king; likewise in the Ras Shamra texts Elohim occurs as the name of a specific deity. When Elohim designates the true God, the modifiers as well as the following verb usually are in the singular (*constructio ad sensum*), but sometimes the plural does occur.[16] In later times the construction with the plural was avoided out of fear of error. When the article occurs, Elohim signifies the true God. Yahweh alone is *ha-ʾelohim,*[17] but the word has the same meaning also without the article.[18] Since Elohim is a very common

1. Transcription difficulties seem to have legitimized various spellings of Semitic words.
2. ZatW 50, 1932, 178-182.
3. Gen. 31:29; Prov. 3:27; Mich. 2:1; cf. Deut. 28:32; Neh. 5:5.
4. Gen. 49:24; Is. 1:24; 49: 26; 60:16; Ps. 132:2, 5.
5. Cf. LXX ὁ ἰσχυρός, the Strong One; ὁ παντοκράτωρ, the Almighty.

6. Ps. 81:10; Deut. 32:12, 21; Mal. 2:11.
7. Ps. 29:1.
8. Ex. 15:11; Dan. 11:36.
9. Gen. 46:3; Pss. 68:20; 77: 15.
10. Gen. 21:33.
11. Jos. 3:10; Pss. 42:3; 84:3.
12. Ex. 34:6.
13. Gen. 16:13.
14. Gen. 35:7; cf. Gen. 31:13; at Ras Shamra there was a god named Bethel

(ThRdsch 13, 86).
15. GK §124e-k.
16. Modifiers: Jos. 24:19; 1 Sam. 17:26, 36; predicate Gen. 20:13; 35:7; 2 Sam. 7:23; 3 Kgs. 19:2; cf. Ex. 32:4, 8; GK §124g, 132h, 145h-i.
17. Deut. 4:35, 39; 3 Kgs. 18:21, 37.
18. Cf. Gen. 1:1; 9:27; Am. 4:11.

name for God, it may also refer to the gods of the Gentiles, in which case the plural form is a numerical plural.[19] Idols too are called)elohim.[20]

Specific gods received the name)elohim, e.g., Dagon,[21] Beelzebul,[22] Chemosh,[23] Milkom,[24] Baal of the Phoenicians,[25] the goddess Astarte.[26] The golden calf was called)elohim.[27] Perhaps the teraphim which Rachel stole and which are called "my gods" by Laban were but a single figure.[28] Unusually impressive is the phrase)elohey ha-)elohim, God of gods, i.e., the true God sovereign over all the gods of the earth.[29]

4. ELOAH is probably related to)el as a further development of the root, or is derived from the plural form)elohim. This title occurs almost exclusively in poetry; in prose it is found only in Nehemias, Chronicles and Daniel, and like El and Elohim is used both of the true God and of false gods.[30]

5. THE MOST HIGH GOD,)el (elyon, ὕψιστος, altissimus; (Elohim Elyon, Yahweh Elyon and Elyon alone also occur). The word is of frequent occurrence, especially in the Book of Ecclesiasticus. The Babylonians, Egyptians and Canaanites honored a "Most High" god,[31] and therefore the name in itself contains no indication of monotheism. In the Scriptures it is found on the lips of non-Jews.[32] When Melchisedech sacrificed to the Most High God and blessed Abraham in his name,[33] his thoughts were centered upon the God whom Abraham adored, and who had accorded victory to the patriarch. Abraham could therefore reply using the same expression.[34] Balaam spoke in the name of the true God when he, as one "who knew the doctrine of the Most High," prophesied the coming King.[35]

6. GOD ALMIGHTY,)el šadday, also šadday alone. This name occurs most frequently in the patriarchal accounts and in Job. Authors generally derive the word from šadad, to be powerful; as evidence note the play on words in Is. 13:6 and Joel 1:15. Also in Gen. 49:24-25 šadday is used parallel to)abbir, the Mighty One. Accordingly the name would mean the "almighty, the all-powerful One." For its equivalent the Vulgate gives omnipotens, the Septuagint frequently renders it with παντοκράτωρ. Some etymologists align it with Accadian šadu, mountain, and see in the name the meaning, sovereign, lord, highest.

7. LORD,)adon (V Dominus), is ordinarily derived from)adan--dun, judge. This name expresses man's dependence upon God. When the word refers to God and has the first person singular suffix the masoretes punctuated it)adonay (an artistic elongation).

8. YAHWEH. This name, called the "tetragrammaton" from its four consonants,[36] is never used of false gods as are the names El, Elohim, Eloah.[37]
a) Meaning. In Ex. 3:14-15 the name is derived from hawah, an older and less frequently used form for hayah, to be; hence, the One Who Is. The more

19. Ex. 12:12; 20:3; 34:15;
    3 Kgs. 11:4; Jer. 2:28.
20. Ex. 20:23.
21. 1 Sam. 5:7.
22. 4 Kgs. 1:2.
23. 3 Kgs. 11:33.
24. 3 Kgs. 11:33.
25. 3 Kgs. 18:21, 24.

26. 3 Kgs. 11:5.
27. Ex. 32:1, 4, 8.
28. Gen. 31:19, 30, 32, 34; cf.
    1 Sam. 19:13, 16.
29. Deut. 10:17; Ps. 136:2.
30. Dan. 11:37-39.
31. § 7:5.
32. Dan. 3:26; 32 Aram.

33. Gen. 14:18-20.
34. Gen. 14:22.
35. Num. 24:16.
36. Philo Vita Mosis II 132,
    cf. 114; Jos. Bell. V 5, 7
    §235.
37. Cf. Is. 42:8.

ancient Hebrew root is used since it sounds more solemn. This meaning is confirmed in Os. 1:9, "You (faithless Israel) are not my people, and I am not 'I AM' (*ehyeh*) for you." As in Exodus the first person is used because God is speaking; He could not say of Himself, "He is," as easily as, "I am." There is allusion to this name also in Is. 43:10-11, "Before me there was no God formed, and after me there shall be none (*lo* *yihyeh*); I, I am Yahweh."

b) *Pronunciation and usage.* The pronunciation of the divine name as "Yahweh" rests upon Samaritan tradition as given by Theodoret (Ιαβέ with β vocalized softly; cf. Δαβίδ),[38] also upon evidence given by Clement of Alexandria (Ιαουέ),[39] by the Elephantine papyri which have *yhw* and *yhh*, by ancient inscriptions which render the name Achaz with Yauhazi, the abbreviated form of the divine name Yah, lastly names like *Abiyahu*.[40] Alongside the name Yahweh which was used not only in literature but also in common ordinary life, as is proven by the Lachish ostraca from the time of Jeremias,[41] Yahu is found as a name in its own right.[42] Most often however this form appears in nominal compounds. The form Ιαώ, found in later writers, shows that it was also vocalized Yaho. From Yahweh too was derived Ya-u which the masoretes pointed as Yo. In postexilic times the use of the divine name Yahweh became less frequent. This may be seen by comparing Chronicles with Samuel and Kings. Nehemias almost wholly shuns its use. In communication with the Persian officials the phrase "God of the Heavens" was used. The word is not found in Ecclesiastes. The Jews feared lest it should be dishonored, and imagined that due to the ever increasing number in the diaspora, the Gentiles would begin to consider the name as that of one of the Jewish gods, rather than the only true God. The Greek translators rendered it with κύριος because they already found God referred to as Lord, *adon*, in the sacred books, and because κύριος like θεός was a common term for God in the Hellenic world. At the time of Jesus Sirach the name Yahweh was uttered at the bestowal of the high-priestly blessing,[43] and at common prayer.[44] The ancient revision of the psalms which frequently replaced Yahweh by Elohim in Pss. 42-72, 73-83, and where Adonai was added after Yahweh,[45] shows that in very early times there had been a tendency to use this divine name in cult.[46] Express proofs for the change from Yahweh to Adonai as a substitute for Yahweh date only from the second century after Christ,[47] but Adonai may have been substituted for Yahweh in the synagogue services already at the time of Philo.[48] This practice gradually exerted an influence upon daily life in that the tetragrammaton was used less and less. For centuries however it persisted in Jewish and half-Jewish circles and that not only in magical formulae, which used the shorter form *yao*,[49] but also in private life.—Our first definite witness to *Jehovah*, which had become very common by Luther's time, is Porchetus a Salvaticis (1303), but the form undoubtedly is considerably older.[50] It is due to a misunderstanding of the masoretic text which vocalized the consonants

38. Quest. 15 in Ex.
39. Str. V 6, §34:5.
40. 2 Chr. 13:20.
41. ZatW 56, 1938, 126-139.
42. Cf. Elephantine papyri.

43. Sir. 50:20.
44. Sir. 50:22.
45. Ps. 130:2, 3, 6.
46. Cf. Herkenne, Die Psälmen.
47. Celsus. Irenaeus.

48. Baudissin, Kyrios II, 176f.
49. E. Shürer, Geschichte des jüd. Volkes III⁴, 1909, 411f.
50. Cf. Alfrink.

YHWH with the vowel points of the word)^adonay (vocal š^ewa instead of hateph-pathah in the first syllable). If Adonai preceded YHWH the points employed are those of the word Elohim; this was done to warn the reader that instead of Yahweh he should vocalize Adonai and Elohim respectively.

c) *Source and age of the name.* Many authors hold that the name YHWH was borrowed from the Kenites, a branch of the Midianites with whom Moses stayed a long time as son-in-law of the priest Jethro. It is stated in the Pentateuch that Moses received valuable advice from Jethro regarding the administration of justice,[51] but there is no indication that he heard the name of his God from the Kenite priest. Jethro first mentions and praises Yahweh after he had heard Moses' account of the deliverance Yahweh had wrought for Israel.[52] In another passage Moses promises Hobab, his kinsman, Yahweh's blessing if he would lead Israel;[53] hence Hobab's knowledge was indirect. Had Yahweh been the God of the Midianites He could not have said, "I have seen the affliction of MY people in Egypt."[54] If *later* Kenites worshipped Yahweh,[55] it was because they had associated themselves with the Israelites and had adopted their religion. In Accadian inscriptions *yau* does not occur as such as a name for a god but only as a component element in personal or geographical combinations. The lack of the usual determinative preceding divine names is evidence that the Accadians did not acknowledge a god with the name *yau*.[56] The Assyrian names Yaubidi (*yau* here having the determinative for God) and Azriyau of Yaudi (both from the 8th century, the former from Hamath, the latter from north Syria?) may be due to Israelitic influence; Azriyau may even be identical with Azarya (Uzziah) of Judah. Whether the divine name Yau occurs in the Sinai inscriptions of Serabit el-Khadem is likewise uncertain.[57] At the present time it is not even definitely probable that the name Yahweh was used as the name of a specific god before the time of Moses or outside of Israel.

In Ex. 6:2-3 God says to Moses, "I am Yahweh. I appeared to Abraham, Isaac and Jacob by the name of God Almighty (*El Šadday*), but my name Yahweh I did not show them." The antithesis of names proves that God did not reveal the name Yahweh to the patriarchs. According to Ex. 3:13-15 it was to Moses that God first manifested His name Yahweh. Passages like, "I, Yahweh, your God from the land of Egypt,"[58] surely allude to the proclamation of that divine name, a name peculiar to the covenant which God ratified with Israel. So when in the Book of Genesis Moses placed the title Yahweh upon the lips of the patriarchs or of God Himself,[59] He did not intend to indicate that the patriarchs knew that name, but rather wished to emphasize that the very same God who manifested Himself on Horeb and there proclaimed His name as Yahweh had previously chosen Abraham, had spoken to the fathers, had directed

51. Ex. 18.
52. Ex. 18:10.
53. Num. 10:29-32.
54. Ex. 3:7.
55. Judg. 5:24f; 4 Kgs. 10: 15f; cf. 1 Chr. 2:55.
56. Hehn 238f; Baudissin, Kyrios IV, 9; Schleiff.

57. Bb 1931, 101. Whether a god YW occurs in the Ras Shamra texts is doubtful; even if granted, scholars would still have to prove that a relationship existed between this god YW in north Syria and Yahweh

the God of Israel (cf. Hempel, ZatW 53, 312; de Langhe EphThLov 16, 281f, 19, 91-101; Les Textes de Ras Shamra-Ugarit I 373).
58. Os. 12:10; 13:4.
59. Gen. 15:2, 7; 21:33; 38:13.

the destinies of mankind from the beginning. For the same reason he noted that at the time of Enos, Adam's grandson, the name Yahweh was invoked.[60] The emphasis does not lie on Yahweh but upon invoke; the name Yahweh appears already in the paradise account. The names Ahiyyah, Bithyah, Abiyyah[61] do not demonstrate the use of the name Yahweh in pre-Mosaic times; *yah* may be an invocative suffix as in the Hittite name Uriyyah. The name Yokebed (Moses' mother)[62] may have been changed at a later period in a similar way as the name Isbaal (man of Baal)[63] was changed to Isboseth (man of shame).[64] Similarly a son of David is called Baalyada (Baal knows)[65] and Elyada (El knows).[66] We may however concede the possibility that Israel was cognizant of the name Yau in pre-Mosaic times. In such a case God could have made use of it, changing the form linguistically to an imperfect, a change without parallel among other divine names in Semitic religions; hence the modification was not due to chance. In any case the fundamental point is that the new name received a very special significance.[67]

9. YAHWEH OF HOSTS, *Yahweh ṣeba'oth, Yahweh 'elohe ṣeba'oth,* or *haṣ-ṣeba'oth* (the phrase [*Yahweh*] *'elohim ṣeba'oth* which occurs in the elohistic psalms, is a textual error). When *Yahweh ṣeba'oth* occurs, *'elohe* is to be inserted. *Ṣaba'* signifies army, the host of heaven, the angelic hosts surrounding Yahweh's throne,[68] the host of heavenly bodies.[69] In the case of the latter the context frequently inveighs against idolatrous worship.[70] The host of heaven and earth in Gen. 2:1 are the stars and all living creatures upon earth. The plural at times refers to the Chosen People,[71] who are also called the "army of Yahweh."[72] The name *Yahweh Ṣeba'oth* denotes Yahweh as Lord of all heavenly and earthly powers. At the time of the Philistine wars Yahweh was regarded as Israel's invisible leader who was fighting for His people,[73] and from this conviction the phrase took its origin.[74] The notion itself however is older. In the canticle of Moses Yahweh is praised as the Victor over the Egyptian armies.[75] To Josue appeared "the captain of Yahweh's host."[76] The stars from the heavens fought on the side of the Israelites against Sisera.[77] There was a "Book of the Wars of Yahweh."[78] In the processional psalm commemorating the entrance of the ark of the covenant into Sion, Yahweh is glorified as "the strong, the mighty, the mighty in battle,"[79] expressions which are parallel to and clarify the name which follows, "Yahweh, God of hosts."[80] The prophets picture Yahweh as a war hero, praise His sword of slaughter;[81] in the Maccabean wars He bestows victory upon the Jews.[82]

By this designation the prophets usually referred to the hosts of heaven, i.e., the angels and stars. In the vision of Isaias the seraphim, who form God's

60. Gen. 4:26.
61. 1 Chr. 2:25; 4:18; 7:8.
62. Ex. 6:20; Num. 26:59.
63. 1 Chr. 8:33.
64. 2 Sam. 2:8.
65. 1 Chr. 14:7.
66. 2 Sam. 5:16.
67. § 6.

68. 3 Kgs. 22:19; 2 Chr. 18:18; Ps. 148:2; Jos. 5:14.
69. Is. 34:4; 40:26; 45:12; Jer. 33:22; Ps. 33:6.
70. Deut. 4:19.
71. Ex. 6:26; 12:17.
72. Ex. 7:4; 12:41.
73. 1 Sam. 17:45; 2 Sam. 5:24.
74. First occurrence, 1 Sam. 1:3, 11.

75. Ex. 15:1, 3.
76. Jos. 5:14.
77. Judg. 5:20.
78. Num. 21:14.
79. Ps. 24:8.
80. Ps. 24:10.
81. Is. 27:1; 34:6; Jer. 34:10; 47:6; Ez. 21:14-22, 33.
82. 2 Mach. 15:22-24, 34.

heavenly court, praise "Yahweh of hosts."[83] Preceding the angels as "Yahweh of hosts," God will smite the faithless Jews, but for the sake of the pious will protect Jerusalem.[84] Nor was this notion foreign to more remote periods. When Jacob met a great multitude of angels in token that divine assistance would not be lacking him, he spoke of the "camps of God."[85] By using the phrase "Yahweh of hosts" the prophets also intended to warn the Israelites against astral worship: Yahweh is Lord of the stars, even the stars must obey him.

10. THE HOLY ONE OF ISRAEL, *qedoš yiśra'el*. This name was devised and used frequently by Isaias.[86] It indicates that God hates sin and demands a holy life.

11. LORD, *ba'al*. This very popular name among the Semites[87] was also frequently used by the Israelites during the period of the Judges and the first centuries of the kingdom as is shown by the many names compounded with *ba'al*. It expressed the votary's conviction that he belonged to the divinity from whom he likewise expected aid and protection. It was easy to call Yahweh Baal, since *ba'al* also meant "spouse" and the relationship between Yahweh and Israel was considered a nuptial one.[88] Later however when the cult of Baal of the Skies (worshipped by the Canaanites as principal god) and of Melkart of Tyre endangered the purity of Yahwistic monotheism,[89] the use of the name Baal, in itself quite legitimate, was proscribed as a name for Israel's God. Names compounded with Baal disappeared already after the time of David. The prophet Osee requested that in the future Israel should no longer use the word *ba'al* to designate Yahweh as her Spouse, but only the word *'iš* (man); in fact, she should no longer use the word at all.[90]

12. KING, *melek*. This name for God is also common to all Semitic languages. The note of kingship is contained in the ancient oriental concept of God. In Israel the name *melek* was applied to Yahweh as early as the time of Moses,[91] and thereafter remained in constant use.[92] For this reason Gideon renounced the proffered dignity of kingship for himself and his descendants, "Yahweh is your king,"[93] and Samuel at first opposed granting the people an earthly king.[94] When the kingdom was established the ruler was Yahweh's representative. Particularly in the psalms is Yahweh lauded as King who rules over Israel, over the nations and over the entire world. This title occurs less frequently in the older prophets, evidently because they had to battle the worship of the Canaanite Melekh.[95] Later it was again used very freely.[96] The idea underneath was: although the Chosen People be oppressed and enslaved by Gentile overlords, Yahweh truly remains Israel's King.

83. Is. 6:2.
84. Is. 31:4-5.
85. Gen. 32:1-2.
86. Cf. also Pss. 71:22; 78:41; 89:19; Jer. 50:29; 51:5; 4 Kgs. 19:22; Sir. 50:17: with slight variations: Hab. 1:12; 3:3; Job 6:10; Prov. 9:10; 30:3; Jos. 24:19; 1 Sam. 6:20.

87. Baudissin, Kyrios III, 19f.
88. § 16:4.
89. Os. 2:10, 15, 19; 13:1.
90. Os. 2:18-19. The names compounded with Baal inscribed upon the sherds found in Samaria and dating to the time of Achab are those of Baal worshippers.
91. Num. 23:21; 24:7-8.

92. Ex. 15:18; Deut. 33:5.
93. Judg. 8:22-23.
94. 1 Sam. 8:6f.
95. § 33:4. The masoretes pointed the word as *molekh* to remind the reader of *bošeth*, shame; whence Moloch.
96. Is. 43:15; Zach. 14:16; Mal. 1:14; 2 Mach. 1:24; Tob. 13:15; Wis. 6:7; 8:3.

13. GOD OF THE HEAVENS, *)elohe haššamayim,* Aram., *)elah šemayya).* This designation for God was used very often during and after the Persian period, especially in intercourse with non-Jews who themselves employed the term; the abbreviated form "Heaven" occurs in Dan. 4:23; 1 Mach. 3:18, 19, 60, etc. Already in Gen. 24:3 we find "Yahweh, God of heaven and earth," and in 24:7 "Yahweh, God of heaven." This name is closely related to the appellation, the "Most High," which also occurs frequently in postexilic times; undoubtedly some influence was exercised by the Persian teaching on Ahura-Mazda, the god who created heaven and earth, and dwells in light.[97]

14. GOD IS ALSO REFERRED TO AS: the Mighty One of Jacob, the Mighty One of Israel, the Rock of Israel, the Fear of Isaac (i.e., whom Isaac fears and honors),[98] the Living One, the Great One, the Glorious One, the Eternal One.[99]

§ 6. GOD'S SELF-EXISTENCE

When God called Moses He said, "I am who am! And he continued saying: Thus shall you say to the children of Israel: 'I am' has sent me to you. God further said to Moses: Thus speak to the Israelites: Yahweh, the God of your fathers, the God of Abraham, the God of Isaac and the God of Jacob has sent me to you. This is my name for all times, and this my memorial unto all generations."[1] The text introduces God as speaking three times, a means to emphasize the importance of the passage. That which God here reveals of Himself by the words, "I am who am," is not merely a divine attribute as His might or goodness, but the very nature of His divine being. The phrase cannot denote that kind of existence which is shared by things in general; it implies that God possesses existence by His very nature, that His existence is from Himself, that His origin is not from some other being. Philosophically expressed He possesses self-existence (aseity—*ens a se*), while everything else outside of Himself does not contain in itself the reason for its being, but derives its being from some One other Being, in other words, has been created. God not only has being, He *is* being. His activity does not consist in self-actualization, His very being *is* actualization itself. When with evident reference to the meaning of the name Yahweh the author of the Book of Wisdom censured those "who through the means of visible things are unable to know him who is (τòν ὄντα), or through meditating upon the work fail to recognize the workman,"[2] he was contrasting the "One who is" with created things. The "One who is" is the creator of all visible things; all things receive existence from Him, nothing is so perfect that it would or could exist apart from and independent of Him. By stressing His self-existence God placed Himself in opposition to the idols who have no existence, hence are "nonentities."

God's self-existence is not a mental abstraction, it is not something impersonal, but rather most active and very personal. Calling Himself, "I am," He

97. Cf. § 5:5.   98. Gen. 31:42, 53.   99. § 10:1.
. Ex. 3:14-15.   2. Wis. 13:1.

spoke to Moses and commissioned him; He recalled the promises He had given
to the fathers and was determined to liberate His people from servitude. Such
personal interest eliminates pantheistic interpretations, and the Septuagint
rightly renders the name by ὁ ὤν (masc.), and not by τὸ ὄν (neut.). The Apoca-
lypse expresses God's transcendence over time and thereby over all things which
wax and wane in the phrase, "Him who is and who was and who is coming."[3]

That Yahweh is a *living* God also flows from His self-existence. Already
Agar called Him such after He had revealed Himself to her.[4] David was indig-
nant over the Philistines who dared defy "the armies of the living God."[5] Osee
foretold how the Israelites would again be called, "Children of the living God."[6]
God swore, "As truly as I live."[7] At the call of Moses this was expressed symbolically by the bush which kept burning but was not consumed.[8] Being the
"One who is," the living God is the source of all life, of physical life as its
creator, of spiritual life as its final reward, "With you is the fountain of life,
and in your light we shall see light."[9]

Because "He is" God remains steadfast in His resolves and does not forget
promises once made. He is the Unchanging One, the Faithful One. From the
implications of the name Yahweh, the Israelites could have deduced His ten-
derness toward the afflicted, but this deduction would not have stemmed directly
from the term itself; for *hayah* means to be, to exist, not: to be here—ready to
help. God is not called the "One who is" because He is faithful, but He is
faithful because He is the "One who is."

The concept of self-existence accordingly is contained in the primitive text
of Exodus and was not first introduced by the LXX translators. Nor did Moses
by speculative thought devise the idea, it rests upon revelation. Yet a person
like Moses—the greatest prophet of Israel, the one who longingly sought to
penetrate the deep secrets of God,[10] the one who was chosen by God to elevate
His people to an extraordinary high place of religious knowledge, to whom
God so often revealed Himself and who was reared in all the wisdom of Egypt
as the adopted son of a princess[11]—was able to grasp a God-given explanation.
To be sure the mass of people did not clearly understand the full significance
of the name upon first hearing or for a long time afterwards. Neither was this
necessary, its deep message was meant primarily for Moses. But the name was
not without import for the Israelites; from it they could derive at least this
much, "The God of times past still is."

The origin of the gods was one of the subjects for speculation among the
priests in the ancient Orient. A certain hymn praises the Babylonian moon-god
Sin as "the fruit which begets itself."[12] A votive inscription of Sennacherib
praises Asshur as the god "who created himself."[13] The Egyptian god Re says,
"I am the great god who gave myself existence."[14] In one of the Osiris mys-

3. Apoc. 1:4.
4. Gen. 16:14.
5. 1 Sam. 17:26, 36; cf. 4
    Kgs. 19:4, 16.
6. Os. 2:1.
7. Num. 14:21, 28; Deut.
    32:40; Jer. 46:18.

8. Ex. 3:2.
9. Ps. 36:10.
10. Num. 12:6-8; Ex. 33:18;
    §4:3.
11. Acts 7:22.
12. AOT 241.

13. Jastrow, Die Religion der
    Babylonier I 532; Dhorme,
    Choix 92f; Hehn, Gottes-
    idee 93.
14. Book of the Dead 17, 6;
    Roeder, 239.

teries a god is called "creator of his own name," i.e., self-begotten.[15] If someone in Egypt wished a deceased person to be transformed into the moon-god,
he would have him cry out, "Through myself have I come into being."[16] So
we find the notion that the gods, or at least certain greater gods, came into
being through self-actualization, that they called themselves into existence. But
self-actualization is not the same as self-actuality. A being, to move itself into
being, must already be extant before its existence, which is impossible. If these
gods called themselves into being, there must have been a time at which they did
not yet exist; accordingly they are not eternal. Actually the oriental religions
do possess a theogony with divine nuptials and divine progeny.[17] These ideas
therefore rest upon mere speculation. The theme in the hymn to Sin is the
increasing moon, and thus this god is as closely bound up with nature as the
sun-god Re, who daily rises in the east. In the case of Sennacherib's inscription
the author may have had in mind Asshur's appearance at the moment the city
was founded. What little religious significance these expressions had may be
deduced from a text in which a third millenium pharaoh says, "As truly as
I live, I am, because I am," words which simply tell his consciousness of absolute power.[18] An inscription in the Isis temple at Sais reads, "I am all that
has been, is and will be; my robe no mortal as yet has uncovered."[19] The
reference here was to a world-soul which cannot be grasped by mortals, not to
a personal God. The passage is pantheistic.

SECTION 2. THE ATTRIBUTES OF GOD

The attributes of God may be divided into a) essence-attributes, e.g.,
unicity, immateriality, perfection, eternity, immutability, holiness, omnipotence,
immensity, omnipresence; b) action-attributes of the intellect, e.g., omniscience,
and of the will, e.g., justice, love, mercy.

§7. UNICITY OF GOD: MONOTHEISM

1. MONOTHEISM, THE FOUNDATION STONE OF OT RELIGION. The fundamental distinguishing characteristic of Israel's religion, that which isolates it
from every other religion of the ancient Orient, is its insistence upon the unicity
of God. ONE God created the world and governs it, ONE God is Lord over the
nations, ONE God revealed Himself to mankind; all peoples some day will
worship the ONE true God. According to the Holy Bible belief in one God goes
back to the very beginning of the human race. The accounts concerning primitive man and concerning the patriarchs take for granted that there is but one
God. In the beginning God manifested Himself as one God, and by the name
Yahweh, i.e., He who is, indicated that all gods worshipped by other nations
"are not."

15. Roeder 38, 44.

16. Book of the Dead 85, 3; Roeder 266.

17. §10:1.

18. A. Alt, ZatW 58, 1940/1, 159f.

19. Plutarch, Isis and Osiris 9.

The decalog began with the solemn proclamation, "I, Yahweh, am your God. You shall have no other gods besides me."[1] Violations of this commandment were to be punished by death, "He who sacrifices to (strange) gods shall be put to death."[2] False gods were not to be invoked in any way, "By the name of strange gods you shall not swear, neither shall it be heard out of your mouth."[3] Taken strictly these texts, it is true, only require that Israel worship Yahweh exclusively (monolatry). It was part of divine pedagogy to proceed slowly. The earlier texts do not expressly accredit a mere imaginary existence to the gods honored by other peoples; yet if the Israelites were not allowed to render them homage, the exclusive cult of Yahweh must logically have led to the conclusion that Yahweh alone is God. Israel's spiritual leaders like Moses always possessed this conviction, but the masses were led to this sublime height only after long and tedious education and many defections.

A passage in Deuteronomy already is quite emphatic, "Hear, O Israel, Yahweh is our God, Yahweh is one."[4] To this is joined the admonition, "You must love Yahweh, your God, with your whole heart, with your whole soul, and with your whole strength."[5] These verses belong to the so-called Shema', the pious Jew's morning and evening prayer in which he daily professes his faith in the one God. Yahweh powerfully demonstrated His right to exclusive worship by forcing Pharoah to let Israel go free, thereby executing judgment upon all the gods of Egypt.[6] Even in their own country they could not protect their devotees.

Further passages from which we may conclude the monotheistic character of the religion practiced by the patriarchs and proclaimed by Moses are those which stress Yahweh's absolute sovereignty, e.g., "judge of all the earth[7].... God of heaven and earth[8].... (to him) belongs the whole world[9].... the God of the spirits of all flesh[10].... when Yahweh, Elohim, made earth and heaven."[11] While the religions of surrounding nations had corresponding feminine terms for female deities, the Hebrews, possessing no such words, had to use El or Elohim when speaking of goddesses.[12] This situation did not change in the course of time, for even after the exile the Jews at Elephantine called the goddess whom they worshipped Anath-Yahu or Anath-Bethel.

Polytheism acknowledged to each god the right to be honored in his own country, but an Israelite, even while sojourning in strange lands, was not allowed to serve the gods worshipped there. In this regard it is noteworthy that the king of Assyria in an official manner ordered the pagan colonists who settled in the northern kingdom after its destruction to be instructed in the Jewish religion.[13] It was common belief that a nation's god battled, conquered or was conquered. After a city or country had been subjugated its god was placed in the pantheon of the victor; though such a god was secondary in rank he still

1. Ex. 20:2-3.
2. Ex. 22:19.
3. Ex. 23:13; cf. Ex. 23:24; 34:14; Lev. 17:7; 19:4; 26:1; Deut. 7:4-6; 12:2-3, 30; 13:2-19.
4. Deut. 6:4.
5. Deut. 6:5.
6. Ex. 12:12.
7. Gen. 18:25.
8. Gen. 24:3.
9. Ex. 19:5.
10. Num. 16:22; 27:16.
11. Gen. 2:4.
12. 3 Kgs. 14:23 (Astarte); 15:13; 4 Kgs. 18:4; Jer. 2:27; 7:18; Ez. 8:5.
13. 4 Kgs. 17:26-28.

remained a god. But Yahweh laid claim to sole dominion over all peoples without allowing any other god to be placed at His side.[14] In polytheistic theology a new god in the pantheon meant a new helper; in the theology of Israel any inclination to a different god implied apostasy from the true faith.

2. THE STRUGGLE TO MAINTAIN THE PURITY OF MONOTHEISTIC BELIEF. The history of Israel from Moses till the end of the Babylonian exile, and even after the exile, is the history of monotheism's struggle to win acceptance. Time and time again the Israelites fell back into the worship of false gods. The decalog injunction to honor Yahweh exclusively was reiterated by Elias, who demonstrated with convincing clarity that Yahweh alone is God and that the gods adopted by Israel do not exist.[15] The words in Deuteronomy are very definite, "Yahweh is God, there is no other beside him."[16] For Osee the worship of strange gods is apostasy, adultery.[17] Isaias proclaims that the gods of the pagans are "things of nought,"[18] and foretells the end of their cult.[19] Already in the time of Judges false gods are called "things of nought,)elilim."[20] Other designations for them are "no-gods[21].... vapour[22].... nothingness[23].... the dead[24].... falsehood[25].... unreality."[26] On the other hand "Yahweh is the God of truth, the living God and eternal king."[27] The prophets present Yahweh as the only God when they proclaim Him God of the world, the God to whom all nations must render obedience and whom all men some day will worship.[28] Their polemic against idols, of course, is directed against faith in false gods.[29]

The doctrine of but one God is taught with extraordinary clarity in the following verses, "To whom then will you liken God? or what image will you make for him?[30].... Before me there was no God formed, and after me there shall be none[31].... I, I am Yahweh, and there is none else; there is no God besides me[32].... Know that I am in the midst of Israel, and I, Yahweh, am your God; there is none besides."[33] The psalmists rejoice that some day Yahweh will be acknowledged exclusively by all nations.[34]

3. KINDS OF POLYTHEISM. In Wis. 13-15 three types of polytheism are distinguished, a) the worship of natural forces and heavenly bodies;[35] b) the worship of images and idols;[36] c) animal worship.[37] The same classification may be found in Philo.[38] Dualism places a second principle alongside of God, i.e., all that which by nature is evil and conflicts with God. It may be doubted whether Isaias was combatting this error when he wrote, "I, Yahweh, and there is none else; I form the light, and create darkness; I make peace, and create evil; I, Yahweh, do all these things."[39] In any case he was opposing that type of demonology which ascribes misfortune and disease to the evil spirits.[40] Since monotheism is found at the very portal of human history, the

14. § 45.
15. 3 Kgs. 18:21f.
16. Deut. 4:35, 39; 32:39.
17. Os. 1-3.
18. Is. 2:8, 18; 18:10; 19:3.
19. Is. 2:18.
20. Lev. 19:4; 26:1; cf. Ps. 96:5.
21. Deut. 32:17, 21; Jer. 2:11; 5:7.
22. 3 Kgs. 16:13; Jer. 2:5.
23. Jer. 10:3; 8:19.
24. Ps. 106:28.
25. Is. 41:29.
26. Is. 66:3.
27. Jer. 10:10.
28. § 45:2; 48:2.
29. § 4:2.
30. Is. 40:18.
31. Is. 43:10.
32. Is. 45:5.
33. Joel 2:27.
34. § 48:3; cf. 2 Mach. 7:37; Wis. 12:13; 14:21f.
35. Wis. 13:1-9.
36. Wis. 13:10-15:17.
37. Wis. 15:18f.
38. De dec. 52-81.
39. Is. 45:6-7; § 7:5.
40. On God as the cause of all things, cf. § 11:4c; 25:6.

sacred writers viewed polytheism as apostasy and error: idol worship and polytheism "came into the world by the vanity of men, and therefore they shall
be found to come shortly to an end."[41] According to the composer of the Book
of Wisdom idol worship arose in the following manner: at the death of a
beloved one a picture was made in remembrance of him. Soon the honor paid
to the picture turned into worship, first by the members of the immediate family,
later by wider circles. The honor rendered to the picture of the ruler was at
first due to motives of affection, but later imposed by law.[42]

4. DID LEGITIMATE EXPONENTS OF OT RELIGION ADMIT THE EXISTENCE OF
GODS? Of course those texts in which non-Israelites speak must be eliminated,
e.g., Ex. 18:11; 1 Sam. 4:8, and those in which the hagiographer only quotes
another's thought. The occurrence at times of Elohim with plural modifiers or
verbs is to be explained on grammatical grounds.[43] The patriarchs did not
worship a number of Elim, but an only God, who had revealed Himself to them.[44]
The names, "God who sees[45].... God of Bethel,"[46] should be compared with
the expressions, "Yahweh of hosts in Shiloh[47].... Yahweh in Hebron;"[48] no
one proposes the existence of several Yahwehs. In a similar way we speak of
our Blessed Lady of Lourdes, of Fatima, of Czenstochau, of Altötting, without
implying several Marys. What is implied is that Mary receives special veneration
in particular places. The expressions "strange gods" or "other gods," in the
mouth of the inspired writer simply implied that the *Gentiles* worshipped gods
other than Yahweh. Exclamations like "God of gods and Lord of lords[49]....
Who is like you among the gods[50].... Yahweh is king over all the gods,"[51]
must be evaluated from the context. Deuteronomy is decisive on the point of
Yahweh's unicity,[52] and according to Ps. 95:4-5 Yahweh is the creator of the
whole universe; Ps. 96:5 declares that "all the gods of the nations are things
of nought;" Ps. 97:7 inveighs against those who adore graven images, "who
glory in their things of nought." When reading such texts we must keep in
mind that reference is being made to gods as imagined by the Gentiles. Passages
like, "Yahweh will hold judgment over all the gods of Egypt,"[53] are to be
explained in a similar manner. At a much later time Jeremias, certainly a mono-
theist, says, "Yahweh will punish Amon in No,"[54] i.e., when Nabuchodonosor
shall have pressed forward as far as No (Thebes) in Upper Egypt, it will be
evident that the god Amon is a phantom.[55] Yahweh challenged the pagan gods
to bring their cause before Him.[56] The author of the Book of Wisdom writes
in the same vein, "Upon the idols of the Gentiles shall judgment come."[57]

"Are not those things which your god, Chemosh, possesses due to you by
right? But what Yahweh, our God, has obtained by conquest shall be our
possession."[58] These words of Jephte may be understood as diplomatic address,

41. Wis. 14:14.
42. Wis. 14:12-30.
43. Cf. § 5:3; cf. § 17 regarding the texts, "Let us make
man" (Gen. 1:26), "Man
is become as one of us"
(Gen. 3:22), "Let us go
down and there confound
their tongue" (Gen. 11:7).
44. § 4:4b.
45. Gen. 16:13.
46. Gen. 31:13; 35:7; § 5:2.
47. 1 Sam. 1:3.
48. 2 Sam. 15:7.
49. Deut. 10:17; Ps. 136:2;
Dan. 11:36.
50. Ex. 15:11.
51. Ps. 95:3; cf. Pss. 82:1;
96:4; 97:7.
52. Deut. 4:35, 39.
53. Ex. 12:12.
54. Jer. 46:25.
55. Cf. Jer. 51:44, 47, 52.
56. Is. 41:21.
57. Wis. 14:11.
58. Judg. 11:24.

i.e., the chieftain is speaking from the viewpoint of his enemies. But as Jephte was not too deeply immersed in the spirit of orthodox religion, as is shown by the sacrifice of his daughter,[59] we may also admit that he believed in the existence of a god, Chemosh, whom the Ammonites could lawfully worship. According to David's complaint his enemies exiled him "in order that he would have no portion in the inheritance of Yahweh, saying: Go, serve strange gods."[60] They wished to place him in danger of apostatizing from Yahweh; for since one was allowed to sacrifice to Yahweh only in Canaan, an Israelite beyond its boundaries was deprived of cult, was deprived of the support of his kinsfolk and so became an easy victim for seduction. David's actual mind is shown in his confession, "You are great, Yahweh, God! No one is like unto you, and there is no god besides you,"[61] and also in his exclamation, "Who is God but Yahweh?"[62] Recall moreover his conduct in Philistine territory where he prayed only to Yahweh and inquired of Yahweh through the priests.[63]

5. ALLEGED MONOTHEISTIC CURRENTS IN THE ANCIENT ORIENT. a) *Although the Babylonians* had many gods, with Marduk at the apex after the time of Hammurabi, the pious petitioner would frequently turn to a specific god and elevate him above all others so that, comparatively speaking, all the others almost vanished in favor of the one then seemingly honored as an only god. In a hymn to the moon-god Sin we read, "In heaven who is exalted? You alone are exalted."[64] The thunderstorm god Adad-Ramman is praised in a hymn, "Before his anger, before his growling, before his roaring, before his thunder the gods of the heavens ascend, the gods of the earth go into the earth, the sun seeks the recesses of the skies, the moon disappears in the heights of heaven."[65] A certain incantation praises Ishtar as "mistress of mistresses, goddess of goddesses, mistress of the heavens and of the earth before whom heaven and earth and the gods themselves tremble," and then concludes, "Irnini, the mighty daughter of Sin, is not comparable to her!"[66] The hymn which celebrates her elevation to queen of heaven proclaims, "Men should regard you as a goddess who has no equal among the gods."[67] Similar expressions may be found in the Babylonian penitential psalms. An inscription of Adad-Nirari I (811-782) concludes with the profession, "I trust in Nebo, I trust in no other god!"[68] None of these passages however may be used as proofs for monotheism, or even for monolatry. The petitioner did not think that Sin or Adad or Ishtar or Nebo was the ONLY god that existed, or the only god that laid claim to worship; he did not deny the might of the other gods, because by the formula used he merely intended to give special emphasis to his trust in the god addressed; his formula was, in fact, mere flattery in order to gain the good will of a specific god. If the petitioner received no answer from the first god invoked he would without hesitation turn to another and direct identical words to him. Although Marduk was the chief god, any other god could be praised as the "Most High."

59. Judg. 11:34; cf. § 20:5.
60. 1 Sam. 26:19.
61. 2 Sam. 7:22.
62. 2 Sam. 22:32.
63. 1 Sam. 30:6-8.
64. AOT 242; AO VII 3, 12.
65. AO VII 3, 12.
66. AO VII 3, 19f.
67. AOT 254.
68. Hehn, Gottesidee 68.

Just as little is there question of monotheism or of any "inclination to monotheism" in the penitential psalms where, e.g., a petitioner prays "to the god whom I know, or do not know." The penitent is simply ignorant which of the many gods afflicted him with disease or misfortune and wants to make absolutely sure to include the god responsible, even though that god be unknown to him.

In a neo-Babylonian text Marduk is lauded as god of all, "Ninurta is Marduk as regards might, Nergal is Marduk as regards war, Enlil is Marduk as regards rule and judgment, Sin is Marduk as regards the illumination of the night, Shamash is Marduk as regards justice, etc."[69] All this merely indicates that Marduk possessed more attributes, was more active than other gods. The final step to honor Marduk alone should have been easy as the remaining gods were relegated more and more to the rear, yet that step was never taken. The thought that Marduk could be god exclusively was wholly foreign to the Babylonian manner of thinking.

Every god had his own peculiar field of operation, e.g., Ninurta and Nergal were gods of the chase and of war, Enlil the god who governs, Sin was primarily the moon-god, and Shamash the god of the sun and of justice. Nergal and Enlil were accorded attributes in the same way as Marduk.[70] A noteworthy but repulsive comparison ascribes to Ninurta bodily parts from various gods, "Anu and Antu are his lips, his ears Ea and Damkina, his cranium Adad, his neck Marduk, his breast Nebo, etc."[71] Such passages show what little part reason played in polytheism. The priests themselves never thought of reforming the state religion or its pantheon, never attained to the knowledge of the existence of one personal God. Had priestly speculation reached this point—which cannot be demonstrated—viz., to dissolve all individual gods and regard them as manifestations of a universal divinity, the result would have been pantheism, not monotheism. Divine might would have become cosmic matter. "The whole tendency of religious belief as well as of cult as it evolved gradually in Babylon excludes an explanation of the universe upon a monotheistic basis."[72]

b) *The Canaanites* too adored many gods with one seated at the zenith. The title, "Lord of gods," given in a letter found at Taanach and dating undoubtedly from the Amarna period, only proves that someone was honoring a specific deity as supreme—in this instance we may single out Hadad, Baal of Aram, without fear of error.[73] The same applies to the expression, "Lord of the heavens," contained in a Phoenician inscription,[74] and to the "Highest god" worshipped at Byblos.[75] Ugarit records list about 100 gods by name, but since many of these names refer to the same god, the actual count is not quite that large. As members of this pantheon R. de Langhe counts 8 Horrite gods, 37 Semite gods, Amon from Egypt and perhaps Ptah. The oldest gods were El (the moon), Ashirat (the sun) and Attar (a star). This pantheon very probably dates back to the time when the Canaanites were still on the march toward Pales-

69. AOT 329.
70. Meissner II, 1925, 48.
71. AOT 250.
72. Jastrow, Die Religion Bab-   yloniens und Assyriens I, 1905, 422; II, 1912, 132f.
73. AOT 371.
74. AOT 443.
75. Euseb. Praep. ev. I 10; § 11. On the "Most High God" of Melchisedech, cf. § 5:5.

tine-Syria-Phoenicia. Baal and his consort Anat (vegetation gods) and Mot (underworld god) were added later.[76] At the time when Israel took possession of the land, the Canaanites worshipped many male Baals and female goddesses to whom they ascribed the fertility of their lands, vineyards, herds and women. The Canaanites were not traveling a road that led to monotheism, rather their pantheon was becoming more crowded, their cult more degrading. May we not surmise that at the source of this progressive degeneration there once had been some type of monotheism? A similar deterioration may be traced at Mari (on the west bank of the middle Euphrates at the beginning of the 2nd millenium), where with the advent of trade and traffic new gods appeared.[77]

c) *Egypt.* Partly from political considerations Pharoah Amenophis IV (c. 1375-1358) introduced a new religion in Egypt. All men are children of the sun-god; the sun-god gave them their various colors and tongues, he provides for all, all should pray to him. The sun-god is not only the chief god but "the only god, besides whom there is no other." Amenophis gave the sun-god a new name, Aton, "sun-disc," and changed his own name to Ikhnaton, "brightness of the sun-disc." The symbol of this new god was the sun-disc from which rays, ending in human hands, proceeded—a sign that the sun confers all good things upon men and accepts their offerings in return. The idea was not totally new, for during the reign of Amenophis III Re was worshipped under the name Aton, and Amon was honored as "the one who created all things, the only one with many hands," just as Ikhnaton later represented Aton. Yet this religion, of which we are informed in a famous hymn to the sun,[78] was not monotheistic but pantheistic in nature. For its proponents claimed that the sun embodies and manifests the energies or forces which permeate the universe, and Aton (the sun) shows himself anew every morning simply by rising over the horizon. Amenophis made no attempt to abolish the idea of Pharaoh's divine sonship, rather stressed it in the song, "No one knows you but your son Ikhnaton, who proceeded from you." He meant to say: the sun gives birth to him daily by conferring upon him its "divinity"; consequently he was not ashamed of accepting adoration. With his death his religion came to an end. The older officials and the people had always opposed it. The palace of the heretic king fell into ruins and was covered with sand; the site became known as Tell el-Amarna. Educated at court Moses could have been aware of the religious innovation of Amenophis IV. But there are no relationships between the impersonal force emanating from the sun and the personal God, who at a definite moment in history spoke to Moses as he had previously spoken to the patriarchs and later spoke to the prophets.

The "great god" mentioned in texts dating from the Old Kingdom is Re, the god of heaven, or in prayers to the dead, Osiris. The ancient Pharaohs sometimes called themselves "great god." The word "god" did not designate "one only God," but was a common noun, and the listeners could restrict their thoughts to some specific deity. There is no proof that in historical times the

76. Langhe II 347f.   77. Bb 21, 1940 193f.   78. AOT 15f; Erman 109f.

Egyptians worshipped a god of the heavens as the one and only God; already the most ancient documents are grossly polytheistic.

d) *Persia.* Among the oriental religions that of Zarathustra ranks as least objectionable. It first appeared however long after monotheism had been proclaimed in Israel, even though its founders be assigned to an early date. Zarathustrianism does not come under consideration as a possible source for Israelitic monotheism; we mention it here only for comparative purposes. The one god Ahura-Mazda personified all that is good; he demanded purity of life. Counter to him stood Angra Mainyu (Ahriman), the evil principle, who would be vanquished at the end of time.[79] The Achemenids Darius I, Xerxes I and Artaxerses I were monotheists of this cloth and sought to repress the polytheistic religion of the Magi. Under later Achemenids however the Magi regained sufficient influence to place Mithra and Anachita in leading positions. Zarathustrianism then declined—another instance of progressive deterioration.

§ 8. GOD'S IMMATERIALITY

1. GOD IS A SPIRIT. Since God is "being itself" and in no way subject to change or dissolution as are all material things, He must be a spirit. And because He is infinitely perfect,[1] He must be a perfectly pure spirit. The OT does not teach this truth as clearly as does the NT,[2] yet it leaves no doubt concerning the attribute itself. God can neither be compared with anything outside of Himself, nor can the human mind comprehend Him;[3] He is not composed of matter, has no body.

The words, "The Egyptians are men, not God; and their horses are flesh, not spirit,"[4] express primarily the impotence of earthly opposition; but inasmuch as the text contrasts the material and transitory with the divine and spiritual, it implies God's immateriality or spirituality. According to Job we must not imagine that God has a body, "Have you (God) eyes of flesh, or shall you see as man sees?"[5] The passage, "Behold, he passes me by and I do not see it, he sweeps on past me and I do not perceive him,"[6] refers principally to the mysterious operations of God, but it also implies God's immateriality.[7] Because He transcends space and time, because He is omnipresent,[8] He cannot be limited by matter, He must be a spirit. All those passages may also be cited in which the prophets and psalmists inveigh against a merely external view of sacrifices, as if God needed sacrifices, or as if God could be placated by them.[9] The commandment, "You shall not make for yourself a graven thing,"[10] was enjoined to forestall ascribing to God any type of bodily form; from the fact that He could not be represented pictorially men should conclude that He was invisible, incorporeal.[11]

For the ancients light was the substance farthest removed from matter. With

79. § 23:4.

1. § 9.
2. Jn. 4:24; 2 Cor. 3:17.
3. Is. 40:18; § 4:3.
4. Is. 31:3.

5. Job 10:4.
6. Job 9:11.
7. Cf. Job 23:8.
8. § 13.

9. Ps. 50:12, 13; Is. 43:23, 24; § 33:7cd.
10. Ex. 20:4-5.
11. Cf. Deut. 4:15, 16; § 28:4.

this in mind, note how God appeared to Moses in a burning bush,[12] and how in visions the prophets beheld Yahweh manifesting Himself in the splendor of light.[13] We read that He is "clothed with light as with a garment,"[14] that He is the "light of Israel,"[15] that He is "light eternal."[16]

2. DIVINE APPARITIONS. The OT tells of many instances in which God revealed Himself in a way perceptible to the senses. The sacred writers take pains to express these objective, mystery-laden experiences in a form adapted to the understanding of the common reader, even though the result be incommensurate and the method anthropomorphical. Many interesting details grace the account of the apparition to Abraham near the terebinths of Mamre. Three men, Yahweh accompanied by two angels, approach the patriarch as he was sitting at the door of his tent, drink and converse with him.[17] The appearances to Agar,[18] to Moses in the inn on his way to Egypt,[19] to Gedeon,[20] to the parents of Samson,[21] are recounted more briefly. On other occasions God manifested Himself in dreams[22] or in visions.[23] Often those to whom God spoke heard only a voice, as Agar when Ismael was dying of thirst,[24] as Abraham when sacrificing Isaac,[25] as the Israelites during the theophany on Horeb,[26] as Elias at Sinai.[27] When the Law was being given on Mt. Sinai, Yahweh appeared in massive clouds amidst thunder, lightning, trumpet calls and quaking mountains.[28] Such phenomena were needed to prove Himself Lord of nature and to impress the people. Storms and particularly earthquakes demonstrate that all the forces of nature are at God's disposal.[29] When God made the covenant with Abraham, a smoking furnace and a flaming torch appeared;[30] the smoke symbolized God's inaccessibility and incomprehensibility, the fire His immateriality. To Elias God revealed Himself not in a storm, not in an earthquake, not in fire, but in a low soft sigh;[31] awe-inspiring disturbances in nature preceded the gentle whisper to teach Elias that God was far mightier than the assaults directed against Himself which had made the prophet so impetuous. The variation in the natural phenomena employed showed a) that God is not identical with such phenomena, b) that any natural phenomena may serve as a medium for conveying messages to His chosen ones, c) that they are in no way essential to divine apparitions.

As far back as pre-Mosaic times the belief was universal in Israel that any person who saw God must die. Agar, filled with amazement, exclaimed, "Have I really seen (God) *and remained alive* while I looked?"[32] Yahweh reminded Moses, "No man looks upon me and remains alive."[33] Isaias in terror cried, "I am lost, for my eyes have looked upon the King, Yahweh of hosts."[34] Although it is impossible for us to determine in every instance what details belong to history and what to the author's method of narration, still the divine appari-

12. Ex. 3:2.
13. Is. 6:1; Ez. 1:27-28; Hab. 3:4.
14. Ps. 104:2.
15. Is. 10:17; 60:1, 19; Mich. 7:8.
16. Wis. 7:26.
17. Gen. 18.
18. Gen. 16:7f.
19. Ex. 4:24-26.
20. Judg. 6:11f.

21. Judg. 13:3.
22. Gen. 26:24; 28:11 (ladder reaching to heaven); 3 Kgs. 3:5f.
23. Is. 6:1f; 3 Kgs. 22:19; Ez. 1.
24. Gen. 21:17.
25. Gen. 22:11, 15.
26. Ex. 19:19; 20:19; Deut. 4:12.
27. 3 Kgs. 19:9f.

28. Ex. 19:16-19; 20:18.
29. 2 Sam. 22:8-15; Pss. 18:8-15; 50:2-3; 68:8-9; 77:17-19; 97:2-5; 144:5-6.
30. Gen. 15:17.
31. 3 Kgs. 19:11-12.
32. Gen. 16:13.
33. Ex. 33:20.
34. Is. 6:5; cf. Ex. 3:6; 24:11; Judg. 6:22; 13:22; 3 Kgs. 19:13; Tob. 12:16.

tions cannot be explained wholly as interior experiences which took place in the mind of those to whom God revealed Himself, or wholly as visions; there are cases in which others besides the person so favored witnessed the event, e.g., Sara and the servant in Gen. 18. The account of the angels' stay in Sodom and Lot's deliverance in Gen. 19 would be difficult to explain as an inner experience, also Abraham's hospitality toward them.

"To see the face *(panim)* of God" does not imply having a vision, but to experience His love,[35] or to visit places of cult.[36] To seek His face means to turn to Him for aid,[37] or to enter the sanctuary.[38] To caress His face means to make efforts to obtain His favor, and if He be angry, to appease Him.[39] When God "hides his face" He is angry,[40] or has withdrawn His love.[41] Cain had to flee from the face of God.[42] If God turns His face away from the sins of men divine forgiveness is implied.[43] The face of God was to accompany Israel during the desert journey, e.g., He would personally go along with the Chosen People.[44] The "glory *(kabod)* of Yahweh" was God manifesting Himself in the brightness of light, revealing His holiness and power to men.[45]

The divine apparitions took place at definite historical moments and were accorded to historical personages, and to such personages as were of extraordinary importance in the history of salvation. Accordingly they are not to be classed with appearances of gods as recounted by other nations nor to be given a like rating. The latter are myths which, far from effecting a deeper and more refined belief in God, turned the gods into men and drew them down to earthly levels.

3. ANTHROPOMORPHISMS. Many passages in the OT speak of God as if He had a human body. Eyes and ears, mouth, heart, arms, hands, fingers and feet are ascribed to Him; He talks,[46] writes,[47] sees and hears,[48] sits and rests,[49] smells,[50] whistles,[51] laughs,[52] walks down (from heaven),[53] sleeps and awakes,[54] claps His hands,[55] has a face and a back side.[56] To Him are attributed human emotions (anthropopathy): He rejoices,[57] grieves,[58] feels regret,[59] is angry,[60] is disgusted,[61] is zealous,[62] hates (sin).[63] Never however is a base passion ascribed to God, one that would conflict with His holiness. God's activity too is graphically delineated: He fashions man out of earth and breathes into him the breath of life;[64] He plants a garden[65] in which at the cool of day He walks about so that Adam and Eve could hear the sound of His tread,[66] He locks the ark,[67] draws His sword from its scabbard,[68] whets the sword and draws the bow,[69] treads the wine press.[70] Anthropomorphism and anthropopathy

35. Ps. 17:15; cf. Num. 6:25-26.
36. Ex. 23:15, 17; 34:20, 23; Is. 1:12; Ps. 42:3.
37. Ps. 27:8.
38. Ps. 24:6.
39. 1 Sam. 13:12; Jer. 26:19.
40. Deut. 32:20; Is. 59:2.
41. Ps. 104:29.
42. Gen. 4:14, 16; cf. Pss. 13:2; 22:25; 27:9.
43. Ps. 51:11.
44. Ex. 33:14; cf. Deut. 4:37; Is. 63:9.
45. Ex. 16:7; 24:16; 40:34;

Lev. 9:6, 23; Num. 14:10; 16:19; 17:7; 3 Kgs. 8:11; Is. 40:5; Ez. 1:28.
46. Gen. 1:3; 8:15.
47. Ex. 31:18.
48. Gen. 6:12; Ex. 16:12.
49. Gen. 2:2; Ps. 47:9.
50. Gen. 8:21; 1 Sam. 26:19.
51. Is. 7:18.
52. Ps. 2:4.
53. Gen. 11:5.
54. Ps. 44:24; 78:65.
55. Ez. 21:22.
56. Ex. 33:14-15, 23; Num. 6:25; Ps. 104:29.

57. Deut. 28:63; Soph. 3:17.
58. Gen. 6:6.
59. Gen. 6:6.
60. Ex. 15:7.
61. Ps. 106:40.
62. Ex. 20:5; 34:14.
63. Deut. 12:31.
64. Gen. 2:7.
65. Gen. 2:8.
66. Gen. 3:8.
67. Gen. 7:16.
68. Ez. 21:8.
69. Ps. 7:13.
70. Is. 63:2-3.

occur more frequently in the older books, though later authors love to write in a similar fashion, especially the poets. The translators of the Septuagint sought to suppress these figures of speech.

The very fact that God is likened to animals should indicate that concrete expressions are to be understood figuratively. God is said to roar like a lion,[71] to act like a lioness and lurk on the wayside like a panther, to attack like a she-bear robbed of her cubs,[72] to resemble a moth,[73] to be an eagle protecting the pious with outstretched wings.[74] He is also likened to fire which consumes the godless,[75] and to dew.[76] On the other hand in certain passages God is said to lack human form, sense perception and emotion. Thus in Pss. 44:24; 78:65 Yahweh sleeps and awakens, but in Ps. 121:4 "he neither slumbers nor sleeps who keeps Israel." Yahweh "faints not, neither is weary,"[77] has no eyes like those of men;[78] He is "not man" to be carried away by passion.[79] Balaam proclaimed, "God is not a man that he keep not his word, nor a son of man that he should repent,"[80] and Samuel reminded Saul, "Israel's trustworthy God does not *lie* and feels no repentance; for he is not a man that he could repent."[81] Previously however God had said, "I regret that I have made Saul king."[82]

One reason why biblical writers employed such expressions lies in man's inability to describe God in an adequate manner. As a being composed of body and spirit man must reason from perceptible objects to spiritual realities, he must use imagery proper to the visible world and the field of human emotional experience when he seeks to discuss God's attributes and activity. The NT does not avoid this method, and theological language itself cannot wholly abstain from employing anthropomorphical expressions. Arms and hands indicate God's might, eyes His omniscience, etc. It is an imperfect method, but it is no sign of a hazy and blurred or, as sometimes claimed, false concept of God. Anthropomorphism does not aim at humanizing God, but—and this is a second reason justifying its use—to bring God close to man as a warm, living person and thus to preserve and strengthen religious life. God must not be regarded as an abstract idea distant from and unconcerned about us, but as a Being who will not remain indifferent if we sin. Punish He will, yet if we repent He will be merciful, always eager to receive us in times of need.[83]

By stressing God's transcendence and human frailty in those very passages which seem ultra anthropomorphistic, Holy Scripture itself guards against possible false notions. In the apparition granted to Abraham Yahweh foretold a remarkable event,[84] showed His omniscience,[85] exercised judgment upon Sodom.[86] Abraham called Him "judge of all the earth."[87] The prophets, who never tired exhorting the people to obey God and proclaiming the coming judgment, unhesitatingly employed anthropomorphism, a proof that they saw no

71. Os. 11:10; Am. 1:2.
72. Os. 13:7-8.
73. Os. 5:12.
74. Os. 8:1; Ps. 17:8.
75. Is. 10:17; 33:14.
76. Os. 14:6.

77. Is. 40:28.
78. Job 10:4.
79. Os. 11:9.
80. Num. 23:19.
81. 1 Sam. 15:29.
82. 1 Sam. 15:11; cf. 15:35.

83. Cf. § 10:2.
84. Gen. 18:10.
85. Gen. 18:13.
86. Gen. 18:20f.
87. Gen. 18:27.

danger to the faith in this type of language. And the Israelites themselves never questioned its wholly figurative character.

§ 9. GOD IS PERFECT

1. GOD'S TRANSCENDENT PERFECTION. That God is perfect is signified by His name Yahweh. Since God is "being" and all creatures apart from Him owe their existence to Him, He must possess in an eminent degree and from Himself all prerogatives imaginable together with all those had by creatures; it is they, not God, who receive their perfections or obtain them through laborious effort. The perfection of God is evident from all those passages which speak of Him as creator of the world and of men or which teach His omnipotence and omniscience, His omnipresence and eternity. He is the source of all that pleases because of its beauty, He is the creator of all that instills admiration because of its power and activity; but He surpasses by far all creatures both in beauty and might.[1] "His greatness is unfathomable[2].... his wisdom is limitless."[3] Next, those passages may be mentioned which celebrate God's superiority over the world. The divine name, "Most High God,"[4] implies that Israel attributed all prerogatives to her God. The same follows from the phrases, "God of heaven and earth[5].... God of all flesh[6].... God of the spirits of all flesh[7].... God over all the kingdoms of earth[8].... Lord of the universe[9].... Lord of all the world."[10] As such He is awe-inspiring, especially in manipulating world events in favor of His people. He shows himself "awe-inspiring through glorious deeds, working wonders."[12] Israel must fear Him,[13] not by remaining at a distance but by obeying Him.[14] "Fear God and keep his commandments for this is of universal application."[15]

The poets never tire praising God's perfection. "Yahweh, the Most High, must be feared; he is the great king over all the world[16].... All the earth is full of his glory."[17] Jesus Sirach regretted that words failed him in his efforts to praise God adequately. "Who shall show forth the power of his majesty?"[18] After he had described the perfection of God as revealed in creation, he acknowledged, "We could still say much, but would not come to an end. The sum of our words is: He is all! We want to continue praising, yet we shall not be able to fathom him because he is greater than all his works. Who has seen him and is able to declare it? Who is able to magnify him as he is?"[19] Animal and inanimate creation should join the chorus of praise to the creator, "Let the heavens rejoice, and let the earth be glad! Let the sea roar together with all that is in it! Let the fields and all things upon them be jubilant!"[20]

Man cannot comprehend God's being. Likewise God's thoughts and decrees

1. Wis. 13:3-5.
2. Ps. 145:3.
3. Ps. 147:5.
4. § 5:5.
5. Gen. 24:3.
6. Jer. 32:27.
7. Num. 27:16.
8. Is. 37:16.

9. Mich. 4:13.
10. Jos. 3:11, 13; Ps. 97:5; Zach. 4:14; 6:5.
12. Ex. 15:11; 34:10; 2 Sam. 7:23; Sir. 43:29.
13. Deut. 10:12, 20.
14. Deut. 10:13; 28:58.

15. Qoh. 12:13.
16. Pss. 47:3; 57:6, 12; 66:5; 95:3; 96:6; 97:9; 106:2; 113:2; 113:4; 147:5.
17. Is. 6:3.
18. Sir. 18:5.
19. Sir. 43:27-31.
20. Ps. 96:11-12.

are unsearchable. Human understanding is not able to scrutinize them, for that would imply becoming equal to God. "How magnificent are your deeds, Yahweh! How unfathomably deep your decrees![21].... How difficult to understand are your thoughts, O God, how great their number. Did I wish to count them, they are more than the sand; had I reached the end, my life's span would be like yours[22]. . . . My thoughts are not your thoughts, and your ways are not my ways, says Yahweh. For as high as heaven is above the earth, so are my ways above your ways, and my thoughts above your thoughts."[23] Man simply lacks the ability to know God perfectly.[24] The entire world is as nothing in the sight of its sovereign Lord who made it; it is passing away while men, all men, are but a breath, "Behold, the nations are as a drop on a bucket, they are reckoned as a dust particle on the balance."[25] Whether or not a drop hanging upon a bucket will fall off and evaporate is indeed a matter of little importance; and in weighing merchandise small dust particles are wholly disregarded, no one even notices them. The author of the Book of Wisdom repeats this comparison.[26] In Job 38:1-42:6 God points out His omnipotence, wisdom and goodness as revealed in the structure of the universe, in atmospheric phenomena, in His care of the animal world. How frail and weak is man in comparison to so many creatures, how defective his understanding which cannot even grasp those few works of God which come under his observation!

2. GOD'S SELF-SUFFICIENCY. Since God created the world, all that exists belongs to Him, "Mine is the whole earth[27].... To Yahweh, your God, belong heaven and the heaven of heaven, the earth and all upon it[28]. . . . In his hands are the foundations of the earth, and the mountain tops are his; to him belongs the sea for he made it, his hands too have fashioned the dry earth."[29] Accordingly God is "wholly independent of every being."[30] He needs no sacrifices, "Lebanon will not suffice for fuel, nor its beasts be sufficient for burnt offerings" worthy of Yahweh.[31] Nor can man increase God's greatness by piety and virtue. A life pleasing to God is not of profit to God whose beatitude is infinite, but to man. "Will man's labor profit God, whether he work wilily or wisely? Is it advantageous for the Almighty if you be just, or to his gain if you keep your ways blameless?[32].... If you act justly, are you giving him something, or will he receive something from your hand?"[33] He who fasts does not fast for God's benefit.[34] Neither can sin harm God nor mar His majesty, "If I sin, do I accomplish anything against him?"[35] asked Job, even before Elihu reproached him, "If you sin, do you accomplish anything against him? If your transgressions be multiplied, do you do anything to (harm) him?"[36] By revolting against God man harms only himself, "If you are wise, it is to your own good; if you are a scorner, you shall suffer the consequences alone."[37] Likewise God could

21. Ps. 92:6.
22. Ps. 139:17-18.
23. Is. 55:8-9; cf. Pss. 40:6; 71:19.
24. § 4:3.
25. Is. 40:15.
26. Wis. 11:22; cf. Is. 40:17-18, 25; 46:5.
27. Ex. 19:5.
28. Deut. 10:14.
29. Ps. 95:4-5; cf. Ps. 24:1.
30. 2 Mach. 14:35.
31. Is. 40:16; cf. Ps. 50:9-13; § 33:7cd.
32. Job 22:2-3.
33. Job 35:7.
34. Zach. 7:5-6; § 37:3.
35. Job 7:20.
36. Job 35:6.
37. Prov. 9:12; Ps. 37:13; cf. Ps. 2:4.

reject even His Chosen People without loss of happiness or of honor; to attain His ends He had no need of Israel.

3. GOD'S PERFECTION, THE FOUNDATION OF HIS LOVING-KINDNESS. Simply because He is perfect, God has compassion upon helpless man, "On high as the Holy One am I enthroned, I am with him of contrite and humble spirit, to revive the spirit of the humble and to revive the heart of the contrite[38]. . . . Who is like Yahweh, our God, enthroned on high, but who condescends to look down upon heaven and earth? He raises up the needy from the dust, and from the dunghill advances the poor to high estate."[39] After the author of the Book of Wisdom had praised the greatness and might of God and had emphasized the nothingness of the world he continued, "You have mercy upon all because you can do all things, and you overlook the sins of men in order that they do penance."[40] And alongside the passage, "Who dares say: What have you done? Or who can withstand your sentence?" he placed the following, "Your power is the foundation of your justice, and because you are Lord of all, you make yourself gracious to all."[41]

§ 10.   THE ETERNITY AND CHANGELESSNESS OF GOD

1. ETERNITY OF GOD. God is eternal, i.e., He is without beginning and without end. The divine name, Yahweh, "the One who is," embodies this truth, as also the title "the Living God."[1] The first verse in Sacred Scripture, "In the beginning God created heaven and earth," implies the eternity of the creator, because all things apart from Him owe their existence to Him, while He alone existed before any creature. The psalmist praises God who was "before the mountains were born, before the earth and the world came into being, even from eternity to eternity."[2] And to give some weak notion of the meaning of eternity he continues, "A thousand years in your eyes are as yesterday after it has passed, yes, it is like a watch in the night on the *following morning.*"[3] The longest period imaginable to the sacred poet was a thousand years, but to God these thousand years are as a day that, when past, appears very brief, briefer too than the few hours of a vanished night watch. Yahweh says of Himself, "I am the first, and with the last I am still the same."[4] How insignificant is the life of a man in comparison with God's! "Are your days like the days of man, your years like those of a mortal?[5] . . . . Inscrutable is the number of his years."[6]

The words for "eternity," *(olam, qedem, (ad, neṣaḥ, tamid,)ethan,* frequently denote nothing more than *a long period of time.* Eternal are the hills which had a beginning,[7] eternal too are periods long since past.[8] To Amos the times of David were "everlasting days,"[9] and by "days of eternity" Micheas understood the period when the northern and southern kingdoms were united.[10]

38. Is. 57:15.   39. Pss. 113:5-6; 138:6.   40. Wis. 11:23.   41. Wis. 12:12, 16.
1. § 5:2.   44:6; 48:12; Sir. 42:21.   8. Gen. 6:4; Deut. 32:7; Ez.
2. Ps. 90:2.   5. Job 10:5.   26:20.
3. Ps. 90:4.   6. Job 36:26.   9. Am. 9:11.
4. Is. 41:4; cf. Is. 43:10;   7. Deut. 33:15.   10. Mich. 7:14.

Moses said the precepts regulating the pasch would last forever,[11] also those regarding the golden lamps,[12] the Sabbath,[13] the showbread,[14] and the contributions assigned to Aaron.[15] The exile would continue forever,[16] but at its end the desolated cities of Judah already were eternal ruins.[17] For Josue Abraham and Nachor lived "from eternity (*me ʿolam*)"[18] on the other side of the Euphrates, i.e., at a time in the dim distant past. A person could become a servant forever, i.e., for the rest of his life.[19] Samuel was dedicated to Yahweh's service "till into eternity,"[20] i.e., all the days of his life.[21] The felicitations extended to kings included the wish that he "live forever."[22] But when *ʿolam* is used of God it receives a more profound connotation. Yahweh was called "the eternal One[23]. . . . the everlasting God[24]. . . . the One who lives forever[25]. . . . the eternal King[26]. . . . the God of old[27]. . . . the Ancient of Days[28] . . . . eternal Light."[29] God's spirit is imperishable,[30] and He swears, "As I live forever . . . ."[31]

The OT teaches that Yahweh had no beginning, while for the Babylonians, Phoenicians, Egyptians and Greeks a complicated theogony is part and parcel of religious lore. For them the gods had a beginning, there was a time when they did not yet exist. The Babylonian creation epic, Enuma elish, begins:

When above the heaven had not (yet) been named,[32]
(And) below the earth had not (yet) been called by a name;[32]
(When) only Apsu primeval, their begetter, (existed),[33]
(And) mother Tiʾamat, who gave birth to them all;
(When) their waters (still) mingled together,
(And) no dry land had been formed (and) not (even) a marsh could be seen;
When none of the gods had been brought into being,
(When) they had not (yet) been called by (their) name (s, and their)
        destinies had not (yet) been fixed:
Then were the gods created in the midst of them.[34]

Hence, in the beginning there existed nothing but chaos, i.e., the primeval waters from which the gods arose in successive generation.[35] The same ideology is found in the cosmogony of Damascius.[36] It is true that in the Enuma elish Apsu was styled the "primeval one," (likewise Tiʾamat), but these primeval principles were not worshipped. They had no beginning, yet met violent deaths at and because of the world's creation. Anu and Enlil conferred upon Marduk "an eternal kingdom."[37] After the formation of the universe the gods praised Marduk's "everlasting rule."[38] Tikultu-ninurta addressed Asshur, "forever be

11. Ex. 12:14.
12. Ex. 27:21.
13. Ex. 31:16.
14. Lev. 24:8.
15. Num. 18:19.
16. Is. 42:14; 57:11.
17. Is. 58:12; 61:4.
18. Jos. 24:2.
19. Ex. 21:6; Deut. 15:17.
20. 1 Sam. 1:22.
21. Cf. Ps. 89:2.
22. 3 Kgs. 1:31; Dan. 2:4; Neh. 2:3; Ps. 21:5.

23. Bar. 4:10, 14, 20; 2 Mach. 1:25.
24. Gen. 21:33.
25. Dan. 12:7; Sir. 18:1.
26. Jer. 10:10; Tob. 13:6.
27. Deut. 33:27.
28. Dan. 7:9, 13, 22.
29. Is. 60:19; Wis. 7:26.
30. Wis. 12:1.
31. Deut. 32:40.
32. I.e., did not yet exist as such.

33. I.e., the begetter of the gods.
34. In the midst of Apsu and Tiʾamat. (Text and Notes taken from: Alexander Heidel, "The Babylonian Genesis," Chicago 1942, p. 7).
35. AOT 109.
36. AOT 138.
37. CH Introd. 1f. AOT 381.
38. Enuma elish VII 134, AOT 128.

your sovereignty."[39] None of these expressions imply eternity in the full sense simply because all the extant gods had a beginning. Consider the text from Nippur published in 1915 by Stephen Langdon under the title, "Sumerian Epic of Paradise, the Flood, and the Fall of Man," which was presented to the world as a parallel to the paradise story. The god Enki (Ea) impregnates the goddess Ninhursag and later the daughter of that union; then he impregnates his grand-daughter and finally his great-granddaughter, who is called Uttu. Uttu produces eight plants which Enki eats, becomes sick and is healed by Ninhursag; Uttu then creates nine gods . . . .[40]

An Egyptian myth describes how the earth emerged from primeval water and how the sun arose from an egg which lay upon it. Another tale tells how from the waters a lotus flower sprouted in which sat the "Sun-Child" who begot the first gods. Another version describes how heaven and earth were not separate before the earth emerged from the waters; Nut, the goddess of the heavens, was still reposing upon her husband Keb, god of earth. Nut's father, Shu, god of the air, pushed himself between them and lifted Nut on high, and with her lifted up on high all that till then was in existence, i.e., every god with his ship.[41] According to another Egyptian story it was Ptah who fashioned the gods.[42] The Egyptians were conversant with divine triads (father, mother, son), even triple triads (without too much concern for numerical exactitude). It was the accepted thing for the gods to beget children. A very ancient origin is meant when they are described as "eternal."

The Phoenicians held that at the beginning there existed chaos and a dark but agreeable breeze. Through the union of these two, Mot, who contained the germ of all things, came into being; thereupon the sun, moon and stars beamed from the sky.[43] At Ugarit tablets were found which describe "The Birth of the Beautiful and Lovable Gods"—another instance of divine beginnings.[44] The Greeks too believed in the temporal origin of their gods; in Homer's mind the gods owed their origin to Okeanos, while Hesiod (who wrote a work called "Theogony") thought they came from Chaos.

2. GOD'S CHANGELESSNESS. Changelessness, the antithesis of mutability, excludes any development or decay, any passing from one condition to another. Since God is eternal He is subject to no progression or retrogression, He is free from all types of change. This too is contained in the name Yahweh, for if God is "being itself," He cannot increase in power or in knowledge, or, for that matter, decrease. This is the teaching of St. Augustine, "What meaning does 'I am who am' have, if not: I am eternal? what meaning does 'I am who am' have, if not: I cannot change myself?"[45] The psalmist sings, "In the beginning you founded the earth, and the heavens are the works of your hands. They shall perish, but you shall remain; all of them shall grow old like a garment and as

39. AOT 264.
40. S.N. Kramer, Enki and Nin-hursag, A Sumerian "Para-dise" Myth, New Haven 1945.
41. Erman 61f.

42. AOT 6.
43. M. J. Lagrange, Etudes sur les religions semitiques,[2] 1905, 405f; V. Zapletal, Der Schöpfungsbericht der Genesis,[2] 1911, 67f.

44. R de Langhe, Les Textes de Ras Shamra II 176f.
45. Sermo 7, 7; cf. Sermo 6, 3; MLP 38:66, 61.

a vesture you shall change them, and they shall be changed. But you are always the selfsame, and your years shall not fail."[46] Like St. Augustine the psalmist places the attribute of eternity alongside that of changelessness.

Personified wisdom, which is by nature like God, also possesses changelessness, "Remaining in herself the same, she renews all things."[47] The decisions of the divine will are immutable, "He does not revoke his words[48]. . . . Indeed I have spoken it and I am not sorry, I have it in mind and will not give it up[49] ....All flesh is grass and all its beauty as the flowers of the field. The grass withers and the flowers fade, but the word of our God remains forever."[50] All earthly things perish like the grass, but what God promises comes to pass. "The heavens shall vanish like smoke, and the earth shall wear out like a garment; its inhabitants shall die like flies, but my salvation shall endure for ever, my righteousness shall never fail."[51] (However the words in Malachy, "I, Yahweh, have not changed,"[52] were not meant to teach that God is changeless by nature; rather that God, the just One who had always punished sinners, now too would chastise the guilty). Because of His changelessness God is frequently called the "Rock," at times the "eternal Rock,"[53] a phrase which implies both concepts, eternity and changelessness.

There are not lacking passages which seemingly predicate to God changes of heart and will, e.g., He forgives and forgets about punishment that had been threatened, He retracts promises given. One of the more significant of these is in Osee, "How could I deliver you over to oppression, Ephraim, abandon you, Israel? My heart turns against me, my mercy too is flaming up. I do not want to act according to my fierce wrath."[54] Yet because of His changelessness God *cannot* regret a decision or an action, a threat or a promise once made. Osee himself continues, "I am God, not man; a Holy One in your midst, *I* do not *destroy*."[55] Evidence that God cannot repent may be found in Num. 23:19; 1 Sam. 15:29. All such passages which imply repentance on God's part are anthropomorphic in nature.[56]

God's changelessness must not be regarded as something inflexible, cold, unyielding, for this would make sinners doubt the value of repentance and amendment, would make the virtuous imagine their piety was a license to sin because they are certain of God's love. The true outlook is developed in Ez. 18:21-29. God in His wisdom foresaw the conversion of sinners, His threats are meant to instill fear and hasten their return.[57] Yahweh determined to destroy Israel after she had worshipped the golden calf, but changed His mind when Moses pleaded fervently.[58] After Amos had petitioned in Israel's favor, "Yahweh relented; it shall not happen, said Yahweh."[59] Such passages demonstrate the power of intercessory prayer and arouse the pious to plead for sinners.[60] Having always known what measure of intercessory prayer would be made in the course of time, God shaped His plan of salvation accordingly from all eternity.

46. Ps. 102:26-28.
47. Wis. 7:27.
48. Is. 31:2.
49. Jer. 4:28.
50. Is. 40:6, 8.
51. Is. 51:6, 8; cf. Is. 46:4.

52. Mal. 3:6.
53. Is. 26:4.
54. Os. 11:8-9.
55. Os. 11:9.
56. Cf. § 8:3.

57. Jer. 18:8, 10; 26:3, 13, 19; 42:10.
58. Ex. 33:12f; cf. Ex. 32:11-14.
59. Am. 7:3, 6.
60. § 35:5.

§ 11. GOD'S HOLINESS

1. GENERAL CONSIDERATIONS. God's holiness is mentioned so frequently and with such emphasis in the OT that some authors have attempted to treat all OT doctrine on God under the one heading: Holiness.[1] The word qadoš, holy, qodeš, holiness, is probably derived from qadad, to cut off, rather than from hadaš, to be new, and accordingly clean, pure. It signifies a) to be separated, removed from all that is profane or unclean (hol), and b) destined for Yahweh's service. There is a relationship between the term "holy" and the term "clean," tahor, yet a "clean" object becomes holy only after it has been removed from profane associations and in some manner dedicated to God.

Holy are those places where God revealed Himself or where He is worshipped, e.g., the spot where Moses heard the voice from the burning bush,[2] Jerusalem,[3] Canaan,[4] the tent[5] of which the first section was called the "Holy Place,"[6] the second the "Holy of Holies."[7] The entrance to this tent too was holy;[8] holy was the temple,[9] its altars,[10] its furnishings.[11] Cult days as the Sabbath[12] and feasts[13] were holy, likewise sacrifices and sacrifice-portions,[14] the showbread,[15] persons and things that had come in contact with the altar.[16] Heaven as the dwelling place of God is holy;[17] holy are the priests dedicated to God's service (on which account they are consecrated, i.e., "made holy"),[18] even their clothing is holy.[19] The pious,[20] the cleansed congregation of the future,[21] the angels are holy.[22] Earthly things become holy only when brought into union with God, but God is holiness itself. He is "separated" from all created things, transcends heaven and earth.[23] He is above all moral evil, He is not only sinless, He is per se impeccable, not able to violate the ethical laws which have their source in Him.

2. GOD'S SINLESSNESS. When called to the prophetical office Isaias heard the seraphim chant, "Holy, holy, holy is Yahweh of hosts."[24] The thrice repeated "holy" together with the words, "the whole earth is full of his glory," expressed Yahweh's absolute holiness.[25] Understanding that God thereby demanded holiness on the part of man, the prophet lamented, "Woe to me, I am lost because I am a man with unclean lips, and dwell in the midst of a people with unclean lips."[26] Not only is he a sinner himself, he belongs to a people who habitually violate the divine precepts. A seraph verifies his conviction by purifying his lips with a glowing coal, "Removed is your guilt, your sin is expiated."[27] Isaias, keenly aware of the gap which separates sinful man from the all-holy and sinless God, coined the divine name, "The Holy One of Israel."[28] He knew that the great mass of people had deserted God. Later on Ezechiel too lamented

1. E.g., Hänel.
2. Ex. 3:5.
3. Is. 27:13; 48:2.
4. Zach. 2:17.
5. Ex. 28:43; 29:30; Ps. 20:3.
6. Ex. 26:33.
7. Ex. 26:33.
8. Ex. 29:31; Lev. 6:9.
9. 3 Kgs. 6:16; Ps. 5:8.
10. Ex. 29:37; 30:10.
11. Num. 4:15.
12. Gen. 2:3; Ex. 35:2.
13. Ex. 12:16; Lev. 23:4f.
14. Lev. 2:3; 6:18; 7:1; Num. 18:9.
15. Lev. 24:9; 1 Sam. 21:5.
16. Ex. 29:37; Lev. 6:11-20.
17. Pss. 114:4; 20:7.
18. Ex. 29:1; Lev. 21:6, 23; 22:9.
19. Ex. 29:29.
20. Pss. 16:3; 34:10.
21. Is. 4:3.
22. § 22:1.
23. § 9:1.
24. Is. 6:3.
25. § 17.
26. Is. 6:5.
27. Is. 6:7.
28. § 5:10.

over Israel who by sin desecrated "the holy name" of Yahweh.[29] A further passage testifying to the sinlessness of God is, "The rock, blameless is his work; for all his ways are just, a God who is faithful without *fail*, just and upright is Yahweh."[30] And it is by His holiness that God swears.[31]

Even as God alone is sinless by nature, so He alone is holy in the full sense of the word. "No one is holy as Yahweh[32]. . . . The stars are not pure in his eyes."[33] The angels owe their holiness to God, and between their holiness and God's there is no comparison.[34] Much less may man boast of holiness, even the most saintly. "Is any man in the right over against God, or shall a mortal prove himself pure before his Maker?[35]. . . . What is man, that he should be stainless?"[36]

3. DUTY OF BEING HOLY. The doctrine of God's holiness is so important because from it flows man's duty to render himself like unto God by a holy life. Before giving the Law on Sinai Yahweh proclaimed, "You shall be to me a kingdom of priests, a holy nation."[37] Later He specifically enjoined this duty upon the Israelites, "Be holy, because I, Yahweh, your God, am holy."[38] The all-holy God loathes sin, "Your eyes are too pure to behold evil[39]. . . . You are not one who takes pleasure in wickedness, evil has no rights to your hospitality. You hate all who practice injustice; those who tell lies and practice deceit Yahweh abhors."[40] No wonder that Isaias feared death as he gazed on God, no wonder that in a symbolical manner his lips had to be cleansed.[41] As God hates sin, so He loves virtue, "He loves righteousness, his countenance beholds the virtuous[42]. . . . Yahweh, who may abide in your tabernacle, who may dwell upon your holy hill? He who lives honestly and acts uprightly, who harbors truth in his heart."[43]

Whoever desecrates God's holiness must expect God's punishment. In the vision in which the seraphim praised Yahweh's holiness, Isaias received the commission to proclaim judgment against his sinful kinsmen.[44] Again and again the prophet found it necessary to refer to God's holiness which had set a day of reckoning for the wicked, "Exalted is Yahweh of hosts (seated) in judgment! The holy God proves himself holy through justice."[45] Yahweh swears "by his holiness" that the voluptuous women who oppressed the poor would not escape punishment,[46] and Josue reminded the people that "the holy God" would not forgive defections from His commandments.[47] Even though not always directly stated, it is God as the all-holy One who hates evil; and when the prophets face king and people for Yahweh's sake, it is to safeguard the worship of the all-holy God. The closer a man approaches God—and this is true particularly of priests[48]—the more holy must he be, and the more severe

29. Ez. 36:20-23.
30. Deut. 32:4.
31. Ps. 89:36; cf. Num. 23:19; 1 Sam. 6:20; 15:29; Pss. 77:14; 145:17.
32. 1 Sam. 2:2.
33. Job 25:5.
34. § 22:3.
35. Job 4:17.
36. Job 15:14; cf. 25:4-6; § 38:3.
37. Ex. 19:6.
38. Lev. 19:12; 11:44; Num. 15:40.
39. Hab. 1:13.
40. Pss. 5:5; 11:5.
41. Is. 6:3-7; cf. Am. 5:21; 6:8; Os. 9:15; Is. 1:16;
42. Ps. 11:7.
43. Ps. 15:1-2.
44. Is. 6:9-13.
45. Is. 5:6.
46. Am. 4:2.
47. Jos. 24:19; cf. Am. 2:7.
48. § 3:1.

the punishment if he stumble. Sudden death consumed Nadab and Abiu, sons of Aaron, because they disobeyed God.[49] Core's band of Levites perished.[50] God's holiness was manifested in His judgment upon the nations, "The light of Israel will become a fire, and her Holy One a flame which will burn and consume his (Assyria's) thistles and thorns in one day."[51] By destroying the hosts led by Gog in the final hostile assault upon the messianic kingdom "God will show his greatness and his holiness."[52]

Divine punishment has as its end the sinner's spiritual renovation, "They who remain in Sion and they who still survive in Jerusalem will be called 'Saints.' "[53] "A holy seed" shall remain after the day of judgment.[54] The coming judgment upon the Gentile nations will make them acknowledge Yahweh as the Holy One.[55] The psalmist urges all to praise the "holy name" of Yahweh who "forgives all your failings, who heals all your infirmities."[56]

Ordinances regarding foods, ritual purifications and sacrifices were not meant as ends in themselves but as means to a moral life, to promote that inner sanctity demanded by God.[57]

The holiness of God as an attribute which is ethical in nature and opposed to sin was proclaimed long before the time of the prophets. Those who maintain the contrary ignore the following facts: that the obligation in Ex. 19:5-6 is closely connected with the decalog and the Book of the Covenant; that Moses covered his face at his call since he considered himself a sinner;[58] that because of sin God punished the Sodomites,[59] Jacob and Jacob's sons, sent the flood, called Cain to judgment and drove Adam from paradise. The concept of God's sanctity is proper to Mosaic religion from its very inception as well as to pre-Mosaic religion. The prophets only stressed this truth to a greater extent in their denunciation of a cult that was wholly external.

4. OBJECTIONS TO GOD'S HOLINESS. a) *He showed favoritism* by espousing the cause of the patriarchs and of Israel whether it was good or bad. While Abraham was sojourning in Egypt he handed Sara over to Pharaoh's agents as his sister from fear of being murdered, but also with the hope of receiving some gain.[60] He acted in similar fashion toward Abimelech, king of Gerar.[61] God preserved Sara from adultery, but seemingly sanctioned the deception. Here we must note that the mind of the sacred writer is to be deduced from the harsh words spoken by Pharaoh to Abraham and from Abraham's expulsion from the country. God expressly acknowledged Abimelech's innocence; and Abraham a second time deserved severe censure. Isaac likewise is blamed for declaring that Rebecca was his sister.[62] Because Jacob had obtained the birthright surreptitiously through lying and deceit, he had to leave home with hardly a hope of seeing his parents again, he was cheated by Laban, had to humble himself before Esau upon his return, lost his beloved son Joseph and was deceived by his own sons. After God had chosen the patriarchs for His high

49. Lev. 10:1-3.
50. Num. 16:4-11, 18-24, 35.
51. Is. 10:17.
52. Ez. 38:23.
53. Is. 4:3.
54. Is. 6:13; § 46:5.
55. Ez. 38:23; § 45:6.
56. Ps. 103:1-3.
57. Cf. Lev. 11:44-45; § 33:1; 34:7.
58. Ex. 3:6.
59. Gen. 18:20f.
60. Gen. 12:10f.
61. Gen. 20.
62. Gen. 26:7f.

purposes He protected them in danger. This protection was not intended for their own personal interests, but for the good of mankind. Moreover God imposed heavy obligations; accomplishments had to correspond to privileges; He put them under strict discipline and made them atone for their sins and failings. In Egypt the Israelitic midwives were rewarded by God not because they lied to Pharaoh but because they failed to execute the decree to murder all male infants among the Hebrews.[63] Israel's rights and privileges had corresponding duties, and God knew how to punish when His ordinances were disregarded.

b) *Yahweh acted capriciously.* This accusation is made because Yahweh slew 70 citizens of Bethshemesh after they had gazed upon the ark of the covenant. Note however that it was not a matter of a pious glance but of inquisitive, disrespectful gazing which lessened the reverence due to Israel's holiest object, one which served as Yahweh's throne and as the symbol of the divine presence. The account states that after this visitation the Bethshemites considered themselves unworthy "to stand before Yahweh, the holy God" and therefore sent the ark to Kiriath-jearim.[64] While the ark was being transferred from this latter place to Jerusalem, Oza died as he tried to hold it from falling off the cart.[65] Because he was not a Levite he had no right to touch the ark; moreover Levites should have been there discharging their obligation. God sent this misfortune as a vivid reminder that cult prescriptions must be scrupulously observed. Oza himself acted in good faith, but in ancient times there was no sharp distinction between formal and material sin, and cult offenses were regarded as punishable by death.[66]

c) *God seemingly caused men to sin.* "God tempted Abraham,"[67] i.e., He tested his love and his obedience. Here an opportunity was given Abraham to overcome himself and to purify and elevate his natural love toward his son above all earthly considerations. The trial also served to sanctify him, and so in reality was a great blessing.[68]

The Israelites were told, "Yahweh, your God, will tempt you (i.e., put you to the test) to see whether you actually love Yahweh, your God, with your whole heart and with your whole soul."[69] The psalmist even implored God to try him in order that he might have the opportunity to demonstrate his faith, his obedience and his love.[70] The long and painful test which Job had to undergo was ordained to purify him through suffering and thus to bring him closer to God.[71]

In a few passages God seemingly deludes men and provokes them to sin. In the vision granted to Micheas at the time of Achab and Josaphat, there came forth a spirit who offered to deceive the (false) prophets of Achab. Yahweh gave him permission, "Deceive you may, you will also prevail."[72] Through Micheas God served notice on Achab; if the king would not listen because the

63. Ex. 1:17f.
64. 1 Sam. 6:19-20.
65. 2 Sam. 6:6-7; 1 Chr. 15:13.
66. § 38:4-5.
67. Gen. 22:1.
68. § 41:5.
69. Deut. 13:4.
70. Ps. 26:2.
71. § 41:5.
72. 3 Kgs. 22:19f; § 23:4a.

words of the false prophets were more acceptable, it was his own fault if he failed. The following passages also are pertinent, "When a (false) prophet is misled and utters an oracle, I, Yahweh, have misled that prophet, and I shall stretch forth my hand against him and destroy him from the midst of my people[73]. . . . Yahweh's wrath flamed up against Israel. He incited David against them by saying: Get up, number Israel and Judah."[74] Soon afterwards Yahweh inflicted heavy punishment, and David acknowledged the scourge as due to his sin.[75] Immediately upon finishing the census the king was filled with remorse, "I have sinned exceedingly by that which I have done."[76] Joab and other officials had been minded against the census.[77] A census was considered to be sinful.[78] God had promised to Abraham innumerable descendants, and no one should try to count them. There was also a certain amount of pride in David's attempt to find out the number of men capable of bearing arms; the king would then consider his own forces sufficiently strong to win victory apart from divine help. When persecuted by Saul David exclaimed, "If Yahweh has incited you against me, let him be given a sacrifice to smell."[79] If God was the cause why Saul was so hostile, David wished to appease Him by sacrifice. True, David did no evil to Saul, but still he was a sinner before God. Semei's curse David regarded as a divine punishment for his sins, "He was ordered to do so by Yahweh."[80]

According to some passages Yahweh made the hearts of Pharaoh and the Egyptians obstinate,[81] while according to others Pharaoh hardened his own heart.[82] Now we should always be mindful of how divine grace and human freedom work together. God knew beforehand how Pharaoh would misuse his freedom and how miracles would merely strengthen him in his opposition. Pharaoh himself admitted his sin,[83] but being stiffnecked refused to amend; he preferred to repeat the same sins, even though the Egyptian magicians recognized "the finger of God" in the miracles performed.[84] Inasmuch as God conferred graces which, as He knew, would be rejected, did He cause Pharaoh's hardness of heart. Pharaoh's fault did not thereby become less great; had he not striven against grace, grace would have aided him; he would have been spared the impending catastrophes and would even have been granted knowledge of Yahweh's preeminence.

The preaching of the prophets produced results quite similar. Israel ignored every exhortation, and persevering in her evil ways alienated herself farther and farther from God until judgment came upon her. Upon the prophet Isaias Yahweh imposed the mission, "Make obdurate the heart of this people, harden their ears and plaster tight their eyes."[85] Yahweh poured out upon Israel a "spirit of insensibility."[86] Other passages according to which God hardens, deceives or incites to sin are: Deut. 2:30; Jos. 11:20; 1 Sam. 2:25; 2 Sam.

73. Ez. 14:9.
74. 2 Sam. 24:1.
75. 2 Sam. 24:17.
76. 2 Sam. 24:10.
77. 2 Sam. 24:3-4.
78. Cf. Ex. 30:12.

79. 1 Sam. 26:19.
80. 2 Sam. 16:10-11; § 35:7.
81. Ex. 4:21; 7:3; 9:12; 10:1, 20, 27; 11:10; 14:4, 8, 17.

82. Ex. 8:11, 28; 9:34.
83. Ex. 9:27; 10:16.
84. Ex. 8:15.
85. Is. 6:10.
86. Is. 29:10.

12:11 (cf. 16:21-22); 16:11; 17:14; 3 Kgs. 12:15; 22:19-23; cf. § 23:4a.

These passages are not to be studied separately, but in the light of the whole teaching of the OT upon God. In an evil act a distinction must be made between the action in itself and its malice. Because man is utterly unable to perform any act, or have even the slightest thought, unless God gives the power for such activity, God is said to cooperate in positing the action, while the evil inherent in it remains the fault of man. OT theology emphasizes God's ultimate causality so strongly[87] that secondary causality, i.e., that due to the human will, recedes into the background. In earlier epochs the Israelites did not discuss the problem whether God caused moral evil directly, or whether He merely permitted man's misuse of free will. In 2 Sam. 24:1 Yahweh incites David to evil, in 1 Chr. 21:1 it is Satan.[88] Even as late as the time of Zacharias Yahweh declared, "I incite all men against one another."[89] The sacred writers did not determine the boundaries between God as first cause and human will with theological precision, but they were fully aware that God's causality did not destroy human freedom and with it personal responsibility. God "commands no one to act wickedly, he gives no man license to sin."[90] This is proven by the commandments as well as the admonitions and threats of the prophets. The paradise story already shows how God hates sin, but will not deprive man of the use of his free will. In Ez. 20:25 we read, "I gave them statutes that were not good," and as an example child-sacrifice is mentioned. God did not enjoin such sacrifices; on the contrary He had forbidden them.[91] But He did permit the people to retain their free wills with which they committed the outrage, and in this sense God did "what was not good." Jesus too preached to the Jews, worked countless miracles to win them over, although He knew beforehand how His preaching and miracle working would occasion their ruin. "If I had not come and spoken to them, they would have no sin. But now they have no excuse for their sin."[92] Jesus chose Judas and dealt patiently with him even though He knew well who would betray Him; neither did He hinder the perfidious act.[93] For further mention of blameworthy opposition to the truth, cf. Matth. 13:13-15; Jn. 12:37-41; Acts 28:25-27 (quoting Is. 6:9-10).

When the OT says that God provokes to sin or hardens the heart, the underlying judgment is quite unlike similar statements found in e.g., Homer. For the Greek poet the gods purposely deluded those upon whom they intended to bring evil. OT thought is also quite unlike that in the Greek tragedies where, e.g., Oedipus is driven by a pitiless fate, or that expressed in the Latin proverb, *Quem deus perdere vult, dementat.* In the OT man remains free in making decisions, he is responsible for his actions; and God is just when He punishes.

According to Ex. 3:18 Moses was ordered to demand permission from Pharaoh to lead the Israelites into the desert for the purpose of offering sacrifice.[94] Yahweh was not thereby directing Moses to lie; He merely wanted to put Pharaoh to the test,[95] although He knew beforehand Pharaoh's course of

87. § 25:6.
88. § 23:4a.
89. Zach. 8:10.

90. Sir. 15:20.
91. § 33:4.
92. Jn. 15:22.

93. Matth. 26:21f.
94. Cf. Ex. 5:1; 7:16; 8:23.
95. Ex. 3:19.

action. There is no case of deceit and robbery maneuvered by Yahweh in Ex. 3:21-22; 11:2; 12:35-36. The Israelites did not "borrow" clothing and valuable articles from the Egyptians with the intention of not returning them; they were to demand them (*ša'al*) "as payment for their labors,"[96] since for many years they had been unjustly deprived of freedom and had been forced to do heavy work without pay. Furthermore because of their hasty departure they left behind their houses and furnishings, they surrendered all claim to grain ripening upon their fields; for these things the articles taken were to some extent compensation. Having been forced to let Israel leave, the Egyptians did not expect them to return to slavery—in this they were not deceived![97]

5. "HOLINESS" OF PAGAN GODS. It is true that the Gentiles equipped their gods with moral virtues, ascribed to them human characteristics such as justice, mercy, love, and when seeking special favors they would raise these attributes to a most eminent degree. Alongside the holiness ascribed to pagan gods there was much that was not holy, alongside the preternatural much that was of the earth, earthy. In the OT holiness is proper to God first and foremost; in the other religions the word "holy" is used primarily with reference to cult objects, very seldom of divinity itself.[98] OT concepts of God are free from the least trace of mythology; in other religions mythology plays a noteworthy role as it attributes to the gods dissension, envy, jealousy, injustice, immorality, greed. In the Bible a holy God sent the flood to punish sinners only after He had given them a time of grace for repentance; the building of the ark was a final warning, and Noe was saved only because he was just. Quite different the Mesopotamian accounts. Utnapishtim, the hero in the Babylonian deluge story, is informed by Ea, who acts without the knowledge of and against the will of other gods. Utnapishtim is told to deceive his fellowmen concerning the purpose of the ship he is to build; the reason for the flood is the whim of the gods, and only at the story's end do we find some indication that it had been intended as punishment upon evildoers. However at the same time Enlil is blamed for having thoughtlessly destroyed the innocent along with the guilty. The gods did not foresee what great evils they occasioned, and, frightened over the consequences, lamented loudly. The epic ends as they greedily assemble "like flies over the sacrifice" to smell the sweet savor.[99]

At the sight of Gilgamesh's beauty Ishtar burnt with lust, having no control over her passion.[100] Even among themselves the gods committed adultery.[101] The gods, Ishtar in particular, took pleasure in obscenities performed in their honor in the temples. In the creation epic Enuma elish, Nudimmud (Ea) through a holy incantation casts a spell upon his ancestor Apsu and then slays him.[102] A Sumerian text recounts how Enki committed numerous acts of incest. An Egyptian myth describes how the goddess Hathor proceeded to murder mankind. To bring the bloody purge to an end Re orders a great mess of beer

96. Wis. 10:17; cf. Jub. 48:18.
97. On atrocities in war, cf. § 32:1e, on physical evils, § 41:1, on "the evil spirit from Yahweh," § 20:7.
98. Hänel 26; Eichrodt I 140.
99. Gilgamesh Epic. 11, AOT 175f.
100. Ibid. 6, AOT 160.
101. Ex Oriente Lux Jaarbericht 4, 1936, 200f.
102. Enuma elish I 55f.

brewed; the goddess drinks till she is drunk and no longer can recognize a human being.[103] In another myth Isis feels her power encroached upon because she does not know Re's secret name. By trick and intrigue she endeavors to discover it, and does not shrink from causing a poisonous snake to bite the father of the gods. Re becomes helpless, he wails; the other gods, ignorant of what counsel to give, simply moan until Re reveals his name to Isis and she condescends to heal him.[104] The Ugarit tablets make frequent mention of the "virgin" Anat, sister and consort of Baal. She was goddess of love and goddess of war, as was Ishtar in Babylon. As war goddess she found great pleasure in smiting the foe till "heads fell like globes, and hands flew like grasshoppers." Savagely she mutilated the fallen, bathing her legs and breasts in blood, and washing her hands in the gore of the slain.[105] Ugaritic records recount battles between the gods, and sacrifices offered by the gods themselves in support of their wishes (e.g., Mot's; also Anat's for the dead Baal).[106] Scenes such as that in which Baal as a bull copulates with Anat in a meadow, or in which El seduces two goddesses would have been utterly abhorrent to the inspired writers.[107] Serious minded men readily admit that the myths of the Greeks and Romans recount much about the gods that was unworthy of them and injurious to the morals of young persons. There have been attempts to concentrate attention on the more ethical and cultural passages while explaining away scandalous sections by allegorical interpretations.

§ 12. GOD'S OMNIPOTENCE

Yahweh alone has existence of Himself, everything outside His divine being rests upon His omnipotent creative act. Divine omnipotence is expressed by the names El (the strong One), Šadday (the Almighty), by phrases like "the mighty One of Jacob,"[1] the "strong One of Israel,"[2] by metaphors referring to Yahweh's hand or arm, symbols of His power.

God manifested His omnipotence by calling the world into existence.[3] He is the "creator of heaven, the moulder and maker of the earth."[4] As creator He is "God of heaven and earth[5].... Lord of all the world."[6] Creation should make us marvel at God's omnipotence, "The heavens show forth the glory of God, and the firmament declares the work of his hands."[7] Even at this very moment all natural phenomena are His work.[8] As we observe how God removes mountains unexpectedly, causes hills to spring up, eclipses the sun, we cannot but conclude, "He does things great and incomprehensible, deeds wonderful and without number."[9] After God had shown Job how His power was manifested in the creation of the world and how it ought to be constantly discernible in

103. AOTB I² 4f.
104. Roeder 138f.
105. Bea Bb 20, 1939, 446; Aistleitner, ZatW 57, 1939, 206f; R. Dussaud, Les combats de 'Anat et le pouvoir universel El, RHR 118, 133-169.
106. ZatW 57, 198F.
107. ThRdsch 13, 1941, 178.

1. Gen. 49:24.
2. Is. 1:24.
3. § 24.
4. Is. 45:16; cf. Is. 44:24; Jer. 27:5; Ps. 135:6; Sir.
43:2; Wis. 11:17.
5. Gen. 24:3.
6. Jos. 3:11, 13; Ps. 97:5; Zach. 4:14; 6:5.
7. Ps. 19:2; cf. Ps. 89:12-13; Sir. 43:29.
8. § 25:1-2.
9. Job 9:4-10; cf. 5:9; 26:5-14.

the phenomena of nature and in the animal kingdom,[10] the patient sufferer confessed, "I acknowledge that you can do all things, no project is impossible for you."[11] A striking aspect of God's omnipotence lies in the fact that He merely has to exercise His will to obtain results. A simple *fiat* brought the universe and all within it into being. "God said: Let there be light! And there was light."[12]

God made man, man consequently is wholly dependent upon God.[13] The might of man is as nothing in God's eyes, "If Yahweh of hosts has decreed, who can disannul it? His outstretched hand, who can turn it back?"[14] When nations rise in revolt against Him, He is able to annihilate them, "Yahweh is riding upon a swift cloud, he is going toward Egypt. Egypt's idols shall reel before him, and the heart of Egypt shall dissolve within her."[15] It will be as easy as play for Yahweh to prepare the destruction of Assyrian world power, for to Him Assyria is nothing more than chaff and dry leaves in the wind.[16] The psalmist admonished all to subject themselves to Yahweh's power, "Say to God: How awe-inspiring are your deeds! Because of your great power your enemies must flatter you."[17] And when the whole world turns into tumult against God—"He who is enthroned in heaven laughs, the Lord makes fun of them."[18]

God showed His omnipotence through many centuries as He guided the people of Israel. The liberation from slavery in Egypt, the journey through the wilderness and the occupation of Canaan were so many manifestations of the might of Israel's God. The miracles performed in Israel's behalf are extolled in Pss. 74:13-15; 77:14-21; 78; 107; Wis. 10:15-11:20; 16:1-19:17. True, the pagans made sport of the Chosen People when they were in distress, "Where is your God now?" Israelitic history however amply demonstrates how God "accomplished whatsoever pleased him," while Gentile gods remained powerless.[19] When God had resolved to lead the exiles back home from Babylon, no power on earth was able to obstruct it.[20] Full of trust Mardochai prayed as annihilation threatened his people, "Lord, almighty king, all things are in your power, and there is no one who can resist your will if you determine to save Israel."[21] Referring to His future work of redemption God said to Zacharias, "If it seem unbelievable in the eyes of the remnant of this people in those days, shall it also seem unbelievable in my eyes?"[22]

The miracles through which Yahweh modified the life story of the patriarchs and of Israel are proofs of His omnipotence; they are termed "mighty deeds."[23] "Is anything impossible for Yahweh?" was the question put to Abraham as God planned to give his aged and sterile wife Sara a son.[24] In the desert Yahweh promised flesh meat to the Israelites and upbraided Moses who at first doubted whether a miracle would be worked, "Is Yahweh's hand too weak?"[25] Centuries later when the Israelites continued their evil ways despite all exhortations,

10. Job 38:1-41:26.
11. Job 42:2.
12. Gen. 1:3; Pss. 33:9; 148:5; Sir. 39:18, 20; Is. 40:28.
13. Deut. 32:39; 1 Sam. 2:6; Tob. 13:2.
14. Is. 14:27; cf. 43:13.
15. Is. 19:1; cf. § 45.
16. Is. 17:12-14.
17. Ps. 66:3.
18. Ps. 2:4.
19. Ps. 115:2-7.
20. Is. 43:13; 46:10.
21. Esth. 13:9.
22. Zach. 8:6.
23. Deut. 3:24; Ps. 106:2; cf. Ps. 118:23.
24. Gen. 18:14.
25. Num. 11:23.

God determined to use His power to destroy their very capital, "Truly I am Yahweh, the God of all flesh. Is there any miracle too great for me?"[26] Treating of God's judgment upon Egypt the author of the Book of Wisdom established the fact that it lay in God's power not only to send a multitude of bears or furious lions against them, but also to create an entirely unknown species of beasts, more dangerous than those already existing, or He could simply "sweep sinners away by the breath of his omnipotence."[27]

§ 13. GOD'S IMMENSITY AND OMNIPRESENCE

Because of His infinite perfection God is not only independent of time, having neither beginning nor end, but He is also wholly free from spatial limitations; He is immense, omnipresent.

1. GOD'S IMMENSITY. Before tangible things came into existence space, in the proper sense of the word, did not exist. Even then God enjoyed the attribute of immensity. In his inaugural vision Isaias saw Yahweh in heaven seated "on a high and elevated throne" with garments flowing down and filling the temple.[1] Well might Yahweh have said, "Heaven is my throne, and the earth a stool for my feet[2]. . . . Heaven and earth, is it not I who fill them?"[3] At the dedication of the temple Solomon humbly admitted, "The heaven and the heaven of heavens cannot contain you, how much less this house that I have built!"[4]

2. GOD'S OMNIPRESENCE. God is creator of the whole world and consequently is not confined to any particular corner. There are indications in primitive as well as in patriarchal history of God watching over all men wherever they might be, aiding them, calling them to judgment. On this subject the author of Proverbs leaves no doubt, "The eyes of Yahweh are in every place, they behold the good and the wicked."[5] Indeed God lives in heaven and has His throne there,[6] and we pray in the Our Father, "Who art in heaven." Heaven however is not to be understood in too spatial a sense. The word implies that God transcends creation and that He beholds all things. "Who is like Yahweh, our God, enthroned on high, but who condescends to look down upon heaven and earth? He raises up the needy from the dust, and from the dunghill advances the poor to high estate[7]. . . . He has looked down from his holy heights, from heaven he has glanced upon the earth to hear the groans of them who are in fetters, to liberate those destined to death."[8] By appearing to the fathers in various localities God showed that He was not confined to any one particular place, heaven for instance. To express God's transcendency the psalmist speaks of the "heaven of heavens," i.e., the highest heaven,[9] and Solomon asserts that the heaven and the heaven of heavens are not able to contain Him.[10]

Because God is present everywhere He is able to summon every sinner to

26. Jer. 32:27.

27. Wis. 11:17-20; on miracles, cf. § 25:6.

1. Is. 6:1f.
2. Is. 66:1.
3. Jer. 23:24.
4. 3 Kgs. 8:27; cf. Deut. 4:39; Job 11:7-9.
5. Prov. 15:3; cf. 5:21.

6. Pss. 2:4; 11:4; 68:6; 103:19; 123:1; Deut. 26:15; 3 Kgs. 8:34, 39f; Am. 9:6; Is. 63:15; Bar. 2:16; Dan. 3:53.

7. Ps. 113:5-6.
8. Ps. 102:20-21; cf. Ps. 11:4-5; Is. 57:15.
9. Ps. 148:4.
10. 3 Kgs. 8:27.

judgment. "None of them who run away will save themselves. If they break into Sheol, from thence my hand will bring them out; if they mount up to heaven, from thence I shall topple them down; if they hide on the summit of Carmel I shall hunt them out and take them away from thence; if they conceal themselves from my eyes on the ocean floor, there shall I bid my serpent to bite them."[11] Nowhere can the sinner find safety, while the just may depend upon God's aid wherever he be and in whatever trouble he find himself, "If you pass through waters, I am with you; if through rivers, they shall not cover you. If you go through fire, you shall not be singed, and the flames shall not burn you."[12] He may trust in God unreservedly, "Do not forsake me, Yahweh, do not remain far away from me; hasten to my aid, O Lord, my salvation."[13]

Jonas was unable to escape from the divine presence although he boarded a ship bound for Tartessus; and as he preached in Niniveh he was instructed and reprimanded by God. God is everywhere and accordingly may be worshipped in any place. Yahweh reproached the Israelites, "I was (waiting) to be sought by those who did not ask for me, I was (waiting) to be found by those who did not seek for me. I said: Here I am, here I am, to a people who did not invoke my name."[14] A classic passage for portraying God's omnipresence is, "Whither can I go from your spirit, whither can I flee from your face? If I ascend to heaven, you are there, if I make my bed in Sheol, behold, you are there! If I arrived at the borders of the dawn, or lived at the limits of the sea, even there your accompanying hand would maintain me, your right hand hold me!"[15]

God is omnipresent not only by knowledge and power but also by nature.[16] In the Book of Wisdom we find this tersely summarized, "The spirit of the Lord fills the whole world, and he who embraces all knows every spoken word[17].... Your immortal spirit is in all things,"[18] i.e., all created things, particularly man. Although omnipresent God ever remains invisible to human eyes.[19]

The doctrine concerning God's omnipresence became more profound under the influence of the author of the Book of Wisdom, who recognized differences in the mode of God's presence. He says of personified wisdom, "(she) permeates all spirits, those intelligent, pure and most refined; for wisdom is more active than all activity, she permeates and penetrates all things by reason of her purity[20].... Full of strength she reaches from one end (of the world) to the other conducting all things excellently."[21] According to Wis. 7:24 everything that exists is permeated by wisdom and preserved thereby,[22] consequently the wicked also. But wisdom will not enter an unclean soul,[23] still less will she abide with evil spirits. Wisdom is present *ratione substantiae* in irrational creatures and in the wicked, but pious souls and the angels are in addition enlightened and sanctified by her, "From generation to generation she enters holy

11. Am. 9:1-3.
12. Is. 43:2.
13. Ps. 38:22-23; cf. Pss. 11:4, 7; 33:13, 18.
14. Is. 65:1.
15. Ps. 139:7-10.
16. Cf. Jer. 23:24.
17. Wis. 1:7.
18. Wis. 12:1.
19. Job 9:11; 23:8; § 8:1.
20. Wis. 7:23-24.
21. Wis. 8:1.
22. Cf. Wis. 7:27; 8:1.
23. Wis. 1:4.

souls and makes them friends of God, and prophets."[24] Divine wisdom, present in the wicked, remains "unstained" because she is holy.[25]

3. PLACES FAVORED BY GOD'S PRESENCE. There is no conflict between the truth of God's omnipresence and the practice of worshipping Him in a particular manner at certain definite places. Cain's complaint, "You are driving me away today from the fields, and I must hide myself from your face,"[26] indicates he believed God could not be worshipped by sacrifice on the distant steppes; yet even there did God will to protect the murderer.[27] When Jacob awoke after dreaming of the ladder which reached to heaven, he said, "Truly Yahweh is in this place, and I did not know it. Here indeed is the house of God, and the gate of heaven."[28] God had revealed Himself in that place and thereby had sanctified it. Likewise Yahweh was present over the cherubim upon the cover of the ark of the covenant,[29] and in the tent of meeting.[30] In Canaan, Yahweh's own land, there were various sanctuaries where He was worshipped in a special manner; of these the more famous were at Shiloh, and after Shiloh's destruction, at Nob and Gibeon. Most illustrious however was the temple at Jerusalem.[31] Yet Solomon acknowledged, "Is it then to be thought that God should indeed dwell upon earth?"[32] The 3rd verse of Ps. 20 implores God to send aid "from his sanctuary, from Sion," but in verse 7 God answers the petition "from his heaven." Everywhere God is close to men, and His worship is not confined to particular localities. Abraham's servant prayed in Mesopotamia,[33] Moses in Egypt[34] and in the wilderness,[35] Samson in Philistia,[36] Absolom in exile at Geshur in Syria,[37] Elias in Phoenicia,[38] Jonas in Niniveh,[39] Ezechias,[40] Sara,[41] Judith[42] and Daniel[43] in their homes. It is true God willed to receive honor at particular places, but this did not imply that He dwelt there. Yahweh appeared to Moses on Horeb,[44] descended upon Sinai when the covenant was made,[45] went forth from Seir as is recounted in the song of Debbora.[46] And Elias made a pilgrimage to Horeb[47] although the temple was located in Jerusalem. A contradiction could arise only in case these passages were interpreted: Yahweh is only in heaven, only in the tabernacle, only on Horeb, i.e., if we attempted to circumscribe Him spatially. Tabernacle and temple were sacred sites where the faithful could turn to God with greater trust; here He had revealed Himself in a visible way and here was reserved the ark of the covenant, His throne on earth.[48] Just as God is present in created things in various ways, so also is He present in various ways at different places of cult. Contrary to what one might surmise, it was only in later centuries when the concepts of God's spirituality together with that of His omnipresence were more clearly understood,

24. Wis. 7:27.
25. Wis. 7:22.
26. Gen. 4:14, 16.
27. Gen. 4:15; concerning God's "face," cf. § 8:2.
28. Gen. 28:16-17.
29. Ex. 25:22; Num. 7:89; 10:35; 2 Sam. 6:2.
30. Ex. 40:34.
31. 3 Kgs. 8:10, 27f; 9:3; Pss.

20:3; 42:3; Am. 1:2; Is. 8:18.
32. 3 Kgs. 8:27.
33. Gen. 24:12f.
34. Ex. 8:8, 25, 26; 9:33; 10:18.
35. Ex. 15:25; 16:4.
36. Judg. 16:28.
37. 2 Sam. 15:8.
38. 3 Kgs. 17:20.

39. Jon. 4:2.
40. 4 Kgs. 20:2.
41. Tob. 3:11.
42. Jud. 8:5.
43. Dan. 6:11.
44. Ex. 3.
45. Ex. 19.
46. Judg. 5:4.
47. 3 Kgs. 19:8.
48. Ex. 40:34-38; 3 Kgs. 8:10.

that His veneration by sacrifice was localized to one definite spot—proof that such practice was in no way opposed to belief in divine omnipresence.

Of course many Israelites thought themselves secure from all enemies simply because the temple was in their midst; they would not acknowledge that divine protection was merited by obeying the commandments. It was these who boasted, "Is Yahweh not in our midst? No evil can come upon us."[49] The prophets thought differently, and foretold the temple's destruction, "Sion shall be plowed as a field, Jerusalem shall become a desolation and the temple hill a wooded height."[50] As the temple and city sank in ruins the masses learnt that Yahweh was nigh to them in foreign lands too. The prophets, who had warned against false confidence in the temple, now after the exile was over strove for its reconstruction,[51] promising Yahweh's return to Sion.[52] And as they prophesied the conversion of the Gentiles in messianic times, they employed the picture of the nations making pilgrimages to Sion and its temple, from which the true religion would have its origin.[53]

According to prevailing pagan views the gods lived in the heavens, yet were intimately associated with and symbolized by the stars. In many localities the cult of celestial Baals gave birth to the notion that many Baals really existed. In Israel however even though Yahweh had revealed Himself at numerous sites and was pleased with sacrifices offered in various places until the centralization of cult was effected, there never arose any tendency to dissect Yahwism in a polytheistic fashion. Ancient oriental thought linked the gods to their temples or idols in a very concrete way. Having captured a city the victorious army took along its idols, certain that the fallen city would thereby be deprived of divine protection and that the captured gods would then direct their aid toward themselves. Only when the images were returned did the gods return.

§ 14. GOD IS ALL-KNOWING

God's knowledge differs from that of His creatures in three ways, a) He possesses it perfectly—it can in no way be increased;[1] b) because He is the eternal One who knows no change, His knowledge is eternally contemporaneous as He surveys the past, present and future;[2] c) His knowledge is absolutely certain knowledge, subject to no doubt or error.

1. DIVINE SELF-KNOWLEDGE. The doctrine of God's self-knowledge is implied in the name, "I am who am," which was revealed to Moses. It also flows from the fact that God has revealed His attributes to man. The fullness of this knowledge can be shared with no creature, since created intellects are and ever remain imperfect.[3]

2. GOD'S KNOWLEDGE OF CREATION. Belief in an omniscient God fills the whole OT. "He beholds the ends of the earth, he *causes* her (i.e., divine wisdom

49. Mich. 3:11.
50. Mich. 3:12;   Jer.   7:4f; 26:6; Ez. 10.
51. Ez. 40-48; Is. 44:28; 56:7; 60:7; Agg. 1:8; Zach. 1:16.
52. Ez. 43:1-4; Is. 52:8.
53. Is. 56:7; 60:10f; Zach. 14:16; § 48:2; 49:3.
1. § 9:2.
2. § 10:1.
3. § 4:3.

personified) to look on all things under the heavens. When he wrought a weight for the wind and weighed the waters according to measure by making a law for rain, as also a road for the rumbling thunder—then did he gaze upon her and proclaim her; he established her, since it also was he who had fathomed her[4]. ... All things were known to him before they were created, so also after they were completed[5]. ... He determines the number of the stars, he calls them all by name; his wisdom is limitless[6]. ... I know every bird in the heights (of heaven), and whatsoever moves in the field is present before me."[7] Not even Sheol, which is far beyond the reach of human vision, is hidden from God, "Sheol lies naked before him, unveiled the Abyss[8]. ... Sheol and the Abyss lie open before Yahweh, how much more the heart of the children of men."[9]

3. GOD'S KNOWLEDGE OF MAN, EVEN OF HIS MOST SECRET THOUGHTS. According to the OT neither the deeds nor the plans of men are hidden from Yahweh, who "proves hearts and reins,"[10] who knows "the secrets of the heart[11]. ... O God, all my desire is manifest to you, my groans are not hidden from you[12]. ... Men glance at the *face*, Yahweh however beholds the heart[13] .... He scrutinizes the hearts of all the children of men."[14] "She (wisdom) knows the past and *discloses* the future. Signs and wonders she knows beforehand, and the results of times and seasons."[15]

God's knowledge embraces every individual. God knows each person before he begins to exist, "Before I fashioned you in (your) mother's womb, I chose you[16]. ... Say not: I am hidden away from God; up there, who thinks about me? Among so many people I shall not be noticed; what am I in this immense creation?"[17] God knows the purpose had in performing an action and thus can better judge one's deed than the person himself, "A man may consider all his ways pure, but it is Yahweh who examines motives."[18]

God's omniscience is denied only by the wicked who do not wish to abandon their sinful ways. Deluding themselves like fools they say while oppressing the innocent and helpless, "God is forgetful, he has hidden his face, he did not even see it[19]. ... Yahweh does not see it, the God of Jacob will keep nought of it in mind."[20]

God's knowledge includes all free acts which men will posit in the future. When Yahweh committed to Moses the task of demanding from Pharaoh leave of absence for the Israelites, He foretold the king's refusal.[21] "He knew beforehand their future behavior," i.e., the Egyptians would pursue the Israelites whom they had just urged to leave.[22] To the Canaanites Yahweh gave an opportunity to repent although He knew their dispositions would never change.[23] "My days were specified even as I was being fashioned, when none of them yet

4. Job 28:24-27.
5. Sir. 23:20.
6. Ps. 147:4-5.
7. Ps. 50:11.
8. Job 26:6.
9. Prov. 15:11; cf. Ps. 139:7-13.
10. Ps. 7:10; Jer. 11:20: 17:10.

11. Ps. 44:22.
12. Ps. 38:10.
13. 1 Sam. 16:7.
14. 3 Kgs. 8:39.
15. Wis. 8:8; cf. Zach. 4:10; Ps. 139:1-4; Prov. 5:21; 15:11; Esth. 14:15; Sir. 15:18; 23:19; 39:19-20; Wis. 1:6.

16. Jer. 1:15.
17. Sir. 16:17.
18. Prov. 16:2; 21:2; 24:12.
19. Ps. 10:11.
20. Ps. 94:7; cf. Is. 29:15; Ez. 8:12; 9:9.
21. Ex. 3:19.
22. Wis. 19:1.
23. Wis. 12:10.

were mine."[24] Susanna prayed in her affliction, "Eternal God, you who know that which is hidden, you who know all things before they come to pass . . . ."[25] Prophecies rest upon divine foreknowledge, "He has revealed his plans to his servants, the prophets[26]. . . . The old (prophecies), behold, they have come to pass; new ones shall I (henceforth) proclaim. Before things burst forth I shall inform you of them."[27]

Because God is omniscient He needs no counsellor. While in the pagan pantheons the gods take counsel, dispute among themselves and contradict each other, in Yahweh's heavenly court the angels simply and humbly receive all divine communiques and commands without question or comment. *"Who as his adviser has taught him? With whom has he taken counsel?"*[28]

4. GOD'S KNOWLEDGE OF FUTURE FREE ACTS. By this is meant that God knows the course of action which would be pursued in any given contingency. David asked Yahweh whether Saul would come to Keilah, his place of refuge. There was always some possibility that Saul would discontinue the pursuit even as he did a short time later in the wilderness of Ziph. On this occasion Saul had almost taken David before calling off the chase because the Philistines were again advancing into Israelitic territory.[29] The oracle's answer was in the affirmative, "He will come up." Then David asked whether the inhabitants of Keilah, whom he had just defended against the Philistines, would deliver him over to the king. Again an affirmative, "They will deliver you over." Thereupon David and his company abandoned Keilah. When Saul was informed he discontinued the trek, and the citizens of Keilah were never asked to betray David to his enemy.[30] God knew beforehand with perfect certainty that Saul would have continued the pursuit had David remained at Keilah, and how the city's inhabitants would conduct themselves when Saul appeared before the gates. As the siege of Jerusalem was nearing its end, Jeremias placed two alternatives before King Sedecias: if he surrendered himself to Nabuchodonosor, his life and family would be spared and Jerusalem would not be destroyed; if he refused to capitulate, the city would be set on fire and he would be taken into captivity. Now the king's great fear was that if he surrendered, Nabuchodonosor would deliver him to the Judeans who would revile and mishandle him. To this Jeremias answered, "They will not hand you over."[31] After the murder of the Babylonian official Godolias, the Jews asked the prophet Jeremias whether they should abandon the land and flee to Egypt. Jeremias told them not to fear the Babylonian king who would do them no harm; but if they betook themselves to Egypt they would perish there.[32] God knew beforehand how Nabuchodonosor would act toward Sedecias if he surrendered himself on his own accord, and how the Jews who remained in Palestine after Godolias' death would be treated. The Book of Wisdom tells us, "(Henoch) was carried off so that wick-

24. Ps. 139:16.
25. Dan. 13:42.
26. Am. 3:7.
27. Is. 42:9; cf. Is. 40:21; 41:22-23; 44:7; 45:21;

46:10; 48:3; Sir. 42:19; § 4:2.
28. Is. 40:13-14; cf. Gen. 19:1; Is. 6:8; Job 1:1f.

29. 1 Sam. 23:27-28.
30. 1 Sam. 23:9-13.
31. Jer. 38:17-23.
32. Jer. 42:1-22.

edness would not pervert his mind or deceit mislead his soul."[33] Had he lived longer upon earth his virtue would have suffered shipwreck. Yahweh said to Ezekiel, "Not to many nations with unintelligible speech and heavy tongue whose words you do not understand (have you been sent) ; if I would send you to them, they would listen to you."[34] (4 Kgs. 13:18-19 can hardly be used as proof for God's knowledge of future contingent acts. Eliseus wanted to discern from King Joas' behavior whether the Arameans would be destroyed; every stroke the king made upon the ground with an arrow would indicate a victory. Joas struck three times, but three victories would hardly break the might of Aram.)

5. REASONS FOR GOD'S OMNISCIENCE. One reason why God is all-wise is His omnipotence. Since He created all things He knew them before they existed, while they were still mere possibilities. He knows not only that which actually exists, but also that which could possibly exist, i.e., future realities and future possibilities, in a word, everything. "He who formed the hearts of every one of them, who gives heed to all their activities[35]. . . . He who constructed the ear, shall he not hear, he who fashioned the eye, shall he not see?[36]. . . . You have formed my reins, have woven me in the womb of my mother. Your eyes beheld *my deeds* (at the time you created me), and in your book they all are written[37] . . . . What happened of old you brought about, and you devised what later came to pass. What you wanted always happened."[38]

A second reason for God's omniscience is his omnipresence. Since God is everywhere, He is able to see all things, "Am I a God only near at hand, and not a God afar off? If one hide himself ever so well, shall I not see him? Heaven and earth, is it not I who fill them?"[39] The psalmist bases God's knowledge of his thoughts and actions upon divine omnipresence, from which no one can escape whether he ascend into heaven, lay down in Sheol or sojourn at the farthest limits of the sea.[40] "The spirit of the Lord fills the whole world, and he who embraces all knows every spoken word."[41]

6. CONCLUSIONS. Since God knows all things, even our most intimate thoughts, we should live in a manner worthy of reward, not punishment, "I, Yahweh, scrutinize the heart and prove the reins to render to every one according to his behavior, and as his deeds deserve[42]. . . . His eyes watch over all the ways of men to requite each according to his behavior and in proportion to the merit of his deeds."[43] This thought gives strength to the virtuous man in time of trial; his prayer is, "You know my weakness and my confusion *before* all my opponents."[44] On the contrary the godless "do not consider in their hearts that I remember all their iniquity."[45] It were well if they called to mind the words of Job, "Will you deceive him as man deceives man?"[46]

7. SELECTED DIFFICULTIES. In certain passages God makes inquiries regard-

33. Wis. 4:11.
34. Ez. 3:6.
35. Ps. 33:15.
36. Ps. 94:9.
37. Ps. 139:13-16.

38. Judg. 9:4; cf. Is. 14:24;
    Sir. 23:20.
39. Jer. 23:23-24.
40. Ps. 139:1-12.
41. Wis. 1:7.

42. Jer. 17:10.
43. Jer. 32:19.
44. Ps. 69:20.
45. Os. 7:2.
46. Job 13:9; 34:21-22.

ing the problem in question, seemingly ignorant of the situation. For instance, in Gen. 11 He descends from heaven to view Babylon and its tower as the latter is in process of construction by proud men.[47] The reader should sense the insinuation immediately: men thought their tower scratched the heavens, but to Yahweh in the heights it was so insignificant it could hardly be recognized, He had to go down to see it! How perfectly God understood the whole undertaking is betrayed by the very manner in which He acted. Later God betook himself to Sodom "to see whether they acted *exactly* as was reported of *them*, or not."[48] He sent ahead two angels;[49] the Sodomites were to receive one last chance to prove they were not wholly depraved; yet God knew well that they would commit further crime. In paradise God asked Adam and Eve where they were and how they came to know their nakedness.[50] Here God's purpose was to move them to confess their fault and to do penance. The words, "Perhaps they will hear and turn away from their wicked behavior,"[51] were meant to prepare the prophet for a fruitless mission.

The case is quite otherwise when lack of knowledge and foresight are ascribed to pagan gods. Injustice, quarrels and immorality were common "divine" vices.[52] In the Adapa legend Ea, not knowing beforehand that Anu would give Adapa the water and food of life, advised him falsely (if through envy he was not seeking to prevent Adapa from obtaining immortality).[53] In the Gilgamesh epic Ishtar solicited Gilgamesh unaware that she would be rejected. The gods were not able to ward off the effects of the flood which they had caused; they blamed Enlil, who had known nothing of the ship or of Utnapishtim's deliverance, for acting imprudently.[54] Isis was anxious to discover Re's secret name, while Re was unaware of the snake coiled to strike him; neither did he know who was to blame for his sufferings or how to allay them; even the remaining gods were ignorant of the calamity that had befallen Re, their father.[55] Hathor mistook beer mixed with pomegranate sap for human blood.[56] Elias' mockery, "Call real loudly, you know he is a god! Perhaps he is engaged, or is gone apart, or is on a journey; perhaps he sleeps just now—but he will awake alright,"[57] affords an insight into pagan attitudes. The priests of Baal thought loud cries punctured with self-incisions were necessary to gain Baal's attention.

§ 15. GOD'S JUSTNESS

1. CONCEPT. Correspondence to a given norm is the essence of justice in common parlance. In the OT however justice *(ṣedeq, ṣedaqah)* almost always implied some action. We arrive closest to the concept which the OT writers had of divine justice if we consider it as God's will accomplishing all the requirements of the moral order, i.e., blessing those who subject themselves to His

47. Gen. 11:5.
48. Gen. 18:21.
49. Gen. 18:22; 19:1.
50. Gen. 3:9-11.
51. Jer. 26:3.
52. § 11:5.
53. AOT 145.
54. VI 7f; XI 114f, 180f; AOT
160, 178f.
55. Roeder 138f.
56. Roeder 142f.
57. 3 Kgs. 18:27.

will and punishing those who oppose Him. In other words God's justice (or, better: justness) consists in rendering to each one his due according to his thoughts, words and deeds, be they good or bad.

Man is "just" if he obeys God and allows his fellowmen enjoy whatever God has allotted to them. An all-holy God must detest sin; for Him to act justly is a way of manifesting His holiness, "Exalted shall Yahweh of hosts be in judgment, the holy God shall prove himself holy by righteousness."[1] The psalmist attempted to describe God's justice more precisely, "To those who are loyal you show yourself loyal, to the blameless, blameless; to the pure you show yourself pure, but toward the perverse you will act accordingly; you will help the *humble* by beating down those with haughty eyes."[2] A similar thought is found in Proverbs, "*Towards* scorners he will be a scorner himself, but to the humble he gives grace."[3] God treats both the sinner and the saint justly, the one by bringing misfortune upon him, the other by flooding him with blessings. (Of course the anthropomorphic character of passages depicting God as "angry" when inflicting judgment or as "hating" evildoers is always taken for granted.[4])

2. THE NOTION OF GOD'S JUSTICE BEFORE THE PERIOD OF THE LITERARY PROPHETS. Belief in God's justice, i.e., that He rewards the good and punishes the wicked, dates to the most ancient ages of mankind. It was not, as claimed by the Wellhausen school, first proclaimed by the literary prophets. Our first parents were driven from paradise because they had disobeyed God's command. Cain was warned by God and, after murdering his brother, was forced to flee because the blood of Abel cried to heaven for vengeance.[5] The flood was sent upon mankind as punishment for having deserted the ways of God; only Noe and his family were spared because they were "upright."[6] Some time later the human race was scattered over the face of the earth because of sin against God. The inhabitants of Sodom and Gomorrah perished because they were addicted to unnatural lusts. Abraham pleaded for the city, "It is by no means your way of acting to smite the good along with the wicked so that the just and the wicked suffer the same lot. By no means is this your way of acting. Should not he who is judge of all the earth show justice?"[7] Abraham appealed to God's righteousness, and Lot with his family, the only ones who had kept themselves free from the sinful practices of the Sodomites, were saved from the catastrophe. There were upright men in Gerar.[8] Rueben reminded his brothers, "For his (Joseph's) blood an account is now being demanded."[9] To make his decisions just Moses used divine authority as the basis for his judgments. The religious and moral precepts of the decalog and the Covenant Code were given by Yahweh.[10] Because David had committed adultery and murder he was censured by Nathan and threatened with punishment from on High.[11] Elias withstood Achab after he had seized Naboth's field through manipulating an

1. Is. 5:16.
2. Ps. 18:26-28.
3. Prov. 3:34.
4. § 8:3.

5. Gen. 4:10.
6. Gen. 6:9; 7:1.
7. Gen. 18:25.
8. Gen. 20:4.

9. Gen. 42:22.
10. Ex. 18:13-26; 20:2-17; 20: 22-23:19.
11. 2 Sam. 12:1f.

unjust sentence.[12] Achab, who had called the prophet "Israel's Destroyer," later heard the prophet's reply, "I have not brought Israel to destruction, but you and the house of your father, by forsaking the commandments of Yahweh and running after Baal."[13] (Concerning God as being temperamental, unjust and showing favoritism toward Israel, cf. § 11:4; 32:1a; concerning the liquidation of the Canaanites, cf. § 31:1e.)

3. GOD AND ISRAEL. Israel's whole history is a manifestation of God's justice. Because a covenant had been made with Yahweh,[14] the people had a right to His protection, but they also had duties. When they became unfaithful to these duties, God inflicted punishment. Assistance and punishment are corollaries to divine justice. While yet in the wilderness Israel was made to experience what it means to oppose God. The prophets heralded her coming judgment; and for the very reason that Yahweh had chosen Israel as His own He was determined to punish her more severely.[15] Suffering produced a better spirit and she acknowledged, "Yahweh, he is just; for I defied him."[16] Then cherishing the expectation of Yahweh's certain forgiveness she prayed, "I will bear Yahweh's anger (because I have sinned against him), until he judges my cause and renders me a just decision, until he brings me forth into the light so that I may behold his justice."[17] God "in righteousness roused up" Cyrus[18] to bring freedom to the reformed people. It is said of the Servant of Yahweh's advent, "I, Yahweh, have called you in justice,"[19] because His mission was to redeem Israel and the nations. The messianic king was to bear the name, "Yahweh, our righteousness."[20] Belief in Yahweh's justice was a source of strength for Israel; in misfortune she clung fast to Him and did not despair.

4. GOD AND THE NATIONS. God rules justly not only over his Chosen People, but over all of mankind. Every person is bound to fulfill God's will; each individual will be made to render an account, because through the natural law every one knows the fundamentals of right and wrong.[21] God punished sin long before there was a Jewish nation. Beginning with Amos, the prophets lifted up their voices to proclaim judgment upon surrounding countries.[22] Like Israel these peoples could ward off the impending doom by determining to amend their evil ways.[23] To the Canaanites "(God) gave an opportunity for repentance by inflicting judgment gradually."[24] Accordingly there is no essential difference between the position which God assumed toward Israel and toward other nations for all are subject to His moral law. God "judges the world with justice, pronounces judgment upon the nations with equity[25].... His judgments come upon all the earth[26].... He comes to judge the earth, and he will judge the world justly and the nations uprightly[27].... As the Just One he governs the world with justice."[28]

5. GOD AND THE INDIVIDUAL. God is a judge who tries the "hearts and

12. 3 Kgs. 21:17-28.
13. 3 Kgs. 18:18.
14. § 2:2a.
15. Am. 3:2; § 46.
16. Lam. 1:18.
17. Mich. 7:9.
18. Is. 45:13.
19. Is. 42:6.
20. Jer. 23:6.
21. § 2:2b; 45:2, 4.
22. § 45:2.
23. Jer. 19:7-8.
24. Wis. 12:10.
25. Ps. 9:9.
26. Ps. 105:7.
27. Ps. 96:13; cf. Ps. 98:9.
28. Wis. 12:15.

reins" of men.[29] He shows no partiality, does not respect a person's social status, considers only his moral condition, "He pays no regard to anyone, and takes no bribes; he obtains justice for the orphan and the widow, and he loves the non-Jew[30].... He is great in counsel, mighty in act; his eyes watch over all the ways of men to requite each according to his behavior and in proportion to the merit of his deeds[31].... *Blessed* is the virtuous man, for it shall go well with him; he shall enjoy the fruit of his deeds. Woe to the godless man, for it shall not go well with him; the misdeeds of his hands shall strike home upon him[32].... According to a man's work will he reward him. Truly God does not condemn their faithfulness, nor does the Almighty pervert that which is right."[33] Good deeds of the past are of no value if a person now walks the way of sin, "If a just man forsake his justice and do evil, he shall therefore die."[34] Severe punishment is in store for sinners, "He who loves injustice, hates his own soul[35].... You hate all who do evil."[36] However if a sinner converts he may with absolute confidence expect forgiveness. With David he may pray, "Deliver me from blood-guiltiness, O God, and my tongue shall rejoice over your justice."[37]

With even greater confidence than penitent sinners the virtuous may seek the justice of God who lovingly receives innocent sufferers, "Yahweh puts righteousness into action, obtains justice for all the oppressed[38].... Yahweh, the righteous, has cut to pieces the cords of the wicked."[39] Full of trust the afflicted may appeal to divine justice, "When I called, my just God replied; he had mercy on me and heard my prayer."[40] The upright, always mindful of God's promises, frequently praised God's righteousness which never allowed his words to fall into disgrace, "I will praise Yahweh for his justice[41].... Yahweh is righteous, he loves righteousness[42].... Justice and judgment are the foundation of your throne, kindness and fidelity precede your face."[43]

The conviction that an omniscient God knows the truth and that a just God will help truth triumph gave rise to various practices of ascertaining the divine will. (Divination, a common practice in ancient times, however never attained much significance in Israel.) To determine whether a suspect was guilty the Urim and Tummim were consulted,[44] or the suspect was made to utter an execration having the form of self-condemnation (e.g., a woman suspected of adultery;[45] a depositary claiming that the goods confided to him had been stolen[46]—perhaps the Urim and Tummim were here employed; a shepherd who lost an animal;[47] a person against whom guilt could not be satisfactorily proven).[48] The ordeal in Israel did not place the accused in danger of losing life or health if innocent, as did the trials by water or fire in adjacent countries.[49]

29. Ps. 7:10; Jer. 11:20; § 14:3.
30. Deut. 10:17-18.
31. Jer. 32:19.
32. Is. 3:10-11.
33. Job 34:11-12.
34. Ez. 33:18.
35. Ps. 11:5.
36. Ps. 5:6.
37. Ps. 51:16.

38. Ps. 103:6.
39. Ps. 129:4.
40. Ps.4:2; cf. Pss. 5:9; 18:21; 31:2; 37:5-6; 62:13; 71:2; 143:11; § 28:2; 41:7.
41. Ps. 7:18.
42. Ps. 11:7.
43. Ps. 97:6; cf. Pss. 33:5; 37:28; 48:11; 71:19; 97:2; 111:3.

44. Ex. 28:30; Jos. 7:16-18; 1 Sam. 14:40-42; § 3:1; 28:1c.
45. Num. 5:11-31; § 31:1a.
46. Ex. 22:7.
47. Ex. 22:10.
48. 3 Kgs. 8:31-32.
49. CH 131, 132; AG 17.

Concerning the virtue of trust in God, cf. § 28:2; concerning the seeming
denial of divine justice and the problem of suffering, § 41:3; concerning communal solidarity and responsibility, § 32:2f; 39:1.

6. JUSTICE AND THE GOODNESS OF GOD. Since God justly avenged violated
rights and thereby brought help and deliverance to an oppressed nation as well
as to an oppressed individual, the OT writers often spoke of divine *justness*
where we would speak of divine *goodness*. For the Israelite God's goodness was
a natural sequel to His justice, inasmuch as the nation as such, the just man,
and the repentant sinner possessed a "right" to rely upon the divine promises.[50]
In messianic times when Yahweh receives the people cleansed in the crucible
of judgment, He will act "rightly." Nevertheless the virtuous man has no strict
right to forgiveness. The penitential spirit is merely a prerequisite on the part
of the sinner to obtain pardon.[51] Yahweh said to Moses, "I shall favor whom
I shall favor, and I shall be merciful to whom it pleases me."[52] Moses had
asked Yahweh to enter more deeply into the mystery of the Godhead and to
forgive the people who had repented of their sin. Yahweh, inclined to grant
the petition, pointed out that neither Moses nor the people had any claim against
Him; His compliance would be a free act of divine goodness. Over against
God man is nothing more than clay in the potter's hand;[53] God is absolutely
sovereign and man has no right to confront Him with any kind of claim. Many
texts emphasize that every person, be he ever so virtuous, is a debtor toward
God. The just man prays, "Do not enter into judgment with your servant, for
no living person appears just before you."[54] In the presence of the All-holy
every man is a sinner and must fear his lot, if the measure of strict justice is
meted out.[55] Our cry must always be, "Yahweh, do not punish me in your
anger or chastise me in your fury. Have pity on me, Yahweh."[56] In the presence of the all-holy God Isaias feared death because he was a sinner;[57]
Jeremias placed himself at the mercy of God, "Chastise me, Yahweh, but according to measure; not in your fury lest you bring me to nothingness."[58] In the
psalms mention is often made of God's justice alongside His goodness and
mercy, "Let your goodness continue toward those who know you, and your
justice toward all who are upright of heart[59].... When need and sorrow come
upon me, I call upon the name of Yahweh. Yahweh is gracious and righteous,
our God is full of mercy."[60]

God's justice, as it reveals itself in the fulfillment of His promises, is called
fidelity. There is a relationship between God's fidelity and His mercy in that
both are oriented toward sinners; God, who is faithful to His promises, has
assured the penitent of forgiveness. Yahweh calls Himself "a merciful and
gracious God, long-suffering and full of goodness and fidelity, showing loving-
kindness to the thousandth time, leaving however no (sin) unpunished."[61]
From God's constant guidance Israel should learn that "Yahweh is the true

50. Mich. 7:9; Ps. 51:16.   54. Ps. 143:2.   58. Jer. 10:24.
51. § 40:4.   55. § 38:3.   59. Ps. 36:11.
52. Ex. 33:19.   56. Ps. 6:2-3.   60. Ps. 116:3-5.
53. Is. 45:9; 64:7.   57. Is. 6:5.   61. Ex. 34:6-7.

God, the faithful God who keeps his covenant and his mercy towards those who love him unto the thousandth generation, but punishes every one who hates him."[62] He is "a God who is faithful without fail."[63] Time and time again God promised to keep the covenant made with Israel. The repentant sinner appeals to God's fidelity, "In virtue of your fidelity hear me, and do not enter into judgment with your servant."[64] God's love and fidelity are often mentioned side by side,[65] as also His justice and fidelity.[66]

The foundation of God's justice is His omnipotence. He need fear no one, while man is often influenced by external circumstances. He is "the mighty, strong and awe-inspiring God[67].... (who) has no respect for princes, does not favor the rich against the poor, for they all are the work of his hands."[68] When God, the just judge, acts kindly, He does so motivated by love.[69] Certain passages seem to state that God hates the sinner,[70] while others declaim His love toward all His creatures, accordingly toward the sinner too.[71] These statements are not contradictory. God hates the sinner inasmuch as he defied and transgressed the divine law; God must abhor sin since it is an assault upon His holiness, but He loves the sinner who always remains His creature. Being merciful God wills the sinner's conversion and therefore delays the punishment deserved.[72]

7. THE GODS AND JUSTICE. The sun-god, Shamash, victor over night and darkness, was honored in a particular manner as the god of justice. This is shown in many hymns written in his honor, for instance the following, "No sinner escapes your net, no evildoer evades your snare. Whoever violates his oath . . . whoever lifts up his eyes toward his neighbor's wife . . . toward him your weapon rushes and there will be no savior. You destroy the horns of everyone who plots a wicked act; the cunning swindler looses ground under his feet; you cause the unjust judge to see chains; you load with punishment those who accept bribes. The one who will not be bribed, who fights for the weak, is pleasing to Shamash and will live for ever."[73] Shamash however was never regarded as wholly distinct from the sun. At the beginning as well as at the end of the hymn the sun is praised for its brilliance which lights up the hills and fills the lands; it is the orb toward which all turn, even "the robber, the thief, the enemy of the sun." In Israel men clearly understood Yahweh's demands. In practice His commandments may have been violated, but there was no doubt regarding their existence and obligation. Though the prophets encountered opposition at every turn, no one, not even the priests who were frequently their most violent enemies, ever accused them of making demands which had not already been sanctioned by God. In Babylon the petitioner, feeling himself a sinner, was often in doubt as to which god had afflicted him with misfortune and by what sin he had transgressed. The formula, "the sin which I committed, I do not know," reoccurs constantly in the Babylonian peni-

62. Deut. 7:9-10.
63. Deut. 32:4; cf. Ps. 33:4.
64. Ps. 143:1-2.
65. Cf. Pss. 25:10; 36:6; 40:11-12; 57:11; 61:8;
66. Pss. 85:11; 89:15; 111:7-8.
67. Deut. 10:17.
68. Job 34:19.
69. Cf. 16:4-5.
100:5; 115:1.
70. E.g., Ps. 5:6.
71. Wis. 11:24.
72. § 16:5-6.
73. AOT 244f.

tential psalms. Ritual faults were emphasized while little importance was attached
to penance and sincere amendment; of significance was the proper pronunciation of words, the right ceremonies and sacrificial offerings. It is true that
observance of ritualistic prescription was strictly enjoined in Israel; such however never constituted an end in itself. The purpose of ceremonial was to educate
the people to obedience and to a moral life; the prophets and sapiential writers
did not stress this point.[74] God would grant a sinner forgiveness and avert the
threatened punishment only when he had abandoned his evil ways; without
a spirit of repentance and betterment the greatest sacrifices had no value.[75]

The gods of Babylonia and of the pagans by and large punished their
devotees and their respective nations, but their justice was not the type that
would go into abeyance in favor of mercy—if it had, no devotees would have
remained to bring sacrifices. Yahweh destroyed His sanctuary, put an end to
the regular sacrificial cult and forced the people to leave their homeland;
apparently this was the end. To Him righteousness was of greater importance
than good fortune, and even of Israel's very existence.[76] And as He punished
the injustices done to His people, He also punished the injustices which they
themselves had committed—sometimes much more severely.

§ 16. GOD'S LOVE AND MERCY

1. General Considerations. The divine attribute which more than any
other serves as a foundation for man's trust in God is God's love, i.e., His
determination to confer natural and supernatural favors upon His creatures.
The word ʾahab, to love, was not used very frequently of God in the older writings. More often throughout the OT we find the word ḥesed, which connotes
God's spirit of helpfulness, His condescension toward men, gathering them
unto Himself, forgiving the sinner his fault—in short, showing *kindness, favor*.
God's mercy toward the poor and needy, as well as toward the repentant sinner,
is designated by *riḥam* and *ḥanan* (*ḥen*). Exact limits regarding the use of
these terms cannot be set. God's mercy manifested in delaying a sinner's punishment was expressed in the words, ʾerekh ʾappayim, long-suffering.

2. The Concept of God's Mercy Before the Period of the Literary
Prophets. Certain scholars of the history of religious development maintain
that Israel in ancient times did not consider God as being righteous, loving,
merciful; in their opinion it was the prophet Amos who first introduced this
theology,[1] and the prophet Osee who (as a consequence of his unhappy marriage!) developed it. Such theories disregard abundant evidence in the OT
indicating the very opposite. In every period, the primitive, the patriarchal and
the Israelitic, we find the conviction of an all-good, merciful, and forgiving
God. This good God placed Adam in a garden planted specifically for him, and
supplied him with a helper.[2] He destined our first parents to bodily immortality

74. § 2:3; 3:3; 30:4; 32:1i.   75. § 33:7; 40:3.   76. Num. 14:12; cf. Ex. 32:10.
   1. § 15:2.   2. Gen. 2:8; 2:18.

and eternal happiness. After they sinned He sought to make them acknowledge their fault, and in the protoevangel gave them hope of again attaining His love.[3] When Cain was harboring hate against Abel, God warned him; even after the assault God listened to the murderer's lament.[4] When men had strayed into evil ways God was deeply moved upon finding it necessary to punish them,[5] and gave them a final warning as Noe was building the ark. He resolved never to send a second flood.[6] Had there been but ten upright souls in Sodom, Yahweh would have spared the Pentapolis.[7] The patriarchs enjoyed His kindly guidance. The history of Israel is a chain of divine favors and blessings. In the Book of the Covenant God forbade receiving in pledge the mantle of a poor debtor, "Wherewith shall he otherwise lay himself down to sleep? And if he cry to me, I shall hear it for I am merciful."[8] When David repented God forgave him;[9] and later when the prophet Gad told him to choose the manner in which he wished to be punished for having ordered the census, the king replied, "We prefer to fall into the hand of Yahweh for his mercy is great; I would not want to fall into the hands of men."[10]

3. GOD AND CREATURES. In Ps. 136:1-9 creation is praised as the work of God's goodness and mercy. "To every being Yahweh is good, his mercy embraces all his creatures[11]. . . . All eyes hope in you, for you give them food in due season. You open your hand and satisfy the desires of all that lives[12]. . . . You love all that exists[13]. . . . The Lord's mercy is toward all men."[14] God's love flows out to all without distinction. True, Yahweh chose Israel, but that did not exclude other nations from His love. Even when chastising them He sought to show His love. Words of comfort are found in the midst of the judgment upon Edom, "Abandon your orphans, I will keep them alive; your widows may well confide in me."[15] By penance and amendment the nations could avert chastisement, "If a people against whom I have spoken repent of their evil, I also shall repent of the evil that I have planned against them."[16] Due to his narrow-mindedness Jonas did not wish to preach penance to the Ninivites; he feared they would repent and God would then forgive them, "I know that you are a kind and merciful God, long-suffering and rich in mercy, one who easily forgives evil."[17] Actually the Ninivites did repent and were pardoned. Even toward the Canaanites God showed "mercy as toward men."[18]

Irrational creatures also come within the ambit of God's love. "He gives to cattle their fodder, and to young ravens that cry to him[19]. . . . Apart from him there is no God who provides for all."[20]

4. GOD AND ISRAEL. Yahweh's covenant with Israel was an act of sheer mercy. It was not due to any virtue or merit of hers that God selected her in preference to some other nation, "Not because you were more numerous than the other nations did Yahweh find pleasure in you and choose you; for you

3. Gen. 3:8f.
4. Gen. 4:6-7, 15.
5. Gen. 6:6.
6. Gen. 8:21; 9:15.
7. Gen. 18:32.
8. Ex. 22:26.
9. 2 Sam. 12:13.

10. 2 Sam. 24:14.
11. Ps. 145:9.
12. Ps. 145:15-16.
13. Wis. 11:24.
14. Sir. 18:13.
15. Jer. 49:11.

16. Jer. 18:8.
17. Jon. 4:2.
18. Wis. 12:8.
19. Ps. 147:9; cf. Pss. 104:14, 21, 24-28; 33:5; 36:7.
20. Wis. 12:13.

are the least of all peoples; much rather it is because Yahweh loved you and
because he wished to keep the oath which he swore to your fathers that Yahweh
delivered you with a strong hand."[21] Already before Esau and Jacob were born
God had revealed how the descendants of Jacob should be more highly privileged
than those of Esau; it was in no way due to the merit of the one or the fault
of the other.[22] The prophet Malachy reminded the Jews of this fact when
they boasted of their selection as if it were a foregone conclusion.[23] On eagle's
wings Yahweh carried the people to Horeb;[24] and as it was from love that
He had mercy on the people suffering servitude in Egypt, so He maintained
a loving intimacy toward them during the whole journey through the desert,
loading them with favors and forgiving them again and again in spite of their
unruly spirit. Because of His goodness He remitted their sins after Moses had
interceded for them.[25] Israel was so stiffnecked that on one occasion Moses
believed Yahweh would work no further miracle in her favor, but that very
thought offended God because it set limits to divine mercy.[26] Reviewing the
desert journey a poet expressed his conclusion in one line, "In your goodness
you led the people whom you saved."[27] In Deuteronomy the Israelites were
reminded how Yahweh had flooded them continually with blessings since the
times of their forefathers.[28]

With the passing centuries Yahweh did not withdraw His love from His
people although very frequently they were unfaithful to Him. The whole story
of Israel is simply the development of the theme, "With an everlasting love
have I loved you."[29] All the warnings of the prophets, all their proclamations
of coming judgment were ordered toward bringing the people to penance so
God could grant pardon. God punished, but only to effect an amendment of
morals.[30] A review of the many offenses which Israel had committed against
Yahweh during the desert journey and in Canaan ends with a reminder of
Yahweh's loving-kindness, "For their sake he was mindful of his covenant; he
had pity in accordance with his great goodness."[31] The exile itself was a proof
of divine love.[32] Under the blows of misfortune those who remained in Judea
saw how their punishment had been deserved and they humbly acknowledged,
"It is due to Yahweh's clemency that we are not annihilated, his mercy is
unfathomable."[33] In captivity the complaint of course was sometimes made,
"Yahweh has forsaken me, the Lord has forgotten about me." But Yahweh's
answer was not slow to come, "Is it possible for a mother to forget her infant,
and to have no pity upon the son of her womb? Even though she forget, I shall
not forget you."[34] God's love is greater than mother love! He bids the people
to convert so that His blessings could be effective, "Return to me for I am
redeeming you[35].... Continually was I holding out my hands to a stubborn,
perverse people."[36] In this wooing of a stiffnecked nation that repeatedly

21. Deut. 7:7-8; cf. 10:15.
22. Gen. 25:23.
23. Mal. 1:2-3.
24. Ex. 19:4.
25. Ex. 32:32; 33:12-19; Num. 14:10-20.
26. Num. 20:2-13.
27. Ex. 15:13.
28. Deut. 4:32-40.
29. Jer. 31:3.
30. Am. 4:6-12; cf. § 39:3; 46:5.
31. Ps. 106:45; cf. Ps. 103:8-13.
32. Deut. 30:2-3; Jer. 29:12-14; Is. 48:10; § 46:5.
33. Lam. 3:22.
34. Is. 49:14-15.

showed herself ungrateful in the presence of countless proofs of mercy is revealed God's abiding love; here the greatest sinner may find a solid basis for hoping to be received back in God's good favor. Whenever Israel in a spirit of penance acknowledged her guilt, her wicked past was wholly forgiven and forgotten, "As I swore that the waters of Noe should never again flood the earth, so I have sworn never again to be angry against you or to reproach you."[37]

Osee very beautifully developed the doctrine of Yahweh's love and mercy toward Israel. By marrying a prostitute Osee showed how greatly Yahweh loved the people with whom He had made the covenant on Horeb. Israel did not deserve His love because she had become faithless and had turned toward strange gods. Then Yahweh deserted her, but only out of love; He would not desert her forever. Yahweh punished with the purpose of moving her to amend, and in the end would make a new covenant with her.[38] Jeremias continued this marriage theme, "I remember your youthful affection, your love as a bride when you followed me in the wilderness, the land unsown."[39] But Israel and Judah, the two sisters whom Yahweh had espoused, became unfaithful. So Yahweh asked reproachfully, "If a man put away his wife and she leave him and marries another person, shall he again return to her? Is not such a *woman* wholly defiled? But you have prostituted yourself with many lovers, and should you be allowed to return to me?"[40] Such a marriage could not again be lawfully consummated, and Israel should keep this in mind. But God's love is so infinitely great that He Himself would remove the difficulty. It ought to have been perfectly clear to Israel that it was an act of boundless and undeserving grace when Yahweh showed mercy to them, "I shall not always be angry—only acknowledge your iniquity."[41] Ezechiel too described the love which Yahweh tendered Israel in terms of the marriage bond, a bond which the people had disgracefully violated.[42] But toward the exile's end when Judah had become humble and repentant she heard God ask, "Where is your mother's bill of divorce with which I sent her away?"[43] A bill of divorce had not been issued, and therefore nothing legally impeded a reunion with the separated spouse. Here the feeling between sinful Israel and Yahweh is a more kindly one than in Jer. 3:1 because the people meanwhile had adopted a different frame of mind. Hence the words of comfort, "As a wife abandoned and deeply afflicted, Yahweh has again called you. The wife of one's youth, shall she be scorned? Only for a moment did I forsake you; with great mercy I shall bring you home."[44]

In the Canticle of Canticles the bridal or marital relationship serves to show God's overwhelming love toward Israel. This affection the people ought repay with their whole heart. The fiery ardor of divine love is "strong as death," its might forces every issue, "Many waters cannot extinguish her."[45]

The intimate bond between father and son also served to portray Yahweh's

35. Is. 44:22.
36. Is. 65:2; 43:4; Jer. 3:4, 12-13.
37. Is. 54:9.
38. Os. 1-3.

39. Jer. 2:2.
40. Jer. 3:1.
41. Jer. 3:12.
42. Ez. 16; 23.

43. Is. 50:1.
44. Is. 54:6-7; cf. Is. 62:4-5.
45. Cant. 8:6-7.

love toward Israel. It had been revealed to Moses that Israel was Yahweh's "first-born son."[46] Having called the Chosen People into existence,[47] Yahweh carried them through the wilderness "as a man carries his son."[48] During their long and painful wanderings in the desert He reared them "as a man rears his son[49]. . . . When Israel was a child, I became fond of him; out of Egypt I called my son."[50] This son proved very disobedient and forgot the blessings with which his forefathers had been laden, "The more I called them, the farther they departed from me; they sacrificed to Baals and offered to idols[51]. . . . I thought you would call me: My Father! and would never turn yourself away from me. Yet *as* a woman proves unfaithful to her love, so you have proven unfaithful to me, O house of Israel."[52] When a husband is wronged as grievously as God was wronged by Israel he does not forgive. But God's fatherly love knows no bounds, "How could I deliver you over to oppression, Ephraim, abandon you, Israel? . . . . I do not want to act according to my fierce wrath (I do not want) to destroy Ephraim again; for I am God, not man; a Holy One in your midst."[53] Israel might act like a *qedešah* (a woman who offered herself as a harlot to honor Astarte),[54] but Yahweh is *qadoš* holy, not subject to human passion and quite able through love to draw a rebellious, erring nation back to Himself again. Divine mercy is ever mightier than divine justice, and Yahweh was minded to call Israel a second time, certain that she then would follow Him.[55]

Israel was obstinate, it seemed she never seriously sought to amend; constantly she was relapsing into old sins. Yahweh Himself became astonished over His love toward such a people, a love so great that it repeatedly let mercy triumph over justice. "Is Ephraim, my dearest son, (indeed) my darling? As often as I threaten him, I must think lovingly of him again! My heart is beating for him, I must have mercy upon him."[56] Even after the exile Israel forgot her debt to God. Yahweh continued His complaint, "A son honors his father and a servant his master. If I be a father, where is my honor? if I be a master, where is my fear?"[57] In the parable of the prodigal son[58] our Savior further developed this thought.[59] Nevertheless in no OT passage does the word "father" have the full meaning which we Christians see in it. It expressed God's status as creator, lord and guardian of His people, as is seen in the parallel use of father and creator in Deut. 32:6; Is. 64:7; Mal. 2:10. God Himself used the title "father," but apart from certain prayers[60] the people did not as yet use this invocation.

God's love toward Israel is also presented under the figure of shepherd and flock,[61] a comparison Jesus too employed.[62] Lastly we may note the allegory of the vine-dresser who cares for his vineyard, "The vineyard of Yahweh of hosts is the house of Israel, and the men of Judah are his cherished planting."[63]

5. GOD AND INDIVIDUALS. To the poor and suffering God always manifests

46. Ex. 4:22.
47. Deut. 32:6.
48. Deut. 1:31.
49. Deut. 8:5; cf. 14:1; Ps. 80:18; Wis. 11:10.
50. Os. 11:1.
51. Os. 11:2.
52. Jer. 3:19-20.

53. Os. 11:8-9.
54. Os. 4:14.
55. Os. 11:11.
56. Jer. 31:20.
57. Mal. 1:6.
58. Lk. 15:11-32.
59. Cf. Is. 1:2, 4; 30:1, 9; 63:16; 64:7; Jer. 31:9;

Tob. 13:4.
60. Is. 63; 64 (63:16; 64:7); Jer. 3:4; cf. Jer. 3:19; 2:27.
61. § 49:1a.
62. Matth. 18:12; Lk. 15:4; Jn. 10:11-16.
63. Is. 5:1-7; cf. Jn. 15:1, 5.

a special love, "He renders justice to the oppressed, distributes bread to the hungry, looses captives from their bonds, makes the blind see, raises up them who are bowed down, safeguards strangers, supports orphans and widows."[64] The prophets never tire advocating the cause of the poor and weak, condemning as grievous crimes against Yahweh all profiteering at the expense of the helpless.[65] When in need individuals should turn to God's mercy, not only for forgiveness from sin but also for aid in the little troubles and cares of daily life. God's love is the reason why one may look up to Him with full confidence and await aid.[66] The terms of course are observance of the commandments, "Yahweh loves the just but confounds the way of the wicked."[67]

God's attitude toward individual persons was likened to that of a father toward his child. Yahweh is "a father to orphans, a defender of widows[68] .... As a father has pity upon his children, so Yahweh has pity upon those who fear him."[69] He said to Solomon, "I shall be to him a father, and he will be to me a son."[70] David was to address Him, "You are my father!"[71] But only in later centuries did certain persons dare to use the name father in speaking of or to God.[72] At the time of Jesus the name occurs somewhat frequently in extracanonical Jewish prayers.[73] Divine love is greater than parental love, "Though (my) father and my mother forsake me, Yahweh nonetheless will receive me."[74] God will love him who is merciful "more than his own mother."[75] In this manner the ground was prepared for the "Our Father." But apart from the few passages cited above, we do not find the expression in the OT prayer formulas; furthermore in the OT Yahweh was the father of Israel and of Israelites, while in the NT he is the father of all nations and all men. First through God's only Son, Jesus our brother, has the full "father-child" relationship been conferred upon us; only now may we call God "Father" in the true sense of the word.[76] (The reference to God as shepherd may be listed here also, "Yahweh is my shepherd, I suffer no want[77] .... He reproves, punishes, instructs and leads back as a shepherd does his flock."[78])

Yahweh manifested His goodness toward David and his house in a special manner because the Messiah was to proceed from his family.[79] Yet the repentant sinner may trust in God's mercy more than any one else.[80] He "forgives guilt, transgression, sin."[81] God takes no pleasure in the death of the wicked, but wills that he be converted and live.[82] Isaias admonished his kinsmen, "Let the godless forsake his way, and the fool his plans; let them betake themselves to Yahweh who will have mercy on them, to our God who is rich in forgiveness."[83] Trusting in divine mercy the repentant sinner ought pray, "Be merciful to me, O God, according to your goodness; according to the fullness of your

64. Ps. 146:7-9.
65. Am. 2:6-7; 5:11-12; Is. 3:14; Ez. 22:7; Mal. 3:5; cf. Prov. 14:31; § 29:5.
66. § 28:2; 35:2e.
67. Ps. 146:8-9.
68. Ps. 68:6.
69. Ps. 103:13.
70. 2 Sam. 7:14.
71. Ps. 89:27.

72. Wis. 2:16; Sir. 23:1, 4; 51:10; cf. Wis. 5:5; 14:3.
73. P. Fiebig, Das Vaterunser, Gütersloh 1927, BFchrTh XXX 3; Strack-Billerbeck I, 1922, 393-396.
74. Ps. 27:10.
75. Sir. 4:10.
76. Matth. 5:48; 6:6; 6:9, 32;

7:11; Rom. 8:15; Gal. 4:6.
77. Ps. 23:1-4.
78. Sir. 18:13.
79. 2 Sam. 7:12-16; 3 Kgs. 3:6; Ps. 89:27-30.
80. § 40:4.
81. Ex. 34:7.
82. Ez. 18:21-23; 33:11.
83. Is. 55:7.

mercy blot out my iniquity.... A humbled heart, O God, you cannot send away[84].... In your goodness, Yahweh, do not remember the sins of my youth or my evil deeds. For your name's sake, Yahweh, forgive all my sins."[85] In the *De Profundis* sin-conscious man—and who is without sin[86]—implores, "If you would remember offences, Yahweh, who could survive? With you indeed there is forgiveness, so that you may be honored."[87] If God always pronounced judgment as a strict judge, we would be forced to despair. But since God is merciful, we may hope in Him who forgives all our guilt, heals all our offences, redeems our life from destruction, crowns us with favors and kindnesses.[88] But we must not abuse divine forbearance, it too has an end. God cannot concede to human fancy the right to decide the moment for conversion, "Do not defer returning to the Lord; do not delay it from one day to another, for suddenly the wrath of the Lord shall break out, and you shall perish on the day of retribution."[89] The evils which God permits to harass a sinner are proofs of His love; for by them He seeks to lead a wayward child to acknowledge its offences and to amend.[90] Even upon the pious, God in His goodness brings trials and afflictions in order to effect greater purity of heart.[91]

6. THE IMMENSITY OF DIVINE LOVE. A love "of which the earth is full,"[92] which embraces all creatures, which does not exclude the sinner or the pagan, must be immeasurably great. Yahweh describes Himself as "a merciful and gracious God, long-suffering and full of goodness and fidelity, showing loving-kindness to the thousandth time."[93] These sentiments are re-echoed in Nahum.[94] According to the decalog God visits the sins of parents upon the children unto the third and fourth generation, but shows His kindness unto the thousandth.[95] Hence humanly speaking His love is infinitely greater than His justice. The prophet may therefore compare the love of God to the love of a mother embracing her child who had provoked her to anger and had strayed from her.[96] God's mercy is simply inexhaustible.[97] "His anger is but for a moment, his loving-kindness endures a lifetime[98].... Your loving-kindness is great, even unto heaven, your fidelity even unto the clouds[99].... As high as the heavens are above the earth, so great has he shown his mercy to those who fear him."[100] There is no end to God's love, "With an everlasting love have I loved you[101] .... Though the mountains be moved and the hills totter, my loving-kindness shall not depart from you or my covenant of peace be broken[102].... His loving-kindness endures for ever, his fidelity unto all generations."[103] The phrase, "his loving-kindness endures for ever," became a liturgical formula by which the Israelites expressed their firm trust in God's mercy.[104] Of course the pious man felt oppressed when misfortune overwhelmed him and his people, and sometimes groaned, "Has God forgotten to be gracious, or because of anger

84. Ps. 51:3, 19.
85. Ps. 25:7, 11, 18.
86. § 38:3.
87. Ps. 130:3-4.
88. Ps. 103:3-4.
89. Sir. 5:7.
90. § 41:2.
91. § 41:5.
92. Pss. 33:5; 119:64.

93. Ex. 34:6-7.
94. Nah. 1:3; Joel 2:13; Jon. 4:2; Pss. 86:15; 103:8; 145:8; Neh. 9:17; Wis. 15:1.
95. Ex. 20:5-6.
96. Is. 49:14-16,
97. Lam. 3:22,
98. Ps. 30:6,

99. Ps. 57:11.
100. Pss. 103:11; cf. Pss. 36:6; 108:5.
101. Jer. 31:3.
102. Is. 54:10.
103. Pss. 100:5; 103:17; Dan. 3:89-90.
104. Pss. 106:1; 117:2; 118:1-4, 29; 136:1-26; 138:8.

suppressed his mercy?" Immediately however he would recall the many favors with which God formerly had flooded his people, "You led your people like little sheep."[105]

Passages which seem to imply a possibility that God might not show mercy throw no doubt upon this doctrine. Take for instance the prophet's exhortation, "Return to Yahweh, for he is merciful and ready to repent of evil. Perhaps he will repent again, and leave blessings behind him."[106] The first verse here contains a firm acknowledgement of God's mercy, the second, understood alongside the first, is a silent petition that, in spite of the insufficient spirit of penance on the part of the people, God might pour forth grace. It expresses that man, even when repentant, has no strict right to a modified or remitted punishment. Moses had pointed out to the Israelites how they deserved no clemency even when God did act kindly toward them, "Perhaps I may obtain remission for you for (your) sin."[107] Similarly the Ninivites acknowledged having no right to God's mercy since it was a free gift, "Perhaps God will repent again and will turn away from his fierce anger, and then we shall not perish."[108] When David had heard from Nathan that the child conceived in adultery would die, he fasted and wept; later he explained, "I thought: Perhaps Yahweh will have mercy on me, and permit the child to live."[109] Though he sought to stave off the deserved and imminent punishment, he was conscious of having no claim to it; God need not leave him the child.[110]

God's love and mercy must never be regarded as untimely impotence or weakness; alongside His loving-kindness there always stands His justice. Indeed it is Osee who proclaimed so stirringly God's love toward Israel who is also most vehement when preaching God's just judgments, "Into the land of Egypt shall she return (Egyptian servitude had become the symbol of exile); and Asshur shall be her king because she refused to amend. The sword shall *rage* in her cities and destroy her children."[111] Jeremias left no doubt in the people's minds that they had been led into exile in punishment for their sins. In Is. 40-66, alongside many consoling words, we find admonitions to abandon sin and to attach ourselves to God with our whole heart. David's descendants lost the throne.

7. THE BASIS AND PURPOSE OF DIVINE LOVE. God loves all creatures because He created them. If a man hesitates before destroying an object he has made, more so God. The prophet Isaias prayed, "Now, Yahweh, you are our father. We are clay and you our fashioner; we all are the work of your hand. Do not be angry beyond measure, Yahweh, and do not keep our guilt in mind for ever."[112] Centuries later we find the same sentiments, "You love all that exists, and abhor nothing you have made; if you hated something, you would not have made it. You practice forbearance toward everything because everything is your

105. Ps. 77:10, 21.
106. Joel 2:13-14.
107. Ex. 32:30.
108. Jon. 3:9.

109. 2 Sam. 12:22.
110. Cf. § 40:4-5; on God's changelessness, § 10:2; on

anthropomorphism, § 8:3.
111. Os. 11:5-6.
112. Is. 64:7.

possession, O Lord, you lover of life. Your immortal spirit is in all things.[113] Men, being so helpless, God has compassion upon them. When Yahweh was minded to destroy Israel Amos implored, "Yahweh, Lord, please forgive! How shall Jacob stand? see, he is so little."[114] Job reminded God how weak, how short-lived he was in his appeal for mercy, "My days are but a breath. What is man that you have such a high regard for him, and that you should set your heart's desire upon him? If I should sin, what would I accomplish against you?"[115] The psalmist develops the same theme, "What is man, Yahweh, that you bother yourself about him, the son of man that you notice him? Man is like a breath, his lifetime a shadow gliding past!"[116] Treating God's mercy Sirach noted the shortness of human life, the agony at death and the joylessness of Sheol.[117] (Concerning man's helplessness as a reason for divine mercy, cf. further, Is. 57:16; Pss. 78:39; 103:14-16.) Moreover, because God is almighty, He can at any time begin acting, and destroy the sinner. He may also postpone action to allow the sinner time for repentance.[118] The Israelite had a very special basis for hope in Yahweh's love and mercy, i.e., he was a citizen of the nation with which God had made a covenant.[119]

A sure way of obtaining God's mercy is to honor Him. When Yahweh wanted to annihilate Israel, Moses advanced two reasons why He should pardon the people: 1. Yahweh's honor demanded that Israel continue to exist; the other nations, not understanding the reason for her destruction, would consider Yahweh impotent; 2. Yahweh Himself had proclaimed His mercy;[120] He had promised to show His might not by destroying, but by showing mercy.[121] Ezechiel informs us that Yahweh had intended to destroy the people while they were still in Egypt. "But I acted for the sake of my own name, that it would not be defamed in the eyes of the nations in whose midst they were."[122] So too the blessings showered upon Israel penitent in exile glorified God.[123] God's mercy moreover gives the sinner time and chance to amend, "Those who err you discipline little by little, and as they recall their sins you admonish them, so that liberated from their transgressions, they may believe in you, O Lord[124].... With you indeed there is forgiveness, so that you may be honored."[125] Whoever has experienced God's mercy will pay his debt of gratitude by saving others, "Then shall I teach evildoers your ways, so that sinners may return to you."[126]

8. PAGAN GODS AND MERCY. Generally speaking, all who believe in higher beings expect aid from them in time of need as well as forgiveness of sin. Now for the few Israelites who had assimilated the true spirit of OT religion, repentance and amendment were indispensable prerequisites for obtaining God's mercy,[127] while for the others as also for the neighboring Gentiles petition and sacrifice were the essentials. Through adjuration pagan divinities could be

113. Wis. 11:24, 26; 12:1.
114. Am. 7:2, 5.
115. Job 7:16-20.
116. Ps. 144:3-5.
117. Sir. 18:9-12.
118. Wis. 12:16, 18.
119. Ps. 22:5.
120. Ex. 34:6-7.
121. Num. 14:13-19; cf. Ex. 32:11-13.
122. Ez. 20:9.
123. § 46:5.
124. Wis. 12:2.
125. Ps. 130:4.
126. Ps. 51:15.
127. § 40.

forced to aid the petitioner; their help consequently was not a free act of love and benevolence as in OT religion. If a polytheist believed he had or could win the love of a specific god, he still was not certain of assistance or deliverance, since some other god or demon might torment him. For Israel the covenant had a very specific significance in that it secured for the people Yahweh's special protection. Similar relationships outside of Israel were of very little importance.[128] In conclusion we might recall how Ishtar-Astarte delighted in lustful loves, how she wished to be honored by "sacred" prostitution.[129]

SECTION 3. PREPARATION FOR THE MYSTERY OF THE MOST HOLY TRINITY

§ 17. EXPRESSIONS EXPLAINED AS CONTAINING INDICATIONS OF THE BLESSED TRINITY

The OT teaches: God is one.[1] It was reserved for the incarnate Son of God to reveal to mankind the mystery of the three Persons in one God. Such teaching would hardly have been intelligible to the Israelites, and because of their polytheistic leanings very easily would have occasioned the worship of three Gods. Nevertheless the greatest mystery of Christian faith should at least have been foreshadowed in the OT. By this however we are not referring to expressions which some Church Fathers and certain theologians have applied to the Blessed Trinity in the light of the NT.

The words, "Let us make man,"[2] do not re-echo an older polytheism among the Hebrews. The singular of the verb and of the pronoun occur in the very next sentences, "Elohim made (sing.) man according to his (sing.) image[3] .... Elohim blessed (sing.) them (Adam and Eve)."[4] There is no reference to the Trinity in these passages. Regarding the plural form of the word Elohim, cf. §5:3; 7:4. The expression, "Let us make man," was meant to indicate that in the case of man's creation, God considered the matter in a most special manner, taking counsel as it were with Himself and not simply issuing an order as had been the procedure in preceding works. A consultation with the angels can hardly be implied since angels are mentioned nowhere in the whole creation story. The passage in the account of the fall, "Man is become like one of us,"[5] may be explained on the basis of the plural form of Elohim present in the writer's mind; or one may think of the angels found in Yahweh's entourage[6] —a few verses later the author introduces the cherubim. The resolve, "Let us descend and confound their speech," is a self-exhortation.[7] At the call of Isaias Yahweh asked, "Whom shall I send, and who will go for us?"[8] Here the plural may include the seraphim—the prophet should promote God's honor even as the seraphim. In the verse, "Yahweh let fire rain over Sodom and

128. Baal-berith at Shechem,   Judg. 8:33; 9:4.   129. Cf. § 11:5.
1. § 7.   4. Gen. 1:28.   32:2.
2. Gen. 1:26.   5. Gen. 3:22.   7. Gen. 11:7.
3. Gen. 1:27.   6. Gen. 18:2; 19:1; 28:12;   8. Is. 6:8.

Gomorrhah from Yahweh,"[9] the second Yahweh is used in place of the personal pronoun, a frequent occurrence.

In the priestly blessing of Num. 6:24-26 the name Yahweh was used *three* times, and the seraphim three times sang "holy."[10] The number three signified perfection, the blessing should draw down upon man all graces; for the same reason Jacob called upon God three times as he blessed his grandchildren,[11] and the seraphim thrice praised God as the All-holy. In Jos. 22:22 the divine names, El, Elohim, Yahweh, follow each other twice. Proof that the threefold repetition simply implies intensification may be adduced from parallel passages: the opponents of Jeremias repeated, "Temple of Yahweh," three times, i.e., the temple would be an impregnable stronghold for them.[12] Jeremias began a sermon, "Land, Land, Land, hear Yahweh's word."[13] Yahweh threatened, "In ruins, in ruins, in ruins will I lay her (the city)."[14] Other passages which could serve to illustrate the significance of the number three are: Gen. 15:9; 30:36; 40:10; 40:16; Ex. 3:18; 19:11; 23:14; Lev. 19:23; Num. 19:12; 22:23f; 31:19; Nah. 1:2. A twofold repetition was also indicative of special emphasis, e.g., God called, "Yahweh, Yahweh,"[15] when He revealed Himself to Moses. To Isaias the Lord said, "I, I am Yahweh[16].... I, I am he who blots out your transgression[17].... Here I am, here I am."[18] The man of God who announced to Jeroboam I the overthrow of the altar began his speech, "Altar, Altar!"[19] (No conclusive argument can be drawn from patristic writings because the Fathers are not of one mind in the interpretation of these and similar passages; many hold the mystery of the Blessed Trinity was not revealed in the OT, but only in the NT; often too they do not give the literal sense but an accommodated one in their interpretations.)

§ 18. "MAL'AKH-YAHWEH"

In many OT narratives we find the words, *mal'akh-Yahweh*, or *mal'akh-Elohim*, which English translations usually render as, "the angel of the Lord." Sometimes an angel in the accepted sense of the word is undoubtedly meant as, for instance, in the case of the angel who after David's census punished Israel,[1] or the angel who appeared to Elias,[2] or the angel who smote the Assyrian army,[3] or the angel in the Susanna account,[4] or the angel who carried Habacuc to Babylon.[5] In other passages, especially in the Pentateuch and in the Book of Judges, there is a real problem regarding the specific meaning intended by the sacred writer.

The *mal'akh-Yahweh* who met Agar in the wilderness addressed her by name and promised her innumerable descendants;[6] she should name the child in her womb Ismael, "God hears;" in v. 13 the expression *mal'akh-Yahweh*

9. Gen. 19:24.
10. Is. 6:3.
11. Gen. 48:15-16.
12. Jer. 7:4.

13. Jer. 22:29.
14. Ez. 21:32.
15. Ex. 34:6.
16. Is. 43:11.

17. Is. 43:25.
18. Is. 65:1.
19. 3 Kgs. 13:2.

1. 2 Sam. 24:16.
2. 4 Kgs. 1:3, 15

3. 4 Kgs. 19:35.
4. Dan. 13:55, 59.

5. Dan. 14:34-39.
6. Gen. 16:7.

alternates with Yahweh used without modifiers. This interchange is also found
in Gen. 21:17, 19, 20 where the *mal'akh-Yahweh* called to Agar from out of
heaven, but Elohim opened her eyes, and Elohim was with the boy. As Abraham
was on the point of sacrificing Isaac, the *mal'akh-Yahweh* called to him from
heaven, "Now I know that you are God-fearing and would not have kept your
son, your only son, from me."[7] Abraham had in mind to sacrifice to Yahweh,
not to a created angel; and after the manifestation he named the place "Yahweh
sees."[8] The *mal'akh-Yahweh* spoke to Jacob in a dream, "I am the God of
Bethel."[9] When Jacob was blessing Ephraim and Manasses he invoked the
mal'akh that had saved him from all evil in parallel terms with the God before
whom his fathers had walked and who had given him protection;[10] the words,
"May he bless," cannot be interpreted as implying an essential distinction
between God and the *mal'akh;* and moreover, where is it recounted how an
angel accompanied Jacob, and that throughout his whole life? When Moses
received his call on Horeb the *mal'akh-Yahweh* appeared to him in fiery flames,
while Yahweh saw Moses approach and Elohim called to him from the thorn-
bush.[11] Yahweh promised the Israelites, "I will send *my mal'akh* before you;
he shall not forgive your infidelity, since my name is in him."[12] Accordingly
the *mal'akh-Yahweh* here led the people,[13] while in Ex. 14:24 Yahweh led
them. In the latter part of the Balaam story Yahweh's *mal'akh* is on the scene
of action,[14] even as previously Yahweh alone had been.[15] The "captain of
Yahweh's host," i.e., the *mal'akh* who appeared to Josue was not one of the
heavenly creatures.[16] In the account of the appearance granted to Gedeon,
the expression, *mal'akh-Yahweh,*[17] alternates with *mal'akh-Elohim,*[18] or with
Yahweh alone.[19] Gedeon addressed the *mal'akh-Yahweh,* "Yahweh, Lord," and
the *mal'akh* requested sacrifice.[20] The *mal'akh-Yahweh* who promised Manue
and his wife a son (Samson) was likewise called Elohim and Yahweh,[21] and
He too accepted sacrifice.[22]

In later centuries the figure of the *mal'akh-Yahweh* appears less often. From
the postexilic period only a few passages can be cited. In a vision described
by the prophet Zacharias the *mal'akh-Yahweh* accuses the high priest Josue
in the presence of Satan. The *mal'akh* orders the angels standing before Him,
i.e., serving Him, to take off Josue's filthy rags and to clothe him with clean
garments after which He forgives him his guilt.[23] In messianic times the house
of David will rule "as God, as the *mal'akh-Yahweh;*[24] the second phrase in
this comparison does not imply a limiting of sovereignty, but rather an elucidation of what precedes. In the passage, "Behold I send my angel to prepare
the way before me, and suddenly the Lord whom you seek will come into his
temple, and the angel of the covenant *(mal'akh habberith)* whom you so ear-

---

7. Gen. 22:11-12.
8. Gen. 22:14.
9. Gen. 31:11, 13.
10. Gen. 48:15-16.
11. Ex. 3:2, 4.
12. Ex. 23:20-21; cf. Ex. 33:
14-15; Is. 63:9; "my"

mal'akh, as in Sam. G V
and v. 23.
13. Ex. 13:21.
14. Num. 22:22-35.
15. Num. 22:9-21.
16. Jos. 5:13-15.
17. Judg. 6:11, 21.

18. Judg. 6:20.
19. Judg. 6:14, 16, 23.
20. Judg. 6:21-22.
21. Judg. 13:22-23.
22. Judg. 13:20.
23. Zach. 3:1-5.
24. Zach. 12:8.

nestly desire,"[25] the "angel of the covenant" is identical with the "Lord" and the God of the judgment in Mal. 2:17; the phrase is applied to Yahweh because He appeared to Moses on Horeb,[26] and led the Israelites to Canaan.[27] (Many see in the "angel of the covenant" the Messiah, cf. § 51:2.)

We may make the following observations from the passages cited: the expression *mal'akh-Yahweh* or *mal'akh-Elohim* is used interchangeably with the divine name Yahweh itself;[28] there is no essential difference between promises made by Yahweh Himself and those made by the *mal'akh-Yahweh*;[29] the *mal'akh* had been Jacob's special protector;[30] Yahweh's "name," i.e., His nature, is in Him;[31] sacrifices are offered to Him;[32] He has the power to forgive sins;[33] the angels are subordinate to Him;[34] Satan must acknowledge His power;[35] He is the angel of the covenant, identical with God;[36] those to whom He appears are convinced of having seen God.[37] A representative may indeed speak in the person of his principal, but a representative will never say, for example, "I am the king of Babylon." Now the *mal'akh-Yahweh* did say, "I am the God of Bethel[38]. . . . I am the God of your father."[39] Would anyone ever address a king's representative, "My king!" Yet Gedeon said to the *mal'akh-Yahweh*, "Yahweh, Lord."[40] The persons to whom the *mal'akh* appeared, as well as the ancient witnesses to the accounts, regarded the manifestation simply as God Himself. Still the term *mal'akh* (messenger?) of Yahweh should imply some difference. It can hardly denote God in the act of revealing Himself, since very many times Yahweh revealed Himself without *mal'akh* implications. The question, how Yahweh could be called *messenger* of Yahweh, did not vex the Israelitic mind; they made no distinction between Yahweh and the *mal'akh-Yahweh*, but simply accepted the essential identity of the two. Concerning the specific character of the relationship between the *mal'akh-Yahweh* and Yahweh, the OT gives no information. Here we have one of those obscurities with which the OT abounds. Ancient patristic writers beginning with Justin saw the Logos in the *mal'akh-Yahweh*.[41] But then, why does the *mal'akh-Yahweh*, who is Yahweh Himself, practically disappear in the more recent books? Because of the greater development in angelology? Because divine wisdom and the spirit of God were regarded as more and more self-subsistent?

No objection can be made by pointing to Marduk as the ambassador of his father Ea, Nebo as the messenger of Marduk, Thot as Re's second, Hermes as the message bearer for Greek gods; all these are independent divinities having their own peculiar functions.

25. Mal. 3:1.
26. Ex. 3:2f.
27. Ex. 23:20f.
28. Gen. 16:7, 13; 21:17, 19, 20; 22:11, 14; 31:11, 13; 48:15, 16; Ex. 3:2, 4; Judg. 6:11, 14, 16, 20, 21, 23; 13:3, 22, 23.
29. Cf. Gen. 16:10; 22:16, 17 with 12:2; 13:16; 15:5, etc.
30. Gen. 48:16; cf. 28:20.
31. Ex. 23:21.
32. Gen. 22:12; Judg. 6:21; 13:20.
33. Ex. 23:21; Zach. 3:3-4.
34. Zach. 3:4.
35. Zach. 3:1.
36. Mal. 3:1.
37. Gen. 16:13; 22:14; Judg. 6:22; 13:22.
38. Gen. 31:13.
39. Ex. 3:2, 6.
40. Judg. 6:22.
41. Dial. c. Tryph. 56, 59, 60.

§ 19. WISDOM

1. GENERAL CONSIDERATIONS. Wisdom may be defined as the ability to recognize a definite end and to discover the means for attaining it, "The wisdom of a discreet man is to understand his way."[1] For the Israelites wisdom was not mere speculation or theory, but fear of God.[2] Wisdom, piety, morality were almost synonymous; profane principles and norms of prudence had a definite part in wisdom. All human wisdom has its source in God who acts according to design and purpose;[3] this is evident from creation,[4] as well as from conservation and the divine government of the world at the present time.[5] Though God's wisdom is not expressly mentioned as frequently as His other attributes, passages stressing it are not wanting, "He is wise in heart, and mighty in strength[6]....With him is wisdom and power, counsel and understanding are his[7]....His wisdom is limitless[8]....The wisdom of the Lord is great,"[9] far surpassing all human intelligence, "Who has directed Yahweh's mind, who as his adviser has taught him? With whom has he taken counsel for enlightenment, or for instruction regarding the path of justice?[10].... My thoughts are not your thoughts, and your ways are not my ways, says Yahweh. For as high as heaven is above the earth, so are my ways above your ways, and my thoughts above your thoughts[11]....To whom has the root of wisdom been revealed, who knows her wise counsels? But one is wise, most awe-inspiring, the Lord seated upon his throne."[12]

2. WISDOM AS SELF-EXISTENT. After the exile, when belief in the unicity of God had triumphed among the masses, divine wisdom was depicted more and more as self-existent. Three stages may be distinguished in the development of the wisdom idea. In Job 28 and Bar. 3:9-4:4 wisdom is still a thing; in Prov. 1-8 and Sirach it is presented as a person, and this tendency becomes more pronounced in the Book of Wisdom. Wisdom itself however always remains intimately united to God in a most mysterious manner.

a) *Job 28 and Bar. 3:9-4:4.* In Job 28 the sacred poet describes how men laboriously seek after precious ore in the mines, but in spite of every effort no one is ever able to find wisdom.[13] Neither the earth nor the sea conceals it; it is other-worldly, no treasure would be sufficient to purchase it. "Only God knows its place."[14] When He created the world "then did he gaze upon her and proclaim her; he established her since it was also he who had fathomed her."[15] Wisdom then is a good outside of God and man, which God possesses. At the creation of the world He made use of it; it served, as it were, as a model which He considered from every side when He called things into being. In Bar. 3:9-4:4 the same thought is developed with this addition: wisdom also

1. Prov. 14:8.
2. Prov. 1:7; 9:10; Job. 28: 28; Sir. 1:14, 20; Ps. 111:10.
3. Ex. 28:3; 3 Kgs. 3:9; 5:9; Is. 28:26; Sir. 38:6.
4. Gen. 1; Job 38-41; Ps. 104:24; Jer. 10:12; Sir. 1:9.
5. § 24; 25.
6. Job 9:4.
7. Job 12:13.
8. Ps. 147:5.
9. Sir. 15:18.
10. Is. 40:13-14.
11. Is. 55:8-9.
12. Sir. 1:6, 8.
13. Job 28:12.
14. Job 28:23.
15. Job 28:27.

manifests herself in the Law.[16] Through the instrumentality of wisdom men reach God.

b) *Prov. 1-8 and Sirach.* In Prov. 1:20-23 wisdom makes a public appearance as a person. She urges all to hear her words, proclaims her intention to destroy those who toss her teaching to the wind, promises success to those who obey her. The poet introduces her again in 3:16-19, "A long life is in her right hand, in her left riches and honor. . . . By wisdom Yahweh founded the earth, and by intelligence he established the heavens." The climax is reached in the pericope 8:22-36 in which wisdom reveals her origin, "Yahweh created me" (*qanani* undoubtedly to be translated in this manner with G S Targ—cf. Sir. 1:4, 9; 24:8-9—as against Aq Sym Th V, "possessed me"). In order to forestall the reader from thinking of a creation like that of matter she adds: I was "poured out, born." While God is without beginning, wisdom has her origin in God. The author did not consider her a creature like other things God called into existence; this is indicated both by the huge number of expressions employed and by the use of words other than *bara')* and *(asah.* We must not expect to find the precise terminology of theologians in an OT sacred author. This mystery-laden truth, i.e., wisdom emanating from God, took place at the very beginning, before the origin of the world, from all eternity.[17] When therefore God began to create the world, wisdom was "present," was "at his side."[18] This can hardly be understood as mere witnessing—it implies rather an active participation in creation; therefore *)amon* (v. 30) is better translated as "overseer" *()omman)* along with G S V than as "nursling, pet" *()amun)* as found in Aq. Already in Prov. 3:19 the author had stated that God had founded the earth "by wisdom." In her activity as "overseer" wisdom was "filled with joy day after day, and at all times she played before God." The work was as easy as a game for her.[19] Wisdom consequently is both eternal and omnipotent. "Before him" she played, i.e., she acted according to God's will; "day after day," i.e., not only at creation but afterwards also. "I have my joy with the children of men," i.e., she loves them and seeks to make them happy by leading them to God.[20]

Sirach was well grounded in the doctrine of the sapiential writers who had preceded him. So for him too wisdom "was created before all, from eternity."[21] He tells us in the section 1:1-10, Yahweh "created her, beheld her and numbered her, and poured her out upon all his works."[22] Here wisdom is presented objectively after the fashion in Job 28 and Bar. 3. However in Sir. 4:11-19 she appears as a person, admonishes, rewards, punishes; likewise in Sir. 14:20-15:10. The most important passage is Sir. 24:1-29. There we hear her say, "I came forth from the mouth of the Most High (v. 3). . . . From the beginning and before the world he created me, and unto the world to come I shall not cease to be (v. 9)." How she "issued" from God is wrapt in mystery; and since this occurred before time began she is not a creature. Her statement,

---

16. Bar. 3:37.
17. Prov. 8:25-26.
18. Prov. 8:27-30.

19. On adults "playing" cf. 2 Sam. 2:14; Prov. 26:19.
20. Prov. 8:35-36.

21. Sir. 1:4.
22. Sir. 1:9.

"As a mist I covered the earth,"[23] does not clearly indicate cooperation in creation, but when aligned with other passages at least intimates it. Dew moistens and causes buds to sprout—wisdom transformed chaos into cosmos. Then wisdom sought a place to dwell and found one in Israel.[24] The liturgy in the holy tent and later in the temple is her work.[25] The concluding words, "All this is the Law which Moses gave," signify that her will is embodied in the Torah. Sirach emphasized the close union between wisdom and Israel because in his day, before the Maccabean uprising, many Jews had become unfaithful to the religion of their fathers.

c) *The Book of Wisdom* presents the climax in wisdom speculation. Note particularly the passage 7:22-8:1. The author describes the "origin" of wisdom[26] as an issuance from God,[27] and as words fail him in the effort to describe this clearly, he calls her "breath of the might of God, an emanation of his glory, the reflection of eternal light, the mirror of his activity, the image of his goodness."[28] Hence she must have a share in the divine nature. She proceeded from God in a marvellous manner, is immaterial, spiritual.[29] She possesses divine attributes, is intelligent,[30] changeless,[31] holy[32] (on which account she hates sin[33]), almighty;[34] accordingly she possesses intellect and will. Her self-existent character, even though joined to God in deepest intimacy, seems indicated in that w) she lives together with Him, enjoys His love,[35] x) she is near God's throne,[36] y) she has been introduced into God's knowledge,[37] z) she was sent from heaven to earth.[38] She was present when God created the world not as a mere spectator,[39] for she acted as His counsellor.[40] The first time she employed her omnipotence[41] was at the world's creation. She operates all things and is able to accomplish all things;[42] she is the creatress,[43] the artist who fashions all.[44] In Sirach's mind wisdom not only created the world, but also governs it. She directs everything,[45] penetrating everything, even spirits.[46] She renews everything,[47] extends herself mightily from one end of the universe to the other and excellently orientates the whole ensemble.[48] Her special love is tendered to mankind.[49] She confers upon men good counsel,[50] and aids them at work.[51] All sciences have their source in her,[52] while rulers and judges are enabled to perform their functions through her.[53] In battle it is she who grants victory.[54] Her primary endeavor is to benefit men spiritually. She teaches all virtues.[55] She knows what is pleasing to God, guides men to Him,[56] and to the extent she enters their souls, makes them holy.[57] She rewards those who listen to her,[58] and saves them from sin and error.[59]

23. Sir. 24:3.
24. Sir. 24:5-8.
25. Sir. 24:10; cf. 4:14.
26. Wis. 6:22.
27. Wis. 9:6.
28. Wis. 7:25-26.
29. Wis. 1:5-6; 7:22; 9:17.
30. Wis. 7:22.
31. Wis. 7:27.
32. Wis. 7:22.
33. Wis. 1:4.
34. Wis. 7:23, 27.
35. Wis. 8:3; 9:9.
36. Wis. 9:4, 10.
37. Wis. 8:4.
38. Wis. 9:10.
39. Wis. 9:9.
40. Wis. 8:4.
41. Wis. 7:23.
42. Wis. 8:5; 7:27.
43. Wis. 7:12.
44. Wis. 7:22.
45. Wis. 7:23.
46. Wis. 7:23-24.
47. Wis. 7:27.
48. Wis. 8:1.
49. Wis. 1:6; 7:23.
50. Wis. 8:9.
51. Wis. 9:10.
52. Wis. 7:17-21; 8:8.
53. Wis. 8:9-15.
54. Wis. 8:15.
55. Wis. 8:7.
56. Wis. 6:19; 8:7; 9:9.
57. Wis. 7:27.
58. Wis. 7:11-12; 8:17-18.
59. Wis. 9:18; on the manner of her presence in creatures, cf. § 13:2.

A comparison of the style in older wisdom books with that in the Book of Wisdom will show how the latter is distinguished by abstract speech and philosophical phraseology. The author makes no attempt to conceal his Hellenistic background and his devotion to Greek learning. According to Prov. 8:31 wisdom loves the children of men, but according to Wis. 7:22-23 there is in her a beneficent spirit lovingly disposed toward men. According to Sir. 24:5 wisdom walks about everywhere, but according to Wis. 7:24; 8:1 she reaches mightily from one end of the universe to the other. And a real advance is made by the author of the Book of Wisdom in presenting wisdom as self-existent.

The OT writers personified wisdom to a strikingly greater degree than other divine attributes. God's justice is said to look down from heaven and to go before Him;[60] the psalmist sings of piety and fidelity meeting each other,[61] and of loving-kindness and fidelity preceding Yahweh.[62] In one passage God's attributes are likened to angels who assist men, "Send forth your light and your fidelity, they shall lead me."[63] "May his loving-kindness approach us[64] . . . . Your mercy and fidelity shall ever protect me[65] . . . . Swiftly let your mercy come to meet us."[66] In these passages the poets merely intended to employ figurative language in order to make the description more vivid; they were satisfied with a short metaphorical turn. The procedure followed in personifying wisdom is quite different, and this is significant.

Why was God's wisdom singled out and depicted so vividly as a person and not, e.g., His omnipotence, His justice or His love? The answer may be simply that it was wisdom teachers who were concerned in the matter. Since they wanted to teach men "wisdom," they meditated at length on this attribute. Thus they discovered how wisdom revealed herself in creation, how she educated men to live according to God's will, moved sinners, aided penitents, consoled the sorrowful.

The sacred writers were constantly striving to present the doctrine of divine wisdom with greater clarity. How then explain the obscurities we sometimes meet? In the first place we must remember that the matter is treated in poetical books where rich imagery and figurative language are in place. In certain passages the sacred authors speak of wisdom as if it were a divine attribute or a good proper to God; compare, for example, Prov. 3:13-15 with 3:16-18; Sir. 1:1-10 with 24; Wis. 7:13-14 with 7:22-8:1. How belief in one God may be reconciled with wisdom as a person possessing divine attributes is not discussed. While wisdom appears as a divine person who espoused the cause of men and conferred all temporal and eternal goods, there is no trace of prayers being directed to wisdom as to a person. Neither is wisdom expressly called a divine person, it is only portrayed as such. The author of wisdom never said, "Wisdom is God," as St. John proclaimed, "The Word is God." All prerequisites

60. Ps. 85:12, 14.   63. Ps. 40:3.   65. Ps. 40:12.
61. Ps. 85:11-12.   64. Ps. 59:11.   66. Ps. 79:8.
62. Ps. 89:15.

seem present, the step needed was not a great one, but no wisdom writer ever took that step. So even in the Book of Wisdom the concept of wisdom hovers between attribute and real person. The OT was ordained to prepare men for the revelation to be given by the second person of the Blessed Trinity, who from eternity had proceeded from Its bosom; He was to appear upon earth to instruct, to console, to warn and to lead to God; the full light first shone in darkness when Wisdom Itself appeared upon earth.

3. WISDOM AS A PERSON IN THE OT AND IN THE NT. In the Gospel Jesus is called "Wisdom" and the "Wisdom of God"[67] without further elucidation. Already in the apostolic Church wisdom and Christ were synonymous. St. Paul called Christ "the first-born of every creature[68]. . . . the image of the invisible God[69]. . . . the power of God and the wisdom of God. . . . God-given wisdom."[70] Through Christ all things have been made,[71] and His activity keeps all things in existence.[72] Christ guided the Israelites in the wilderness, preserved them from destruction.[73] In Heb. 1:3 He is designated the "brightness of his glory and the image of his substance."[74] The Logos doctrine in the first chapter of St. John's Gospel agrees remarkably well with the teaching contained in the Book of Wisdom; compare but the first passage, "In the beginning was the Word, and the Word was with God. . . . all things were made through him," with Wis. 7:12, 22; 8:5; 9:4, 9, 10.[75] Patristic writers, beginning with Justin,[76] identified wisdom with Christ.[77]

In later Jewry wisdom as a person received increasingly less attention. Commentators were satisfied to compare it with the Law,[78] and glorified the Torah in the way the sapiential writers had glorified wisdom. The basis for this change lies in Jewish antagonism toward Christians who saw Christ personified in the OT wisdom teaching, as well as in the hostile attitude of the Rabbis toward all "profane" knowledge.

4. WISDOM AMONG ISRAEL'S NEIGHBORS. a) *Oriental wisdom gods.* In Babylon Ea, Marduk, Nebo and Ishtar received special praise as "wise" gods. Alongside these Nina and Nisaba (originally grain gods) took a secondary position, as also Chasisu (i.e., thought or intelligence). Among the Egyptians Ptah was regarded as particularly wise; being a craftsman he was believed to have been the creator of the world. The Greeks compared Thot, the god of arithmetic and writing, to Hermes, and praised him as Trismegistos; Isis was the outstanding personage in the Egyptian pantheon during the Graeco-Roman period. For the Persians Ahura-Mazda was the "wise" god, but he proceeded from a divinity no more than did Ea. His heavenly household, the six Amesha Spenta, are personifications of moral concepts, of which one was Spenta Armatay, interpreted (first by Plutarch!) as "consummate wisdom."

67. Matth. 11:19; Lk. 11:49;
    cf. Matth. 23:34-36.
68. Col. 1:15; cf. Prov. 8:22;
    Sir. 1:4.
69. Col. 1:15; cf. Wis. 7:26.
70. 1 Cor. 1:24, 30.
71. Col. 1:16; cf. Prov. 8:30;
    Wis. 7:22; 8:4.
72. Col. 1:17; cf. Wis. 8:1;
    7:27.
73. 1 Cor. 10:4; cf. Wis. 10:
    17-18; 11:4.
74. Cf. Wis. 7:25-26.
75. Cf. Prov. 8:22, 30.
76. Dial. c. Tryph. 129.
77. Hudal 106-124.
78. Cf. Bar. 4:1; Sir. 24:23.

Now Darius, Xerses and Artaxerses I were the only Zarathustrian monarchs,[79] and it may be doubted whether the religious ideas which they sponsored became popular, and whether the Jews were influenced to any extent by them.

The Babylonians and the Egyptians accordingly regarded various individuals as wisdom gods. In the OT wisdom is always one. The wisdom divinities arose from forces inherent in chaos, e.g., Ea was and ever remained a personification of water, Marduk of the morning and springtime sun; but Wisdom was in no way earthly. Spenta Armatay had been a nature goddess, a characteristic she never quite outgrew. Ea and Marduk were invoked in oath formulae and in atonement rites, and as patrons of the lowest forms of superstition. Ishtar was honored chiefly as a mother-goddess. Upon moral living these wisdom gods exercised no influence. OT wisdom transcends the wisdom gods of the ancient Orient as monotheism transcends polytheism. There can be no question of borrowing. It has not even been proven whether the wisdom teachers received incentives from the oriental religions in developing the concept of wisdom. They possessed the notion of an omniscient God who had made and who governs the world, who confers wisdom upon men to enable them to attain the love of God. Wisdom is depicted as a person during a period in which the Babylonian religious ideas no longer enjoyed the same importance for Israel as previously. The Egyptian gods likewise had lost their power of attraction after the exile. As there was no danger that the Jews would adopt Persian, Babylonian or Egyptian gods, the wisdom teachers had no reason for counterposing the wisdom of Yahweh against that of false wisdom gods.

b) *Greek philosophy*. Speculation upon wisdom in Israel hardly arose under the influence of Greek thought. Hellenistic influences upon the Orient surely antedate the triumphal march of Alexander the Great, but Stoic itinerant philosophers certainly did not appear in Palestine before chapters 1-8 of Proverbs had taken form. Now the style and method in which wisdom speaks in the older proverb literature justifies the conclusion that this was not the first time wisdom was personified; the author proceeds as if the reader were very familiar with his method.

The Greek philosophers preceding the Stoics directed their efforts primarily toward explaining the order revealed in the universe. Although this problem was not disregarded by the sapiential writers, they much preferred to regard wisdom as a means toward living in harmony with God's holy will. To Greek thinkers wisdom was a cosmological principle, to Jewish teachers it was primarily ethical. Although Jesus Sirach was reared in a Hellenistic environment, he adhered strictly to traditional Jewish belief and considered Hellenism an enemy. In his doctrine on wisdom he relied upon older sapiential writers. Greek sources may have contributed certain expressions but not fundamental ideas. The author of the Book of Wisdom lived in Alexandria, a center of Hellenistic culture, a treasure house of Greek science. He described wisdom

79. RHR 113, 1936, 21-41;
    § 7:5d.

in terms Anaxagoras had depicted *nous* (viz., reason as revealing itself in
the world). For the one *nous*, for the other wisdom is the most excellent and
purest of all things, has no connection with matter, is motionless, gave matter
motion, and penetrates all. The sacred writer thus compares the *nous* of the
Greeks with the wisdom of the OT. Plato elevated ideas to realities of which
the highest, the idea of the good, is *nous*, *logos*, or wisdom. It is the world-soul,
extends over all matter, is the source of all motion and life, possesses mobility
but itself is incorporeal. The similarity with wisdom in Wis. 7:22f is evident;
the hagiographer compares wisdom with the world-soul of Plato, but does not
identify them. OT wisdom is not an indispensable intermediary whose services
God was forced to employ in creating and governing the world; nor does it
unite itself to matter or abandon its place at the throne of God. In addition
scriptural wisdom has a very important duty: to direct mankind to the good.
The *logos* of the Stoics is well explained as a personalization of the order ruling
in the world; it is the world-soul vivifying and permeating the universe; and
as it operates in nature by necessity, so in the moral order it decrees the activity
of men. There may appear to be little difference between the Stoic's doctrine
of the *logos* and OT wisdom teaching, yet the concepts in the two systems are
contradictory; the Stoic doctrine is pantheistic, the difference between God
and the world being only relative; it knows nothing of a personal God. OT
wisdom and the world stand in opposition to each other as creator and creature,
the one is spirit, the other matter; Yahweh is a personal God with wisdom
present at His throne. The *logos* indwells in all men in a uniform way, but
wisdom makes a distinction in the mode of indwelling.[80] The Stoics might
praise their *logos* ever so highly and glorify its might and providence, yet when
affliction came they turned to a personal god from whom they expected compassion in trial and sorrow. Impersonal power penetrating the world as *logos*
left them cold; it probably satisfied the intellect, but brought no peace to
yearning hearts.

When we accordingly find the author of the Book of Wisdom portraying
wisdom with terminology borrowed from Greek philosophy, we must distinguish
between content and form, between the thoughts advanced and the figures with
which such thoughts are clothed. The sacred writer does not want his words
understood in the pantheistic sense accorded them in the various philosophical
systems; and perhaps he became familiar with many such terms by way of
popular use when their original signification had already been profoundly modified. He employed philosophical expressions to depict wisdom not only because
he was thinking in Greek channels, but because he had the definite purpose of
informing the educated reader among his Hellenistic kinsmen as also all interested Greeks that in the OT were hid treasures having some similarity with
the doctrine of Greek philosophy, indeed that Jewish wisdom was far superior
to the *logos* of the Stoa, that it bestowed peace on one's soul and led to moral

80. § 13:2.

living. By his doctrine of personalized wisdom he did not seek to explain away
monotheism or to transform it into pantheism; on the contrary he endeavored
to deepen faith in the one, personal, omnipotent and transcendent God.

The very fact that wisdom speculation avoided the pitfalls of error and
that OT belief in God suffered no harm demonstrates the great vitality and
clarity of OT concepts about God. This orthodoxy can hardly be adequately
accounted for without positing divine guidance. A glance over the religious
philosophy of Philo, who wrote in Alexandria only a few decades after the
composition of the Book of Wisdom, will corroborate this. Philo too strove
to be a faithful adherent of his fathers' religion; he too knew Greek thinkers,
being even more deeply immersed in their doctrine than the sacred writer;
he too wished to win pagans for the God of Israel. But while the author of
the Book of Wisdom culled certain terms from the teaching of Anaxagoras,
Plato and the Stoics and filled them with new content, Philo sought to reconcile
Jewish belief and Greek knowledge, to harmonize the personal God of Israel
with the impersonal pantheistic doctrines of the philosophers. He separated
God and the world, while OT wisdom teaching ever maintained the closest
union between God and creation.

The wisdom gods of oriental religions have disappeared. Reason immanent
in the universe as propounded by the Stoa, may still have proponents—at least
a few—who after denying a personal God acclaim it as the highest principle.
Philo's *logos* is of interest to some scattered scholars. But divine Wisdom of
the OT assumed human flesh, is and ever remains the Alpha and the Omega,
the first and the last.[81]

§ 20. THE "SPIRIT" OF YAHWEH

1. THE EXPRESSION. Like the Greek word *pneuma* and the Latin *spiritus*,
the Hebrew word *ruaḥ* signifies primarily blowing, wind, secondarily breath of
life, breath, spirit. In certain passages the *ruaḥ* of God is nothing more than
wind, air in motion.[1] There are a few references to the "holy" spirit of Yahweh;[2]
(cf. the expression "spirit of the holy gods" in Dan. 4:5, 6, 15; 5:11 (14).
The specific implications of the phrase "spirit of God" must be deduced from
the operations ascribed to it in the OT.

2. CREATION. God's power as manifested in the world was frequently a
theme for the psalmist, "You send forth your breath, things are created (anew),
it is as if you remade the face of the earth."[3] All that lives in the world can
continue to exist only because God wills to send forth His life-giving breath.
Creatures die as soon as He recalls this breath of life to Himself.[4] Successive
generation in the animal kingdom accordingly resembles creation continually
repeated. Man has spirit from Yahweh, and consequently life;[5] likewise do

81. Apoc. 1:8, 17.
1. Gen. 8:1; Ex. 15:8, 10; Is.   2. Is. 63:10, 11; Ps. 51:13;   4. Ps. 104:29.
   40:7; 59:19; Os. 13:15;   Wis. 1:5.   5. § 26:3c.
   Job 37:10.   3. Ps. 104:30.

animals.[6] The author of Gen. 1:2 imagines the spirit of God hovering over chaos and by its vivifying might producing "heaven and earth and all their host,"[7] just as an eagle with extended wings slowly hovers above its young.[8] The spirit of God is not mentioned in the work of the six days where all is produced through the creative word, but for the Hebrews there was no strict distinction between *word* and *breath*. With Gen. 1 in mind the psalmist sang, "By the word of Yahweh the heavens were created, and all their host by the breath *(ruaḥ)* of his mouth."[9] The creative command, "Let there be," and the psalmist's phrase, "breath of his mouth," are parallel; in Babylonian too the latter is equivalent to *word*. In ordinary usage spirit and word often appear parallel.[10] The significance of the spirit of God in creation is referred to in the Book of Judith.[11] According to the author of the Book of Wisdom, "the spirit of the Lord fills the whole world, and he (i.e., the spirit) who embraces all knows every spoken word."[12] Since the beginning the spirit of God is present everywhere in the universe, and to it creation must be grateful for further existence. "Your immortal spirit is in all things,"[13] i.e., all creatures have a share in the life-bestowing spirit of God.

3. ISRAEL. In order to bring deliverance to the Chosen People in times of crisis, or to lead them back again after they had apostatized, Yahweh equipped certain individuals with "spirit" in a special manner. This spirit roused up the will to fight in the judges Othoniel, Gedeon and Jephte and enabled them to muster the people humbled by their enemies and thus free them from further oppression.[14] By the spirit of God Samson was enabled to exercise preternatural strength;[15] Saul, the son of a farmer and from a family of small repute, quickly rallied the Israelites to battle when the spirit of God had come upon him.[16] The artisans who constructed the tabernacle and its appurtenances owed their skills to a divine spirit.[17] The spirit of God brought a state of ecstatic rapture upon certain individuals, e.g., the 70 elders selected to aid Moses in governing the people,[18] Balaam,[19] the prophets at the time of Samuel,[20] Saul,[21] the servants of Saul.[22] In an ecstatic state Ezechiel was seemingly transported from Babylon to Jerusalem and brought back again, and on another occasion saw the field of dead bones.[23] The prophets could be carried away bodily by the spirit of God, as for instance, Elias,[24] while Ezechiel was lifted up by it and set upon his feet.[25]

During the Exodus journey Yahweh promised to take some of the spirit which rested upon Moses and bestow it upon the 70 elders.[26] This spirit of God however is not to be regarded as something material, and therefore divisible; the expression simply implies that Moses possessed the spirit of God in a superabundant measure and the 70 elders were to receive it through Moses,

6. Gen. 6:17; 7:15, 22.
7. Gen. 2:1.
8. Deut. 32:11.
9. Ps. 33:6.
10. 2 Sam. 23:2; Is. 42:1; 59:21; Agg. 2:5; Zach. 7:12; Neh. 9:20.
11. Jud. 16:14 (17).

12. Wis. 1:7.
13. Wis. 12:1.
14. Judg. 3:10; 6:34; 11:29.
15. Judg. 14:6, 19; 15:14.
16. 1 Sam. 11:6.
17. Ex. 31:3; 35:31.
18. Num. 11:25-26.
19. Num. 24:2-3.

20. 1 Sam. 19:20.
21. 1 Sam. 10:6, 10.
22. 1 Sam. 19:20.
23. Ez. 8:3; 11:1, 24; 37:1.
24. 3 Kgs. 18:12; 4 Kgs. 2:16.
25. Ez. 2:2; 3:24.
26. Num. 11:17.

since they were inferior to him and subject to his instructions. Eliseus wished that two-thirds of the spirit which rested upon Elias be transferred to himself, since he did not consider himself worthy to receive the whole ensemble of graces with which his master was endowed.[27] Individuals whom God had called to a specific office came under the influence of the divine spirit during the duration of their mission. This is true not only of Moses but also of the 70 elders, of Josue,[28] of Saul till the spirit of God departed from him,[29] of David.[30] According to Aggeus the spirit of God was still abiding in Israel's midst after the exile,[31] and with its assistance the construction of the temple was to be brought to completion.[32] Prophecy, however, was the spirit's greatest work to the Israelitic mind.

4. THE PROPHETS. The false prophets followed their own spirit,[33] the true prophets were conscious of being filled with the spirit of Yahweh.[34] Already Joseph, according to the judgment of Pharaoh whose dream he explained and whom he counselled, possessed the spirit of God.[35] Moses was filled with the spirit of God.[36] Accordingly centuries later the people prayed that Yahweh would raise up for them a prophet as in the days when their great leader possessed the spirit.[37] Balaam prophesied when the spirit of God came upon him.[38] David likewise was prophetically inspired.[39] Elias and Eliseus possessed the spirit of God.[40] When a prophet proclaimed judgment the people sometimes scoffed, "The prophet is a fool, mad is the spirit-man."[41] The spirit of God came upon Azarias,[42] Jahaziel,[43] and Zacharias, the son of Joiada the priest.[44] Sedecias, the lying prophet who opposed Micheas, claimed to have the spirit of Yahweh.[45] Since Daniel knew how to interpret dreams, Nabuchodonosor and Baltassar declared that he possessed the "spirit of the holy gods."[46]

Every prophet was enlightened and enabled by the spirit of God to perform his office of preaching truth and counselling virtue, but in a special manner this would be true of the Messiah whom they foretold.[47] When He would appear the grace of God's spirit would not be limited to a small, select group, but all men would receive it in superabundant measure.[48]

5. RELIGION AND MORALS. The prophets were enlightened by the spirit of God to proclaim to the people God's will, "You bestowed upon them your good spirit to instruct them."[49] Moses wished every one of his nation were a prophet who under the influence of the spirit might cling to Yahweh and obey His commandments.[50] However to be caught up by the spirit of God did not always result in spiritual enlightenment and a virtuous life. Gedeon tore down his father's Baal-altar, but sinned by making an ephod after which "all Israel went astray."[51] Jephte sacrificed his daughter,[52] Samson associated with

27. 4 Kgs. 2:9.
28. Deut. 34:9.
29. 1 Sam. 16:14.
30. 1 Sam. 16:13.
31. Agg. 2:5.
32. Zach. 4:6.
33. Ez. 13:3.
34. Mich. 3:8; Is. 48:16; 61:1; Zach. 7:12; cf. Neh. 9:20, 30.

35. Gen. 41:38.
36. Num. 11:17.
37. Is. 63:11.
38. Num. 24:3.
39. 2 Sam. 23:2.
40. 4 Kgs. 2:9.
41. Os. 9:7.
42. 2 Chr. 15:1.
43. 2 Chr. 20:14.

44. 2 Chr. 24:20.
45. 3 Kgs. 22:24; 2 Chr. 18:23.
46. Dan. 4:5, 5, 15; 5:11, 14.
47. Is. 11:2; 42:1; § 51:2.
48. Joel 3:1, 2; § 49:1b.
49. Neh. 9:20.
50. Num. 11:29.
51. Judg. 6:25; 8:27.
52. Judg. 11:39.

Philistine women and committed himself in such a way that he lost the super-human strength which he owed to the spirit of God.[53] Saul acted imprudently,[54] ignored the instruction which Yahweh had given him through Samuel.[55] David sinned, and that by adultery and murder.[56] The spirit of God did not in every instance effect an interior change, even though it enabled the judges to perform acts which strengthened popular faith in God's power and providence, thereby preserving Mosaic religion. Beginning with Moses however all those commissioned as prophets must be regarded as morally upright individuals, for their authority among the people rested upon the fact that no one was able to accuse them of violating God's commandments. As numerous passages indicate, Israel recognized that the spirit of God sanctified men. The author of the *Miserere* prayed, "Do not thrust me away from your presence, or withdraw your holy spirit from me."[57] The spirit of God impels the sinner to repent, transforms him, enables him to persevere, "Create a clean heart within me, O God; instil a new, a stable spirit within my breast."[59] When Isaias said in his prayer for the people, "They became rebellious and grieved his holy spirit,"[60] he implied that the spirit of God guides men to virtue. The spirit's significance for moral living is shown by the author of the Book of Wisdom, "The holy spirit of discipline flees from falsehood, withdraws from an imprudent course, is frightened away when evil approaches."[61] Since the spirit is holy, it sanctifies men, hates sin; it is the spirit of discipline, of upright moral conduct. Without light and strength from the spirit of God we would be unable to observe the commandments, "Who would have known your will, if you would not have given him wisdom, and sent your holy spirit from above?"[62]

Most important will be the inner transformation which the spirit of God will effect in messianic times, a transformation not only of Israel but of the whole world. Of course sinful Jerusalem will first be purified "by the spirit of judgment and the spirit of destruction,"[63] which will exterminate those who have sinned against God's holy will. But after this spirit has re-enlivened Israel languishing death-like in exile, the spirit from on High will be poured out and it will transform the wilderness into a paradise[64]—a picture of the spiritual operations of grace as it transforms and enables men to live in a manner pleasing to God.[65] God will then put "his spirit within them"[66] whom He sanctifies and say, "No longer shall I hide my face from them, because I have poured out my spirit over the house of Israel."[67] The operations of the spirit of God will extend into the most distant future[68] because the messianic age will be characterized by it,[69] and through it the Gentiles will be led to the knowledge of the one true God.[70]

Thus the concept of the operation of the spirit of God deepened as centuries slipped by. The spirit had been the power which produced all that lives upon

53. Judg. 16:19.
54. 1 Sam. 14:36-46.
55. 1 Sam. 13:7-15; 15:9-31.
56. 2 Sam. 11.
57. Ps. 51:13.
58. Ps. 51:12.
59. Ps. 143:10.

60. Is. 63:10.
61. Wis. 1:5.
62. Wis. 9:17.
63. Is. 4:4
64. Ez. 37:1-14.
65. Is. 32:15-18; 44:3-4; § 49:2a; 49:6ef.

66. Ez. 36:27; 11:19.
67. Ez. 39:29.
68. Zach. 12:10.
69. Cf. 59:21.
70. Is. 44:3-5; § 48; § 49:1b.

earth; it awakened champions in Israel; it enabled the prophets to fulfill their religious tasks and in the messianic era will sanctify all mankind after it descends in its plenitude upon the Messiah. Apart from its power to produce life upon earth, it was a vocation-grace which gave certain individuals, e.g., judges, artisans, kings and prophets, a special position in Israel, and enabled them to lead the people politically and spiritually. Later the pious became eager to acquire the spirit, and in the messianic era all members of God's new kingdom will possess it, lastingly. Just as all men have physical life through the spirit of God, so through it all will be brought near to God and strengthened to live virtuously and in Yahweh's love.

6. THE SPIRIT OF YAHWEH PERSONIFIED. According to the passages already noted the "spirit" belongs to Yahweh and is bestowed by Him; there is a distinction between it and God. The spirit has a share in the work of creation[71] and conservation;[72] it is omnipresent,[73] sanctifies men.[74] If the older hagiographers had considered it as a person they could hardly have said that God placed "a portion of the spirit" of Moses upon the elders,[75] or that Eliseus begged for two-thirds of Elias' spirit.[76] Moreover they attributed certain operations of the spirit to the "hand of Yahweh," e.g., Elias ran a great distance before Achab when the hand of Yahweh came upon him (superhuman strength);[77] upon Isaias the hand of Yahweh lay heavy as he was admonished not to tarry upon the crooked way of Israel (grace of encouragement);[78] Jeremias was forced by the hand of Yahweh to live as a solitary;[79] upon Ezechiel the hand of Yahweh came as he was called to the prophetic office (vision)[80] and rested heavily upon him as he began to realize the responsibility of his calling (inner illumination);[81] again it came upon him while having the vision of the abominations performed in the temple.[82]

The spirit is a power emanating from God which gives life, confers strength, enlightens, and spurs on to virtue. The words, "Josue was filled with the spirit of wisdom,"[83] mean he was enabled to lead the people prudently. In the vision of the dead bones[84] the spirit is the breath of life as in Gen. 2:7, even though the prophet speaks to it. Ezechiel's words, "There came upon me the spirit of Yahweh,"[85] precede the phrase, "and he spoke to me"; now the spirit did not speak, Yahweh did. The passage, "The Lord, Yahweh, has sent me, and his spirit" (V spiritus eius—Is. 48:16) means: He has equipped me with His spirit. To bring home that the prophets were organs of God's spirit the Jews were told how Yahweh gave oracles "through his spirit by the hand of previous prophets,"[86] how "the spirit of the Lord Yahweh" was upon them.[87] While he was praying, "Do not withdraw your holy spirit from me,"[88] the psalmist had in mind God's love and aid. In other passages the spirit is personified, e.g., "May your good spirit direct me[89].... My spirit abides in your midst[90]

71. Ps. 33:6.
72. Ps. 104:29-30.
73. Ps. 139:7.
74. Ps. 51:13.
75. Num. 11:17.
76. 4 Kgs. 2:9.
77. 3 Kgs. 18:46.

78. Is. 8:11.
79. Jer. 15:17.
80. Ez. 1:3.
81. Ez. 3:14.
82. Ez. 8:1.
83. Deut. 34:9.
84. Ez. 37:1-14.

85. Ez. 11:5.
86. Zach. 7:12.
87. Is. 61:1.
88. Ps. 51:13.
89. Ps. 143:10.
90. Agg. 2:5.

.... Whither can I go from your spirit, whither can I flee from your face?"[91]
The statement, "The spirit of Yahweh speaks through me,"[92] is followed by,
"his word is upon my tongue."[93]

The following passages tend toward personifying the spirit of God, "They
became rebellious and grieved his holy spirit."[94] Accordingly the spirit seems
to possess intelligence and moral discrimination. The passage continues, "So
Yahweh changed and became their enemy, and himself fought against them."
Neh. 9:19-20 enumerates what Yahweh did for Israel in the wilderness: He
gave them the pillar of cloud and fire, He gave them His good spirit to teach
them, He gave them manna and water; this synthesis may occasion the thought
of a very definite self-existence for the spirit, but all the author is actually
describing is Moses' enlightenment from on High. Another pertinent passage
is from Judith's song of praise, "Your whole creation ought serve you; for
you spoke and they were created, you sent forth your spirit and it fashioned
them; there is no one who can oppose your work."[95] This text is not unrelated
to Gen. 1:1-2 and Ps. 104:30 (concept of sending), and may seem to present
the spirit acting as a self-subsistent being; the thought however is not developed
further as the following line treats God's omnipotent word. According to the
author of the Book of Wisdom God's spirit possesses omniscience[96] and holiness,[97] and guides men morally.[98] In Wis. 1:3 God's "power, when provoked,
casts the fool away from his presence," but in 1:6 wisdom too punishes the
wicked. What the writer has to say concerning the spirit is predicated likewise
of wisdom. In wisdom is a spirit which penetrates and fills the universe[99] even
as does the spirit of God;[100] it is a "breath" of divine omnipotence.[101] In
1:4 wisdom, in 1:5 the holy spirit seeks to shun intercourse with the wicked,
and in 9:17 wisdom and the holy spirit are placed parallel to each other, almost
identified. Evidently the sacred writer did not distinguish clearly between
wisdom and the spirit of God. Compared to the concept of wisdom that of the
spirit of God is significantly recessive in the Book of Wisdom; nevertheless
in personifying the spirit the Book of Wisdom does show an advance over
earlier works, but not to the degree earlier works had personified wisdom. It
was reserved for the NT to reveal the mystery of the Holy Spirit. On Pentecost[102] Peter saw fulfilled Joel's prophecy concerning the pouring out of the
spirit,[103] and thereafter he was convinced that the spirit of God which spoke
in the OT through the prophets is the third Person of the Blessed Trinity.[104]
The same is proclaimed in the Creed of Constantinople: *Credo in Spiritum
Sanctum, qui locutus est per prophetas.*

7. THE EVIL SPIRIT FROM YAHWEH. God's spirit can only be good,[105]
holy,[106] because God Himself is good and holy. Yet we find "an evil spirit
from Yahweh" tormenting King Saul after the spirit of Yahweh had departed

91. Ps. 139:7.
92. 2 Sam. 23:2.
93. Cf. personification of di-
    vine attributes, § 19:2.
94. Is. 63:10.
95. Jud. 16:14 (17).

96. Wis. 1:7.
97. Wis. 1:5.
98. Wis. 1:5.
99. Wis. 7:22-24; 8:1.
100. Wis. 12:1.
101. Wis. 7:25.

102. Acts 2:16-18.
103. Joel 3:1-2.
104. 2 Pet. 1:21.
105. Ps. 143:10; Neh. 9:20.
106. Ps. 51:13; Is. 63:10-11;
     Wis. 1:5.

from him.[107] Whenever this "spirit of Elohim" came, David would play upon
the zither, and "the evil spirit" would leave the king.[108] Once as the "evil
spirit of Elohim (or Yahweh)" came upon him, Saul attempted to transfix
David with a javelin.[109] As he became more certain of his rejection, he was
seized by fits of melancholy, which at times approached the stage of advanced
spiritual despondency and precipitated a persecution complex. The explanation
that Yahweh permitted Saul to be tormented by a demon, as Job was afflicted
by Satan, has little probability—a parallel case occurs in David's life, i.e., in
the older account of David's census recorded in 2 Sam. 24:1f, where Yahweh
Himself incited the king; in the later account by the Chronicler the temptation
is attributed to Satan.[110] The OT also mentions a "spirit of jealousy" which
may come upon a married man,[111] a "spirit of fornication," i.e., apostasy from
Yahweh,[112] a "spirit of perversity" which Yahweh brought upon the leaders
of Egypt so that they led their people into misfortune,[113] a "spirit of deep
sleep," which Yahweh poured out upon Israel, i.e., insensibility as to the consequence of and punishment for sin,[114] a "spirit of uncleanness," i.e., prophecy
in the service of false gods or efforts toward leading the people away from the
true God;[115] and "a spirit" was permitted to come upon Sennacherib which
made him hear a report of bad news from Assyria.[116] Just as little as the "spirit
of judgment and destruction,"[117] or the "spirit of grace and petition,"[118] or
the "spirit of wisdom,"[119] or the "spirit of Elohim" which rendered the craftsmen able for their work,[120] refer to actual spirits or to chastising or guarding
angels, do the passages in question imply that the "spirit" is an independent
creature and not a disposition or condition. By saying that Yahweh allowed
such a "spirit" to come upon an individual, the hagiographer simply wished
to emphasize the fact that every event, whatever the circumstances, has been
willed by God and must be traced back to God as its final cause.[121] God willed
and caused Saul's sufferings as punishment, for he had proven himself unworthy of his high calling.[122] Thus too in Judg. 9:23 Yahweh sent an evil
spirit between Abimelech and the citizens of Shechem. By this we are to understand that a dissension arose by means of which, as the account immediately
shows, Yahweh punished Abimelech for the murder of his brothers, as well as
the citizens of Shechem who had aided him. Regarding the lying spirit in
3 Kgs. 22:19ff., cf. § 23:4a.

    8. NON-BIBLICAL PARALLELS. In Israel the spirit of God tended to be con-
sidered as a self-subsistent being very slowly and never attained that status in
any satisfactory manner. In Babylonian religion we find no parallel to this,
for there divine attributes very easily developed into real persons. The *pneuma*
of the Stoics was earthly in nature, and their world-soul pantheistic.[123] One
should not even suppose that the OT writers were moved by the Stoics to depict

107. 1 Sam. 16:14.
108. 1 Sam. 16:23.
109. 1 Sam. 18:10; 19:9.
110. 1 Chr. 21:1; § 23:4a.
111. Num. 5:14, 30.
112. Os. 4:12; 5:4.
113. Is. 19:14.
114. Is. 29:10.
115. Zach. 13:2.
116. 4 Kgs. 19:7.
117. Is. 4:4.
118. Zach. 12:10.
119. Ex. 28:3.
120. Ex. 31:3; 35:31.
121. § 25:6.
122. Cf. § 11:4c.
123. § 19:4b.

the spirit of God as realistically as they did, for it is in Sirach and Wisdom where Hellenistic influence is strongest that relatively little is found on this subject. The Gathas of the Avesta refer to a "holy spirit," Spenta Mainyu, but the OT was describing the operations of the spirit of God in the world and among men at a time previous to any possible contact with Persia. In the Iranian system the "holy spirit" eventually resolved itself into Ahura-Mazda; thus the course of development proceeded in a direction exactly counter to that in the OT, where the spirit of God tended at least somewhat toward a subsistent being.

§ 21. THE WORD OF GOD—THE NAME OF GOD

1. THE WORD OF GOD IN ITS CREATIVE ASPECT. To the common ancient Oriental even as to any Israelite a person's word was not a mere sound; rather as soon as it was uttered it took on existence, became effective, and constituted the initial phase of action. *Dabar* meant both "word" and "act," e.g., *dibre šelomoh,* "the deeds of Solomon." God acted when He said, "Let there be light!"—there was light.[1] God created the world through His word, and through His word conserves and governs it; this truth is constantly recurring in the OT. "By the word of Yahweh the heavens were created."[2] The psalmist graphically describes how the earth emerged from the primeval waters, "At your rebuke they had to yield, at the sound of your thunder they fled in terror."[3] "He determines the number of the stars, he calls them all by name . . . . You have made all things by your word."[4] Our daily weather is due to His commanding word, "He sends forth his decree to the earth, his word runs with greatest haste and causes snow, hoarfrost and hail to appear, and then to vanish."[5] Frequently in her long history Israel witnessed how the forces of nature acted as servants to God's word, "He ordered the Red Sea, and it dried up."[6] By the miracle of the manna they were to learn that everything on which man lived is produced by the word of God.[7]

2. THE WORD OF GOD AS THE MEANS OF SALVATION. The will of God is manifested through His word. Upon Sinai He spoke the "Ten Words," the decalog.[8] The Deuteronomic Code concludes, "This is no empty word for you, rather it means life for you; for through this word you will abide a long time in the land."[9] The psalmist prayed, "Your word is a lamp for my foot, and a light on my path."[10] By the words, "I have *taught* them with the words of my mouth," Osee (6:5) was referring to the instructions given by Moses and succeeding prophets. God "proclaimed his word to Jacob, his precepts and judgments to Israel."[11]

Through His word Yahweh revealed Himself to the prophets. Yahweh spoke "mouth to mouth" to Moses. "Adonai, Yahweh, has spoken, who shall refuse

1. Gen. 1:3.
2. Ps. 33:6.
3. Ps. 104:7.
4. Ps. 147:4; Wis. 9:1. Cf. Is. 40:26; Sir. 42:15; 43:5,
5. Ps. 147:15-18.
6. Ps. 106:9.
7. Deut. 8:3.
8. Deut. 4:13.
9. Deut. 32:47.
10. Ps. 119:105.
11. Ps. 147:19.

to become a prophet?"[12] The word of the prophets was God's word, and of this the prophets were not unaware.[13] Accordingly their words of commination as well as their words of consolation were no empty echo, but power unto the nation's doom or good fortune. The sure hope of liberty came to the exiles through the word of Yahweh, "He accomplishes the word of his servants (i.e., the prophets); he says to Jerusalem: 'It shall be inhabited again,' and to the cities of Judah: 'They shall be rebuilt.'"[14] Through His word He will eliminate all obstacles, and if necessary, will drain the very Euphrates to make an easy path for the people upon their return to Canaan—as He once dried up the Red Sea.[15] As certainly as rain and snow bring fruitfulness to the earth, God's word brings salvation.[16] According to the author of the Book of Wisdom the Israelites should learn from the miracle of the manna that they are kept alive less by the products from their fields than by the word of God, for God's word produces all food, whether through the normal processes of nature or through miraculous processes when necessary.[17] When the Israelites were bitten by poisonous snakes in the wilderness, "neither herbs or plaster cured them, but your word, O Lord, which heals all things;" natural remedies were ineffective, God's mighty word saved them.[18] For penitent sinners the word of God was likened to a saving angel, "He sent his word which healed them, and saved them from their graves."[19] The pious man prayed, "Enliven me according to your word.... Through your *word* give me vitality."[20]

God also punished through His word, "Adonai has sent a word against Jacob, it has fallen upon Israel."[21] As a hostile or chastising angel the word was commissioned to scourge the people, to smite them as a bolt of lightning. Yahweh was determined to make His word in the mouth of Jeremias a fire, and the people wood for its consumption.[22] Jeremias preached against the false prophets whose words were without meaning and power, "Is not my word as a *scorching* fire, and as a hammer which shatters rocks?"[23] The death of the first-born of the Egyptians was caused by "the almighty word" of God, which "leapt down from heaven, from the royal throne, a fierce warrior into the midst of a land destined to destruction. He carried a sharp sword, your irrevocable order. He took position, and spread death everywhere. He touched the heavens although he strode upon the earth."[24] Here the word of God is depicted as an active person. The description has points in common with that of the pest-angel in 1 Chr. 21:16. Since the writer is describing divine wisdom as a warrior, he places a sword in its hand, and to emphasize its might, attributes to it a giant-like stature. The messianic king too will be a warrior who "shall smite the *oppressor* with the staff of his mouth, the evildoer he shall slay with the breath of his lips."[25]

3. THE WORD PERSONIFIED. Every Israelite believed there was in the word of God a power which manifested itself a) in creation, b) in the order of grace

12. Am. 3:8.
13. Am. 7:15-16; Is. 2:1; Jer. 1:4, 11.
14. Is. 44:26.
15. Is. 44:27; 50:2.
16. Is. 55:10.
17. Wis. 16:26; cf. Deut. 8:3.
18. Wis. 16:12.
19. Ps. 107:20.
20. Ps. 119:25, 37.
21. Is. 9:7.
22. Jer. 5:14.
23. Jer. 23:29.
24. Wis. 18:14-16.
25. Is. 11:4.

by guiding the nation as a whole as well as each individual. At times the prophets and psalmists describe God's word and its power as if it operated as a distinct person. The inclination toward personalizing it may already be observed in the phrase, "the word of Yahweh went forth." The same is true of expressions as, "I have awaited your word[26].... My eyes languish for your words,"[27] by which is simply meant the fulfillment of the divine promises. In various passages God's word is likened to a stroke of lightning,[28] to scorching fire,[29] to a hammer which shatters rocks;[30] to it are ascribed eternity[31] and omnipotence.[32] It appears as a messenger who executes God's command,[33] heals,[34] and preserves alive.[35] These passages are but lively personifications, a literary method used when telling of God's might and benevolence toward men. Human words have no ontological existence even though we use phrases as, "his word can move mountains"—neither does God's word have actual existence. It must always *be* spoken because it can never speak for itself. This is true even of the divine word which punished the Egyptians (Wis. 18:14-16). In this passage the description is more lively, more realistic than usual, yet there is no progression in thought content beyond that which the writer already had said on the subject. The word which brought destruction upon the Egyptians was the same through which all things had been created,[36] which conserves all,[37] which heals,[38] and which can annihilate the godless in an instant.[39] In Ex. 11:4; 12:12, 27, 29 Yahweh Himself goes about to smite the Egyptians, in Ex. 12:23 He employs a "destroyer," while according to the poetic description in Wis. 18:14-16 (where the night too is personified) He sends forth His word. In Wis. 16:12 our hagiographer personifies divine benevolence, in 18:14-16 divine chastisement.

Philo sought to correlate OT teaching concerning wisdom and God's word with the teaching of Greek philosophy, in particular with that of Plato on ideas and of the Stoics on the *logos*. According to Philo God could operate upon the world only through the *logos* who recapitulated the powers of God and who served as world-reason; the role of the "word" as a direct manifestation of Yahweh's mind was decidedly recessive. Philo hardly considered the *logos* as subsistent, even though he depicted it as the son of God or as a second God, for he likewise described it as "idea" and as "force." In the prolog to his Gospel St. John countervailed the *logos* speculation of the Graeco-Roman world (including Philo's *logos* doctrine and that of Thot-Hermes) by the true Logos who created all things, who became flesh in the person of Jesus and who redeemed the world. In this he builds upon the doctrine of wisdom and of the word of God found in the OT. However, only after the appearance of the "Word" upon earth did these OT expressions take on new and clarifying light. In the OT the word of God and the spirit of God are repeatedly used as parallels,[40] likewise wisdom and spirit.[41] Only from NT revelation do we know that Jesus

26. Ps. 119:74, 81, 114, 147.
27. Ps. 119:82.
28. Is. 9:7.
29. Jer. 5:14.
30. Jer. 23:29.
31. Is. 40:8.
32. Wis. 18:14.

33. Is. 9:7; 55:10, 11; Ps. 147:15-18; Wis. 18:14-16.
34. Ps. 107:20; Wis. 16:12.
35. Wis. 16:26.
36. Wis. 9:1.
37. Wis. 16:26.
38. Wis. 16:12.

39. Wis. 12:9.
40. Is. 11:4; 59:21; Pss. 33:6; 147:18; Jud. 16:14; cf. Agg. 2:5; Zach. 7:12; 2 Esdr. 9:20, 30; § 20:2.
41. Sir. 24:3; Wis. 7:25; § 20:6.

accomplished His work by the power of the Holy Spirit and that in the Church the Holy Spirit is continuing that work, bringing it to perfection.

(The term, "Memra," found in ancient Aramaic translations, does not denote a hypostasis distinct from God which mediated between God and the world or between God and Israel; it was inserted into the text or substituted for certain words, or used to circumscribe anthropomorphisms without wholly obliterating them. Memra signified Yahweh's word or will, and replaced the name Yahweh or its corresponding pronoun.[42])

4. THE WORDS OF PAGAN DIVINITIES. The Babylonians praised the mighty words of their gods which made the world, conserved things in existence, interfered with the course of world affairs, punished, aided and healed the sick. In the Enuma elish we read how Marduk's word was able to destroy a garment as well as to restore it.[43] Divinized, though not a god in its own right, it was present at his court. In Egyptian mythology the utterance of a word fashioned the gods, the world, and mankind. Through the words of the gods things are kept in existence and men are preserved from sickness and misfortune. Even the words of the dead can create and destroy. Thot was the god of speech, yet he more often appears as god of wisdom than as "word"-god. To ḤW (the creating word) a real existence was assigned. When the Gathas were composed, the "word" had not yet evolved into a person for the Persians, and thereafter continued to vacillate between attribute and person.

In Babylon, Egypt and Israel, then, the divinity acts through "words." The explanation is simple: a higher being realizes his will through effortless command. A consequent common inclination of poets was to glorify the divine word which could do all things so easily, viz., to personify it. The prophets both before and during the exile painted in magnificent colors the power of Yahweh's word, perhaps with the purpose of counterbalancing the word of Yahweh against that of Babylon's gods. The latter's words were "a thing of nought" even as the gods who uttered them, while the word of Yahweh was power and permanence.[44] Yahweh's word is not only creative, it also conducts mankind heavenwards. In Babylon and Egypt the words of the gods served for purposes of sorcery and magic, in Israel the word of Yahweh served to save the nation and the world.

5. THE NAME OF GOD. The "word" of God is a term denoting God's will, the "name" of God is a term denoting God's person. Upon hearing it the Israelite would think of God Himself, His nature and attributes. In the places where Yahweh permits "his name to dwell" sacrifice should be offered.[45] Yahweh wished that "his name might abide" in the temple at Jerusalem.[46] Sion therefore is "the city of the name of Yahweh of hosts."[47] "His name dwelt" in the sanctuary at Shiloh.[48] By Moloch worship the name of Yahweh was desecrated.[49] In visible creation the name of God reveals itself, "How glorious is your name in the whole world[50].... Tabor and Hermon rejoice at your

42. Strack-Billerbeck II, 1924,   45. Deut. 12:5, 11, 21.   48. Jer. 7:12.
     302-333, Hamp.   46. 3 Kgs. 8:16, 29; 11:36.   49. Lev. 18:21.
43. IV 19-26, AOTB I², 117.   47. Is. 18:7.   50. Ps. 8:1.
44. Is. 40:8.

name."[51] The exalted character of the divine name (i.e., God's nature) may be deduced from the wondrous events in sacred history, e.g., "In Israel holy is his name," because Yahweh aided Jerusalem against hostile attack.[52] "Yahweh's name comes from afar" to visit judgment upon the nations.[53] Here Yahweh's name implies His justice, at other times it indicates His might and mercy, e.g., "As his name, so also are his works."[54]

Identity between the name of Yahweh and Yahweh Himself is also indicated by the equation between the name of Yahweh and the "angel of Yahweh" in Ex. 23:21; here God was revealing Himself through the "angel of Yahweh" who accordingly could claim unqualified obedience.[55] Phrases like that sung by the three men in the fiery furnace, "Give glory to your name,"[56] or by the psalmist, "To your name accord the honor,"[57] simply mean: glorify Yourself. The name of Yahweh, like Yahweh Himself, is "great, awe-inspiring and holy[58].... exalted and awful,"[59] and to it are due divine honors.[60] The just man praises, fears, loves, seeks, calls upon God's name; he is sure the name of God will help him in need.[61] To blaspheme the divine name is a crime deserving death;[62] the decalog expressly forbade profaning Yahweh's name.[63] The Rabbis referred to God by the term "Name." In the NT too the word "name" is equated with God Himself. We say in the Our Father, "Hallowed be your name."[64] Jesus prayed, "Father, glorify your name,"[65] and by declaring, "I have manifested your name to the men whom you have given me out of the world,"[66] showed how He had caused the little group which had gathered about Him to enter more deeply into the knowledge of God and His plan of salvation.

Concerning the prophecies which portray the Messiah as God yet distinct from God, cf. § 50:5. The "face" of God and the "glory" of God are not subsistent entities in the OT; cf. § 8:2. The "shekina," i.e., God manifesting Himself in a cloud, and the "voice of mystery" (bath qol) speaking from heaven belong to later Jewish speculation.

51. Ps. 89:13.
52. Ps. 76:2.
53. Is. 30:27.
54. Sir. 2:18(S).
55. § 18.
56. Dan. 3:43(G).

57. Ps. 115:1.
58. Ps. 99:3.
59. Deut. 28:58.
60. Ps. 29:2.
61. Pss. 20:2; 54:3; 124:8;
    Prov. 18:10.

62. Lev. 24:11, 23.
63. Ex. 20:7.
64. Matth. 6:9.
65. Jn. 12:28.
66. Jn. 17:6, 26.

PART II

CREATION

SECTION 1. THE SPIRIT WORLD

§ 22. THE ANGELS

1. EXISTENCE AND ATTRIBUTES OF ANGELS. Belief in angels permeates the whole OT. The cherubim are present in paradise after the fall and receive the task to guard God's garden.[1] Accompanied by two angels Yahweh appeared to Abraham at the terebinths of Mamre; the angels then continued on to Sodom.[2] Angels appeared to Jacob[3] and were not absent from the lives and writings of the prophets[4] or of the sacred writers in the time after the exile. At the time of Christ only the Sadducees denied their existence.[5]

The OT does not expressly declare that God created the angels, but this truth is implicitly contained in those passages which speak of God as creator of all that exists.[6] God "made heaven and earth, the sea and all that is in them,"[7]—which certainly includes the angels who dwell in the heavens. The reason why the angels, the sun, moon, stars, the heavens and the water over the heavens are urged to praise Yahweh, i.e., "He commanded and they were created,"[8] is that the angels are God's creatures as truly as the heavenly bodies. Regarding the time when angels were created nothing can be deduced from Job 38:7, according to which the sons of God, i.e., the angels, shouted for joy when God made the earth; for this passage includes the stars too as present when the earth was made. The angels however already existed when man sinned in paradise.

The endowments which the angels received from God raise them far above mankind. To incline Esau toward a gracious and forgiving disposition Jacob compared him to an angel.[9] The superior character of angelic intelligence may be deduced from the flattering words which the wise woman from Tekoa addressed to David, "My lord is wise as an angel of God, so that he knows all that happens on earth."[10] Angels are "giants in strength" as they accomplish God's commands.[11] Because of their moral perfection they are often called "holy ones."[12] When the elder Tobias questioned Raphael concerning his family, Raphael described himself as "Azarias, the son of the great Ananias."[13] These two names occur frequently in the OT, e.g., Azarias in 3 Kgs. 4:2, 5;

1. Gen. 3:24.
2. Gen. 18:19.
3. Gen. 28:12; 32:2-3.
4. 3 Kgs. 19:5; 22:18; Is. 6:2.
5. Acts 23:8.

6. Gen. 1:1.
7. Ex. 20:11.
8. Ps. 148:2-5.
9. Gen. 33:10.
10. 2 Sam. 14:20; 19:28.
11. Ps. 103:20; cf. Gen. 19:11.

12. Ps. 89:6, 8; Job 5:1; 15:15; Dan. 4:10, 14, 20; 8:13; Zach. 14:5; Sir. 42:17.
13. Tob. 5:13.

128

Jer. 43:2; Dan. 1:6; Ananias in Jer. 37:13; Dan. 1:6, etc. Upon hearing these names Tobias thought of persons he knew and remained ignorant about his son's guide until the latter revealed his true nature when they had returned. The author and readers of the account knew that the names had symbolic meanings, viz., Raphael, "Yahweh heals," Azarias, "Yahweh helps" (through Raphael who accompanied Tobias' son to Media, effected his marriage with Sara and healed his father). Raphael could call himself the son of the great Ananias ("Yahweh is merciful") because as an angel he was one of the "sons of God" who assist man upon orders from a "merciful God." The designation, "Sons of God" *(beney)elohim),*[14] is good evidence for showing their intimate relationship to God. Since they are superior beings they may be called "Elohim."[15] Upon his return from Paddan-aram Jacob encountered and wrestled with an Elohim, i.e., an angel.[16]

The angels, who appeared in human form handsome and youthful, were at times not immediately recognized as heavenly visitors.[17] Only the cherubim and seraphim are described as having wings. Angels ascended (they did not fly) and descended the ladder in Jacob's dream. According to 1 Chr. 21:16[18] David saw a "destroying angel standing between earth and heaven;" wings need not be added. The author of the Book of Wisdom, with 1 Chr. 21:16 in mind, described the "word" of God as a warrior who leapt down from heaven upon earth, but did not picture this "angel of destruction" as winged.[19] We may imagine the angel Gabriel as having wings because we find the words, "flying swiftly,"[20] in Daniel; but the author could also have meant motion without wings. Angels appeared to Daniel in a vision of indescribable magnificence.[21] Being incorporeal they do not eat or drink; such actions when attributed to them are only apparent; the food consumed is not changed into the substance of the consuming body.[22] The manna was called "bread of angels"[23] because it fell from heaven, the dwelling place of the angels;[24] for the same reason it was described as "bread of heaven."[25] The word *spirit* in the verse, "wisdom permeates all spirits, those intelligent, pure and most refined,"[26] refers to the souls of men and to created spirits, i.e., angels. God is the "Lord of spirits," i.e., of angels.[27]

2. THE NUMBER OF ANGELS is incomparably great. At Mahanaim Jacob saw such a multitude that he called them "camps of God."[28] Daniel gazed while a thousand thousands served Yahweh, while ten thousand times ten thousand ministered before Him.[29] Aptly then are they called the "host of heaven"[30] or the "host of Yahweh."[31]

3. ANGELS AND GOD. The mission which angels accomplish is expressed by

14. Job. 1:6; 2:1; 38:7; *beney)elim* in Ps. 29:1; 89:7.
15. Gen. 33:10; cf. 1 Sam. 28:13 on the ghost of Samuel called *)elohim.*
16. Gen. 32:29; Os. 12:5.
17. Gen. 18:19; Tob. 5:5f; in the vision, Ez. 9:2f; cf. the *Mal)akh-Yahweh,* Judg.

6:11f; 13:3f.
18. Cf. 2 Sam. 24:17.
19. Wis. 18:15-16.
20. Dan. 9:21.
21. Dan. 10:5-6; cf. 2 Mach. 3:25-26.
22. Tob. 12:19.
23. Ps. 78:25; Wis. 16:20.
24. Ex. 16:4.
25. Ps. 105:40.

26. Wis. 7:23.
27. 2 Mach. 3:24.
28. Gen. 32:2-3.
29. Dan. 7:10.
30. 3 Kgs. 22:19; Ps. 149:2.
31. Jos. 5:14-15; Ps. 103:21; cf. Ps. 68:18 and the divine name, *Yahweh seba)oth,* § 5:9.

their name *malʾakh,* i.e., messenger. They fulfill God's commands and there-fore are called "his servants, executors of his will[32]. . . . performers of his word[33]. . . . his servants."[34] They stand at His throne surrounding Him like courtiers awaiting orders;[35] they are witnesses to His decrees, "a council of holy ones."[36] They continuously praise God;[37] they observe events upon earth and report them to God in order to receive further orders.[38] The two angels who had accompanied Yahweh on His visit to Abraham continued on to Sodom to investigate conditions there.[39] In Dan. 4:10, 14, 20 angels are called "watchers" *(ʿirin),* as in the book of Henoch.[40] If one could add the words, "they who never sleep praise you" (Hen. 39:12), to these passages in Daniel, the "watchers" would then have received their name because they unceasingly praise God. Isaias uses the word "watchers" *(šomerim)* for angels, because they should constantly remind Yahweh to restore Jerusalem.[41]

Although the angels surround the heavenly throne as "holy ones," the abyss between them and God is unbridgeable. He is their creator, they His creatures who as "God's holy ones are incapable of proclaiming Yahweh's marvellous. deeds. (Yet) God grants strength to his hosts to enable them to stand before his majesty."[42] Not even the angels are capable of praising God adequately![43] This difference between God and the angels is well pointed out in Job, "Shall a mortal prove himself pure before his Maker? Behold, he does not even trust in his servants, his messengers, whom he created for *glory!"*[44] Not only is every human being a sinner, but even the angels are not perfect when there is question of God's holiness. "What is man, that he should be without spot? or upright, he that is woman-born? Behold, he does not trust in his holy ones, the heavens are not pure in his eyes."[45] In 4:18 and 15:15 Job hardly refers to the fall of the angels, although the passage does concern the spirit world (recall that only a certain number of angels rebelled against God). Neither is there any reference to the fall of the angels in the passage, "Yahweh shall requite the host of the heights on high, and the kings of the earth upon earth;"[46] rather this verse tells of the judgment which will be passed upon the stars, the hosts of the heights, because worship was directed to them. They are presented as living beings as in Judg. 5:20, where the stars fought for Israel, or as in Job 38:7, where the morning stars shouted for joy.[47]

4. ANGELS AND MEN. a) *Angels aid men.* Two angels saved Lot from im-pending destruction.[48] When Abraham sent his servant upon a mission he was confident that Yahweh would send along an angel.[49] On his flight to Mesopo-tamia Jacob was comforted by the dream of the ladder reaching to heaven: descending the angels bring graces and come to aid, ascending they bear man's prayers and petitions before God.[50] Returning to Canaan he again saw angels

32. Ps. 103:21.
33. Ps. 103:21.
34. Job 4:18.
35. 3 Kgs. 22:19; Job 1:6; 2:1; Dan. 7:10.
36. Ps. 89:9; cf. Job 15:15.
37. Pss. 29:1; 89:6; 103:20; 148:2; 150:1; Tob. 8:15.

38. Job 1:2; Zach. 1:7-13.
39. Gen. 19.
40. Hen. 12:3; 13:10; 15:9.
41. Is. 62:6.
42. Sir. 42:17.
43. § 11:2.
44. Job 4:17-18.

45. Job 15:14-15; cf. Sir. 17:32.
46. Is. 24:21.
47. Cf. § 43:4.
48. Gen. 19:15-22.
49. Gen. 24:7, 40.
50. Gen. 28:12.

in great number, a sign that he was never without divine assistance.[51] After the Israelites had sinned at Sinai Yahweh determined not to accompany them personally to Canaan, yet promised to send an angel before them.[52] To the prophets God delivered messages through angelic instrumentality. When a plague was raging in Israel, an angel in Yahweh's service sent the prophet Gad to David with the order to build an altar; the scourge would then come to an end.[53] An angel ordered Elias to meet the messengers of King Ochozias and to appear before the king himself.[54] While he was fleeing from Jezabel, an angel provided him with food and drink.[55] To Ezechiel an angel explained the new temple's structure,[56] and to Zacharias the mission of the four horses.[57] Gabriel committed to Daniel the revelation on the 70 weeks of years[58] and on another occasion explained to him a vision.[59] Later an angel revealed to him the future lot of his nation,[60] and when confined to the lions' den carried Habacuc from Judea to Babylon with nourishment.[61] The "man of God" who heralded judgment upon Jeroboam I was directed by God to accept no hospitality while accomplishing his mission; however another prophet invited him and overruled his objection by saying, "An angel spoke to me in the name of Yahweh" rescinding the injunction.[62] Although a lie, this appeal to an angel's words does witness to the common belief that angels conveyed messages from God to men.

Belief in guardian angels characterizes the Book of Tobias. The elder Tobias besought God to prosper the journey of his son and to send His angel as a companion for the journey.[63] He comforted his weeping wife with the words, "A good angel shall accompany him."[64] An angel protected the three youths in the fiery furnace,[65] and Daniel in the lions' den.[66] Judith was convinced an angel of God had accompanied her into the Assyrian camp and had safeguarded her purity from every stain.[67] The God-fearing need fear no danger, because "Yahweh's angel encamps about those who reverence him and delivers them[68]. . . . He will give his angels charge over you, to keep you in all your ways. Upon their hands they will carry you, lest you strike your foot against a stone."[69] The angel Raphael gave testimony to the guardian angel's duty as intermediary,[70] "When you and your daughter-in-law, Sara, were praying I brought your mementos before the Holy One."[71] In postexilic times it was part of Jewish belief that angels could act in an intercessory capacity before God on man's behalf; recall in particular Zacharias' vision in which an angel pleaded the cause of Jerusalem.[72]

Nations too have guardian angels. Michael, the patron-spirit of the Jewish people,[73] will be present on the last day to deliver them.[74] This concept was not new to exilic Jewry, since such an angel is mentioned in the Exodus story.[75]

51. Gen. 32:2-3.
52. Ex. 33:2.
53. 1 Chr. 21:18.
54. 4 Kgs. 1:3, 15.
55. 3 Kgs. 19:5.
56. Ez. 40:3f; 47:1.
57. Zach. 1:8f.
58. Dan. 9:21-27.
59. Dan. 8:16.

60. Dan. 10:1-12:13.
61. Dan. 14:34, 39.
62. 3 Kgs. 13:18-19.
63. Tob. 5:17.
64. Tob. 5:22.
65. Dan. 3:49-50.
66. Dan. 6:23.
67. Jud. 13:20.

68. Ps. 34:8.
69. Ps. 91:11-12.
70. Gen. 28:12.
71. Tob. 12:12, 15.
72. Zach. 1:12.
73. Dan. 10:13, 21.
74. Dan. 12:1.
75. Ex. 23:20.

Persia and Greece also enjoyed angelic guardianship.[76] The conflict between the angel who instructed Daniel and the angels of Persia and Greece is well resolved as a symbol indicative of the relationships between world kingdoms and their destinies. Already Deut. 32:8G refers to the angels as spirit-guardians of individual nations. When in Maccabean times the oppressed Jews were praying, "May God send a good angel to deliver Israel," an angel appeared in their midst.[77] Jerusalem, the capital city, had a special guardian.[78]

b) *Angels punish men*. Two angels struck the Sodomites with blindness.[79] An angel, "the destroyer," slew the first-born of the Egyptians.[80] At the time of David an angel smote the people by means of a plague.[81] An angel destroyed the Assyrian host encamped about Jerusalem.[82] In a vision Ezechiel witnessed how angels executed judgment over Jerusalem and Judah.[83] Jeremias warned the exiles that the angel of God who was with them would punish them if they apostatized.[84] When Heliodorus sought to plunder the temple at Jerusalem he was whipped by angels.[85] The psalmist petitions for an angel to drive his enemies like dust before the wind.[86] Likewise the composer of Ps. 78:49 believed angels could smite one's enemies upon God's command.

5. RANK AND NAMES. The more ancient writers of the books of the OT recognized no differences in rank among the angels, the "captain of Yahweh's host"[87] being of course the "Mal)akh-Yahweh."[88] In Ezechiel's vision of Jerusalem's imminent destruction an angel scribe appeared leading six others who delivered the virtuous, while glowing coals were scattered upon the wicked city.[89] In the Book of Daniel Michael ("Who is like God?") is called "one of the chief princes[90].... your prince[91].... the great prince."[92] The guardian angels of Persia and Greece also are called "princes."[93] Gabriel ("Man of God") explained a vision to Daniel.[94] Raphael ("God heals") was sent by

76. Dan. 10:13, 20. (This traditional interpretation does not seem to give satisfactory answers to two difficulties: a) how could misunderstanding arise between angels in regard to the welfare of God's Chosen People, misunderstanding which resulted in a state of conflict between them; b) was it not as far removed from Jewish mentality to think that Yahweh had placed a beneficent spirit-guardian over the uncircumcised Gentile Persians and Greeks in their opposition to the Jews as it is for Christians to believe that God maintains beneficent spirit-guardians over, *e.g.*, the Mohammedans, Buddhists, or godless nations in their opposition to Christianity?

Both of these difficulties however may be eliminated and a reasonable historical interpretation be given the passage in question by a simple emendation of the text. It is common knowledge that a frequent pre-masoretic transcription error was the confusion of *Daleth* and *Reš* because of orthographic similarity. Hence, if for the

consonants *šr* we read *šd* (no differentiation having been made in pre-masoretic (Śin and Šin), we obtain a word used in the Bible and common in Accadian [*šedu*] for demon, tutelar demonic deity, jinni. This would not imply that the author of Daniel believed in mythological genii; rather his mind was like that of St. Paul, "I say that what the Gentiles sacrifice, 'They sacrifice to devils and not to God' (Deut. 32:17; Ps. 106:37); and I would not have you become associates of devils" (1 Cor. 10:20). In this verse the Apostle quotes a passage from the Old Testament having the word *šedim*, and explains it as meaning devils. If sacrifice was made to them, some sort of help or deliverance must have been expected from them by their devotees. In the passage in Daniel the angels Gabriel and Michael fight off the evil influences of the *šedim* of Persia and Greece who were hindering the welfare of the Jewish people. This harmonizes well with the services accorded by angels to the Israelites

throughout their long history; it agrees perfectly with the interpretation St. Paul gives to the *šedim* and their functions in the pagan world; it removes the disturbing proposition that pagan nations acting against God's Chosen People are assisted in their efforts by good angels ignorant of the full plan of divine Providence. Cf. *Angelology of the Old Testament*, Washington 1949, p. 56f.—*Translator's note*.)

77. 2 Mach. 11:6-10.
78. Zach. 1:12.
79. Gen. 19:11.
80. Ex. 12:23.
81. 2 Sam. 24:15-17.
82. 4 Kgs. 19:35.
83. Ez. 9:5-7; 10:2.
84. Bar. 6:6.
85. 2 Mach. 3:24-26.
86. Ps. 35:5.
87. Jos. 5:13-15.
88. § 18.
89. Ez. 9:2-4; 10:2.
90. Dan. 10:13.
91. Dan. 10:21.
92. Dan. 12:1.
93. Dan. 10:20-21.
94. Dan. 8:16; 9:21.

God to heal Sara, whose spouses had been slain by an evil spirit,[95] and to restore eyesight to the elder Tobias.[96] Hen. 40:9 tells us that Gabriel "is placed over all diseases and wounds." Raphael says of himself, "I am one of the seven holy angels who carry the prayers of the saints on high, and have access to the majesty of the Holy One."[97] Special importance is attached to the number seven in connection with the angels. Whether the digit is numerically specific, or whether it was chosen because of its symbolic character is difficult to say; perhaps the seven angels in Ezechiel's vision[98] and the seven princes near the throne of the Persian king[99] exerted some influence. The vision in Zacharias chapter 4 also makes reference to seven angels and an indication of rank would not be wanting if the two olive trees from which oil flowed into the lamps signified angels.[100]

The word "archangel" does not occur in the OT. Hen. 9:1 mentions four archangels: Michael, Uriel, Raphael, Gabriel. Hen. 20 lists six: Uriel, Raphael, Raguel, Michael, Sariel, Gabriel (to which the Greek text adds Jeremiel as a seventh, who also appears in 4 Esdr. 4:36). In other discourses the following four archangels appear: Michael, Gabriel, Raphael, Phanuel (e.g., in Hen. 40:9; 54:6; 71:8, 13). Influenced by the account of the vision of the fiery chariot in Ez. 1:15, a class of angels appear in Hen. 61:10; 71:7 called Ophanim (wheels), alongside the cherubim and seraphim. And in Hen. 61:10; Apoc. Bar. II 1; Test. Jud. 3 we find mention of Dominations and Powers (cf. Eph. 1:21; Col. 1:16).

6. THE CHERUBIM. The word is of Babylonian origin. The best etymology is that which aligns it with Accadian *karabu*, to bless, to pray. The *karibi* were doorwatchers and intercessors (secretaries?) in the service of higher divinities. The Biblical cherubim never appear as mediators or as intercessors. Their *raison d'etre* is indicated by their function as a) throne-bearers, b) custodians of sacred places. Never do they serve as God's messengers to men. As guardians of holy places they first appear at the gates of paradise.[101] According to Ez. 28:14, 16 the king of Tyre dwelt in a paradise in the company of a cherub, who drove him out when he had sinned (text corrupt). The two cherubim on the lid of the ark of the covenant indicated Yahweh's presence;[102] above them "from the space between the two cherubim" God revealed Himself.[103] From this arose the expression, "Yahweh enthroned upon the cherubim."[104] Since Yahweh dwelt in the sanctuary, the inner curtains of the tabernacle and the veil before the Holy of Holies were adorned with cherubim.[105] Within the Holy of Holies of Solomon's temple two cherubim stood upright with outspread wings.[106] The cherubim in the passages so far noted had human face and form, excluding wings. There were cherubim carved upon the temple's wooden walls.[107] Alongside lions and oxen cherubim were engraved upon the bases supporting the molten sea in the temple courtyard.[108] In Ezechiel's vision the cherubim

95. Tob. 3:8.
96. Tob. 3:17; 12:15.
97. Tob. 12:15.
98. Ez. 9:2f.
99. Esth. 1:14.
100. Cf. Junker.

101. Gen. 3:24.
102. Ex. 25:18-22.
103. Ex. 25:22; Num. 7:89.
104. 1 Sam. 4:4; 2 Sam. 6:2;
   4 Kgs. 19:15; Is. 37:16;

Pss. 80:2; 99:1.

105. Ex. 26:1, 31.
106. 3 Kgs. 6:23.
107. 3 Kgs. 6:29.
108. 3 Kgs. 7:29.

had four faces, a human face indicating intelligence, a lion's symbolizing sovereignty, an oxen's signifying irresistibility, an eagle's signalizing all-embracing vision, speed and freedom from the limitations of space. Their number four, as well as their four faces and wings, express perfection. Since Ezechiel did not at first recognize the four creatures that carried Yahweh's throne as cherubim, and since he described them so minutely, the Israelites till then probably had imagined and pictured them in some other way. The cherubim of the tabernacle and temple, at least of the Holy of Holies, had only one face, a human one, and two wings. Their appearance in Ezechiel as a combination of man and animal was occasioned by the Babylonian composite creatures representing gods of a secondary rank which the exiles saw daily; and certainly they had heard the songs in which the Babylonians recounted the prerogatives of their gods. Ezechiel's vision was meant to show the Jews that all the attributes which the Babylonians ascribed to their gods were had by Yahweh's servants and that Yahweh possessed in a most eminent degree all the perfections of His creatures. The cherubim on the walls of Ezechiel's temple had two faces, a human face and a lion's face, because they stood between palm trees, and the artist simply orientated them in both directions. In the Apoc. 4:6-8 the four faces are distributed among four cherubim, each however having six wings as the seraphim in Isaias; since angels are spirits they can appear in different forms. In Ez. 1 and 10 Yahweh sat upon a throne carried by cherubim; in Ps. 18:11 and 2 Sam. 22:11 He rode upon a cherub while "thick darkness was under his feet." Though Yahweh rode upon a cloud,[109] there are no grounds for regarding the cherubim as merely personifications of clouds; in Ez. 1:5 they are described as living creatures, while at the entrance of paradise and upon the ark there can be no cloud implications.

7. THE SERAPHIM are mentioned only once in the OT, viz., in the account of Isaias' call to the prophetical office.[110] They stood upright before Yahweh and had six wings; with two they covered their face (out of fear of God upon whom they dared not gaze), with two they covered their feet (out of reverence, for they should not appear naked before Yahweh), and with two they flew. They praised God chanting the trisagion. The poisonous serpents which bit the Israelites in the wilderness were called seraphim,[111] and a seraph, i.e., the bronze serpent, was set up by Moses. Household mythology recognized creatures such as flying serpents and associated them with basilisks.[112] The seraphim which stood before God were not serpentine in form since they possessed hands and feet, and moreover could think and speak. Whether śeraph in Is. 6 is etymologically related to śaraph in Num. 21 and Is. 14:30 is questionable. The serpents are called "burning" because their bite caused a burning pain. In case the roots of the two words are identical, the angels of Is. 6 are called seraphim because one of them burnt away as it were the uncleanness of sin with a glowing coal.

109. Ps. 104:3; Is. 19:1   110. Is. 6.   111. Num. 21:6-9.   112. Is. 14:29; 30:6.

8. Source and Significance of the Doctrine on the Angels. The angels are not degraded gods. Moses and the prophets never looked askance at faith in angels; rather they opportunely sanctioned it. And it was in later times, when monotheism had triumphed among the people,[113] that angelology came into full flower. By no stretch of the imagination are angels personified physical forces; they are not personifications of physical phenomena but personal beings. The "seven" angels in Tobias did not owe their origin to the seven planetary gods. [114] For among the planetary gods there was a female, Ishtar; moreover the angels of Sacred Scripture had no connections with the stars. Since seven had always been a sacred digit in Israel, we need not seek its origin in star worship. If Ezechiel referred to Nebo, a Babylonian scribe-god, in the account about the scribe angel (9:2), it was only to discredit him in Jewish eyes. Isaias too ridiculed Nebo whose might would soon be destroyed.[115] Some scholars have added the six Amesha Spentas to Ahura-Mazda in order to obtain seven and then concluded that Persian influence is responsible for the seven chief angels in Tob. 12:15. Angels however do not fluctuate between attributes and real beings, but are spirits created by God and capable of independent activity. Furthermore there can be found no connection between the Amesha Spentas and the angels Michael, Gabriel and Raphael relative to name or duties. Belief in angels antedates the time of Moses; indeed it begins with the very dawn of human history in paradise. It is a belief which rests upon revelation, as is shown by the inclusion of the cherubim in the paradise story and by the angelophanies granted to the patriarchs and prophets.

Monotheism was in no way endangered by faith in angels. Indeed their subordinate position throws Yahweh's transcendence into greater relief. Rather than separating men from God, angels have aided men to become more conscious of God's mercy and justice. His omnipresence, omniscience and omnipotence. Man's moral fibre is strengthened by knowing that God has placed angels at his side to guard him from sin and misfortune and to punish him for doing evil.

§ 23. DEMONOLOGY

1. Demons. In the pre-Mosaic period as well as in later times the Israelites feared evil spirits. a) *The Se(irim.* During the journey through the wilderness they propitiated the Se(irim by sacrifice,[1] a practice which was again resorted to during the reign of Jeroboam I in the northern kingdom[2] and in the southern kingdom under King Manasses.[3] As the word indicates (*śa(ir:* hairy he-goat), these demons were visualized as having a goat's body. Describing Babylon's impending destruction Isaias said, "Ostriches will dwell there, and satyrs will dance there."[4] Likewise in ravished Edom, "Desert dogs and hyenas will meet,

113. § 7:2.   114. Tob. 12:15.   115. Is. 46:1.
1. Lev. 17:1-7.   3. 4 Kgs. 23:8.   4. Is. 13:21.
2. 2 Chr. 11:15.

one satyr will encounter another."[5] In the popular mind the desert and desolate places served as the usual habitat of demons.[6]

b) *The word Shedim* brings to mind Accadian *šedu*, but Babylonian *šedim* were regarded not only as harmful spirits but at times also as protective spirits. The word is derived from *šud* (equivalent to *šadad*) and means "mighty one"; nevertheless the Israelites may have connected it with the root *šadad*, to destroy, for euphonic reasons. Deut. 32:17 contains evidence that the Israelites sacrificed to the Shedim, likewise Ps. 106:37 (cf. Bar. 4:7).

c) *Lilith* was a female night demon; (note Hebrew for night *layil*).[7] The Babylonian *lilitu* was originally a storm demon. In one of Zachary's visions evil is personified as a woman shut up in an epha and carried to Babylon by two winged women. This picture implies some notion of female demons. The ʿaluqah,[8] according to the Targum, are beings who roam about and vampire-like suck human blood. Whether demons are meant by the spies in 2 Chr. 20:22, as has been maintained, is very doubtful.

d) *Demons and Mosaic Law.* Certain laws stem from very old pre-Mosaic customs and ultimately rest upon belief in demons.[9] Here we may list the prohibition to eat certain animals, e.g., swine, asses, snakes (and eels because of similarity to snakes), which once served as means of contact with demons; various birds that dwell in ruins, the habitat of demons; the law of uncleanness of women in childbirth[10] (a big family was a sign of God's good pleasure in Israel); the ceremonies following the healing of a leper;[11] the bells on the robes of the high priest;[12] the prohibition to boil a kid in the milk of its mother[13] (originally a kind of sacrifice made to the fertility gods); perhaps too the prescription to offer the first fruits at the sanctuary[14] (thus withdrawing them from the power of the harvest genii). Likewise certain funeral practices arose from fear of demons. Between the sin "which couches at the door" (*robeṣ*, Gen. 4:7) and the demon Rabiṣu there is some relation. The "evil spirit from Yahweh" however is not a demon, but simply the personification of human passion.[15]

e) *The Septuagint*, influenced by Greek demonology, translated ʾelilim, things of nought, no-gods, with the word demon; Gad, the god of fortune, received similar treatment, which shows how Gentile gods and demons were placed in the same category although the OT had distinguished them.[16] The Septuagint also rendered ṣiyyim, desert dogs, by demons,[17] and for ostriches we find sirens, i.e., demons whose primary interest was to inflict death.[18] In the verse: You need not fear "the pest that creeps in the darkness, the pestilence that rages at noonday,"[19] pest and pestilence are personified in the Septuagint (and therefore in V) as the "noonday devil," i.e., a demon who is inimical to good health.

5. Is. 34:14; cf. v. 12G.
6. Cf. Bar. 4:35; Tob. 8:3; Matth. 12:32; Apoc. 18:2.
7. Is. 34:14.
8. Prov. 30:15.
9. § 2:2b.
10. Lev. 12:1-8.
11. Lev. 14:1-46.
12. Ex. 28:33-35.
13. Ex. 23:19.
14. Ex. 23:19.
15. § 20:7.
16. Ps. 96:5 (G95:5); Is. 65:11.
17. Is. 34:14.
18. Is. 13:21; Jer. 50:39 (G27:39); cf. also Mich. 1:8, and the translation given for "jackals" in Is. 34:13; 43:20; Job. 30:29.
19. Ps. 91:6.

f) *Conclusion.* In Babylonia all evils, particularly disease and death, were attributed to demonic influences. It was believed they could afflict men with or without the permission of the gods, in fact they could torment the gods themselves. Accordingly all feared them greatly and sought to break their power and evil influences by incantations and magic, and by amulets to protect themselves against attack. While incantations formed a major part of Babylonian official cult, any such practice in Israel was a grave transgression. The Pentateuch contained laws against incantation and magic;[20] Israelitic cult possessed no prayer formulas against demons, the pious man made no cry to Yahweh against them. Customs which originally were linked with belief in demons, particularly those on sexual uncleanness and the lamentations over the dead, were orientated to Yahweh, and this eliminated all danger to the purity of Mosaic religion. Yahweh, the true and only cause of all, sent misfortune, disease and death,[21] and if spirits led man into evil ways, punishment was meted out by angels sent by God.

2. AZAZEL. On the day of Atonement[22] Jewish ritual called for two he-goats, one to be sacrificed to Yahweh, the other, the scapegoat, destined for Azazel.[23] The significance of the name Azazel (G apopompaios) is not evident. But since Azazel was given a goat he must have been regarded as a personal being; and since the sins of the people were consigned to him, a demon. He stands opposed to Yahweh as Satan does in Job 1 and 2 and the serpent in Gen. 3. Because the people thought that demons dwelt in desert places, the scapegoat was driven out into the wilderness. And because it was a goat that was given to Azazel, Azazel was believed to be goat-like in form, similar to the Se'irim.[24] Animal sacrifices necessarily required the sprinkling of blood, a fact which would exclude the notion that the scapegoat was a sacrifice to Azazel; besides the Law had condemned such practice.[25] Post-Biblical Judaism considered Azazel a leader of the fallen angels.[26]

3. ASMODEUS. A demon named Asmodeus, mentioned in the Book of Tobias, slew Sara's seven husbands "on their first going in unto her."[27] It was rumored that Asmodeus himself was inflamed with lust toward Sara.[28] By following directions given by the angel, viz., to burn the heart and the liver of the fish, Tobias sent him scouring to the deserts of Upper Egypt where Raphael bound him.[29] Asmodeus appears as the demon of lust, who had power over Sara's seven husbands because they wished merely to satisfy base passion; against Sara and Tobias this demon had no power. He was a sinister, malicious creature and may well be classed with the Se'irim, Shedim and Lilith; the word δαιμόνιον points in the same direction, and hence he is to be distinguished from Satan. The author of the book was cognizant of belief in harmful demons and sought to impress upon the reader not to fear them but to confide in God and to live in such a way as not to come under their power. The name Asmodeus was not

20. Ex. 22:17; Deut. 18:9-14; Lev. 19:26; on the attitude of the prophets, cf. Is. 2:6; Ez. 13:18.
21. § 25:6; 41:1.
22. § 34:5.
23. Lev. 16.
24. § 23:1a.
25. Lev. 17:1-7.
26. Hen. 6:7; 8:1; 9:6; 10:4f.
27. Tob. 3:8.
28. Tob. 6:15.
29. Tob. 6:8; 8:3.

used by the persons who appear in the story, but was introduced when the
traditional material was put into writing. It is related to *šamad*, destroy, hence
the Destroyer, Devastator of Sara's marital happiness. He was the counterpart
to Raphael, "God heals." Whether there is a connection between Asmodeus
and the Iranian Aeshma daeva, the most baneful demon next to Angra Mainyu,
may be doubted. The Persian demon was a wrath demon; he receives no mention in the Gathas, the oldest sections of the Avesta.

4. SATAN. a) *Development of the concept*. The word *śaṭan* means to be
hostile towards, to attack, to accuse.[30] Satan, true to etymology, appears as
an individual who causes trouble, makes hostile attacks, is an adversary in
war.[31] Moreover the term was used of David by the Philistines,[32] of the *Mal-
ʾakh-Yahweh* as Balaam's opponent,[33] of the sons of Servia in their antagonism
toward Semei,[34] of an accuser at court.[35] In the OT it is always a question of
an occasional appearance, never of continued activity.

The concept of Satan as a creature opposed to God was to some extent
aided by the vision of Micheas.[36] The prophet saw "Yahweh sitting upon his
throne, and the whole host of heaven standing before him, at his right and at
his left." When Yahweh inquired who would be willing to deceive Achab,
"there came forth a spirit" (the article is to be explained as in GK § 126q)
who volunteered, "I will go and be a lying spirit in the mouth of all his
prophets." Yahweh consented and "therefore, Yahweh placed a lying spirit in
the mouth of all your prophets, for Yahweh has decreed evil upon you." To
understand this passage remember that the OT frequently ascribed moral evil
to God, who is the ultimate cause of all things, without distinguishing between
direct active causality and indirect permissive causality.[37] Yahweh willed to
punish Achab for his sins by having him smitten during battle with the
Arameans. The king had declared war, and the court prophets strengthened
him in his resolve by promising victory. Achab listened to them rather than
to the warning given by God's prophet Micheas. Their false predictions and
Achab's subsequent delusion are ascribed to Yahweh as to the ultimate cause.
As a tool to make the king persist in his erroneous decision and thereby to
bring on his own punishment Yahweh employed a spirit. His court was formed
of angels.[38] Although Micheas beheld them in a vision they were real, had
actual existence, even as the seraphim which Isaias saw and heard in his
inaugural vision.[39] So too the spirit who came forth and proffered his service
to Yahweh was a real angel, though not a good one, for a good angel could
not have "become a lying spirit." The adversary in Job was already evil as
he stepped forward, the spirit in Micheas was merely willing to do evil; Yahweh
allowed Satan to harm Job, while in Micheas the spirit carried out Yahweh's
designs by deceiving Achab's court prophets. The narrative does not distinguish
too clearly between good and evil spirits, but it is easy to sense the course of
future development.

30. Pss. 38:21; 71:13; 109:4,
    20, 29; Zach. 3:1.
31. 3 Kgs. 5:18; 11:14, 23,
    25.
32. 1 Sam. 29:4.
33. Num. 22:22.
34. 2 Sam. 19:23.
35. Ps. 109:6.
36. 3 Kgs. 22:19-23.
37. § 7:4; 11:4c.
38. § 22:3.
39. Is. 6; 22:7.

In the first chapters of Job God's adversary is called Satan for the first time.[40] Here the article indicates an individual already known to the reader. Satan seeks to make Job despair and then to curse God. He is filled with glee at the thought that Job might not remain steadfast—evidently a malicious fellow. The author allows him to appear in a dramatic way before the throne of God among the angels, for he must converse with God and receive from Him permission to inflict great suffering upon Job. It was part of God's plan[41] that Job be tempted, for God knew Job would stand the test and triumph over all misfortune.[42] Though God tried Job to make him perfect, Satan sought to hurl him into destruction. Satan is the enemy not only of man but also of God, because he endeavored to falsify God's judgment concerning Job. He is the *diabolus* (source for the word devil), the slanderer *par excellence*.

In Zachary's vision[43] Satan (with the article) accuses the high priest Josue.[44] Here it is not a case of personal sin, for Josue represents the priests who before the exile had sinned grievously. If the high priest be condemned, he could no longer absolve the people, and God's wrath would remain upon them. Satan was seeking to destroy not only Josue but all Israel. Then Yahweh, "who has chosen Jerusalem" (this very expression indicates that it was a matter not merely of Josue but of the whole nation), commanded Satan to be silent, and forgave the high priest's guilt. In Job Satan strove against an individual man, here against all God's people endeavoring to undo the divine plan of redemption.

According to 2 Sam. 24:1 Yahweh incited David to order a census of the people; according to 1 Chr. 21:1 it is Satan who tempts David.[45] In the latter passage the word Satan does not have the article; hence it is a proper name. He is not only an accuser, but incites to sin.

Sir. 21:27, "If a godless one curse Satan, he curses himself," i.e., although tempted by Satan you remain responsible for your evil deeds; you may not cast all the blame upon the devil.

Wis. 2:24, "Through the envy of the devil death has come into the world, and those who belong to him experience it." Death is here the loss of the state of grace. For those who have become Satan's servants physical death opens the door to eternal death, damnation.[46] According to Gen. 3 the serpent induced our first parents to commit sin in order to rob them of God's love, and death resulted. The first instance in which Satan is expressly singled out as the tempter of Adam and Eve occurs in Wisdom 2:4. Just as Satan expected to ruin Job's trust in God, just as Satan incited David to sin by numbering the nation,[47] so the serpent stirred up evil thoughts in Eve to make her disobey God. Satan accused Job falsely, just as already in paradise the serpent endeavored to discredit God by implying that the enjoyment of certain fruit had been forbidden through divine selfishness. The serpent hated God and envied man; the serpent sought to rob Adam and Eve of their good fortune and to

40. Job 1:6-12; 2:1-7. 43. Zach. 3:1-5. 46. § 43:5.
41. Job 38:2. 44. Cf. Ps. 109:6. 47. 1 Chr. 21.
42. § 11:4c. 45. Cf. § 11:4c.

frustrate God's designs; hence the serpent must have been an intelligent being, though very hostile toward God. That a demon from the netherworld was involved is indicated by the words "eat dust."[48] Truths implicitly contained in Gen. 3 are stated explicitly in Wis. 2:24. The Book of the Life of Adam and Eve (10, 16, 18) and the Slavonic version of the Book of Henoch (31:6 Rec. A) also ascribe the temptation of our first parents to the devil; hence this teaching was a part of Judeo-Palestinian theology.[49]

The concept of a creature hostile to God who seeks to turn men from God existed already during most ancient times, as is shown by the Genesis account. However, since it was customary to accredit all things to God, even moral evil,[50] it was not necessary to explain the origin of evil; accordingly anyone who now seeks to distinguish clearly between direct divine causality and permissive divine causality, finds relatively few pertinent passages. Those which may be adduced emphasize the truth that man is wholly subject to God, that man is always able to resist evil. Thus the idea never gained ground that Satan's might was irresistible, while the opposition between good and evil was put into sharper relief. Perhaps Sir. 21:27 gives a pointer as to why Satan so seldom was mentioned, viz. in order to guard against the spread of the false idea that Satan is to blame for violations of God's commandments.

The question, "Whence Satan, if God created all things good,"[51] did not bother the Israelites. Nevertheless from the viewpoint of the OT all beings now inimical to God once had been good. Ancient apocryphal works link Satan's fall with Gen. 6:1-4 by identifying angels with the "sons of God" who seduced the "daughters of men" (and who communicated to them heavenly secrets).[52] In the "Life of Adam and Eve" the angels proudly endeavor to elevate themselves above God, for which they are driven from heaven.[53] But Gen. 6 is as little implicated with the fall of the angels as is Job 4:18.[54] The "sons of God" were the descendants of Seth, at least those who remained pious;[55] these entered into polygamous marriages with depraved women, whereupon the fear of God vanished from the earth and immorality prevailed.

"How you have fallen from heaven, you brilliant star, son of the dawn!"[56] These words Isaias addressed to the king of Babylon, who proudly strove to ascend the heavens, set up his throne on the divine mount, and ride the clouds pretending equality with God. The Vulgate translates, *Lucifer, qui mane oriebaris,* and many Church Fathers interpreted *lucifer* as Satan. Because he had proudly exalted himself, the king of Tyre deserved to be tumbled off the divine mount and cast upon the earth.[57] These passages can be applied to Satan only in the typical sense; perhaps however the picture would be easier to explain if the prophet had had in mind an angel who had exalted himself against God and was punished by being hurled into hell.[58] The envy of the devil is expressly mentioned in Wis. 2:24, but we should not overlook it in Job

48. Gen. 3:14.
49. F. Weber, Jüd. Theologie², 218.
50. § 11:4c.
51. Gen. 1:31.
52. Hen. 6:7; Jub. 5, etc.
53. Life of Adam and Eve, 12ff.
54. Also Job 15:15; cf. § 22:3.
55. Cf. 16:4, 5.
56. Is. 14:12.
57. Ez. 28:16-17.
58. Cf. Luke 10:18.

and in Zacharias; in Gen. 3 Satan begrudges man God's love. Such a mentality is most easily accounted for if Satan once possessed divine favor, and later lost it through his own fault. Lucifer is a later name for Satan. The NT also calls him Beelzebub (Beelzebul), i.e., "Baal of flies,"[59] an oracle-god honored by the Philistines at Ekron.[60]

b) *Satan and Angra Mainyu.* Among the Persians the god of light and goodness, Ahura-Mazda, was opposed by the evil spirit, Angra Mainyu (Ahriman), the cause of all evils: poor land, poisonous insects, the sins of men, etc. Azhi-Dahaka, a serpent demon and tool of Angra Mainyu, robbed Yima, the first man, of his Hraovena, i.e., the divine glory rendering Iranian kings invincible. Persian dualism was somewhat modified in that the power of evil was limited spatially and temporally—Ahura-Mazda would finally triumph over his adversary. In the Bible however Satan is always subject to God and cannot harm those who resist him. Ahriman was evil from the beginning, while according to Genesis all things were created good. Satan fell by sin and became evil, just as the first man who had been created perfect fell by sin. Since opposition to God is found already in Genesis, there is little logic in deriving the antithesis between good and evil from the Persians. Biblical demonology would have developed without the concurrence of Persian concepts and would have developed in the very manner it did. Nevertheless contact with Iranian demonology may have occasioned the more accurate exposition of true doctrine,[61] e.g., the express exclusion of every vestige of dualism.

SECTION 2. THE WORLD

§ 24. THE CREATION OF THE WORLD

1. ISRAELITIC IDEAS ON THE STRUCTURE OF THE UNIVERSE. There is no special word in the OT for "world" corresponding to the Greek "cosmos," i.e., an ordered universe. The parts of the universe are called heaven, earth and sea in Ex. 20:11; heaven, earth and water under the earth in Ex. 20:4; heaven, earth, sea and the deep in Ps. 135:6; heaven, earth and underworld in Job 11:8-9; simply heaven and earth in Gen. 1:1 and in most other passages. For the Israelites the earth was the center of the universe. It resembled, so they said, a saucer surrounded by water and resting upon water,[1] or better, resting upon pillars sunk in the waters of the deep.[2] These pillars are the hills.[3] From the "lower waters" arise springs and rivers;[4] at the time of the deluge all the fountains of the deep broke open.[5] Above the earth and its surrounding sea is the vault of the firmament which also rests upon pillars, in this case upon the mountains at the rim of the earth.[6] In Job the firmament is said to be hard as a molten mirror,[7] but other poets compare it to a fine cloth or tent covering.[8]

59. Matth. 10:25; 12:27.
1. Gen. 7:11; 49:25; Ex. 20:4; Prov. 8:27; Pss. 24:2; 136:6; Job 26:7.
2. Prov. 8:29.
60. 4 Kgs. 1:2ff.
3. Prov. 8:25; Ps. 46:3.
4. Gen. 49:25.
5. Gen. 7:11.
61. Cf. § 23:3.
6. Job 26:11.
7. Job 37:18.
8. Is. 40:22; Ps. 104:2.

Above the firmament is more water, hence it serves to separate the earthly from the heavenly oceans.[9] The firmament has doors and windows; if these be opened, rain spurts out to water the earth.[10] Above the heavenly ocean God dwells as in a balcony;[11] this is the "heaven of heavens" or the "highest heaven"[12] (which the OT does not distinguish numerically). The underworld, the abode of the dead, is located in the depths of the sea,[13] or in the deepest part of the earth.[14]

Such ideas on the structure of the world were common to all ancient peoples. They were not derived from primitive revelation but simply from appearances. The Biblical writers used current thought as a means to express religious doctrine. In the natural sciences the hagiographers were children of their times. For obtaining profane knowledge God endowed man not with the Bible but with the ability to do research work. And every attempt by "concordists" to harmonize the details of scientific data with the Bible has resulted in lowering esteem for the inspired Word.

2. CREATION IN TIME AND "EX NIHILO." By creation in the strict sense of the word is understood producing an object without employing prejacent material. Only God has existence from Himself and therefore all things existing outside of God have in God the reason for their existence. The first verse in the Bible, "In the beginning God created heaven and earth,"[15] proclaims that God created the world. The word *bara'*, to make, create, is used exclusively of divine activity in the Qal and Niphal, and directs attention to the fact that what is being effected is something admirable, something new.[16] Though the word in itself does not necessarily imply creation *ex nihilo* since man,[17] the stars,[18] the people of Israel,[19] and miracles[20] were also "created" by God, nevertheless in Gen. 1:1 creation *ex nihilo* is meant because the verses which follow describe how formless matter, chaos, became cosmos. The author uses *bara'* in 1:21 to emphasize God's power in making great sea-monsters, and in 1:27 to show that man is the crown of creation. Certain OT passages point to an antithesis between God and the world, between the creator and created things, and this indicates that God alone created the world and excludes all notion of a demiurge. "It is I, Yahweh, who created all things, who stretched out the heavens alone, who spread out the earth[21].... Heaven is yours, yours too is the earth, you have founded the earth and all that it contains."[22] Truly Yahweh is the sole creator of all things, revealing His omnipotence in creation.[23] Since the world was created, it had a beginning; at the moment of its creation time began,[24] while God alone is eternal.[25]

Did God also create chaos or unformed matter from which the world was fashioned? Yes, inasmuch as the OT offers no evidence of anything existing

9. Gen. 1:7; 7:11; Ps. 104:3.
10. Gen. 7:11; 8:2; Ps. 78:23.
11. Ps. 104:3, 13.
12. § 13:2.
13. Ps. 88:7.
14. Job 26:5-6; § 42:1.
15. Gen. 1:1.
16. Num. 16:30; Am. 4:13; Is.

40:26; 41:20; 48:7.
17. Gen. 1:27; 5:1-2.
18. Is. 40:26.
19. Is. 43:15.
20. Num. 16:30.
21. Is. 44:24.
22. Pss. 89:12; 33:6, 9; 95:5;

Is. 40:12, 26, 28; 45:18; 48:13; 66:1-2; Jer. 10:11, 12.
23. Sir. 24:8; 2 Mach. 1:24; § 12.
24. Ps. 90:2; Prov. 8:22-24.
25. § 10:1.

alongside or independent of God. Every passage points to God as the one absolute creator, whose power knows no bounds. As Moses was writing the introductory words to the paradise story, "When Yahweh, Elohim, made earth and heaven,"[26] he was not thinking of the creation of primeval matter, but if questioned on the subject he undoubtedly would have affirmed that it too was created by Yahweh; for thereafter Yahweh appears as a God with limitless sovereignty. The author of Gen. 1 however did have primeval matter in mind as that from which the universe would be fashioned. According to Gen. 1:2 the world was *tohu wabohu, inanis et vacua,* void and empty; it lacked differentiation and living beings, was covered by raging primeval waters and by thick darkness. The story then tells how the universe as we know it was formed. Consequently the initial verse, "In the beginning God created heaven and earth," informs us that unformed primeval matter was called by God into existence from nonexistence. Moreover God is antecedent to all that exists, including formless matter, and therefore must have been responsible for its creation. There may be an allusion to the creation of primal matter in Isaias, "(Yahweh) did not make the earth for chaos (tohu), he fashioned it for a dwelling place."[27] The author of Prov. 8:22-24 was not ignorant of the fact that chaos was once nonexistent. In the second century before Christ the belief that God created the world, formless matter included, out of nothing was common among pious Jews and shared by the inspired author of 2 Mach. This is evident from the words spoken by the mother of the seven martyred sons, "Look upon the heavens, look upon the earth, consider all things which are therein contained and know that God made them from nothing."[28] We find the author of the Book of Wisdom saying, "Your almighty hand created the world from formless matter;"[29] here he was merely using the phraseology of the Platonic eclectics, the Stoics (and Philo), to designate matter still awaiting form, i.e., *tohu wabohu.* He himself however did not doubt that God had made this matter too, for He is almighty;[30] He created all that exists (including formless matter),[31] has dominion over everything (which would only be true if He also created primal matter from which all things were later fashioned),[32] and has power to annihilate the world in an instant (implying that He also had the power to call it into existence out of nothing).[33] In one passage even Philo, who considered matter to be eternal, asserts that God is not only the fashioner of the world but also its creator.[34]

3. CREATION A FREE DIVINE ACT. If there was a time when the world did not as yet exist, if God's position relative to the world is that of creator, then God is in no way dependent upon the world nor is the world necessary for His well-being.[35] He can "annihilate it with a single wink."[36] Its existence continues only as long as and because God wills it, "What permanency would anything have had, had you not willed it?"[37] God's freedom in the creation of the

26. Gen. 2:4.
27. Is. 45:18.
28. 2 Mach. 7:28.
29. Wis. 11:17.
30. Wis. 11:17.
31. Wis. 11:24; 1:14.
32. Wis. 11:26.
33. Wis. 11:25.
34. De Somn. I, 76.
35. § 9:1-2.
36. 2 Mach. 8:18; Wis. 11:22.
37. Wis. 11:25.

world is the primary message in passages where God is said to create "by his word."[38]

4. THE WORD, THE SPIRIT, AND THE WISDOM OF GOD IN THE WORK OF CREATION. The world was called into existence through God's word, "He spoke and they were made, he commanded and they were created."[39] The function of the spirit of God is pointed out in the story of creation, "The spirit of God hovered over the waters."[40] Divine wisdom is glorified in a special way when linked to the work of creation, viz., as divine attribute, as prototype which God, so to say, had in mind in the act of creating, and as being itself active in creation.[41]

5. PURPOSE OF CREATION. After each day's work in the creation account we find the phrase, "And God saw that it was good," and at the end of the sixth day, "... it was very good." Creation extolls God's power and wisdom. The psalmist was alluding to the order reigning in the world when he declared, "The Lord rejoices in his works."[42] The sapiential writers were of the same opinion, "All the works of the Lord are good, and for every necessity he provides in its time[43].... He has made everything excellent in its season[44].... You have ordained everything according to measure, number, and weight."[45] In the psalms we praise God's greatness as manifested in nature, "How admirable is your name throughout the whole earth[46].... The heavens show forth the glory of God, and the firmament declares the work of his hands."[47] Other passages seek to arouse nature itself to chant the praises of its creator and king.[48] Mankind should join this chorus of praise; God has given men understanding in order "to show them the greatness of his works that thereby they may praise the grandeur of his works and laud his holy name."[49] And yet all nature's glory can convey nothing more than a weak idea of God because "What may be seen is but like a spark."[50]

Creation should not only reveal God's greatness but also serve mankind. Gen. 1 teaches that God has subjected all things to man as the crown of creation, a fact which is developed in Gen. 2:4f. Paradise was planted for man and the animals were made for his benefit. "The heaven of heavens is for Yahweh, but the earth he gave to the children of men."[51] Man's sovereignty over creatures however is not absolute since God remains Lord over all, "The earth is Yahweh's and all that it contains, the world and all who dwell therein."[52]

6. THE GENESIS OF THE WORLD. Excluding many brief references to creation, there remain four passages which treat the manner in which the world came into being, viz., Gen. 1:1-2:4a; Gen. 2:4b-25; Job 38-39 and the creation hymn, Ps. 104.

a) *According to Gen. 1:1-2:4a* God first created primeval chaos and then by eight acts fashioned the universe in six days. He made light and distinguished

38. § 21:1.
39. Ps. 33:9; cf. Pss. 33:6; 148:5; Is. 48:13; § 21:1.
40. Gen. 1:2; cf. Ps. 104:30; § 20:2.
41. § 19:1-2.
42. Ps. 104:31.
43. Sir. 39:33-34; cf. 16:26-27; 42:23-25.
44. Qoh. 3:11.
45. Wis. 11:20.
46. Ps. 8:2.
47. Ps. 19:2; Sir. 42:15-43:33.
48. Pss. 96:11-12; 97:1; 98:3;
103:22; 148:3-10; Dan. 3:57-90.
49. Sir. 17:8-10.
50. Sir. 42:22; § 9:1.
51. Ps. 115:16; Is. 45:18.
52. Pss. 24:1; 50:10-12; 89:12.

between day and night; He made the firmament and distinguished between the upper and lower waters; He distinguished water from land and made the plants; then He made the stars, fish, birds, beasts and man. The first three days were devoted to the work of separation, while on the last three days the localities prepared by that separation were adorned in various ways. There is an evident equation between a) the 4th and 1st day (the celestial bodies and light), b) the 5th and 2nd day (the fish enlivening the water and the birds the air under the firmament), c) the 6th and 3rd day (plant and animal life and man). Plant life was assigned existence to the third day because of its close union with the earth which emerged from the waters on that day. Two works were performed on the third day and on the sixth day. It is impossible to overlook how harmoniously these works are related to one another. Note too the use of number symbolism. Seven in Israel was the number for completeness, perfection, consummation; four was significant as implying the four regions of the earth—the author twice mentions four works; there is a thrice given blessing (Gen. 1:22, 28; 2:3), and, "God spoke," is repeated ten times. Evidently this account of the world's origin is due to the author's fine artistic sensibilities. The dissimilar accounts in Gen. 2:4b-25 and Job 38-39 (and Ps. 104 whose author freely employed Gen. 1) amply prove this. The essential here is not the sequence of the works of creation, for it was the author's primary intent to give religious truths, e.g., 1. God alone created the world, not a demiurge; the world did not emanate from God by a natural process; it is not identical with Him in nature. 2. By His spirit and His word God called the world into existence; He is almighty and omniscient. 3. God existed prior to the world, the world had a beginning. 4. Stars, plants and animals may not be proffered divine veneration since they too were created. 5. The visible things about us are part and parcel of God's great plan of salvation; they are "good." 6. Man is the crown of creation because he bears the divine likeness within him. 7. God made one man and one woman and destined them for monogamous marriage. 8. The earth was made and equipped for man's benefit; therefore man owes God gratitude. 9. Man is duty bound to sanctify the Sabbath by abstaining from work.

b) *Ps. 104* describes the creation of light (v. 2a; 1st day's work in Gen. 1), the division of the upper and lower waters by means of the firmament with mention of clouds, winds and lightning (vv. 2b-4; 2nd day in Gen. 1), the separation of solid earth from the sea, with irrigation by means of fountains and brooks (vv. 5-9; 3rd day, 3rd work), the creation of plants, distinguishing between domestic and wild (vv. 14-16; 3rd day, 4th work), the creation of the moon and sun, without mentioning the stars (vv. 19-23; 4th day), the creation of aquatic life, listing one or the other specifically (vv. 24-26; 5th day). Various beasts and birds are named in the course of the description and man receives special attention. The psalmist concludes by praising God's kindly care over creation and bids Him to "rejoice in his works."[53] The latter phrase is a poetic

53. Ps. 104:31.

enhancement of, "It was good . . . very good." Though the psalmist took the six day account of creation as his topic, his development is considerably different. His presentation is enriched by many details; he does not assert that God made the world in six days, nor does he assign any importance to each day's work as such; he does not speak of "separation." As in Gen. 1 the psalmist praises God as the omnipotent and omniscient creator who made all things good, and in addition singles out for prayerful praise God's loving providence toward His creatures.

c) *Gen. 2:4b-25* makes no attempt to describe the whole sequence of creation, but gives only sufficient detail to understand the paradise story. That this section is due to another author and does not constitute a continuation or supplement to Gen. 1 is almost universally recognized. Also according to this author, whom we believe to be Moses, the earth at the beginning was in a chaotic condition, every type of life being at first absent. After water rose from the earth and moistened the ground, Yahweh fashioned man and planted a garden in which to place him. Then He made the animals and lastly woman. No mention is made of the creation of the stars or of the sea; 2:19 presumes the creation of forage since animals need fodder; there is no reference to distinct days of work or to the number six or seven. Although in this pericope the earth was arid at the beginning and beings come into existence according to a different sequence, the religious doctrine propounded is identical: God is the sole creator of all, the world had a beginning, creation is *ex nihilo*, God is almighty, His work is good, man is the crown of creation, the earth is equipped for man's benefit, the sexes were created by God and intended for monogamous union. Gen. 1 stresses the power of God, Gen. 2 His love.

d) *Job 38-39.* Since Job had questioned the ways of God, God sought to teach him how to act in suffering by showing him his insignificance in the face of creation. All the works of creation are not mentioned, and the sequence is a free one due to the moral purpose at hand. God is said to have laid the foundation of the earth as one would a building; having made the blueprints, He measured off the ground and placed the cornerstone (i.e., the firmament).[54] When the earth was being created, the stars were present watching joyfully (according to Gen. 1:14 they were made only on the 4th day), and likewise the angels.[55] Although according to ancient notions the earth rested upon water, the poet only now begins to speak of the creation of the primeval sea, which he describes as an issuance from a womb. This newborn giant had clouds as clothing and darkness as swaddles (cf. the darkness of chaos in Gen. 1:2, which however existed before the formation of the world).[56] God hemmed in the sea by placing bounds between land and water (Gen. 1:9) and made the day and the night and the sun (Gen. 1:3, 14).[57] Then the author speaks of the lower waters (2nd day) and the netherworld (not referred to in Gen. 1),[58] of light and darkness[59] (Gen. 1:3; 1st day), of the storehouses for snow, cold, rain and

54. Job 38:4-6.   56. Job 38:8-9.   58. Job 38:16-17.
55. Job 38:7.   57. Job 38:10-15.   59. Job 38:19.

hail;[60] he lists certain constellations and the seasons of the year[61] (cf. Gen. 1:14; 4th day), makes allusion to the changes of rainy and dry weather[62] and tells of God's care for beasts and birds. A long section is devoted to the habits and peculiarities of certain beasts and birds,[63] but no mention is made about the creation of plants and aquatic animals (the crocodile is described in another setting, i.e., 40:25-41:26); neither is man's creation treated. The poet's purpose was to glorify God's omnipotence, omniscience and love as revealed in creation; he brings out more strongly than Gen. 1 and 2 how insignificant man is over against creation; man must therefore subject himself to God. At the end of his account the sufferer bows down before God even though he does not comprehend God's ways.

7. THE BIBLICAL DOCTRINE ON CREATION AND BABYLONIAN COSMOGONY. a) *The epic Enuma elish.* Outside of Israel too there were attempts to describe the origin of the world. The most important document for comparison with Biblical concepts is the Babylonian creation epic Enuma elish. According to this poem there existed in the beginning two principles, Apsu, the personification of sweet water, and Tiamat, the personification of salt water—the former male, the latter female. Apsu was called "the knowing (begetting) father," Tiamat "the mother of heaven and earth as well as of the gods ... the creatress of the universe." A third party named Mummu appears in lines 30f as vizier to Apsu. The two primal principles are presented as persons, distinguished sexually. Through the union of Apsu and Tiamat arose the gods in successive generations. The first "divine" pair were Lachmu and Lachamu, according to Deimel "Light" and "Mother of Light" (i.e., the darkness from which light is born). The next pair of gods were Ansar and Kisar (i.e., the upper and lower world). Then came the great gods Anu, the god of heaven, and Nudimmud (Ea), the god of wisdom and of the deep; after him further divinities. When the gods sought to put order into universal chaos, Apsu and Tiamat objected. Thereupon Ea seized and slew Apsu and fashioned the "sweet water ocean" from his carcass. A number of the gods allied themselves with Tiamat as she sought to avenge Apsu's murder; of these she took Kingu as her consort and made him the leader in the impending war; to him she gave the tablets of fate and fashioned eleven monsters to assist him in battle. Meanwhile in the other camp Marduk received from the gods the commission to fight Tiamat, for which he was promised world sovereignty together with the tablets of fate. Marduk captured Tiamat in a net, sent a mighty wind into her mouth, slew her. After he had vanquished the gods who were her allies and the eleven monsters, he clove Tiamat in two and from one half fashioned the firmament and from the other half the earth. Then he made the heavenly bodies, determined the year and the months, ordered the moon and sun to shine, produced plants and animals and last of all formed mankind, upon whom he laid the task to serve the gods. The seventh tablet describes Marduk's glorification by the gods.

60. Job 38:22-30.   62. Job 38:36-38.   63. Job 38:39-39:30.
61. Job 38:31-35.

A late witness to this cosmogony is Berossos,[64] a priest at Marduk's temple in Babylon at the time of Antiochus I (281-261 B.C.). According to his account there existed in the beginning darkness and water, i.e., chaos. Then came various composite creatures over whom a woman, Θάμτε (Tiamat), reigned. Bel (i.e., Marduk) clove this woman in half and fashioned the earth from one part and the sky from the other; then he formed men, animals and stars, the sun, the moon and the five planets. A certain Babylonian didactic poem relates how there was nought but sea, *tamtu*, in the beginning; after the holy places were established came men, and then animals and plants.[65]

The similarities between Biblical and Babylonian cosmogony consist primarily in that the world was fashioned from primeval matter through a series of divisions, e.g., God separated the upper and lower waters by setting up the firmament, Marduk split Tiamat and constructed the firmament from the upper half of her body. This parallelism however may reflect nothing more than the prevailing popular notions regarding the world's structure. The Egyptians believed that the sun-god Re sailed in a boat across the upper ocean during the day to give light to men upon earth, and during the night across the lower waters to bring joy to the dead in the netherworld with his rays. In Gen. 1 the primeval waters are called *tehom*, in Enuma elish (also in Berossos) *tiamat*; both words may be traced to a common Semitic root. The creation of light is the first day's work in Genesis, likewise in Enuma elish the formation of the universe begins with light, symbolized mythologically by Lachmus; Lachmu and Lachamu, light and darkness, correspond to the difference between day and night in Gen. 1. This agreement follows from the fact that in the popular mind darkness had to yield to light before the things made could be seen. Such incidental similarities do not prove literary dependence of the Biblical creation account upon Enuma elish as has been claimed.

There are also very important dissimilarities. In Babylon primal matter existed at the beginning, from which the gods arose. There was no god prior to, above or apart from the world acting as its creator; there was no creation *ex nihilo*. This holds not only for the epic Enuma elish, but for all Babylonian literature on the gods or on creation. In Babylon Apsu and Tiamat, sweet and salt water, are distinguished; in Gen. 1 *tehom* constitutes the whole mass of water. In Babylon chaos is personified and sex is ascribed to it; in Gen. 1 it is non-living matter. In Babylon chaos is a force opposed to god; in Gen. 1 it is created by God. In Babylon the primal principles had to be vanquished in mighty conflict by the higher gods before the universe was fashioned from them. In Genesis God commands, and one object after another leaps into existence. In Babylon the stars are gods, in Gen. 1 they are sources for light created by God. In Babylon the gods, one after the other, proceed from primal matter through carnal generation and war among themselves; the Bible shows no trace of a theogony, no trace of a theomachy. The Babylonians recognized that the universe followed design and order and that law prevails, but it orig-

64. AOT 137. 65. AOT 130.

inated from conflict between various natural forces. And the gods remained nature forces or heavenly bodies; because these are multiple, there must be an assortment of gods. In the Bible all is subject to one God. In compliance to His will the stars follow their courses and even the unusual and harmful phenomena in nature, storms, hail, earthquakes, are due to Him and serve His ends. In Babylon men were made for the sake of the gods who were seeking worship; Gen. 1 and 2 points out clearly how all creation was made for the sake of man and should serve him. In the Bible the work of creation falls into a definite scheme, the week; the Sabbath must be kept holy, for God worked six days and rested on the seventh. That the epic Enuma elish was written upon seven clay tablets simply reflects the significance which the digit seven had throughout the Fertile Crescent. There is no agreement between Gen. 1 and Enuma elish as to the number of works or their sequence. In its present form the Enuma elish dates to Hammurabi's Amorite dynasty and was given the form in which we know it to prove that world sovereignty belonged by right to Babylon. It assigned the role of creator to Marduk, Babylon's city god, who thereupon became a national god (previously Ea had been accredited with the formation of the world, Ea the god of boundless wisdom). The epic therefore had a political purpose, was nationalistic in character. The Biblical account has a universal character and glorifies the power and the love and the wisdom of the one only God—it is religious in character.

b) *Mythological expressions in the OT.* The epic Enuma elish tells of a titanic struggle between Marduk and the primeval waters, Tiamat and her colleagues. In the OT too there are passages which tell of God's triumph over the sea at the dawn of time, "You remain Lord over the raging sea; when its billows roar, you silence them. You dashed Rahab to pieces like one who has been smitten, with your strong arm you have scattered your enemies."[66] Since the next two verses treat of creation, Rahab must be the primeval waters which were dashed to pieces at their division, and the "enemies" the monsters in allegiance to Tiamat. Job reproached God, "Am I the sea or the dragon *(tannin)* that you have ordered a watch over me?"[67] God was treating him like Marduk treated Tiamat. For after Marduk had triumphed he fixed the bar and posted guards to prevent her escape.[68] On another occasion Job lamented, "God does not withdraw his anger, Rahab's helpers bow themselves beneath him;"[69] here we have an obvious reference to Tiamat's helpers whom Marduk defeated. "By his tact he crushed Rahab, his hand slew the flying serpent."[70] As in Ps. 89:10-11 Rahab's dissolution is the division of the upper and lower waters, the smiting of the serpent, the separation of the sea from dry earth. The sacred writers are reminding us that even now the sea is a mighty power which God holds in subjection. According to Job 3:8 there were magicians "ready to awake Leviathan." "The tortuous" was a mythological name for the sea because its billows when they are quiet seem asleep, but when awakened through storms

66. Ps. 89:10-11.   68. Enuma elish IV, 139-140.   70. Job 26:12-13.
67. Job 7:12.   69. Job 9:13.

rage violently. With similar phraseology OT poets color their description of the miracle at the Red Sea, "By your power you have split the sea, you have shattered to pieces the dragon's head upon the water. You have smitten the head of Leviathan, have given him as savoury food to the beasts of the desert."[71] The dragon *(tannin)* and Leviathan refer to the crocodile as symbolizing Egypt.[72] The bodies of the drowned Egyptians floating in the Red Sea were eaten by desert animals. The account of Yahweh's battle with chaos in primeval times supplied the psalmist with color for this picture. Isaias too referred to the triumph over the Egyptians, "Was it not you who cut Rahab in pieces, who smote the dragon?",[73] by alluding to the triumph over the primeval waters. Also when painting the judgment which Yahweh will hold over the world powers, Isaias used phraseology proper to the subjugation of chaos, "With his hard and great and strong sword Yahweh will requite Leviathan, the flying serpent, and Leviathan, the tortuous serpent, and will slay the dragon that dwells in the sea."[74] The dragon in the sea is Egypt, while Leviathan, the flying serpent, is the Tigris with its rapids, and Leviathan, the tortuous serpent, is the Euphrates with its frequent meanderings. Hence the author is simply thinking of Egypt and Mesopotamia. The serpent in the depths of the sea, to whom God gives the command to bite those who flee before Him in Am. 9:3, may refer to this same Leviathan.

These mythological concepts of a struggle between the gods and the powers of chaos were spread far and wide. The version at Ugarit (Ras Shamra) recounted the annihilation of "Lotan (Leviathan), the flying serpent, the tortuous serpent, the mighty seven-headed one."[75] These figures bring to mind the monsters who assisted Tiamat in her conflict with Marduk. In a myth circulating at Ugarit they appeared as agents of Mot, god of the underworld, in his struggle against Baal.[76] Another Ugaritic story told how Baal, the god of solid earth, fought the attacks of the prince "Sea" and the judge "River." There is no doubt that there is some dependence between these Phoenician myths and Enuma elish. And the prophet who spoke of Leviathan, the flying serpent, and of Leviathan, the tortuous serpent and the dragon,[77] was not unfamiliar with Phoenician mythology. The Israelites must have been acquainted with such myths ever since they had wandered into Canaan. Commerce with Phoenicia especially at the time of Solomon and during the dynasties of Amri and Achab, when the northern kingdom was in league with Tyre, had opened the door to constant Phoenician influence in cultural and religious spheres. St. Gregory of Nyssa stated his opinion on the problem whether an inspired writer may use mythological expressions and concepts, "Sacred Scripture often indulges in culling from matter that is definitely mythological to attain its own purposes; without blushing the sacred writers employ certain mythological names in order to emphasize more strongly the thoughts at hand.... Did the sacred writers

71. Ps. 74:13-14. 73. Is. 51:9. 76. Bb 20, 1939, 477.
72. Cf. Is. 27:1; Ps. 104:26; 74. Is. 27:1. 77. Is. 27:1.
   Job 40:25; Ez. 29:3; 32:2. 75. ZatW 55, 1937, 296.

believe these myths? By no means!"[78] The mythological allusions to the triumph of the gods over the forces of chaos are not the essential elements in the mind of the hagiographer but only ornamentation intended to express more forcibly Yahweh's might. These figures, when employed in the Bible, are not real gods or living monsters, but simply symbolize forces of nature subject to Yahweh. Profane poets have sung the glories of the gods of Greece without believing in their actual existence. The Biblical authors know nothing about a difficult and dangerous conflict between Yahweh and primeval water, as that between Marduk and Tiamat and her colleagues, but only speedy and easy mastery. God ever remains the sovereign Lord against whom every other power fades into nothingness. Job 38:8-11 teaches that God created the primeval waters; in Ps. 89:12 Yahweh is the creator of heaven and earth; in Gen. 1 He has no rival. The figurative character of the allusion to the triumph over the primeval waters becomes more apparent if we keep in mind those passages which extol Yahweh's might at the Red Sea and at times of judgment over nations. In these cases such figures represent the water which obeyed God's command, or enemies powerless before God's Chosen People. Mythological allusions were very easily employed by poets and the prophets were poets—and they loved personification; spontaneously they would regard Yahweh's word as a person that subdued the sea and consigned it to fixed boundaries.[79]

§ 25. THE CONSERVATION AND GOVERNMENT OF THE WORLD

1. THE CONSERVATION OF CREATION. All that exists owes to God its being and its continuance in being. An object would instantly drop back into nothingness if God failed to conserve it, and this is true not only in the sense that God wards off harmful influences, but that God by acting positively preserves it in existence. Consequently every atom is dependent upon God at every moment. The conservation of the world may be regarded as creation constantly continued,[1] which manifests God's omnipotence and goodness even as the act of creation itself. Creation and conservation are therefore often spoken of together. "Who provides for the earth with him, and who founded the world as a whole? If he obliterate his spirit in it, or draw back his breath to himself, at once all flesh would die, and man return to dust[2]. ... What permanency would anything have had, had you not willed it? or how would anything have been preserved, had it not been called forth by you?"[3] It was God's omnipotence which "made all things be;"[4] it is God's love toward His creatures which prompts Him to hold them in existence, "You practice forbearance toward everything because everything is your possession, O Lord, you lover of life."[5] Creation owes its

78. In Cant. Cant. Hom. 9; MG 44:973.
79. Pss. 65:8; 104:7; Job 38:11; Jer. 5:22; cf. Ps.
1. Cf. Ps. 104:29-30; § 20:2.
2. Job 34:13-15.

18:16 (storm); Ps. 106:9 (Red Sea); Is. 50:2 (marvels at the return of the exiles); Ps. 90:2 (hills
3. Wis. 11:25.
4. Wis. 1:14.

"are born"); Job 38:8-9 (primeval waters called an "infant giant"); § 24:6d.
5. Wis. 11:26.

conservation to God's immortal spirit present in all things.[6] His love also provides for dumb animals and inanimate creation.[7]

Some OT passages predict a dissolution of the world, but this must not be understood in the sense of an annihilation, "The heavens shall vanish like smoke, and the earth shall wear out like a garment[8]. . . . I create a new heaven and a new earth."[9] Isaias was only foretelling the renewal that would take place at the advent of messianic times,[10] while the author of Ps. 102:27-28 ("The earth and the heavens . . . . shall perish, but you shall remain; all of them shall grow old like a garment and as a vesture you shall change them, and they shall be changed. But you are always the selfsame. . . .") juxtaposes the transitory character of earthly things with God's immutability.

2. THE WORLD AS GOVERNED BY LAW. In the very act of creation God endowed His creatures with the power to perpetuate themselves. Plants were to produce fruit and seed, aquatic life and birds received the command, "Be fruitful in order to multiply yourselves,"[11] as also did man and indirectly the beasts.[12] God ordered sun and moon to run their courses regularly in the firmament.[13] The stars were shown their orbits in heaven's vault;[14] wind, rain, snow, even the thunderclaps had set norms to follow.[15] Migratory birds, vultures, storks, doves, swallows are guided by God-given instinct; at the proper season they fly to warmer climates and in due time return again.[16] With the deluge chaos seemed to have returned, but God promised that such a catastrophe would not again occur.[17] The psalmist stood amazed before the order governing the world, "sun, moon and stars should praise God . . . . he has granted them lasting continuance in existence; he has given them a harmonious order which shall never fail."[18] Jesus Sirach eulogized the sun, moon and stars, the rainbow, clouds, hail, storms, snow, rain, dew, flood and ebb tide, and then concluded, "By his word are all things regulated."[19] Qoheleth, who found so much dissonance in the world, observed how constant change follows a regular, definite sequence.[20] To encourage his kinsmen in misfortune Jeremias reminded them of the order governing the world, for God will fulfill His promises as certainly as He will continue to maintain this order.[21]

3. GOD'S GUIDANCE OF MEN. God not only conserves His creatures in existence; He guides those endowed with intelligence to their proper end, i.e., His glory and their own happiness. He placed Adam and Eve in paradise[22] and cared for them after their fall.[23] He saved Noe from the flood and protected the patriarchs. He arranged that Rebecca came to the well at which Abraham's servant was waiting.[24] The providence of God is very beautifully shown in the Joseph story, "God sent me out ahead to preserve your family upon earth, to keep you alive, to rescue you in a remarkable manner. Therefore you have

6. Wis. 12:1.
7. § 16:3.
8. Is. 51:6.
9. Is. 65:17; 66:22.
10. § 49:5.
11. Gen. 1:22.
12. Gen. 1:11, 22, 28.
13. Gen. 1:14; Ps. 19:6.
14. Is. 40:26; Job 38:31-32.
15. Job 28:25-26; 38:24-30; Is. 55:10.
16. Job 39:26; Jer. 8:7.
17. Gen. 8:22.
18. Ps. 148:6; cf. Ps. 119:89-90.
19. Sir. 43:1-26.
20. Qoh. 1:4-6.
21. Jer. 31:35; 33:25.
22. Gen. 2:15.
23. Gen. 3:19-21.
24. Gen. 24:12-15.

not sent me here, but God."[25] God arranged events so Moses would be rescued from the river and reared in the royal court; thereby he would gain the knowledge necessary for leading his people.[26] The story of Tobias, Judith and Esther have as leit-motif God's disposal of all things unto good when human strength and prudence fail. And not only those who worship Him come under His care, but even idolators. By disobedience Jonas had brought his ship into distress, yet Yahweh preserved both.[27] The same holds for every ship and sailor on the stormy seas.[28] To each person comes "good and evil, life and death, poverty and wealth from the Lord."[29] No one should say, "I am hidden away from God; up there, who thinks about me? Among so many people I shall not be noticed; what am I in this immense creation?"[30] For God is not absent from any human act, "The heart of man determines his course, but Yahweh guides his steps."[31] Hence the proverb, "Man proposes, God disposes." When a person is practicing his art or trade he is under divine influence. To the king God grants wisdom and turns his heart as a brooklet.[32] He fills the artist with His spirit;[33] He teaches the farmer how to cultivate his fields;[34] He instructs the doctor and druggist.[35] God watches over man from the first moment of his existence, "as he was fashioned in secret, moulded out of the elements of the earth."[36] He protects the pious as a bird protects its young.[37] God even knows how to make error and sin serve His purposes. At the end Joseph could say to his brothers who had sold him into Egypt, "You schemed evil against me, but God turned it to good, so He could accomplish what today is manifest: to keep alive a numerous nation."[38]

The practice of casting lots rests upon the conviction that human destinies are in the hand of God. People believed God would manifest His will through this means, "You may cast the lot into the lap, but from Yahweh alone comes the decision."[39] In important matters the Israelites resorted to the Urim and Tummim.[40] The division of Canaan among the tribes was regulated by lot;[41] by lot Saul was chosen king[42] and Matthias selected as an apostle.[43] Quarrels too were settled in this manner.[44]

Although we find the word "providence" for the first time in the Book of Wisdom,[45] belief in divine providence is contemporaneous with primitive revelation. It rests upon faith in God's omnipotence,[46] upon faith in God's omniscience which foresees future contingent acts,[47] and upon faith in God's justice.[48] Above all however it rests upon God's love which, though embracing all creation,[49] is tendered primarily to men[50] and is able to make evil itself serve a higher end.[51]

25. Gen. 45:7-8.
26. Ex. 2.
27. Jon. 1.
28. Wis. 14:3.
29. Sir. 11:14; cf. 1 Sam. 2:6; Deut. 32:39; Wis. 16:13.
30. Sir. 16:17.
31. Prov. 16:9; cf. 16:1; 19:21; 20:24.
32. 3 Kgs. 3:12-28; Prov. 21:1.
33. Ex. 35:30.
34. Is. 28:26.
35. Sir. 38:1, 8.
36. Ps. 139:15.
37. Pss. 17:8; 36:8; 57:2; 63:8; 91:4; cf. Ex. 19:4.
38. Gen. 50:20.
39. Prov. 16:33.
40. 1 Sam. 23:2, 11; 30:8; 2 Sam. 2:1; 5:19.
41. Num. 26:55; 33:54; Jos. 14:2.
42. 1 Sam. 10:20-21.
43. Acts 1:26.
44. Prov. 18:18.
45. Wis. 14:3; 17:2; cf. 6:7 (with which compare pequd-dah, care, in Job 10:12).
46. § 12.
47. § 14:3-4.
48. § 15:5-6.
49. § 16:3.
50. § 16:5.
51. § 39:3; 41.

4. GOD'S GUIDANCE OF ISRAEL AND OTHER NATIONS. Israel's history is the story of God providing for and guiding a people. In times of misfortune God espoused their cause; when they fell by the way He punished them in order to lead them back on the right path. In the interest of humanity God tendered them a most special love.[52] Moses reminded the people of the marvels Yahweh had worked for them and gave them the reason for such marvels, "that you might not think within yourselves: my own strength and the power of my hand has wrought for me this good fortune; that much rather you remember Yahweh, your God, for it is he who gives you strength to bring about good fortune."[53] All that Israel accomplished, Yahweh, in the last analysis, did for Israel. Therefore the prophet Isaias prayed, "Yahweh, procure peace for us, for you have done all our works for us."[54] Israel was wholly dependent upon God, "as clay in the hand of the potter"[55]—which is likewise true of every one of us.[56]

The Gentile nations too came under the supervision of God who extended His benevolence to them although they did not worship Him.[57] The table of nations in Gen. 10 should demonstrate how mankind is one great family and how no people is excluded from God's loving care. It was Yahweh who led Israel out of Egypt, who brought the Philistines out of Caphtor and the Arameans out of Kir to new habitats.[58] He used the Gentiles to punish the faithless Israelites. This happened already during the wanderings in the wilderness,[59] then again during the period of the Judges. To punish Solomon Yahweh permitted Adad the Edomite and Razon the Aramean to foment trouble.[60] By Yahweh's order Hazael was anointed king of the Arameans in order to afflict the northern kingdom.[61] Assyria was "the rod of his wrath and the staff of his fury"[62] commissioned to punish the Israelites.[63] He engaged the people of the northern kingdom to chastise Judah.[64] In a vision Ezechiel saw angels commissioned by God to beat the inhabitants of Jerusalem to the ground and set fire to the city;[65] they represented the Chaldeans whom God summoned against Judah.[66] The Gentile kings also stand at Yahweh's beck and call and unconsciously fulfill His prophecies. He called Nabuchodonosor of Babylon His servant,[67] gave him the kingdom of Syria, led him against Judah and then against Tyre, and finally down to Egypt.[68] Cyrus began his triumphal march under Yahweh's direction; and by His order would give Israel liberty and ordain Jerusalem's reconstruction.[69] Even Gog will be obeying the command of Yahweh when he discontinues the siege of Jerusalem.[70] God punishes nations which rise up against Him. The Canaanites were dispossessed because of their sins.[71] If Yahweh does not consent, all the world powers can accomplish nothing against His people, "Go and make plans, they shall be broken; give

52. § 16:4.
53. Deut. 8:17-18.
54. Is. 26:12.
55. Jer. 18:6.
56. Is. 45:9; Sir. 33:13.
57. § 16:3.
58. Am. 9:7.
59. Num. 14:42f.

60. 3 Kgs. 11:14-23.
61. 3 Kgs. 19:15; 4 Kgs. 8:11-12; 13:3.
62. Is. 10:5.
63. Is. 5:26; 7:18; 8:7; 28:1-4.
64. Jer. 25:9.
65. Ez. 9:1-11; 10:6-7.

66. Cf. Ez. 6:3; 16:37; 23:22.
67. Jer. 25:9; 27:6; 43:10.
68. Jer. 25:9; 27:1f; 43:10; Ez. 29:18-20; 30:24-25.
69. Is. 41:25; 45:1-7; 46:11.
70. Ez. 38:4.
71. Gen. 15:16; Lev. 18:24-28; Deut. 12:29-31.

commands, they shall not be carried out."[72] Sennacherib failed in his attack against Jerusalem.[73] Yahweh will smite to the ground the king of Babylon;[74] Gog will meet destruction when attacking the People of God.[75] All the fulminations of the prophets against the Gentiles may be taken as proof for the proposition that all nations are subject to Yahweh and must obey Him.[76] Punishment should aid men and nations in finding the way to God.[77]

5. TRUST IN GOD. Since man at each moment of his life is under the direction of divine providence, he has every reason (apart from the obligation) for trusting in God.[78] Whatever may be the circumstances, he must abandon himself to God's guidance, "Yahweh is my shepherd, I suffer no want. And had I to wander in the valley of gloom, I would fear no evil."[79] His prayer, whether it be of thanks or petition, will be borne along by trust.[80] Even the sinner, instead of despairing, will pray with sinful Israel, humbled but full of trust: *De profundis!* "Out of the abyss I cry to you, Yahweh. O Yahweh, hear my voice! With you is forgiveness. Upon Yahweh my soul relies; he will redeem Israel from all her sins."[81] Of course trust in God may not degenerate into passivity, or lead to self-sufficiency which expects all from God, and does nothing itself. Only he has a right to God's assistance who gives himself to God and obeys His commandments; and if he has sinned, he must do penance for the offence. The same holds for nations. Israel perished because she had deluded herself into thinking that God could not reject her, that she had, as God's people, unconditional claim to His protection. Divine guidance does not eliminate human freedom, but puts it on the right path. Man must use his faculties; for that reason God gave them. Noe built the ark,[82] Jacob endeavored to appease Esau,[83] Moses accepted good advice from his father-in-law,[84] David acted very cleverly in escaping his pursuers and seeking safety with Philistines. Divine guidance does not do away with sin; even those to whom God had assigned special duties in the work of salvation fell into sin.[85] Balaam, whom God had guided and enlightened, counselled the Midianites how to destroy Israel.[86]

Genuine supernatural hope sufficiently strong to sustain us when bowed under the burden of life must rest upon faith in a God who transcends the world, whose will is free and moral, who is responsible for nature's laws, and who takes action when His designs for our salvation demand it. A person who adores many gods always remembers how these gods work against one another, and since they are nothing more than nature forces, they can do nothing entailing a modification of natural law. The Stoics indeed praised "wise providence," to whose guidance man might confide himself. But this acceptance of providence consisted in nothing else but weak acquiescence to fate. The same criticism may be made against those religions which divinize the forces of nature and assign to "destiny" the highest rung. Fate is impersonal, and a

72. Is. 8:10.
73. Is. 37:33-35.
74. Is. 14:4f.
75. Ez. 38-39.
76. § 45:2.

77. § 45:6; 48:4.
78. § 28:2.
79. Ps. 23:1, 4.
80. § 35:3e.
81. Ps. 130.

82. Gen. 6:14f.
83. Gen. 32-33.
84. Ex. 18:17-26.
85. § 32:1a.
86. Num. 31:16.

moral relation between it and man is impossible; it is unreasonable to tender lifelong obedience to a "destiny" which never hears a prayer. Belief in blind fate can confer no consolation or strength in time of trouble.[87]

6. GOD, THE FIRST MOVER. Overlooking secondary causes, the religious spirit of the OT sees the hand of God in everything. God brought the waters over the earth[88] and ordered them to recede.[89] He caused sulphur and fire to rain upon Sodom and Gomorrha,[90] gave the Egyptians fruitful and fruitless years,[91] sent the plagues over their land.[92] He sets limits for the sea,[93] causes grass to sprout, snow to fall; He spreads the hoarfrost, lets it hail and brings the thaw.[94] It is He who bestows rain,[95] makes lightning and sends the wind;[96] He topples mountains, causes earthquakes, eclipses,[97] droughts, cloudbursts.[98] He is responsible for pregnancy[99] as well as for sterility.[100]

Though as a rule God uses the forces which He Himself has placed in nature to accomplish His plan of salvation,[101] still at times He takes exception and works miracles, for He is omnipotent.[102] Isaac was given to the aged Abraham and sterile Sara to strengthen their faith, but more so to make their descendants realize that they owed their existence wholly to God's good favor and that they had a special mission to fulfill. The power of miracles was given to various prophets to help them get a hearing. Because the purpose of miracles is God's greater glory, miracle-workers who preached heresy were to be avoided and cut off from the people as false prophets.[103]

On physical evils, which also come from God, cf. § 41:1; on the problem whether God is the cause of moral evil, cf. § 11:4c; 20:7.

SECTION 3. MAN

§ 26. THE CREATION AND NATURE OF MAN

1. THE ORIGIN OF MAN. The first chapter of the Bible teaches that the first human beings, Adam and Eve, were created by God.[1] The Paradise Account,[2] which abounds in anthropomorphisms, tells how Yahweh fashioned the body of man from earth and breathed into his nostrils the breath of life. Then He caused him to fall into a deep sleep and took one of his ribs, with which He made woman. Man's soul is something essentially different from the body; it is of divine origin, brought forth by a special act of creation, and because man has a reasoning soul he is God's image.[3] The men of the Old Stone Age, as science presents them to us, were endowed with reason; they were not animals or creatures intermediate between animals and men. So the problem is: did God create man's body immediately, or mediately by placing the soul into a body already organized.

87. § 19:4b.
88. Gen. 6:17; 7:4, 12-17.
89. Gen. 8:1-2.
90. Gen. 19:24.
91. Gen. 41:25f.
92. Ex. 7-10.
93. Prov. 8:29; Ps. 65:8.
1. Gen. 1:27.

94. Ps. 147:8, 16-18.
95. Ps. 65:10-12.
96. Jer. 10:13.
97. Job 9:5-7.
98. Job 12:15.
99. Gen. 15:4; 18:10; 25:21;
2. Gen. 2:4b-3:24.

29:31f; 30:6; Ex. 1:21;
Ruth 4:13; 1 Sam. 2:5.
100. Gen. 15:3; 30:2.
101. Wis. 16-19.
102. § 12.
103. Deut. 13:2-6; § 2:3a.
3. Gen. 1:26.

Such evolutionism as claims that life upon earth arose spontaneously from dead primeval matter, and that the forms extant today developed from lower forms during the course of thousands or millions of years by inherent natural powers alone, must be discarded on basis of human reason. The riddle of life can only be solved by accepting it as wrought by God, an all-wise and all-powerful creator; for it is a fundamental *biological* principle that life comes only from life. Undiluted Darwinism, which claims that species result from natural selection or the struggle for existence, is now almost universally discarded. Certainly God as the prime mover could have employed secondary causes in the work of creation; He could have placed forces in nature which would produce effects according to His designs. Some Church Fathers too, who knew nothing of evolution in the sense that we understand it today, were not adverse to this position. When God created matter, says St. Gregory of Nyssa, plants and animals existed *in nuce*, virtually, not actually; they came into being through a divine stimulus.[4] St. Augustine distinguished between creation *qua tale*, i.e., matter only, and the formation or evolution of the world; for God had placed forces in nature which gradually became operative.[5] On problems proper to paleontology, biology and morphology the Bible gives no information; it never crosses over into the field of science to make statements on scientific aspects relating to the origin of living beings, even of men. Accordingly there is no irreconcilable opposition between the dogma of creation by a personal, supramundane God and the teaching of many men learned in the natural sciences that plant and animal life in the course of many millenia developed from a few simple forms.

Relative to the human body the exegete need not reject as contrary to Sacred Scripture the teaching that God equipped an organized body with a reasoning soul after the former had undergone a long period of development. Surely such development had been willed and effected by God, and it was destined to be perfected immeasurably as God endowed the organism with a reasoning soul. Man is man because of his mind, not his body. It was spirit which transformed the living organism into an *animal rationale*, a reasonable being—and constituted the *peculiaris creatio*.[6] With this backlog you can easily explain why the human body possesses vestigial remains which betray an evolutionary development, why between man, particularly the more primitive types, and the great man-apes there exist numerous similarities, why after the first sin in paradise baser inclinations and animal tendencies soon made themselves felt.

Be there ever so many reasons advanced by science postulating the infusion of the soul into a ready-made body, no scientist of repute would point to a known or an existing species of ape as the direct source for man's body—the differences are too many, and up to the present there have not been found sufficient links to bridge the gap adequately. Not a few scientists therefore hesitate to view the present status of the human body as the last phase in

4. In Hexaemeron Liber, Migne 44:77. 5. De Gen ad Lit VII 28, Migne 34:571. 6. Decision of Biblical Commission, June 30, 1909.

a long evolutionary process. "The countless investigations on the origin of the human body have as yet offered nothing clear, specific, positive," our present Holy Father said some years ago.[7] There have been no authoritative pronouncements by the Church on the meaning of the Biblical passages in question; nor has evolutionary teaching, which acknowledges God as creator, been proscribed. Natural science has an open road for further investigation.

In the verses touching the creation of Eve the sacred writer aims to teach a) woman is sexually different from man, yet b) she enjoys an equal status with him, c) man and woman should be joined to one another in love, d) marriage is by nature monogamous and can never be dissolved, e) the man is the head of the family.

Not only Adam and Eve were created by God, but each person owes his life to God because no one has the power to call forth life of himself.[8] The soul of each newborn individual comes from God who creates it.[9] The Maccabean mother protested that God, not she herself, gave spirit and life to her children.[10] In the womb man is wondrously formed,[11] whether he be servant or master.[12] From the very beginning mothers were grateful to God when a child was born.[13] God is able to awaken life in a sterile womb,[14] but how the formation of a child in the womb takes place is a great mystery,[15] one in which the Biblical writers shared the popular notions of their day.[16] When they speak of the origin of man, it is to point out God's might, wisdom and goodness.

2. THE BODY OF MAN. Man's body, *basar*, flesh, was fashioned out of the earth in the case of the first man. The name Adam should be a reminder that man is derived from ʾ*adamah*, earth;[17] he is the "one born of earth."[18] When he dies his body returns to earth[19] because its constituent parts are "dust and ashes."[20] When Sacred Scripture wishes to point out man's frailty and transitoriness, it frequently refers to him as made of flesh.[21] Concerning the relation between body and soul the author of the Book of Wisdom says, "The corruptible body is a load upon the soul; the earthly tent is a burden upon the thinking spirit."[22] It is as if the spirit would gladly lift itself to God, but the body, being material, "corruptible," hinders him. Though the body is not evil in itself, it still possesses the tendency to sin, because it seeks pleasure in earthly goods.[23] In developing this idea the author of the Book of Wisdom uses certain expressions current in popular philosophy without making his own Plato's notion of the body as the soul's prison-house.

3. MAN'S SPIRITUAL ELEMENT. Though the body is essential to man, nevertheless it is the spiritual element which makes him what he is, and which bestows life and self-consciousness. This spiritual element has various designations in

7. Pius XII's Academy Address, Nov. 30, 1941; AAS 33, 1941, 504f.
8. Gen. 30:2.
9. Is. 57:16; Zach. 12:1.
10. 2 Mach. 7:22-23.
11. Pss. 119:73; 139:13; Job 10:8.
12. Job 31:15; 33:4.

13. Gen. 4:1, 25; 29:32-35; 30:6.
14. Gen. 18:10f.
15. Sir. 11:5; 2 Mach. 7:22.
16. Job 10:9-11; Ps. 139:15-16; Wis. 7:1-2.
17. Gen. 3:19.
18. Wis. 7:1.
19. Gen. 3:19; Qoh. 12:7.

20. Gen. 18:27; Ps. 103:14; Sir. 10:9; 17:32; Wis. 15:10.
21. Gen. 6:3; Is. 40:6; Pss. 56:5; 78:39; Job 10:4; Sir. 14:17; 28:5.
22. Wis. 9:15.
23. Cf. Rom. 7:23; Gal. 5:17.

the OT, viz., *nešamah, nepheš ruah;* certain parts of the body also stand for spiritual or psychological functions.

a) *Breath, nešamah.* When Yahweh created the first man, He breathed "the breath of life" into a body formed from the earth, and thus man became a living being.[24] All men have this breath of life,[25] which makes them intelligent;[26] therefore the word can be used as a term for man.[27]

b) *Soul, nepheš,* means primarily gullet or throat like the Accadian *napištu;* this is its meaning in Is. 5:14; 29:8; Hab. 2:5; Jon. 2:6; Ps. 69:2; Prov. 16:24; 28:25. A second meaning of the word is the breath coming out of the throat.[28] The *nepheš* is responsible for physical life and therefore like *nešamah* can be ascribed to animals.[29] It is not identical with the breath coming out of one's mouth, for it is *in* man.[30] The blood was considered the seat of the *nepheš,* since the ancients observed that man lived as long as blood pulsed through his body, but died when the blood had flowed from it.[31] Because the *nepheš* belongs to God who gave it,[32] the use of blood is prohibited,[33] and the most important act at a bloody sacrifice was the sprinkling of blood.[34] Blood is even called *nepheš.* If the *nepheš* be preserved, man stays alive;[35] if it leave the body, man dies;[36] if it return, he lives again;[37] if it has been "poured out," he is dead.[38] The law of retaliation declared, *"Nepheš* for *nepheš"*—whoever killed a man must die himself.[39] The soul will be summoned back again by God.[40] A person who wishes to kill another sets a trap for his soul.[41]

Because the soul *(nepheš)* enlivens man, the lower functions of life also proceed from it. The *nepheš* hungers, thirsts,[42] satisfies its hunger,[43] defiles itself with forbidden food.[44] But above all it is the soul that is responsible for intelligence and free will. For it loves,[45] longs,[46] rejoices,[47] seeks revenge,[48] experiences grief.[49] The soul is the source of religious life;[50] it seeks God,[51] lifts itself up to God,[52] cries to Him,[53] thirsts for Him,[54] praises Him,[55] fears Him,[56] thirsts for wisdom,[57] is holy,[58] is stainless.[59] Idols are a scandal to the soul,[60] which after death is in God's hand[61] and comes before Him for judgment.[62] On the other hand it is also the *nepheš* that sins,[63] thinks evil,[64] is led astray,[65] refuses to believe,[66] abandons evil ways.[67]

Lastly *nepheš* is a common term for person.[68] Animals too are called *nepheš.*[69] And there are instances in which a corpse is styled a dead *nepheš.*[70]

24. Gen. 2:7.
25. 3 Kgs. 17:17; Is. 2:22; Job 33:4.
26. Job 32:8.
27. Deut. 20:16; Jos. 10:40.
28. Gen. 35:18; Jer. 15:9; Job 11:20.
29. Lev. 24:18.
30. 2 Sam. 1:9; 3 Kgs. 17:21-22.
31. Lev. 17:11; Deut. 12:23.
32. Ps. 104:29-30.
33. Gen. 9:4; Lev. 3:17; 7:26-27; 17:10-14; 19:26; cf. §30:6.
34. § 33:1.
35. Lev. 17:14; Deut. 12:23; Gen. 19:20; 32:31.
36. Gen. 35:18; 2 Sam. 1:9.
37. 3 Kgs. 17:21.
38. Is. 53:12; Ps. 141:8.
39. Ex. 21:23.
40. Wis. 15:8.
41. Sir. 51:3.
42. Prov. 10:3; 27:7; Prov. 25:25.
43. Prov. 27:7.
44. Ez. 4:14.
45. Gen. 34:3; Cant. 1:7.
46. Ps. 42:3.
47. Ps. 86:4.
48. Pss. 27:12; 41:3.
49. Job 19:2; cf. Ex. 23:9.
50. 1 Par. 28:9; Ps. 139:14.
51. Deut. 4:29.
52. Ps. 25:1.
53. Ps. 42:2.
54. Ps. 63:2.
55. Ps. 119:175.
56. Sir. 34:17.
57. Sir. 51:24.
58. Wis. 7:27.
59. Wis. 2:22.
60. Wis. 14:11.
61. Wis. 3:1.
62. Wis. 3:13.
63. Lev. 4:2; Num. 5:6.
64. Wis. 1:4.
65. Wis. 4:11.
66. Wis. 10:7.
67. 3 Kgs. 8:48.
68. Gen. 2:7; 12:5; Ex. 1:5; 12:4, 15; Lev. 4:2; Jos. 10:28.
69. Gen. 1:21, 24; 2:7; Lev. 24:18.
70. Lev. 19:28; 21:11; Num. 6:6.

Therefore when we read that the soul dies[71] or is killed,[72] we must not infer that the spiritual element in man is actually destroyed or ceases at death.[73]

c) *Spirit, ruah,* is not only used of God's spirit[74] but also of the spiritual principle operative in man. The *ruah* is given man by God;[75] it is "his spirit,"[76] and consequently He is "God of the spirits of all flesh."[77] Physical life is dependent upon the *ruah.* If God recalls His *ruah,* all things die.[78] Idols are dead because they have no *ruah* in their mouths.[79] *Ruah* is responsible for sensation and emotion; it grieves,[80] is patient,[81] loses heart,[82] is prudent,[83] humble,[84] proud;[85] on this account Sacred Scripture speaks of the *ruah* of jealousy,[86] fornication,[87] perversity.[88] All decisions depend upon the *ruah*[89] for it possesses intelligence.[90] Religious life too has its source in the *ruah,* which meditates upon God's providence[91] and serves God[92] in penance.[93]

d) *Other terms.* To designate the spiritual element in man certain parts of the body are also used in a figurative sense. Strong emotions affect the heart *(leb)* so that its beat is slowed down or accelerated; therefore the heart was considered not only as the seat of life in that it revives,[94] is sick,[95] wilts like grass,[96] but also as the seat of love,[97] trust,[98] respect,[99] joy,[100] sadness,[101] contrition.[102] Moreover the heart is the organ which wills or decides,[103] thinks, knows[104] and judges between right and wrong.[105] The reins *(kelayoth),* the seat of feeling and affection, are said to languish from ardent desire. God proves the reins and the heart.[106] The entrails *(rahamim)* are the seat of compassion, love, mercy.[107] Practically synonymous with *rahamim* are *me(im*[108] and *qereb.*[109]

The word glory *(kabod)* is frequently used for soul.[110] In these instances some commentators prefer reading *kabed,* liver, which was also associated with the functioning of the emotions.[111]

4. DICHOTOMY OF TRICHOTOMY? According to the OT, does man consist of body, soul and spirit, or simply of body and a spiritual principle? The expressions "soul" *(nephes)* and "spirit" *(ruah*—only seldom is *nesamah* used) fluctuate in the various authors, and even in the same author are not clearly distinguished. In Job 12:10 *nephes* and *ruah* are parallel, and signify physical life. The "breath of life" *(nephes hayyah)*[112] is identical with the "spirit of life" *(ruah hayyim)*[113] and "soul" *(nephes).*[114] The spirit of God and the

71. Num. 23:10; Judg. 16:30.
72. Lev. 24:17; Wis. 12:6.
73. Cf. § 26:6; 42:1.
74. § 20.
75. Is. 42:5; Zach. 12:1.
76. Gen. 6:3.
77. Num. 16:22.
78. Ps. 104:29; Job 34:14; 2 Mach. 6:30; Ez. 37:8; *ruah* however is never used of the soul after separation from the body.
79. Ps. 135:17; Hab. 2:19.
80. Gen. 26:35; Is. 65:14.
81. Qoh. 7:8.
82. Is. 61:3.
83. Prov. 17:27.
84. Prov. 29:23.
85. Prov. 16:18.
86. Num. 5:14.

87. Os. 4:12; 5:4.
88. Is. 19:14; § 20:7.
89. 1 Chr. 5:26; 2 Chr. 21: 16; Agg. 1:14.
90. Ex. 28:3; Job 20:3; 32:8; Is. 29:24.
91. Ps. 77:7.
92. Ps. 51:12.
93. Ps. 51:19.
94. Ps. 22:27.
95. Is. 1:5.
96. Ps. 102:5.
97. Judg. 16:15.
98. Prov. 31:11.
99. Prov. 5:12.
100. Ps. 104:14.
101. Prov. 13:12.
102. Pss. 51:19; 109:16.
103. 1 Sam. 14:7; Is. 10:7.
104. Ex. 28:3; Job 9:4; 34:

10; Ps. 19:15; Prov. 15:32.
105. Pss. 15:2; 51:12; 101:4; Ez. 11:19; Lev. 26:41.
106. Job. 19:27; Pss. 16:7; 73:21; Jer. 11:20; 17: 10; Ps. 7:10.
107. Gen. 43:30; 2 Sam. 24: 14; Jer. 16:5; Am. 1:11; Os. 2:21; Prov. 12:10.
108. Is. 16:11; Ps. 40:9; Job 30:27.
109. Pss. 5:10; 64:7; 103:1.
110. Gen. 49:6; Pss. 7:6; 16: 9; 30:13; 57:9.
111. Lam. 2:11.
112. Gen. 2:7.
113. Gen. 6:17; 7:15, 22; Job 27:3.
114. Gen. 35:18; 2 Sam. 1:9.

breath of the Almighty are parallel in Job 33:4, likewise spirit and soul in Wis. 16:14. The soul is said to have its seat in the blood, so too the spirit. Soul is used more commonly when there is question of lower functions of life, spirit on the other hand when there is question of activity proper to the mind, of thinking and willing, without however implying an absolute distinction. Higher spiritual activities and religious life are ascribed to the soul and to the spirit in parallel passages.[115] In Wis. 9:15 the body is considered a source of obstacles to the soul and to the spirit; this book almost exclusively uses the word soul when there is question of man's relation to God. The author of the Book of Wisdom makes no distinction between soul and spirit, as may be concluded from his constant practice of acknowledging only two constituent elements in man, the body and a spiritual principle.[116] Of like mind was the author of 2 Mach. 6:30; 15:30. The words, spirit and life,[117] are simply equivalent to "breath of life." Hence a survey of OT doctrine shows no evidence for considering man trichotomous.

5. MAN MADE IN THE LIKENESS OF GOD. As far as the body is concerned there is no essential difference between man and animal. Both are *basar*, flesh.[118] Just as man animals have life through the spirit which God gives them.[119] Man is a *nephes hayyah* (living soul)[120] just like the animals.[121] The end of man and beast is the same, at least according to appearances, for they return to the earth from which they were taken;[122] God withdraws the spirit of animals just as He recalls man's.[123] Nevertheless the OT points out a fundamental difference between man and beast. Man is the crown of creation as indicated in Gen. 1; he is fashioned only when everything has been prepared to welcome him. In the Paradise Account however man is created first, whereupon all other things are called into being for his benefit. According to Gen. 1 all things came into being at God's simple command, but when man was about to be created God took counsel with himself.[124] In the Paradise Account the creation of man is told in greater detail than the creation of the animal world;[125] in addition Yahweh made Adam realize he could find no being like himself among all the animals.[126] Man is destined to rule over the animal world, a truth expressly stated in Gen. 1:28 and indicated by man's naming the animals.[127] Man retains this superiority over animals and inanimate creation after his fall and ejection from paradise.[128] The psalmist thanks God for having made man "ruler over the works of his hands;"[129] the sapiential writers are mindful of man's dominion over the rest of God's creatures.[130]

The basis for man's sovereignty over animals lies in his creation "in the image of God, conformable to his likeness."[131] This can refer only to man's spiritual endowments; it consists in intelligence which distinguishes man from

115. Job 7:11; Is. 26:9; Bar. 3:1.
116. Wis. 1:4; 8:19-20; 15:8, 11, 16; 16:14.
117. 2 Mach. 7:22-23.
118. Gen. 6:13, 17; 7:15; 9:11; Ps. 136:25; used of animals only, Gen. 7:21.
119. Gen. 6:17; 7:15, 22; Ps. 104:29-30; Sir. 3:19, 21.
120. Gen. 2:7.
121. Gen. 1:20, 21, 24; 2:19; 9:10; Lev. 11:46; 24:18.
122. Sir. 3:19-21.
123. Ps. 104:29; Job 34:14-15.
124. Gen. 1:26; § 17.
125. Gen. 2:7, 19.
126. Gen. 2:20.
127. Gen. 2:19-20.
128. Gen. 9:2-3.
129. Ps. 8:7-9.
130. Sir. 17:4; Wis. 9:2.
131. Gen. 1:26.

the remaining visible creation. Man excels not in bodily strength, in fact he is inferior in this to many animals, but in mental capabilities. Man's likeness to God was not lost by the fall.[132] Ps. 8:6f and Sir. 17:3 re-echo this sublime truth of man's likeness to God and his consequent dominion over lower creation. The words in the Book of Wisdom, "He made him the image of his being,"[133] in context imply that man should share in God's beatitude even as in His perfections. The author is here developing ideas contained in older books.

The Babylonian epic Enuma elish describes how man was made from the blood of the slain god Kingu mixed with clay;[134] Kingu had been the leader of the gods who fought Marduk. In Berossos' account Bel (Marduk) had one of the gods beheaded; and we find the author's elucidating remark, "Therefore they (men) are endowed with reason and share in divine insight." Because of his ability to reason the Babylonian believed himself essentially different from animals and like the gods; nevertheless because he was fashioned from clay, earth, he must die. We read in the Gilgamesh story how Ishtar gave birth to various persons, another indication of mankind's oneness with the gods.[135] The Babylonians however diluted this sublime truth with much mythology. No Babylonian tablet claims that a single pair of human beings were created. In the Enuma elish Marduk made mankind, and since the task of offering sacrifice in the place of the lower gods and of building temples was imposed upon mankind, two individuals would hardly have been sufficient. According to a fragment of the 7th tablet of the same epic four men were made, a like number occur in other songs.[136] This number represents the four regions of the earth, and hence must be understood symbolically. When mankind had been destroyed, the mother goddess Mami created seven males and seven females, again a symbolic digit indicating a considerable number.[137]

Man possesses intelligence and consequently free will. Biblical proof for this is had in the command enjoined in paradise[138] as well as in all later injunctions, threats and promises. Just a few quotations, "Behold, I place before you today blessing and cursing; blessing if you are obedient to the commands of Yahweh, cursing if you are not obedient to the commands of Yahweh[139] .... Behold, I place before you the way of life and the way of death[140].... If you want to, you are able to keep the commandments, and to act faithfully is matter for your decision. He has placed fire and water before you; toward which you choose, stretch out your hand. Life and death lie before a man, whichever he selects, will be given him."[141]

6. IMMORTALITY OF THE SOUL. Israel at all times firmly believed that the soul, when separated from the body, does not cease to exist. Common opinion consigned the soul of the deceased to the netherworld, Sheol.[142] The very fact that the body was given burial is a sure sign of belief in some kind of

132. Gen. 5:1-3; 9:6.
133. Wis. 2:23.
134. AOT 122; Berossos, AOT 137; other creation stories, AOT 134-135.
135. 11, 123.

136. JEOL 4, 1934, 195; Th. C. Vriezen, Onderzoek naar de Paradijsvoorstelling, Wageningen 1937, 99.
137. Ea und Athrahasis 4, 25f, AOT 206.

138. Gen. 2:16.
139. Deut. 11:26-28; 30:15-20.
140. Jer. 21:8.
141. Sir. 15:15-17.
142. § 42:1.

afterlife. It was always lawful to kill animals, but not man—another indication
that man was conscious of an essential difference between human and animal
souls. The patriarchs believed that after death they would be gathered to their
fathers and kinsmen. But this expression did not imply interment in a family
grave, as is easily seen from the following: Abraham received the promise
that he would "go unto his fathers in peace."[143] His ancestors were buried
in Mesopotamia, while he "was gathered unto his people,"[144] although interred
in the cave at Machpelah. Nor was Isaac buried in the family tomb, although
the same phrase occurs again in his case.[145] Thinking a wild beast had de-
voured his son Joseph, Jacob wished to descend in sorrow to him in the underworld.[146] When Jacob died in Egypt he was "gathered to his people,"[147] but
only seventy days later was his body taken to Canaan.[148] The death of Aaron
was recorded by the same words;[149] words by which the death of Moses too
was foretold.[150] David, Amri, Manasses were "gathered to their fathers," yet
they did not rest in a single family sepulchre.[151] Attempts were sometimes made
to contact the souls of dead persons by necromancy. Samuel's spirit, called
up by the witch of Endor, told Saul, "Tomorrow you and your sons shall be
with me;"[152] this has no reference to their burial which occurred much
later,[153] but to their meeting in Sheol. A psalmist[154] and the author of Job
34:14-15, according to whom God received back the spirit of man and beast at
death, believed in afterlife. Qoheleth is very outspoken concerning the fates of
men and beasts, "One fate do they have. As one dies, so dies the other. Who
knows whether the spirit of man ascends on high, and whether the spirit of the
beast descends to the earth?"[155] Their apparently similar lots constitute for
him an insoluble riddle, yet he maintains an afterlife for the soul in Sheol
whither all men go.[156] The faithless Jews of the Egyptian diaspora, on whose
lips the author of the Book of Wisdom placed the "Rose-Song," roundly denied,
it is true, the immortality of the soul, "By chance have we come into existence,
and afterwards we shall be as if we had not been; for the breath in our nostrils
is smoke, and thought is a spark begotten by the beat of our heart; when it is
extinguished, the body will disintegrate into ashes and the spirit will vanish as
thin air."[157]

7. PRE-EXISTENCE OF THE SOUL? The OT speaks of the soul as created by
God and bound to the body; we find no indication of belief in the soul's existence
before this union. The author of the Book of Wisdom puts these words on King
Solomon's lips, "I was a goodly child, and had received a good soul. Or rather,
being good I entered a spotless body."[158] Many exegetes err in finding here the
Platonic doctrine of the soul's pre-existence. For Plato the entrance of the soul
into a body was a punishment, or at least implied a defilement, in any case it
was unfortunate. According to the author of the Book of Wisdom the body is

143. Gen. 15:15.
144. Gen. 25:8.
145. Gen. 35:29.
146. Gen. 37:35.
147. Gen. 49:33f.
148. Gen. 50:3f.
149. Num. 20:24.
150. Num. 27:13; 31:2; cf.
     Deut. 31:16; 32:50.
151. 3 Kgs. 17:21-22; 4 Kgs.
     4:34-35; 13:21.
152. 1 Sam. 28:19.
153. 1 Sam. 31:8f.
154. Ps. 104:29.
155. Qoh. 3:19-21.
156. Qoh. 2:15; 9:10; § 42:2.
157. Wis. 2:2-3.
158. Wis. 8:19-20.

spotless and hence cannot defile the soul; neither is the union of body and soul a regrettable event nor a punishment. Although he uses platonic terminology, he simply is making Solomon explain that as a youth he led a virtuous life with the best predispositions (v. 19), and that his two constituent parts, body and soul, were good at conception (v. 20). He does not declare that his soul entered a spotless body because it had been good, for the author of Wisdom does not consider the body evil any more than the soul.[159]

§ 27. THE FIRST COUPLE

1. THE UNITY OF THE HUMAN RACE. God made the first human beings "man and wife," a couple, whom He blessed "to be fruitful in order to multiply and fill the earth."[1] From this couple all men are descended through physical generation. According to Gen. 2:7, 21 Yahweh formed one man and one woman, whom the man named Eve "because she became the mother of all the living."[2] Wis. 10:1 calls Adam the "first-formed father of the world." The Bible makes no allusion to pre-Adamites. The table of nations in Gen. 10 teaches that all peoples are related to one another. The doctrine of the unity of the human race is implied in the flood account, even though the flood be limited both geographically and anthropologically; if men existed who were not destroyed by the deluge, they and their descendants would have been related to Noe's posterity by common blood descent from Adam. Anthropologists too at the present time hold as scientifically certain the unity of the human race in the sense that it appeared with uniform characteristics at a specific time and in a definite place. Differentiation which gave rise to the various races is evident already among the Neanderthals. Distinctive groups within a race presuppose the unity of the original constituents. The universal fertility among human beings points to the same conclusion. Regarding the number of the first human beings natural science can offer no positive information, but it does not require a large number, a single pair suffices. We can see no reason why God should have performed this marvel, the creation of reasonable beings, in various places and at different times. The Bible tells of a single first pair and thereby complements profane science.

2. PRIVILEGES OF ADAM AND EVE IN PARADISE. In paradise Adam and Eve enjoyed God's love in a most special measure. They were allowed greater intimacy with Him than any prophet, even Moses, received. After they had sinned they hid themselves from Yahweh,[3] indicating that previously they had approached Him without inhibitions. They had been free from lustful concupiscence, since "they were both naked, the man and his woman, without being ashamed of themselves before each other."[4] After the fall "their eyes were opened and they saw that they were naked,"[5] but before they had been as

159. Wis. 1:4.
1. Gen. 1:27-28.
2. Gen. 3:20.
3. Gen. 3:8.
4. Gen. 2:25.
5. Gen. 3:7.

innocent children to whom the feeling of shame is foreign. They also possessed the gift of bodily immortality, i.e., not the impossibility of dying, *non posse mori,* as the angels have and men will have after the resurrection (for man is made from earth and therefore death comes natural to him), but a state in which through obedience to God's command they could safeguard themselves from death. Their bodies were not subject to the natural disintegrating effects of time, because they were endowed with what theologians call *posse non mori.*[6] The knowledge of our first parents embraced those things necessary and useful for them to fulfill the essential tasks entrusted to them by God, e.g., to till the garden, to attain their supernatural end, to maintain love and increase it. It was the will of God that they should develop the faculties natural to body and soul through practice and experience, and in this manner to make progress. Lastly, they were not subject to pain and sorrow. Joined in love to one another,[7] they were destined to attain the highest rung of perfection by subjecting themselves to God's will in all fidelity.

3. SIN. Gen. 3 explains how the first man and woman, whom God had privileged with a life of good fortune and freedom from death, became subject to afflictions, trials and death—misfortunes which they bequeathed to all their descendants. God had forbidden them to eat of the tree of the knowledge of good and evil.[8] Tempted by the serpent, the woman disobeyed this command and induced her husband to eat of the fruit.[9] Like the creation of the first man, the author presents the temptation and fall most realistically. The one fact which stands out most clearly is this: the first sin consisted in an act of disobedience against God's command; it proceeded from pride, for they wished to be like God. The specific nature of the act which they committed cannot be deduced from the Biblical account. If the sin had consisted in sexual intercourse forbidden to them at first, one would reasonably expect the prohibition to be placed after 2:24, i.e., after Eve's creation and the institution of marriage—not previous to the woman's creation. After sinning they were ashamed of their nakedness not because they had associated sexually, but because by their rebellion they had unchained the lower physical impulses which previously had been under perfect control. Note too that first the woman *ate,* and *then* she gave to the man *and he ate;* it does not say *both* ate simultaneously; Eve seduced Adam after she herself had been disobedient. Sexual relations between Adam and his wife are first mentioned in Gen. 4:1 where the act is indicated in clear terminology. Eve rejoiced as she gave birth to her first child and thanked Yahweh who had given it to her.[10] Had sexual intercourse deprived her and her descendants of the happiness of paradise, she would have in some way recalled that fact and uttered words of repentance. Still less could it have been a sex sin consisting in the refusal of intercourse so as not to have children, or in preventing conception itself. The Israelites regarded marriage and large families as the greatest good fortune, and any intimation that the first woman

6. Gen. 2:17; 3:3.   8. Gen. 2:17.   10. Gen. 4:1.
7. Gen. 1:27; 2:24.   9. Gen. 3:6.

had obstructed the purpose of marriage (and succeeded in making her husband partner to the act) would have sounded preposterous to them. The base practices of the Kedeshim arose only after belief in the one God had vanished and esteem for marital chastity and moral living had been lost. Should the first man and woman, who stood in the most intimate relationship with God and knew no inordinate passions, have committed a sin which was not even ascribed to the men whose evil conduct occasioned the flood? The paradise serpent was not a symbol of sensual love and unclean lust, but a very real creature cunning and full of hatred toward God.[11]

The death penalty was the sanction attached to the command not to eat. After the sin conscience made itself felt. The words, "knowledge of good and evil," refer to moral conduct and its implications: man was destined to experience the results of obedience or disobedience. If he had listened he would have experienced how good obedience was; God would have bestowed His love upon him in still greater measure. Because he disobeyed he experienced how terrible it is to rise up against God. By obedience he would have merited the happiness of paradise which had been accorded him gratis. Since the expression "know good and evil" may also mean, "know everything,"[12] the temptation was a strong one; and the serpent used the phrase in this sense: you shall be as God.[13]

4. PUNISHMENT. One effect of their sin was the unleashing of sinful concupiscence,[14] another the loss of immortality. Out of His infinite goodness God had made immortality possible to a creature who by nature was mortal. Through disobedience our first parents foolishly threw away this treasure; death was now their lot—would God have reacted differently had they pleaded for forgiveness? Death followed sin as its punishment,[15] "Through a woman sin had its beginning, and because of her we must all die."[16] In the Protoevangel however God consoled them.[17] By bearing sorrow and physical suffering[18] with minds directed toward God,[19] they atoned for their sin and so Wisdom "saved the first-formed father of the world from his fall."[20]

The descendants of Adam and Eve were destined to share their sufferings, sorrow and death. Theirs too is the duty of serving God and attaining happiness in His love. What God demands can be known by reason, but He has manifested His will in a special way through His messengers. The memory of a lost paradise in which mankind had once lived happily and without sin was never utterly lost. And in Israel the prophets kept alive a desire for redemption from the sins which had caused all present affliction.[21] (On the problem of original sin, cf. § 38:3.)

5. EXTRA-BIBLICAL PARALLELS. The words, ʿeden, the land in which paradise was situated, and gan, garden, are Accadian. Up to the present time no one has found a Babylonian text which tells of a paradise, a tree of knowledge, a temptation, a sin by the first man and woman which was punished with death

11. § 23:4; 50:2.
12. Cf. 2 Sam. 13:22; 14:17;
    19:36; Deut. 1:39; Is.
    7:15.
13. Gen. 3:5.

14. Gen. 3:7.
15. Gen. 3:19, 22.
16. Sir. 25:24.
17. Gen. 3:14-15; cf. § 50:2.

18. Gen. 3:16-18.
19. Gen. 4:1.
20. Wis. 10:1.
21. Cf. § 49.

and suffering. Wholly foreign to Babylonian thought was the doctrine that man according to God's plan should never die or that man by knowingly transgressing a command brought death upon himself, "When the gods made man they imposed death upon him; life however they kept in their own hands."[22] Of the myths in which reflections of the paradise story are commonly seen, the Adapa story is the most important.[23] It tells how Anu offered Adapa "the food of life" and the "water of life," but Adapa refused to eat and drink because he believed Ea who counselled the contrary. Accordingly he remained mortal. Adam lost immortality because he sinned, Adapa failed to acquire it because of an error in judgment. Adam died because he ate of the forbidden fruit, Adapa died because he did not eat of the proffered food. Certain passages refer to a life-giving plant, e.g., in the Gilgamesh epic Utnapishtim, the Biblical Noe, gives such to the hero; on the way a snake snatches it from him.[24] The point in the story is that no one is able to acquire immortality for himself. Adam and Eve were enabled by God to retain this grace. In Semitic literature a "life-giving plant" is one which prolongs physical life; it has no moral implications.

Neither were the Egyptians conscious of a fall through sin, although from their folklore they knew of a snake, Apophis, hostile to the gods. Jima, the first man in Persian mythology, lived happily with the god Ahura-Mazda; death and old age did not exist before he spoke the untruth which brought suffering upon the earth. According to a very late myth Jima was bested by a serpent demon, Dahaka. The Persians also spoke of a tree, Gokart, which existed in the heavenly paradise and conferred immortality and superhuman knowledge. Indic mythology describes how in the first age man lived without suffering like the gods; Brahma, the first man, sinned by fancying himself like God, prodded on by his wife. The Chinese tell of a mountain in paradise upon which are wonderful fountains and trees; there you would find a tree of life and a fountain of immortality. Primitive peoples believe that God gave laws to the first men; most of them are of the opinion that originally man was not destined to die. Some tribes hold that an evil being prompted man to rebel against God and that death and suffering are punishment for sin.

Most interesting is the role assigned to serpents among the various peoples. In the Bible the serpent appears as an evil creature; in Babylonia a serpent robs Gilgamesh of the plant of life. Serpents were regarded as diabolical among the Egyptians, the Arabs, the Indians, and the Chinese.

Only isolated fragments from the traditions of various nations have any relation to the Biblical account of paradise and the 'fall. Some of these "parallels" come from peoples who had no contact with Israel or with sources from which Israel drew; yet the question whether these similarities are due to a primitive tradition cannot be answered with an absolute affirmative. The Biblical account itself does not give every detail of the story as it circulated in the earliest Israelitic circles, for in Genesis Moses showed his literary talents: note the play

22. Gilgamesh epic, AOT 194.   23. AOT 143f.   24. 11, 282f; AOT 182.

on words, the anthropomorphisms and the relation between the creation of
Eve and the creation of the animals. And Moses enjoyed very special divine
illumination, since the Genesis account was destined to be of tremendous importance for the religious teaching of the OT and of Christianity. Upon this
illumination the text of the Protoevangel also depends.

PART III

HUMAN ACTS

SECTION 1. MORALITY

§ 28. DUTIES TOWARD GOD

1. FAITH. a) *Insistence on faith in one God.* Upon Sinai Yahweh reserved all honor and worship to Himself. In the course of time the practice of worshipping Yahweh alone influenced the mass of the people to regard Yahweh as the *only* God, the one God whom the prophets untiringly proclaimed.[1] During the exile or soon thereafter the desired result was finally achieved. The youngest of the Maccabean brothers boldly asserted that Israel's God "alone is God."[2] Jesus Sirach wrote, "There is but one from eternity;"[3] and the author of the Book of Wisdom considered polytheism "a silly delusion."[4] Faith is strengthened by meditating on creation, by reflecting upon the history of the nation, by miracles and fulfilled prophecies.[5]

b) *Types.* Abraham was a man of indomitable faith.[6] By faith Sara too became certain that she would give life to a son in her nineties, "Is anything impossible for Yahweh?"[7] Men of faith were the prophets, staunch defenders of the things of God in the face of popular unbelief.[8] For his faith Zacharias, the son of the high priest Joiada, shed his blood,[9] likewise the martyrs in the time of Manasses[10] and numerous Jews in the persecution of Antiochus Epiphanes, e.g., Eleazar, the seven Maccabean brothers and their mother.[11] A false zeal for the faith was shown by the Hasmonean leaders who forced Gentiles to be circumcised;[12] they made an external sign the essential of religion and regarded inner sanctity as secondary.

c) *Sins against faith.* There were no persons in Israel who theoretically denied God's existence.[13] The struggle of the prophets from Moses to the close of the exile was not a struggle against unbelief, but against the tendency to worship idols, i.e., to deny strict Yahwistic monotheism.[14] Balaam's observation, "In Jacob there is no divination, no soothsaying in Israel,"[15] did not always hold true. When it became necessary to discern the future in an important matter, recourse could have been had in the period till David to the Urim and Tummim.[16] In spite of this legitimate means[17] the Israelites did resort to magic, sorcery, necromancy.[18] The ephod mentioned in Judges was an occasion

1. § 7:1-2.
2. 2 Mach. 7:37.
3. Sir. 42:21.
4. Wis. 14:14, 27, 29.
5. § 4:2.
6. Gen. 13:4f; 17:15.
7. Gen. 18:10f.
8. § 41:5.

9. 2 Chr. 24:20-21.
10. 4 Kgs. 21.16.
11. 2 Mach. 6:8-11, 18-31; 7:1-42.
12. § 48:5.
13. § 4:1.
14. § 7:2; 23:1a.

15. Num. 23:23.
16. § 3:1; 25:3.
17. Deut. 33:8-11.
18. Ex. 22:17; Lev. 19:26, 31; 20:6, 27; Deut. 18:9-14; 1 Sam. 28:3, 9; Os. 4:12; Is. 2:6; 3:3; 8:19.

to sin since the Israelites used it to obtain oracles.[19] When afflicted the Israelites were not permitted to trim their beards and hair after the fashion of pagan Bedui, nor were they allowed to make incisions, because originally any blood that flowed was offered to demons.[20] At the time of Jeremias this connection with demon worship was no longer remembered.[21] Tatooing too was taboo[22] because it implied acting as servants to a Canaanite god or a spirit of the dead; again in this instance the primitive significance was forgotten in later times.[23] It was believed one could protect himself[24] against demons and witches and ward off misfortune by using amulets; an example of this occurs as late as the Maccabean wars.[25] Some kind of superstition will be found in every nation, but in Babylon and Egypt it was an essential ingredient of religion.

2. HOPE AND TRUST. a) *Hope a duty.* A firm and joyous faith in God as one, almighty, all-good and provident engenders the hope and trust that He will come to one's aid.[26] How closely faith and trust are related is indicated by the word *he)emin,* which has both meanings. Though childless and aged, Abraham believed when Yahweh promised him direct posterity, i.e., he was confident that God's word would come to pass.[27] When the Egyptians overtook the Israelites at the Red Sea, Moses buoyed up their drooping spirits,[28] and when the enemy had perished in the waters, "the people feared Yahweh, trusted in Yahweh and in his servant Moses."[29] When Jerusalem was threatened by Damascus in league with the northern kingdom, Isaias challenged the disheartened king and people, "If you do not believe, you shall not abide."[30] Later he labored to prevent an alliance with the Egyptians which was designed to free them from the Assyrian yoke, "By retreat and quiet you shall find deliverance, in remaining still and in trust lies your strength."[31] At some future time the Messiah would bring deliverance, "Whoever trusts in him (the stone, i.e., the Messiah) shall not *stagger.*"[32] When the southern kingdom collapsed, faith in God's power and trust in His mercy was put to a severe test. Through Ezechiel's vision of the revival of the dead bones, the despondent were filled with hopes for a national restoration; and Isaias, the other great prophet of exilic times, promised speedy deliverance and a return home in the midst of marvels (ch. 40-55). An earthly object upon which men place their hopes is at best ephemeral. "Cursed is the man who trusts in man or relies on flesh; blessed is the man who relies on Yahweh, makes Yahweh his trust."[33] The just man regards Yahweh as his rock, his mountain, his shield. Indeed at times God may seem very distant, but then he consoles himself by the knowledge that in spite of all God is very near. "Why are you despondent, O my soul, and why do you groan within me? Trust in God. I shall yet praise him as my helper and as my God."[34] He recalls how God will reach out to embrace him even if father and mother abandoned him;[35] when downcast he prays, "My soul,

19. Judg. 8:27; 17:5; 18:14.
20. Lev. 19:27-28; 21:5; Deut. 14:1.
21. Jer. 16:6; 41:5.
22. Lev. 19:28.
23. Is. 44:5.
24. Gen. 35:4.
25. 2 Mach. 12:40.
26. § 16:3, 5; 25:3-5.
27. Gen. 15:4-6.
28. Ex. 14:13.
29. Ex. 14:31.
30. Is. 7:9.
31. Is. 30:15.
32. Is. 28:16.
33. Jer. 17:5, 7; Ps. 52:9; Prov. 11:28; Job 31:24-28.
34. Ps. 42:43.
35. Ps. 27:10.

trust quietly in God alone, for from him hope comes to me! He alone is my rock, my help, my stronghold, I shall not waver."[36] *In te, Domine, speravi; non confundar in aeternum.*[37] The sinner too must trust in God's mercy,[38] and the man bowed down by sorrow may give doubt no admittance.[39] Without confidence a life of prayer is simply impossible.[40] The sages tell you, "Commit your works to Yahweh, then shall your plans prosper[41]. . . . Trust in God, and he will espouse your cause[42]. . . (while the wicked) do not hope for virtue's reward."[43]

b) *Types of hope.* We have as types of firm trust the patriarchs and the prophets; in the blackest hour they did not despair, but "delivered Jacob by strong faith."[44] When falsely accused, Susanna "trusted in God,"[45] as did the three men in the fiery furnace,[46] Daniel in the lions' den,[47] and many martyrs in time of persecution, for "their hope was full of immortality."[48]

c) *Sins against hope.* Frequently during the journey through the wilderness the Israelites sinned through lack of trust in God's guidance. Toward the end of the wanderings Moses himself doubted whether Yahweh would work any further miracles[49] for a people who had revolted so often, who so seldom were grateful for benefits received or amended when punished. The other extreme is presumption, relying upon God yet offending Him continually. Some Jews felt certain of Yahweh's protection while leading an immoral life. A greater sin however is despair, i.e., refusing to believe that God is ready to forgive a contrite soul; of this Cain was guilty.[50]

3. LOVE AND FEAR. Divine love which "drew them with cords of *kindness,* with bands of love and was to them as one who presses an *infant* to his cheeks,"[51] demands human love in return. "You must love Yahweh, your God, with your whole heart, with your whole soul, and with your whole strength."[52] The pious man begins his prayers with a profession of love, "I love you, Yahweh, my strength."[53] And what intimacy reveals itself in the cry, "Whom else have I in heaven beside you, upon earth no *good* pleases me."[54] In the Canticle of Canticles the bride protests her love of Yahweh in multiple metaphors, expressions designed to spur the pious man to pour out his whole heart in love to God.[55]

With love comes fear. Preceding the command to love Yahweh,[56] we find the injunction to fear Him.[57] "Israel, what does Yahweh, your God, demand of you? that you fear Yahweh, your God, by keeping straight upon his way, and that you love and serve Yahweh, your God, with your whole heart and with your whole soul."[58] Love remembers favors received, especially God's mercy stooping down to us sinners; fear prevents us from forgetting the great distance between Creator and creature, between divine holiness and human sinfulness. After promulgating the decalog in the midst of thunder and lightning Moses

36. Ps. 62:6-7
37. Ps. 31:2; 71:1.
38. § 16:5.
39. § 41:3.
40. § 35:2e.
41. Prov. 16:3.
42. Sir. 2:6; cf. 2:7-8; Wis. 1:2.

43. Wis. 2:22; 3:18; 5:14.
44. Sir. 49:10.
45. Dan. 13:35.
46. Dan. 3.
47. Dan. 6
48. Wis. 3:4.
49. Num. 20:2f.
50. Gen. 4:13.

51. Os. 11:4; § 16:5-6.
52. Deut. 6:5.
53. Ps. 18:2.
54. Ps. 73:25.
55. Cf. § 16:4.
56. Deut. 6:5.
57. Deut. 6:2.
58. Deut. 10:12.

warned the Israelites, "God has come that he might try you, and that his fear may abide with you lest you sin."[59] Job "feared God and avoided evil[60]. . . . The fear of the Lord is wisdom, and avoiding evil (is) understanding[61]. . . . The beginning of wisdom is the fear of God."[62] Fear and love are two excellent incentives to keep God's commandments, "They who fear the Lord do not disobey his words, and they who love him follow his ways."[63] Only the impenitent sinner has reason to dread the wrath of God.[64] Hence on this point there exists no essential difference between the teaching of the OT and that of Jesus; the NT does stress love to the point of casting out slavish fear,[65] but this type of fear was nowhere enjoined in the OT. The OT did not demand the blind obedience of a dull servant toward a haughty master, but an obedience stemming from love and gratitude, like that of a child toward parents or benefactors. And this theology was not advanced first by the prophets, it is found in the oldest psalms, in the lives of the patriarchs and David, in the challenge to Israel to become a holy nation, in the liberty granted to Israel to accept or reject the covenant with its high moral requirements. And Jesus Himself admonished us to fear him who is able to cast body and soul into hell.[66]

4. PICTURELESS CULT. The second commandment of the decalog forbade using any type of representation in divine worship—God is a pure spirit.[67] The Israelites committed a grave sin when they set up a golden bull to honor Yahweh;[68] Michas was guilty of the same crime,[69] and also Jeroboam, who placed bulls at Bethel and Dan.[70] This proscription by the Law and the prophets included idols and symbolic representations of the gods because such objects led to or implied apostasy.[71] The maṣṣebah erected by the patriarchs[72] were innocent expressions of piety[73] at which the sacred writers took no offense.[74] For the Canaanites however the maṣṣebah represented Baal, and on this account the Law ordered their demolition.[75] A much greater scandal were the ashera, the cultic poles which symbolized Astarte, goddess of fertility and lust.[76] The teraphim, or hearth-gods, fell under the general proscription because of their idolatrous implications.[77]

5. SANCTIFYING THE DIVINE NAME. According to ancient ideology name and nature could not be separated;[78] consequently God's name must be kept holy. Oaths, prohibited except in conjunction with the name of Yahweh,[79] followed given formulae, e.g., "Truly as Yahweh lives[80]. . . . May Yahweh do unto me (you) this and that. . . ."[81] Thus oaths involved a solemn acknowl-

59. Ex. 20:20; cf. Deut. 6:13.
60. Job. 1:1.
61. Job 28:28.
62. Sir. 1:14; cf. Prov. 1:7; 3:7; Sir. 1:12, 16; 7:29-30.
63. Sir. 2:15.
64. Sir. 5:6; 16:11.
65. 1 Jn. 4:18.
66. Matth. 10:28.
67. Ex. 20:4-5; § 8:1.
68. Ex. 32.
69. Judg. 17.
70. 3 Kgs. 12:28-29; Os. 8:5-6.
71. Ex. 20:23; Lev. 19:4; 26:1; Num. 33:52; Deut. 4:16, 28; Is. 2:8, 18, 20;

10:11; 30:22; Mich. 5:12; Ez. 8:1f; § 4:2.
72. Gen. 28:18; 31:45; 35:14, 20.
73. § 4:4a.
74. Is. 19:19 (in messianic times there will be a "sacred pillar" at the borders of Egypt to show that Egypt worships the one true God).
75. Ex. 23:24; 34:13; Deut. 12:3.
76. Ex. 34:13; Deut. 7:5; 12:3; Judg. 6:25f; 3 Kgs.

15:13; 4 Kgs. 18:4; 23:6, 15.
77. Gen. 31:19, 30-36; 35:2-4; Judg. 17:5; 18:14; 1 Sam. 15:23; 19:13; Os. 3:4; Zach. 10:2.
78. § 5:8a; 21:5.
79. Deut. 6:13; Jer. 4:2.
80. 1 Sam. 14:39, 45; 20:3; 3 Kgs. 2:24; Jer. 4:2; 5:2 (cf. Lachish letters 3:9; 6:12; 12:3—ZatW 56, 1938, 126-139).
81. 1 Sam. 3:17; 14:44; 3 Kgs. 2:23.

dgement of God as omnipotent, omniscient, and all-just. The decalog forbade
uttering Yahweh's name irreverently. This included all types of profanity, par-
icularly swearing falsely,[82] rash oaths,[83] breaking a promise given under
oath,[84] thoughtless vows.[85] Blaspheming the divine name was punished with
death.[86] The random use of God's name desecrates His holiness. In postexilic
imes arose the usage of avoiding the divine name altogether and substituting
words such as Lord, the Eternal, the Highest, the Holy One, Heaven, the
Place, etc.[87]

Faith, love, and fear of God are shown in a morally upright life[88] and in
such external acts as sacrifices, sanctifying the feasts, prayer, mortification.[89]

§ 29. DUTIES TOWARD FELLOW MEN

1. HUMAN LIFE. a) *Murder.* The criminal character of murder is clear from
the account of Cain and Abel;[1] after the deluge God imposed the death penalty
for shedding blood.[2] The decalog prohibits taking another man's life,[3] and
in the Covenant Code[4] and other sections of the Pentateuch the same injunction
is repeated.[5] To punish a murderer was a religious duty,[6] one to be accomplished by the relatives of the murdered man; the avenger of blood was not
allowed to rest satisfied with a ransom as a substitute.[7] Even an animal that
had caused the death of a man was to be killed.[8] Blood revenge as the expression of justice becomes a necessity when people have no civil arrangements for
executing justice; certain unbridled elements can be restrained from shedding
blood only through the fear of bloody reprisals. In Israel blood revenge remained
customary for a long time, was sanctioned and enjoined by the Law since a
responsible government was not at first extant, and legitimate authority in
later times neglected its duty of safeguarding rights. Under exceptional circumstances the king could pardon a murderer.[9] Blood revenge could be resorted
to legally only in case of premeditated murder. For a person implicated in the
death of another only slightly or not at all, or in a case of homicide through
negligence or accident, the Law provided an asylum.[10] The Law even attempted
to protect a thief's life in the act of housebreaking.[11]

b) *Physical injuries.* Ex. 21:18-27 gives the laws governing bodily injuries.
If one suffered a permanent bodily injury just requital was in place *(lex
talionis)*: Eye for eye, tooth for tooth.[12] Theoretically this may be taken in
a strictly literal sense expressing the ancient notion that an offense must be
atoned for by an identical punishment, a procedure paralleled in the laws of
other nations. In practice however these cases were settled by compromise.
Equitable resolution lay in the spirit of Mosaic jurisprudence, which called

82. Lev. 5:22; 19:12; Os. 10:4; Jer. 7:9; Ps. 24:4.
83. Lev. 5:4.
84. Ps. 15:4; Ez. 17:18.
85. § 36.
86. Lev. 24:10-16; 3 Kgs. 21:13.
1. Gen. 4.
2. Gen. 9:6.
3. Ex. 20:13.
4. Ex. 21:12-14.
5. Lev. 24:17; Num. 35:16-21, 30, 31; Deut. 19:11-13.
6. Ex. 21:12, 14.
7. Num. 35:31; Deut. 19:13.
8. Ex. 21:28-32; cf. Gen. 9:5; § 29:8.
9. 2 Sam. 14:1f.
10. Ex. 21:13; 3 Kgs. 1:50;
87. § 5:8b.
88. § 29-31.
89. § 33-37.
2:28; Num. 35:9-15, 22-29; Deut. 4:41-43; 19:1-13; Jos. 20.
11. Ex. 22:1-2.
12. Ex. 21:23-25; Lev. 24:19-20; Deut. 19:21.

for punishment by physical deformation only in a few specific cases.[13] In daily life one had to employ all reasonable care to prevent injury to another, e.g., vicious oxen were to be kept in a place of safety,[14] railings were to be put around flat roofs,[15] etc. Feminine health benefited by the ordinance declaring a woman unclean for seven days each month[16] and for seven or fourteen days after the birth of a boy or girl respectively; then for an additional 33 or 66 days she was to stay at home.[17] Regard for bodily integrity is reflected in the ordinance denying a castrated person admission into an Israelitic community.[18] This ruling was directed against the widespread Oriental practice of making eunuchs serve in palace or temple (e.g., in Asia Minor in the Cybele cult). Toward those mutilated against their own will a more lenient spirit prevailed in later centuries.[19]

c) *Personal liberty.* Capturing a man for the purpose of selling him into slavery was a capital crime.[20] Concerning slaves, cf. § 31:4; 32:1d, 2h.

2. PROPERTY RIGHTS. The decalog is specific, "You shall not steal."[21] This commandment forbade thievery, robbery, unjust acquisition of goods, e.g., through usury, fraud, and all wanton destruction. In addition we find special enactments against embezzlement,[22] against false weights and measures,[23] against theft and fraud,[24] usury,[25] changing landmarks,[26] profiteering on hired help.[27] Regulations on security and indemnification sought to safeguard private property.[28] Disregard for these laws is evident from complaints by the prophets accusing the Israelites of theft and robbery, fraud and usury.[29] The sapiential writers commend honesty and condemn theft, usury and fraud.[30] Because men are so easily disposed to enrich themselves at another's expense, a merchant's trade brims with moral dangers, "Hardly will a merchant remain innocent of crime, and the shopkeeper clean of sin[31].... Between sale and purchase sin tarries."[32] Jesus Sirach admonished the debtor to repay promptly any loan he has made.[33] The source of all these sins is inordinate desire, which if nurtured, easily passes into action.[34]

3. RIGHT TO A GOOD NAME. The command, "Do not bear false witness against your neighbor,"[35] may not be limited to testimony given at court; its purpose is to outlaw lies and safeguard your fellow man's good name from all harm through calumny.

a) *Truthfulness in court.* A false statement in court may cost the life of the defendant in a criminal process; in a civil process it may entail great financial loss or deprivation of liberty—in both cases loss of status in the community. Therefore the Covenant Code obligated witnesses to speak only the absolute truth, and judges to pronounce sentence only in accordance with

13. Deut. 25:11-12.
14. Ex. 21:28-32.
15. Deut. 22:8.
16. Lev. 15:19-24.
17. Lev. 12:1-5.
18. Deut. 23:2.
19. Is. 56:3-5.
20. Ex. 21:16; Deut. 24:7; cf. Am. 1:6, 9; Joel 4:2-3.
21. Ex. 20:15.

22. Ex. 22:6-8; Lev. 5:20-26.
23. Lev. 19:35-36; Deut. 25:13-16.
24. Ex. 21:37-22:2; Lev. 19:11.
25. Lev. 25:36.
26. Deut. 19:14; 27:17.
27. Lev. 19:13; Deut. 24:14-15.
28. Ex. 21:33-22:14.
29. Am. 8:5; Os. 4:2; 12:2,

8-9; Is. 5:8; Mich. 2:2,9; 3:2-3; 6:10-11; Ez. 22:12; Jer. 5:27; cf. Neh. 5:1-5.
30. Prov. 19:22; 20:10, 17,23; 28:8; 30:9; Sir. 40:12.
31. Sir. 26:29.
32. Sir. 27:2.
33. Sir. 29:4-6.
34. Ex. 20:17.
35. Ex. 20:16.

right and justice. Neither witnesses nor judges may allow themselves to be moved by bribes or false compassion.[36] When the death sentence was imposed, the witnesses were obliged to cast the first stone upon the guilty, and thus assume the responsibility for the decision;[37] in case their statements were proven false during the hearings or later, they incurred the death penalty as just punishment for their malicious testimony.[38] The prophets preached justice,[39] denounced the unjust decisions so frequently rendered in the courts and the ease with which judges were bribed.[40] They proposed as an ideal the messianic king who would rule in justice and speak righteousness.[41] The sapiential writers reiterated the duty of judges to judge strictly according to justice,[42] and excoriated unjust decisions.[43]

b) *Truthfulness in personal matters.* The Law and the wisdom writers condemned lying.[44] "Lying lips are an abomination to Yahweh;"[45] but worse still is slander and talebearing, which destroy your neighbor's good name.[46] Slander frequently causes irreparable damage, "Town talk, mob uprising, slander: all these are worse than death."[47] Wives were accorded some protection against unjust accusations by their husbands.[48] Hypocrisy and dissimulation likewise offend against the virtue of truthfulness,[49] but the most grievous offense is a false oath, for it dishonors God's holy name.[50]

4. GOOD EXAMPLE. By example man deeply influences his environment for good or for evil. "Whoever misleads a just man into wicked ways, himself will fall into the snares he laid."[51] The aged Eleazar preferred to die rather than afford young men an occasion to waver in their faith.[52] Because of their calling priests are dedicated to sanctity; they give far greater scandal than others by godless or immoral lives; Malachias charged them with having made many fickle in observing the Law.[53]

5. CARE OF THE POOR. Here the ideal was, "There ought to be no poor man in your midst."[54] Prov. 39:8-9 set a happy mean, and the Jubilee year ordinance was designed to eliminate permanent poverty.[55] The latter decreed that plots of land which the owner through need had alienated should be returned to him (or to his heirs) without payment in the fiftieth year, i.e., in the seventh Sabbath year. The family should retain possession of land allotted to it, and thus the inordinate differences between poor and rich would not develop. The Law, recognizing that some poor would always remain, enjoined consideration for the stricken, for widows, and for orphans.[56] These had a right to a portion, even though small, of the land's produce;[57] in their favor the fields and gardens should not be completely harvested, nor should

36. Ex. 23:1-3, 6-9; cf. Lev. 19:15-16,35; Deut. 16:18-20.
37. Deut. 17:7.
38. Deut. 19:18-19.
39. Am. 5:24; Mich. 6:8; cf. Ps. 15:5.
40. Am. 2:6; 5:7, 10; Is. 10:2; 29:21; Mich. 3:9,11; 7:3; Jer. 5:28; Ez. 22:12.
41. Is. 11:2-5; Jer. 23:5-6; Ps. 72:4,12-14; § 50:1.
42. Prov. 24:23-25; 31:5; Sir.

7:6; Prov. 16:12.
43. Prov. 17:15,26; 18:5; 24:24.
44. Lev. 19:11; Prov. 4:24; 12:17,19; 16:13.
45. Prov. 12:22.
46. Lev. 19:16; Ps. 15:3; Prov. 11:13; 16:28; 20; 19; 30:10; Sir. 5:14; 11:31; 19:14-15; 26:13-26.
47. Sir. 26:5.
48. Num. 5:11-31; Deut. 22:13-21; cf. § 31:1-2.

49. Prov. 26:23-26; Sir. 12:16-17; 27:22-23.
50. Cf. § 28:5.
51. Prov. 28:10.
52. 2 Mach. 6:24-25.
53. Mal. 2:8.
54. Deut. 15:4.
55. Lev. 25.
56. Deut. 15:11; Ex. 22:21-26; Deut. 10:18; 24:17.
57. Lev. 19:9-10; Deut. 24:19-21.

gleanings be made. The tenth each third year was allotted to them,[58] and profitable work was to be provided.[59] The poor had first claim to whatever grew in field or garden during the Sabbatical year.[60] Israelites were not to pay interest on loans,[61] for in pre-exilic times they were not merchants but small farmers and cattle raisers; they did not contract debt to begin business but to stave off starvation or to meet serious household needs, e.g., purchasing seed grain, cattle (after an epidemic), etc. On the other hand foreigners, Canaanites and Phoenician traders, who profited on borrowed money, could be charged interest.[62] The good Israelite must not force his debtor to repay at an unseasonable time,[63] not at all during a Sabbatical year when he received no return from his fields and day labor was not easily obtainable.[64] Rich and selfish Israelites gave no loans in the time immediately preceding a Sabbatical year.[65] In the Hellenistic era, when the Jews no longer were primarily agriculturalists, they insisted upon the right to demand payment on debts at any time.[66] As surety the Jew could not take an article which his debtor needed, e.g., his handmill, the upper millstone,[67] his mantle,[68] any object particularly dear to him.[69] Among those toward whom special love must be shown were the aged and the infirm, who could not take care of themselves. Respect was due older persons.[70] It was considered rude and heartless to take advantage of or to ridicule the blind and deaf.[71] The Law summarized all duties in the verse, "Love your neighbor as yourself. I am Yahweh!"[72]

The practice of brotherly love toward the poor involves sacrifices repugnant to a greedy and avaricious person who inconsiderately seeks to profiteer on another's need. The prophets were a prick to many such consciences, "Charity pleases me, not (bloody) sacrifices."[73] Judgment will overtake those "who sell the just man for money, and the poor man for a pair of shoes[74].... who gorge themselves on the flesh of Yahweh's people, skin off their flesh and mangle their bones."[75] With eyes plastered over by evil conduct, they sprawl beside the altar on cloth pitilessly taken in pledge from the poor and drink wines purchased with fines unjustly extorted.[76] Our duty toward fellow men is summarized briefly in the prophet's admonition, "Learn to do good, strive after justice, help the *oppressed*, see that orphans get their rights, champion the widow's case."[77] Only he is upright "who oppresses no one, who *conscientiously* returns his pledge, who does not appropriate another's goods, who donates bread to the hungry, clothes to the naked, and does not lend for usury or accept interest."[78] Isaias emphasized the corporal works of mercy, breaking bread for the famished, sheltering the homeless, clothing the naked.[79] The sages taught, "Poor and rich are bound together in one unit: Yahweh has

58. Deut. 14:28-29; 26:12.
59. Lev. 25:35.
60. Ex. 23:11; Lev. 25:6.
61. Ex. 22:24; Lev. 25:36; Deut. 23:20-21.
62. Deut. 23:21.
63. Ex. 22:24.
64. Deut. 15:1-5.
65. Deut. 15:7-9.
66. E. Shürer, Geschichte des

jüd. Volkes II² 1907, 427f.
67. Deut. 24:6.
68. Ex. 22:25-26; Deut. 24: 12-13.
69. Deut. 24:10-11.
70. Lev. 19:32.
71. Lev. 19:14; Deut. 27:18.
72. Lev. 19:18.

73. Os. 6:6.
74. Am. 2:6.
75. Mich. 3:3.
76. Am. 2:8.
77. Is. 1:17; 10:1-3.
78. Ez. 18:7-8, 16-17.
79. Is. 58:7; cf. Mich. 3:2-3; Ez. 22:7,12; Zach. 7:9-10; Mal. 3:5.

made them all[80]. . . . Whoever oppresses the poor insults his creator; on the other hand whoever shows mercy to the needy, honors him[81]. . . . Whoever has pity on the poor, loans to Yahweh, and he will compensate him for his kindness[82]. . . . but he who stops his ears to the poor man's cry, he too shall cry and get no answer."[83] An almsgiver never becomes poor because God blesses him, "Some give alms liberally and only become the richer, some retain even that which is due, and only become the poorer."[84] The virtuous housewife "stretches out her hand to the poor, her arm she extends to the needy."[85] Alms should be given willingly, without demur, "Do not say to your neighbor: Now go, and come again later; or: I'll give you something tomorrow, if you are able to do so today."[86] Jesus Sirach urges us to give alms, to console the sorrowing, visit the sick, bury the dead.[87] The aged Tobias counselled his son to feed the hungry and to clothe the naked, to pay laborers immediately, to give alms even when in want.[88] The poor have a right to earn a living and whoever hinders them in this or deprives them of wages is no better than a murderer.[89] We should lend to the needy even though they often are ungrateful, neglect to repay at the time stipulated, and sometimes become abusive to their benefactors.[90] Nevertheless in going surety prudence is always in order lest some thoughtless spendthrift waste all one's goods.[91]

To stimulate a merciful spirit in the reader the OT recalls how the Israelites suffered while still in Egypt,[92] how all men without distinction have in God the same creator and father (and so are brothers),[93] how charitable acts blot out sin,[94] and how God abundantly rewards the virtuous.[95] The value placed upon almsgiving in later times is clear from the meanings accruing to the word justice *ṣedaqah*, e.g., mercy, love and finally alms.

6. RELATIONSHIP TO STRANGERS. On this topic a distinction must be made between the attitude of the OT toward nations taken as units and toward individual persons. Close communication with foreign nations was frowned upon,[96] but a different attitude is apparent when there was question of individuals. As far back as Exodus times strangers joined the ranks of the Israelites.[97] The commandments against murder, adultery, theft, false testimony and lust bound everyone, Israelite and non-Israelite. The Law distinguished the stranger, *ger*, from the foreigner, *nokri* or *ben-nekar*. The *ger* was a non-Israelite who for a shorter or longer time lived among the Israelites; ordinarily he was a Canaanite, while the *nokri* tarried in Canaan as a traveller or more often as a merchant. The sojourner, *tošab*, was one who had placed himself under the protection of the Israelite upon whose property he was squatting; he would be a stranger, *ger*, or a poverty stricken Israelite. The *rea* usually was a fellow countryman,[98] since the Israelites were brothers by common blood and com-

---

80. Prov. 22:2.
81. Prov. 14:31.
82. Prov. 19:17.
83. Prov. 21:13.
84. Prov. 11:24.
85. Prov. 31:20.
86. Prov. 3:28; Sir. 4:1-10.
87. Sir. 7:32-35.

88. Tob. 4:7-11,14,16; cf. Job 29:12-13; 31:16-21.
89. Sir. 34:25-27.
90. Sir. 29:1-13.
91. Sir. 29:16-20.
92. Deut. 10:18-19; 15:15.
93. Job 31:15; Mal. 2:10.

94. Prov. 16:16; Tob. 4:10-11; Dan. 4:24; Sir. 3:14-15, 30.
95. Ex. 20:6; Ps. 62:12-13.
96. § 32:1ef.
97. Ex. 12:38.
98. Lev. 19:18.

mon religion. A stranger could become a man of means,[99] but the majority remained poor, day laborers, artisans, tillers of a small plot; therefore they are frequently mentioned alongside the poor, the widows, and the orphans. Yahweh "loves the stranger also, and gives him food and clothing. So too you ought to show love toward the stranger, for you were strangers in the land of Egypt[100].... You must not hate the Edomites, for they are your brothers; you must not hate the Egyptians, for as strangers you tarried in their land.... Consider the stranger who resides with you as one born in the midst of your land; love him as you love yourself."[102] Passages in which the term neighbor is not limited to the Israelites by the context may well be given a universal application, "Cursed be he who kills his neighbor clandestinely[103].... Cursed be he who perverts the rights of the stranger, the orphan, and the widow."[104]

To recapitulate, the same regulations bound strangers and born Israelites; both classes were subject to the penal code, to certain cleanliness prescriptions, and both were permitted to offer sacrifices.[105] The stranger and the Israelite had to rest on the Sabbath[106] and on the feast of Atonement.[107] They were forbidden to blaspheme,[108] and to eat blood[109] and leavened bread on the Passover;[110] of the Passover meal however only the circumcised could partake.[111] The towns of refuge served as havens for strangers as well as for Israelites;[112] if they were wage earners, they were protected against the retention of wages and profiteering,[113] and had the right, if poor, to the gleanings from field and garden[114] and to that which grew there during the Sabbatical year.[115] They took part in the offering of the firstfruits,[116] participated in the rejoicing on the feast of Tabernacles.[117]

The prophets preached judgment upon nations hostile to Israel, yet prophesied their final conversion and reception into the new kingdom of God.[118] God's mercy embraces non-Israelites, both as individuals and as nations.[119] Elias assisted the widow of Sarepta,[120] Eliseus healed the Syrian Naaman.[121] With a like spirit Solomon besought Yahweh at the consecration of the temple to listen kindly to strangers from distant lands who had come to adore.[122] In postexilic times Zacharias[123] and Malachias[124] inveighed against the oppression of strangers, and the Book of Jonas teaches how God's care embraces distant Gentiles. A spirit of bigheartedness toward strangers pervades the Wisdom literature. Job protests he always provided shelter for the stranger.[125] Wisdom heralded her appeal to all the children of men[126] and emptied herself upon all flesh.[127] God Himself treated the Canaanites with forbearance.[128]

7. LOVE OF ENEMIES. To practice kindness toward a personal enemy is

99. Lev. 25:47; Deut. 28:43-44.
100. Deut. 10:18-19.
101. Deut. 23:8.
102. Lev. 19:34.
103. Deut. 27:24.
104. Deut. 27:19.
105. Lev. 24:22; 17:15; Num. 19:10; 15:10-16.
106. Ex. 20:10; 23:12.
107. Lev. 16:29.
108. Lev. 24:16.
109. Lev. 17:10.
110. Ex. 12:19.
111. Ex. 12:48.
112. Num. 35:15.
113. Deut. 24:14-15.
114. Lev. 19:9-10; Deut. 24:19.
115. Lev. 25:6.
116. Deut. 26:11.
117. Deut. 16:13-14.
118. § 45:2-5; 48:2.
119. § 25:3-4.
120. 3 Kgs. 17:8f.
121. 4 Kgs. 5:1f.
122. 3 Kgs. 8:41-43.
123. Zach. 7:10.
124. Mal. 3:5.
125. Job 31:32.
126. Prov. 8:4.
127. Sir. 1:10.
128. Wis. 12:8.

incomparably more difficult than keeping on friendly terms with a stranger who may benefit you directly or serve as your hired man. Insults, property damage, bodily injuries easily occasion a demand for revenge. The *lex talionis* gave the right to inflict due punishment. Nevertheless the OT points out a higher ideal than legitimate reprisals. Joseph forgave his brethren from his heart.[129] Moses prayed for the people as they were attempting to stone him.[130] David spared Saul who was pursuing him to death,[131] was solicitous about Absolom who had rebelled against him,[132] and forgave Semei's abusive conduct.[133] Eliseus espoused the cause of the Arameans.[134] Jeremias prayed for his enemies.[135] The psalmist protests his willingness to save even those who harassed him without cause.[136] The Law directed, "Do not bear hate in your heart against your brother; do not be revengeful or resentful toward your fellow men, but love your neighbor (who has wronged you) as yourself. I am Yahweh!"[137] The person offended should desist from revenge and should show love toward an adversary from a sense of religious duty. The sages admonish not to rejoice over the misfortune of an enemy, "If your enemy falls, do not rejoice; if he stumbles, do not let your heart be merry, lest Yahweh see it and it displease him."[138] Job confessed he never experienced joy when misfortune overtook his enemy; he did not requite evil with evil, but left revenge to God.[139] He considered it sinful to wish death upon an enemy out of a spirit of revenge.[140] The faithful Israelite was enjoined to aid an enemy when the occasion arose,[141] "If your enemy be hungry, nourish him with bread, and if he be thirsty, give him water to drink; for by this manner of acting you gather fiery coals upon his head, and Yahweh will repay you."[142] Such conduct will make your enemy feel ashamed, will touch his heart and thereby end all ill feeling. Indeed Jesus Sirach advised, "Give to the God-fearing, but take no interest in the wicked; do good to the humble, but to the godless give nothing,"[143] yet this counsel presupposes that the good done to such as these would bring in return nothing but harm and would confirm the wicked in their wickedness. In other chapters he inveighs against evil gossip[144] and inculcates forgiveness of wrongs, for "then at your petition will sins disappear from you. Think on the commandments and bear no ill will against your fellow man, remember the covenant with the Most High and forgive a mistake."[145] When his enemy is sick, the pious man will grieve and fast, imploring his recovery.[146] This effort to inculcate kindness toward enemies is also found in certain laws referring to the conduct of war.[147] Jeremias made a signal contribution in the year 597 by counselling the Judean deportees to pray for the Chaldeans who were enslaving them.[148] The motives given indeed pointed to personal interests, e.g., their own prosperity would depend upon the prosperity of the land in which they were to live; nevertheless it must have been exceedingly

129. Gen. 45:1f; 50:15f.
130. Num. 14:10f.
131. 1 Sam. 24:1f; 26:1f.
132. 2 Sam. 18:5.
133. 2 Sam. 16:5f (cf. § 34:7).
134. 4 Kgs. 6:22.
135. Jer. 18:20.

136. Ps. 7:5.
137. Lev. 19:17-18.
138. Prov. 24:17-18.
139. Job 31:29; cf. Prov. 20: 22; 24:29.
140. Job 31:30.
141. Ex. 23:4-5.

142. Prov. 25:21-22.
143. Sir. 12:4.
144. Sir. 19:15-17.
145. Sir. 28:2, 6-7.
146. Ps. 35:13.
147. § 32:1e.
148. Jer. 29:7.

difficult for captives to comply with his request to quiet the spirit of revenge
and to wish good upon the enemies who oppressed them because of the aver-
sion—understandable, it is true—which they as exiles cherished against the
Babylonian overlords.[149] Alongside this admonition we find violent outbursts
of hostile spirit.[150] Concerning the treatment of women captured in war, cf.
§ 31:1a,2b.

8. CONSIDERATION FOR ANIMALS. Even toward animals men should act
considerately according to the proverb, "The just man provides for the needs
of his cattle;"[151] moreover God's good providence includes irrational creation.[152] The commentary on the third commandment expressly states that
the Sabbath rest was also for the benefit of the beasts.[153] The ox must not be
muzzled while treading out the grain on the threshing-floor,[154] but should be
privileged to take a mouthful of the fodder lying at his feet. Ox and ass should
not be yoked together, lest the weaker animal, the ass, be overworked.[155] It
was allowed to take only the eggs or the young birds from a nest, the mature
birds were not to be harmed—a precept ordained to develop a more humane
disposition.[156] Later Jewish exegesis found a similar purpose in the prescriptions, a) to leave a young animal with its mother seven days before it was
sacrificed (an animal only a few days old would not have been a gift worthy
for Yahweh),[157] b) not to boil a kid in its mother's milk (a superstitious
practice),[158] c) not to sacrifice a sheep or cow on the same day as its young.[159]
Any animal that killed a man or served to gratify unnatural lust was to be
killed;[160] animals were created for man's benefit, but no longer fulfill that
purpose when they become a source of physical or moral evil.

§ 30. DUTIES TOWARD SELF

1. HUMILITY is the first and most important virtue which we must practice. Why? Because we are infinitely inferior to God. God would not need
us even if we possessed all virtue, knowledge and wealth, or occupied the most
responsible positions.[1] The precept, "Love your neighbor as yourself,"[2] however implies an ordered self-love. Man bears in himself God's image[3] and
should remember it was God who placed him over all irrational creation. The
author of Psalm 8 was aware of this, yet in that same psalm his thoughts are
principally upon his own nothingness and weakness: how insignificant he feels
in the presence of God's mighty wonders! "What indeed is mortal man that
you are mindful of him."[4] He has every reason "to live humbly before his
God."[5] He need but recall his origin, realize his frailty, meditate on his end,
"Why are dust and ashes boastful? A little sickness—the doctor's face beams—
king today and dead tomorrow! When a man dies he becomes the proprietor

149. Ps. 137:8-9.
150. Cf. § 32efg; 45:1-2.
151. Prov. 12:10.
152. § 16:3.
153. Ex. 20:10; 34:21.

1. § 9:2.
2. Lev. 19:18, 34.

154. Deut. 25:4.
155. Deut. 22:10.
156. Deut. 22:6-7.
157. Ex. 22:29; Lev. 22:27.
158. Ex. 23:19.

3. Gen. 1:26-27.
4. Ps. 8:5.

159. Lev. 22:28; cf. Philo, De
     Virt. 125f.
160. Gen. 9:5; Ex. 21:28-32;
     Lev. 20:15.

5. Mich. 6:8.

of mould and maggots, of dirt and worms."[6] Since earthly goods, health and riches are so much vanity, let him humble himself, "Haughtiness does not become a man, or wrathful insolence those born of women."[7] O that man would be mindful of his sinfulness! "Do not justify yourself before *God.*"[8]

Humility endears us to our fellow men, "Comes pride, comes disgrace, but with the prudent there is wisdom[9]. . . . A man's pride will humiliate him, while the humble will obtain honor[10]. . . . My son, do your work humbly, and you will be loved by men who are pleasing to God."[11] We find the same idea put negatively in the verse, "Do not exalt yourself lest you fall and cover yourself with shame."[12] The humble man's greatest glory is God's good pleasure, "*Towards* scorners he (God) will be a scorner himself, but to the humble he gives grace."[13] God is "glorified by the humble,"[14] and "he teaches the humble his way."[15] The prophets and psalmists exhort us to practice humility, to subject ourselves to God's will and to feel ourselves His slaves.[16] The humble are promised possession of the land.[17] The sacred writers in every century reminded their fellow men of their many sins past and present; and if they were delivered out of Egypt and still enjoyed good fortune, it was not due to their own might or merit but only to the infinite mercies of God. There exists also a false humility which in reality is nothing but hypocrisy, e.g., when a person acts very modestly while asking for a loan, but becomes insolent toward his creditor as soon as payment is due,[18] or when an enemy dons the mask of a friend.[19]

A humble person will not overrate his own abilities; he will always remain conscious of his own frailty. "What is too difficult for you, do not petition, and do not probe into what is above your ability[20]. . . . We hardly have an idea of the things at hand. Who then can fathom the things that are in heaven?"[21] The humble man prays like the psalmist, "Yahweh, my heart does not reach out for lofty things, nor does my glance rove about haughtily. I do not entertain presumptuous plans, or things beyond me."[22] The humble man is aware of his inability to know the will of God and his absolute incapacity to fulfill it if God does not enlighten him.[23] What God sends he will try to bear, "Accept whatever happens to you, and be patient in the midst of your changing humiliations."[24] In all things the honor goes to God, "Not to us, Yahweh, not to us, but to your name accord the honor."[25] In none of these passages however is there any undercurrent of quietism or of slothfully sitting by and awaiting the good which God gives. Rather OT religious spirit is most active and positive; it incites to action with promises, as if God were awaiting everything from man.[26]

A humble man will be discreet in giving judgment and guard himself from

6. Sir. 10:9-11.
7. Sir. 10:18.
8. Sir. 7:5; cf. Job 15:14.
9. Prov. 11:2.
10. Prov. 29:23; cf. 15:33; 18:12.
11. Sir. 3:17.
12. Sir. 1:30.

13. Prov. 3:34.
14. Sir. 3:20.
15. Ps. 25:9.
16. Soph. 3:12; Is. 41:17; 49: 13; 61:1; Pss. 10:16-17; 22:27.
17. Ps. 37:11.
18. Sir. 29:5-6.

19. Sir. 12:11.
20. Sir. 3:22.
21. Wis. 9:16.
22. Ps. 131:1.
23. Wis. 9:17-18.
24. Sir. 2:4.
25. Ps. 115:1; cf. Ps. 8:2.
26. § 30:7.

sins of the tongue, "Death and life proceed from the tongue, and they who use it much *partake* of its fruit[27].... Where there is much speaking sin will not be wanting; therefore he who is wise guards his tongue."[28] Conscious of his littleness a humble person will not be easily moved to anger; he will remain gentle even when insulted. "A gentle tongue is a tree of life, its perversity breaks (one's) heart[29].... A hothead stirs up strife, a patient man quiets quarrels."[30] Particularly those whom God blessed superabundantly teach us humility. Abraham, chosen in preference to all other men, regarded himself dust and ashes, not worthy to speak with God.[31] Jacob deemed himself unworthy of the graces and the fidelity God had tendered to him.[32] Before Pharaoh Joseph acknowledged, "I am capable of nothing."[33] Moses, though well educated, did not believe himself equipped for the mission Yahweh assigned to him;[34] the judgment of fellow Israelites was, "He was exceedingly humble, more so than any other man on earth."[35] David did not feel worthy of God's favor.[36] Solomon confessed that without God's help he was unable to govern the people.[37] At his call Jeremias objected, "I am not even able to speak, I am yet so young."[38]

Pride stands at odd's end to humility. Pride is mutiny against God to whom it refuses submission, "The beginning of pride is the acquisition of power, then does the heart turn away from its creator."[39] But the proud man will not triumph for long, "Pride goes before destruction, and haughtiness before a fall."[40] Those who after the deluge proudly sought to construct a tower high as heaven were scattered.[41] Nabuchodonosor became delirious because he exalted himself.[44] The proud women of Jerusalem, mincing along and parading their apparel with outstretched necks, were to be humbled to the very dust.[45] God is never at a loss for ways to break the spirit of pride, "for all pride is an abomination to Yahweh, truly it shall not go unpunished."[46] No human power will endure before God, "The thrones of the arrogant God tumbles over, and he stations the oppressed in their place."[47] Some day Yahweh will hold judgment "over everything proud and exalted, over everything that exalts itself and domineers."[48] Then "shall he bring to an end the pride of the insolent, he shall bring low the arrogance of the mighty."[49] In their comminatory speeches against the nations and their rulers, the prophets inveighed continually against their arrogance, for they imagined themselves to be like God (cf. § 45:4). In the next world too pride will not go unpunished. "What did pride profit us, and what has riches with vain boasting brought us!"[50]

2. MAINTAINING SELF-RESPECT. A consciousness of our own nothingness does not eliminate the duty of maintaining that self-respect upon which good standing with our fellow men depends. "A good name is preferable to great

27. Prov. 18:21.
28. Prov. 10:19; cf. 13:3; 17: 27.
29. Prov. 15:4.
30. Prov. 15:18; cf. Prov. 14: 17, 29; 15:1; 22:24.
31. Gen. 18:27.
32. Gen. 32:11.
33. Gen. 41:16.
34. Ex. 3:11.
35. Num. 12:3.
36. 2 Sam. 7:18.
37. 3 Kgs. 3:7.
38. Jer. 1:6.
39. Sir. 10:12.
40. Prov. 16:18.
41. Gen. 11:1-9.
44. Dan. 3:98(31)-4:34.
45. Is. 3:16-24.
46. Prov. 16:5.
47. Sir. 10:14.
48. Is. 2:12.
49. Is. 13:11.
50. Wis. 5:8.

riches, better than gold and silver is popularity[51]. . . . Man and his body will pass away, but the name of a virtuous man shall not vanish. Safeguard your name, for it shall remain with you longer than a thousand *precious* treasures."[52] Popularity depends upon a virtuous life, "The just will be mentioned for blessing, the name of the wicked will be *cursed*."[53] True honor does not flow from position or wealth but from piety, "The rich, the illustrious, and the poor, their glory is the fear of Yahweh."[54]

3. PRUDENCE IN FRIENDSHIP. Friendship is necessary, for we need friends in order to develop a rounded out character. "Every being loves its like, and every man one who resembles himself."[55] You are most fortunate if you have a sincere friend, "A faithful friend cannot be bought, his value is above price."[56] True friendship however is possible only among the God-fearing, "He who fears the Lord finds true friendship, for as he is, so is his friend[57]. . . . There are friends who are friends in name only[58]. . . . for in the day of need he will not be present."[59] Often one who is presumed a friend and given confidences turns out to be an enemy.[60] Therefore hesitate before striking a friendship; seek to live peaceably with everyone, but be intimate only with a chosen few;[61] before your associate has proven himself genuine, remember the warning, "Be on guard against your friends."[62] For the godless too seek intimacies with the pious—with the same purpose as wolves descending upon lambs.[63] The danger of seduction is always great, "Who touches pitch soils himself, and who associates with a scoffer will become like to him."[64] But if you find a true friend, "love (him) and remain faithful to him."[65] Friendship is ruined by gossip, which tends to blab confidential matter.[66]

4. PURITY OF BODY. Natural bodily disturbances or diseased conditions pertaining to sex rendered a person unclean.[67] Of course this did not imply moral guilt, yet an unclean person was not allowed to take part in liturgical functions. Women with child were required to remain separate,[68] not because they had produced new life, but because of their physical condition. The legislator simply retained rights which women had by prescription and orientated them to Yahweh; these prescriptions tempered male concupiscence and benefited women's health.[69]

Uncleanness also resulted from contact with the carcass of a beast and various kinds of creeping things, or eating the flesh of an animal that had died.[70] Ordinary daily life provided the Israelite with many occasions for practicing obedience to Yahweh. The laws concerning the uncleanness of a human corpse and the purifications which every one had to undergo who touched a corpse, whether accidentally or necessarily,[71] could not but remind the Israelite that he was a sinner; and the wages of sin is death.[72] A leper was

51. Prov. 22:1.
52. Sir. 41:11-12.
53. Prov. 10:7.
54. Sir. 10:22.
55. Sir. 13:15.
56. Sir. 6:15.
57. Sir. 6:17.
58. Sir. 37:1.

59. Sir. 6:8.
60. Sir. 6:9; 37:4.
61. Sir. 6:6.
62. Sir. 6:13; 6:7.
63. Sir. 13:17.
64. Sir. 13:1.
65. Sir. 27:17.

66. Sir. 27:16-21.
67. Lev. 15.
68. Lev. 12.
69. § 2:2b; 29:1b.
70. Lev. 11:24f.
71. Num. 19.
72. Gen. 2:17; 3:19.

considered as dead.[73] In case he was healed a purification ceremony was performed symbolizing his resurrection to new life and re-entry into Yahweh's service.

5. SICKNESS AND HEALTH. Health was esteemed as the most precious earthly good, "More fortunate is the poor man who is well and healthy, than the rich man who is stricken in body[74]. . . . Health and a strong constitution are better than gold."[75] An ailing rich man derives no benefit from his goods.[76] Accordingly take proper care of your health, live temperately,[77] do not permit yourself to be overcome by anger or cares; even at the death of a near and dear relative or friend you should not grieve excessively or protractedly because such practice harms your health and weakens your vitality.[78]

Sickness often follows sin as punishment.[79] "Who sins against his creator, *falls* into the hands of the physician."[80] Enemies scoff when one becomes sick;[81] Tobias' wife had no compassion upon her distressed husband, even less so the wife of Job.[82] Later generations however were more inclined to recognize that God permits sickness to come upon upright men in order to prove and purify them; the sick man should bear patiently what God sends him.[83] The most thorough and profound treatment of this problem occurs in the Book of Job. The virtuous man may be so overcome by pain as to desire death, particularly if he has no hope of recovery, e.g., Job[84] and blind Tobias.[85] The good man will sympathize with and console the sick, "Do not delay in visiting the sick, for by it you will harvest love."[86]

During sickness the invalid should pray and have sacrifices offered.[87] The pious King Ezechias prayed to be healed,[88] while the Chronicler notes how King Asa, who had been zealous for the cause of true religion,[89] failed to seek the Lord when ill.[90] Nevertheless the sick man may not omit using the natural means which God has placed at his disposal. Isaias applied a plaster upon Ezechias.[91] "The Lord causes the earth to produce medicines, and the reasonable man will not disregard them."[92] He will also consult the physician, for "he too is needed[93]. . . . (he) quiets the pain"[94] by means of the medicinal herbs which God permits to bud. Still the physician himself ought to turn to God in prayer to obtain the desired cure.[95] "Honor the physician, for the Lord has made him too."[96]

Suicide is indirectly forbidden in the passage, "You shall not kill."[97] Since the Israelites were a happy people and feared Sheol,[98] only a few instances of suicide are recounted. Saul wounded himself mortally by falling upon his sword to avoid being taken captive, scoffed at and tortured by the Philistines; his armour-bearer followed him in death not wishing to outlive his master.[99]

73. Lev. 13.
74. Sir. 30:14.
75. Sir. 30:15; cf. 30:16.
76. Sir. 30:18-20.
77. Sir. 37:27-30.
78. Prov. 15:13; Sir. 30:21-23; 38:17-18.
79. Lev. 26:16, 25; Deut. 28: 21-22, 27-28, 35, 59; Pss. 38:3, 5; 41:5.
80. Sir. 38:15; § 41:2.
81. Pss. 38:13, 17; 41:6.
82. Tob. 2:14; Job 2:9.
83. Tob. 2:10; 12:13; 41:4-5.
84. Job 3:13-19.
85. Tob. 3:6; § 42:3.
86. Sir. 7:35.
87. Sir. 38:9-11.
88. 4 Kgs. 20:2.
89. 3 Kgs. 15:11; 2 Chr. 14:2.
90. 2 Chr. 16:12.
91. 4 Kgs. 20:7.
92. Sir. 38:4.
93. Sir. 38:12.
94. Sir. 37:7.
95. Sir. 38:14.
96. Sir. 38:1.
97. Ex. 20:13.
98. § 42:2-3.
99. 1 Sam. 31:4-5.

Achitophel hanged himself when he foresaw he would have to pay for his treachery.[100] Zambri of Israel burned himself in his palace to avoid falling into the hands of Amri.[101] During the Maccabean wars the pious Rages killed himself rather than suffer a disgraceful death.[102] The Biblical writers report the act, and they endeavor to give all the circumstances, but their words contain nothing indicating they considered the act itself objectively permissible.

6. TEMPERANCE IN EATING AND DRINKING. God bestows bread for nourishment and also wine "which gives joy to the human heart."[103] Wine sweetens life[104] and makes sorrow more bearable.[105] But only the moderate use of food and drink is good, "Woe to them who are heroes as winebibbers, gallant people in mixing drinks[106]. . . . who stagger from wine, and reel from cocktails," with whom "all tables are full of vomit."[107] The wisdom teachers admonish, "Do not enjoy anything immoderately[108]. . . . Do not be numbered among winebibbers, among those who gorge themselves with meats, for the drunkard and the glutton become impoverished."[109] Jesus Sirach warns about unbridled appetites at banquets, "Do not say: How well it's heaped!"[110] A person in a responsible position will easily become remiss in his official duties if he is an intemperate eater.[111] The greatest damage to health results from gluttony.[112] The evil effects of drunkenness are pointed out in Prov. 23:29-35; Sir. 31:20.

In the Pentateuch we find very detailed regulations that had been taken from ancient customs and further amplified by the legislator.[113] Their purpose was to remind the Israelites that before Yahweh they were unlike any other nation and accordingly had to observe special restraints.[114] In the persecution under Antiochus Epiphanes fidelity to Yahweh was tested by means of these laws.[115] The prohibitions placed upon the use of blood and of bloody meat[116] derive from the ancient notion that life is in the blood, and life belongs to God.[117] The use of specific cuts from certain animals was forbidden, since such were to be given to Yahweh in sacrifice.[118] The precepts regarding the use of meat from dead animals were intended to remind the Israelite to keep himself legally undefiled. By means of these varied restrictions he was led to subject his will to God's and was afforded opportunities for self-denial; the laws on fasting have the same purpose.[119]

7. EVALUATION OF EARTHLY GOODS. The differences between the rich and the poor have been ordained by God and are reflected in His good providence.[120]
a) *Riches*. The rich have many advantages; they are secure from the changing vicissitudes of life;[121] they may permit themselves many joys,[122] are easily able to make legal compensation when found at fault,[123] have friends and influence.[124] Yet riches do not necessarily imply happiness, "Better to have a

100. 2 Sam. 17:23.
101. 3 Kgs. 16:18.
102. 2 Mach. 14:37-46.
103. Ps. 104:15; cf. Judg. 9:13.
104. Sir. 31:27-28; Qoh. 9:7.
105. Prov. 31:6-7.
106. Is. 5:22.
107. Is. 28:7-8; cf. Is. 5:11-12; Mich. 2:11.
108. Sir. 37:29.
109. Prov. 23:20-21; cf. Prov.

20:1.
110. Sir. 31:12; 31:16-19, 25.
111. Prov. 31:4-5.
112. Sir. 37:30-31.
113. Cf. § 2:2b; 4:4a.
114. Cf. Ez. 4:9, 14; Dan 1:8, 12; Tob. 1:11; Jud. 10:5; 12:2.
115. 2 Mach. 6:18-19; 7:1.
116. Gen. 9:4; Lev. 3:17; 7: 26-27; 17:10-14; 19:26.

117. § 26:3b.
118. Lev. 7:23-25.
119. § 37.
120. Prov. 22:2; cf. 14:31; 17:5; Sir. 11:14.
121. Prov. 10:15.
122. Sir. 31:3.
123. Prov. 13:8.
124. Prov. 14:20; 19:4, 6; Sir. 6:7-8; Prov. 22:7.

humble home in the fear of Yahweh than rich possessions with anxiety."[125] Riches bring many troubles.[126] In spite of his riches the miser is miserable, he allows himself no enjoyments, makes no one happy.[127] Moral dangers too accompany riches. Riches easily open the way to avarice, self-esteem and intemperance, to a false confidence in God's patience and thereby to impenitence.[128] Often they are obtained unjustly,[129] and with such goods there is no lasting fortune. The rich man may rejoice over ill-gotten goods, but misfortune will overtake him in the end;[130] he will die prematurely; he will take none of his money with him to the grave.[131] What good are stolen goods if they cannot prolong life? "They put their trust in their possessions, and vaunt themselves over their great wealth. *Yet* the aristocrat will not be able to redeem *himself* or count out a ransom to God for himself."[132] And when he dies his property goes to another.[133] Even during lifetime the rich man cannot rest secure in his wealth, "He lies down rich, but shall not *harvest*, he opens his eyes, it no longer exists."[134] Most plainly however will it be shown at the judgment in the next world how vain are ill-gotten goods.[135]

The rich should use their wealth in a prudent way, taking lawful enjoyment and aiding the poor.[136] They should keep in mind that riches have only a relative value. Better than wealth is health, "No wealth is as great as bodily health, no possession as great as cheerfulness."[137] A happy home life should be esteemed more highly than riches, "Better is a piece of dry bread and peace than a house full of meat-offerings and strife" (Prov. 17:1). Prudence too is a possession more valuable than any earthly treasure, "To what purpose anyway has the fool money in his hand? To buy wisdom? he has no judgment."[138] A good name is a treasure more precious than gold,[139] while fear of God ranks far above all. Tobias taught his son, "Do not fear because we have become poor. You are rich if you fear God, if you keep yourself from all sin and do that which is pleasing to him."[140] "Better are the trifles which the poor man has than the vast riches of many sinners."[141]

From these considerations we should see the folly of striving inordinately for riches, particularly by crooked ways.[142] It is far wiser to pray, "Give me neither beggary nor riches; but let me enjoy my needed nourishment lest perhaps being filled I should become a liar and say: Who is Yahweh? or being impoverished I should become a thief and offend the name of my God."[143] The jubilee year law pointed out clearly that the purpose of life was not to accumulate earthly goods,[144] and the Sabbatical year ordinance, which forbade the sowing of fields, reminded the landholder that he had only a limited right to his possessions.

125. Prov. 15:16.
126. Sir. 31:1.
127. Sir. 14:3-10.
128. Am. 6:3-6; Is. 3:16; 5: 22-23; Sir. 4:31-5-7.
129. Is. 10:1-2; Jer. 6:13; Prov. 19:1; 28:6, 20; Sir. 31:5, 8.
130. Prov. 20:17.
131. Jer. 17:11; Ps. 49:18;

Prov. 10:2.
132. Ps. 49:7-8.
133. Pss. 49:11; 39:7; Sir. 11: 18-19; 14:4.
134. Job 27:19; Prov. 23:4-5; 27:24; Sir. 5:1.
135. Wis. 5:8.
136. Sir. 14:11-16.
137. Sir. 30:16; § 30:5.

138. Prov. 17:16.
139. Prov. 22:1.
140. Tob. 4:21.
141. Ps. 37:16; Sir. 40:26; Wis. 7:8.
142. Prov. 23:4; Qoh. 2:4-11; 5:9-11.
143. Prov. 30:8-9.
144. Lev. 25:8-55; § 30:5.

b) *Poverty.* In the OT poverty is regarded as a great evil, "The misfortune of the needy is this: their poverty."[145] A poor man is subject to every stroke of fate. If he be sentenced and cannot pay the fine, he becomes a slave;[146] no friend appears,[147] not even his relatives give him support.[148] The rich use him to advantage;[149] his rights are disregarded;[150] and when he is treated unjustly he must bear it—and act all the more humbly.[151] A dark picture of the lot of the poor is painted in Job 24:4-13: they must seek food in deserted places, are allotted only the gleanings in the gardens of the wealthy, go half naked and freeze when it is cold, are taken as security, and their children sold into slavery. Poverty is not free from moral dangers. A hungry man is easily tempted to steal[152] or to make promises which he cannot fulfill.[153]

Poverty often results from sloth,[154] from love of liquor,[155] sumptuous living,[156] foolish exploits,[157] unthriftiness,[158] stubbornness, refusing advice.[159] At times poverty is a punishment which God inflicts upon those who strive to become rich quickly and by unjust methods.[160] Other reasons which lead to impoverishment are droughts, crop failures, cattle plagues, war, disease, fraud and usury; these evils reduce the poor to still greater indigency and aid the concentration of great possessions in one hand.[161]

Though poverty is an evil it is not the greatest evil. A poor man who is healthy is better than a rich man who is ill[162] or who lives in a constant unrest.[163] A poor man will not sin so frequently by frivolous speech, since he does not ramble about in public places.[164] A poor man who is virtuous must be regarded as far more fortunate than a rich man who is godless.[165] A wise man receives honor even though he is poor,[166] "Better is a poor but wise youth than an old but foolish king who accepts no further counsel."[167] A poor man living in his own country is more lucky than a person who must reside in a foreign land, even though he seems to prosper, "Better a poor man's life under a protecting roof than tempting titbits among strangers." The foreigner will be reminded that he is roving about, he will be unable to voice an opinion without immediately hearing insulting words at which he has to keep silent; he will be used to advantage and will be given to understand that his departure would be very welcome.[168]

The poor man ought not be sad; if he is of a happy disposition his lot will be much less burdensome.[169] The real needs of life are indeed few, "The necessaries for life are water, bread and clothing, and a house to hide one's nakedness."[170] Inner peace of heart seasons the simplest meal.[171] If you are wealthy and misfortune suddenly strikes, submit to the will of God, "Yahweh gave, Yahweh took, may Yahweh's name be blessed."[172]

145. Prov. 10:15.
146. Prov. 13:8.
147. Prov. 14:20; 19:4.
148. Prov. 19:7.
149. Sir. 13:18-19.
150. Sir. 13:22-23.
151. Sir. 13:3.
152. Prov. 30:9.
153. Sir. 20:23-24.
154. Prov. 6:11; 10:4; 23:21; 24:30-34.
155. Sir. 19:1.
156. Prov. 21:17; 23:21.
157. Prov. 12:11; 28:19.
158. Sir. 19:1.
159. Prov. 13:18.
160. Prov. 20:21; 28:22.
161. Is. 5:8; Mich. 2:2.
162. Sir. 30:14-16.
163. Prov. 15:16-17; 17:1.
164. Sir. 20:21.
165. Tob. 4:21; cf. Prov. 16:8; 19:1, 22; 28:6; Ps. 37:16.
166. Sir. 10:30.
167. Qoh. 4:13.
168. Sir. 29:22-27.
169. Prov. 15:15.
170. Sir. 29:21.
171. Prov. 15:16-17; 17:1.
172. Job 1:21.

A final observation which should comfort the poor and reconcile him to his lot is this: God takes a special interest in the poor, they are "His" poor.[173] For this reason the Law, the prophets and the wisdom writers exhort us to be charitable toward the poor out of religious considerations.[174] Though the poor man may be despised, though he may not obtain justice in the courts, with God "there is no respect of persons; he does not side against the poor, but hears the prayers of the oppressed."[175] The Messiah will be particularly solicitous for the poor.[176] Because the poor are so beloved by God, the expressions, *to be poor* and *to be pious*, are often used interchangeably, particularly in the psalms, with the result that the words, *poor, oppressed,* receive a good moral connotation along with their primary meaning. And the poor, feeling themselves God's favorites, regarded the propertied class, who were only too eager to despoil them, as godless. In spite of this attitude toward poverty we find no recommendation to donate all one's goods to the poor. The reasons were: 1. poverty itself is an evil which is not to be brought upon oneself; 2. to be occupied with the Law, which was esteemed most highly in later times, presupposed a certain amount of economic freedom; 3. some material goods are needed to fulfill the demands of God more easily, "only he who is relieved of his business can become wise."[177]

Though the poor are loved by God and are commended to the charity of others, they must not abandon themselves to the support of their fellow men and pass their days begging. "It is better to die than to beg."[178] A beggar's life is unworthy of a man; only he who lacks all sense of honor is unashamed to beg; but he is not happy, for the envy which he experiences against the rich is like a fire smouldering in his breast.[179] As long as a person has the strength and the chance he should gain his livelihood through work. Already in paradise some work was imposed upon Adam.[180] And when driven out he was told, "In the sweat of your face you will eat your bread."[181] Ever since, this has been the law of life.[182] Stated positively, the seventh commandment reads: *Work!* Work has been willed by God and therefore it is honorable, "Do not despise hard work or the tilling of the land because it has been ordained by God."[183] Whoever works will not go hungry, rather he will become wealthy.[184] The lazy man should learn from the ant that he must work.[185] Work keeps one well.[186] One may enjoy the fruit of his labor for it is God's gift.[187] We should remain mindful that it is God who blesses our work, "If Yahweh does not build the house, in vain do they labor who build it."[188] Work may never become an end in itself; we must never lose ourselves in our work, for we have not been created for self or for this world, but for God. And that we may ever remain conscious of this, God ordained the Sabbath.[189]

173. Ps. 72:2; cf. Pss. 10:14, 18; 68:6; 69:34; Prov. 14:31; Sir. 35:17; § 16:5.
174. § 29:5.
175. Sir. 35:15-16; Prov. 22: 22-23; Job 5:15.
176. Ps. 72:4, 12; § 51:1.
177. Sir. 38:24.

178. Sir. 40:28.
179. Sir. 40:29-30.
180. Gen. 2:15.
181. Gen. 3:19.
182. Ps. 104:23.
183. Sir. 7:15.
184. Prov. 10:4; 11:16; 12:11, 24; 28:19; Sir. 10:27.

185. Prov. 6:6-11.
186. Qoh. 5:11.
187. Qoh. 2:24; 3:12; 5:18; 8:15; Ps. 128:2.
188. Ps. 127:1; Prov. 10:22; Sir. 11:11-13.
189. Ex. 20:8-11.

§ 31. FAMILY DUTIES

1. MARRIAGE. a) *Holiness of the married state.* The continuance of human society depends upon the sanctification of marriage. Even the most savage tribes esteem the bond which unites man and woman. The purpose of marriage is not to appease lust but to preserve the human race. Upon our first parents in paradise and upon Noe after the deluge God pronounced the blessing, "Be fruitful in order to multiply and fill the earth."[1] Because marriage was instituted and blessed by God in paradise,[2] it does not rest upon human caprice; it is a "covenant with God .... (a covenant at which) Yahweh is a witness."[3] Tobias prayed, "Not out of sinful lust do I take my sister (to wife), but out of fidelity to the Law."[4] The married couple should act with reserve in the presence of each other, "A modest wife experiences shame even in the presence of her husband."[5] Because marriage is "God's covenant," the prophets loved to depict the relationship between Yahweh and Israel in terms of marriage.[6]

The decalog's injunction, "You shall not commit adultery,"[7] flows from the sanctity of marriage. Adultery is a sin against God.[8] Even evil desire is grievously sinful, "You shall not lust after your neighbor's wife."[9] Intercourse with a foreigner violates God's laws, as Joseph told Putiphar's wife.[10] Since polygamy was permitted in the OT, a married man committed adultery by having relations with a married woman, but not with an unmarried woman; on the other hand intercourse between a married woman and a married or unmarried man was adultery. The punishment for adultery was death in all cases.[11] However if the woman (or a betrothed person) was not free to marry, death was not inflicted, but inasmuch as the Law inflicted punishment upon the guilty (a fine for the man, a sound beating for the woman) and imposed a guilt-offering, this act too was a grievous insult to God's holiness.[12]

We find marital fidelity highly praised. Piety in a wife was esteemed higher than external charm, which quickly fades.[13] Susanna preferred to die rather than commit adultery.[14] Job protested that "his heart never set itself foolishly upon a woman ... or glanced at the door of his friend;" he condemned adultery as "a shameful act, a crime which rages like fire and devours down to Sheol."[15] The sapiential writers frequently and forcefully inveigh against this sin;[16] it may remain hidden among men, but it is never concealed from the eyes of God.[17] An adultress defiles herself in a threefold way: she impairs God's holiness, she deceives her husband, she introduces strangers into the family circle.[18] Yet withal she experiences no remorse of conscience, "She eats and wipes her mouth and says: I have done nothing evil."[19] More despicable however is an old man whose pleasure is lust.[20] The wisdom teachers admonish

1. Gen. 1:28; 9:1; Tob. 8:6-7.
2. Gen. 2:23-24.
3. Prov. 2:17; Mal. 2:14.
4. Tob. 8:7.
5. Sir. 26:24.
6. Os. 1:2; Is. 50:1; 54:5; 62:5; Jer. 2:2; the theme of Cant.; § 16:4.
7. Ex. 20:14.
8. Gen. 20:6; Prov. 2:17.
9. Ex. 20:17.
10. Gen. 39:9.
11. Gen. 38:24; Lev. 18:20; 20:10; Deut. 22:22-27; Dan. 13:22; Jn. 8:5.
12. Lev. 19:20-22.
13. Prov. 5:15-19; 31:30; Sir. 26:23; Tob. 3:11f.
14. Dan. 13:23.
15. Job 31:9, 11-12.
16. Prov. 2:16f; 5:3f; 6:25f; 7:10f; 9:18; 23:27.
17. Sir. 23:18-19.
18. Sir. 23:23.
19. Prov. 30:20.
20. Sir. 25:2.

husband and wife to enjoy the privileges of marriage instead of wandering into forbidden ways; they should fulfill their marital duty lest one or the other be tempted to infidelity.[21] The prescriptions of the cleanliness code aided self mastery in matters of sex.[22]

If a husband accused his wife of adultery she could vindicate herself by a self-imposed curse.[23] This law too reflects the holiness of marriage and God's concern over it. The wisdom writers exhort husbands to guard against the spirit of jealousy, otherwise their wives would likewise become jealous or grow cold toward them.[24]

The religious character of marriage is manifested by such laws as forbid union between those related by consanguinity or affinity.[25] These laws tend to preserve the natural love between relatives and to eliminate lustful affections. An exception was made only when a married man died without leaving a son. Then his brother (in case there was none, the next of kin to the deceased) was bidden to marry the widow (levirate marriage, from Latin *levir*, brother-in-law). The first son of this union was regarded as the child of the deceased.[26] The purpose of the law was to prevent the family from dying out, while at the same time the livelihood of the widow was made secure. This institution accordingly had an ethical foundation. The relative who married the widow did not profit financially. In the oldest times levirate marriage was a duty, but the Law already took into consideration instances in which the relatives of the deceased refused to marry the widow. The practice was still in vogue at the time of Christ.[27]

Canaanite, Moabite and Ammonite women were not to be taken in marriage[28] because there was imminent danger that the wife would lead the husband into idolatry.[29] Religion was to be placed above personal wishes and interests. When foreign women interiorly embraced Yahwism, as did Rahab and Ruth, the bann no longer held. The sacred historian expressly blamed Solomon's marriages with pagan women as the reason why he sacrificed to strange gods in his old age.[30] Esdras and Nehemias took strong positions against mixed marriages,[31] and Malachias regarded marriage with a pagan woman as a breach of the covenant.[32] The Law made an exception when the woman was a prisoner of war; still the man had first to examine himself whether he was marrying solely to appease his passion.[33] Likewise marriages with foreign slaves were permitted because such cases presented no danger to the faith.[34] David's retention of Bethsabee, whose husband he caused to be slain, is not censured by the narrator, neither did Nathan demand a dissolution of the union.[35] According to Canon Law a person guilty of adultery and the murder of his consort's partner is under a diriment impediment relative to the proposed marriage.

The purpose of marriage is to insure racial continuity, and hence any in-

21. Prov. 5:15-19.
22. § 30:4.
23. Num. 5:11-28.
24. Sir. 9:1.
25. Lev. 18:6-18;   20:11-21;
    Deut. 27:20-23.
26. Deut. 25:5-10; Gen. 38:8;

Ruth 4:10.
27. Matth. 22:23-28
28. Ex. 34:11-16; Deut. 7:3;
    23:4.
29. Ex. 34:16; Deut. 7:4; cf.
    Gen. 24:3; 27:46; 28:1.
30. 3 Kgs. 11:1-8.

31. Esdr. 9:1; 10:3-44; Neh
    13:23-28.
32. Mal. 2:11.
33. Deut. 21:10-14.
34. Ex. 21:4.
35. 2 Sam. 11:12.

tentional prevention of conception is a most grievous crime, worthy of death. From the very beginning parents rejoiced at the birth of a child and were grateful to God.[36] Childlessness was equivalent to misfortune[37] and regarded as a punishment from God.[38] The sapiential writers however decry boasting over a big family when the children lack every semblance of virtue, "Better is one (son) who fears God than a thousand, and to die childless than to have godless offspring."[39] The Book of Wisdom praises "the sterile who is unstained, who has had no sinful relations" and sees a blessing in "childlessness with virtue." The woman who preserves marital fidelity, and the man who though childless leads a pure life are already honored upon earth and their example will be imitated; in the next world they will be amply rewarded, while godless adulterers derive no happiness from their children in this life and in the next will be severely punished.[40]

b) *Monogamy and polygamy.* Among the ancient Israelites pious persons practiced polygamy, e.g., Jacob,[41] Elcana the father of Samuel,[42] David,[43] and the Law admitted polygamy as a fact.[44] But the feeling was always current that such a practice was not from the beginning; it was not willed by God as was monogamy. In paradise God had instituted marriage monogamous.[45] Lamech's bigamy appears as a departure from the primitive ordinance, an act of a vulgar and godless person.[46] As the depravity of mankind became universal before the flood, polygamy became the norm.[47] Noe and his sons lived monogamously.[48] Abraham had intercourse with Agar only because Sara was sterile, and Yahweh had promised him posterity; it was his belief that God intended to fulfill His promise in this manner.[49] Isaac appears to have had but one wife.[50] Osee, Isaias, and Ezechiel lived monogamously. The prophet's love of presenting Yahweh's relationship to Israel in terms of marriage also pointed to monogamy as God-willed, for with Israel only and not with any other nation did Yahweh make a covenant. The prescription directing the king to limit his harem[51] was at least an effort to curtail excess. The regulation enjoining the high priest to "take to wife a virgin from his own people"[52] had a monogamous slant. In the course of time monogamy became the accepted practice and the proverb composers regard it as the normal form of marriage.[53] This development was of tremendous importance in raising the position of woman. The marriages of Tobias and Judith were monogamous. It was Jesus however who first decreed monogamy as the only licit form of marriage and placed polygamy in the same category as adultery.[54]

c) *Divorce.* Deut. 24:1-4 allowed a man to dismiss his wife "on account of an odious thing;" hence guilt was required on the woman's part, and in

36. Gen. 4:1, 25; 29:32-33, 35; 30:18, 20; Pss. 113:9; 127:3-6; Prov. 17:6.
37. Gen. 15:2; 30:1; 1 Sam. 1:5f; Is. 4:1.
38. Os. 9:12; Jer. 18:21.
39. Sir. 16:1-3.
40. Wis. 3:15-19; 4:1-6.
41. Gen. 29:30.
42. 1 Sam. 1:2.
43. 1 Sam. 19:27; 25:39-43; 2 Sam. 3:2-5; 5:13; 11:27.
44. Lev. 18:18; Deut. 21:15.
45. Gen. 1:27; 2:24.
46. Gen. 4:19.
47. Gen. 6:2.
48. Gen. 6:18; 7:7, 13; 8:16, 18.
49. Gen. 15:5, 13; 16:1-2.
50. Ex. 2:21.
51. Deut. 17:17.
52. Lev. 21:13-14.
53. Prov. 5:15-20; 12:4; 18:22; 19:14; 31:10-31; Qoh. 9:9; Sir. 7:19; 9:1; 25:1, 8; 26:1-27; cf. Ps. 128:3; Job 31:10; Mal. 2:14-15.
54. Matth. 19:4-9.

this way the Law protected her against her husband's whims. The husband alone had the right to dissolve the marriage,[55] not the wife. The ordinance forbidding a man to remarry his dismissed wife, if in the meantime she had married another,[56] was a warning not to dissolve marriage precipitously. Divorce was rendered difficult inasmuch as the woman retained the right to her bridal gift, and hence the man suffered financially if he dismissed his partner. The Law denied the right of divorce to one who falsely accused his bride of not being a virgin,[57] and to one who violated her before marriage.[58] Dismissal of a secondary wife was easier; she usually came from a poorer family and accordingly the husband would lose only the sum which he had given to her father.[59] A man who discontinued married life with a woman captured in war was not allowed to sell her or degrade her to slave status.[60]

In more ancient times divorces seem to have occurred seldom, but after the exile they became frequent and without weighty reasons, as is shown by Malachy's denunciation of those who rashly broke the marriage bond.[61] Jesus Sirach frowned upon divorce[62] but counselled separation from a wife who was so unruly as to make marital life unbearable.[63] At the time of Christ the schools of Shammai and Hillel disputed whether the "odious thing" in Deut. 24:1 referred to shameful conduct or to some defect, e.g., a physical deformity, failure to care for the family, etc. How opposed to the prevailing Jewish notions on marriage Jesus' stand outlawing divorce and limiting dismissal to cases of adultery was,[64] we easily see from the reaction of the disciples; they considered it better to remain single under such circumstances than to marry.[65]

2. SAFEGUARDING CHASTITY. a) *Sin and the occasion of sin.* As the Paradise Account teaches, lust is the consequence of original sin. After our first parents had violated God's command, they made aprons for themselves to cover their nakedness.[66] In this action is contained an admonition to repress unchaste glances and to afford others no opportunity to be scandalized. Bethsabee's wanton conduct as she bathed in a place easily seen by David, and David's lustful glances quickly led to adultery and murder.[67] Quite otherwise Susanna, who locked herself in when she wished to bathe.[68] Even accidental and unintentional nudity was regarded as shameful, and immodest conduct grievously sinful.[69] The prohibition to ascend an altar on steps, "so that your nakedness may not be disclosed on it,"[70] was designed to insure proper decorum at divine services by eliminating accidental exposure, which could lead those present into temptation or make the ceremonies repulsive. Modesty was highly esteemed in Israel. Job's conscience accused him of no sins of unchaste desires and glances.[71] Jesus Sirach exhorted youths to keep themselves pure[72] and to avoid looking at immodest objects,[73] because looks lead to lust and lust to actions. Do not be dazzled by a woman's beauty; avoid personal confidences

55. Jer. 3:1; Sir. 25:26; 42:9.
56. Deut. 24:1-4; cf. Jer. 3:1.
57. Deut. 22:13-19.
58. Deut. 22:28-29.
59. Ex. 21:11.
60. Deut. 21:10-14.
61. Mal. 2:13-16.

62. Sir. 7:26.
63. Sir. 25:26.
64. Matth. 5:31-32; 19:3-9.
65. Matth. 19:10.
66. Gen. 3:7.
67. 2 Sam. 11.

68. Dan. 13:15f.
69. Gen. 9:22.
70. Ex. 20:26.
71. Job 31:1.
72. Sir. 26:19.
73. Sir. 9:5.

with another's spouse.[74] A female slave too had rights which her master should respect.[75] Many a danger to the chastity of a young man was removed by the limitations on harlotry[76] and by the bann on religious prostitution.[77] Despite the horrors of war, captive women were not forced to go naked before Israelitic conquerors, as they were obliged to do before the Assyrians and Babylonians.[78]

b) *Virginity*. Every maiden in Israel looked forward to marriage and the joys of motherhood. The OT lists no example of virginity freely embraced out of love toward God, though it is true that Judith[79] and Anna renounced a second marriage in order to serve God more perfectly.[80] All things considered, virginity was highly esteemed in OT times. The high priest was permitted to marry none but a virgin.[81] Feast day processions held to honor Yahweh included "virgins striking tambourines."[82] Jerusalem was the "Virgin daughter of Sion;"[83] and the Canticle, as it hymns Yahweh's love toward Israel and Israel's love toward Yahweh under the form of nuptial love, praises the purity of the future bride.

The Law sought to safeguard the virginity of young women. Whoever seduced an unbetrothed virgin was obliged to pay the dowry and take her as wife[84]—a girl no longer a virgin did not easily find a husband. The dowry was insisted upon to afford the woman some financial security in case her husband died or abandoned her. For violating a maiden the offender had to compensate her father with a dowry of 50 shekels, was obliged to marry her and lost the right of divorce.[85] Inability to pay did not free the oppressor from punishment; in such case he could be treated like the thief unable to meet an imposed fine;[86] i.e., he could be sold as a slave for six years.

The great importance attached to virginity in a bride is shown by the remark "(Rebecca) was a virgin with whom no man had yet had relations,"[87] and by Lot's reference to the virginity of his daughters.[88] A priest was forbidden to marry a harlot, a divorced woman or one who had been violated.[89] Thamar was despondent when her brother Amnon had violated her.[90] Sirach describes the anxiety parents have lest a daughter lose her integrity.[91] If without good evidence a husband accused his wife of not being a virgin at the time of marriage, he was fined and scourged, and he lost the right of divorce.[92]

c) *Sexual immorality*. Like onanism self-pollution was regarded as a sin which brought down God's wrath.[93] It was a despicable act for a woman to sell herself for money.[94] No priest was allowed to marry a harlot, "for he is holy to his God."[95] The daughter of a priest who became a harlot was to be burnt alive.[96] The wisdom writers repeatedly inveighed against immorality, they tried to appeal to reason by pointing out how a wayward woman inconsiderately squandered the family income[97] and endangered her consort's life.

74. Sir. 9:3, 8-9.
75. Sir. 41:22.
76. Lev. 19:29.
77. Deut. 23:18.
78. Is. 3:17; 47:2; Jer. 13: 22, 26; Nah. 3:5; cf. § 32:1e.
79. Jud. 8:4; 16:23.
80. Lk. 2:36-37.

81. Lev. 21:13-14.
82. Ps. 68:26.
83. Is. 37:22; cf. 23:12; 47:1.
84. Ex. 22:15-16.
85. Deut. 22:28-29.
86. Ex. 22:2.
87. Gen. 24:16.
88. Gen. 19:8.
89. Lev. 21:7.

90. 2 Sam. 13:11-19.
91. Sir. 42:9-14; cf. 7:24.
92. Deut. 22:13-19.
93. Sir. 23:16.
94. Lev. 19:29.
95. Lev. 21:7.
96. Lev. 21:9.
97. Prov. 6:26; 23:27; 29:3; Sir. 9:6; 23:17.

The sinfulness of lust may be seen in the tendency to regard idolatry as adultery[98]—faithless Jerusalem was called the "Harlot."[99]

Particularly reprehensible was religious prostitution, whether practiced by men or women.[100] This perversion was widespread in the Orient[101] and was resorted to by the Israelites when they fell away from Yahweh and served Baal and Astarte.[102] Under Manasses and Amon even the sanctuary at Jerusalem was desecrated by such immoral practices.[103]

The Law condemned sodomy as an abominable practice[104] and forbade a man to wear female clothing or a woman male clothing,[105] as happened in pagan liturgies, the scene of the most degrading practices. The fate of Sodom and Gomorrha[106] stood as a continual warning to the Israelites.[107] (The crime at Gibeah[108] consisted in the brutal violation of a woman by the town's inhabitants; their effort toward having immoral relations with her consort is an interpolation from Gen. 19.) Bestiality was punished with death.[109]

Adultery, incest, onanism, sodomy and bestiality are forbidden by the natural law, since by such acts the sanctity of marriage, the foundation of human society, is destroyed. These sins accordingly were proscribed already before Moses.

3. PARENTS AND CHILDREN. a) *Rights and duties of parents.* Since marriage is a divine bond and children a divine gift, the family is a spiritual unit. On the feast of the Pasch the family as such offered the sacrifice, and the father of the house, who (in more ancient times) killed the lamb and sprinkled the blood, functioned as priest.[110] In common the family made the pilgrimage to the temple.[111] The mother was not excluded from the liturgy; she partook in the sacrifice banquet, offered sacrifice,[112] prayed—as did Rebecca[113] and Anna,[114] Susanna and Judith—was allowed to make vows with her husband's approval.[115] Deut. 31:12, Jos. 8:35 and Neh. 8:2 expressly included women under the Law.

Over children who were still living at home the father possessed unrestricted authority, save in the matter of life and death. It is of special note that never is there mention of parents killing a newborn child; not even the Law refers to this crime. A poor man could sell his children into slavery (for six years)[116] or pledge them to a fellow Israelite.[117] If he was not able to give his daughter a dowry, he could "sell" her to a respectable person with the stipulation that she become his maid-servant.[118] The vow of a girl (and of a minor son) was valid only if the father explicitly or implicitly approved it.[119] In the selection of a bride the father usually had a part;[120] for a son to marry without his father's approval was looked upon as improper.[121] The mother's influence was

98. Ex. 34:15-16; Lev. 17:7; 20:5; Deut. 31:16; Judg. 2:17; Ez. 16; 23.
99. Is. 1:21.
100. Deut. 23:18-19.
101. § 11:5.
102. 3 Kgs. 14:24; 15:12; 22:47; Am. 2:7; Os. 4:14; cf. Gen. 38:21.
103. 4 Kgs. 23:7.

104. Lev. 18:22; 20:13.
105. Deut. 22:5.
106. Gen. 19.
107. Is. 1:9.
108. Judg. 19:22f.
109. Ex. 22:18; Lev. 18:23; 20:15-16; Deut. 27:21.
110. § 34:4a.
111. 1 Sam. 1.
112. Lev. 12:15.

113. Gen. 25:22.
114. 1 Sam. 1:9f.
115. § 36:2.
116. Ex. 21:2-6.
117. Neh. 5:5.
118. Ex. 21:7.
119. Num. 30:4-6; § 36:2.
120. Gen. 24:2f; 28:1f; 38:6; Judg. 14:3; Ex. 21:9.
121. Gen. 26:34-35.

felt in the choice of a daughter-in-law.[122] When a daughter wished to marry, she needed the consent of her father who usually selected her bridegroom.[123] Ordinarily parents accorded great consideration to the wishes and inclinations of their children; the Hebrew maiden did not live in utter isolation.

Parents were reminded of their duties toward their children. They were obliged to nourish them and to train them to live God-fearing lives, a task belonging to father and mother.[124] They were obligated to instruct them in the commandments of God, particularly in the commandment to love Yahweh with their whole heart.[125] Religious training was to begin in early infancy, and the children were to be accustomed to a moral way of life.[126] Strict parents were a special blessing.[127] Parents who train their children well will be gladdened by them, will be praised by acquaintances, and even when dead their instruction will continue to produce good results; but parents who are remiss will suffer much grief.[128] A terrifying example was the conduct of Heli, who did not correct his sons when he was fully aware of their wicked deeds.[129]

b) *Duties of children.* Children were commanded, "Honor your father and your mother."[130] This natural duty God imposed as a religious obligation. Though the father had the greater power in the family, yet the mother had a like claim to honor and obedience from the children, and the proverb poets insist that she be honored even as the father.[131] Rising up against one's parents was a crime deserving death.[132] The child who by a dissolute life brought grief to his parents and disgrace upon the family sinned grievously.[133]

Children are to be grateful toward parents, for without them they would have no existence.[134] What hardships every mother suffers as she carries a child in her womb![135] God Himself is the source of parental rights,[136] and therefore children are in duty bound to obey their instructions.[137] When parents become old and feeble the children must provide for them in a kindly way;[138] they sin grievously if they refuse them the needs of livelihood.[139] God rewards piety toward parents, "Who honors his father, expiates sins, and he who respects his mother is like one who hoards up treasures."[140] He will be gladdened by his own children; God will hear his prayer,[141] and he will experience the truth of the words, "A father's blessing will establish (his) children's homes."[142] On the other hand, "He who mistreats his father and drives out his mother is a worthless and shameless son"[143] who will not prosper.[144] "A mother's curse destroys the houses of her children to their very foundations."[145] "The eye which mocks a father or dishonors a *grayhaired* mother the ravens at the brook will peck out, the young eagles will devour,"[146] i.e., he will be denied burial, his corpse will become spoil for birds of prey.

122. Gen. 21:21; 27:46-47.
123. Gen. 29:18-30; Jos. 15:16-17; Judg. 1:12-13; 1 Sam. 18:27; 25:44; cf. Ex. 22: 15-16; 2:21.
124. Prov. 1:8; 6:20; 31:1f.
125. Ex. 12:26; 13:8, 14-15; Deut. 4:10; 6:7, 20; 11: 19; Ps. 78:5-8.
126. Prov. 22:6; 23:13-14.
127. Prov. 13:24; Sir. 30:2.

128. Sir. 30:1-13.
129. 1 Sam. 3:13.
130. Ex. 20:12; Lev. 19:3.
131. Prov. 1:8; 6:20; 23:22; Sir. 3:3-16; 7:27-28; cf. Tob. 4:3.
132. Ex. 21:15, 17; Lev. 20:9; Deut. 27:16.
133. Deut. 21:18-21.
134. Sir. 7:27-28.
135. Tob. 4:4.

136. Sir. 3:2.
137. Prov. 1:8; 6:20.
138. Prov. 23:22; Sir. 3:12-15.
139. Prov. 28:24; Sir. 3:16.
140. Sir. 3:3-4.
141. Sir. 3:5.
142. Sir. 3:9.
143. Prov. 19:26.
144. Prov. 20:20.
145. Sir. 3:9.
146. Prov. 30:17.

Disregarding this teaching the Scribes and Pharisees declared it permissible to designate as a temple offering what parents could justly demand—even though such dedication would deprive them of support.[147]

4. SLAVES. In Israel slaves were adjudged part of the family. For an Israelite servitude could last only six years,[148] and upon obtaining freedom he was to be provisioned liberally by his master for immediate needs.[149] Being sold or selling oneself into slavery (for debts) entailed in practice nothing more than a labor contract for six years, with the stipulations, of course, that during the period he was subject to the will of the employer, had to accept reproofs, and had no right to terminate his services and choose another employer. If the jubilee year occurred during the six year period, he regained liberty with its inception and recovered the property he or his fathers had alienated in time of need.[150] Slaves of non-Israelitic origin were received into the community of God's people by circumcision.[151] All slaves benefitted by the Sabbath day rest,[152] partook in the Paschal celebration and ate of the sacrifice banquet,[153] while the slaves of priests enjoyed the right to eat of the sacred offerings,[154] a privilege denied to lay persons.

Ex. 21:5-6 and Deut. 15:17 cover the case in which an Israelite male or female slave freely desired to remain with his or her master after the expiration of six years—an indication of kindly treatment. And custom conferred upon the slave more privileges than the Law. Abraham entrusted his slave with the task of courting a wife for Isaac.[155] A slave gave Saul good counsel when they were seeking the lost asses, and had money at his disposal.[156] Nabal's slave informed his mistress Abigail how unbecomingly her husband had treated David.[157] A slave could take to wife the daughter of his master,[158] inherit the property of a childless master[159] and, even when sons were present, be numbered with the heirs.[160] The counsel of a wise servant was often willingly heard.[161] The proverb writers warn against treating slaves too indulgently lest they become domineering,[162] while they also advise to act friendly toward a trustworthy servant.[163] A good wife provides sufficient help to do the family work.[164] This good treatment of slaves in Israel resulted from the common religion which brought master and slave together in close union. In addition, for born Israelites, there were the ties of common blood and common deliverance from Egyptian bondage.[165] Moreover there was a consciousness that master and slave possessed the same human dignity. These truths inspired Sirach to write, "If you have a slave, treat him as yourself *and do not be furious against your own blood.*"[166] And though he gives a very practical reason, viz., to keep the slave from running away if mishandled, the fundamental principle is not invalidated. Job said in his last apology, "I have not cast aside the rights

147. Matth. 15:5; Mk. 7:11.
148. Ex. 21:2-3.
149. Deut. 15:12-18.
150. Lev. 25:40-41.
151. Gen. 17:12; Ex. 12:44.
152. Ex. 20:10.
153. Ex. 12:44; Deut. 12:12, 18; 16:11, 14.
154. Lev. 22:11.
155. Gen. 24:2f.
156. 1 Sam. 9.
157. 2 Sam. 25:14f.
158. 1 Chr. 2:35.
159. Gen. 15:2.
160. Prov. 17:2.
161. Sir. 10:25.
162. Prov. 29:19, 21; Sir. 33: 33-38; 42:5.
163. Sir. 7:20-21.
164. Prov. 31:15, 21.
165. Lev. 25:39-46.
166. Sir. 33:30.

of my slaves, male or female, *because I had the power*. What could I do if God would arise? and if he would inquire about it, what could I answer him? Did not my creator fashion him also in the womb? did not he form each one of us in (our) mother's belly?"[167] Actual cases of course did not always reflect the demands of the Law or the ideals of the wisdom teachers; it did happen that Israelites were retained as slaves beyond the legal six year limit and lawful authority would not interfere.[168]

§ 32. CRITIQUE OF OT MORALITY

1. OT Ethics in the Light of the NT. a) *Sins and weaknesses of eminent personages*. Since the OT is only an anteroom to the NT, the same demands cannot be made upon OT saints as upon those for whom the teaching of Christ serves as the rule of conduct. But some of their actions cannot be approved even from the standpoint of OT ethics. We find this to be the case with the patriarchs,[1] with Moses who killed an Egyptian taskmaster,[2] with David who sinned by adultery and murder.[3] Other actions are, to say the least, unworthy of imitation. In Egypt Joseph capitalized on the famine: by selling the grain taken from the Egyptians as tax, he first obtained their money for Pharaoh, then their cattle and lastly title to their fields, and thereby reduced the people to serfdom.[4] By a trick Jacob succeeded in acquiring a large part of Laban's herds, though it should be noted that the latter had taken unfair advantage of Jacob and had tried to cheat him of his wages.[5] The OT historians recount the facts, but usually in the presentation they make quite clear their disapproval of all unethical implications; and they keep on showing how God always punishes sin. Even the apostles, who were reared in the school of Jesus till the descent of the Holy Ghost, were not paragons of virtue in every respect, and saints commit sins for which they are sorry and do penance.

b) *Mosaic Law verses Semitic customs*. When Yahweh ratified the covenant with the Chosen People, many of their habits were so deeply ingrained as to make changes very difficult. These habits, together with the customs current in the neighboring nations, had to be taken into consideration by Moses.[6] Only gradually did the Israelites accept the precepts of Yahwistic religion and develop a moral sense. In this way may be explained some of the cruelties and improprieties, as well as practices such as polygamy, *herem*, recourse to lies and deception toward enemies, which are recorded in the OT. Neither did Christianity transform pagan morality in a day—centuries passed before Rome was educated to a Christian way of life. The preaching of the prophets and the teaching of the sages contributed immensely to the final triumph of Mosaic morality by deepening the religious insight of the people and by arousing their spirit to overcome inveterate evil habits.

167. Job 31:13-15.   168. Jer. 34:9-22.
  1. § 9:4a.   3. 2 Sam. 11.   5. Gen. 31:7.
  2. Ex. 2:11f.   4. Gen. 41:56; 47:13f.   6. § 2:2b; 23:1d; 30:6.

c) *The OT marriage* ideal does not stand on a par with that of the NT, since polygamy and divorce were permitted.[7]

d) *Slavery* goes contrary to the individual's right of personal freedom.[8] In Israel a slave's lot was not an unmitigated misfortune; a poor man would even willingly sell himself into slavery, and some slaves refused the freedom to which they were entitled after six years.[9] A thief who could not pay his fine was sold[10] and thus forced labor took the place of imprisonment.

e) *By ḥerem* persons and things were proscribed because they were odious to Yahweh. In its strictest form men, women and children were put to death, and cattle too; inanimate objects were burned.[11] *Ḥerem* of this nature was pronounced against the Amalekites.[12] On occasion God "enjoined" *ḥerem* and punished violators;[13] if individuals disobeyed, the whole nation sometimes suffered, e.g., Jos. 7:11f. This severe measure was part of the divine economy of salvation: a) it was meant to safeguard the Israelites from fusion with the Canaanites and from apostasy;[14] b) it was a manifestation of divine justice: by their sins the Canaanites had deserved annihilation[15] (the Amalekites were robbers,[16] the Midianites led Israel into idolatry and immorality).[17] The Hebrews were God's agents as they proceeded against sinful nations. *Ḥerem* was not an ethically perfect norm, or one worthy of imitation; nor may it be judged from the viewpoint of present day military law—still less in the light of the Sermon on the Mount. It falls into proper perspective against the background of the rules of war then in vogue, rules which deprived the conquered of the right to life, even women and children; the vanquished considered it a favor to be made slaves. Yahweh gave these traditional "rights" a nobler purpose. Israel should feel she was fulfilling God's holy will; to Him she was responsible. This tended to soften the desire for personal revenge or enrichment, and moreover taught the people the lesson of divine retribution. Israel herself was not exempt; *ḥerem* would be visited upon her too if she strayed from Yahweh or abandoned herself to immoral ways.[18]

Ḥerem was one of the imperfections of the OT. But already in the earliest periods it was not carried out in all its severity. Women and children, or at least young girls, were not put to death.[19] David ordered two-thirds of the captured Moabites slain (2 Sam. 8:2), but after this *ḥerem* was no longer resorted to; its purpose, the supremacy of the Chosen People over the Canaanites, ceased to be endangered. By the time the mighty northern nations arose and Israel became dependent, the practice of *ḥerem* was a thing of the past. We meet it but once again, in the Maccabean struggles, when from a spirit of vengeance *ḥerem* was inflicted in all its severity (1 Mach. 5:5).

Otherwise Israel's conduct in war was gentle compared with the war ethics of neighboring nations. The kings of Israel were known to be merciful. Muti-

7. § 31:1.
8. § 29:1c.
9. § 31:4.
10. Ex. 22:2.
11. Deut. 13:16-18; 1 Mach. 5:5.

12. Ex. 17:14; Deut. 25:19; 1 Sam. 15:3.
13. Deut. 7:2; 20:16f; Jos. 7:25-26; 1 Sam. 15:28; 28:28.
14. Deut. 7:2-5; 20:18.
15. Gen. 15:16; Lev. 18:25-26.

16. Ex. 17:14; 1 Sam. 15:2.
17. Num. 31:2; cf. 25:1-2.
18. Deut. 13:13-19; Judg. 20:12f; 21:8f.
19. Deut. 20:14; Num. 31:18; Judg. 21:11f.

lation and torture of enemies seldom occurred.[20] The violation of women and girls was forbidden,[21] a law which was easy to keep because they refrained from marital relations while in military service.[22] Captive women's sense of shame was respected.[23] Fruit bearing trees were not to be cut down during a siege, so as not to inflict lasting damage upon the enemy.[24] If a city opened its gates when terms of peace were offered, the Israelites were to rest satisfied with the payment of tribute.[25] In this point their conduct in war could well have served as a model for their age—and for ours.

f) *Hatred of foreign nations.* Alongside of admonitions to love and assist foreigners living in their midst,[26] there are passages which reflect a hostile spirit toward outside nations. The Law forbade assimilating Ammonites and Moabites into the Israelitic community and contained these strong words, "As long as you live you shall never be concerned about their peace or their well-being."[27] The memory of the Amalekites was destined to extinction.[28] The prophets gave comminatory speeches against foreign nations and prophesied their dissolution.[29] The judgment upon Edom was pictured as a great feast at which so many steers, lambs and goats would be slaughtered for the sacrifice that the land would become saturated with blood and dunged with fat.[30] How hostile these nations were against each other is described in drastic words, "I shall cause your tormentors to eat their own flesh, and with their own blood they shall intoxicate themselves as with new wine."[31] The author of the Lamentations hopes, "You shall requite them and blind their hearts, you shall pursue them in wrath and destroy them."[32] The psalmists petition Yahweh to hold judgment upon the enemies of Israel.[33] With rejoicing the just will "take vengeance upon the heathen, punish nations, bind their kings with chains and their princes with iron bonds."[34] Then there are the cursing or imprecatory psalms. Sirach has immortalized his abhorrence of the Edomites, Philistines and Samaritans in a famous verse.[35] Wis. 11:5-20 and 16:1-19 describes how God punished the Egyptians in a just manner. In the Book of Esther Christian sensibilities are gravely wounded at the joy which the Jews showed when they were enabled to revenge themselves upon their enemies, and at the conduct of Mardochai and Esther, who used royal power to inaugurate a pogrom against their enemies.[36] Here the OT is definitely inferior to the NT. This cannot be denied. Still some reasons may be adduced to make this feeling among the Jews, even pious Jews, appear more intelligible.

When Israel first entered into Canaan, she had to struggle at great odds in deadly conflicts against the inhabitants of the land, and later against the Philistines and other neighbors. In the next centuries she was oppressed by Arameans, Assyrians, Babylonians. During the exile she was beset by an

20. 4 Kgs. 15:16 (whether 2 Sam. 12:31 recounts the torture and death of war captives in very questionable); 3 Kgs. 20:31.
21. Deut. 21:10-14.
22. 1 Sam. 21:5-6; 2 Sam. 11:11; cf. Deut. 23:10-12.
23. § 31:2a.
24. Deut. 20:19.
25. Deut. 20:10-11.
26. § 29:6.
27. Deut. 23:4-7.
28. Deut. 25:19; cf. Ex. 17:16.
29. § 45:2.
30. Is. 34:6-7; cf. Ez. 39:17-20.
31. Is. 49:26.
32. Lam. 3:64-66.
33. Pss. 68:22-24; 83:10-19; 129:5-8.
34. Ps. 149:7-8.
35. Sir. 50:25.
36. Esth. 8:9.

overpowering homesickness for home and temple,[37] and, when allowed to return, the Edomites and Philistines had appropriated a portion of her territory. The prophets repeatedly proclaimed that Israel deserved judgment and that foreign nations were merely instruments in God's hands, as they rushed in upon the land and finally carried Israel away captive.[38] Israel learnt slowly to recognize a divine punishment in misfortunes. The people were inflamed particularly against Babylon and Edom, because they capitalized upon the visitation which had come to Israel;[39] and because the Edomites were regarded as relatives,[40] they became still more furious.[41]

Furthermore, the Israelites judged that since they were Yahweh's Chosen People, an offense against them was an assault against God Himself. They prayed, "Do I not hate those who hate you, and are not your adversaries nausea to me?"[42] Every insult and humiliation was regarded as an attack upon God's honor, "I have heard the reviling of Moab and the blasphemy of the Ammonites because they reviled my people and dealt wantonly against *my* domain."[43] In the Egyptians Jeremias beheld Yahweh's enemies, and their defeat by the Chaldeans for him was "a day of revenge, to avenge oneself upon his enemies."[44] Israel's foes were Yahweh's foes,[45] against Him they leagued,[46] Him they derided, His name they blasphemed.[47] When they attacked Israel they overran Yahweh's meadows,[48] descended upon Yahweh's property, desecrated Yahweh's holy temple.[49] The heathens had sinned against God, and justice demanded that they be punished in accordance with OT standards, i.e., the *ius talionis*.[50] They themselves must experience the horrors they perpetrated in war, and therefore the Jews rejoiced in the thought of some day being able to sell the sons and daughters of their enemies;[51] and the psalmist blessed him who would seize and dash the Babylonian children against the rock[52]—an action proclaimed against Babylon by the prophets.[53] That they oppressed Israel was not the only or even the most important reason why the nations were to be punished.[54] Remember too how in a similar way the prophets threatened *Israel* with utter destruction,[55] a proof they judged from a religious and not from a political viewpoint. Whenever the prophets or psalmists spoke about judgment upon the Gentile nations, they did not forget how this would lead to their conversion and how a great kingdom of peace would arise upon the earth.[56]

g) *Hatred.* In the OT we frequently cross passages in which someone asks God to put to shame and humble an enemy or even to destroy him.[57] The just man will beg that coals and fire might fall upon his adversary, or that his enemy tumble into the pit[58] and go down alive to Sheol.[59] He rejoices as he pictures his enemy nearing his end and would love to "bathe his feet in the blood

37. Cf. Ps. 137.
38. § 46:4.
39. Abd. 14; Jer. 49:7f; Ez. 25:12.
40. Deut. 2:4, 8; 23:8; Am. 1:11; Abd. 10.
41. Ps. 137:7.
42. Ps. 139:21.
43. Soph. 2:8; Zach. 1:15.
44. Jer. 46:10.
45. Ps. 74:23.

46. Ps. 83:6.
47. Pss. 74:18; 79:12; 139:21.
48. Ps. 83:13.
49. Ps. 79:1; cf. Lam. 3:59; 1 Mach. 4:30-33; 2 Mach. 14:35-36; 15:22-24.
50. Cf. Judg. 1:6-7.
51. Joel 4:8.
52. Ps. 137:7-9.
53. Is. 13:16; 14:22; cf. 4 Kgs. 8:12; Os. 14:1; Nah. 3:10.

54. § 45:4.
55. § 46.
56. §45:6.
57. Pss. 5:11; 6:11; 7:10, 16; 10:12; 28:4; 31:19; 35:4-6; 40:15 (70:3); 54:7; 139:19; 141:10; 143:12.
58. Ps. 140:9-11.
59. Ps. 55:16, 24.

of the wicked."[60] Ps. 109:6-19 seems to express a prayer for speedy death to one's opponent, a wish that his children become orphans and be forced to beg, that his property be seized and all should forsake him, that he have no descendants and his name be blotted out by the next generation. Granted that these words expressed God's sentence of punishment (but compare v. 15 and v. 20), they nevertheless manifest a spirit of deep hatred; and if v. 6-13 constituted the enemy's curse upon the psalmist, the latter returned the curse in v. 17. The just man would even request to execute revenge with his own hands, "Yahweh, be merciful to me and lift me up again that I might repay them."[61] Elias caused lightning to strike the captain and the soldiers who came to arrest him because they approached in a haughty, arrogant manner. Eliseus cursed the boys of Bethel who mocked him, whereupon 42 of them were mangled by bears. The priest Zacharias was stoned because he admonished the people to amend; at the point of death he implored God to avenge the crime (2 Chr. 24:22). Nehemias petitioned divine chastisement upon the Samaritan governor Sanaballat, the Ammonite Tobias, and the false prophets who had placed numerous difficulties in his way (Neh. 4:1f; 6:14). Jeremias, a man of truly tender disposition, implored God to destroy his enemies and their accomplices,[62] and desired to witness their destruction.[63] Though Jesus' quotation, "Love your neighbor and hate your enemy" (Matth. 5:43), is not found in this form in the OT, it does echo a sentiment found on many of its pages.

Such effusions of hostility, wholly contrary to true Christian piety, we must first of all remember flow from the mouths of Orientals who do not easily control their feelings and who use hyperbole in a way unintelligible to Occidentals. Secondly, an injured person ordinarily does not distinguish too clearly between the person who injured him and the injury itself—this holds true in any age. And with this we come to the most important point, which for a criticism of such passages is decisive: every violent word reflects the consciousness of an intimate union with God and a living faith in His justice. The hatred of the pious, whose sentiments the OT hands down to us, is directed primarily against sin, and thereby is elevated above a merely personal or natural spirit of revenge. The pious man believed his enemies to be Yahweh's enemies,[64] who violated His law by committing crimes against God and man.[65] But wickedness must not triumph; of God's justice one should expect such action as to confound the sinner[66]—otherwise the sinner would be confirmed in malice, would believe God could or would not punish.[67] Punishment therefore should pave the way to conversion[68] and effect the acknowledgment of God's justice.[69] Because Yahweh had promised His blessing to the obedient, the just man could expect divine intervention against a sinner who persecuted him or hindered him from fulfilling the commandments.[70] Jeremias was aware that he suffered because he pleaded the cause of Yahweh; his enemies made it impossible for him to

60. Ps. 58:7-11; cf. Ps. 69:23-29.
61. Ps. 41:11.
62. Jer. 15:15; 17:18; 18:21.
63. Jer. 11:20.
64. Pss. 9:18; 55:20; 139:21.
65. Pss. 17:9; 40:15; 54:5; 55:24; 59:3; 5:10; 31:19; 35:11.
66. Ps. 41:12.
67. Pss. 10:4, 11; 35:25; 64: 6; 94:7.
68. Cf. § 39:3; 41:2.
69. Ps. 58:12.
70. Pss. 35:27; 40:17.

perform his duty in God's service and on this account God was obliged to espouse the cause of His servant.[71] The punishment, which was to follow in accordance with the *ius talionis*, was placed in the hands of God. The psalmist too who sought to requite his adversary[72] felt himself as God's instrument. There was a prototype for the cursing psalms in the curses which were pronounced upon transgressors of the divine law at the solemn ratification of the covenant at Shechem.[73] These imprecations were uttered at a holy place during a very impressive ceremony. Another parallel to the cursing psalms is David's malediction against Joab after the latter had murdered Abner (2 Sam. 3:27-39). Because the circumstances in which David found himself prevented him from bringing the murderer to justice, he delivered him over to divine judgment.

OT passages which wish evil upon others, whether it be just punishment or not, mirror the imperfection of the Old Law and the maxim, "Eye for eye, tooth for tooth."[74] These texts do not stand on a par with Christ's sublime teaching, "If someone strike you on the right cheek, turn to him the other also .... Love your enemies, do good to those who hate you, and pray for those who persecute and calumniate you."[75] They do not reflect Jesus' prayer on the cross, "Father, forgive them, for they do not know what they are doing,"[76] which found an echo in St. Stephen's petition, "Lord, do not lay this sin against them."[77] Remember however how our Savior pronounced *woe* upon those who showed themselves blind to every admonition.[78]

h) *Sanctions.* Since the idea of a blessed afterlife remained imperfect till long after the exile,[79] the religious leaders held out temporal rewards for observing God's commandments, and temporal punishments for transgressions; loftier sanctions however are not wanting, especially during the last centuries before Christ.[80] The Christian too may turn to God for the necessities of life, e.g., in the Our Father he petitions for daily bread, and Christ aided the cause of the hungry, the sick, and poor. The challenge, "Ask, and it shall be given you,"[81] must not be limited to spiritual needs. Yet there is an undeniable difference between the Old and New Law. If our Savior stresses reward and punishment, He leaves no doubt that this life will bring His disciples suffering and persecution and that only hereafter will matters be balanced.[82] He spoke but once of compensation in this life,[83] and then He promised rewards of a spiritual rather than a material character.

i) *Purificatory and food laws.* Purificatory laws, which determined cases of defilement and cleansings that effected only an external, physical purity, were not strictly differentiated from laws governing moral purity—as was common in antiquity. In the NT religion, embracing as it does the whole world, these injunctions are obsolete, but they did have a purpose for Israel and her needs.

71. Jer. 15:15; 18:23.
72. § 41:2; cf. Ps. 41:11.
73. Deut. 27:15-26; Jos. 8:30-35.
74. Ex. 21:23-25.
75. Matth. 5:39, 44.
76. Lk. 23:34.
77. Acts 7:59.
78. Matth. 11:21f; 23:13f.
79. § 42.
80. § 2:2b.
81. Matth. 7:7.
82. Matth. 15:4; 19:19; Mk. 7:10; 10:19; Lk. 18:20.
83. Lk. 18:29-30.

For the external practice was designed to lead to an inner religious spirit. The prophets, psalmists and wisdom teachers pointed out how these precepts possessed only an accidental importance in the face of basic moral laws. The Pharisees and Scribes equated their fulfillment with the essence of religious life and disregarded interior holiness in favor of preoccupation with external purifications.[84]

j) *Working for reward.* To seek reward is spontaneous to human nature. Unlike the Stoics or Kant, Jesus did not preach virtue merely for virtue's sake. He emphasized the reward which would be given those who lived according to God's holy will, "Be glad and rejoice for your reward is great in heaven."[85] The faithful and exact observance of the Law which characterized postexilic Jewry may not be condemned as "pure externalism." People did believe they were fulfilling God's will as revealed in the Law and were thereby making themselves worthy of His love. Never however does faithful performance of duty confer a right to demand reward from God. The Creator is far too exalted above the creature; the creature owes everything to Him and can only strike his breast confessing his unworthiness. He must not be like the Pharisees who boasted about their observance of the Law and regarded God as their debtor.[86] Evaluate OT religion apart from phariseeism and apart from the standards set up after the Maccabean revolution when the influence of the Scribes was on the increase.

2. ISRAEL'S NEIGHBORS. In order to arrive at a correct estimate of OT morality we must not merely compare OT teaching with that of the New, but also with the morals of those peoples with whom Israel had relations and by whose culture they were influenced. a) *Murder.* The laws of every nation protect human life, proscribe and avenge murder. Now while the Mosaic Law unconditionally imposed the death penalty for premeditated murder, Hittite law[89] imposed, practically speaking, only a fine. Ex. 22:2-3a acknowledged self-defense as licit only if the owner of the house was in danger, while the Code of Hammurabi[90] decreed that a thief be killed on the spot. Mosaic Law valued human life higher than other ancient Oriental codes. The Babylonian and Hittite codes made no mention of blood revenge, a fact explicable from the conditions of civilization, for when authority has assumed the responsibility of avenging murder, the citizen no longer has a right to do so. Because of the fluid state of society in Israel blood revenge could not be outlawed, but it was restricted through the right of asylum.[91]

b) *Chastity.* Theoretically marriage was monogamous in Babylon, polygamous in Israel. This too was in part due to the cultural backgrounds. But in Babylon the ideal remained theoretical, secondary wives were allowed, and also intercourse with slaves. Adultery was punished more severely in Israel than in Babylon or Assyria.[92] In Israel complicated impediments deepened esteem for marriage, in Egypt brother-sister marriages were permissible. Sacred prosti-

84. Matth. 15:2; 23:25; Lk. 11:38-39.
85. Matth. 5:12; 19:27-29.
86. Lk. 18:9f.
89. HL 1:1-5.
90. CH 21, 22, 25.
91. § 29:1a.
92. CH 129, 130; AL 12-16, 24.

tution was an abomination in Israel,[93] in Babylon it formed part of the temple service, it was officially protected and fostered;[94] harlotry likewise received due recognition and protection.[95] Neither did Assyrian law regard as criminal the services of hierodules and prostitutes.[96] In Israel a girl who let herself be seduced was looked upon with contempt, while otherwise in the Orient extramarital relations were not regarded as dishonorable; and for this reason Deut. 22:13-19, which protected the young wife from false accusations of intercourse before marriage, has no parallel. Women captured in war could not be violated according to the usual practice.[97] Sodomy, which had been accorded a place in Oriental cult, was a capital offense in Mosaic Law. Beastiality, not considered sinful in Egypt as it occurred in cult forms,[98] was punished by death in the Hittite and Mosaic codes.[99]

c) *An offense against parental authority* was more severely punished in Israelitic than in Babylonian law.[100]

d) *Violations of property rights* were more heavily punished in Babylon than in Israel. The Covenant Code recognized fourfold, at times fivefold or twofold compensation,[101] and if the thief could not pay, he was to labor six years as a slave (but was allowed to purchase freedom before the expiration of his term). Hammurabi's code imposed a thirtyfold or tenfold fine upon thievery, and if the fine could not be met, the thief was put to death.[102] Assyrian law threatened with mutilation the woman who pilfered an article from her husband and, under certain circumstances, with death;[103] the same sanctions held for concealing stolen property.

e) *Punishments.* While Deut. 25:1-3 set the maximum number of strokes for a flogging at forty and allowed mutilation in but a single instance,[104] Assyrian and Babylonian law listed many offenses punishable by cudgeling and mutilation,[104] e.g., cutting off the tongue, ear, breast (of wet-nurses), tearing out eyes, death by fire in Babylon, in Assyria cutting off the nose, ear, finger, lower lip, tearing out the eye, piercing the ear, castration (though actual practice may have been more humane). Mosaic Law never resorts to the rack to obtain evidence, and it contains no indication of allowing torture previous to inflicting the death penalty.

f) *Communal responsibility.* Oriental codes acknowledge the common responsibility of the members of a family for a crime committed by one of their number.[105] Nevertheless Deut. 24:16 expressly directs the judge to punish only the guilty person, not his relatives. Of course a debtor took his family along into servitude;[106] but when a man has become impoverished his children also suffer, and it was better that the family stay together and get bread from some master than to be separated. Blood revenge did not extend to the murderer's family as it did among many other nations. For children to suffer with

93. § 31:2c.
94. CH 153, 182, 187, 137, 144.
95. CH 108f.
96. AL 40.
97. § 31:2a; 32:1e.
98. E.g., Mendes' goat.
99. HL 2:73, 74, 85, 86; cf. § 31:2d.
100. CH 168, 169; SL 3, 4; SFL 1, 2; cf. § 31:3b.
101. Ex. 21:37-22:2.
102. CH 6, 8.
103. AL 1:3-5.
104. I.e., Deut. 25:11-12.
105. CH 116, 210, 230; AL 23, 49, 54; HL 1:19a; 2:58.
106. Ex. 21:2-6.

the guilty was exceptional in Israel. Amasias' refusal (797 B.C.) to execute the sons of his father's murderers along with the murderers themselves was looked upon as an act of exceptional leniency,[107] but this was a case of treason and conspiracy. Achab had Naboth's sons slain along with their father[108] because he wished to remove all heirs to the estate. David delivered seven of Saul's descendants to the Gibeonites to expiate Saul's blood-guiltiness and to ward off divine punishment.[109]

g) *Economics.* Hammurabi sought to safeguard free workers and craftsmen from profiteering capitalists by fixing wages,[110] by legislation against usury[111] and by granting deferments to debtors who fell under adverse circumstances.[112] Hittite law likewise sought to guarantee a minimum standard of living to workers and craftsmen.[113] These measures were enacted in the interest of the common good which suffers whenever large groups of civilians are in want. The Pentateuch provided for the poor out of religious motives.

h) *Slaves.* Hittite law punished slaves with mutilation and even with death for offenses which freemen could rectify by a money payment.[114] Aiding a runaway slave was severely punished, while rewards were offered for capturing one.[115] In Israel the slave belonged to the family and often remained with his master of his own free will. If a slave ran away he was protected by the Law.[116] In the Book of the Covenant the ordinances concerning slaves come at the beginning and confer rights upon male slaves and female slaves; in the Code of Hammurabi the laws concerning slaves come at the end and are treated from the aspect of the owner's rights.

i) *Love of enemies.* Unique and indicative of OT spirit are the admonitions to love enemies contained already in the Pentateuch; outbursts of hatred however are not wanting.[117]

j) *Sin.* Babylonian priests directed their efforts toward delivering the sick man not from his sins but from his sufferings.[118] According to the Book of the Dead nothing was more important for a person after death than to protest his innocence of all the sins enumerated—the whole procedure being in fact a mere formality. Quite otherwise among the Israelites; they believed that sin was not remitted unless a person was contrite and made amends.[119] And where in the ancient Orient did men like the prophets arise demanding social justice and the practice of loving-kindness from the mighty, protesting the oppression of the poor, condemning all profiteering upon the economically weak, men who would not shrink from upbraiding kings, Nathan David,[120] Ahias Solomon,[121] Elias Achab,[122] Amos Jeroboam,[123] Isaias Achaz,[124] Jeremias Joakim and Sedecias?

k) *Spirit of OT law.* The ancient Oriental codes (like that of Moses) were

107. 4 Kgs. 14:5-6.
108. 3 Kgs. 21:13; 4 Kgs. 9: 26.
109. 2 Sam. 21:1-9; on collective guilt, cf. § 39:1.
110. CH 257, 258, 261, 273, 274.
111. CH 66f.
112. CH 48.
113. HL 2:39, 43-46.
114. HL 1:96, 100; 2:55.
115. HL 1:22-24; CH 15, 16, 17, 226.
116. Deut. 23:16-17; cf. § 31:4.
117. § 29:7; 32:1g.
118. § 14:7.
119. § 38; 40.
120. 2 Sam. 12; cf. 2 Sam. 24:11 (God and David).
121. 3 Kgs. 11:11f, 26f.
122. 3 Kgs. 18:17f; 21:17f.
123. Am. 4:1f.
124. Is. 7.

promulgated in the name of a divinity, yet in reality (unlike that of Moses) reflect merely the will of the ruler; none of them command the worship of only one God or require faith, hope, love. OT law binds even the king, and the warning, "Love justice, you rulers of the nations,"[125] was in force from the moment Yahweh proclaimed His will on Horeb. Unlike other codes, Mosaic Law involves more than external actions only, it demands an inner spirit; it governs relationships between man and man not only with reference to the common good, but assumes as fundamental that each man enjoys the love of God who is father to all. Again and again one is reminded how Yahweh avenges all violations, even such as cannot be punished through a legal process. Thus in Israel law and religion were much more closely united than among other Oriental peoples. Moreover one should not overlook how the historical books presented characters whom the Israelites had to regard as models: Abraham, in his obedience to God's promises, even though these promises were not easy to understand and occasioned great suffering; Jacob, who did penance in all patience for his injustices and never lost trust in God; Joseph, who gloriously preserved his virtue, who remained humble even when exalted, who bigheartedly forgave those who had gravely wronged him; David, who when persecuted without cause let pass the opportunity to liquidate his most bitter enemy, who later resignedly accepted punishment from God's hand; Moses and the prophets, who sacrificed themselves in God's service on behalf of an ungrateful people.

SECTION 2. DIVINE WORSHIP

§ 33. SACRIFICES AND OFFERINGS

1. WHY SACRIFICE? A man who is interiorly conscious of union with God and of duties toward Him will feel compelled to express his sentiments in an external manner. A vigorous religious spirit must show itself in action, and such action must not be frowned upon as superfluous is man's relation to God. Various external acts are common to all religions, still similarity of action should not blind us to dissimilarity in underlying theological content. In OT cult the most important act was sacrifice, as in practically all ancient religions. Here too the Israelites assimilated certain practices from neighboring cultures, were stimulated by them, purified and harmonized them with Yahwistic religion.

The common word for sacrifice was *minḥah*, gift, which in a narrower sense was applied to unbloody food and drink offerings. The word *qorban* (etym., a bringing near), an oblation, i.e., for Yahweh, was a generic term for sacrifice. Sacrifice involved giving a portion of one's personal goods to God. By it the offerer showed he belonged to God with all that he possessed, he owed to God all, life included. The most important sacrifices were the bloody because in them the idea of oblation was most realistically expressed. The sprinkling of blood was essential; the blood was dedicated to Yahweh because it was consid-

125. Wis. 1:1.

ered the seat of life.[1] Man owes his life to God, but in its stead he offers an animal's life. The dedication of the sacrificial gift was consummated by burning it wholly or in part; the smoke ascended to heaven, God's dwelling place, and if the sacrifice had been presented with the proper disposition, the offerer could hope God would respond mercifully. Before the animal was slain the offerer would lay his hands upon it; this signified a relationship between himself and the animal—by giving the animal to God he was giving himself. At an atonement sacrifice the sins of those making the offering were symbolically laid upon the beast;[2] by sin man had deserved death, but out of mercy God allowed Himself to be appeased with an animal's life and blood.

2. SIGNIFICANCE OF SPECIFIC SACRIFICES. a) *At a holocaust* or burnt-offering (*'olah* from *'alah*, to ascend, because the animal ascended the altar, or (better) because the smoke went up to heaven; or *kalil*, whole-offering) the entire animal was burnt except the hide, which was not dedicated to God since it could not be used at the sacrificial banquet. To a greater degree than other sacrifices it symbolized how man ought to give himself wholly to God.[3] The community did homage to Yahweh as its God by immolating a lamb each morning and evening as a burnt-offering.[4]

b) *Peace-offering.* The main characteristic of a peace-offering, also known as a thank-offering or welfare-offering *(zebah, zebah šelamim,* or merely *šelamim,* plu. of intensity, the sing. *šelem* only in Am. 5:22) was the sacrificial banquet at which Yahweh was host and the immolator was guest at the "Lord's table."[5] Yahweh returned part of the sacrificed animal to the individual who had offered it, a sign of the bond of peace and friendship that had arisen between them. Peace-sacrifices were made to God from motives of gratitude, petition, praise, or to fulfill a vow. It was holy flesh the offerers were eating, and accordingly only the ceremonially clean could partake of it.[6] The Israelite who offered a sacrifice had to examine himself on how he was keeping God's command to live a holy life. Since slaves, Levites, the poor and strangers should also be included in the sacrificial banquet,[7] the occasion reminded him of the duty to love subordinates and to be generous toward the needy.

c) *Atonement sacrifices.* In Arabic *kipper* means to cover—so that God will not see the sin; a better derivation is from Accadian: to wipe away—with the result that sin is blotted out. The effect of an atonement sacrifice was to appease God and thereby ward off the punishment due to sin, "If they make atonement, they will be forgiven."[8] In each instance it was necessary to admit having sinned and to make reparation for any damage done.[9] The sin-offering at the consecration of Aaron and his sons,[10] who were God's own choice, and Aaron's sacrifice after his consecration,[11] indicate no man is perfectly pure in the presence of God. The practice of making sin-offerings in cases of external

1. Gen. 9:4; Lev. 17:11, 14; Deut. 12:23; § 24:3b.
2. Cf. Lev. 16:5, 10.
3. Lev. 1:3.
4. Ex. 29:38-42.
5. Cf. Ps. 23:5.
6. Lev. 7:19-21.
7. Deut. 12:12, 18; 16:11, 14.
8. Lev. 4:20; 5:13; 9:7; cf. § 40:4.
9. Cf. § 34:5 on expiatory sacrifice and the Day of Atonement.
10. Lev. 8:14-17.
11. Lev. 9:8.

defilement,[12] rooted as it was in the notions of the age,[13] was orientated toward God in the Torah and served to put consciences at ease. The paschal lamb, an expiatory sacrifice[14] at which the sins of the family were blotted out by the sprinkling of blood, appeased the wrath of God so that He passed by and spared all homes marked by its blood.[15] In the time of the Maccabees expiatory sacrifices were offered for the dead.[16] However only the sins committed through error or weakness were effaced by atonement sacrifices, not sins committed "with uplifted hand," i.e., with full reflection and malice.[17] This limitation was a warning not to overestimate the efficacy of expiatory sacrifice. Moreover each offense required a specific sacrifice, and this did much to eliminate any thought that one expensive sacrifice could appease God without interior personal amendment. The OT recognized confession of sins without an accompanying sacrifice.[18] The tendency to overrate expiatory sacrifice was also curbed by the existence of other ways to atone for sin and regain God's good favor.[19]

d) *By food and drink offerings* the good Israelite thanked God for his daily nourishment. The bread for such sacrifices was made of unleavened dough to remind him to live a spotless life.[20] A covenant confirmed by eating salt was held inviolable.[21] Salt therefore served as a concomitant offering at unbloody sacrifices: the union between God and His servant must never be broken.

e) *Showbread.* Bread is essential to human existence—showbread was regularly placed in the sanctuary.[22] Israel ought to remain conscious of how she depended upon Yahweh for her continued existence and how necessary it was to petition Him for her daily bread.

f) *Incense-offering.* The ascending cloud of an incense-offering symbolized prayer.[23] Accordingly the people prayed before the Holy of Holies while the priest within was making the sacrifice.[24]

3. SACRIFICES NOT OFFERED TO NOURISH GOD. In many passages offerings are designated as "God's food,"[25] while others describe how Yahweh "smelt the sweet (or soothing) odor" of the sacrifice.[26] Now only if you imagined God as having a body of flesh would He need earthly food—a very unrefined theological conception. "Do I eat bull meat, or drink goat blood?"[27] Such expressions occur in the latest as well as in the oldest books, a good indication of their figurative character.[28] It was not the smell that was pleasing to Yahweh, but the spirit with which he who sacrificed offered his gift. The expression, "God smelt the odor," is good anthropomorphism,[29] and simply indicates God's pleasure in the action.

4. HUMAN SACRIFICE. Since by sacrifice man wishes to show that his whole life belongs to God, the thought would arise on occasions of special need or rejoicing to present God with a human life. Sometimes any person would be taken, sometimes the death of the ruler's own child was in order. Human sacri-

12. Lev. 12:6; 15:14.
13. § 30:4.
14. Ex. 12:27; 34:25.
15. Ex. 12:13, 27.
16. 2 Mach. 12:43.
17. Num. 15:30-31; § 38:4-5.
18. § 40:2.
19. § 40:3.

20. Cf. 1 Cor. 5:7.
21. Num. 18:19.
22. Ex. 25:22-30; 1 Sam. 21:7.
23. Ps. 141:2.
24. Lk. 1:10.
25. E.g., Lev. 3:11, 16; 21:6, 8, 17; 22:25; Num. 28:2.

26. Gen. 8:21; Lev. 1:9; 3:16; 6:8; 25:13; 1 Sam. 26:19, etc.
27. Ps. 50:13.
28. Cf. Ez. 44:7; Mal. 1:7; Num. 28:2.
29. § 8:3.

fice was practiced among many ancient peoples, Sumerians, Egyptians, Greeks, Romans, Germans. Sacred Scripture and archeology record how the Canaanites sacrificed human beings, especially children. The danger was great that the Israelites would be infected by their environment. Abraham already had been instructed to regard human sacrifice as unacceptable. For Yahweh directed him to immolate Isaac his son, but then in a marvellous manner rescinded the order.[30] The Law strictly forbade human sacrifice.[31] Indeed God laid claim to the first-born son,[32] but the legislator clarified this in the "redemption" legislation.[33] The Law did not reflect a custom of actual sacrifice, as may be deduced from the patriarch's high esteem for a first-born son,[34] Jacob's efforts to obtain for himself the right of the first-born,[35] and Esau's lament over the loss of that right.[36] Jephte sacrificed his daughter because he believed it necessary to fulfill his ill-considered vow; even as he made it he had reckoned with the possibility of human sacrifice.[37] When beginning the reconstruction of Jericho, Hiel sacrificed his eldest son, and his youngest at the erection of the gates.[38] This occurred during the reign of Achab. Achab favored the cult of Baal of Tyre (Melkart), who was fond of foundation sacrifices. In Hiel's action the Israelites saw fulfilled the curse Josue placed upon anyone who would rebuild Jericho's walls.[39] During the eighth and seventh century there was a place of sacrifice to Melekh (Moloch) in the valley of Ben Hinnom; there Achaz and Manasses sacrificed their sons.[40] With all vehemence the Law and the prophets inveighed against this crime,[41] and the author of the Book of Kings regarded child sacrifice as one of the reasons why the northern kingdom perished.[42]

5. THE PLACE OF SACRIFICE. During the journey through the wilderness sacrifices were permitted only at the site of the tabernacle; by this temporary centralization Moses sought to safeguard the Israelites from sacrificing to desert demons.[43] The court which surrounded the tabernacle served to remind the Israelites to put away earthly thoughts when they approached God. The most Holy Place was shrouded in darkness, a sign that divinity was full of mysteries unfathomable by man. They were not allowed to set foot in the tabernacle proper to keep them mindful that their sinfulness prevented access to the God of holiness.[44] In Canaan many abominations took place at the high place sanctuaries; the worship of Yahweh was intertwined with the worship of Baal and usually occasioned gross immoral excesses. Ezechias and Josias sought to eradicate these practices by forbidding sacrifice in the high places and designating the temple at Jerusalem as the one center for sacrifice.[45] Regarding false reliance upon the temple and the position taken by the prophets in this matter, cf. § 11:3.

6. CULT IN POSTEXILIC TIMES. Centralization of sacrifice in Jerusalem

30. Gen. 22.
31. Lev. 18:21; 20:2-3; Deut. 12:31; 18:10.
32. Ex. 22:28.
33. Ex. 13:13; 34:20.
34. Gen. 48:18; 49:3; cf. 27:4, 19.
35. Gen. 25:27-34.
36. Gen. 27:36.
37. Judg. 11:29f.
38. 3 Kgs. 16:34.
39. Jos. 6.
40. 4 Kgs. 16:3; 21:6.
41. Mich. 6:7; Jer. 7:31; 19:5; 32:35; Ez. 16:20, 21; 20:26.
42. 4 Kgs. 17:17; cf. Ps. 106:37-38.
43. Lev. 17:1f.
44. Cf. Num. 17:27-28.
45. Cf. Deut. 12; 4 Kgs. 18:4; 22:23.

should have shown clearly that cult was not the one essential in religion, since Israelites who dwelt at a distance seldom had the opportunity of attending services there. During the exile religious life suffered no harm by the cessation of the customary sacrificial cult, but rather attained a spiritual character which enabled Jewry to survive even the destruction of the nation under Titus. For in the hard school of reality the Jews learnt that the external act of sacrifice is not decisive in man's religious formation—essential is a spiritual attitude and a morally upright life. In exile they assembled on the Sabbath and on the feasts and recalled Yahweh's mighty deeds at the Exodus and during the wilderness journey, read the sacred books, sang psalms and listened to a priest's comments. This was the beginning of synagogue services. In prayer they manifested reverence toward God, by fasting they gave expression to a spirit of penance.[46] Nevertheless when the exiles returned under Zerobabel, the regular sacrificial cult in Jerusalem was immediately reinaugurated. The Jews, scattered far and wide in the diaspora, regarded the temple at Jerusalem as their center of unity and to it they made pilgrimages and sent rich gifts. In the last period before Christ the Scribes and Pharisees endeavored to heighten the significance of ceremony by devising minute refinements, just as they multiplied to an unreasonable degree the prescriptions for the Sabbath and feasts. They again fostered what the prophets had condemned for centuries: external display devoid of inner sincerity and sanctity. While these externalists were still at work, Malachy's prophecy was fulfilled; bloody sacrifices ceased, their place was taken by the one new sacrifice, a clean and lasting oblation.[47]

7. EVALUATION OF OT SACRIFICES. a) *Significance for spiritual life.* The sacrificial oblations were a means of rousing up the people to love God with renewed fervor and to serve Him by a virtuous life. External cult did not injure personal piety or suffocate it, as is evident from the lives of David and Solomon, who were zealous in promoting the solemnity of sacred service while remaining most intimately united with God and experiencing His love in the deepest degree. In Maccabean times too religious spirit burned brightly and yet the greatest interest was taken in the temple and temple sacrifices. The psalms, written primarily for temple service, stem from deeply religious souls. A pious Jew was fortunate to have the privilege of visiting God in His sanctuary and sharing in the liturgical solemnities. Many would travel a great distance. Sometimes for years they longed to tread on the ground where Yahweh had revealed Himself. Then the occasion came. They would see the priests whom God had chosen for His service at the altar, hear the elevating music, the hymns of the choirs, themselves joining in the alternate chant. Now he was experiencing what it meant to be near to God.[48] Deeply moved he repeated after the psalmist, "One thing I have asked of Yahweh, that do I want, that I might dwell in the house of Yahweh all the days of my life, that I might pasture myself upon Yahweh's loving-kindness and visit his temple[49] . . . . How lovely

46. Is. 58:3; Dan. 9:3; Zach.   47. Mal. 1:10-11; § 49:1b.   49. Ps. 27:4.
    7:3; Tob. 3:11; 12:8.   48. Sir. 50.

are your dwellings, Yahweh of hosts! My soul longs, my soul wastes away for the courts of Yahweh. Surely the sparrow has found a house and the swallow a nest for itself! Blessed are they who dwell in your house, who may praise you constantly. For better is a day in your courts than elsewhere a thousand."[50] When forced to live away from the temple, he would recall in the midst of tears the time when he "advanced *in the procession of princes* to the house of God with jubilation and song of praise" and pray, "When may I come and appear before the face of God? Ah, that I would arrive at the altar of God, of God *my* fountain of joy."[51] If persecuted without cause, his prayer in the temple would be, "In innocence I can wash my hands and thus stand near your altar. I love your *lovely* house and the place where your glory dwells."[52] No one was excluded from these spiritual transports because of position, family or age; lay people shared in the divine services as well as priests, wives as well as husbands; only the actual performance of ceremonies was reserved to Levites.

True, the Israelites at their sacrificial banquets at times forgot the sanctity of the place as well as the sanctity of an action designed to unite man with God. Already in the wilderness they fashioned a Yahweh-idol and kept the sacrificial banquet with unrestrained merriment.[53] Osee complained how sacrifice amounted to nothing further in their eyes than an opportunity to feast sumptuously;[54] and drunkenness in the sacred places was not rare.[55] Yes, the most sacred things can be misused by men; similar aberrations crept in during apostolic times at the agape.[56]

b) *Cult and morals.* Though cult had tremendous significance in Israel's religious life, it did not take first place amid the duties man owed to God. In the decalog but one commandment is concerned with cult, that of the Sabbath observance. By far the majority of ordinances in the Covenant Code concern morals, and the bulk of Deuteronomic Law is ethical rather than ritual. Moses himself was not a priest, and the prophets and psalmists were primarily concerned about morality, not ceremonial. Samuel said, "Obedience is better than sacrifice,"[57] and Psalm 15 admitted into the sanctuary only those who led a holy life. Many Israelites adopted pagan attitudes in the matter of offering sacrifice. They cared little for what sacrifice implied, viz., an oblation of self to God, abandonment of sinful habits, and believed they could pacify Yahweh and get His help simply by presenting fatter and bigger bulls. The story of Cain and Abel's sacrifice should have shown them that the essential is not the gift but the heart of the offerer.[58]

c) *Attitude of the prophets.* God wanted sacrifice. This is shown by His benevolent acceptance of the sacrifices made by Abel and Noe;[59] the covenant with Abraham was inaugurated with sacrifice;[60] Moses was enjoined to outline

50. Ps. 84:2-5, 11; cf. Pss. 15; 23; 24; 122.
51. Pss. 42:3, 5; 43:4.
52. Ps. 26:6, 8.
53. Ex. 32:6.
54. Os. 8:13.
55. 1 Sam. 1:13.
56. 1 Cor. 11:17f.

57. 1 Sam. 15:22.
58. Gen. 4:3-5. (Many readers will not agree with the author's interpretation of what is primary in OT religion. This view would lead to divorce sacrifice from morality and, in our times,

nourish a prevalent moralizing attitude at the expense of the religious-liturgical which is primary in both OT and NT.—Trans.)
59. Gen. 4:4; 8:20-22.
60. Gen. 15:7f.

a ritual of sacrifice for his people; the covenant with Israel was sealed with a sacrifice;[61] fire came down from heaven upon Aaron's first sacrifice and consumed it.[62] Heavenly fire enveloped Gedeon's gifts[63] and Elias' bullock,[64] the latter having been a sacrifice designed to bring Israel back to true Yahweh worship. Sacrifices however must represent the overflow of love toward God, a love proven by obedience to His commands. This the prophets emphasized when they preached to a people who "honor me with their lips, but keep their heart distant from me."[65] In the struggle against false popular concepts, they at times expressed themselves so bluntly as to leave the impression of contemning sacrifice itself, "I hate and abominate your feasts, I prefer not to smell your solemnities; for you offer me burnt-offerings—in your oblations I have no pleasure and in the peace-offerings of your stall-fed cattle I take no delight. Take away from me the noise of your songs, I do not want to hear the strumming of your harps! Rather ought righteousness flow as water, and justice as a perennial stream."[66] "Charity pleases me, not sacrifices; knowledge of God rather than burnt-offerings."[67] Yet by no means did they reject ceremony as such, for they sought to establish the Mosaic Law, which certainly included sacrifices. They attacked cult, as the passage from Amos manifestly shows, as wrongly understood and practiced by the masses. Their sharp language is to be understood in a way similar to Paul's when he says Christ sent him not to baptize but to preach;[68] the apostle merely wished to stress his principal task, i.e., preaching; on occasion he himself baptized, as he recalls in the same passage. Isaias did not oppose the reform of King Ezechias, Jeremias did not oppose the reform of King Josias and yet the efforts of these rulers for the most part were concerned with public worship. Samuel, who condemned the sacrifice of Saul,[69] himself offered sacrifice.[70] Osee prophesied the cessation of sacrifice in exile as part of Israel's impending punishment.[71] Isaias compared the joy which the Israelites were to experience at the destruction of their enemies with the joy had upon visiting the house of God,[72] and painted the messianic era as a pilgrimage of the nations to the temple at Jerusalem.[73] And Ezechiel, who foretold the end of the temple and its ceremonial, unfolded a program for the cult of the future.[74]

d) *Psalmists and wisdom teachers.* The disparaging statements of certain psalmists must be understood as directed against false notions concerning the value of sacrifices, "From your stables I need receive no steers, nor any bucks from your flocks. Surely all the beasts of the forest are mine, the animals upon *my* hills I can multiply a thousand*fold*. Should I become hungry, I would not need to tell you; for mine is the earth, and that which fills it."[75] It is a great error, the poet wishes to say, to think God can be pacified with gifts, He who created all. Sinners must not approach Yahweh without giving up the ways of

61. Ex. 24.
62. Lev. 9:24.
63. Judg. 6:21.
64. 3 Kgs. 18:38.
65. Is. 29:13.
66. Am. 5:21-24.

67. Os. 6:6; cf. Is. 1:11-14; Mich. 6:7; Jer. 7:21-22.
68. 1 Cor. 1:14-17.
69. 1 Sam. 15:22.
70. 1 Sam. 7:9, 17; 9:14; 16:2, 5.

71. Os. 3:4; 9:4.
72. Is. 30:29.
73. Is. 2:2-4.
74. Ez. 40-48.
75. Ps. 50:9-12.

sin, "As an offering to God, an avowal of guilt."[76] The penitent who prays, "Since you ask no sacrifice—I would give a burnt-offering if it would please you—my sacrifice is a contrite spirit; a humbled heart, O God, you cannot send away,"[77] undoubtedly has the right approach, for sacrifice is but the sign of repentance. The same spirit is found in Pss. 40:7-8 and 69:32. In Sirach's assertions, "A *burnt-offering* in injustice is a mock gift, the *gifts* of evildoers are unacceptable[78]. . . . who obeys the Law brings many gifts: a *peace-offering*, he who heeds the commandments; he who shows mercy brings a food-offering; he who bestows alms a sacrifice of praise,"[79] there is no element of contempt for sacrifices; indeed in other passages he urged his readers to be zealous in the matter;[80] he counselled the sick to offer sacrifices to obtain from God the gift of health;[81] he spoke with enthusiasm on the installation of Aaron as high priest[82] and considered it an incomparable privilege to have been present at sacrifices offered by the high priest Simon in Jerusalem.[83]

8. Value and Typical Significance of OT Sacrifices. Imposed by Yahweh Himself, the OT sacrifices were meant to remind the Israelites of their dependence upon God; their purpose was to foster a yearning for God, to promote friendship with God by a perfect giving of self; at the same time they benefitted the sinner by evoking a consciousness of guilt and urging him to do penance and amend. Sacrifice blotted out sin, for according to 1 Sam. 3:14, "The guilt of the house of Heli (could) not be expiated by sacrifices and offerings;" hence, such must have been possible in other instances. Forgiveness always presupposed that the sin in question did not belong to a class of exceptionally grievous transgressions committed in open defiance of God,[84] and that the sinner with sincere sorrow had abandoned his evil ways. Levitical defilement was removed by offerings, e.g., those prescribed for women in childbed,[85] for cured lepers,[86] for sexual disturbances.[87] The water needed to cleanse defilement consequent upon touching a corpse was obtained by a sin-offering.[88]

OT sacrificial cult accordingly had its own specific purpose, i.e., to rear a holy people. Of themselves however sacrifices had no power to blot out sin. Only in view of grace did an angry God allow Himself to be appeased by them. "The Law had but a shadow of the good things to come[89]. . . . it is impossible that sins should be taken away with blood of bulls and of goats,"[90] and sacrifices immolated by OT priests could "never take away sins."[91] The imperfect sacrifices of the old covenant pointed to the one perfect sacrifice of the new covenant, the sacrifice which the son of God "offered for sins" on the cross for all time[92] by immolating His blood to the heavenly Father.[93] In anticipation of this future sacrifice God looked favorably upon holocausts offered as a sign of devotedness, upon atonement sacrifices offered to obtain forgiveness of sins, upon peace-offerings given by the virtuous to strengthen friendly relations with

76. Ps. 50:14, 23.
77. Ps. 51:18-19.
78. Sir. 34:21-22.
79. Sir. 35:1-4; cf. 34:24.
80. Sir. 7:31; 35:6-9.
81. Sir. 38:11.

82. Sir. 45:6-22.
83. Sir. 50:1-21.
84. § 33:2c.
85. Lev. 12.
86. Lev. 14.
87. Lev. 15.

88. Num. 19.
89. Heb. 10:1.
90. Heb. 10:4.
91. Heb. 10:11.
92. Heb. 10:12.
93. Heb. 9:28; § 50:3; 52:1.

God and renew divine love—all three classes being foreshadowed and fulfilled in the perfect sacrifice, the sacrifice of Mass and its eucharistic banquet.[94] No bone of the paschal lamb was to be broken;[95] only those could share in the meal who belonged to the Chosen People and were purified of every stain;[96] it saved Israel when Yahweh slew the first-born of Egypt, and opened for them the way from servitude to liberty. St. Paul instructed the Corinthians on the typical character of this lamb, "Christ, our Passover, has been sacrificed."[97] On the cross no bone of Christ's body was broken;[98] He offered the true expiatory sacrifice for the sins of the world; His blood preserves men from eternal death and delivers them from the servitude of Satan; a share in His eucharistic Body is permitted to those only who belong to the Chosen People of the New Kingdom and possess interior purity, and these He unites most intimately with the Father. The sin-offering of the red cow that was killed outside the camp and whose ashes were used in preparing the purificatory water[99] was a type of the sacrifice of Golgotha in which the blood of Christ removed sin[100] and imparted to the waters of baptism the power to wash away sin.[101] On the typical implications of Yom Kippur, cf. § 34:5.

9. TITHES. When offering the firstfruits and tithes all Israelites were to remember (as they regularly protested in prayer),[102] that it was Yahweh who freed them from Egyptian bondage and gave them Canaan. The same legislation admonished them to overcome selfishness and avarice and to practice charity toward the poor.[103] "With all your gifts show a cheerful face, and with joy dedicate your tithes. Give to the Most High as he gave to you, and with a gracious eye as much as you are able; for he is a Lord who repays, and sevenfold will he reimburse you."[104] The Pharisees and Scribes collected tithes on mint, dill and cummin, articles not included by the Law.[105]

§ 34. FEASTS

1. THE SABBATH. Israel's most important religious festival was the Sabbath. To keep holy the Sabbath was the only cult law contained in the decalog.[1] No kind of work was permitted on this day. Man arranges his labors more or less for his own interests and profit; on the Sabbath the Israelite should abstain from all work to show that God has full and complete right to his time.[2] The Sabbath day rest thus was an acknowledgment of Yahweh as supreme Lord. In six days God had made the world, by resting on the seventh He blessed and sanctified it.[3] The Sabbath served as a memorial of the great act of creation and inculcated the truth that man's activity must always harmonize with God's. The religious observances consisted in special sacrifices, and assemblies marked by common prayer and mutual edification.[4] If there was a prophet in the neigh-

94. Cf. Ps. 22:17; § 52:2b.
95. Ex. 12:46; Num. 9:12.
96. Ex. 12:43-45; Num. 9:7-11.
97. 1 Cor. 5:7.
98. Jn. 19:33-36.
1. Ex. 20:8-11.
2. Cf. § 30:7b.

99. Num. 19.
100. Heb. 9:13-14.
101. Barn. ep. 8, Migne 2:747; Aug. qu. 33, in Num., Migne 34:733; Ephrem expl. in Lev. 10; Gregor.
3. Ex. 20:11; 31:17; Gen. 2:2-3.

M. expos. quarti psalmi poen. Migne 79:588.
102. Deut. 26:5-10.
103. Deut. 26:12-13.
104. Sir. 35:11-13; 7:31.
105. Matth. 23:23; Lk. 11:42.
4. Lev. 23:3; Num. 28:9-10.

borhood, the people would gather about him for instruction in spiritual matters.[5] During the exile the Sabbath together with circumcision and the food laws[6] served to distinguish the Jews from Gentile neighbors, kept alive in them the consciousness of their providential selection and gave them a sense of national unity. Antiochus Epiphanes proscribed circumcision and Sabbath day observances in his efforts to destroy the Jewish religion.[7]

The Sabbath day restrictions were not designed to weigh upon Israel as a heavy yoke. To observe the Sabbath was a great blessing joyfully accepted.[8] First through the casuistry of the Scribes and Pharisees did it become an intolerable burden. According to their perverted notion the Sabbath was not ordained for man's benefit, but man was ordained for the Sabbath.[9] Propounding a spirit of empty formalism they regarded the cure of the sick as a violation of the Sabbath, even if it was effected by a mere word. This attitude frequently brought them in conflict with our Blessed Savior.[10] Likewise they were scandalized when the disciples broke off heads of wheat on the Sabbath to appease their hunger because they considered this action to be manual labor![11] Proscriptions and prescriptions multiplied to such an extent in the course of time that the rabbis themselves had to devise ways and means to circumvent their own directives without formal violation.[12]

2. THE NEW MOON FEAST. At the end of each week the Israelite thanked God for the blessings received in the course of the week; at the beginning of each month he implored God's protection for the coming four weeks.[13] There were offered holocausts in Yahweh's honor, and expiatory sacrifices to atone for sins committed since the last New Moon Feast. At the holocaust offering the priests blew trumpets "to remind Yahweh" of His people[14] and to implore Yahweh to espouse their cause. As on the Sabbath, the people assembled for spiritual instruction at a holy place[15] or at the feet of a prophet.[16]

3. "DAY OF BLOWING THE HORN." The beginning of the seventh month was celebrated in an exceptionally festive manner with holocausts and atonement sacrifices, abstention from work and sacred convocations.[17] It was the "day of blowing the horn" to implore Yahweh to show mercy toward His people and to remind the people of benefits received. If, as the Mishnah says, this was the original New Year's feast, it was an occasion to be grateful for the blessings of the past year and to petition protection for the year just beginning.

4. THE THREE GREAT FEASTS. The Covenant Code prescribed three feasts having a predominantly joyous spirit, the feast of Unleavened Bread, the feast of the (wheat) Harvest and the feast of the Vintage or Tabernacles.[18] On these occasions all adult males were to gather at the sanctuary. The communal character of these celebrations heightened national and personal enthusiasm and made the Israelites more conscious of being God's own people.

5. 4 Kgs. 4:23.
6. § 30:6.
7. 1 Mach. 1:41f; 2 Mach. 6:6.
8. Os. 2:13; Is. 58:13.
9. Mk. 2:27.
10. Matth. 12:10f; Lk. 13:10f;

14:1f; Jn. 5:1f; 9:14f.
11. Matth. 12:2; Mk. 2:23f.
12. Cf. Tractate Schabbath, Erubin and Besa, E. Schürer, Gesch. des jüd. Volkes II Leipzig 1907, 551f, 574f,
13. Num. 28:11-15.

14. Num. 10:10.
15. Is. 1:13; 66:23; Ez. 46:3.
16. 4 Kgs. 4:23; cf. Agg. 1:1.
17. Lev. 23:23-25; Num. 29: 1-6.
18. Ex. 23:14-17; cf. Ex. 34: 18, 22-23.

a) *The feasts of the Passover and of Unleavened Bread.*[19] The feast of the Passover occurred on the evening of the 14th of Nisan, the first month in springtime.[20] The celebration commemorated the deliverance of the Hebrews from Egypt. Pasch *(pesaḥ)* means to spare, pass over; Yahweh spared the houses of the Hebrews when He slew the first-born of Egypt.[21] With the lamb bitter herbs were eaten as a remembrance of the bitter slavery in Egypt.[22] Later a broth, charoseth, by its yellowish brown color brought to mind the work of brick-making. Gratefully the Israelites recalled the time when Yahweh freed their fathers from oppression.[23] Gratefully they sang the Great Hallel, Pss. 113-114, before the meal strictly so-called and Pss. 115-118 after the meal. The feast of Unleavened Bread *(Maṣṣoth)* began on the fifteenth of the first month and lasted seven days.[24] It owed its origin to the manner in which the Israelites left the land of Egypt. Because of their hasty departure there was no time to leaven the dough, and therefore they had to bake it unleavened.[25] The people recalled Yahweh's mighty deeds at the Exodus[26] and celebrated Massoth with great joy.[27] Abstention from work, assemblies on the first and seventh day and sacrifices helped to solemnize the commemoration. After the Sabbath which fell during the octave, the first sheaves of the new harvest were brought to the sanctuary; solemn thanksgiving was made for the blessings bestowed upon the fields[28] together with the petition that the harvest now beginning be successfully completed.

b) *The feast of Weeks*[29] received its name from being celebrated seven weeks after the feast of Unleavened Bread; it was also called the feast of Harvest,[30] the Day of Firstfruits,[31] and finally Pentecost.[32] It was a "thanksgiving day" at the end of the wheat harvest.[33]

c) *The feast of Tabernacles* was celebrated in autumn during grape gathering time;[34] it lasted seven days beginning with the fifteenth of the seventh month; later, perhaps at the time of Solomon, the eighth day too was kept as a feast. The people thanked God for all the fruits of nature, particularly for the grape harvest. It was *par excellence* the feast of rejoicing, "Be joyous before Yahweh, your God."[35] At times it was simply called the "Feast."[36] Yet in the midst of jubilation the people were not to forget that they had often offended Yahweh in the course of the year; therefore an atonement sacrifice was offered daily. Furthermore they should recall how Yahweh preceded and led them in the wilderness. As their fathers had lived in tents, they too should live in tents—a second motive for gratitude and trust in God. In postexilic times a further expression of joy consisted in a water libation at the morning sacrifice on all seven days and a torch dance after the evening sacrifice on the first day. As soon as the priest appeared in the court with the water, the verse, accompanied

19. Cf. Ex. 12:1-14, 21-27, 43-50; Num. 9:1-14.
20. Concerning the paschal lamb sacrifice, cf. § 33:2c, 8.
21. Ex. 12:13, 27, 29.
22. Cf. Ex. 1:14.
23. Ex. 12:26-27.
24. Ex. 12:15-20; 13:3-10; Lev. 23:4-8; Num. 28:16-

25; Deut. 16:1-8.
25. Ex. 12:34, 39.
26. Ex. 12:17.
27. 2 Chr. 30:21; Esdr. 6:22.
28. Lev. 23:9-14.
29. Ex. 34:22; Deut. 16:10, 16.
30. Ex. 23:16.
31. Num. 28:26.

32. 2 Mach. 12:32.
33. Lev. 23:15-21; Num. 28:26-31.
34. Ex. 23:16; Lev. 23:33-44; Num. 29:12-38.
35. Lev. 23:40; Neh. 8:9-12.
36. 3 Kgs. 8:2; 12:32; Ez. 45:25.

with music, was intoned, "With joy you shall draw water from the fountains of salvation."[37] The words pointed forward to the blessings of messianic times and backward to the miraculous flow of water in the desert.[38] Jesus used the opportunity afforded by this water libation on the seventh day to manifest Himself as the fountain of living water flowing eternally.[39]

5. THE DAY OF ATONEMENT was kept on the tenth of the seventh month.[40] It was a day of penance characterized by expiatory sacrifices and confession of sins. Priest and people stood before Yahweh as sinners. The high priest, himself a penitent, appeared clad only in the ordinary priestly garb which was made of common linen. The most important liturgical action was the sprinkling of blood in the Holy of Holies upon and before the ark of the covenant; and with ascending clouds of incense there went up a petition for forgiveness. After this the high priest acknowledged "all the transgressions and all the infidelities of the Israelites"[41] over a goat and symbolically consigned them to the animal[42] which then carried them into the wilderness.[43] This goat belonged to Azazel.[44] To transfer sins, diseases, curses and religious uncleanness from one person to another or to an animal was a very ancient custom common to many peoples. In Israel, for instance, a bird was let fly at the reinstatement of a cured leper or at the purification of a house defiled by leprosy.[45] The scapegoat ceremony was a forceful way of teaching the Israelites to remove themselves as far as possible from sin and all its implications. On the Day of Atonement the Israelites were not allowed to work; they were to dedicate themselves wholly to a serious examination of conscience and to the keeping of a strict fast.[46]

No day was more sacred than the Day of Atonement. In later times it took precedence over all other feasts; even at the present time it enjoys a pre-eminent position in the Jewish calendar and is referred to simply as *yoma*, "The Day," or *yoma rabha*, "The Great Day." Inasmuch as it was the day upon which Israel as a covenanted people made atonement to their God, it was the Good Friday of the OT (Delitzsch) and prefigured that Good Friday on which Christ as high priest accomplished the great atonement by His own blood, blotted out sin and reconciled mankind with the eternal Father.[47] We may even note a further relationship between type and fulfillment, e.g., on the Day of Atonement the flesh of the expiatory sacrifice was burnt outside the camp,[48] while our Redeemer died outside the walls of Jerusalem.[49]

6. POSTEXILIC FEASTS. a) *The feast of Purim* on the 14th and 15th of Adar (March) commemorated the deliverance of Jews in Persia from the massacre planned by Aman, as narrated in the Book of Esther. Gratitude toward God and trust in His protection was the dominant religious spirit on this feast. The joy over deliverance was superseded by jubilation over the enemy's destruc-

37. Is. 12:3.
38. Ex. 17:5-6; Num. 20:11.
39. Jn. 7:37f.
40. Lev. 16:23, 26-32; Num. 29:7-11.
41. Cf. Mishna, Joma 6, 2.
42. Lev. 16:21.
43. Lev. 16:22.
44. § 23:2.
45. Lev. 14:7, 53; cf. the deportation of the woman symbolizing sin in Zach.
5:5-11.
46. § 37:1.
47. Heb. 9:7, 11-12.
48. Lev. 16:27.
49. Heb. 13:11-12.

tion and thus Purim became more of a civil celebration than a religious one. Feasting and revelry took the first place, yet the poor were not forgotten.[50]

b) *Chanukkah.* For the assistance granted during the Syrian persecutions the Jews were grateful on the feast of the re-dedication of the temple, Chanukkah, held on the 25th of Kislev (December),[51] on Nicanor Day, the 13th of Adar (March), which commemorated the glorious triumph over the Syrian general,[52] and on a feast kept on the 23rd of Iyar (May) in commemoration of the capture of the citadel of Jerusalem.[53]

7. GOD'S ATTITUDE TOWARD FEASTS. What was said concerning sacrifice holds true also of feasts. The essential was not the external celebration, but the spirit in which the feast was kept, the readiness to be edified spiritually and to be filled with gratitude, penance and fidelity toward God. Against festivity which did not express an inner life of union with God the prophets inveighed as much as against merely external sacrifice, "My soul hates your New Moons and your feast days, they have become a burden for me of which I am tired carrying."[54] In punishment God would change Israel's feasts into mourning and her songs into lamentations;[55] exile would end all celebrations.[56] However since religious feasts as such were not odious to God—He Himself had instituted them—the people, purified by exile, would again keep festivals in Yahweh's honor.[57]

§ 35. PRAYER

1. GENERAL CONSIDERATIONS. Man acknowledges God as his creator and supreme Lord and praises His power manifested in creation and in the providential care of the world. Man is grateful to God for the blessings conferred upon him, begs forgiveness of sin and assistance in time of trouble. Prayer ranks with sacrifice as the oldest and chiefest means to honor God; it is common to all religions.

a) *Praise.* God's power revealing itself in creation is an oft-recurring theme in Israel's prayer.[1] The Hebrew poets glorify God's intervention in the history of His people, particularly in the marvels during the Exodus from Egypt;[2] they acknowledge that they owe all to God with whom they are conscious of being closely associated. "With you I have taken refuge; I have said to Yahweh: You are my Lord, *apart from you* I have no good. Yahweh is the portion of my inheritance and my cup."[3]

b) *Thanksgiving.* Israel was grateful to God for preservation from evils, for triumph over enemies,[4] for the deliverance of the Holy City,[5] and for her own gracious selection as the Chosen People.[6] The first prayer mentioned in

50. Esth. 9:17-22.
51. 1 Mach. 4:52-59; 2 Mach. 10:5-8.
52. 1 Mach. 7:48-49; 2 Mach.
1. Pss. 8; 9; 33; 74; 104; 148; Sir. 42:15-43:33.
2. Ex. 15; Pss. 68; 77; 105; 111; 114; 136.
15:36-37.
53. 1 Mach. 13:51-52.
54. Is. 1:14; cf. Am. 5:25.
3. Ps. 16:1-2, 5; cf. Ps. 73: 23, 25-26.
4. Ex. 15; Pss. 18; 21; 47;
55. Am. 8:10.
56. Os. 9:5-6.
57. Ez. 45:18-46:7; Soph. 3:18.
66.
5. Ps. 48.
6. Ps. 100.

the Bible, Eve's cry at the birth of Cain, was an expression of gratitude.[7] And the sinner upon becoming reconciled with God was grateful for forgiveness.[8]

c) *Petition*. In ordinary prayer-life petition occupies a foremost place. Pious persons asked for children,[9] good crops,[10] deliverance from dangers,[11] from persecution and calumny.[12] They implored recovery during sickness[13] (when ill Job's friends urged him to pray[14]), long life,[15] strength and courage,[16] aid in time of need.[17] Elias asked for the revival of a dead child,[18] Tobias prayed when he became blind,[19] Sara upon falling into disgrace.[20] As with individuals, so Israel as a nation turned to Yahweh in time of affliction, especially when besieged by hostile armies,[21] and begged for victory.[22]

Prayers of petition usually request deliverance from earthly affliction, because trouble and sorrow are very hard to bear. Hebrew history gives many examples illustrating the axiom, "Necessity teaches how to pray." Requests for spiritual blessings were not absent from their prayers. Moses asked to be enlightened about God's designs in the work of salvation;[23] he implored Yahweh to give him a worthy successor,[24] and once he even dared to ask for the privilege of beholding His glory.[25] Solomon asked for wisdom to govern his people,[26] and the author of the Book of Wisdom places upon his lips a petition for the fear of the Lord.[27] In the psalms the pious man asked for the virtue of trust in misfortunes[28] and for strength to lead a virtuous life.[29] Very often we find the people as a whole requesting divine forgiveness even as individuals did.[30] Pleas ascended to God for strength to avoid sin and to be preserved from temptation.[31] Moving penitential prayers are found in Esdr. 9; Neh. 9; Dan. 9; Bar. 1:15f.

Prayers of petition become more efficacious if accompanied by tears, fasting, and signs of grief, such as sitting on the ground, wearing mourning apparel, laying aside all finery, etc.[32] Petitions accompanied by vows[33] or a sorrowful acknowledgment of having sinned are practically always answered.[34]

By petition the pious man makes a glorious avowal of faith in God's providence. He appeals to God's omnipotence to help him,[35] he reminds God of being the "God of the spirits of all flesh;"[36] he is not unmindful of God's justice[37] or the promises made to the patriarchs;[38] he is convinced that Yahweh's honor compels Him to uphold Israel and humble her enemies.[39]

7. Gen. 4:1, 25.
8. Ps. 32:1-5.
9. Gen. 15:3; 24:60; 25:21; 1 Sam. 1:10-11.
10. Gen. 27:28; 49:25.
11. Gen. 32:12; Pss. 3; 10; 17.
12. Pss. 7; 12; 13; 17; 35; Jer. 15:15f; 17:14f.
13. 4 Kgs. 20:3; Ps. 38.
14. Job 5:8; 8:5; 11:13.
15. Ps. 61;7; Tob. 8:7.
16. Jud. 9:14.
17. Ex. 22:22, 26; Sir. 35:16-21.
18. 3 Kgs. 17:20.
19. Tob. 3:1f.
20. Tob. 3:11f.
21. Judg. 20:25f; 3 Kgs. 8:33-34; 2 Chr. 20:6f; Joel

2:15f; Jud. 4:10f; 7:19f; Esth. 13:18; 1 Mach. 3:44f.
22. Judg. 10:10f; Ps. 20.
23. Ex. 33:13.
24. Num. 27:16.
25. Ex. 33:18.
26. 3 Kgs. 3:9.
27. Wis. 9:1f.
28. Pss. 42; 43.
29. Pss. 5:9; 119:33-35.
30. 1 Sam. 7:2f; 2 Sam. 12:13; 24:10, 17; Jer. 14:7; Dan. 9:4-16; Lam.; Ps. 25:7; Sir. 39:5; the penitential psalms 6; 32; 38; 51; 102; 130; 143.
31. Prov. 30:7-9; Sir. 22:27-23:6.

32. Ex. 33:4; Deut. 1:45; 1 Sam. 7:6; 2 Sam. 12:16; 2 Chr. 20:3; Dan. 9:3; Tob. 3:11; Jud. 4:8; Esth. 14:2.
33. Gen. 28:20; 1 Sam. 1:11.
34. Ex. 32:31; Num. 14:19; 1 Sam. 7:6; 2 Sam. 12:13; Dan. 9:5.
35. 2 Chr. 20:6; Neh. 1:5; Esth. 13:9; Jud. 9:4f.
36. Num. 16:22.
37. Num. 16:22; Pss. 30:2; 35:24.
38. Gen. 32:13; Ex. 32:13; 3 Kgs. 8:23f; Neh. 1:5.
39. Ex. 32:12; Num. 14:13-17; Jud. 6:17; 9:9-11.

All this followed from the terms of the covenant.[40] The pious man knows that God is merciful and wishes to help,[41] that He seeks above all to espouse the cause of the poor and needy.[42] Frequently we find the just man mentioning his virtues and good qualities to move God to hear his petition;[43] this has its root in the firm belief that God is just and glorifies Himself when He helps the innocent secure his rights.[44]

2. QUALIFICATIONS FOR PRAYER. a) *Good moral life.* God inclines His ear to the prayers of none but those who lead a good moral life. Only "the prayer of the upright is pleasing to God."[45] If you have helped your neighbor in need, if you have fed the hungry, clothed the naked, redeemed captives, "if then you call, Yahweh will answer you. If you cry for aid, he will say: Here I am[46] . . . . Who honors his father will find a hearing when he prays."[47] Judith was urged to intercede "because she was a God-fearing woman."[48] To the question, "Who may ascend Yahweh's mount, and who may stand in his holy place?," the psalmist replied, "He who has clean hands and a pure heart!"[49] Contrariwise, one who has strayed from the paths of virtue need not expect his wish to be granted from on High. That was why Moses told the disobedient Israelites, "You weep before Yahweh, but Yahweh does not listen to you or take notice of you."[50] "Who turns away his ear so as not to hear the Law, even his prayer is an abomination."[51] The prophets gave the same interpretation, "When you stretch out your hands, I cover my eyes from you, and though you pray ever so much, I shall never answer you because your hands are full of blood[52] . . . . This people draw near to me with their mouth and honor me with their lips, but they keep their heart distant from me."[53] An unkind person "who stops his ears to the poor man's cry, he too shall cry and get no answer."[54] The sinner must first repent before he may hope for help in his needs.[55] As long as he remains obstinate he will get no assistance, even if a prophet pleads for him.[56] Yahweh forbade Jeremias to intercede for impenitent Israel, "I shall not listen to you."[57]

b) *Reverence.* The physical positions taken during prayer should be such as to indicate an acknowledgment of God as Lord. Special postures, of course, are not essential, but externals are not to be contemned. They indicate inner spirit, or aid in awakening proper dispositions. At prayer one may stand as a servant before the Lord, alert to do His wishes,[58] or kneel to show dependence;[59] a greater degree of subjection is manifested by squatting[60] or prostrating.[61] Ezechias prayed while lying upon his sickbed.[62] Priests showed reverence by performing their duties barefoot. Changing one's clothes or wash-

40. 3 Kgs. 8:23.
41. Ex. 34:6-7; Ps. 103:8-11; Dan. 9:18; Tob. 3:15.
42. Num. 11:11; Ps. 6:3.
43. Pss. 17:1-5; 18:21-28; 26: 1-6; 44:18-19; Jer. 12:3; Neh. 13:14, 22, 29.
44. Cf. § 15:6.
45. Prov. 15:8, 29.
46. Is. 58:6-9.
47. Sir. 3:5.
48. Jud. 8:31.

49. Ps. 24:3-4; cf. Pss. 15:1-5; 50:15.
50. Deut. 1:45.
51. Prov. 28:9; Deut. 31:18; 1 Sam. 8:18.
52. Is. 1:15.
53. Is. 29:13; Am. 5:21; Prov. 1:28.
54. Prov. 21:13.
55. Sir. 17:25.
56. Jer. 15:1.
57. Jer. 7:16; 11:14; 14:11.

58. Gen. 18:23; 1 Sam. 1:9, 26; 3 Kgs. 8:22; Jer. 18:20.
59. 3 Kgs. 8:54; Is. 45:23; Dan. 6:11; Ps. 95:6; Esdr. 9:3.
60. 2 Sam. 7:18.
61. Gen. 24:26; Num. 14:5; 16:22; Jos. 7:6; 1 Sam. 1:3, 19; Jud. 9:1.
62. 4 Kgs. 20:2.

ing them before entering the temple was also indicative of a reverential spirit.

c) *Humility.* Before God man is nothing, "a dust particle on the balance[63] .... a torn off leaf, a dried up stalk."[64] By raising or extending hands man shows that he awaits all things from God. This gesture is so characteristic of prayer that "to extend hands" is synonymous with "to pray."[65] The sapiential writers advise us to remain humbly aware of the distance that separates us from God.[66]

d) *Devotion.* To eliminate external distractions, which so easily destroy recollection at prayer, the pious man withdraws from noise, preferably to the roof or upper chambers.[67] Elevated places are excellent spots for prayer because one gets the feeling of being closer to God.[68] A sanctuary where God manifested Himself[69] is always well adapted to further devotion.[70] In the temple the Israelite turned toward the Holy of Holies,[71] away from the temple he longed for Jerusalem and its shrines.[72] Sirach's advice, "Do not multiply words at prayer,"[73] did not imply a criticism of repetition as expressive of zeal or need for help,[74] but was directed against the notion that words are more essential than recollection and good will. Lengthier prayers could be said with great interior devotion, witness the psalms, Moses' plea that Yahweh spare the people,[75] Solomon's prayer at the dedication of the temple,[76] the prayer in Is. 63:7-64:11, Daniel's petition for the deliverance of the people,[77] the cry of the exiles,[78] Israel's confession of sin through the mouth of Esdras.[79] Familiarity with meditative prayer is reflected in the psalms which tell of God's operations in nature and in the history of Israel, or describe His power, wisdom, mercy.

e) *Trust.* Since God rules the world and is deeply concerned in every one's well-being,[80] we have every reason to look up to Him with confidence.[81] We ought see in Him our father,[82] and at prayer express our childlike trust.[83] Every appeal to God's omnipotence, justice, or mercy reflects a spirit of trust. To strengthen our confidence in God we should love to meditate upon the divine help tendered to men in times past and upon the divine promises.[84]

f) *Resignation.* God is absolutely free, His decisions are unconstrained. He need not and does not always hear the just man's cries. In vain Moses petitioned Yahweh to be allowed to enter the land of his desires.[85] Anna besought a child at many pilgrimages.[86] In vain Samuel prayed for Saul the whole night through.[87] David's child died in spite of his pleadings.[88] The author of Ps. 39 implored help without seeing the end to his sufferings. Job contended with

63. Is. 40:15; Wis. 11:22.
64. Job 13:25; § 9:2.
65. Cf. Ex. 9:29; 3 Kgs. 8:22, 54; Is. 1:15; Pss. 28:2; 63:5; 119:48; 134:2; 141:2; Sir. 48:20.
66. Qoh. 5:1; § 30.
67. Dan. 6:11; Tob. 3:11; Jud. 8:5.
68. 1 Sam. 9:12; 3 Kgs. 18:42.
69. Cf. § 11:3.
70. 1 Sam. 1:9; 9:12; 3 Kgs.

8:29-30; 4 Kgs. 19:14f; Is. 56:7; § 33:7a.
71. Pss. 5:8; 28:2; 138:2.
72. 3 Kgs. 8:38, 44, 48; Dan. 6:11.
73. Sir. 7:14.
74. Cf. Pss. 136; 148-150.
75. Num. 14:13-19.
76. 3 Kgs. 8:22-53.
77. Dan. 9:4-19.
78. Bar. 1:15-3:8.
79. Esdr. 9:6-15.
80. § 25:3, 5.

81. § 28:2.
82. § 16:4, 5.
83. Pss. 3:3-5; 9:10-11; 13:6; 23:1-4; 25:2, 11; 27:10; 46:2-3, 8; Jud. 9:17; 130.
84. Gen. 32:10; 48:15; 49:24; Ps. 22:4-5.
85. Deut. 3:23-28; Num. 20:12.
86. 1 Sam. 1:4f.
87. 1 Sam. 15:11.
88. 2 Sam. 12:18.

God till he was exhausted.[89] In similar cases we must make an act of trust realizing that God's ways are not our ways, and God's thoughts are not our thoughts.[90] We cannot comprehend God's decrees,[91] for He has His own prudent purposes when He delays the fulfillment of a petition or denies it altogether. Perhaps the reason is to punish us, as was the case with Moses and David, or to prove our perseverance, as with Anna and Job;[92] perhaps He has decreed to grant our plea in other and better ways, as when He empowered Samuel to give Israel a king who would act after God's own heart.[93] Judith criticized the suggestion to surrender the city after five days in case no deliverance came—as if men were permitted to determine the time when God should intervene.[94]

g) *Perseverance.* Because your prayer is not immediately answered is no reason to discontinue. God first granted Abraham's petition for a son after all human hope had vanished. The Israelites entreated Samuel to pray for them without ceasing.[95] Nehemias prayed day and night for Israel.[96] Besieged by Holofernes the Israelites besought God for help the whole night long.[97] In distress the pious man prays "day and night,"[98] or "at morning and at evening,"[99] i.e., perseveringly.

3. TIME OF PRAYER. Though no particular time is specified for prayer, the pious man feels himself moved to thank God already "in the middle of the night"[100] and praises Him "seven times a day,"[101] i.e., continually. He takes daily prayer for granted.[102] Daniel prayed three times daily.[103] The psalmist asserts, "In the morning I carry my cry before you[104].... Already at dawn I arise."[105] Esdras[106] and Daniel[107] prayed at the time of the evening sacrifice in accordance with the sentiments expressed in Ps. 141:2. Every morning and evening a burnt-offering and an incense-offering were made in the temple for the people;[108] every morning and evening the Levites prayed in the temple.[109] At these hours zealous Hebrews visualized themselves in the Holy Place and participated in the sacrifice and the common prayer. In apostolic times prayer was made at the sixth and the ninth hours.[110]

4. COMMON PRAYER. As the expression of one's inner spirit, prayer is a very personal act. As examples of individuals at prayer we may recall Eve, the patriarchs, Agar,[111] Abraham's servant,[112] Lea and Rachel,[113] Moses, Anna,[114] Elias, Jeremias. In the psalter the Israelite found prayer forms in which he could give expression to his joy in God, his gratitude, his repentance, his afflictions. Because Israel was God's people she should serve Him, praise Him, thank Him, petition Him as one body. The psalter contains hymns composed for common use in the temple; in many hymns the people as a whole

89. Cf. Joel 2:14; Jon. 3:9.
90. Is. 55:8-9.
91. § 9:1.
92. § 41:4-6.
93. Cf. 1 Sam. 16:1f.
94. Jud. 8:12-17.
95. 1 Sam. 7:8.
96. Neh. 1:6.
97. Jud. 6:21.
98. Ps. 88:2.

99. Ps. 92:3; cf. Ps. 55:18.
100. Ps. 119:62.
101. Ps. 119:164.
102. Ps. 145:2.
103. Dan. 6:11, 14.
104. Ps. 5:4; cf. Pss. 59:17; 88:14; Sir. 39:5.
105. Ps. 119:147; cf. Ps. 57:9; Jud. 12:5; Wis. 16:28.

106. Esdr. 9:5.
107. Dan. 9:21.
108. Ex. 29:38-42; 30:7-8.
109. 1 Chr. 23:30.
110. Acts 3:1; 10:3-4, 9.
111. Gen. 16:11.
112. Gen. 24:12.
113. Gen. 30:1.
114. 1 Sam. 1:9.

could pour forth their heart with the same intensity as individuals. In the Gradual psalms, 120-134, they could mutually edify themselves, and heighten their longing to approach God's holy city. At common prayer a leader formulated the general sentiment and the people responded "Amen!" or "Praised be Yahweh!"[115] In Ps. 136 the congregation added to each invocation, "For his mercy endures forever."[116]

At common divine service the chant and music introduced by David tended to increase devotion.[117] Religious dances witnessed to the spirituality of their emotions and edified the bystanders.[118] Recall how the psalms frequently urge praising Yahweh "with dance and song."[119]

5. INTERCESSION. The pious man may plead with God in behalf of others— every one feels closely linked to his family and country.[120] Abraham prayed for sinful Sodom and Gomorrha,[121] and for Abimelech.[122] Isaac prayed for Rebecca.[123] God instructed Eliphaz, Baldad, and Sophar to betake themselves to Job and seek his intercession.[124] Judith demanded that the elders pray for her, and the elders requested her to pray for them.[125] The physician prays for his patients.[126] Prayer was offered for the king,[127] for the sick,[128] and the priests prayed for the heavily oppressed people.[129] The Jews of Palestine prayed for their brethren in the diaspora.[130] Prayer, like sacrifice, could be offered for pagans.[131] The intercession of a prophet was particularly efficacious.[132] Pharaoh requested Moses to ask Yahweh to turn away the plagues.[133] Moses interceded for his sister Mary,[134] and frequently in behalf of the people.[135] The Israelites asked Samuel to intercede for them.[136] Elias besought Yahweh in favor of the widow of Sarepta,[137] Jeroboam sought the services of a man of God,[138] Ezechias the aid of Isaias,[139] and Sedecias that of Jeremias.[140] Samuel was convinced that Yahweh had imposed upon him the duty of interceding for the people.[141] Daniel besought deliverance for the Jews.[142] Moses, Aaron, and Samuel continued to live in the popular mind as men whose intercession was extraordinarily effective.[143] Whenever the prophets interceded for the people or for individuals in earthly needs, their real purpose was to lead them away from sin and to strengthen their faith; thus they remained faithful to their higher mission.

During the postexilic period the belief arose that man could turn to the angels and obtain their intercession before God.[144] In Hellenistic times the Jews believed that those who had died in God's friendship could aid men here on earth. In a vision Judas Maccabeus saw the deceased high priest Onias interceding for Israel, as well as the prophet Jeremias "who prayed much for

115. 1 Chr. 16:36; Neh. 8:6.
116. Cf. the song of the three men in the fiery furnace (the *Benedicite*), Dan. 3:51-88; Tob. 8:4-8.
117. 1 Chr. 25:1f; cf. Am. 6:5.
118. Ex. 15:20; 2 Sam. 6:5, 14, 21.
119. Pss. 149:3; 150:4.
120. § 26:5.
121. Gen. 18:22-31.
122. Gen. 20:7, 17.
123. Gen. 25:21.

124. Job 42:8.
125. Jud. 8:35, 31.
126. Sir. 38:14.
127. Ps. 20.
128. Ps. 35:13.
129. Joel 2:17.
130. 2 Mach. 1:6.
131. Bar. 1:11; 1 Mach. 12:11.
132. 3 Kgs. 17:1f.
133. Ex. 8:4; 9:27; 10:17.
134. Num. 12:13.
135. Ex. 5:22-23; 32:11-14,

30-32; Num. 11:2; 14:13-19; 16:22; 21:7.
136. 1 Sam. 7:8; 12:19.
137. 3 Kgs. 17:20.
138. 3 Kgs. 13:6.
139. 4 Kgs. 19:4.
140. Jer. 37:3.
141. 1 Sam. 12:23.
142. Dan. 9:7.
143. Ps. 99:6; Jer. 15:1; Sir. 46:16; Wis. 18:21.
144. § 20:4a.

the people and the holy city."[145] We have specific information that the living offered expiatory prayers and sacrifices for the dead in the Maccabean era.[146]

6. VALUE OF PRAYER. Prayer was highly esteemed in Israel. A sinner who failed to obtain forgiveness by sacrifices could become reconciled with God through prayer or through the intercession of an upright man.[147] From the very beginning prayer had its place alongside sacrifice; for sacrifice and prayer are complementary, not mutually exclusive. Sacrifice itself is a prayer even when not accompanied with words; by prayer and sacrifice man expresses his subjection to God's will and makes known to Him his anxieties. The expression, "to call upon the name of Yahweh," simply refers to prayer made at places of sacrifice.[148] Sacrifice was accompanied with prayer, e.g., before going out to battle,[149] at thank-offerings,[150] on the feast of Tabernacles,[151] at the fulfillment of a votive-offering,[152] at the morning sacrifice.[153] Job 42:8 shows the close relationship between sacrifice and prayer. The pious Israelite yearned to be present at the sanctuary to sacrifice and pray.[154] Apart from the psalms and the priestly blessing,[155] the OT contains relatively few prayer forms. Deuteronomy gives a specific formula for use at the payment of the firstfruits[156] and of third year tithes.[157] The "Shema(" and the "Shemone (esre" belong to NT times. When the regular sacrificial cult ceased during the exile, prayer assumed a more prominent role. After the exile this continued to be true in the diaspora.

The Pharisees overemphasized the externals of prayer. During prayer they fastened on the left arm and forehead little leather strips, phylacteries,[158] upon which were written the four passages, Ex. 13:1-10, 11-16; Deut. 6:4-9; 11:13-21, to show they observed literally the injunction, "Let it be a sign on your hand and a mark between your eyes."[159] The meaning actually intended however was that man should obey the Law and always be mindful of it. Moreover to gain public attention they loved to pray in public places, with loud voices,[160] for long periods.[161] If only their lives had harmonized with their prayers![162]

7. BLESSINGS AND CURSES AS PRAYER FORMS. A blessing consists in beseeching God to grant a particular person or group of persons temporal or spiritual benefits. Those who held an official position in the family or state had a special right to bless, viz., fathers, e.g., Noe,[163] Isaac,[164] Jacob;[165] relatives, e.g., Rebecca's family;[166] kings, e.g., Melchisedech,[167] David,[168] Solomon;[169] prophets, e.g., Moses,[170] Balaam;[171] priests.[172] According to Oriental and Israelitic conceptions a blessing had a certain power by and of itself, particularly if God was expressly invoked; Isaac therefore would not recall the blessing he had spoken over Jacob.[173]

---

145. 2 Mach. 15:12-14.
146. 2 Mach. 12:42-46; § 43:5.
147. § 33:2c.
148. Gen. 4:26; 12:8; 13:4; 21:33; 26:25.
149. Ps. 20.
150. Pss. 21; 66; 116.
151. Ps. 118.
152. Ps. 65.
153. Ps. 5; 1 Sam. 7:9; 2 Chr. 29:27f; 1 Mach. 12:11; Job 42:8.

154. § 32:7a.
155. Num. 6:24.
156. Deut. 26:3-10.
157. Deut. 26:13-15; another example is had in Deut. 21:7-8.
158. Matth. 23:5.
159. Ex. 13:9, 16; Deut. 6:8; 11:18.
160. Matth. 6:5.
161. Matth. 23:14.
162. Matth. 15:7-9.

163. Gen. 9:26-27.
164. Gen. 27:28.
165. Gen. 48:15; 49:1-28.
166. Gen. 24:60.
167. Gen. 14:19.
168. 2 Sam. 6:18.
169. 3 Kgs. 8:54-61.
170. Deut. 33.
171. Num. 23; 24.
172. Num. 6:24-26.
173. Gen. 27:33, 37.

God's mercy is appealed to when blessings are invoked, God's justice when
a curse is imposed. A curse once uttered was believed to have a certain efficacy
in itself. The Moabites sought to curse Israel through the person of the seer
Balaam and thereby to destroy them.[174] When Semei cursed David, David did
not allow his companions to avenge the act; he accepted the humiliation as if
willed by God and hoped to gain mercy by bearing it, "Perhaps Yahweh will
take note of my *distress* and recompense me with good in place of the curse
which today has come upon me."[175] Nevertheless he feared that after his death
the curse would be effective upon his children if Semei continued to live.[176]
When a thief remained undetected the injured person took vengeance by calling
down God's punishment upon the guilty person.[177] The Law instructed priests
how to impose a curse upon women suspected of adultery; the curse would be
effective only if the sin had been committed.[178]

In all cases blessings and curses were conditional. The blessing of a father
did not benefit children who led evil lives and deserved their mother's curse.[179]
Nor did the blessing of a bad priest have any value.[180] Long before the time
of the exile people knew that an undeserved curse need not be feared, "Like
a sparrow that escapes, or a swallow that soars away, so is an unjustified curse:
it shall not take effect."[181] The text listing the blessings and curses in Lev. 26
and Deut. 28 adequately shows the intimate relationship between observance
of the Law and God's intervention for good or evil. The pious man does not
fear the curses of the godless, "When they curse, may you bless."[182]

No magical power was ascribed to blessings and curses. Imprecations and
benedictions did not produce their effects infallibly; they did not force Yahweh
to act pro or con. OT prayer forms were not incantations. Against such interpretation note that God does not answer every prayer[183] and that legitimate
proponents of OT religion always inveighed against incantation and magic.[184]

§ 36. VOWS

1. GENERAL CONSIDERATIONS. A vow is a freely made promise to dedicate
oneself or part of one's possessions to God, or to deny oneself some legitimate
pleasure, such as wine or marital intercourse. An Israelite could dedicate himself by a vow to serve God at the sanctuary; parents could vow their children
to God, as did Anna who brought her boy Samuel to the tabernacle at Shiloh.[1]
Jacob vowed to offer the tenth of his possessions.[2] In Ps. 76:12 the citizens of
Jerusalem are urged to make a vow, in this instance, a thank-offering. Regulations
for votive-offerings are given in Lev. 7:16; 22:21. Vows were more readily
made on occasions when trouble threatened, e.g., when Jacob was forced to
flee to Mesopotamia,[3] when the Israelites were harassed by the Canaanites,[4]

174. Num. 22:6, 15, 37.　　178. Num. 5:19f.　　　　182. Ps. 109:28.
175. 2 Sam. 16:5-12.　　　 179. Sir. 3:9.　　　　　 183. § 35:2f.
176. 3 Kgs. 2:8-9.　　　　 180. Mal. 2:2.　　　　　 184. § 28:1c; on the cursing
177. Judg. 17:2; cf. Lev. 5:1;　181. Prov. 26:2.　　　　　　psalms, cf. § 32:1fg.
　　　Prov. 29:24.
1. 1 Sam. 1:11, 22.　　　　3. Gen. 28:20.　　　　　4. Num. 21:2.
2. Gen. 28:20-22.

when Jephte was about to go into battle,[5] when the tempest struck Jonas' boat,[6] when Anna saw her misery,[7] when the just man fell into misfortune.[8] Vows by sick persons and those in distress were generally conditional: if God aided them they in return would make an offering. Effects already belonging to Yahweh according to the Law, e.g., the first-born, could not serve as matter for a vow;[9] excluded too were seriously deformed animals[10] and the wages a harlot obtained for sin.[11]

2. OBLIGATORY CHARACTER. Before a vow bound it had to be clearly formulated; the mere thought was not sufficient.[12] According to the Law and the sages no one was in any way obliged to make a vow; both stressed prudence and reserve, but insisted that vows once made must be kept.[13] Jephte's was an example of an ill-considered vow.[14] If anyone rashly made a vow and then discovered it was impossible for him to keep it, he was bound to offer an expiatory sacrifice.[15] Whoever could dispose of property in his own name, viz., a male adult, a widow, a divorced woman, was bound by the vows he had made.[16] Fathers retained the right to annul the vows of children still under their care.[17] If a girl had made a vow of chastity before marriage, her husband had the right to declare it void.[19] Silence was considered as consent; objections had to be voiced within a day in order to nullify the vow. It was permitted to change the content of a vow, to give a substitute for the thing promised. A person who had dedicated himself, his child or a slave to God (apart from a Nazirite vow) could fulfill his promise by giving to the sanctuary an amount in accordance with the age and sex of the one so offered.[20]

3. NAZIRITE VOWS. From motives of divine love the Nazirite (from *nazar*, to cut off, keep oneself from) vowed to lead a life of self-denial and mortification. Women too could bind themselves by this type of vow,[21] but, as with every vow, were bound to obtain the consent of their husbands.[22] This vow could be made for life (Samuel,[23] Samson,[24] John the Baptist[25]) or for a specified time; later law required a minimum of thirty days.[26] Mention is made of temporary Nazirite vows in 1 Mach. 3:49. The Nazirite was obliged to avoid the use of wine and intoxicating drink and model his ways upon the simple life of the Israelites in the wilderness. He was not permitted to cut his hair (hair being regarded as a sign of vitality), for he had vowed his life and all his strength to Yahweh—Samson's strength went with his hair.[27] Lastly a Nazirite was not permitted to approach a corpse, not even at the death of his nearest relatives, because such an act would render him unclean.[28] Dedication to Yahweh rated higher than piety towards parents, brothers and sisters; in

5. Judg. 11:30.
6. Jon. 1:16.
7. 1 Sam. 1:11f.
8. Ps. 116:18; cf. Ps. 22:26.
9. Lev. 27:26.
10. Mal. 1:14.
11. Deut. 23:19.
12. Num. 30:3, 7, 13; Deut. 23:24.
13. Deut. 23:22-24; Prov. 20-
25; Qoh. 5:3-4; Sir. 18:22-23.
14. Judg. 11:30; § 33:4.
15. Lev. 5:4-6.
16. Num. 30:3, 10.
17. Num. 30:4-6; § 31:3a.
18. Num. 30:7-9.
19. Num. 30:11-16.
20. Lev. 27:1-8.
21. Num. 6:2.
22. Cf. Jos. Bell. 2, 15, 1 § 310.
23. 1 Sam. 1:11.
24. Judg. 13:5, 7.
25. Lk. 1:15.
26. Bell. 2, 15, 1 § 313.
27. Judg. 16:17-20.
28. § 30:4; 32:1i.

this he resembled the high priest.[29] Concern over external cleanliness should effect a still greater concern for inner purity of heart.

4. EVALUATION OF VOWS. A vow implies the acknowledgment of God as supreme Lord. To supplement a petition with a vow is not tantamount to mistrust or selfishness. When Anna vowed to dedicate to God the son she was seeking,[30] she showed the greatest selflessness, being willing to forego the joys of motherhood as soon as the child could serve in the tabernacle. Her petition was accompanied by a great spirit of self-denial. Upon having his petition answered, the pious man is grateful to God for the opportunity of fulfilling his vow. In Ps. 65 the people gratefully paid their vow to Yahweh for having terminated a great drought; in Ps. 116:18 the psalmist is grateful for having been delivered from death, and in v. 10 tells how great his trust had been during the trial, how he had relied not upon man but only upon God. Since vows are an excellent form of prayer, they will continue to be made and kept in messianic times.[31] The object of a Nazirite vow was the greatest good man possesses: one's own person, and therefore Philo rightfully called it "the great vow."[32] The decision to make a Nazirite vow rested upon divine grace.[33] Instances of this vow are not absent from the New Testament.[34] Later OT writers inveighed against vows which went counter to natural law or to moral duties imposed by the covenant.[35]

§ 37. FASTING

1. PURPOSE. There is frequent mention in the OT of abstinence from food and drink for a shorter or longer period due to motives of penance.[1] The Law however prescribed but one general fast day, the Day of Atonement.[2] It afforded the Israelites an occasion for private and national penance, an occasion for heartfelt contrition and resolute amendment. In Babylon the exiles introduced new fast days to commemorate the destruction of Jerusalem and the temple, since they were aware of having caused that tragedy by their sins.[3] "Esther's Fast" before the feast of Purim[4] quite probably was not observed in Biblical times. Apart from these regular fast days the people abstained from food on special occasions to ward off just punishment, for instance, after a sermon on penance by Samuel,[5] during the exile,[6] because of a locust plague.[7] The fasting of the Ninevites deserves special mention.[8] Fasting was resorted to as a means to reinforce prayers of petition, for example, before the exiles began their homeward march under Esdras,[9] before great battles,[10] while the Jews were being threatened with massacre in Persia.[11]

29. Lev. 21:11.
30. 1 Sam. 1:10f.
31. Is. 19:21.
32. De Spec. Leg. I 247, 248;
1. Concerning the non-use of certain foods, cf. § 30:6; § 32:1i.
2. Lev. 16:29; 23:26-32; Num. 29:7; § 34:5.
3. Zach. 7:5; 8:19.

Leg. Alleg. I 17; Quod Deus Sit Immut. 87.
33. Am. 2:11.
4. Cf. Esth. 4:16; 9:31.
5. 1 Sam. 7:6.
6. Bar. 1:5.
7. Joel 1:14; 2:12.
8. Jon. 3:5-7.

34. Acts 21:23f; cf. Acts 18:18.
35. Cf. § 31:3b; concerning oaths, § 28:5.
9. Esdr. 8:21.
10. Judg. 20:26; 1 Sam. 14:24; 2 Chr. 20:3; Jud. 4:12; 1 Mach. 3:47; 2 Mach. 13:12.
11. Esth. 4:3, 16.

Individuals fasted in order to gain God's good favor, e.g., Achab, when Elias foretold his punishment,[12] Esdras, when sorrowing over the sinfulness of the returned exiles,[13] David, when his child lay grievously ill,[14] Nehemias, upon receiving the news that enemies had torn down the walls of Jerusalem and burnt the gates,[15] Esther, while preparing for the audience upon which the fate of her nation hung,[16] the psalmist, when petitioning health for sick enemies.[17] By a life of penance Judith sought to honor God and to gain His good pleasure.[18] Fasting prepared the soul for divine enlightenment, as is shown in Daniel's life.[19] Moses fasted for the forty days during which he enjoyed intimate intercourse with God on Mt. Horeb.[20] Before the paschal meal a fast was kept in order to prepare for the celebration.

Fasting was commonplace at the death of someone near and dear. The inhabitants of Jabesh fasted after they had buried Saul and his sons.[21] David fasted when notified of the deaths of Saul and Jonathan[22] and after the death of Abner.[23] These fasts had no religious significance; they followed from natural sorrow over the deceased, the survivors simply had no appetite for food. With this kind of fasting pious Israelites may have subconsciously wished Yahweh to show mercy and preserve them from an early or untimely death.

2. DURATION. The ordinary fast lasted one day, from evening to evening (since the Hebrew day began with sunset). This held for the fast on the Day of Atonement[24] and for all general and private fasts.[25] No food or drink was taken. If the fast was of longer duration only so much was eaten as was needed to keep alive, the food being of the simplest kind.[26] The symbolic numbers 3 and 7 usually determined the length of these fasts.[27] Longer ones are mentioned in Neh. 1:4; Jud. 4:12; Dan. 10:2-3. Exceptional are the 40 day fast of Moses[28] and the lifelong fast of Judith.[29]

3. VALUE. Fasting is found in very many religions. It satisfies the need of voluntarily assuming mortification in order to appease an angered God, or to implore help in misfortune. By fasting the Israelites sought to satisfy divine justice, for while fasting they often acknowledged having sinned, shed tears of contrition and wore penitential garb.[30] Since this grave spirit could not be harmonized with the joyous spirit of feasts, fasting was not in order on the Sabbath and on feasts.[31] As a penitential act fasting had great spiritual value, and through the prophets God sought to encourage its practice.[32] When Achab showed his repentance by fasting, Yahweh softened the punishment.[33] To the Ninevites He showed mercy when by fasting they manifested a spirit of penance.[34] "Prayer is good with fasting and almsgiving and righteousness."[35]

12. 3 Kgs. 21:27.
13. Esdr. 10:6.
14. 2 Sam. 12:16, 22.
15. Neh. 1:4.
16. Esth. 4:16.
17. Ps. 35:13.
18. Jud. 8:6.
19. Dan. 9:3; 10:2.
20. Ex. 24:18; 34:28; Deut. 9:9.

21. 1 Sam. 31:13.
22. 2 Sam. 1:12.
23. 2 Sam. 3:35.
24. Lev. 16:29.
25. Judg. 20:26; 1 Sam. 7:6; 2 Sam. 1:12; 3:35.
26. Cf. Dan. 10:3.
27. Esth. 4:16; 2 Mach. 13:12; 1 Sam. 31:13.
28. Ex. 24:18.

29. Jud. 8:6.
30. 1 Sam. 7:6; 3 Kgs. 21:27; Joel 1:13; Jon. 3:5f; Ps. 35:13; 1 Mach. 3:47.
31. Jud. 8:6.
32. 1 Sam. 7:2f; Joel 2:12.
33. 3 Kgs. 21:27-28.
34. Jon. 3:10.
35. Tob. 12:8.

Jesus fasted,[36] counselled fasting as meritorious and pleasing to the Father,[37] foretold that His disciples would fast.[38] However only such fasting as is done in a spirit of penance or humbly to beg some favor has value, not the act in itself. Nevertheless many Israelites believed God could be appeased simply by offering sacrifices, or by abstaining from food and drink without inner conversion from sin and vice. Jeremias was given an unpleasant reception when at a fast sponsored by the authorities he ordered Baruch to read a comminatory speech in which he reminded the Jews of their sins and urged them to do penance—he and Baruch were obliged to hide in order to escape the wrath of the king, while the people remained untouched.[39] Fasting with such a spirit is worthless before God.[40] Equally worthless is it to fast for the purpose of obtaining wealth, or to fast while exploiting laborers of due wages, or while harboring an angry, resentful spirit. Fasting must be interlarded with works of brotherly love.[41] Zacharias reminded those who had returned from Babylon how they had sought their own interests by the fasts introduced during the exile—what God really wanted was justice, mercy, love.[42] The same theology is found in wisdom literature: the sinner gets no benefit from fasting if he does not amend his ways.[43] Worse still was the fasting of Pharisees done in order to be seen and honored as pious by the populace.[44]

SECTION 3. MAN AND GOD'S COMMANDMENTS

§ 38. SIN

1. THE NATURE OF SIN. Because man is a creature he is duty bound to obey God; any disregard of this duty involves sin. As shown in the Paradise Account sin is not an imperfection inherent in nature, but a conscious and considered act against God's authority. To the injunction and warning of the prophets the Jews replied, "We do not wish to follow it (the path of the just), we do not wish to listen."[1] The root of sin is pride. Our first parents let themselves be beguiled by the promise, "You shall be like God."[2] At Babylon proud men strove to build a tower whose top would reach heaven.[3] Isaias characterizes sin as pride; the proud will not humble themselves before God, and accordingly will be smitten to the dust—"Yahweh alone will be exalted on that day."[4] When Yahweh comes to judge, prophesied Sophonias, "he will liquidate the haughty boasters from Israel's midst, and pride no longer will be nurtured upon his holy mount."[5] The principal sin for which the nations will be punished is pride.[6]

An offense against one's neighbor is also an offense against God. Violating another's wife is a crime against Yahweh.[7] David's adultery "displeased Yah-

36. Matth. 4:2.
37. Matth. 6:17-18.
38. Matth. 9:14-15; cf. Acts 13:2-3; 14:22.
39. Jer. 36.
40. Jer. 14:12.
41. Is. 58:3-7.
42. Zach. 7:5; 8-10.
43. Sir. 34:30-31.
44. Matth. 6:16; Lk. 18:12-14.

1. Jer. 6:16-17.
2. Gen. 3:5.
3. Gen. 11:4.
4. Is. 2:11, 17.
5. Soph. 3:11.
6. § 45:4.
7. Judg. 19:25; 20:6, 13.

weh;"[8] the king acknowledged, "I have sinned against Yahweh."[9] Since the whole man belongs to God, even thoughts against Him and His commands are sinful.[10]

Sin is rebellion against Yahweh,[11] apostasy from Yahweh,[12] contempt for Yahweh,[13] infidelity,[14] violation of the covenant.[15] Because God's relationship to Israel was regarded as a marital one,[16] sin was equivalent to adultery[17] and harlotry.[18] Sin is foolishness because it contradicts an omniscient and omnipotent God and produces the very opposite of what man wishes[19]—the sinner is a fool.[20] Every sin goes counter to God's truthfulness and accordingly shares in the nature of a lie or of deceit.[21] God is continually granting us many benefits; to oppose Him is base ingratitude.[22]

The more common words for sin are: *het)*, *hatta)th*, *hatta)ah* (derived from *hata)*, to miss the mark, to err from the right way, to do what is forbidden, to omit what is prescribed). Of frequent occurrence are: *(awon* (from *(awah*, to bend, twist, err from the right way through evil disposition) translated as iniquity, guilt; *(awel* and *(awlah* (from *(ul*, to corrupt,) perversity, falsehood; *pesa(* (from *pesa(*, to be rebellious), apostasy, rebellion, infidelity. The latter word points to the violation of the covenant relationship;[23] the same is true of *ma(al*, treachery, infidelity. The sinner revolts, *marad;* he is obstinate and stubborn, *sarar, marah.* Other common words are *ra(* and *ra(ah*, evil, wickedness, *)asam*, trespass, fault, *)wen*, vanity, iniquity, *nebalah, sikhluth;* foolishness (cf. *nabal, sakhal,* fool), *resa(, ris(ah*, evil, wickedness; the word *rasa(*, evildoer, is frequently used of habitual sinners.

2. RESPONSIBILITY FOR SIN. Since man has free will,[24] he can subject himself to God or can act counter to God's wishes. Adam and Eve should and could have obeyed the divine command, but they chose to follow their own desires. Yahweh said to Cain, "If you do not act uprightly, will not sin lurk at the door and its demands pursue you, over which you ought to be master?"[25] From the "heart" of man, the seat of his thinking and emotion,[26] arises sin.[27] Man may be moved to sin from without, but the decision to yield comes from within, and accordingly he is responsible. The leaning toward sin which every one experiences is in itself no sin; it can be overcome. Satan has no power to force us to do evil;[28] if God "tempts" it is only to give us an opportunity to prove our worth, and the phrase, "he blinds," is only an expression for the misuse of divine graces.[29] No man may blame God for his sins.[30] Lack of grace is not the reason for sin or for persevering in sin, but evil will, "You do not heed my cry, no one notices my outstretched hand; my every counsel you cast to

8. 2 Sam. 11:27.
9. 2 Sam. 12:13.
10. Ex. 20:17.
11. Num. 14:9; Deut. 28:15, 45; Is. 30:9; Ez. 2:3, 8; 3:9; 44:6.
12. Is. 1:4; 46:8; Jer. 2:5; Os. 4:12.
13. Is. 1:4; Mal. 1:6.
14. Is. 48:8; Jer. 3:20; 9:1.
15. Is. 24:5; Jer. 11:10; Ez. 16:59; Os. 6:7; Mal. 2:10.

16. § 16:4.
17. Jer. 3:8; 13:27; Ez. 16:32; 23:43.
18. Lev. 17:7; 20:5-6; Deut. 31:16; Ez. 6:9; 23:30.
19. Gen. 34:7; Deut. 32:6; Jos. 7:15; Judg. 20:6, 10; Jer. 29:23.
20. Is. 32:5-6; Pss. 14:1; 39:9; 53:2.
21. Is. 57:4; Os. 12:1; Pss. 4:5; 5:7.

22. Is. 1:2-3; Am. 2:9-11; Os. 11:1-4.
23. L. Köhler, ZatW 46, 1928, 213-218.
24. § 26:5.
25. Gen. 4:7.
26. § 26:3d.
27. Gen. 6:5; 8:21; Jer. 4:4; Ez. 11:19; Ps. 51:12.
28. § 23:4.
29. § 11:4c; 20:7; 25:6.
30. Sir. 15:11-17.

he wind, you accept none of my reproof."[31] God reproached obstinate Jerusa-em, "I have endeavored to cleanse you, but you would not become cleansed rom your uncleanness."[32]

3. UNIVERSALITY OF SIN. When man fulfills God's will, he feels himself ust *(ṣaddiq)*, morally upright *(tam, tamim)*, good *(yašar)*, like Henoch, Noe, ob. This serves as a basis for distinguishing between the good and the wicked. However because of the infinite distance between the all-holy God and His creatures,[33] the man who strives to fulfill God's will in all things still is reckoned as a sinner, not even the angels being pure before their Maker.[34] The Israelites believed all men were sinners. Solomon prayed, "There is no person who does not sin."[35] At his call Isaias lamented, "Woe to me, I am lost, because I am a man with unclean lips," and an angel confirmed his confession by touching his lips with a burning coal, "Removed is your guilt, your sin is expiated."[36] The psalmist besought Yahweh, "Do not enter into judgment with your servant, for no living person appears just before you[37].... If you would resent mis-deeds, who could last?"[38] The sages were very explicit, "Who is able to say: I have purified my heart, am free from my sins? .... No one upon earth is so good as to do only good and never sin."[39] Eliphaz confronted Job with the question, "Is any man in the right over against God, or shall a mortal prove himself pure before his Maker?"[40] To which Baldad agreed, "How can one born of woman be pure?"[41] Job himself asserted, "There is not one who is pure among the impure."[42] "What is brighter than the sun, and even it suffers eclipses—more so *man, fashioned* from flesh and blood[43] .... Do not laugh at someone who turns away from sin; remember that we all are guilty."[44] Not even Henoch, Noe or Job should be regarded as perfectly free from sin.[45] This consciousness of sin, even when persons were unable to recall specific transgressions, gave rise to the notion that some misfortunes came as punish-ment for forgotten sins or sins not recognized as such.

As a basis for this universal sinfulness the OT does not expressly single out the fall of our first parents, but points principally to the weaknesses of men, who are "maggots[46].... dwellers in clay houses, whose foundations rest on dust."[47] Not that the body by nature is sinful, but since man is so frail, he may overcome temptation frequently, and that severe temptations, but still he will not triumph during his whole life. Upon such weakness God has com-passion and therefore forgives.[48] Yahweh "did not let them perish but fre-quently restrained his wrath; he remembered that they were flesh, merely a breath which vanishes without return[49].... He is ever mindful that we are dust."[50] The OT is very much aware that mankind is inclined to rebel, that human hearts harbor not only good but evil thoughts as well. Sinful desires

31. Prov. 1:24-25.
32. Ez. 24:13.
33. § 11:2.
34. § 22:3.
35. 3 Kgs. 8:46.
36. Is. 6:5-7.
37. Ps. 143:2.
38. Ps. 130:3.
39. Qoh. 7:20.
40. Job 4:17; cf. 15:14.
41. Job 25:4.
42. Job 14:4.
43. Sir. 17:31.
44. Sir. 8:5.
45. Gen. 5:24; 6:9; Job 1:1, 8; 2:3.
46. Job 25:6.
47. Job 4:19.
48. § 16:7.
49. Ps. 78:38-39.
50. Ps. 103:14.

are forbidden in the same way as actual sins are;[51] for this reason God "tries" the heart[52] and notes human thoughts,[53] while the sinner asks for a clean heart and a stable spirit.[54] Only those remain sinless whom God preserves[55] and whom His good spirit guides.[56] The evil man devises evil, "Deceitful beyond all measure is the heart, and full of evil. Who can fathom it?"[57] "The human mind is fully set to do evil."[58] With the Israelites it was as if a "spirit of harlotry" had taken possession of them[59] when they strayed from Yahweh;[60] they resembled animals in the time of heat, not able to withstand the surgings of lust, when in spite of all admonitions they persevered in evil.[61] As the Ethiopian cannot change his color or the panther his stripes, so the Israelites were not able to return to Yahweh; evil in them had become a second nature.[62] Ezechiel called Israel a "house of perversity" that stiffened itself against all God's efforts to effect a change of heart. Time and time again the Law and the Prophets exhorted them to circumcise their hearts, yet it became evident that for messianic times God would have to create a new spirit and new hearts.[63]

The inclination to sin appears already during youth;[64] the child is always more ready to do evil than good. It is a tendency received with birth, an inheritance as it were, "Behold, with guilt was I born, and with sin did my mother conceive me."[65] Man is descended from sinful parents and concupiscence transplants itself from them to their children, "The wicked are degenerate already from their mother's womb, even from birth liars tread evil paths."[66] This tendency to sin showed itself in the first descendants of Adam and Eve: Cain murdered his brother Abel, his posterity practiced bigamy, revenge, polygamy, and finally apostatized completely from God. In Israel too later generations imitated the evil practice of their forefathers, "Your first father already sinned, and your mediators have transgressed against me."[67] The people were "rebellious from birth."[68] Likewise the origin of the Canaanites was marked by sin, their malice inborn; the author had in mind their descent from Cham, whose sin is recounted in the deluge account.[69]

The above passages refer only to concupiscence inherited from parents. To the question, "What is the origin of this inclination to sin?" the only possible answer is: since God made man good, the tendency to sin which forms part of his inheritance must be traced back to the disobedience of the first couple in paradise, from whom all are descended. Intercourse, conception, and birth rendered individuals unclean in matters of cult,[70] but were not regarded as sinful in themselves or able to produce the tendency to sin. We all are doing penance for the sin of our first parents by suffering and dying, since "through a woman sin had its beginning, and because of her we all must die[71].... through the envy of the devil death has come into the world;"[72] easily and

51. Ez. 20:17.
52. Ps. 17:3.
53. Ps. 94:11.
54. Ps. 51:12.
55. Ps. 19:14.
56. Ps. 143:10.
57. Jer. 17:9.
58. Qoh. 8:11; Ps. 73:7.

59. Os. 4:12; 5:4.
60. § 20:7.
61. Jer. 2:23-25.
62. Jer. 13:13.
63. § 47:3.
64. Gen. 8:21.
65. Ps. 51:7.

66. Ps. 58:4.
67. Is. 43:27.
68. Is. 48:8; cf. Ez. 16; 23.
69. Gen. 9:22.
70. Lev. 12:1f; 15:16-18.
71. Sir. 25:25.
72. Wis. 2:24.

logically then we arrive at the conclusion that the sin in paradise is imputed
to all men as guilt and is the reason why we carry in ourselves the inclination
to evil. There is no reference to original sin in Jer. 1:5, "Before I fashioned
you in the womb of your mother, I chose you, and before you left the womb
I sanctified you;" *sanctify* here parallels *chose* and is to be understood in the
common meaning of *dedicating, equipping.* Sir. 49:7M only implies that Jeremias was marked for the office of a prophet from the womb. Wis. 8:20,
"Being good I (i.e., the soul) entered a spotless body," presents no difficulty
against the doctrine of original sin because the author was simply describing
Solomon's innocence from personal sin at conception.

4. DISTINCTIONS BETWEEN SINS. Apart from the division, sins of thought,
word, and deed, the OT distinguished between sins of omission and sins of
commission. Heli sinned by not correcting the evil acts of his sons.[73] To omit
circumcision or to fail to keep the paschal meal was morally wrong.[74] More
important is the distinction between greater and lesser sins. "Faults" and
"hidden sins"[75] were such as every one committed from human weakness, from
lack of advertence or from inadequate knowledge of the Law. Over against
this class were those sins committed "with uplifted hand,"[76] i.e., with full
deliberation, with malice, in open revolt against God. Such "deserved death,"[77]
and persons who transgressed in this manner should "be cursed."[78] Misleading
another into idolatry or oppressing a woman rendered one a "son of Belial,"[79]
i.e., thoroughly depraved (Belial may also refer to an evil spirit).[80] The sons
of Heli were "sons of Belial,"[81] also the false witnesses responsible for Naboth's
death.[82] The phrase, "daughters of Belial," designated women who became in-
toxicated at peace-offerings.[83] The death penalty by stoning was to be exacted
by the people as the divinely appointed authority; this showed that they were
not to condone grave crimes, "You must blot out evil from your midst."[84] In
other cases the Israelites expected that God would bring a speedy death upon
the sinner. Catastrophe came to the Sodomites because their sins were "very
great."[85] The sin of the sons of Heli was "very great before Yahweh"[86] before
they fell in battle. Because the service of idols in the temple was a "great
abomination,"[87] Jerusalem perished and the temple was destroyed.

Grave sins included the worship of idols,[88] tempting others to idolatry,[89]
magic,[90] divination and the use of mediums,[91] blasphemy,[92] violation of the
Sabbath,[93] working on the Day of Atonement,[94] honoring images,[95] observing
pagan practices,[96] omitting circumcision[97] or the celebration of the Pasch.[98]
using leavened bread on the Pasch,[99] violating the fast on the Day of Atone-

73. 1 Sam. 3:13.
74. Gen. 17:14; Num. 9:13.
75. Ps. 19:13.
76. Num. 15:30.
77. Num. 18:22.
78. Deut. 26:15-26.
79. Deut. 13:14; Judg. 19:22;
    20:13.
80. P. Joüon, Bb 5, 1924,
    178-183.
81. 1 Sam. 2:12.

82. 3 Kgs. 21:10; cf. 1 Sam.
    1:16; 25:17, 25.
83. 1 Sam. 1:16.
84. Deut. 13:6; 17:7; 19:19;
    22:21-24; 24:7.
85. Gen. 18:20.
86. 1 Sam. 2:17.
87. Ez. 8:6.
88. Ex. 22:19; Lev. 20:2;
    Deut. 13:13-18; 17:2-7.
89. Deut. 13:2-12.

90. Ex. 22:17; Lev. 20:27.
91. Lev. 19:26, 31; 20:6, 27.
92. Lev. 24:11-16.
93. Ex. 31:14; Num. 15:32-
    36.
94. Lev. 23:30.
95. Ex. 20:4; 32:1, 21.
96. Lev. 19:27.
97. Gen. 17:14.
98. Num. 9:13.
99. Ex. 12:19.

ment,[100] eating blood, portions reserved for the altar[101] or flesh offered while unclean,[102] omitting purification after touching a corpse,[103] using the oils for anointing and sacred incense for profane purposes.[104] Other transgressions serious enough to be punished by death included murder,[105] rebelling against parents,[106] kidnapping,[107] giving false testimony in criminal cases,[108] defying the decision of the highest priestly court,[109] adultery and other serious sins of impurity, marrying near relatives,[110] certain forms of harlotry,[111] unnatural lust.[112] Transgressions not punishable by death but regarded as grave sins: stealing,[113] inflicting serious physical injury,[114] slandering one's wife,[115] attacking another by the sex organs during a fight,[116] slandering another,[117] sinning against purity.[118] Lust for another's wife or for the property of a neighbor was gravely sinful because forbidden in the decalog;[119] jealousy and hate was condemned in the story of Cain and Abel.[120] The gravity of sins varied, murder and murder of parents were not equally grave, lust on the part of unmarried girls and adultery were less grievous than the crime of those who had intercourse with the prostitutes at Canaanite temples, for the latter act implied apostasy from Yahweh.[121] We find the four sins crying to heaven for vengeance: murder ("Loudly the blood of your brother cries to me from the earth"[122]), sodomy ("The complaint against Sodom and Gomorrah—indeed it is great"[123]), oppression of the poor, widows and orphans ("If she [he] cry to me, I shall hear it for I am merciful"[124]), withholding wages from laborers ("He may cry to Yahweh against you"[125]).

Sins committed in youth belong to the class of lesser sins. A young man is inexperienced, passions run rampant within him, he is easily tempted and violates God's commands not from malice but from weakness. The psalmist implores, "Do not remember the sins of my youth or my evil deeds,"[126] as he counterposes the lighter sins of youth with the more grievous sins of manhood. The "hidden" sins[127] and the "secret" sins[128] are sins which only God knows and which man is hardly conscious of—forgiveness of which he may hope for. Another cause for sin to appear in a milder light is an imperfect knowledge of the divine law; younger persons do not easily have time to meditate upon their duties and cannot evaluate the repercussions of their actions; they violate God's command but not with full knowledge and reflection.[129]

Transgressions not committed with full malice could be expiated by an atonement sacrifice or a guilt-offering.[130] For sins to which the death penalty was attached these means were insufficient. Nor were the rites on the Day of

100. Lev. 23:27-29.
101. Lev. 7:25-27.
102. Lev. 7:20-21; 22:3.
103. Num. 19:13, 20.
104. Ex. 30:33-37.
105. Ex. 21:12-14.
106. Ex. 21:15, 17; Lev. 20:9; Deut. 21:18-21.
107. Ex. 21:16; Deut. 24:7.
108. Deut. 19:16-21.
109. Deut. 17:12.
110. Lev. 18:6-23; 20:10-21; Gen. 20:9; 38:24; 39:9.
111. Lev. 21:9.
112. Ex. 22:18; Lev. 20:13, 15-16.
113. Ex. 21:37-22:3.
114. Ex. 21:23-25.
115. Deut. 22:13-19; § 31:2b.
116. Deut. 25:11.
117. § 29:3.
118. § 31:2bc.
119. Ex. 20:17.
120. Gen. 4:6-7.
121. Cf. Os. 4:14.
122. Gen. 4:10; Ex. 20:13; 21:12, 14.
123. Gen. 18:20; Lev. 18:22; 20:13.
124. Ex. 22:21-23, 26; cf. Deut. 10:18; 24:17.
125. Deut. 24:14-15; Lev. 19:13.
126. Ps. 25:7.
127. Ps. 19:13.
128. Ps. 90:8.
129. Jer. 5:4.
130. § 33:2c.

Atonement efficacious against them.[131] However the mercy of God is often
emphasized in the OT, mercy without bounds, mercy that does not stop before
sins upon which the Law laid the death sentence, and Israel in spite of all
perversity very frequently experienced that even the greatest sinner could hope
in divine mercy if only he abandoned his sin.[132] God gave our first parents
time and opportunity to do penance; He let David atone for murder and adultery,[133] and a great prophet proclaimed, "If the wicked man turn away from
the sins he has committed, and heeds my precepts and acts uprightly and justly,
he shall certainly live—he shall not die. Do I take pleasure in the death of
the godless?"[134] There were however men of "a hard forehead and an obstinate heart"[135] who did not want to know Yahweh and His will.[136] Such
were not sorry for their sins and would not stop doing evil.[137] No longer
ashamed of their wickedness[138] they felt safe despite their sins and boasted of
their sinfulness.[139] So enamored of sin did they become that "it would be an
abomination for them to reject it."[140] "They take joy in doing evil, pleasure
in malicious perversity[141].... They find no rest when not doing evil, their
sleep is gone when not misleading another[142].... Deeply imbedded in their
heart is sin."[143] They mock sacred things and holy persons[144] and boast of
their wickedness.[145] These habitual sinners who listen to no admonition will
"not be forgiven."[146] We may see in Pharaoh's case the consequences of the
misuse of grace and how one by so acting becomes hardened and will not re-
linquish evil ways. In spite of many miracles Pharaoh did not convert, he
violated his pledged word as soon as the plagues which had oppressed him
ceased, and he pursued the Israelites although he must have realized a higher
power would again intervene.[147]

5. CONSCIOUSNESS OF SIN. The nature of sin consists in rebellion against
God; the action or the omission of the action is not essential, the act of the
will is; and therefore one must know beforehand what is forbidden, what is
prescribed. The Paradise Account with striking finesse shows how doubting
God's love and truthfulness led to lust and how lust led to disobedience.[148]
Lev. 4:1-6 mentions sins which are committed "through inadvertence"
(bišegagah, from šagag, to err), i.e., at the moment when the act is posited,
the agent is unaware of violating a commandment, for example, contact with
human uncleanness or the carcass of an unclean animal.[149] In such cases an
atonement sacrifice was prescribed. Even today the uneducated find it difficult to
distinguish between formal and material sins—lying is often confused with error.
If Pharaoh and Abimelech had had relations with Sara, whom Abraham had
designated as his sister,[150] it would have been adultery objectively, not sub-
jectively, since they did not know she was married. In Gen. 26:10 Abimelech

131. § 34:5.
132. § 16:4-6; 40:3-4.
133. 2 Sam. 12:13-14.
134. Ez. 18:21-23.
135. Ez. 3:7-9.
136. Jer. 9:5.
137. Jer. 8:6.
138. Os. 4:14.
139. Am. 6:1; Is. 32:9, 11; 3:9.
140. Prov. 13:19.
141. Prov. 2:14; 15:21.
142. Prov. 4:16.
143. Ps. 36:2.
144. Ps. 1:1.
145. Wis. 2:10f.
146. Is. 22:13-14.
147. Ex. 7-10; 13-15.
148. Gen. 3:1-7.
149. Lev. 5:2-3.
150. Gen. 12:17-19; 20:1-7.

charges Isaac with presenting Rebecca as his sister, "How easily one of the people could have slept with your wife, and so you would have brought guilt upon us." Here too no distinction is made between material and formal sin. Saul pronounced the death sentence upon Jonathan who, not knowing of the abstinence vow the king and people had made, had eaten some honey; his kinsmen however espoused his cause and saved him.[151] After her son had died, the widow of Sarepta believed Elias had reminded God of sins which she herself did not know.[152] Yet in the most ancient times there are indications that distinctions were made between formal and material sins, sins committed with and without advertence. In the Abimelech story it is pointed out that the intention of committing adultery really constitutes the sin; God would have caused the king's death in case he did not return Sara after he clearly understood her condition.[153] In the Covenant Code a distinction is made between premeditated murder and unintentional homicide.[154] If a murderer was not apprehended, the community in whose territory the act was perpetuated was obliged to perform an atonement ritual because the land had been stained by the shedding of blood; but they incurred no guilt.[155] If with the best of good will one could not fulfill a promissory oath or vow, he committed no serious sin,[156] although perjury and vow breaking were grave transgressions.

§ 39. THE SEQUEL TO SIN

1. GUILT: INDIVIDUAL AND COLLECTIVE. Rebellion against God, or sin, necessarily entails guilt. Sin is a passing act, guilt is durative. Many words denoting sin are also used for guilt, e.g., ḥaṭṭa'th, 'awon, peša'. The phrases, to load oneself with sin . . . to bear evil, picture the sequel to sin as a burden—the guilt which the sinner loads upon himself weighs him down. Guilt is not limited to personal sin; the guilt of one's family and of one's country for many generations may lie heavily upon the individual, while an individual's guilt may be imputed to his family and his fellowmen. All mankind has been burdened by the sin of Adam and Eve.

The individual frequently benefits from the good fortune of his family or community. In OT times God blessed piety "unto the thousandth generation." Noe's family escaped the flood due to the uprightness of their head; the call and assistance granted Abraham greatly benefited his descendants, and experience shows what a great blessing it is to be born of morally upright parents. There is a similar solidarity in evil fortune. The individual must suffer because of the sins of the community in which he lives, and the community suffers because of the evil lives of its members. God punishes sin unto the third generation.[1] As examples we may point to inherited physical defects, evil propensities or national disasters resulting from false political philosophies.

151. 1 Sam. 14:24-45.
152. 3 Kgs. 17:18; compare § 11:4b with 2 Sam. 6:7.
1. Ex. 20:5-6; 34:7; Num. 14:18.
153. Gen. 20:6-7.
154. Ex. 21:12-14.
155. Deut. 21:1-9.
156. Lev. 5:4.

In ancient times community solidarity was a far more vivid reality than in our own highly individualistic society. If Abimelech had actually sinned with Sara, not only he himself but also his people would have been punished.[2] Had illicit relations occurred between Rebecca and Abimelech, there would have been serious repercussions in the entire community.[3] Joseph's brothers were willing to become servants along with Benjamin, in whose possession the cups were found.[4] Isaias lamented, "I am a man with unclean lips, and dwell in the midst of a people with unclean lips,"[5] as he felt himself stained with the sins of his people. Among the Chosen People religious solidarity cemented together blood relationships. On Sinai Yahweh had made a covenant with the assembled Israelites; this was renewed under Joiada and Josias,[6] and again after the exile the whole nation bound themselves to faithful performance of the Law.[7] Represented by the heads of families the Chosen People gathered at the sanctuary; on specified occasions they offered sacrifices, were blessed, and on the Day of Atonement cleansed from sin. The land of Canaan was theirs as a family heirloom. In the figure of marriage used to express Yahweh's relation to Israel, the concept of collective solidarity is fundamental.[8]

Because of this solidarity arising from blood and religion, Yahweh accepted the penances offered by family or people when an individual had sinned gravely, particularly if he had an official position. Because Achan appropriated articles that should have perished in the destruction of Jericho, the Israelites were defeated at Hai.[9] The guilt incurred by the sons of Heli through their crimes at the place of sacrifice and that of Heli himself by cooperating through silence brought disaster upon the community.[10] The bloodguiltiness which hung heavy on the house of Saul after he slew the Gibeonites was finally expiated by a three year famine during the reign of David.[11] David sinned by ordering a census, and the people were smitten by plague.[12] Jeroboam's family was destined to extinction because he had erected images in the temples at Bethel and Dan.[13] As sequel to Achab's sin neither rain nor dew fell, and famine plagued the nation.[14] Manasses' godlessness brought down Yahweh's wrath upon Judah.[15]

Yahweh expected the penitent Israelites to acknowledge not only their own, but also their fathers' guilt for which they were being punished, "I shall repay their iniquity and their fathers' iniquity as well."[16] At times Israel did pray, "We confess our wickedness, our fathers' guilt,"[17] and acknowledged "their sins and the transgressions of their fathers."[18] The prophets viewed the misfortunes Yahweh sought to inflict upon Israel as due punishment for the guilt of the people. Particularly the leaders, the king, the nobility, the priests, and the false prophets were responsible for the evil in the nation, but the people were not innocent because they willingly followed evil suggestion. At the time

2. Gen. 20:7-9.
3. Gen. 26:10.
4. Gen. 44:16.
5. Is. 6:5.
6. 4 Kgs. 11:17; 23:3.
7. Neh. 10.
8. § 16:4.
9. Jos. 7.
10. 1 Sam. 2:27-36; 3:11-14.
11. 2 Sam. 21:1.
12. 2 Sam. 24:10-17.
13. 3 Kgs. 14:10.
14. 3 Kgs. 17:1.
15. 4 Kgs. 21:10-15; 23:26.
16. Is. 65:7; cf. 14:21.
17. Jer. 14:20.
18. Neh. 9:2.

of Achab the people vacillated thoughtlessly between Yahweh and Baal, and there remained only 7000 who had not bent their knee before the idol.[19] The pagan practices sponsored by Manasses met no resistance on the part of the people. The prophets took pains to arouse the consciousness of guilt in the hearts of the people; they strove to disabuse them of the idea that the impending judgment was unjust or that Yahweh was too weak to protect them against enemies; as did the Law, they too sought to instruct the people's consciences regarding Yahweh's promises and threats, reminding in particular those who were in authority of their social responsibilities.

The fact that the individual was a member of a community, a family and a nation did not eliminate private responsibility. In the decalog the fourth and following commandments are personal obligations, while even the first three, which concern divine worship, affected the individual Israelite; and the same held for the prescriptions in the Covenant Code. The individual had to decide whether he wished to serve Yahweh or some alien god; the individual prayed, the individual brought sacrifice, offered the first fruits, made vows. In the penitential psalms the community acknowledged collective guilt, but still more emphatically does the individual confess personal guilt. The patriarchal accounts relate how God guides and cares for individual persons and how God reckons with individuals who sin. Already in most remote times people felt confident that a just God would not punish the good on account of the sins of the community. Abraham interceded for Sodom and Gomorrah, "Do you really wish to blot out the just along with the wicked?"[20] When Core and his crowd became rebellious Moses prayed, "Are you going to vent your wrath upon the whole community?"[21]

Among the prophets Ezechiel ranks first among those who stressed individual responsibility. The value of the individual before God is shown in the vision of the destruction of the temple in which the scribe-angel puts a mark upon the foreheads of the just to save them from the common destruction.[22] Each soul is responsible to God,[23] the individual is punished for his sins, no one may depend upon the piety of another. Even if such saintly men as Noe, Daniel and Job lived in a sinful city, the inhabitants of that city would perish if they did not repent.[24] Ezechiel developed this theme when some of the people were already in exile and the full destruction of the state was imminent. The Jews thought that their punishment was due solely to the sins of earlier generations and accused Yahweh of injustice; they would not admit that they were no better than their forefathers, that their obstinacy in the face of constant prophetical warning called down punishment upon themselves. They clothed their self-righteous thoughts in the proverb, "The fathers ate sour grapes, and the children's teeth are set on edge;"[25] and after the demolition of Jerusalem complained loudly, "Our fathers sinned and are no longer, while we are bearing their guilt."[26] Only in messianic times, Jeremias pointed out, would it come to

19. 3 Kgs. 18:21; 19:18.   22. Ez. 9:4-6.   25. Jer. 31:29; Ez. 18:2.
20. Gen. 18:24-25.   23. Ez. 18:4.   26. Lam. 5:7.
21. Num. 16:22.   24. Ez. 14:12-20.

pass that each would be punished only for his own faults.[27] Ezechiel was well conversant with the implications of communal responsibility. He himself was taken into exile without sharing the guilt of the politicians; this misfortune he did not regard as a punishment for personal failings, for he realized that in the destruction of Jerusalem the pious too would meet death or be carried into captivity.[28]

2. THE VOICE OF CONSCIENCE. In order that we may more easily fulfill God's will and repent more quickly when we have failed, God has endowed us with conscience. In scriptural language our "heart" admonishes us to observe the divine law and upbraids us when we have failed. In paradise Adam and Eve perceived the voice of conscience: they experienced fear and shame and hid themselves from God's presence.[29] Cain was admonished to resist temptation, and after he yielded became despondent.[30] David was "smitten in heart" after he had cut off a corner of Saul's mantle[31] and after he had ordered a general census.[32] Aaron felt guilty after he had fashioned the golden calf, as is shown by his futile attempt to place the major portion of the blame upon his fellow men.[33] In the time of Osee God determined to let the Israelites shift for themselves, to aid them no longer "until they felt themselves guilty," until their consciences goaded them to penance.[34] How conscience leaves no rest to the just man who happens to fall into sin is described in Ps. 34, "While I was silent my bones wasted away with my continual groaning; for during the day as well as during the night your hand lay heavily upon me."[35] It is the same with the godless, "The sound of terror rings in his ear, while at rest the destroyer comes upon him[36].... The sinner *flees* though no one is pursuing him[37].... There is no peace, says my God, to the wicked."[38] The anxieties consequent upon sin are described in the Pentateuch with the purpose of inculcating fidelity to the commandments, "You tremble during the night and during the day, and you do not feel safe of your life. In the morning you say: If it were only evening! and at evening: If it were only morning! because of the pangs of conscience which you experience."[39] The stings of conscience suffered by the Egyptians are dramatically described in Wis. 17:3-18. And in the next life the wicked will suffer eternal remorse.[40]

The fear which a person experiences after a sinful act is not awakened first by the consciousness of punishment. Adam, Eve and Cain trembled at the voice of conscience even before God imposed penance. Nor does conscience always become active immediately after the act. Jacob's sons first realized how seriously they had sinned against their brother Joseph and their father when misfortune began to fall.[41] Conscience does not raise its accusing voice after every transgression; in confirmed sinners it seems to sleep,[42] since after most horrible crimes they simply say, "Yahweh does not see it, the God of Jacob

27. Jer. 31:30.
28. Ez. 5:1-3; 7:10-16; 15:1-8.
29. Gen. 3:7, 10.
30. Gen. 4:7f.
31. 1 Sam. 24:6.
32. 2 Sam. 24:10; § 11:4c.
33. Ex. 32:22-24.
34. Os. 5:15.
35. Ps. 34:3-4.
36. Job 15:21.
37. Prov. 28:1.
38. Is. 57:21.
39. Deut. 28:66-67.
40. Wis. 3:14.
41. Gen. 42:21.
42. Zach. 11:5.

will keep nought of it in mind."[43] Surely this is sin's worst sequel, because as long as it continues conversion is rendered impossible. A tender conscience on the contrary is revealed if one, like the psalmist, asks pardon even for venial faults.[44] Happy the man whose conscience does not reproach him,[45] who may say with Job, "My heart does not blame *me* because of my days."[46]

3. PUNISHMENT. For keeping His commandments God promises reward, for violating them punishment; this is demanded by divine justice.[47] God may intervene immediately, He may patiently abide His time; He may act kindly or severely since He is sovereign. The scouts who excited the people to rebel died suddenly;[48] Dathan and Abiron were swallowed by the earth,[49] while toward common people Yahweh was wont to act most indulgently. Upon hearing God's judgment Heli humbly answered, "He is Yahweh, may he do what is good in his eyes."[50]

Every sinner hopes to obtain some good from violating the divine command, "Stolen water is sweet, and bread eaten in secret tastes good[51].... Evil tastes sweet in his mouth."[52] Soon however things change, "His food turns topsyturvy in his bowels, gall from adders he has in his intestines; the poison of asps he sucks, the viper's tongue will slay him,"[53] for the godless "sow wind and reap a storm."[54] They are, so to speak, punished by their own sins, since God abandons them "to the power of their own evil deeds[55].... Your malice chastises you, and your apostasy punishes you."[56] No sin remains unpunished, "Do not entangle yourself twice in sin, for even from one you will not go free!"[57]

The means which God uses to chastise sinners are: hardships, pain, suffering and death,[58] the common destiny of men from which no one can escape.[59] A long life is promised as reward for virtue.[60] Abraham died "at a ripe old age,"[61] likewise Isaac,[62] Job[63] and David.[64] On the contrary a premature death "before half their days"[65] comes as a punishment for sinners. We find this was the case with Her and Onan,[66] with Nadab and Abiu,[67] with the scouts,[68] with Core and his companions,[69] with Dathan, Abiron,[70] and the sons of Heli.[71] The psalmists and wisdom teachers develop the same viewpoint: as a reward the virtuous will enjoy a long life, while the godless will die early. This theology underlies the frequent petitions found in the psalms for the speedy death of enemies.[72] In time however the sages realized that an early death is not always a punishment for personal sin.[73]

Alongside premature death God sends various misfortunes as punishment

43. Ps. 94:7.
44. Pss. 19:13; 25:7.
45. Ps. 26:1-7.
46. Job 27:6.
47. § 15:4-5.
48. Num. 14:38.
49. Num. 16:32.
50. 1 Sam. 3:18.
51. Prov. 9:17.
52. Cf. Prov. 30:20.
53. Job 20:12-16; 15:35.
54. Os. 8:7.
55. Job 8:4.

56. Jer. 2:19.
57. Sir. 7:8.
58. Gen. 3:19; cf. 2:17; 3:22.
59. Jos. 23:14; 3 Kgs. 2:2; Sir. 14:17; 25:24; Qoh. 12:7.
60. Ex. 20:12.
61. Gen. 25:8.
62. Gen. 35:29.
63. Job 42:17.
64. 1 Chr. 29:28.
65. Pss. 55:24; 102:24-25; Is.

38:10; Jer. 17:11.
66. Gen. 38:7.
67. Lev. 10:1-2.
68. Num. 14:37.
69. Num. 26:10.
70. Num. 16:20-35.
71. 1 Sam. 2:25; 4:11.
72. Cf. Pss. 52:7, 10; 54:7; 63:10; 91:8; 109:8; 139:19; Prov. 3:2; 10:27; Sir. 40:9.
73. § 41:4.

for sins. Jacob was obliged to flee to a foreign land and humble himself; Mary, Moses' sister, was stricken with leprosy,[74] Saul lost the royal throne,[75] David had serious family troubles,[76] Roboam witnessed the division of his kingdom and the incursion of Sesac,[77] Jeroboam lost his son and his family perished.[78] The rich who by unjust means had obtained possession of extensive landholdings were threatened with drought and crop failure, while revellers faced death through thirst.[79]

At times God punished by granting evildoers their own way. The Israelites who refused to journey to Canaan and wished they had died in the wilderness were condemned to wander about in the desert and die without being allowed to enter Canaan.[80] Balac insisted that Balaam journey to Moab and curse Israel although the seer had informed him that Yahweh had forbidden this move; when with Yahweh's assent Balaam finally did go, it was to bless Israel and announce Moab's destruction.[81]

Worse than earthly misfortune is the loss of citizenship in the kingdom of God. Sinners are "blotted out of the book of the living, are not inscribed with the just[82].... are not inscribed in the book of the house of Israel."[83] When thus excluded from the list of the elect,[84] God does not answer them[85] or permit a prophet to petition in their name.[86] "All the good works which the sinner performed shall not be remembered;"[87] thus he loses the reward of previous service. To which add the torment of an unquiet conscience. To climax all comes the blindness which God inflicts upon those who constantly oppose the operation of grace.[88] And in the next life ignominy, vain sorrow, despair.[89]

Even in the very act of punishing God manifests His mercy. Punishment is not meted out in proportion to the grievousness of the offense; rather the sinner is chastised in a human way, as it were, with rods and stripes.[90] God's wrath was heavy upon Judah because of Manasses' wickedness, yet for David's sake He repeatedly showed mercy to the people and to the royal family.[91] The primary purpose of punishment however was to effect conversion.[92] By incarcerating his brothers and imposing demands upon them, Joseph sought to make them realize their sinful action; what he made them suffer was nothing in comparison to that which they had done to him, and he forgave them when they acknowledged their sin.[93] Should God be less generous with His mercy? "My son, do not despise discipline, and do not be vexed at his correction; Yahweh chastises him whom he loves, and upon the child in whom he delights *he inflicts pain.*"[94] The prudent man will quickly see the truth in the words, "It was good for me that I was afflicted, so that I could learn your precepts."[95]

74. Num. 12:9-10.
75. 1 Sam. 15:23-26.
76. 2 Sam. 12:10-14.
77. 2 Chr. 12:5.
78. 3 Kgs. 14:10-18.
79. Is. 5:8-13; Am. 4:1-2.
80. Num. 14:2, 20.
81. Num. 22-24.
82. Ps. 69:29; cf. Ex. 32:32.
83. Ez. 13:9; cf. Is. 4:3; Dan. 12:1.
84. Cf. § 43:2.
85. 1 Sam. 14:37.
86. Ez. 20:31; Lam. 2:9.
87. Ez. 18:24; 33:13.
88. § 38:4.
89. Wis. 5; § 42:4; 43:4-5.
90. 2 Sam. 7:14; Ps. 89:32-34.
91. 3 Kgs. 11:12, 36; 4 Kgs. 8:19, 34; 20:6; Is. 37:35; 55:3.
92. § 16:5-6.
93. Gen. 42:45.
94. Prov. 3:11-12; Ps. 119:75; Sir. 18:13.
95. Ps. 119:71.

Do not conclude however that God punishes to force repentance. Free will always remains, and with it you may refuse all God's proofs of loving-kindness. Every divine admonition begins with the words, "Who wants to hear, let him hear, and who wants to decline, let him decline."[96]

§ 40. THE RETURN TO GOD

1. SORROW. As often as Israel strayed from God, God chastised her and raised up men who clarified the reason for the affliction, who exhorted her to penance and conversion, "Go back to him from whom you have fallen so fully away."[1] Full of confidence any sinner might turn again to the God whom he has offended because divine mercy "has no pleasure in the death of a sinner."[2] It was this divine mercy which the prophets emphasized when exhorting Israel to repent.[3] In the same vein the psalmist prayed, "You, O Yahweh, are good, you are ready to forgive, and full of mercy toward all who call upon you."[4] Conversion consists in an act by which the will firmly resolves to shun all that is evil, an act which proceeds from sorrow at having offended God. Only this spiritual disposition is able to give worth to the words and actions by which the sinner expresses his hatred for sin, e.g., weeping, rending garments, wearing penitential garb, sprinkling ashes on the head, fasting, etc. "Rend your hearts and not your garments."[5] God demands a deeply contrite spirit and a broken heart.[6] The sinner must take pains to form a new heart and a new spirit,[7] to keep himself clear from evil,[8] to cast off his offenses,[9] to set his heart upon God[10] and abandon evil ways and habits.[11] Since sin is a type of apostasy, the sinner must "return" to God, must "seek" God.[12] These expressions show that conversion implies a break from one's former mode of life. It must be genuine "with all one's heart and with all one's soul"[13]—an external acknowledgment of having sinned is wholly insufficient. Saul regretted not having observed Yahweh's command and Samuel's directions, but his sorrow proceeded merely from the evil consequences of his actions.[14] There is no conversion without abandoning sin because sin breaks intimacy with God, "We do not want to sin because we know that we are accounted yours."[15] The recidivist resembles one who "having touched a corpse washes himself, and then touches it again. What benefit does he derive from washing?"[16]

The admonitions to penance show that man is able to abandon sin and remain on friendly terms with God. From another viewpoint conversion is the work of God, accomplished by His spirit, "Create a clean heart within me, O God; instill

96. Ez. 3:27.
1. Is. 31:6; Ez. 18:30-31; Joel 2:12; Mal. 3:7.
2. Ez. 18:32; § 16:5-6.
3. Joel 2:13.
4. Ps. 86:5.
5. Joel 2:13.
6. Ps. 51:19.
7. Ez. 18:31.
8. Ez. 18:21; Sir. 17:26.
9. Ez. 18:31; Sir. 17:25.
10. 1 Sam. 7:3.
11. Jer. 18:11; 25:5; Ez. 18:23; 33:11; Jon. 3:8.
12. Deut. 4:29; Os. 10:12; 14:2-3; Am. 5:4-6; Is. 26:16.
13. Deut. 4:29; 30:10; 1 Sam. 7:3; 3 Kgs. 8:48; Joel 2:12.
14. 1 Sam. 15:24.
15. Wis. 15:2.
16. Sir. 34:30-31.

a new, a stable spirit within my breast."[17] The same is true on a national scale, "Convert us, Yahweh, in order that we may convert."[18] Here we have an instance of God's prevenient grace cooperating with the human will, the latter remaining wholly responsible for its activity since it can accept or reject the divine advances.[19]

2. CONFESSION OF SIN. The penitent sinner humbles himself and admits having offended God. At atonement sacrifices,[20] and at guilt-offerings[21] a humble admission was expressly required in addition to repairing the damage done.[22] We read how the psalmist regretted not having declared his sin sooner, "I should have made known to you my sin, I should not have concealed my guilt. But finally I said: I shall accuse myself of my iniquity before Yahweh."[23] "Who conceals his sins obtains no blessing, but he who acknowledges and abandons them receives mercy."[24] For this reason Eliphaz and his partners, who viewed Job's trials as punishment for unacknowledged sin, insisted continually upon a full and open confession; only then, they thought, would God forgive and terminate his sufferings. At Mizpah the Israelites confessed they had sinned against Yahweh.[25] We are edified by David's *Peccavi Domino.*[26] By donning a penitential garb, fasting and showing an afflicted appearance Achab showed openly that he was grieving for his sins.[27] After Solomon's prayer at the dedication of the temple the Israelites acknowledged, "We have sinned, we have acted wickedly, godlessly."[28] In the name of all the people Moses made a confession of sin before Yahweh,[29] likewise Daniel,[30] Esdras,[31] Nehemias.[32] On the days prescribed by Nehemias the Jews acknowledged their sins,[33] and the Levites led the people in penitential prayer.[34] Ps. 106 is a prayerful admission of sin. On the Day of Atonement the high priest confessed that he and the priesthood had offended Yahweh and then consigned the sins of the people to Azazel's goat.[35] This acknowledgment of sins had a wholly different purpose than the enumeration of evil acts in the Babylonian incantation rituals and in the Egyptian Book of the Dead.[36]

3. ACTS OF EXPIATION. In addition to our admission of having sinned we must make efforts to expiate our guilt before God. Expiatory acts prescribed for definite days were: applying the blood of the paschal lamb[37] and offering a sacrifice on the Day of Atonement.[38] By the former the guilt of the family was atoned for, by the latter that of the people. For minor faults special atonement sacrifices and guilt-offerings were prescribed.[39] Holocausts too expiated guilt.[40] In accordance with Yahweh's injunction, Job's friends offered a great holocaust to atone for their imprudent discourses; this sacrifice received atoning

17. Ps. 51:12; § 20:5.
18. Lam. 5:21; Jer. 24:7; 31:33; 2:19; Soph. 3:11-13.
19. § 26:5; 38:2, 4.
20. Lev. 5:5.
21. Num. 5:7.
22. § 33:2c.
23. Ps. 32:5; cf. Pss. 38:19; 51:4-5.
24. Prov. 28:13.
25. 1 Sam. 7:6.
26. 2 Sam. 12:13.
27. 3 Kgs. 21:27-28.
28. 3 Kgs. 8:47.
29. Ex. 32:31; Num. 14:19.
30. Dan. 9:4.
31. Esdr. 9:6-11.
32. Neh. 1:6-8.
33. Neh. 9:1-2.
34. Neh. 9:5-37.
35. Lev. 16:6, 21; § 34:5.
36. § 15:7; 32:2k.
37. § 33:2c.
38. Lev. 16; § 34:5.
39. § 33:2c.
40. Lev. 1:4.

efficacy before God only through Job's intercession.[41] When the people murmured against Moses because Core's band was destroyed, "Aaron burnt incense at the direction of Moses and made atonement for the people."[42] At Mizpah the Israelites showed their spirit of penance by a water libation, the water, as it were, washing the sin away.[43] (The washings prescribed by the Law aided in awakening a consciousness of spiritual defilement.) By wearing a penitential garb the Israelite showed externally that he had sinned,[44] while by fasting he mortified himself in order to make satisfaction.[45] Yet by themselves these actions had no efficacy. Any sinner who believed that God could be appeased by sacrifice and ritual without moral betterment deceived himself. Boldly the prophets, psalmists and wisdom teachers attacked that attitude[46] and insisted on the necessity of sorrow for sins committed, a sorrow which was so much more genuine when penance preceded God's intervention with punishment. "Before you become ill (in punishment for sin) humble yourself, and in the hour of sin show repentance."[47] The sinner makes satisfaction to God by obeying His commands, "Who honors his father, expiates sins."[48] Also through patiently bearing suffering are sins expiated, "I have become weak through my groaning, every night I moisten my bed with tears."[49] Charitable works blot out sin, "By genuine acts of mercy guilt is expiated[50] .... Alms deliver from death and preserve from darkness."[51] Any good man may effect the reconciliation of a sinner with God[52] by intercessory prayer, by offering up his work and suffering.[53]

4. FORGIVENESS OF SIN. God's mercy is so boundless that He is always prepared to forgive; He is indeed a father who is ever willing to extend love to His children, a shepherd who receives "the sheep of his pasture" despite their wanderings.[54] When God forgives a penitent, he is forgiven, he is clean once more; it is not as if God merely overlooked his sins. "Blot out *(mahah)* my iniquity," the psalmist implored,[55] "wash me wholly from my guilt and cleanse me of my sins[56] .... Make atonement for me with hyssop that I become clean, wash me that I become whiter than snow."[57] Isaias's words have become classic, "Though your sins are as scarlet, they shall become white as snow! Though they are red as purple, they shall become as wool."[58] Sins as grave as murder will be forgiven, for God "forgives all your failings . . . heals all your infirmities[59] .... As far as the east is from the west he removes our sins from us."[60] The sinner may feel confident that God "hurls into the depths of the sea all his sins,"[61] where they disappear forever. In the light of the above passages we must understand those texts in which God "covers" *(kasah)* sins so as not to see them, or does not "impute" *(hašab)* guilt. "Turn your face

41. Job 42:7-9.
42. Num. 17:12; Wis. 18:21.
43. 1 Sam. 7:6.
44. 3 Kgs. 21:21, 27; Joel 1:13; Jon. 3:5-6; Neh. 9:1.
45. § 37.
46. § 33:7cd; 34:7; 37:3.
47. Sir. 18:21.
48. Sir. 3:3.
49. Ps. 6:7; § 41:2.
50. Prov. 16:6.
51. Tob. 4:10; § 29:5.
52. § 35:4.
53. § 41:6; 52:1a.
54. Deut. 8:5; Os. 11:1f; Jer. 3:19; 31:20; Pss. 74:1; 77:20; 78:51, 72; 80:2; Jer. 31:10; Ez. 34:12f;
§ 16:4-6.
55. Ps. 51:3.
56. Ps. 51:4.
57. Ps. 51:9.
58. Is. 1:18.
59. Ps. 103:3.
60. Ps. 103:12.
61. Mich. 7:19.

from my sins, and blot out all my offenses,"[62] i.e., may God turn away His wrath, not in the sense of merely overlooking sins, but as the parallelism shows in the sense of actually liquidating them. "Blessed *the man* whose offenses are forgiven, whose sins are covered! Blessed the man to whom Yahweh no longer imputes guilt,"[63] the psalmist prayed at the beginning of Ps. 32, but in verse 5 he exclaimed, "You have forgiven (my) guilt." Ezechiel first comforted his readers, "All the sins which (the sinner) committed shall no longer be remembered,"[64] before admonishing them to repent and strive for a new heart and a new spirit.[65] We must not think that God forgives sin because the penitent has a claim or right to it. Forgiveness is a free act of divine love and mercy. Man is too insignificant, too poor and God is too transcendent to be adequately compensated when offended. Forgiveness does not stem from any human merit or service—the sinner really has neither—it is to manifest God's mercy,[66] "For your name's sake Yahweh, forgive my guilt."[67]

5. FORGIVENESS AND PUNISHMENT. With God's forgiveness sin vanishes, and the penitent again enjoys God's love. Because of his temporal outlook the Israelite when reinstated in divine favor expected a return of the good fortune which God had withdrawn in punishment for his sins, viz., health, honor, property, rich harvests, many children. But God did not always grant earthly goods to the penitent. When Ezechiel was urging the exiles to comply with God's will, he did not promise them a speedy cessation of the exile,[68] nor did Jeremias give them to understand that the return home would soon occur.[69] God's justice demands that He impose punishment upon repentant sinners both as penance and as a warning not to relapse. In theological terminology this is called "temporal punishment for sin." Yahweh assured Jacob of His love and protection as he fled to Mesopotamia, but what suffering his sins occasioned! When Moses pleaded in Israel's behalf, he was instructed on how Yahweh "forgives wickedness and sin, without however leaving it unpunished."[70] Later when the people again revolted and Yahweh determined to annihilate the nation, Moses expected God would punish; accordingly he only pleaded for the revocation of the death sentence decreed against them. Yahweh did relent, He resolved not to annihilate His Chosen People, but to keep them wandering in the wilderness till all who had sinned had died there.[71] He forgave Moses for having called into doubt the magnitude of divine mercy and favored him with the grace of mystical union, yet did not permit him to enter Canaan.[72] God forgave David the crimes of adultery and murder, but as a punishment inflicted death upon Bethsabee's child.[73] Absolom's revolt was part punishment for David's former sins.[74] After the census David was truly sorry and implored God for forgiveness, yet he did not escape due punishment.[75] When Achab did penance, Yahweh mitigated but did not revoke the promised punishment.[76]

62. Ps. 51:11.
63. Ps. 32:1-2.
64. Ez. 18:22.
65. Ez. 18:31; cf. § 33:2c.
66. § 16:6.
67. Pss. 25:11; 79:9; § 16:7.

68. Ez. 18:30-32.
69. Jer. 29:10-14.
70. Ex. 34:7.
71. Num. 14:18f.
72. Num. 20:12; Deut. 3:23-28; 32:48-52.

73. 2 Sam. 12:13-15.
74. 2 Sam. 12:11-12.
75. 2 Sam. 24.
76. 3 Kgs. 21:29.

§ 41. SUFFERING

1. THE ORIGIN OF SUFFERING. When God made the world and man, all was good, very good.[1] The sacred writers recognized this fundamental truth,[2] yet were not unaware that "great troubles come to every man, and a heavy yoke weighs upon the children of men from the day *they* leave their mother's womb till the day *they* return to the mother of all."[3] Innumerable physical evils are the portion of every creature, "Upon all flesh from man to beast, and upon sinners seven times more, come plague and bloodshedding, fever and sword, destruction and corruption, *famine* and death."[4] Now because God is the ultimate cause of all that happens upon earth, because all physical and moral dispositions depend upon His will, evil too must stem from Him.[5] Amos asked rhetorically, "Does evil happen in the city and Yahweh does not do it?"[6] A wisdom teacher declared, "Yahweh has made all things for his (own) purpose, the evildoer too for the evil day."[7] Even those who make their fellow men suffer fulfill God's plan, e.g., the sons of Jacob by selling Joseph into Egypt,[8] Semei by cursing David.[9] When pagan nations oppressed Israel they were acting as God's agents.[10] We know how angels were sent to punish sinners,[11] and how evil spirits like Asmodeus and Satan were able to do harm to the extent and at the time God permitted.[12]

2. SUFFERING AS PUNISHMENT FOR SIN. Suffering is the lot of every individual as a result of original sin. For personal sins too God's punishing hand presses heavily. This theme, so deeply imbedded in the OT, is founded upon belief in God's infinite justice.[13] God repays "each according to his behavior and in proportion to the merit of his deeds."[14] "Woe to the godless man, for it shall not go well with him; the misdeeds of his hands shall strike home upon him."[15] Yahweh "lets fiery *coals* and brimstone rain upon evildoers, scorching winds are the portion of their cup."[16] Elihu continued the argument of Job's three friends, viz., that God punishes sinners justly, "According to a man's actions he repays him, he lets things happen to each according to his way."[17] Job and Sirach reached the same conclusion, "Is not misfortune for the wicked, and disaster for evildoers?[18] . . . . There are winds that have been ordained to punish. Fire and hail, *hunger* and pestilence, these too have been made to punish, preying animals, scorpions and asps and the sword of vengeance to destroy the godless."[19] The Book of Judges shows how world history is world judgment; the Books of Kings and Chronicles endeavor to demonstrate how God punishes individuals and nations for violating His law and likewise how He rewards its faithful observance.

According to the law of just retribution[20] punishment should be commen-

1. Gen. 1.
2. E.g., Sir. 39:16.
3. Sir. 40:1.
4. Sir. 40:8-9.
5. § 11:4c; 20:7; 25:6.
6. Am. 3:6.
7. Prov. 16:4.
8. Gen. 45:7-8; 50:20.
9. 2 Sam. 16:11; cf. 2 Sam. 12:10-11.
10. Is. 7:18; 10:5; § 25:4.
11. § 22:4b.
12. § 23:3-4.
13. § 15:5; 39:3.
14. Jer. 32:19; Ps. 62:13; Job 34:11.
15. Is. 3:11.
16. Ps. 11:6.
17. Job 34:11.
18. Job 31:3; cf. 27:7-23.
19. Sir. 39:28-30; cf. 40:8-10.
20. Ex. 21:23-25.

surate to the offense, "Who digs a ditch for another, falls into it himself; who rolls a stone upon another, it shall come back upon himself."[21] Of this proverb history affords copious examples: Jacob first deceived his father, was then cheated by Laban and deceived by his sons; Joseph was sold into slavery by his brothers and later imprisoned; later they themselves feared retention in Egypt as slaves; Adonibezec's thumbs and big toes were cut off because he had thus maltreated his captives;[22] those who were responsible for casting Daniel into the lion's den were thrown to the lions themselves;[23] Amon ordered a gibbet constructed for Mardochai and was hanged upon it himself;[24] Jason drove many from their native country, and himself was slain in a foreign land;[25] because Antiochus tortured those who remained faithful to the Law, he was stricken with indescribable pains.[26] The author of the Book of Wisdom lays down the principle, "By the things a person sins, by the same also he is punished,"[27] and proves his words true from the history and fate of the Egyptians.[28]

3. SEEMING MISCARRIAGE OF DIVINE JUSTICE. Because God is just we may hope that He will punish the wicked and reward the good. The psalmist voiced a common experience when he said, "I was young, now am old, but never have I seen a just man abandoned by God. Observe the pious, how fortunate are all their children. But evildoers are blotted out, and the offspring of the wicked cut off."[29] Nevertheless observation also shows that frequently the godless do enjoy good fortune, that "the sinner does evil a hundred times and still gets old,"[30] while the just man may not have an easy day all through life. Here the pious man consoled himself by recalling that every man is a sinner, hence justly punished by God. Eliphaz stressed this idea in order to induce Job to confess his guilt.[31] The good man should also remember that the wicked man's fortune is transitory, and that soon, perhaps quite soon, his punishment will come, "Quickly like grass they wither, and wilt like the green on plants[32].... Yet a little while and the evildoer will be gone; if you note where he is, he is there no longer."[33] The evildoer marks the good fortune of the pious, frets, and passes from the scene.[34] Referring to the inevitable punishment for sin Jesus Sirach wrote, "Call no one happy before (his) death, for at his end is man known."[35] An early and sudden death is the fate reserved for the godless, "O God, you will bring them down to the pit of corruption, men who shed blood and deceive will not live out half their days[36].... Be not bent on evil, be not senseless lest you die inopportunely."[37] If the evildoer remains prosperous to his very death, it is his children who will suffer. They may die prematurely,[38] so that his memory will perish,[39] or they may become poor and fall into disgrace for which they "will curse their godless father."[40] The author of the Book

21. Prov. 26:27; Sir. 27:26-27;
    Pss. 7:16;   9:16;   35:8;
    37:14-15.
22. Judg. 1:6-7.
23. Dan. 6:25.
24. Esth. 7:9-10.
25. 2 Mach. 5:9.
26. 2 Mach. 9:5-6.
27. Wis. 11:16.

28. Wis. 12:23-27; 16:1; 17:3,
    8; 18:5.
29. Ps. 37:25, 37-38.
30. Qoh. 8:12.
31. Job 4:17-19.
32. Ps. 37:2.
33. Ps. 37:10, 35-36.
34. Ps. 112:10; Prov. 10:25,

27, 30; 12:7; 14:11; Job
    8:11-19.
35. Sir. 11:28.
36. Ps. 55:24; § 39:3.
37. Qoh. 7:17.
38. Ps. 37:28; Job 18:5, 19.
39. Job 18:17.
40. Sir. 41:6-7.

of Wisdom counsels a virtuous life so that posterity need not suffer, "Gone are
the children (of the godless), cursed their generation."[41] Centuries earlier the
decalog had clearly proclaimed that God visits the sins of fathers on their
children to the third and fourth generation,[42] a passage which Jeremias utilized.[43] At the time of Christ many believed, as also did the disciples, that
every misfortune came as punishment either for the sin of the individual concerned or of his forefathers, "Master, who has sinned, this man or his parents,
that he was born blind?"[44]

Nevertheless the view that sinners die early or would be punished in their
descendants, while the just are delivered from affliction quickly or at least
before death, could never serve as a final and satisfying solution to the problem
of suffering. Many evildoers did remain fortunate to the very day of death, and
their children retained places of honor; on the other hand saintly men suffered
to the very last day of their lives and died without vindication. Job had this
in mind as he complained, "The good and the guilty he destroys,"[45] and
pointed out the hard truth, "The one dies with all his faculties intact; he lived
with the full measure of success and happiness, his life aboundingly rich in
luxury, his bones saturated with marrow; the other dies in desperate straits,
having experienced nothing good. Alike they rest in the dust and have decay as
their covering."[46] When Habacuc wrestled with the problem how a just God
could permit the pious to be oppressed,[47] Yahweh comforted him by saying: the
Chaldeans will come to chastise evildoers.[48] But this occasioned new difficulties
because the Chaldeans would commit still greater atrocities; full of anxiety he
asked why these things were permitted.[49] Yahweh replied: the Chaldeans too
would be destroyed while "the upright man stays alive through his faith."[50]
Yahweh's answers however did not settle the problem, for the just were afflicted
first by the godless and then by the Chaldeans, and many lost their lives. What
compensation to them was the assurance that brutal foreigners too would be
punished?[51] Jeremias could not understand why the wicked and their families
prospered; the only comfort he found was in the thought that they did not
possess Yahweh's love.[52]

The objection against the view that children would be obliged to atone for
their parents' sins is easy to see: those who were actually guilty went unpunished,
while those not guilty suffered. "Let him make recompense himself, that he may
experience what it is; for what interest has he in his house after him?"[53] In
the case of national calamity there was little comfort in the thought that one
had to suffer simply because he was a member of the community. Prior to the
exile the Jews resented being punished for the sins of their forefathers.[54] After
the return many took offense at the prosperity of the wicked and its lack among

41. Wis. 3:12; cf. 3:16-17;
    4:3-6.
42. Ex. 20:5; 34:7; Num.
    14:18.
43. Jer. 32:18.
44. Jn. 9:2.

45. Job 9:22.
46. Job 21:23-26; cf. 12:6;
    21:8-14; Ps. 10:1-5.
47. Hab. 1:2-4.
48. Hab. 1:5-11.
49. Hab. 1:13.

50. Hab. 2:4.
51. Cf. § 43:2.
52. Jer. 12:1-2.
53. Job 21:19-21.
54. Jer. 31:29; Ez. 18:2; cf.
    Lam. 5:7 § 39:1.

the law-abiding.[55] Qoheleth found it impossible to explain why "the evildoer lives long in his wickedness,"[56] and why "a like lot awaits every one;"[57] the many riddles of life forced from his anguished mind the cry, "Futility, nothing but futility, all is futility!"[58] The wisdom teachers constantly admonished their disciples not to lose confidence in God when they saw how successful the wicked were, "Do not envy the violent man[59].... Let not your heart grow warm toward sinners."[60] In the psalms a most difficult problem is the relationship between God's justice and the prosperity of the wicked, "Look, these are godless people and yet forever at ease, they even have gathered together great wealth. Really for nothing have I kept my heart pure and washed my hands in innocence!"[61] The psalmist could not understand why God permitted such conditions and almost began to doubt the existence of a moral order.[62] In another verse we hear the unreasoning rabble say, "Why should God bother himself about this; after all does the Most High know everything?"[63] But deliverance did come when God intervened and sent destruction;[64] then the psalmist marvelled that he had ever had such difficulties as he felt himself in permanent possession of God's love.[65] Belief in God's justice and love was greatly confirmed with the spread of the hope that due reward and punishment would be meted out after death.[66]

4. SUFFERING AND SPIRITUAL PURIFICATION. No man is sinless, not even a saint.[67] By enduring trials a person is cleansed spiritually and becomes minded to avoid smaller imperfections. Through the suffering which Yahweh permitted, Jacob was punished and likewise was taught to place himself confidently under God's guidance. In times of persecution David dedicated himself to God with an ever increasing degree of attachment. "The crucible is for silver and the furnace is for gold, but Yahweh tries the hearts,"[68] i.e., through the fire of suffering He burns out the slag and secures the genuine metal in all its purity. Hence the admonition, "Accept whatever happens to you, and be patient in the midst of your changing humiliations, for gold is proven by fire and the man pleasing to God in the crucible of humiliations."[69] To encourage her people Judith recounted the trials of the patriarchs, "As God tried them to test their hearts, so neither does he punish us now; no, as a warning the Lord chastises those who stand close to him."[70] The author of 2 Machabees sees in misfortune a proof of God's kindness, calls it "a useful reprimand."[71] The poor man has climbed high upon the ladder of perfection if he is convinced that earthly goods have only a relative value, that riches often lead to sin, that God hates the wicked but loves the poor man who is virtuous.[72] Sickness is not only a punishment, it is also sent by God as an opportunity for man to overcome himself and triumph over self-love.[73] Even death while one is still young or in the prime of life is not always a punishment. When the prophet proclaimed, "From

55. Mal. 2:17; 3:14-15.
56. Qoh. 7:15; 8:12.
57. Qoh. 9:3.
58. Qoh. 1:2.
59. Prov. 3:31; 24:1.
60. Prov. 23:17; 24:19; Pss. 37:1, 7-8; 49:6-7, 17.
61. Ps. 73:12-13.
62. Ps. 73:2-3.
63. Ps. 73:11.
64. Ps. 73:19.
65. Ps. 73:21-26.
66. § 43; 44.
67. § 38:3.
68. Prov. 17:3.
69. Sir. 2:4-5; cf. Ps. 66:10.
70. Judg. 8:27.
71. 2 Mach. 6:12-16.
72. § 30:7.
73. § 30:5.

(impending) calamity the just man is snatched away and enters into peace,"[74] he insinuated that an early death is not a misfortune under all circumstances; it may be a proof of God's love, and the author of the Book of Wisdom shows how it can be a great blessing.[75]

5. THE TRIALS OF THE JUST MAN. It seems that those who serve God particularly well are sent special sufferings; this is to afford them the opportunity to show that they love God disinterestedly. The more intimate one is with God, the more joyfully he will subject himself to God's will, even when he fails to understand it. Wisdom "tests him through her discipline and tries him through her precepts until she can trust him."[76] When God called, Abraham had to abandon home and relatives and wander into unknown parts.[77] Then he was commanded to sacrifice his son and heir, Isaac, whom he had so long awaited and who finally had been granted him in a marvellous manner—this, his only son he was to immolate with his own hand.[78] By triumphing over the natural love he bore toward his child and obeying God, the patriarch demonstrated he was worthy of God's special love.[79] Joseph was thrown into prison because he resisted the advances of Putiphar's wife; as a result of this his trust in God shines much more brightly. Moses encountered opposition from the people at the very first exercise of his mission[80] and throughout the whole journey in the wilderness; once they even sought to stone him.[81] Elias was forced to flee in order to escape the persecution of Achab and Jezabel.[82] Micheas was mistreated and imprisoned,[83] Amos was ordered to leave the land,[84] Urias was murdered,[85] Osee's married life was anything but pleasant. A prophet's life was one of suffering, a martyr's life, Jeremias taking the foremost place. They suffered interiorly, since they recognized the futility of their warnings and saw how their preaching was even accelerating judgment because the stubbornness of the people increased guilt.[86] Susanna was condemned as an adulteress because she preserved herself inviolate.[87] During the persecution of Manasses[88] and later that of Antiochus Epiphanes, many who remained loyal to God were martyred.[89] And a famous prophecy described how the Servant of Yahweh would meet a violent death in His work of bringing salvation to Jew and Gentile.[90]

The most thorough and comprehensive treatment of why the just must suffer, and suffer so intensely, is found in the Book of Job. The problem is formulated very precisely in the prolog: Job was not an Israelite and hence did not share in the guilt of "the fathers" as did the Chosen People. His virtue is acknowledged by God Himself in the presence of Satan, and yet Job loses all his possessions, his children and lastly his health. He suffers most violent pain and death stares him in the eyes. All this he bears patiently, "Yahweh gave, Yahweh took; may Yahweh's name be blessed."[91] Even when his wife

74. Is. 57:1-2.
75. Wis. 4:7-15.
76. Sir. 4:17.
77. Gen. 12:1.
78. Gen. 22.
79. § 11:9c.

80. Ex. 5:20f.
81. Num. 14:10.
82. 3 Kgs. 17:3; 19:3.
83. 3 Kgs. 22:24f.
84. Am. 7:12.
85. Jer. 26:20-23.

86. § 11:4c.
87. Dan. 13.
88. 4 Kgs. 21:16.
89. § 28:1b.
90. Is. 53; § 52:1a.
91. Job 1:21.

began to murmur, he remained loyal, "Surely we have accepted good fortune from God. Shall we not accept misfortune from him as well?"[92] Only when his friends made him reflect upon his horrible lot did he become restless, and through their speeches interiorly disturbed. His friends were convinced that a person's fortune always reflected his relationship with God. So they regarded Job's afflictions as punishment for his sins, and because Job would not admit this assumption, they accused him of impenitence.[93] Moreover Job believed that posterity would judge him as a great sinner—he regarded himself a sinner in the sense that all men are sinners[94] but denied that he deserved the extraordinary trials which had come upon him. Since God's designs were hidden to him, he gave way to bitter complaints and longed for death, or better, wished never to have been born. He challenged God to come to court against him, yet in spite of all excesses he remained loyal to God. Abstracting from his fidelity, Job showed that he still had many human failings and weaknesses; he became bitter, impatient, angry, uncharitable in his criticisms, even dared to criticise God's ways. He had not yet learnt the lesson of self-mastery. He had not yet learnt that a virtuous man will love God without receiving tangible benefits, will remain steadfast even under most annoying vexations. When God appeared and confronted him with his failings, Job acknowledged his sinful murmuring and sought to do penance in dust and ashes.[95] Humbly accepting his lot, he no longer demanded health and public vindication. This marks the triumph of love, when man forgets himself and wills but one thing: whatever God wills. Thus Job emerged victorious from all his trials, he overcame his failings, his love to God grew stronger, he became more closely united to God than before, his love toward his fellowmen was purified and ennobled. Now he interceded for his friends who were so vehement against him and who had caused him hours of severest mental anguish, who had occasioned his murmuring against God, whom he regarded as his enemies and upon whom he invoked God's punishment.

The Book of Job accordingly teaches that a man may be enjoying God's love even when straightened by misfortune, and that through misfortune a man draws closer to God. With these thoughts he can console himself when appearances are against him and circumstances condemn him. The first readers of Job of course were not wholly satisfied with this solution. Since at the time the book was written no one expected a just requital after death, the reader would be inclined to demand that Job's virtue receive its reward in this life. And the author had to meet this requirement. Therefore already upon earth Job was blessed: he became physically well again, rich in possessions, reared a fine family, reached a ripe old age, and his friends saw and admitted their unjust criticisms of him.

6. SUFFERING IN THE SERVICE OF GOD. The principal purpose of the exile was to bring the people to a realization of their sinfulness, but God also sought to make the Gentiles conscious of His power, justice and love through the chas-

92. Job 2:10.
93. Job 11:10-11.
94. § 38:3.
95. Job 42:6.

tisement and reinstatement of Israel.[96] True, this expectation as expressed in Ezechiel was not realized immediately; while the people were exiles in Babylon only a few pagans deserted their gods in favor of Yahwistic monotheism. But the dispersion did prepare the ground for the spread of the Gospel; in the course of centuries, many pagans became familiar with Jewish services and accepted belief in one God, many more heard of the messianic prophecies and thereby of their own conversion and redemption from sin.[97]

God often permits suffering to afflict an individual in order to realize the divine plan of salvation. This is true not only of sinners who are moved to penance through punishment,[98] but more especially of the innocent. Abraham had to prove himself by severe trials before becoming a model for posterity. Jacob lost his cherished child and was obliged to sojourn in Egypt in order that his family would grow into a nation there. Joseph was harassed by his brothers, then sold into slavery; his suffering resulted in his brethren finding support in time of need.[99] During his sojourn in strange territory Moses realized that he was not able to save his kinsmen by his own strength; it afforded a good opportunity to prepare for the mission to which God had predestined him. Certainly the innumerable hardships which the prophets had to endure in the course of their missions served God's plan of salvation. From his dissolute wife Osee learnt how immeasurably great is God's love toward His wayward people; this truth was meant to give the Israelites strength and hope during the impending visitation. Isaias wore slave's clothing for three years to warn his people against alliances with Egypt and rebellion against Assyria.[100] Jeremias was obliged to forego marriage in his efforts to impress upon the Jews that the impending catastrophe would bring death to countless families.[101] Ezechiel was enjoined to lie motionless first on one side, then on the other—certainly a most unpleasant penance—to indicate how long the exile would last; and his severe fasting was intended to convince them of the horrors of Jerusalem's impending siege.[102] The youngest of the Maccabean brothers petitioned God to accept his sufferings and death as expiation for the sins of the people. Eleazar endured tortures to afford youth an example of how they should "with courage and enthusiasm die an honorable death for the venerable and holy laws."[103] Leprosy brought Naaman to the knowledge of the true God.[104] Daniel's three companions were condemned to suffer along with their leader so that by their miraculous deliverance Babylon's king would acknowledge Yahweh sovereign.[105] Job advised upright men to become models for others in affliction. The Servant of Yahweh would endure willingly the most excruciating tortures and give His life to blot out the sins of mankind.[106] This revelation gave rise to the practice of offering to God all one's sufferings for the salvation of others—the theology of vicarious expiation. "Upon him did Yahweh let fall all our guilt. ... He bore the sins of many and made intercession for evildoers."[107]

96. Ez. 12:16; 17:24; 21:10; 36:23, 36; 37:28; § 46:5; 48:4.
97. § 48:5.
98. § 39:3.
99. Gen. 45:5; 50:20.
100. Is. 26.
101. Jer. 16:1-4.
102. Ez. 4.
103. 2 Mach. 6:28.
104. 4 Kgs. 5:15, 17.
105. Dan. 3:28(95); 6:27-28.
106. Is. 53:11-12.
107. Is. 53:6, 12; § 52: 1a.

7. CONDUCT IN SUFFERING. When a person is stricken with suffering or misfortune he should regard it as an admonition to examine his conscience seriously. He will quickly see that he deserved the visitation and should then accept it in a thankful mood, aware that it smoothens for him the way back to God. Thus the author of Ps. 38 saw God's punishing hand in a serious illness which caused his friends and relatives to leave him and his enemies to ridicule him. He begged, "Do not punish me in your anger, or chastise me in your wrath." He confessed having sinned and asked forgiveness, "Do not remain far away from me, hasten to my aid!"[108] Likewise the author of Ps. 39 acknowledged that he deserved punishment because of his sins, while at the same time he humbly petitioned God to act mercifully. As soon as he became certain that he had remained faithful to God, he, like Job and many other psalmists, left his ultimate deliverance in the hands of God.

God's plans for the salvation of men are at times unfathomable.[109] Full of trust Sirach advises abandonment to divine guidance, "Do not ask for that which is too difficult for you, and do not search into that which is beyond your powers."[110] God is good and merciful, a child must confide himself wholly to Him and say, "I have silenced my soul as a weaned child that clings to its mother."[111] A heroic act of confidence in God will tide one over dark hours, "Why are you depressed, O my soul, and *why* do you groan within me? Trust in God, for I shall yet praise him as my helper and my God."[112] Even Job finally abandoned himself unreservedly to God's will.[113] Every one whom God tempts may be certain of enjoying divine protection, "Ever so much misfortune may menace a just man, Yahweh shall deliver him from it all. *Yahweh* protects his every bone, not one of them shall be broken[114].... Put your lot into Yahweh's hands and confide in him; then he will see to it and make your justice (shine) like sunlight at (mid) day."[115] Qoheleth too is certain that God made all things beautiful in their season[116] and that divine justice and love will finally triumph, "God judges the good and the wicked, for *he has appointed* a time for every cause and every act."[117] In every vicissitude for which he gives maxims this rule of life holds, "Fear God and keep his commandments, for this is of universal application."[118]

What, however, if God does not rectify matters in this life, if the just man actually dies in misfortune and shame? Job, for instance, found himself faced by this situation. With no fear of death the poet of Ps. 16 prayed, "You are my Lord, *apart from you* I have no good."[119] Another psalmist, who indeed asked God to destroy his enemies, esteemed as far more important the realization of inner union with God, "Would that I could in justice gaze upon your face, that I could satiate myself *with beholding* (G Th) your form."[120] The just man, who almost had lost faith while considering the actions of sinners, saw

108. Ps. 38:2, 22, 23.
109. Is. 55:8-9; § 4:3; 19:1; 34:2f.
110. Sir. 3:21.
111. Ps. 131:2.
112. Pss. 42:6, 12; 43:5; cf. Sir. 2:4.
113. Job 42:2-6.
114. Ps. 54:20-21.
115. Ps. 37:5-6.
116. Qoh. 3:11.
117. Qoh. 3:17; 8:12-13.
118. Qoh. 12:13; § 25:3; 28:2.
119. Ps. 16:2.
120. Ps. 17:15.

his greatest good fortune in God's love, "I shall remain forever united to you, you have grasped my right hand. Whom else have I in heaven beside you, upon earth no *good* pleases me."[121] Perhaps only a few extraordinarily blessed souls attained such selfless love of God. For the great majority the problem of suffering was satisfactorily solved only with the unfolding of belief in just retribution after death and in resurrection. The author of the Book of Wisdom tells how at death the transitory suffering of the just is transformed into eternal joy by union with God; this consoling truth, frequently forgotten in time of affliction, is particularly true of those who experience the most severe trials; after death they are God's favorites blessed with eternal beatitude.[122]

To be sure nature sometimes rebels and even good people believe that God makes demands beyond their strength. In their despondency some desire death.[123] Jeremias was so dejected that he accused Yahweh of deceiving him when calling him to the office of prophet: Yahweh was like a brook with water flowing only intermittently, "With fury you filled me[124].... you deluded me, Yahweh, and I let myself be deluded."[125] Then like Job he cursed the day of his birth[126] and called down divine vengeance upon his enemies.[127] But, as in the case of Moses, the grace of state preserved him from becoming unfaithful to his mission; with bleeding heart he persevered, a voice preaching in the wilderness. The author of Ps. 88 showed a different spirit. Seriously sick, he felt completely abandoned by men and by God; moreover it seemed that God was pursuing him with great fury. He was unable to account for God's hostility; in vain he implored, he received no comfort. From the brink of the grave he shrank in fear, because afterlife held nothing in store for him; and his prayer ends without an explicit act of hope or trust.

The OT does not fully solve the problem why the just must suffer. But the cross on Golgotha invites us in time of visitation to look upon the guiltless Son of God who suffered and died for us. The OT saint could not readily arrive at the sentiments voiced by our Savior on Mt. Olivet, "Not my will be done, but thine."[128] Even Jesus had a severe struggle, His human nature revolting against the impending storm. In the hour of suffering God may deny a Christian that inner solace without which he will cry with the suffering Christ, "My God, why have you forsaken me?"[129] Let him then remember how this very lamentation changes into a prayer of praise to God; let him direct his glance to the cross and listen to God's Son who urges him to persevere, even though he may not understand the reason underlying his sufferings. Let him think of eternity with its joys, a comfort granted to the OT saint only in the final era before Christ. Nevertheless in such hours the prayer, "Thy will be done,"[130] will not come easy.

121. Ps. 73:23-25.
122. Wis. 2-5; § 43:5.
123. § 42:3.
124. Jer. 15:17-18.

125. Jer. 20:7.
126. Jer. 20:14.
127. Jer. 15:15; 17:18; § 32: 1g.

128. Lk. 22:42.
129. Ps. 22:2.
130. Matth. 6:10.

PART IV

LIFE AFTER DEATH

§ 42. SHEOL

1. SHEOL. Like modern primitive peoples and like their neighbors in the
ancient Orient, the Israelites always firmly believed that after death man in
some way continues to live, that the soul after its departure from the body
remains in existence.[1] Death was the end of physical life, but not the end of
the human personality. At death the body returned to the dust from which it
had been taken,[2] while the non-physical component, the ego or person, went to
the netherworld, Sheol. The etymology of the word $še^{)}ol$ is not apparent; it
has been related to $ša^{)}al$ (compare $ša^{(}al)$, to be hollow, empty, and $ša^{)}al$, to
inquire, i.e., Sheol as a place of inquiry; however the questioning of the spirits
of the dead never gained importance. In the deuterocanonical books and in the
Septuagint the abode of the dead is called "Hades," translated by Jerome with
infernus, inferi or *inferus*. In some passages *bor*, pit, occurs as a parallel
term;[3] on the other hand, in Ez. 32:17-32 a distinction is made between $še^{)}ol$
and *bor:* heroes who receive honorable burial go to Sheol, while Pharaoh and
the Gentiles descend into the pit.

Sheol is located in "the depths,"[4] which gives rise to the expression "depths
of the underworld,"[5] "depths of the earth."[6] Some passages locate it beneath
the waters which are under the earth,[7] and thus it would lie at the opposite
extreme to heaven.[8] Into this "deepest pit"[9] man "is led down,"[10] or must
"descend."[11] Sheol accepts all without distinction, kings and beggars, masters
and slaves, old and young, innocent and evildoers, "Who is the man who shall
remain alive without seeing death, who can deliver his soul from the power of
Sheol?"[12].... All go to one place[13].... the gathering place of all the living."[14]
Being a very large "land,"[15] it was described as having divisions, and stories
located on various levels.[16] Because no one could escape its clutch, the poets
compared it to a monster with wide open jaws ready to gulp down everything
within reach[17] without being filled, "Sheol and Abaddon are never satisfied."[18]
Sheol is also compared to a hunter who lays snares and traps.[19] There is no
return once one has entered its doors, "Whoever has descended into Sheol will
not ascend again; he shall not return to his house or see his city again[20].... Till

1. § 26:6.
2. Gen. 3:19; Qoh. 3:20.
3. Is. 14:15; 38:18; Pss. 30:4; 88:5.
4. Deut. 32:33; Is. 14:9; 57:9; Am. 9:2.
5. Prov. 9:18.
6. Ps. 63:10; cf. Num. 16:32-33.
7. Job 26:5; 38:16; Ps. 88:7.
8. Am. 9:2; Job 11:8; Ps. 139:8.
9. Ps. 88:7.
10. Gen. 42:38; 1 Sam. 2:6; Is. 14:15; Wis. 16:13.
11. Gen. 37:35; Num. 16:30, 33.
12. Ps. 89:49; Job 3:13-19.
13. Qoh. 6:6.
14. Job 30:23.
15. Job 10:21, 22; Ps. 88:13.
16. Is. 14:15; Ez. 32:23.
17. Is. 5:14; Hab. 2:5; Ps. 141:7; Prov. 1:12.
18. Prov. 27:20; 30:15-16.
19. Pss. 18:6; 116:3.
20. Job 7:9-10.

255

heaven falls to pieces he shall not awake[21]. . . . He shall not see the light forever."[22] Sheol keeps its victims "obstinately, pitilessly."[23] Since no one can
escape, it was described as a prison with doors and bars.[24]

2. ABODE IN DEATH'S KINGDOM. All earthly life comes to an end in Sheol,
a fact which accounts for its descriptive titles, such as "Destruction," "Abyss,"
"Abaddon" (from)abad, to perish).[25] The inhabitants of Sheol are called
methim, "The Dead,"[26] more commonly however repha)im, "The Languid" or
"The Weary" (from rapheh, because of their shadowy existence), at times also
)elohim ("Higher Beings," e.g., 1 Sam. 28:15, of Samuel's spirit).[27] In Sheol
man has rest, the striving for riches comes to an end, the godless cease their
fury. Captives are content, since they no longer are obliged to work, and slaves
are free from their masters.[28] There is no suffering. Neither is there any
happiness. It is "the land of darkness and the shadow of death, the land of
darkness dense as at midnight."[29] Life in continual darkness implies the
absence of all joy.[30] Such an existence can hardly be called "life," and therefore Sheol stands at opposite poles to life here on earth in "the land of the
living."[31] After death no one remembers what happened in this life because
he is in the "land of forgetfulness[32]. . . . the land of silence,"[33] where the shades
can at most only "hiss and mutter"[34] in an existence which resembles sleep.[35]
They know nothing of what is happening in the world, neither are they concerned about it, "If his children are honored, he does not know about it; if they
lose popular esteem, he pays no attention to them."[36] Not even the patriarchs
cared about their descendants.[37] All mental activity ceases in the netherworld,
"The dead know nothing at all, their love as well as their hatred and jealousy have
long disappeared."[38] There is "no work or thought or knowledge or wisdom
in Sheol whither you are going."[39] Sheol lets no one escape; to hope for
amelioration is futile. Because of this dismal view on afterlife, death was
"the king of terrors,"[40] and "a living dog . . . better than a dead lion."[41] Life
grants to all men, even to the poor, certain enjoyments; in afterlife even the
wealthiest and most aristocratic get no special consideration because all are
treated alike.

Alongside these notions we find others which attribute at least a modicum
of activity to the dead. After death man is "gathered to his fathers;" friends
and relatives are united and know each other.[42] Rachel's weeping over the
Israelites of the northern kingdom as they were being led into captivity is
indeed a picture,[43] but a picture which would scarcely have been possible if
people did not believe that their ancestors had some interest in the destiny of
their descendants. The dead also are said to mourn over their lot which allows

21. Job 14:12.
22. Ps. 49:10, 12; Job 10:21;
      Ps. 78:39; 2 Sam. 12:23;
      14:14; Qoh. 12:5.
23. Cant. 8:6.
24. Is. 38:10; Jon. 2:7; Job
      38:17; Pss. 9:14; 107:18;
      Wis. 16:13.
25. Ps. 88:12; Job 26:6; 28:
      22; Prov. 5:11.

26. Is. 26:14.
27. Is. 8:19.
28. Job 3:13-19.
29. Job 10:21-22; cf. Job 3:5;
      17:13; Pss. 88:13; 143:3;
      Wis. 17:14, 21.
30. Qoh. 11:8.
31. Is. 38:11.
32. Ps. 88:13.
33. Pss. 94:17; 115:17.

34. Is. 8:19.
35. Job 14:12.
36. Job 14:21; Ps. 88:13.
37. Is. 63:16.
38. Qoh. 9:5-6.
39. Qoh. 9:10.
40. Job 18:14.
41. Qoh. 9:4.
42. Cf. Gen. 37:35.
43. Jer. 31:15-17.

em no happiness.[44] When the king of Babylon would enter Sheol, the shades ould rise to mock him;[45] this however may be viewed as exceptional in so r as they would be aroused by the fall of the world's mightiest sovereign ho now had become as helpless as they. The Law forbade necromancy,[46] a gn that extraordinary knowledge was ascribed to the dead.[47] Perhaps the eople imagined that in specified instances the dead awoke from their apathy. he practice of placing food on the graves of the dead bespeaks some activity.[48] was assumed that the deceased lived in the grave, even as it was believed at they partook in the funeral banquet. Contradictions between these ideas nd notions concerning the status of the dead in Sheol did not arise for the raelites, their concepts of the grave and netherworld being rather fluid.[49] or do these ideas betray any veneration of the dead. The "offering to the ead"[50] was made to Baal of Peor.[51] Ancestor worship was not an earlier age in Israel's religion.[52] Though some references are made to meeting loved nes in afterlife,[53] there was no thought of happy meetings. The funeral lamenta- ons praise the dead man's deeds and are full of regrets over the deceased's eparture, but they make no attempt to console the survivors by referring to onditions in Sheol.

3. GOD AND THE DEAD. God's might extends into Sheol, as is shown by e instances where the dead through His power are recalled to life.[54] "Sheol s naked before him, unveiled the Abyss."[55] Sheol hides no secrets from im. Everyone there knows God's power.[56] When God shakes the earth, the ades quiver before Him.[57] But they do not enjoy His good providence, for he no longer thinks of them, because they are cut off from his hand."[58] He o longer performs any marvels for them;[59] they are in no condition to praise im.[60] Therefore the just man laments, "In Sheol, who is going to praise ou?[61].... The dead in Sheol do not render honor to the Lord, or extol his ghteousness."[62] No one in Hades recounts Yahweh's loving-kindness and delity, since in the land of forgetfulness no news arrives of His mighty deeds r His justice. Man might have lived forever in God's company; by sin he ot only threw away the gift of immortality, but also that of eternal companion- ip with God.

No wonder then that even the pious man drew back in fear from the presence f death. Jeremias, for example, did not relish the thought of dying although e suffered persecution on every side.[63] Frequently in the OT we find petitions or a long life,[64] but never a prayer for a happy death. Whatever a man has e will give for his life.[65] Only when a man became very old and was unable enjoy what life offered, as was the case with the octogenarian Berzellai,[66] was

. Job 14:22.
. Is. 14:9-10.
. § 28:1c.
. 1 Sam. 28:7f; Is. 8:19; Sir. 46:20.
. Deut. 26:14; Tob. 4:17; Sir. 7:33; 30:18G.
. Cf. Ez. 32:17-32.
. Ps. 106:28.
. Num. 25:2-3.

52. Cf. 4:4a.
53. Gen. 37:35; 2 Sam. 12:23.
54. § 44:1.
55. Job 26:6; 14:13; Prov. 15:11.
56. Ps. 139:8; Am. 9:2.
57. Job 26:5.
58. Ps. 88:6.
59. Ps. 88:11.

60. Is. 38:11.
61. Pss. 6:6; 30:10; 115:17.
62. Bar. 2:17.
63. Jer. 37:20; cf. Ps. 39:13-14.
64. Pss. 21:5; 119:17; 143:11; Is. 38:9f.
65. Job 2:4.
66. 2 Sam. 19:36.

death welcome. A person had to be wholly despondent before he longed fo
the grave. Sorrowing over the loss of Joseph, Jacob wished to die.[67] Jo
desired death when he no longer expected to recover;[68] also Moses,[69] Elias[7]
and Jonas[71] when they believed they could no longer bear the burden God ha
laid upon them, yet they would willingly have lived longer if conditions im
proved. Tobias and Sara desired to die because kinsmen despised them in thei
misfortunes.[72] Jesus Sirach considered death better than constant sicknes
or loss of honor through calumny and slander and a desirable good for on
who is senile or weighed down with afflictions.[73] And Qoheleth, reviewing th
endless miseries of mankind, praises death as better than life and those a
most fortunate who were never born.[74]

These dreary ideas remained current in Israel till the beginning of th
second century before Christ. Qoheleth could not resolve his interior difficultie
because he did not know about future retribution. Jesus Sirach tells us, "It i
impossible to seek after bliss in Hades,"[75] and then asks rhetorically, "Who i
able to praise the Most High in Hades?[76].... On the part of the dead, the
who no longer live, praise is past."[77] Chapters later where he admonishes no
to fear death, he gives no reasons other than that death is the common lot o
all and that it is not becoming to contradict God's will.[78] Man accepts lif
as an unmerited gift from God, he should also be satisfied that its end too ha
been divinely ordained.

4. DIFFERENCES AT AND AFTER DEATH. While the dead in Sheol experience
no comfort or joy, all did not meet an absolutely identical fate. The greates
misfortune was to remain uninterred, leaving the body become the prey of wil
animals. Rispa, Saul's concubine, guarded the corpses of Saul's sons fron
such a fate.[79] This was the punishment in store for Joiakim,[80] for Jeroboam'
descendants,[81] and in general for Jews who sinned grievously.[82] It was regarde
as a divine judgment when someone did not receive "an honorable burial."[8]
Isaias prophesied that Babylon's king, who had brought destruction upon hi
nation, would go tombless.[84] In an appalling prophecy Jeremias describe
how enemies would take from their graves the bones of the kings of Juda
and of the inhabitants of Jerusalem and scatter them under the stars—the ver
stars they had worshipped during life.[85] To bury the dead as did Tobias wa
an act of virtue.[86] The expression, the pious man dies in peace,[87] implie
real differences between the lot of one who lived virtuously and of one wh
lived wickedly. Balaam wished "to die the death of the righteous,"[88] i.e., o
an Israelite who enjoyed Yahweh's love. While other kings in Sheol reste
in peace sitting on thrones, the king of Babylon would have maggots and worm
for his couch and be mocked by those about him.[89] The same notions are foun

67. Gen. 37:35.
68. Job 3:13, 21; 6:9.
69. Num. 11:15.
70. 3 Kgs. 19:4.
71. Jon. 4:3.
72. Tob. 3:6, 13.
73. Sir. 30:17; 28:21; 42:2.
74. Qoh. 4:2-3; § 30:5.

75. Sir. 14:16.
76. Sir. 17:27.
77. Sir. 17:28.
78. Sir. 41:3-4.
79. 2 Sam. 21:10f.
80. Jer. 22:19; 36:30.
81. 3 Kgs. 14:11.
82. Jer. 7:33; 16:4.

83. Is. 34:3.
84. Is. 14:20.
85. Jer. 8:1-2; cf. Am. 2:1.
86. Tob. 1:17-18; 2:3-7.
87. Gen. 15:15; 4 Kgs. 22:20
    Is. 57:2.
88. Num. 23:10.
89. Is. 14:3-21.

in Ez. 32:17-32: at his death Pharaoh would be relegated to the deepest abyss, the abode of all the enemies of God's people, of the uncircumcised and the uninterred who, struck by the sword, must "carry their disgrace" into the next life. Brave men will scoff at Pharaoh and refuse to speak with him.

These notions constituted the kernel from which developed a more profound theology on retribution after death.

§43. RETRIBUTION IN THE NEXT LIFE

1. HENOCH AND ELIAS. A cryptic verse in Genesis recounts how Henoch "walked with God and was seen no longer for God had taken him away."[1] Since he had lived in a manner particularly pleasing to God, he did not die as did the other patriarchs, but was "taken away" in reward for his virtue.[2] Elias too was "taken away," riding in a fiery chariot toward heaven,[3] "because of his great zeal for the Law he was taken away into heaven."[4] During his struggles for God's honor Elias reaped nothing but persecution; finally he obtained a fitting reward.

2. LIFE AS A REWARD, DEATH AS A PUNISHMENT. In the pages of the OT those who obey God's commandments are frequently promised "life" as a reward, while sinners are threatened with "death" as a punishment. "I have placed before you life and good, death and evil[5].... Seek me that you may live[6] .... I place before you the way of life and the way of death[7].... The upright man stays alive through his faith."[8] Ezechiel promised "life" to the man who fulfilled God's commands faithfully and likewise to the sinner who converts, but "death" to the sinner who remained in sin. God has "no pleasure in the death of one who must die" (i.e., a sinner).[9] Surely the prophet was aware that good men and wicked men would be slain in the destruction of Jerusalem which he was prophesying.[10] The concepts of "life" and "death" accordingly should not be limited to physical life and death, but extended to include some reference to the relationship between man and God in the next world.

Very often the proverb writers urge us to merit "life" by practicing virtue and warn us to regard "death" as punishment. "Prudence and discretion will be life for your soul."[11] An adulterer "shall not reach the paths of life[12].... Upon the path of righteousness is life, the way of foolishness leads to death."[13] Without doubt the rewards promised refer primarily to earthly goods[14] and "life" signifies a ripe old age.[15] But "life" also implies God's good pleasure[16] and peace of conscience,[17] while "death" results from God's wrath; consequently the Israelite must have asked himself whether the word "life" embraced nothing more than great age and temporal goods, and whether God in His justice and love did not keep in store another "life" for the just man who on this

1. Gen. 5:24; Sir. 44:16.
2. Cf. Wis. 4:10.
3. 4 Kgs. 2:3-12.
4. 1 Mach. 2:58.
5. Deut. 30:15; 19; cf. Lev. 18:5; Deut. 4:1; 8:1, 3.
6. Am. 5:4, 6, 14.
7. Jer. 21:8.
8. Hab. 2:4.
9. Ez. 18:32; 33:10f.
10. Ez. 15:1-3; 12:7, 10-16; 15:1-8; 21:3, 8, 9; §39:1.
11. Prov. 3:22.
12. Prov. 2:19; 5:6.
13. Prov. 12:28; cf. 4:22; 6:23; 8:35-36.
14. §32:1h.
15. Prov. 16:31.
16. Prov. 8:35.
17. Prov. 3:21-26.

earth experienced only hardships and died at an early age. "The intelligent man takes the path of life (which leads) upwards to escape Sheol below."[18] Virtue however cannot preserve from death and frequently not even from an early death. And how is "death" a punishment for the wicked if they have lived long and enjoyed every earthly luxury? These considerations troubled many[19] and were of such a nature as could have occasioned the conclusion that earthly existence was not "life" in the full sense and that the soul's departure from the body was not "death." Was there not a higher life, a life in the love and friendship of God? Frequently there is mentioned "a book of the living" in which the just are inscribed and from which the godless are stricken.[20] Here too the primary consideration is preservation from an early and sudden death and a long earthly life, but the notion of sharing in blessings promised to the virtuous, particularly God's love, is not totally absent; the good man might well wonder whether he would be stricken out of this book when he died, especially if he died young. These expressions then do not refer directly to the beatitude of the elect in heaven or the punishment of the damned in hell, but they do prepare the ground for the theology of just retribution after death.

3. HOPE IN ETERNAL HAPPINESS. In certain psalms we find the author awaiting eternal beatitude in union with God. The composer of Ps. 73 was convinced that his union with God would last beyond the grave, "Afterwards you will receive me in honor. Flesh and heart may vanish from me, still *Yahweh* remains my portion forever."[21] Quite otherwise with the godless who enjoy every luxury during life: just as a dream disappears from human memory they are forgotten by God the moment they die.[22] The author of Ps. 49 is certain that a just requital will take place at the time of death; the rich man trusting in his goods and remaining estranged from God will die and Sheol will hold him fast never to release him; the virtuous too will die, but "God shall redeem my soul, from Sheol indeed he shall get me."[23] Death and Sheol have no power over the good man, God intervenes and frees him from their terrors. Here we meet the idea of Sheol being a place of punishment where the wicked must ever remain, while the virtuous man has a different lot: after death he meets God who favors him with His love. There is as yet no thought of bodily resurrection. V. 5 expressly says that this doctrine is something new; the psalmist did not obtain it through reflection but through divine enlightenment. According to v. 2 this good news should be shared with all. Beatitude in afterlife was not limited to the sacred writer but extended to all who in this life keep the grace of union with God. Other pious men had the same problem as the authors of Pss. 49 and 73, and for some strong faith may have awakened a longing for lasting union with God. The request in Ps. 16:9-11 for everlasting intimacy with God and preservation from bodily corruption found its fulfillment pre-eminently in Jesus.[24] But the pious OT reader could conclude

18. Prov. 15:24.
19. § 41:3.
20. Ex. 32:32; Is. 4:3; Ez. 21. Ps. 73:24-26.
13:9; Ps. 69:29; Dan. 12:1.
22. Ps. 73:19-20.
23. Ps. 49:16.
24. § 53:2c.

that he need not fear death, rather that at death he would be rewarded for his virtuous life.

4. SHEOL AS A PLACE OF PUNISHMENT. We cannot conclude from the words, "A fire blazed up in my wrath and burnt to deepest Sheol,"[25] that God, whose power reaches down into the netherworld,[26] punishes the guilty there; in this text we simply have a picture which describes the severity of the divine judgment from which no sinner can escape; and the following verses enumerate earthly punishments. The assertion that Sheol will not "free" the adulterer[27] implies that retention there is a punishment willed by God. The poet of Ps. 49 hopes the evildoer "will come to his fathers' generation who never will see the light."[28] He is convinced that the godless are consigned to Sheol forever as punishment. Because Jerusalem remained deaf to all the admonitions of the prophets, she would be cast into the netherworld.[29] The proud king of Babylon "shall be hurled down into Sheol, to the bottommost pit."[30] In another psalm we read, "May evildoers descend to Sheol, all the *arrogant* who forget Yahweh."[31] In the kingdom of the dead the worst offenders will be mocked and scoffed at.[32]

Belief in retribution after death did not become common until the second century before Christ. The prophets Aggeus, Zacharias and Malachias make no reference to it, and when Qoheleth speaks of judgment, he is speaking of retribution in this world.[33] Only hesitatingly and incidentally does Jesus Sirach allude to "the depths of Sheol" where sinners go,[34] or console the God-fearing by declaring, "On the day of his death he shall be praised."[35] His admonitions to remain loyal to the faith and to obey God's will[36] are not supported by sanctions effective in eternity; in other passages he awaits adequate requital in this life.[37]

5. BELIEF IN RETRIBUTION DURING THE LAST TWO CENTURIES BEFORE CHRIST. When many Jews were dying as martyrs in the religious persecutions of Antiochus IV, the question arose whether their blood and lives were offered to God in vain. What once only a few pious persons had hoped for, now became the belief of wider circles. Thus oppression effected a deepening of the theology of afterlife. When the aged Eleazar was urged to simulate compliance with the king's command, he objected, "Even though at this moment I might be able to escape tortures from the hands of men, I would never, living or dead, be able to flee from the hands of the Universal Ruler,"[38] i.e., in eternity God would punish him because of having saved his life by deception. The mother of the Maccabean martyrs encouraged her youngest son, "Accept death so that I may again find you with your brothers on the day of mercy."[39] She believed that after death martyrs would be rewarded for their constancy. And her son addressed the tyrant, "After enduring short affliction our brothers now share

25. Deut. 32:22.
26. § 42:3.
27. Prov. 2:18-19; 5:5; 7:27.
28. Ps. 49:20.
29. Is. 5:14.
30. Is. 14:15.

31. Ps. 9:18.
32. § 42:4.
33. Qoh. 11:9; 12:14.
34. Sir. 21:10.
35. Sir. 1:13.

36. Sir. 2:3.
37. Sir. 9:11; 11:26-28; 51: 30; cf. § 42:3.
38. 2 Mach. 6:26.
39. 2 Mach. 7:29.

in the eternal reward promised by God, but at God's judgment you, on account of your pride, will receive due punishment."[40] As the context shows, he had in mind the punishment which would come upon the king in the next life.[41] When it was discovered that those who had fallen in the battle against Gorgias had carried amulets, "the Jews took to prayer and implored that this violation might be wholly forgiven." Judas had a "sacrifice offered for the sins," because "he believed a truly glorious reward awaited those who had died virtuously;" and the hagiographer endorsed his belief.[42] Hence virtue will be rewarded in the next life, while evil will be punished; one whose sins are not grave will not have to suffer for all eternity, and the living may aid in shortening his time of penance. Here in substance we have the doctrine of purgatory.

In the Book of Wisdom we find clearly expounded the doctrine of just retribution in afterlife. "Righteousness is immortal."[43] Death is a misfortune only for him who dies in sin; for the pious man it opens a way to blessed immortality, to communion with God who rewards piety.[44] Man was created for union with God[45] and all who sacrifice their lives in persecution may hope for this blessed union with absolute certainty;[46] when they die they "are in peace[47].... at rest[48].... after a little affliction they shall experience great blessings."[49] Death for them is a token of divine favor,[50] an early death[51] merely an apparent death.[52] On earth they may have lacked many things which are regarded as blessings, like money and children, but they will receive adequate compensation "in the temple of the Lord," i.e., in heaven.[53] At times beatitude is viewed as a grace[54] and at times as a reward;[55] the deduction to be made is that the reward of eternal happiness is God's free gift, beyond anything one may truly merit.[56]

For the wicked "death" implies loss of grace and God's good pleasure. By their acts of unbelief, their lust for pleasure and their persecution of the just they "entice death,"[57] at which moment they become subject to eternal damnation.[58] A great separation takes place as God judges individual after individual. The just are received into God's presence[59] while the wicked are consigned to Hades, which thereby becomes hell, the habitat of sinners. The older notion of Sheol had prepared the way for this development.[60] The damned will find the pains of hell everlasting and will cry out in vain at the Last Judgment as they witness the blessedness of the elect.[61]

The doctrine on afterlife contained in the Book of Wisdom goes far beyond what older Biblical writers had held. Fundamental differences however keep the Biblical doctrine distinct from that advanced in the Hellenic world and by the mystery religions. The author of the Book of Wisdom may indeed have been stimulated by outside influences as he developed the more ancient Biblical

40. 2 Mach. 7:36.
41. Cf. 2 Mach. 7:17-19.
42. 2 Mach. 12:42-45.
43. Wis. 1:15.
44. Wis. 3:9; 4:10; 6:19.
45. Wis. 1:14.
46. Wis. 3:4.
47. Wis. 3:3.

48. Wis. 4:7.
49. Wis. 3:5.
50. Wis. 4:7, 14, 15.
51. Wis. 4:11.
52. Wis. 3:2.
53. Wis. 3:13-14.
54. Wis. 3:9; 4:15.

55. Wis. 2:22; 3:13-15; 5:15.
56. Wis. 3:5.
57. Wis. 2:1-20.
58. Wis. 1:11-12.
59. Wis. 3:1-9.
60. Ps. 49; Is. 66:24.
61. Wis. 5:3-13.

teachings. However at every step he was under the guidance of divine providence which sought to prepare the Jews in the diaspora (and with them the Gentiles who had become acquainted with Israel's religion) for the revelation which in the fullness of time would soon be proclaimed. This revelation would also shed final light on the theology of future life and eternal retribution.

§ 44. RESURRECTION

1. RAISING THE DEAD TO LIFE. One of the favorite expressions of OT sacred writers to show God's power was the following: Yahweh kills and restores to life, He leads men down to Sheol and brings them back again.[1] The thought underlying this phraseology was deliverance from the danger of death. There are however three passages which do treat of the restoration to life of a deceased person. In answer to Elias' prayer God restored life to the son of the widow of Sarepta,[2] in answer to Eliseus' prayer the son of the Shunammite came to life again,[3] and a dead man arose after the bones of Eliseus had touched him.[4] God would have restored life to one in "the depths of Sheol," had Achaz requested this from Isaias as a sign.[5] According to prophecy the Servant of Yahweh would die, be buried, and rise again,[6] likewise the Man of Sorrows.[7] The pious man of Ps. 16:10 begged for preservation from corruption, i.e., speedy resurrection (which was fulfilled in the Messiah).[8] These instances of raising the dead to life witness God's power over Sheol.[9]

2. NATIONAL RESURRECTION. The prophet Osee foretold how the people of the northern kingdom would be led into exile because of their wickedness. When a sufficient number had repented, Yahweh would deliver them, "From the power of Sheol I shall free them, I shall deliver them from death. *Where are your epidemics, O death? Where is your pest, O Sheol?*"[10] There is question here of several mataphors: the exile is "death," the land of exile is "Sheol," the return from exile "resurrection." Already in 6:2 Osee had re-echoed the people's sentiments, "After two days he shall re-enliven us, on the third he shall cause our resurrection so that we may live before him." This text does not refer to an exile, the prophet is comparing the sinful condition of the people to death and their restoration to divine favor to resurrection.

Centuries after Osee had announced "resurrection" to the northern kingdom, Ezechiel in a vision beheld the "resurrection" of the Judeans actually detained in bondage.[11] In a valley before him were lying a great mass of dead bones, wholly desiccated. Yahweh asked, "Shall these bones live again?" In the circumstances this seemed utterly impossible, but the prophet prudently answered, "Lord, Yahweh, you know!" Upon Yahweh's bidding he then prophesied over the bones. Thereupon they joined themselves together, the skeletons covered themselves with flesh and skin, breath entered the bodies and they

1. Deut. 32:39 (here of the nation); 1 Sam. 2:6; 4 Kgs. 5:7; Pss. 18:6-7; 30:4; 71:20; 86:13; Jon. 2:7; Tob. 13:2.
2. 3 Kgs. 17:17-24.
3. 4 Kgs. 4:31-37.
4. 4 Kgs. 13:21.
5. Is. 7:11.
6. Is. 52:13-14; 53:10.
7. Ps. 22:23f.
8. § 52:2c.
9. Cf. § 42:3.
10. Os. 13:14.
11. Ez. 37:1-14.

stood erect. To the exiles the destruction of the kingdom and the captivity was
like death, the forced retention in Babylonia resembled an abode in a grave.
Yahweh promised "to bring them out of their tombs and to lead them into the
land of Canaan." The good Jew would think of Os. 13:14 and Ez. 37:1-14 when
he prayed, "*If it pleases* you to revivify us, the people will rejoice in you."[12]

3. INDIVIDUAL RESURRECTION. According to Ezechiel's prophecy the Jews,
although living as it were in a grave, would rise to new life; and this prophecy
was fulfilled when they returned from Babylon to their native land. Will the
individual remain forever in the grave where he was buried? Will the good
fortune of being freed from the hands of death be given only to the Servant of
Yahweh,[13] to the Man of Sorrows,[14] and to the just man of Ps. 16? A definite
answer finally came during the Syrian persecutions. After the description of
the afflictions suffered by the Jews under Antiochus IV, Daniel prophesied
national deliverance and added a famous passage on personal resurrection (the
prophets had no perspective in messages about the future),[15] "Many of those
who sleep in the dust shall awake, some to eternal life and others to disgrace,
to everlasting shame. And the wise shall shine as magnificently as the firmament, and those who convert many, as the stars for ever and ever."[16] Not only
the virtuous shall arise but the wicked also. Even if the word "many" be
understood in the sense of "all," this text from Daniel does not tell of a universal resurrection but of one embracing only the Chosen People, since according to v. 1 only these are saved. The resurrection will mark a division between
the good and the bad, the former will enter into the joys of heaven, the latter
into the torments of hell, and that for all eternity. There will be differences
too in the rewards meted out. All will indeed partake in the glory of heaven,
but those who labored in a special manner to strengthen others in virtue by
word or good example, or inspired them to perseverance by suffering martyrdom,
will enjoy greater beatitude in eternity.

Ps. 17:15M, "Would that I could in justice gaze upon your face, that upon
awakening I could satiate myself with your form," is not to be understood
of awakening from the sleep of death, i.e., of a resurrection; there is nothing
about dying in this passage which is concerned about retribution while on
earth.[17] Perhaps the more probable reading is that of G, Th, "*with beholding
your form*,"[18] instead of "upon awakening."

The difficult and critically uncertain text of Job 19:25-27 reads, "I know
that my vindicator lives, and as the last (One) he will raise himself up upon
the dust (v. 25), and in my skin, *bruised indeed*, and in my flesh I shall see
God (v. 26). Then I shall see (to my joy) and my eyes *shall* see, and not
another (v. 27)." G and It understood these verses of physical recovery. Most
of the fathers did not use the passage to prove the resurrection of the body.
Jerome's Vulgate reads, "I know that my Redeemer lives and on the last day
I shall rise from the earth (v. 25). And I shall again be covered with my skin and

12. Ps. 85:7. 15. § 49:6c. 17. Ps. 17:13-14.
13. Is. 52; 53. 16. Dan. 12:2-3. 18. § 41:7.
14. Ps. 22.

shall see my God in my flesh (v. 26). I myself shall see him, and my eyes shall see him, and not another; this hope is stored up in my bosom (v. 27)." From this translation a well-nigh universal but very late interpretation arose ascribing to the passage the doctrine of the resurrection. Actually the idea of bodily resurrection after death never entered the mind of suffering Job.[19] For Job there was no hope in Sheol. He imagined how beautiful it would be if he were like a tree that, when hewn down, sprouts forth new shoots, but rejects the thought as impossible; for there is no return from Sheol.[20] He was willing to bear present suffering and the sorry lot awaiting him in Sheol if he could look forward to a revival after death. In the discourses following the controverted passage there is no allusion to belief in resurrection.[21] Even at the very end of the book we find no reference to retribution in the next world. If Job 19:25-27 expresses belief in bodily resurrection, the passage would constitute the climax of the book and all the discussion which follows would become meaningless. Job's friends did not understand the words as indicating hope in a future resurrection, or they would have in some way modified their replies. Job's desire to see God, as stated in v. 26, is simply an expression of his hope to experience God's intervention while life still remains in his ailing body.[22] So vehement is his longing that he already rejoices in the moment when this blessing will be accorded him.[23] He himself and not another after his demise, will be present when God will attest his innocence.[24] While he is yet alive, God as his vindicator will uphold the sinlessness of Job, which had been so bitterly attacked by those endeavoring to comfort him.[25] God is "the last" since He gives the final decision; "the dust" is the earth. Because God will justify him, Job admonishes his friends to discontinue reproaching him[26] lest they bring down divine wrath upon themselves. Actually God did appear during Job's lifetime; as his vindicator, as "the last," He settled Job's case favorably, proclaiming his innocence in the presence of his friends,[27] returning fortune and health, and thus justifying him before all the world.[28] Some exegetes explain the passage as a vision of the next life, others of bodily resurrection. The Vulgate reading serves as a proof for the resurrection of the body by force of ecclesiastical tradition. A similar witness is the addition to 42:17 in the Septuagint, "But it is written, that he (Job) will again rise with those whom the Lord will awaken."

As late as the year 200 B.C. belief in bodily resurrection was not accepted by and large. It formed no part of the Qoheleth discussions, and Jesus Sirach made no mention of it when he sought to comfort the survivors of a deceased person.[29] Sirach pointed out the glory of leaving behind a good name.[30] The statements "May their (the Judges') bones sprout up from their (resting) places, and renew their fame for their sons[31].... May the bones of the twelve prophets sprout up from their (resting) places,"[32] do not refer to a bodily

19. Job 7:9-10; 10:21; 16:22; 17:13-16.
20. Job 14:7-22.
21. Job 19:25-27, cf. especially Job 21:23-26; 30:33.
22. Cf. Job 8:2.
23. Job 19:27.
24. Job 19:27.
25. Cf. Dhorme, Peters.
26. Job 19:28-29.
27. Job 42:7-9.
28. Job 42:10-17; § 41:5.
29. Sir. 38:16-23.
30. Sir. 39:9; 41:11-13.
31. Sir. 46:12.
32. Sir. 49:10.

resurrection but to the continuation of the family tree. (Sir. 48:10G, "And we too shall have life," is a later addition.)

During the persecution of Antiochus Epiphanes pious Jews began to believe in a resurrection of the body as well as in the doctrine of retribution in the next life. The second Maccabean brother cried out while being tormented, "You evildoer! Truly you are taking away our mortal life, yet the King of the universe shall awaken us who die for the Law to a resurrection in eternal life."[33] The words of the third brother, whose tongue and hands were cut off, "These things *I received* from heaven and I hope to obtain again from him these very same things,"[34] may be a later addition. But the fourth made a similar statement, "Willingly does one die at the hands of men if he cherishes the God-given hope to be reawakened by him. But for you there shall be no resurrection unto life!"[35] The emphasis is upon the last words; our martyr does not deny that the wicked will rise, but resurrection for them will not be a blessing,[36] because they will arise "to disgrace, to everlasting shame,"[37] not "unto life." The youngest brother expressed his belief that those martyred before him had merited resurrection unto eternal life by enduring bitter torture to the very end.[38] At the moment of death Rages asked God to "restore again" his torn body.[39] When Judas offered the sacrifice for the slain, "he took into consideration the resurrection."[40]

The author of the Book of Wisdom does not expressly teach the doctrine of the resurrection, perhaps because he had in mind Gentile readers who were not well disposed toward this doctrine; he does not reject it however and it harmonizes well with his general mentality. God does not rejoice over the destruction of the living.[41] The words, "You have power over the living and the dead, you lead down to the gates of Hades and up again,"[42] not only reflect the most ancient Biblical teaching on preservation from death, but ascribe to God the power to awaken the dead to life, as shown by the following verse, "Through his wickedness a man may indeed murder another, but he cannot bring back the departed spirit or liberate the soul imprisoned (in the netherworld)." There is some relation between, "the just shall shine at the time of their visitation,"[43] and Dan. 12:2-3, which tells of the resurrection. The description of the general judgment in Wis. 4:20-5:14 seems to imply that our author was conversant with the notion of bodily resurrection. Sinners appear as the accused,[44] sins as the accusers,[45] and the just as witnesses.[46] God is judge and the guilty recognize their guilt.[47] Judgment is held over persons who have long since died,[48] and illegitimate children give testimony against immoral parents.[49] Many are judged at the same time, since they speak with one another.[50] Consequently it is not the judgment which follows immediately after death. Many good persons appear before God who have preceded the

33. 2 Mach. 7:9.
34. 2 Mach. 7:11.
35. 2 Mach. 7:14.
36. 2 Mach. 7:36.
37. Dan. 12:2.
38. 2 Mach. 7:36; cf. Bückers Bb 21, 1940, 406-412.

39. 2 Mach. 14:46.
40. 2 Mach. 12:44.
41. Wis. 1:13.
42. Wis. 16:13.
43. Wis. 3:7.
44. Wis. 4:20.

45. Wis. 4:20.
46. Wis. 5:1.
47. Wis. 3:1-13.
48. Wis. 4:19.
49. Wis. 4:6.
50. Wis. 5:3.

wicked to the grave.[51] Till then the godless were scoffed at in Sheol,[52] but now they experience new degradation and shame, "They have no hope and no consolation on the day of decision."[53] But the just shall "shine" before all the world, their virtue shall be manifest as they are glorified,[54] and they shall pronounce judgment upon the wicked by "passing like sparks through underbrush[55].... they shall judge nations and govern peoples, and the Lord shall be their king forever." In heaven untold power and glory will be theirs. But the supreme blessing will consist in "remaining in God's love" forever.[56] They will then "recognize the truth,"[57] the mysteries of divine providence will be disclosed to them, and they will see why God permitted them to suffer while sinners enjoyed the good things of earth.

Most of the OT apocrypha contain descriptions of a general resurrection followed by a universal judgment. The Book of Henoch offers a most vivid and detailed account. At the time of Christ the Pharisees defended the doctrine of a resurrection,[58] while the Sadducees denied it.[59] Martha's reply shows that pious Jews commonly believed in a resurrection, "I know that he will rise at the resurrection on the last day."[60]

4. FOREIGN INFLUENCES? Modern efforts to derive much of Israel's religious doctrine from other Oriental peoples do not leave untouched belief in bodily resurrection. The rationalists point out an Egyptian myth in which Osiris is slain, rises again and attains eternal life; they say his lot became a type for the common man. Actually Osiris did not return to the world; he remained in Hades as its sovereign with only a hope of attaining beatitude at some future time. A true resurrection does not form part of the myth. Moreover, in case there were Egyptian influences, we should expect such to appear long before the exile.

The Oriental vegetation deities reflected nature in her twofold cycle of dying and reawakening. In Israel women wept over the Sumerian-Babylonian god Tammuz.[61] During the fourth month (June/July), which is named after him, Tammuz descended into the netherworld as the grain was cut and the stalks dried in the summer heat; he remained there till spring when nature reawakened. Parallel to Tammuz in Phoenician-Canaanite lands, was the god Adonis.[62] In the Ras Shamra texts Baal and Aliyan are nature deities who die only to come to life again.[63] But this in no way implies that the Babylonians and Canaanites believed in a personal resurrection; though the death of the god was lamented, his reawakening was not celebrated. Moreover the cycle of plant life is a natural process, while Israel's "dying" was a punishment; Israel was to "rise again" after she had performed due penance,[64] and this ethical concept is emphasized particularly in those passages which herald a personal resurrection. Job expressly rejected the notion of comparing man to a tree which when cut

51. Wis. 2:20; 3:2-3; 4:15; 5:4.
52. Wis. 4:19.
53. Wis. 3:18.
54. Cf. Dan. 12:3.
55. Cf. Abd. 18.
56. Wis. 3:7-9.
57. Wis. 3:9.
58. Acts 23:6; 24:15.
59. Matth. 22:23; Mk. 12:18; Lk. 20:27; Acts 23:8.
60. John 11:24.
61. Ez. 8:14.
62. Is. 17:10; (Os. 6:2?).
63. Dussaud RHR 118, 1938, 133-169; Baumgartner ThRdsch 13, 1941, 92.
64. Os.; Ez.

down sends out sprouts and grows branches;[65] hence the reawakening in nature was hardly the source for Israelitic doctrine on the final destiny of man.

Certain Babylonian songs describe a sick or suffering man approaching the doors of the underworld; from thence a god leads him back to life. This only means that the individual concerned became well again; there was merely a danger of death, not actual death, and accordingly a resurrection from physical death is excluded. With these passages texts like Deut. 32:39 and 1 Sam. 2:6 stand comparison. The Persians believed in bodily resurrection at the end of time, but the antiquity of their doctrine is doubtful. At first the Jews believed in the resurrection of good Israelites, then of all Israelites, and only later of all men. Persian *apokatastasis*, according to which the wicked too would be saved after they had passed through a fire that burnt away all dross, is traceable only to comparatively late times and contradicts their older doctrine, according to which the wicked would be eternally rejected at the resurrection. OT eschatology developed gradually under divine guidance; it rested upon faith in the power and justice of God and the retribution of good and evil; it came to crown the doctrine of God's universal sovereignty which must include the dead. Since the OT itself presents all the preliminary steps, there is no valid reason to regard the doctrine of resurrection as a borrowing from Persian sources, even if those sources were proven more ancient than those in the Bible. It is not even probable that a knowledge of Persian ideas hastened the evolution of OT theology on these points, since the major developments first appeared during the Maccabean revolution.

65. Job 14:7-9.

PART V

REDEMPTION

SECTION 1. JUDGMENT

The blot of sin stains the very first page of human history. At first individuals strayed from God, then whole nations. Even Israel frequently became unfaithful. But should the nations remain cut off from God? Should Israel prove continually rebellious? Should there not come a time when men could live free from sin, as was possible for our first parents in paradise? Thus sin gave birth to the desire to be free from sin, to the desire for strength to do God's will at all times; likewise there budded the hope that nations would place themselves wholly at God's service. God had planted in the hearts of Adam and Eve a willingness to obey His commands and, through the preaching of the prophets and Mosaic cult, this willingness was kept awake and increased in Israel. But the Gentile nations must be brought to acknowledge their own helplessness and their dependence upon the one true God, and Israel must be disciplined that she might turn to Yahweh with purified heart. Then would the road be clear for God to enter a new covenant with Israel and mankind. Thus judgment was a preparation for, or an initial stage in the redemption from sin. The prophecies against the nations came before those against Israel, and following this order we shall consider first the judgments against the Gentiles. According to the prophets however the reinstatement of Israel in God's favor precedes the conversion of foreign peoples.

The prophecies which foretell the coming redemption are called "messianic," even when they do not refer to a specific person, the Messiah, who brings salvation. The salvation proclaimed by the prophets will be apportioned to Israel and the world in "messianic times." On the designation "Messiah," cf. § 50:1.

§45. JUDGMENT UPON THE GENTILES

1. ISRAEL AWAITING JUDGMENT UPON HER FOES. At the Red Sea Moses promised, "Yahweh shall battle for you,"[1] and after the crossing he praised Yahweh as the Warrior whose right hand crushed the enemy.[2] Upon breaking camp in the wilderness the Israelites prayed, "Arise, Yahweh, in order that your foes may be scattered as dust, in order that those who hate you may flee before your face."[3] The Chosen People had received the assurance, "I shall

1. Ex. 14:14.   2. Ex. 15:3, 6.   3. Num. 10:35.

269

be hostile to your enemies and oppress your oppressors,"[4] and were convinced that victories on the field of battle were due to Yahweh's intervention. The triumphs over the Canaanites were acts of Yahweh,[5] the stars fought for Israel from heaven[6] as the poet sang, "Thus should all your enemies perish, Yahweh!"[7] There was extant a "Book of the Wars of Yahweh,"[8] and David led the battles of Yahweh.[9] Israel considered her bond with Yahweh so strong as to have no doubts about Yahweh's assistance in time of war.[10] Actually Yahweh's promises of espousing the cause of Israel against enemies held only in case they observed His commandments;[11] this however did not hinder the Israelites, particularly in times of foreign oppression, from longing for the "Day of Yahweh," which would bring light and salvation to themselves, but darkness and misfortune to the Gentiles. The phrase, "Day of Yahweh," used first in Am. 5:18, at times indicated judgment upon a specific people, at other times a series of judgments inflicted by Yahweh, again at other times the final judgment at the end of the world. Since the prophets used the phrase or its shorter equivalent, "that day," without clarification, we may reasonably conclude that they did not create the underlying notion of eschatological judgment but adopted current ideas.

2. COMMINATORY PROPHETIC DISCOURSES. An indication that nations guilty of sin against God will be punished appears already in Noe's prophetical blessing: Cham's posterity would become servants to the posterity of Sem and Japhet.[12] Yahweh promised to curse anyone who wished evil upon Abram.[13] Since the context treats of Abram's descendants, this threat was pointed more directly toward the future than toward the present; attacks upon Abram's children would be judged as attacks upon Yahweh's plan of salvation. In Balaam's prophecy drastic judgment was proclaimed against foreign nations. Israel could be certain of triumph in battle,[14] the star and sceptre arising in Israel would smash the temples of Moab and strike to the ground "all the sons of warmongers."[15]

There are countless prophecies of judgment in the literary prophets. Their judgments are directed in the first place against the smaller neighboring nations, Israel, Edom, Moab, Ammon, Philistia, then against Aram, Tyre, Sidon, against the great world kingdoms of Assyria, Babylon, Egypt, Cush (Ethiopia), Arabia,[16] Elam,[17] Yawan (Greece),[18] and finally against the nations of the north in league with Gog.[19] Another simpler approach taken by the prophets was to pronounce judgment against "the peoples,"[20] against "many peoples,"[21] against "all peoples,"[22] against "all the kingdoms of the earth,"[23] or against "the earth with all its inhabitants."[24] Being already assigned to the mission of prophet over the nations at the time of his call, Jeremias noted how his

4. Ex. 23:22; Deut. 32:41.
5. Judg. 5:11.
6. Judg. 5:20.
7. Judg. 5:31.
8. Num. 21:14.
9. 1 Sam. 18:17.
10. § 32:1f.
11. Ex. 23:22.
12. Gen. 9:26-27.
13. Gen. 12:3.
14. Num. 23:24.
15. Num. 24:17; § 51:1.
16. Jer. 25:24; 49:28-33.
17. Jer. 49:34-39.
18. Zach. 9:13.
19. Ez. 38; 39.
20. Mich. 5;6f; 7:11f.
21. Mich. 4:11f.
22. Is. 34; Abd.; Joel; Agg.; Zach. 12; 14.
23. Agg.; Jer. 25:26.
24. Is. 24-27; 34; 35; Mich. 7:11f; Agg.

predecessors had foretold war, famine, and pestilence upon "many lands and against many kingdoms."[25] Thus they spread the truth that the whole world is guilty before Yahweh.

3. GENERAL JUDGMENT. Isaias described the judgment over Jerusalem and Judah in a way which might lead one to think of a judgment over all mankind.[26] In his prophecies on the downfall of Assyria, the one invincible nation at the time,[27] we must not miss the lesson that any nation which rebels against Yahweh will be annihilated. When Yahweh holds judgment, nature too is drawn into the crucible of suffering: the sea dries up, the mountains quake, the hills reel, rocks burst asunder.[28] Judgment is painted by Habacuc as a great catastrophe in nature[29] during which even the sun and moon will lose their brightness. In Sophonias everything is blotted off the face of the earth, men and cattle, the birds of the heavens and the fish of the sea,[30] and the inhabitants of the earth suddenly perish.[31] According to Jeremias destruction will stalk from nation to nation, mighty storms will rush in from the ends of the earth, and Yahweh's dead victims will lie from one end of creation to the other.[32] In Abd. 16 the judgment upon Edom widens out to become a universal judgment. In Ezechiel the visitation upon Egypt is a type of the final judgment which all nations should expect, "the time of the nations."[33] The judgment upon Edom becomes a universal judgment;[34] so great will be the number of the slain that the mountains and hills will be soaked with blood. Likewise the judgment upon Edom in Is. 63 becomes a judgment upon all nations.

The most detailed description of the final judgment is found in Ezechiel: "After many days" Gog shall come at the head of all the northern peoples "like a storm" upon Israel. An earthquake will strike terror into all; the fish of the sea, the birds of the heavens, the animals of the field, all creeping things and man will tremble before Yahweh; hills will fall, cliffs tumble, walls collapse. Then Yahweh will send pestilence and the sword, floods and hail, fire and brimstone.[35] According to Is. 13:5-11 Yahweh will transform the whole earth into a wilderness and will cleanse it from sin; the stars of heaven will shed light no longer, neither will the sun and moon continue to shine. In Is. 34:4 the stars fall from heaven like withered foliage from trees. According to Joel there will be signs in heaven and upon earth, blood and fire and columns of smoke; the sun will become dark and the moon will take on a deep red hue.[36] Ps. 2 describes how the nations that rebel against Yahweh and His Anointed One will be crushed with an iron sceptre and shattered as so many clay pots.[37] Dan. 7 tells of a conflict not between the Jews and Gentiles but between the just and the godless. The scene of judgment is in heaven, the elements in the world hostile to God are destroyed, and the kingdom of the Son of Man begins. The little horn which raises itself up against the messianic kingdom is Antiochus

25. Jer. 1:5; 28:8.
26. Is. 2:6-21.
27. Is. 10:12-19.
28. Nah. 1:3-6.
29. Hab. 3:3-11.

30. Soph. 1:3.
31. Soph. 1:18; 3:8.
32. Jer. 23:32-33.
33. Ez. 30:3.

34. Is. 34.
35. Ez. 38:19-22.
36. Joel 3:3-4.
37. Cf. Ps. 110:5; Zach. 14;
    Is. 24-26.

IV, here serving as a type of anti-Christ. After describing the general judgment at the end of time,[38] the author of the Book of Wisdom paints the great final conflict with God's enemies and the earth's devastation; here too the opposition is not between Israel and the Gentiles but between the good and the wicked.[39]

4. THE GUILT OF THE GENTILES. Judgment was heralded principally against nations hostile to Israel. They will be punished because they inflicted evil upon God's people. "In wrath you pace through the earth, in fury you crush the nations; you have set out to deliver your people."[40] Nevertheless the nations are punished not solely because they have oppressed Israel, their own guilt is a weightier reason, "Gentile land will be devastated because of its inhabitants, because of the fruit of their deeds[41].... Yahweh has a complaint against the nations, he holds judgment upon all flesh, the godless he delivers to the sword[42].... According to deeds he repays, fury upon opponents, retribution upon enemies."[43] He will "requite the Gentiles, and repay men according to their actions."[44] Judgment is an expression of God's justice and holiness, it restores His honor.

First among the sins of the nations was lust for war and plunder. True, Yahweh employed the Gentiles to punish Israel for her sins,[45] but in that mission they were to observe certain limits; they were not to murder, plunder or destroy wantonly. Assyria "does not think in this manner, nor does his heart plan in this manner, but his mind is bent upon destruction."[46] The Chaldeans likewise went too far in punishing Israel, "I was angry with my people, I desecrated my portion and delivered them into your hand; you had no compassion upon them, the aged you allowed to be weighted down with your all too heavy yoke."[47] Peaceful men would be attacked by Gog and robbed;[48] certain kingdoms were constantly plotting evil against others. Assyria sought to liquidate neighboring nations,[49] Niniveh brought untold suffering upon many peoples,[50] and Babylon plundered countless countries.[51]

Very frequently nations are censured for their pride. Assyria ascribed all success to herself, "By the strength of my hand I have accomplished it and by my wisdom, because I am clever."[52] The Chaldeans regarded their strength as godlike.[53] The king of Babylon strove to resemble God, "I shall ascend to heaven, above God's stars I shall erect my throne and shall sit on the Mountain of Gathering in the farthest north; I shall scale the highest clouds, act like the Most High."[54] He was hurled into the abyss. Yahweh determined to bring the king of Tyre down into the depths of Sheol, "Because your heart exalted itself, because you said: I am a god, I live in a godlike dwelling in the midst of the sea! while you are but a man and not a god, and nevertheless you imagine yourself to be like a god...."[55] Moab "made herself great against Yahweh."[56] It was a common saying among hostile sovereigns, "There is no one besides

38. § 44:3.
39. Wis. 5:16-23.
40. Hab. 3:12; Mich. 4:11f; Ez. 38; Zach. 12; 14.
41. Mich. 7:13.
42. Jer. 25:31.
43. Is. 59:18.

44. Sir. 35:23-24.
45. § 25:4.
46. Is. 10:7.
47. Is. 47:6; Zach. 1:15.
48. Ez. 38:10-12.
49. Is. 10:7.
50. Nah. 3:19.

51. Hab. 2:8.
52. Is. 10:13.
53. Hab. 1:11.
54. Is. 14:13-14.
55. Ez. 28:2.
56. Jer. 48:42.

us,"[57] while they defiled themselves with idolatry and image worship. The prophets roundly condemned this foolish error.[58] When Yahweh comes to chastise the nations, He will cause "all the gods of the earth to vanish."[59] They will be unable to deliver their devotees and thereby will show themselves as helpless as "things of nought." When Babylon falls, her gods will perish[60] and their divinations proven fraudulent.[61] It was a judgment upon all Egypt's gods when Yahweh slew the first-born.[62] Ps. 97:7 tells us, "Every image worshipper who glories in his thing of nought shall be put to shame. All you gods bend down before him."[63]

There was moral guilt too on the consciences of the nations. On the day of judgment offenses and offenders will be swept away[64] because "the inhabitants of the earth violated Yahweh's instructions, contemned the Law, and broke the eternal covenant"[65] which God had made with Noe after the flood.[66] There is a natural moral law to which all peoples are bound.[67] Damascus was slated for punishment because she cruelly massacred the captives from Gilead, Ammon for having inhumanly tortured captive women, Moab for having burnt the bones of the kings of Edom, not even allowing their dead enemies to rest in their graves.[68] Nahum addressed Niniveh, "Woe to the city guilty with blood! Everything about her is deceit, she is full of violence, she never stops plundering."[69] Habacuc accused the Chaldeans of murder and plunder.[70] Edom would be chastised because of her bloodguiltiness[71] and because she reduced escaped Jews to slavery,[72] crimes which were committed also by the Phoenicians and Philistines.[73] The king of Babylon "destroyed his land, murdered his people"[74] by despoliation, constant wars, and unjust legal decisions.

5. JUDGMENT FULFILLED. Assyria was destined to fall "by a 'no-man's' sword, and by a 'no-men's' sword,"[75] i.e., through God's immediate intervention.[76] When God was executing judgment upon Edom, He proclaimed, "The wine press I have trodden alone, and of the nations none stood at my side."[77] At times He delivered a nation into the power of Israel, the very people whom they had oppressed. Edom would be punished when "the house of Jacob becomes a fire and the house of Joseph a flame, but the house of Esau stubble which they ignite and consume."[78] When Israel first occupied Canaan, she inflicted ḥerem upon the inhabitants of the land.[79] Sometimes Yahweh ordained one Gentile nation to punish another. At Yahweh's command Nabuchodonosor subjected the nations bordering Judah,[80] besieged Tyre, and proceeded against Egypt.[81] Commissioned by Yahweh Cyrus liquidated the Babylonian kingdom.[82] Yahweh summoned the Medes against the Chaldeans, calling their

57. Sir. 36:12; Zach. 1:15.
58. § 4:2; 7:2.
59. Soph. 2:11.
60. Is. 21:9; 45:16; 46:1; Ps. 97:7.
61. Is. 47:12.
62. Ez. 12:12.
63. Ps. 97:7.
64. Soph. 1:3.
65. Is. 24:5.

66. Gen. 9:12.
67. § 2:2.
68. Am. 1:3, 13; 2:1-2.
69. Nah. 3:1.
70. Hab. 2:8.
71. Ez. 35:6; Abd. 14; Joel 4:19.
72. Abd. 14.
73. Joel 4:6.
74. Is. 14:20.

75. Is. 31:8.
76. 4 Kgs. 19:7, 35.
77. Is. 63:3.
78. Abd. 18; cf. Ez. 25:14; Zach. 9:13; 12:6.
79. § 32:1e.
80. Jer. 27:1-7.
81. Ez. 29:18; 30:24-25; 32:11f.
82. Is. 41:25; 45:1-3; 46:11.

warriors His "anointed."[83] At times the Gentiles would war among themselves,[84] as in the case of the Midianites versus the Philistines.[85] In the description of judgment found in the Book of Wisdom, God employs various inanimate agents to punish the godless, e.g., lightning, hail, floods, storms. Even the angels are pressed into service to punish the nations.[86]

6. PURPOSE OF THE JUDGMENT. The judgment inflicted upon the nations served to glorify God. By it His honor, violated through sin, was again repaired. His holiness[87] and His justice[88] demands that sinners be punished; accordingly the fire which destroyed Asshur proceeded from Sion, the holy City.[89] In every judgment God's omnipotence is manifested; no power in the world can withstand Him, "He changes princes into nonentities, makes judges of the earth powerless. Hardly are they planted, hardly are they sown and he blows upon them; they wither and a wind carries them away like chaff."[90] The afflicted shall recognize God's omnipotence manifested by the judgment and accept Him as king,[91] for "He shall be king over the whole earth. On that day Yahweh alone and his name alone shall stand erect."[92] Sirach petitioned, "Lift up your hand against foreign peoples so that they may see your power."[93] Judgment is also a manifestation of divine mercy, for through punishment nations are led back to God. Judgment is not designed to destroy but to save. "Yahweh will strike Egypt, he will strike in order to heal; if they return to Yahweh he will listen to their entreaties and heal them," and Assyria would share the blessing.[94] According to Sophonias it is by judgment that God brings the nations to true understanding.[95] Jeremias was assured by God that the nations would be forgiven when they converted;[96] and he informed Egypt, Moab, Ammon and Elam that Yahweh would better their lot after He had chastised them.[97] According to Ezechiel Ammon would acknowledge Yahweh's greatness when judgment came, likewise Moab, Edom, Philistia, Tyre, Sidon, Egypt.[98] Ezechiel does not declare that whole nations actually would draw the proper conclusions viz., abandon their gods, serve Yahweh, and thus attain salvation. But he does teach that some Gentiles would find their way to the one true God.[99] Those who would escape judgment might be very few,[100] but "all who have been left over from all the nations shall year after year ascend to adore Yahweh, King of hosts[101].... Every one who calls upon the name Yahweh shall be saved[102].... and they shall lift up their voices and rejoice over Yahweh's majesty."[103]

§ 46. JUDGMENT UPON ISRAEL

1. COMMINATORY ADDRESSES OF PRE-EXILIC PROPHETS. When the inhabitants of the northern kingdom demanded a "Day of Yahweh," i.e., a favorable

83. Is. 13:3, 17.
84. Ez. 38:21; Is. 49:26; Agg. 2:22; Zach. 14:13.
85. Judg. 7:22; 1 Sam. 14:20.
86. Joel 4:9, 13.
87. § 11:3.
88. § 15:4.
89. Is. 31:9.
90. Is. 40:23-24.
91. § 48:4.
92. Zach. 14:9.
93. Sir. 36:2.
94. Is. 19:22-23.
95. Soph. 3:20.
96. Jer. 18:7-10.
97. Jer. 46:26; 48:47; 49:6,
39.
98. Ez. 26-32; cf. 36:36.
99. Ez. 17:22-24; cf. 16:53-61; § 48:2.
100. Is. 24:6, 13.
101. Zach. 14:16.
102. Joel 3:5.
103. Is. 24:14.

and decisive intervention of God against their enemies, Amos warned them, "Woe to those who desire the Day of Yahweh! What shall the Day of Yahweh bring you? It shall be one of darkness, not of light!"[1] Yahweh would intervene, but not in favor of persons who in spite of admonitions and punishments obeyed none of His laws. Since they had strayed from Him, He "directed his eyes upon them unto evil and not unto good[2]. . . . in order to blot out entirely from the face of the earth the sinful kingdom."[3] The Israelites felt certain of Yahweh's protection because they offered the prescribed sacrifices; yet the injunction to abolish the high places meant little to them.[4] They were not impressed when the prophets described how their cities and proud palaces would sink in ruins,[5] how whole families would meet death,[6] or how those escaping massacre would be herded off into captivity.[7] When Amos with prophetic certainty saw the end, he intoned the celebrated lamentation, "She is fallen! The virgin Israel shall not rise again, she is prostrate upon her land; there is no one who shall raise her up."[8] The southern kingdom too would be destroyed: David's tent would decay and fall into ruins,[9] his dynasty disappear. Amos had in mind the exiles of the southern kingdom when he spoke of a return from captivity.[10] His married life showed Osee that Yahweh could not abide with His people. Just as the prophet was obliged to dismiss his adulterous wife, so Yahweh must dismiss Israel from her home in Canaan.[11] And the southern kingdom would suffer a similar fate.[12] Isaias proclaimed a memorable "woe" over "the sinful nation, the people laden with guilt, the brood of evildoers, the wicked sons who abandoned Yahweh."[13] It was due wholly to God's boundless indulgence that Israel remained in existence, that she had not been totally destroyed like Sodom and Gomorrah.[14] Micheas prophesied judgment upon the northern kingdom, and still more vividly upon Jerusalem.[15] When Manasses was furthering idol worship, prophets arose who proclaimed the destruction of the southern kingdom and exile for the people.[16] In His wrath Yahweh was preparing a day of judgment for the nations,[17] but His fury would blaze more violently still upon Judah and Jerusalem.[18] Jeremias never tired speaking of the impending judgment, the "Day of Affliction,"[19] and Ezechiel preached the same theme from the beginning of his ministry to the downfall of Jerusalem. The people tried hard not to understand their message. They regarded as insurgents and traitors those who, unlike the false seers, spoke only of evil days and divine punishment.[20]

2. Prophecies of Judgment During and After the Exile. What the prophets had been constantly proclaiming had come to pass. In the year 721 the northern kingdom came to an end, in the year 587 the southern. The temple was destroyed, Jerusalem burnt, the people exiled to Babylon. On the point of

1. Am. 5:18.
2. Am. 9:4.
3. Am. 9:8.
4. Am. 7:9.
5. Am. 6:8-11.
6. Am. 6:9.
7. Am. 7:11, 17.

8. Am. 5:1-2.
9. Am. 9:11.
10. Am. 9:14.
11. Os. 1-3; 9:15.
12. Os. 5:12, 14.
13. Is. 1:4.
14. Is. 1:9.

15. Mich. 1:5, 9.
16. 4 Kgs. 21:10-15.
17. Soph. 1:2-3.
18. Soph. 1:4.
19. Jer. 18:17.
20. § 2:3de.

despair the Jews found in Ezechiel a comforter gently reminding them that
Yahweh is not only a Judge who punishes sinners, but also a Savior who forgives penitents.[21] Even this heavy scourge was not sufficient to make them do
better, and he was obliged to proclaim that the obstinate would not return to
"the land of Israel."[22] The bucks who unmercifully trampled the sheep would
be sorted out.[23] While the threats of an earlier period were directed against
the people as a whole, now we find that the good are distinguished from the
wicked; in the new kingdom of God sinners have no place.

The postexilic prophets continued speaking of a Day of Yahweh, a judgment which still hung over Israel but which would not affect all the Jews, only
evildoers. They warned against a feeling of false security arising from the
presence of the temple in their midst and the fact that idols were no longer
worshipped. In the judgment to come perjurers and thieves would be sloughed
off,[24] false prophets and the spirit of uncleanness would perish,[25] two-thirds
of the inhabitants of the land would die, while the third part Yahweh would
purify by fire.[26] For Joel the great grasshopper plague served as a type
and preview of the frightful Day of Yahweh,[27] "a day of darkness and gloom,
a day of clouds and dense darkness."[28] Because this judgment was destined
for the wicked, Yahweh pleaded, "Return to me with your whole heart,"[29] for
then only will salvation come to Sion.[30] Prophesying the Ruler's advent in
judgment, Malachias asked, "Who shall endure the day of his coming? For
he is as the fire of the smelter and as the lye of a fuller," i.e., He would wash
out all dross, cleanse every stain. This purificatory judgment would in the first
place affect the sons of Levi, it would also strike all magicians, adulterers,
perjurers and those who oppressed their economically and socially weaker neighbors.[31] There is reference to this judgment in postexilic Ps. 1, "The godless
shall not stand in the judgment, or sinners in the community of the just."[32]

3. ISRAEL'S GUILT. The prophets never tired repeating how the people
deserved judgment because of their sins. Israel perished in order to atone for
her guilt.[33] Again and again and again the prophets had condemned idolatry
and image worship.[34] Nevertheless in the northern kingdom Yahweh was honored in the form of a bull.[35] At feasts in Yahweh's honor the people abandoned
themselves to debauchery and immorality.[36] The Sabbath rest was not observed,[37] or observed with grumbling over the loss of profit entailed.[38] Against
fellow men the Israelites sinned by murder, adultery, immorality, perjury, lies,
fraud, usury, theft.[39] Parents were despised,[40] judges accepted bribes, judged
unjustly[41] and were hardhearted toward the poor.[42] Gluttony and drunken-

21. Ez. 33:10; cf. Lam. 1:8, 22.
22. Ez. 20:32-38.
23. Ez. 34:17-22.
24. Zach. 5:1-4.
25. Zach. 13:2; 5:5-11.
26. Zach. 13:9.
27. Joel 1:15.
28. Joel 2:2.
29. Joel 2:12.
30. Joel 3:5; 4:16-17.
31. Mal. 3:1-5, 19.

32. Ps. 1:5.
33. Os. 5:5.
34. Am. 2:4; 4:3; 5:26; Os.
    2:7, 15; 4:17; 8:4; 11:2;
    12:1; 13:1; Is. 2:8, 20;
    Soph. 1:4-5; Ez. 6:4; 8:3,
    10, 14, 16.
35. Am. 8:14; Os. 8:5-6; 10:5;
    13:2.
36. Os. 4:13-14; 6:10; 7:14;
    9:1.

37. Jer. 17:21-22; Ez. 20:12;
    22:8, 26.
38. Am. 8:5.
39. Am. 2:8; 3:9-10; 8:5; Os.
    4:2; 6:8-9; 12:8; Ez. 11:7;
    22:2, 7, 29; Mal. 3:5.
40. Ez. 22:7.
41. Am. 2:6-7; 5:7, 10-12; Is.
    1:17, 23; 3:14; 5:7, 23.
42. Am. 2:6; 3:9; 8:4, 6; Is.
    1:17; Mal. 3:5.

ness were common,[43] the higher classes were obsessed by their riches.[44] Ezechiel accused his kinsmen of violating the cleanliness code and the laws on foods;[45] Malachias scored them for negligence in bringing the sacred gifts,[46] for offering unfit animals,[47] for allowing mixed marriages[48] and easy divorce.[49] These sins implied a further sin, that of rank ingratitude toward Yahweh who had overwhelmed His people with blessings.[50] Moreover every sin reflected a spirit of pride, a rebelling against God's holy will.[51] Yahweh must intervene, "Then will the haughty eyes of men drop and human pride cower, and Yahweh alone will be exalted on that day."[52]

4. JUDGMENT FULFILLED. In the minds of the pre-exilic prophets the exile would be the final punishment before the beginning of the messianic era; they saw in one picture events widely separated in time.[53] Actually the exile was a preparation for the day of salvation. The postexilic prophets spoke of the judgment at the end of time. Stiffnecked the people stood firm against every appeal and threat, and even preliminary judgments did not effect amendment. This attitude evoked God's complaint, "However you did not return to me."[54] Jeremias was told that his hearers would reject all his admonitions.[55] Already at his call Ezechiel was informed that God was sending him to "an obstinate generation."[56] Therefore God had to act violently. Because He has the right to claim obedience, judgment is designated as a "time of right" by the prophets. Yahweh is the plaintiff, the nation the defendant, the evil deeds the witnesses against Israel. "Yahweh must law with the inhabitants of the land because there is no more fidelity and no more love and no more knowledge of God in the land[57]. . . . Yahweh is having a lawsuit with *Israel* in order to visit Jacob according to his activity."[58] Yahweh challenged the people to answer for themselves, "We are lawing against each other."[59] In the parable of the vineyard He addressed the citizens of Jerusalem, "Judge now between me and my vineyard."[60] In Micheas Yahweh laments, "My people, what have I done to you, and in what have I been oppressive toward you? Answer me!," and then recounts the benefits He conferred upon them.[61] The kinds of punishment enumerated by the prophets are the same as those listed in the Law, viz., hunger, epidemics, hostile attacks, incursions of predatory animals and finally exile.[62]

No one would be able to escape judgment[63] and only a wretched remnant would remain,[64] "a gleaning as when one shakes an olive tree: only two or three berries remain on top, only four or five on the branches of the fruit tree."[65] So many men would be slain in battle that seven women would besiege one man for marriage;[66] hunger and sword would take so heavy a toll as to leave none to bury the dead.[67] The country side would become a desert, the

43. Is. 5:11, 22.
44. Is. 3:16; 9:8-9.
45. Ez. 22:26.
46. Mal. 3:8.
47. Mal. 1:7, 14.
48. Mal. 2:11.
49. Mal. 2:14.
50. Is. 1:2.
51. § 30:1; 38:1.
52. Is. 2:11, 17.

53. § 49:6c.
54. Am. 4:6-11.
55. Jer. 18:11-12.
56. Ez. 2:3-7; cf. Is. 5:19; 29:9-10; Soph. 3:2.
57. Os. 4:1.
58. Os. 12:3.
59. Is. 1:18; 3:13.
60. Is. 5:3.
61. Mich. 6:2-5.

62. § 2:2b; Is. 8:21; Jer. 14:12; 15:2-3; 21:7; 24: 10; 29:17; Ez. 5:2, 12; 6:12; 14:13f.
63. Am. 5:19; 8:1-3; Is. 5:14; Ez. 7:4, 16; 21:3, 8.
64. Am. 3:12.
65. Is. 17:6; cf. 30:17.
66. Is. 4:1.
67. Jer. 14:16; Am. 6:9-10.

cities would fall to ruins.[68] The temple too would be destroyed,[69] and the
few who survive the catastrophe would be hurried off to exile.[70] Yahweh intended to punish Israel so severely as to terrify even the Gentiles.[71] Sorrowing
over the impending evil which he could not avert, the prophet Micheas began
to "moan and grieve, go barefoot and naked (as a sign of mourning), lament
like jackals and mourn like ostriches."[72] Jeremias suffered horribly when he
was obliged to announce judgment, "Misery prostrates me, my heart is sore.
Because of the collapse of (my) daughter, my people, I am collapsing, I am
sad, fright seizes me. Oh, who is making my head into water, my eyes into
a fountain of tears that day and night I weep over the slain of (my) daughter,
my people![73] . . . . My eyes stream with tears because Yahweh's flock has been
driven off into captivity."[74]

The intercession of a prophet would be of no avail in the day of visitation
because the people refused to amend their ways. In a vision Amos twice pleaded
for the people, first as locusts menaced every green leaf, then as a drought was
scorching the land. Yahweh heard, but at the third vision said, "I will not
forgive him any more."[75] Yahweh directed Jeremias, "Do not pray for this
people or plead with me, for I shall not listen to you."[76] Even if Moses and
Samuel intervened in favor of Israel, Yahweh wanted no further commerce with
them. Jeremias received strict orders, "Take them away from before my eyes,
have them leave!"[77] Mere fasting would not benefit the people because they
had no spirit of penance.[78] If someone sought to implore Yahweh, he would
not be heard, "Silence. Don't even mention the name Yahweh!"[79] For the
prayer had come from an impenitent heart, a heart seeking merely to stave
off punishment; such prayer was no proof of sincere repentance.[80] Therefore
Yahweh became "like a lion toward Ephraim, like a young lion toward the house
of Judah; like a panther he lurks for them on the way, and falls upon them
like a bear robbed of her whelps . . . . and there is none to rescue."[81] Jerusalem's transgressions must be judged more severely than those of Sodom and
Gomorrah because Yahweh had loaded His people with special privileges.[82]
Israel's punishment was just: she had abandoned Yahweh, had served strange
gods in His land, and consequently she must be driven from the land to serve
strangers in strange lands.[83] Israel separated herself from Yahweh; therefore
Yahweh must withdraw from her[84] and deliver her and all her possessions into
the power of nations whose gods she had worshipped.[85]

In describing the judgment impending over Israel the prophets used language
which reminds us of world judgment.[86] They sought to direct attention to
God's power, which has at its disposal all the forces of creation, as well as to

68. Am. 6:8; Os. 2:5; 5:9;
    9:6; Is. 6:11; 7:18-25;
    32:13-14; Mich. 1:6, 8-16;
    3:12; 6:13, 16; Jer. 4:27;
    6:8; 7:34; 18:16; Ez.
    6:14.
69. Mich. 3:12; Jer. 22:5; Ez.
    10.
70. Am. 9:14; Os. 9:3, 6, 15;
    Is. 5:13; 7:16.

71. Jer. 18:16; 24:9; Ez. 5:15.
72. Mich. 1:8.
73. Jer. 8:18, 21, 23.
74. Jer. 13:17.
75. Am. 7:1-9.
76. Jer. 7:16; 11:14; 14:11.
77. Jer. 15:1.
78. Am. 5:22; Os. 6:6; Jer.
    14:11.

79. Am. 6:10.
80. Cf. § 35:2a; 40:1, 3.
81. Os. 5:14; 13:7.
82. Ez. 16:47-58; cf. Am. 3:2.
83. Jer. 5:19.
84. Jer. 15:6; 16:11-13; Os.
    1:2, 8; 2:4; 3:3.
85. Ez. 23.
86. § 45:3.

recall the grievousness of sin and the severity of its punishment. Micheas called upon "all peoples" to witness the event;[87] Isaias addressed the "heavens and the earth" when proclaiming punishment.[88] When Yahweh will appear to judge His people, the hills will melt away and valleys crack asunder.[89] According to Jeremias the whole world will be drawn into sympathetic suffering, the heavens and the hills, men and birds.[90] Because the judgment upon Jerusalem would resemble a world catastrophe Ezechiel began a sermon, "An end is coming, the end to the four ends of the earth!"[91]

The prophets foretold a visitation of Israel, first by the Assyrians, then by the Babylonians. Assyria put an end to the northern kingdom; the majority of its inhabitants were led into captivity never to return. The southern kingdom too was heavily oppressed by the Assyrians, but it was permitted to remain in existence and quickly recovered. Under Nabuchodonosor about 30,000 persons were transported to Babylon in the year 597, as may be deduced from the Bible. We must make our own estimates for the catastrophe of the year 587. Some 60,000 Jews may have been exiled, to which may be added those who escaped to Egypt. At the most only about 40,000 remained in Palestine. Yet these figures show that an almost complete annihilation of the people, as Jeremias and Ezechiel had foretold, did not occur. The land was greatly ravaged by the invading army, the cities lay in ruins, but it was the design of Nabuchodonosor that those whom he allowed to remain in Judah should have sufficient income to make a normal living through industry and thrift. These considerations enable us to evaluate more accurately the threats of the prophets. First of all their task was to shock the people and move them to repentance and conversion of morals. Secondly, lacking perspective, they did not distinguish the judgment which Yahweh would inflict within a few years or months from the great judgment at the end of time.[92] Lastly, their comminatory speeches almost always end with comforting words on the messianic era as they proclaim a bright future once the people have been purified by punishment.

5. THE POINT AND PURPOSE OF JUDGMENT. By disciplining Israel to the brink of annihilation, satisfaction was made to Yahweh's holiness and justice.[93] God's honor demands that He accomplish His plan of salvation. Therefore Israel was not to perish utterly, a remnant was to remain, and this remnant would amend because of the judgment. The lawgiver knew that those who escaped the catastrophe would "confess their sins and the sins of their fathers. Then their uncircumcised heart will humble itself, then will they do penance for their sins and I shall be mindful of my covenant with Jacob."[94] Amos prophesied that the judgment would effect a division, and Yahweh would receive into favor those who had been purified.[95] Osee said that the Israelites will "seek his (Yahweh's) face, in their trouble they will look for him."[96] When adulterous Israel realized what it meant to stray from God, she would

87. Mich. 1:2.   91. Ez. 7:2.   94. Lev. 26:40-42.
88. Is. 1:2.   92. § 49:6c.   95. Am. 9:8-15.
89. Mich. 1:4.   93. Is. 5:16; § 11:3.   96. Os. 5:15.
90. Jer. 4:23-26.

say, "I will get myself ready to return to my first man."[97] She would exclaim, "My husband!," and no longer, "My Baal!"[98] In a picture which was also used to describe the chastisement and purification of individuals,[99] Isaias showed that judgment would cleanse Israel, "I shall smelt out *in the furnace* (of tribulation) all your dross and separate all your lead."[100] "A remnant shall amend, a remnant of Jacob to the strong God."[101] "A remnant of his people" will remain loyal, will seek their glory in the service of Yahweh,[102] and therefore Isaias named one of his sons Shear-yashub ("a remnant will amend"[103])—a mere remnant indeed, yet still a remnant! Likewise according to Sophonias "A remnant from the house of Judah" will abide, they will become better through the judgment, they will sin no longer.[104] Jeremias made no secret of his belief that in the judgment the majority of men would be sloughed off as dross, while only a small portion of genuine metal would remain.[105] Ezechiel was the first prophet commissioned to labor for the welfare of this remnant; he foresaw that they would understand and be ashamed of their sins.[106] In Babylon God proved the people "in the furnace of tribulation."[107] There they re-echoed the words of Osee, "Come, let us return to Yahweh, for he has torn, yet he will heal us; he has smitten, yet he will bind up our *wounds*."[108] They repented as Jeremias had foreseen, "Upon the heights one may hear weeping, the sons of Israel suppliantly crying for having followed crooked ways, for having forgotten Yahweh, their God."[109] After the return Israel was grateful to God for all the suffering He had sent, "O God, you have tried us, melted us as silver is melted, you have brought us into safety. We had fallen into fire and water, but you led us into *freedom*."[110] She returned in sorrow to Yahweh and heard the comforting words, "Yahweh, your God, is a merciful God; he will not abandon you or let you perish; he will not forget the covenant which he made upon oath with your fathers."[111] Nevertheless, even as Osee's wife had no right to her previous intimacies with the prophet, so it would be an act of sheer grace if Yahweh again regarded Israel as His people.[112] God's forgiveness was a manifestation of His mercy and love.[113] So good is He that He considered the punishment imposed far more than sufficient; Israel had "received from Yahweh's hand double for all her sins."[114] The humbled people prayed with full confidence, "Where is there a God like you, who pardons guilt and forgives iniquity! *You* will again show us mercy."[115] Also the difficult passage, "A woman courts a man,"[116] refers to Israel's conversion.[116]

The reinstatement of Israel was designed to further God's glory. At Moses' time Yahweh spared Israel for His own name's sake;[117] but the Gentiles should know that Israel was now taken into exile because of her sins.[118] After she has atoned for her evil deeds, God "will be zealous for his holy name" and

97. Os. 2:9.
98. Os. 2:18.
99. § 41:4.
100. Is. 1:25.
101. Is. 10:21.
102. Is. 28:5-6.
103. Is. 7:3.
104. Soph. 2:7, 9; 3:10-15.

105. Jer. 9:6; 23:3; 31:7.
106. Ez. 16:61, 63; 20:43; 36:31-32.
107. Is. 48:10.
108. Os. 6:1.
109. Jer. 3:21; 31:18.
110. Ps. 66:10-12.
111. Deut. 4:31.

112. Os. 2:8-9, 16-25; 3:3-5.
113. § 15:6; 16:4.
114. Is. 40:2; cf. 61:7.
115. Mich. 7:18-19.
116. Jer. 31:22.
117. § 50:3.
118. Ez. 39:23; cf. 48:4.

"change the lot of Jacob."[119] "When he brings them back from the nations he shall show himself holy through them in the eyes of many nations."[120] If Yahweh were to refuse all further show of favor toward Israel, the Gentiles would think Him weak, "For my own sake, for my own sake I shall act (by showing mercy during judgment) ; for otherwise how *my name* would be desecrated! My honor I concede to no one."[121] Joel urged the postexilic priests to pray in the same tone, "Spare your people, Yahweh, and do not abandon your inheritance to derision, that the Gentiles may scoff over her. Why should it be said among the nations: Where is their God?"[122]

The false prophets foretold good fortune and confirmed the people in their sins,[123] Yahweh's prophets proclaimed judgment. The latter were scoffed at and persecuted as "doomsday prophets."[124] Nevertheless through their sermons on judgment they actually did effect Israel's salvation, inasmuch as they kept alive the notion of God's holiness and justice, confirmed belief in God's existence and prepared for the conversion of the non-Jewish world.

SECTION 2. THE NEW KINGDOM OF GOD

§ 47. THE RESTORATION OF ISRAEL

1. THE RETURN FROM EXILE. Jacob's prophecy over Judah[1] and Balaam's blessing upon Israel[2] revealed to the people a glorious future; the former promised peace and abundance, the latter Yahweh's assistance enabling them to triumph over all enemies and to make them a great nation. There is no contradiction between these and later prophecies, for a timely defeat was in fact an excellent preparation for messianic peace. Judgment was proclaimed but the restoration following upon judgment was also kept in view. Collapse of the kingdom did not imply the end of the nation, still less the end of Yahwistic religion. Jeremias received the commission to tear down *and* to build up,[3] likewise the other prophets. When the exiled people had amended, God would again favor them with His graces,[4] "They should reconstruct and inhabit the destroyed cities and plant vineyards."[5] After completing their term of exile they would "convert and seek Yahweh, their God, and in fear hasten to Yahweh and his blessing in the end of days."[6] Then Yahweh would "free them from the power of Sheol, deliver them from death,"[7] and the nation would arise to new life.[8] According to Isaias Yahweh would "redeem the remnant of his people that still remains,"[9] and from the stump of the fallen terebinth holy seed would sprout;[10] from the four corners of the earth He would bring home the dispersed of Israel and the scattered of Judah.[11] Micheas announced that Yahweh would gather together the dispersed and fashion the new people of God.[12]

119. Ez. 39:25.
120. Ez. 39:27.
121. Is. 48:11.
1. Gen. 49:8-12.
2. Num. 23:10, 24; 24:8.
3. Jer. 1:10.
4. Os. 2:17-25.

122. Joel 2:17.
123. § 2:2e.
5. Am. 9:14.
6. Os. 3:5.
7. Os. 13:14.
8. § 44:2.

124. 3 Kgs. 18:17; 22:8; § 2:2f.
9. Is. 11:11.
10. Is. 6:13.
11. Is. 11:12.
12. Mich. 2:12; 4:6; 7:11-12.

Jeremias foretold that their servitude would last for seventy years,[13] after which the might of Babylon would come to an end and Yahweh would lead the exiles home.[14] The restoration of Israel is the theme in Ezechiel's vision of the field of dead bones.[15] Yahweh would gather the dispersed from out of the nations and lead them back to their land.[16] The details for this are given in Isaias: the procession passes through the wilderness and is accompanied by miracles; mountains and hills disappear, valleys become plains; Cyrus is the agent who performs Yahweh's plans.[17] With this return the messianic age begins, for the prophets behold in one perspectiveless silhouette events that are temporarily distinct.[18] At the same time the punishment of the northern kingdom will come to an end, "The people who escape the sword will find favor in the desert[19].... From a distance Yahweh will manifest himself: With an everlasting love have I loved you, therefore have I kept mercy in store for you a long time."[20] The prophets are happy as they describe the return,[21] "The day has come, watchers on the hills of Ephraim are calling: Arise! let us proceed to Sion to Yahweh, our God."[22] For from all the world, from the east to the west the dispersed are coming home.[23]

When however the liberation from slavery in Babylon became a reality, it proceeded along lines quite unlike those the prophets had foretold: no miracles on the way, no return of the northern tribes. This made them realize that certain prophecies actually had been oriented toward a more remote future, that the messianic age was still to come. The postexilic prophets were aware of this as they prophesied the homecoming from exile which should introduce the messianic era. Zacharias preached the return of the dispersed from the east and west;[24] he promised that Yahweh "for the sake of the blood of the covenant (which he once had made with Israel[25]) would liberate his captives from the pit,"[26] and summoned "the prisoners of hope" who awaited liberation, to return home.[27] According to Joel Yahweh would assemble all the dispersed and restore the people of God.[28] Is. 27:12 tells how Yahweh will assemble the pious Israelites and lead them back home from Assyria and Egypt. On the basis of these prophecies a large circle hoped for a return of the dispersed after the exile. The author of Tobias expected a return to Palestine and the construction of a new and more beautiful sanctuary than that of Zorobabel.[29] Jesus Sirach petitioned, "Gather all the tribes of Jacob and give them the inheritance as in the days of old."[30] According to one of the letters contained in the introduction to 2 Machabees, the Jews at the time of Nehemias prayed, "Lead us again together out of the dispersion, liberate those in servitude from the lands of the Gentiles."[31]

2. Unification of the Separated Kingdoms. Because Solomon had

13. Jer. 25:11; 29:10.
14. Jer. 33:7; 32:42.
15. Ez. 37:1-14; § 44:2.
16. Ez. 11:17; 20:34; 28:25; 36:24, etc.
17. Is. 40:1-5; 44:28; 46:10-11.
18. § 49:6c; 50:3.

19. Jer. 31:2.
20. Jer. 31:5.
21. Is. 11:15-16; cf. Jer. 3:12-13.
22. Jer. 31:6-10; 23:8.
23. Bar. 4:36-37.
24. Zach. 8:7.

25. Ex. 24:8.
26. Zach, 9:11.
27. Zach. 9:12; 10:6.
28. Joel 4:1-2.
29. Tob. 14:5; cf. 13:10, 13.
30. Sir. 36:13, 16.
31. 2 Mach. 1:27; cf. 2:7.

proved unfaithful to Yahweh, the kingdom of David was divided.[32] In the coming day of salvation northern and southern kingdoms were to be united again under one ruler from the house of David. When Amos promised that Yahweh would rebuild the fallen house of David as in time past,[33] he was indicating that the future kingdom would embrace all the tribes. According to Osee Israel and Judah would some day be united under a descendant of David and thus united constitute Yahweh's beloved people.[34] Isaias speaks of the harmony which will reign between Ephraim and Judah.[35] Jeremias sees the day coming when Judah and Israel will find themselves in agreement[36] and forming a kingdom under one of David's offspring.[37] United they would advance against enemies.[38] In an allegory Ezechiel speaks of the kingdoms as two sisters redeemed by Yahweh[39] and, by holding two staffs together in one hand, shows in symbolic action how they will form one kingdom under one king, David.[40] After the exile Zacharias assured his fellow men that the northern and southern kingdoms would eventually be restored and reunited.[41]

3. INTERIOR RENOVATION. In messianic times Israel will no longer stray away from God. Just as Gomer belonged to Osee forever after she was sorry and did penance, so Israel too will remain faithful to Yahweh, "I shall remove the names of the Baals from her mouth so that they shall no longer be invoked by their names."[42] The worship of idols will cease; to Yahweh alone will Israel say, "My God!"[43] The Israelites will be called, "Children of the living God,"[44] because Yahweh will "heal their defection, and willingly love them."[45] Yahweh will forgive Israel's sins, He will "wash off the refuse"[46] and "they who remain in Sion and they who still survive in Jerusalem will be called 'Saints'."[47] Israel will say, "We shall live in the name of Yahweh, our God, for ever and ever."[48] Yahweh will destroy all charms, idols, images, sacred pillars and poles, lest His loved ones fall down before them.[49] It will be "a poor and insignificant people" who remain after the judgment, but "they will put their trust in the name of Yahweh; they will do injustice no longer, they will tell lies no more."[50] Yahweh will "cleanse them from all their sins[51]. . . . and give them such a heart and a mode of life that they will reverence him at all times[52]. . . . a heart that they may know him," and they will be "his people, and he will be their God."[53] "All will know Yahweh from the smallest to the greatest; for I shall forgive their guilt and shall no longer remember their sins."[54] Once again the invocation will be heard, "May Yahweh bless you, meadow of righteousness, holy mountain."[56] The great marvel which Yahweh aimed to accomplish would not exclude the northern kingdom.[57] According to Ezechiel Yahweh will grant forgiveness of sins in the messianic era;[58] He will "sprinkle pure water upon them to cleanse them."[59] This water will not

32. 3 Kgs. 11:9; 12:16f.
33. Am. 9:11.
34. Os. 2:2-3; cf. 3:5.
35. Is. 11:12-13.
36. Jer. 3:18.
37. Jer. 23:5-6; 30:3, 9.
38. Abd. 18.
39. Ez. 16:53-64.
40. Ez. 37:15-28.
41. Zach. 10:6; cf. 9:13.

42. Os. 2:19.
43. Os. 2:25.
44. Os. 2:1.
45. Os. 14:5.
46. Is. 4:4.
47. Is. 4:3.
48. Mich. 4:5.
49. Mich. 5:11-13.
50. Soph. 3:12-13.

51. Jer. 33:8.
52. Jer. 32:39.
53. Jer. 24:7; 32:38.
54. Jer. 31:34.
55. Jer. 3:22.
56. Jer. 31:23.
57. Jer. 31:22; § 50:3.
58. Ez. 16:61, 63; 37:23.
59. Cf. Ez. 36:25.

merely symbolize the forgiveness of sins as the purifications ordained by the Law, but actually effect it. Then will God "bestow upon them a new heart and place a new spirit within them, and give them a heart of flesh." Accordingly there will be a true interior change; the human heart, till then callous to every admonition, will belong henceforth to God; men will "live in accordance with his decrees and heed his rights." The new kingdom will be Yahweh's people and He will be their God.[60]

The morals of those who returned from exile very soon did not tally with the resolutions they had first made. They were not a holy people and Jerusalem was not an upright and holy city.[61] The prophets insisted that the true and lasting conversion of the people was yet to take place. There would come a time when Yahweh "would eliminate the guilt of the land on a (specific) day."[62] In the vision of the flying scroll Zacharias was shown how Yahweh would liquidate sinners and create a holy people;[63] in the vision of the epha, that sin itself, and even sinful impulses, would be done away with.[64] Yahweh would yet turn toward Sion and dwell in the midst of Jerusalem, and Jerusalem would be called "the faithful city."[65] Israel would become God's people and God would be her God in truth and in justice.[66] Yahweh would give them the grace to bereave their sins, and they would beg Him for mercy.[67] There would then flow "a fountain against sin and defilement;"[68] idolatry would come to an end, false prophets who bewilder the people would be slain,[69] and the redeemed would joyfully acknowledge themselves as belonging to Yahweh.[70] Jerusalem becomes a sanctuary.[71] Godlessness and injustice comes to an end and the sun of justice rises.[72]

4. THE NEW COVENANT. The conduct of Osee and Gomer had prepared the people for Yahweh's promise, "I will espouse you to myself forever, I will espouse you to myself with regard to righteousness and justice, loving-kindness and mercy."[73] Jeremias and Ezechiel loved to dwell on the theme of the new covenant relationship between Yahweh and Israel. The old covenant was inaugurated after the liberation from earthly slavery in Egypt. The new covenant will be inaugurated with the liberation from the slavery of sin. In the old covenant individuals were appointed to give instructions concerning God and His holy will; in the new covenant all will possess the knowledge of divine things. Through the tablets of the Law the old covenant made men conscious of obligations toward Yahweh; the new covenant written in the heart will tell how God's grace leads to higher things.[74] No longer will anyone yearn after the ark of the covenant which was lost in the catastrophe of 587[75]— that was only an external sign of the relationship between Yahweh and Israel. In the new covenant God Himself will dwell in men's midst, and Jerusalem will be called "the throne of Yahweh."[76]

60. Ez. 36:25-28; 11:19-20; 37:27.
61. Cf. Is. 56:6-57:13.
62. Zach. 3:9.
63. Zach. 5:1-4.
64. Zach. 5:5-11.
65. Zach. 8:3.
66. Zach. 8:8; 10:6.
67. Zach. 12:10-14.
68. Zach. 13:1.
69. Zach. 13:1-6.
70. Zach. 13:9; 14:20-21.
71. Joel 4:17.
72. Mal. 3:18-20; Dan. 9:24; cf. § 50:4.
73. Os. 2:21.
74. Jer. 31:31-34; 32:38-40.
75. Jer. 3:16.
76. Jer. 3:17; cf. 14:21; 17:12; § 49:1.

§ 48. THE CONVERSION OF THE GENTILES

1. THE EARLIEST PROPHECIES. As God of the universe and as the Lord who determines the destinies of all nations,[1] Yahweh did not choose to limit His worship forever to a small and isolated people. In the protoevangel He gave every man the hope of attaining divine love,[2] and from the oldest times He revealed that at some future day all nations would serve Him. In Noe's blessing[3] Yahweh is called "the God of Sem," and among Sem's descendants the knowledge of God would never be lost entirely. Japhet would live in Sem's tents, i.e., share in his blessings—hence through him would retain faith in the one true God. Cham's children were to serve Sem and Japhet, but since servants know their master's God, true religion would come to Cham through his very position. When mankind apostatized, God chose Abram and his descendants as the means for spreading ethical monotheism among men, "In you all the nations of the earth shall be blessed."[4] God repeated this promise to Isaac[5] and Jacob,[6] and the latter foresaw the Savior arising from the tribe of Judah.[7]

2. THE PROPHECIES OF THE LITERARY PROPHETS. The judgments which the prophets proclaimed upon the nations were designed to prepare mankind for the things of God.[8] Some day the conversion of the pagan world would come to pass. Amos foretold how the nations which once had come under David's sceptre would form part of the new kingdom;[9] messianic blessings would not be restricted to nationality. During the council of the apostles St. James appealed to this passage as he spoke in favor of missionary work among the Gentiles.[10] Amos spoke only of nations bordering on Israel; Isaias drew all mankind into the ambit of his vision. He saw every nation ascending the mountain of Yahweh and demanding "that he teach them his ways."[11] They would abandon their gods to worship the true God and integrate their faith with every act of daily life.[12] Yahweh would "judge between the nations and decide what is right for many peoples." The same prophecy forms part of the Book of Micheas.[13] In the messianic kingdom therefore there will be various nationalities, even as there will be room for earthly kings beneath the sovereignty of God and His Messiah.[14] These ideas receive further development in Is. 11:10-12: the root of Jesse, the Messiah, will take the position of standard bearer for the nations, calling and inviting them to assemble about Himself; and "the nations shall seek him." Then "Adonai once more will *lift up* his hand to redeem the remnant of his people" still in exile; He will "raise a standard to the nations and assemble the dispersed of Israel and bring home the scattered of Judah from the four ends of the earth." According to God's plan of salvation the nations must cooperate in the return of Israelites dwelling in distant places. The prophets do not relate the events of messianic times in strict historical sequence; may this passage then not imply that the conversion of the Gentiles will precede that of

1. § 14:3; 23:4.
2. Gen. 3:14-15.
3. Gen. 9:24-27.
4. Gen. 12:3; 18:18; 22:18.
5. Gen. 26:4.
6. Gen. 28:14.
7. Gen. 49:10; § 50:2.
8. § 45:6.
9. Am. 9:12.
10. Acts 15:16-17.
11. Is. 2:3.
12. Is. 2:2-4.
13. Mich. 4:1-4.
14. Ps. 2.

Israel, leaving Israel to find admission to the messianic kingdom at the end of time and through the efforts of Gentile-Christians? The thought of Yahweh employing converted nations in His efforts to bring Israel home undoubtedly was in St. Paul's mind as he wrote to the Romans, "A partial blindness only has befallen Israel, until the full number of the Gentiles should enter (the Church), and thus all Israel should be saved."[15] Here again the Gentiles are converted first and then only Israel as a nation. Isaias develops this idea: Egypt will be chastised but also blessed; then Yahweh will be honored throughout the country; in the middle of Egypt will be an altar to His honor and monuments at her borders; everyone who enters the land will immediately see that Yahweh is worshipped there.[16] The Egyptians who practiced the basest type of idolatry will experience Yahweh's love, even as Israel did. Assyria too will turn to serve the one true God. And Israel, the bone of contention between Assyria and Egypt, Israel, the land that had been oppressed by both these nations and that had followed their idolatrous example, will be united with them in adoring Yahweh. Thus the messianic kingdom will consist of Gentile nations, represented by Assyria and Egypt, the contemporary world powers, and the children of Israel. Yahweh will call Egypt "my people," as previously He called Israel, and Assyria the "work of my hands," because He made her and spiritually refashioned her. Israel of course will hold a primacy of honor: Yahweh will call her "my portion," because He selected her as the fountain from which blessings might flow. Nevertheless Isaias refers to her expressly as the "third" party in the new covenant. Shall Israel hold herself aloof from messianic teaching indefinitely while the Gentile nations accept it?

According to Sophonias God "will cause all the gods of the earth to vanish, and every one from his own home will adore him, all the islands of the nations."[17] Then He will "give to the nations purified lips to invoke the name of Yahweh together and to serve him in harmony."[18] Jeremias foresaw how the nations would swear, "As truly as Yahweh lives," and how they would then be restored in the midst of His people.[19] They would come to Yahweh from the ends of the earth acknowledging, "Our fathers possessed nothing but illusion, vanity, and what was of no benefit."[20] "No longer will they follow the stubbornness of their evil hearts."[21] Ezechiel speaks of Sodom, the symbol of a morally corrupt world, being presented to Jerusalem by Yahweh as a daughter of the new Jerusalem.[22] In another passage he speaks of an insignificant looking sprout growing into a tree upon whose branches nest birds of every species,[23] i.e., all peoples will find lodging in the messianic kingdom—it is universal. In 47:22-23 the same prophet directs that after the return from exile (which he regarded as the beginning of the messianic era) foreigners who dwelt among the Jews should have equal rights with Jews in the division of the land; he presumes they have accepted Israel's God. Accordingly descent from Abraham

15. Rom. 11:25-26.   18. Soph. 3:9.   21. Jer. 3:17.
16. Is. 19:16-24.   19. Jer. 12:14-17.   22. Ez. 16:53-61.
17. Soph. 2:11.   20. Jer. 16:19.   23. Ez. 17:22-24.

will not be the norm entitling one to share in the blessings of messianic times.

The second section of the Book of Isaias consoled the oppressed by assuring them of the conversion of the Gentile world. "Every knee shall bend before Yahweh, every tongue shall swear[24]. . . . Those from the west shall fear Yahweh's name, and those from the east his glory."[25] Egyptians, Ethiopians, Sabeans will come to Israel convinced that "only among you is God, otherwise there is none, no other sort of gods."[26] The belief in the conversion of the Gentile world inspired Isaias to address the Jerusalem of messianic times, "Arise, shine, for your light is come, and the glory of Yahweh is beaming upon you!"[27] Estranged from God darkness hung heavily over the nations; the light of the true faith now comes to illumine them and show them the way.[28] Then the prophet saw the Gentile nations, even the most distant, pilgrimage to Sion.[29] They call themselves "Jacob" or "Israel,"[30] they consider it their greatest glory to belong to the people of God and enjoy equal rights with Israel; some of their number are chosen as priests and levites![31] In those passages therefore where the prophet told how the Gentiles would bring home the dispersed Israelites upon Yahweh's command,[32] do we not have further instances showing how the Israelites will not be converted prior to or independently of the Gentiles?

When the Jews were obliged to surrender all claim to political independence, Aggeus foretold how the treasures of the nations would be brought to a temple which in beauty would far surpass the earlier one.[33] Zacharias beheld how "many peoples would attach themselves to Yahweh and be numbered with his people,"[34] and how earnestly they would demand a share in Israel's blessings, "Ten men from every tongue of the nations would seize one Jew at the edge of his cloak and say: We wish to accompany you, for we have heard that you have a (true) God."[35] Realizing the vanity of their gods non-Jews will desire to join the Jews as they journey to Jerusalem. Yahweh will then abolish all sacrifices to idols, and the pagans will be "as a *tribe* in Judah" having equal rights with the Israelites.[36] Salvation will be apportioned to everyone who invokes Yahweh's name,[37] and consequently there will be no distinction between Jew and Gentile. In every country a pure sacrifice will be offered.[38] The messianic kingdom will resemble the stone in Nabuchodonosor's dream: without the cooperation of human hands it loosens itself from the mountain, shatters the statue and becomes a mountain filling the entire earth.[39] It embraces all nations, never to be destroyed.[40] Loudly, from the east to the west, resounds the happy voices of men enjoying themselves in God.[41]

The belief that at some future date all nations would worship one God was unique to Israel. Such a conviction was possible only in a religion which taught the existence of but one God and condemned the gods of other nations as nonexistent phantoms. Polytheism is not exclusive; on principle the gods of other

24. Is. 45:23.
25. Is. 59:19; cf. 51:4-5.
26. Is. 45:14.
27. Is. 60:1.
28. Is. 60:2.
29. Is. 60:14; cf. 2:2-4.

30. Is. 44:5.
31. Is. 66:21.
32. Is. 49:22-23; 60:9.
33. Agg. 2:6-9; § 49:2d, 6d.
34. Zach. 2:15.
35. Zach. 8:20-23.

36. Zach. 9:7.
37. Joel 3:5.
38. Mal. 1:11; § 49:1b.
39. Dan. 2:34, 44.
40. Dan. 7:13-14.
41. Is. 24:14-16.

nations are accepted and accorded the right of worship, because every god is operative in his own locality.[42] This theology was in the mind of Sargon of Assyria when, after the deportation of the northern kingdom, he ordered the non-Israelites who colonized Samaria to honor Yahweh alongside their own tribal deities.[43] Rome made room for the gods of all the peoples whom she ruled. During the Hellenistic era, when nations exchanged gods with one another, no one held the notion that one and only one God must be worshipped by the whole world. The religion of Amenophis IV[44] was designed to serve political purposes by furthering the unification of the kingdom. According to this religious innovator the god embodied in the sun-disc (Aton) extended his sway only as far as did the might of Pharaoh. In Israel the belief that Yahweh would some day be worshipped by all nations did not evolve from speculation although the ground was prepared for such development through faith in God as creator of the world and ruler of mankind; it was a belief resting upon divine enlightenment.

3. MESSIANIC HOPES IN WISDOM LITERATURE. Here we find the Gentile world called upon to praise God[45] along with similar appeals to inanimate and irrational animate creation.[46] The Gentiles will behold Yahweh as their king[47] and worship him,[48] while pagan gods will bow down before Him,[49] i.e., idolatry will cease. Israel was commissioned to proclaim to the nations the majesty of her God, so that He would be praised[50] and honored everywhere.[51] Upon their conversion the nations would become citizens of the new Jerusalem.[52] In the psalms Yahweh is acknowledged as ruler by the nations, foreign princes do Him homage,[53] all kingdoms serve Him[54] and His praise re-echoes through all the earth.[55] The new kingdom of God extends from sea to sea and from the river to the ends of the earth, and from afar kings come to bring tribute.[56]

The Book of Tobias does not lack passages manifesting hope in a conversion of the Gentiles, e.g., "All the nations will be truly converted to fear the Lord God, and they will bury their idols."[57] The principal character in the Book of Job is a man who honors the true God without belonging to the Chosen People or observing the Mosaic cult, and his piety is praised by Yahweh Himself. Without difficulty the reader should have concluded that all men must serve God, that the Mosaic Law cannot be binding upon every nation, nor can it last forever. In the Book of Proverbs personified wisdom bids all men to strive after her.[58] The contrast is not between Jew and Gentile, but between love for wisdom and disregard for wisdom.[59] Jesus Sirach may have been more nationalistic as a result of the danger which threatened the Jewish religion through the influx of Hellenistic ideas; yet he also speaks of the promises made

42. § 7:1.
43. 4 Kgs. 17:26-28.
44. § 7:5c.
45. Pss. 117; 150:6.
46. Pss. 69:35; 89:13; 98:7-8; 148.
47. Pss. 47:2f; 68:32-33; 98:4; 99; 102:16.
48. Pss. 22:29; 97:1; 98:4, 9; 99:1-2; 145:13; 146:10.
49. Ps. 97:7.
50. Pss. 9:12; 18:50; 57:10; 96:3; 105:1.
51. Pss. 86:9; 96:7f.
52. Ps. 87:4.
53. Ps. 47:8-10.
54. Ps. 102:23.
55. Pss. 48:2, 11; 66:4-5; 67:4; 86:9.
56. Ps. 72:8-11.
57. Tob. 14:6; cf. 13:11.
58. Prov. 1:20f; 8:1f; 9:1f.
59. Prov. 8:17; 9:16.

o Abraham[60] and of the Gentiles attaining the knowledge of the one true God.[61] The author of the Book of Wisdom realized that "the gods will not last forever"[62] and that through Israel the world will be given "the incomparable light of the Law,"[63] i.e., true religion.

4. INCENTIVES TO CONVERSION. Having found their way back to God, the Gentiles will be very grateful;[64] they will realize it was divine mercy which enlightened them regarding their previous erroneous ways.[65] The Messiah, sent by God, will be like a standard bearer pointing out the way to God's kingdom.[66] "Whom Yahweh calls will be numbered among the escaped."[67] Judgment had as its principal purpose the moving of nations to penance.[68] The plagues which came at Moses' bidding should have taught the Egyptians that the God of Israel was the true God;[69] finally Pharaoh did admit that Yahweh was mightier than the gods of Egypt.[70] In messianic times Yahweh will obliterate every trace of idolatry and then the inhabitants of the islands will adore Him.[71] God's judgments will be "as *light* which scatters the darkness, and through them the earth's inhabitants (will) learn righteousness."[72] Reflection upon God's intervention in the destiny of nations makes it evident that pagan gods can offer no aid.[73] The sudden and unexpected destruction of Assyrian world power will make a nation as distant and warlike as Ethiopia tremble.[74] The fall of Babylon will prove no god exists save Yahweh.[75] The catastrophe about to overwhelm Gog will bring to the eyes of the nations the greatness of Yahweh.[76] At the destruction of the southern kingdom a few Jews were spared in order to inform the nations that God punished justly.[77] The restoration of Israel should be a sign to the nations that Yahweh, who had willed Jerusalem's fall, now intended to show His power by protecting His people against the Chaldeans.[78] When Israel was allowed to return home, she should proclaim to the whole world that it was Yahweh who redeemed her.[79] In fact the Gentiles did remark on the occasion, "Marvellously has Yahweh intervened in their behalf."[80] The reconstruction of Sion was designed to impress the pagans so deeply that they would seek to serve Sion's God.[81] All this history prepared the Gentiles for salvation, for the universal movement back to God to be inaugurated by the Messiah.[82]

Since the prophets foretold the conversion of the Gentiles with such assurance and since the psalmists and wisdom teachers yearned so ardently for this happy consummation, it would seem plausible that some few at least should have undertaken missionary work. There are passages which seem to indicate missionary propaganda. In Isaias the redeemed proclaim Yahweh's deeds to the nations,[83] the psalmist urged Israel to recount to the Gentiles God's great-

60. Sir. 44:21.
61. Sir. 36:5.
62. Wis. 14:13.
63. Wis. 18:4.
64. Ps. 72:10-11.
65. Jer. 12:15-16.
66. Is. 11:10.
67. Joel 3:5.
68. § 45:6.
69. Ez. 7:5.

70. Ex. 8:4, 24; 9:27; 10:16; cf. 12:12.
71. Soph. 2:11; 3:8-9; Is. 59:18-19; Zach. 14:16; Wis. 14:13.
72. Is. 26:9.
73. Ps. 97:1-7.
74. Is. 18:7.
75. Is. 45:6, 20.
76. Ez. 38:23; 39:7, 21.

77. Ez. 12:16.
78. Ez. 20:41; 28:25; 36:36; 37:28; 39:27; § 46:5.
79. Is. 48:20.
80. Ps. 126:2.
81. Ps. 102:16, 23; cf. Soph. 3:20.
82. § 51; 52.
83. Is. 12:4-5.

ness and to invite them to praise Him.[84] Yet these statements are in themselves nothing more than poetic expressions, showing that the poet was inspired by the majesty of Yahweh and believed it his duty to write in that particular manner. For the Israelites such prayer effected a strengthening of faith, since it kept alive the hope that eventually the whole world would profess Yahwistic monotheism. A contrary opinion cannot be deduced from Isaias' statement "You shall summon nations whom you do not know, and those who do not know you, shall run to you,"[85] because the parallelism shows he was not referring to active missionary work. The pagans who will seize Jews by the hem of their garments and ask the privilege to pilgrimage with them to Jerusalem[86] already are believers. The words of Tobias, "O sons of Israel, make him known in the presence of the nations, for it was he who scattered us among them,"[87] reflect the Israelite's duty to profess his faith and to praise God in pagan environment even in times of calamity as during the exile when he was far from the homeland. Here we have an idea to which Ezechiel also refers, viz. through the dispersion of the Israelites God sought to spread the true faith among the Gentiles, an ideal which was never realized in practice. In the booklet of Jonas God sent a prophet to pagans who willingly heeded His message.[88] Certainly no Israelite was prevented from converting his pagan neighbor to Yahwistic religion. A sincere effort was made by the author of the Book of Wisdom, the last book of the OT, to enlighten the educated Greeks for whom apart from the Jews, he developed these three points, a) their gods were non entities, b) they were in error if they deified nature, c) the God of Israel is the one true God whom all men should honor.[89]

The message of the prophets and the songs of the psalmists contain no directives for missionary work, not even an express admonition to instruct the pagans in the things of God during the time in question or in the immediate future. True, Israel was Yahweh's servant[90] and had a task to fulfill in His service. But this did not consist in active mission work among the Gentiles, rather in compliance with God's holy will and in preserving monotheism so that at some future date she could share her treasure with the Gentiles. There is no passage telling of pagans accepting monotheism because Jews had instructed them. In Is. 2:2-4 the nations encourage each other to journey to Sion. Mission activity is the theme in the text, "I shall assemble all nations and tongues, and they shall come and behold my glory. And I shall perform a sign in their presence, and send some of them who have escaped to the nations who have not yet received news of me and have not yet seen my glory, and they shall proclaim my glory among the nations."[91] However those who set out to preach are not Jews, but converted Gentiles to whom God has revealed His glory, for whom He had worked a sign by favoring them and calling them to this special mission. The apostles were the first to receive the command to do

84. Cf. § 3.
85. Is. 55:5.
86. Zach. 8:23.
87. Tob. 13:3.

88. Ez. 3:6.
89. § 4:2.
90. Is. 41:8-9; 42:19; 44:1-2,

21; 45:4; 48:20; Jer
30:10; Ez. 28:25; 37:25
91. Is. 66:18-19.

mission work, to teach all nations.[92] Isaias certainly intimated[93] that first the pagan world will be converted and then only the Jewish people; for this final conversion the Gentiles will be responsible and they will be grateful to God for the graces and privileges granted.[94]

5. THE SPREAD OF MONOTHEISM. Most foreigners who lived among the Israelites would have been willing to honor Yahweh as the territorial god[95] along with their own tribal deities.[96] Some would have considered Yahweh as the only God who should be worshipped, as Abraham's servant,[97] Agar,[98] Hobab (Moses' brother-in-law),[99] Rahab,[100] the Gibeonites,[101] Obededom[102] and Ittai (two Philistines),[103] the Hittite Urias,[104] Jonadab[105] and his children.[106] The widow of Sarepta accepted Yahwism[107] and likewise the Syrian Naaman after his cure.[108] At King Ezechias' invitation to celebrate the pasch in Jerusalem, strangers appeared from parts of the northern kingdom as well as non-Jews from Judah.[109] Aliens who wished to partake in the paschal meal first had to be circumcised;[110] the same held for slaves.[111] This regulation implies that there were some who honored Yahweh before becoming formally naturalized Israelites through circumcision. In his prayer at the dedication of the temple Solomon besought Yahweh to hear the prayers of strangers, "who come from distant lands for your name's sake and pray in this house."[112] Because those who dwelt among the Israelites were obliged to keep the Sabbath and the feasts, many non-Jews naturally made close contact with OT religious practices.[113]

Any alien who during the exile attached himself to a Jewish circle and observed its religious practices was to remain a member of the community.[114] Circumcision is not expressly mentioned but surely was presupposed. The Book of Esther takes for granted that non-Jews joined in with the Jews in celebrating the feast of Purim,[115] and the Book of Judith recounts how Achior, the leader of the Ammonites, professed faith in Yahweh and had himself circumcised.[116]

In Hellenistic times the Jews developed a vigorous religious propaganda and did not shrink from making forced conversions. John Hyrcanus imposed circumcision upon the Edomites, Aristobulus I upon the Itureans, Alexander Janneus upon the inhabitants of many Syro-Greek cities.[117] The Pharisees journeyed through lands and over seas to make a single proselyte.[118] Palestinian Jews however would not consider proselytes 100% orthodox, even after they had formally accepted Judaism; all such remained *gerim*, strangers,[119] and their children became full-fledged Jews only through marriage with true sons of Abraham. Hellenistic Jews were more bighearted. It was part of God's good providence to prepare pagans for the glad tidings of Christianity. Many

---

92. Matth. 28:19.
93. Is. 11:12; 19:24-25; 49: 22; 60:4, 9; 66:20.
94. Is. 61:9; 66:22.
95. Cf. 4 Kgs. 17:26-28.
96. Cf. 3 Kgs. 11:8.
97. Gen. 24:1.
98. Gen. 16:7-13; 21:17.
99. Num. 10:29-32.
100. Jos. 2:11.

101. Jos. 9.
102. 2 Sam. 6:10-11.
103. 2 Sam. 15:19-22.
104. 2 Sam. 11:11.
105. 4 Kgs. 10:15.
106. Jer. 35:1f.
107. 3 Kgs. 17:8f.
108. 4 Kgs. 5:15.
109. 2 Chr. 30:25.
110. Ex. 12:48-49.

111. Ex. 12:44.
112. 3 Kgs. 8:41-43.
113. § 29:6.
114. Is. 56:3-7.
115. Esth. 9:27.
116. Jud. 14:10.
117. Jos. Ant. XIII 9, 1; 11, 3; 15, 4; § 258, 318, 395ff.
118. Matth. 23:15.
119. Cf. Mischna Bikkurim I 4.

non-Jews numbered among their acquaintances men who worshipped but one God and led morally upright lives. The Jew in the diaspora was conscious of his religious superiority, he was confident of being "a leader of blind men, a light to those who walk in darkness."[120] Theoretically these Jews retained every detail of the Law and all the Rabbinic additions, in practice however they disregarded as unessential points which seemed difficult or ridiculous to the Greeks; they stressed the worship of one God whose might is not restricted by other gods, a God who is spiritual and therefore cannot be represented by the figure of man or beast, a God who demands a virtuous life, who rewards the good and punishes the wicked. They were aided by the philosophers who had proven polytheism erroneous and thereby severed the bond between pagan religion and the common people; this led many to adopt a religion from the East which made ascetical demands and promised liberation from sin. The task for the Jewish propagandist was lightened through the Greek translation of the OT (Septuagint) which was read at the synagogue services, since non-Jews also attended these meetings. Furthermore some energetic Jews reworked Biblical material and did not hesitate to publish books under famous pagan names, e.g., Sibylline books, Letter of Aristeas. According to the reckoning of J. Belochs[121] and Ad. Harnack[122] there were about 4 to 4½ million Jews in the Roman empire, i.e., 7-8% of the population. Neither natural fertility nor emigration from Palestine is able to account for this figure—there must have been very many non-Jews who adopted the Jewish religion. The principal motive which incited the Jews to continue propaganda was more the desire to enhance their own influence and reputation than to win souls for God. The proselytes made by Palestinian Pharisees were ordinarily trained in pharisaical self-righteousness and they would esteem pharisaical externalism higher than inner spirit;[123] like the Pharisees they took a hostile position toward Christ and His followers. The proselytes of the diaspora who were not entangled in Rabbinic narrowmindedness accepted with an open heart the glad tidings of salvation, while genuine Jews on the whole refused the message of the Gospel and persecuted its apostles. After the wars against Rome, 66-73 A.D., and the rebellions under Trajan and Hadrian, hatred toward everything foreign flared up in all their activities, and Roman authority forbade any further spread of Jewry; soon the missionary zeal of the Jews flickered out while the infant Church flourished in every way.

§ 49. THE GLORY OF THE MESSIANIC KINGDOM

The glory of the messianic kingdom far transcends that of the old covenant made at Sinai. The new covenant enables man to live without sin; it embraces all nations; the happiness it realizes in men's hearts and the privileges it grants cannot be compared with the blessings accorded the people of old. When the prophets described the glory of Israel, they did not refer to contemporary

120. Rom. 2:19.
121. Die Bevölkerung der griech.-röm. Welt, 1886,
122. 242f, 258f, 292f.
Die Mission und Ausbreit-
ung des Christentums I,
123. 1924, 9f.
Matth. 23:15.

Israel but the Israel of messianic times, that Israel which is intimately united with God and which includes all Gentiles converted from paganism.

1. SPIRITUAL BLESSINGS. a) *God's love.* The greatest blessing tendered to man in the messianic age is God's intimate love. Like Osee who again extended to his wife the fullest measure of intimacy—he had never hated her—so henceforth Yahweh will ever remain lovingly united to the new Israel.[1] The new people of God will cry rejoicingly, "Yahweh is our ruler! Yahweh is our sovereign! Yahweh is our king! He brings salvation to us."[2] From most ancient times Yahweh was honored as king in Israel,[3] but according to the prophets He would reign as king in a still higher sense during the messianic age.[4] Wis. 3:8 speaks of God reigning as king over the saints in heaven. As king Yahweh will dwell in the midst of His purified people unto the end of time;[5] forever will He remain Israel's God and Israel remain His people.[6] He will be Sion's unfailing light, while the sun shines only by day and the moon only by night;[7] He will protect Sion "as a cloud by day and the flame of a flickering fire by night"[8] and "be for her a fiery wall all about and as glory in her midst."[9]

The love Yahweh will tender to the new people will resemble that of a shepherd who anxiously cares for his flock,[10] one who is interested primarily in the sheep neglected by careless shepherds.[11] The Messiah will be commissioned to care for the flock in Yahweh's name.[12]

b) *Holiness of men.* Members of the messianic kingdom will possess a knowledge of God amply adequate to live according to His holy will, "Full is the land of the knowledge of Yahweh, as water covers the sea[13]. . . . In the plains justice shall dwell, and righteousness shall abide in the gardens."[14] The new kingdom will consist only of virtuous men,[15] men willing to be Yahweh's servants,[16] Yahweh's disciples.[17] The new Jerusalem will be named: City of Righteousness, Faithful City,[18] City of Yahweh, Sion, Sion of the Holy One of Israel,[19] Holy City,[20] The Peace of Righteousness, the Glory of the Fear of God.[21]

According to Joel this inner transformation will be effected by the spirit of God that will be poured out upon all without distinction as to age or social position.[22] On the first Pentecost St. Peter quoted this prophecy.[23] While in the past the prophets so frequently had found it necessary to complain about the godlessness of the rulers, the injustice of officials and the corruptibility of judges, in the future God will grant the people, "shepherds after his own heart, to pasture them with wisdom and prudence."[24] All members of God's new

1. Os. 2:21-22; 14:9; § 47:3.
2. Is. 33:22.
3. Num. 23:21; Deut. 33:5; Is. 6:5; Pss. 24:7; 29:10; § 5:12.
4. Cf. Mich. 2:13; 4:7; Soph. 3:15, 17; Abd. 21; Is. 41:21; 43:15; 44:6; 52:7; Zach. 14:9, 16; Is. 24:33; Tob. 13:15.
5. Jer. 3:17; Ez. 37:26; 43:4-9; 48:35; Is. 57:15; 60:14; 62:4; Agg. 2:9; Zach. 2:9,

14-16; 8:3; Mal. 3:17; Joel 4:21; Is. 24:23.
6. Jer. 31:33; Ez. 11:20; 36:28; 37:27; Zach. 8:8; 13:9.
7. Is. 60:19-20.
8. Is. 4:5.
9. Zach. 2:9.
10. Mich. 2:13; 4:6-7; Soph. 3:19; Jer. 23:3; 31:10; Is. 40:11; 49:9-10.
11. Ez. 34:7-22.
12. Ez. 34:23-24; 37:24; Zach.

11:7-9; § 51:1.
13. Is. 11:9.
14. Is. 32:16.
15. Is. 60:21.
16. Is. 54:17; 61:6.
17. Is. 54:13.
18. Is. 1:26.
19. Is. 60:14.
20. Is. 52:1.
21. Bar. 5:4; § 47:3.
22. Joel 3:1-2; § 20:5; 47:3.
23. Acts 2:16-21.
24. Jer. 3:15; 23:4.

people will be "priests of Yahweh," they will stand close to Him and live holy lives.[25] The Aaronic priesthood will have no further significance, still less the sacrifices prescribed by Mosaic Law, "for from the rising of the sun to its setting my name is great among the nations; in every place there shall be sacrifice, to my name men shall offer and that a clean oblation, for great is my name among the nations."[26] *Minhah* in this passage does not have the restricted meaning of *grain offering*, but is used in the wider sense of *oblation* as the context shows. Nor is it a question of sacrifice in a figurative sense, of prayer, for that would not have been anything new. Neither will this sacrifice be restricted to one place, the temple at Jerusalem. Malachy's prophecy is fulfilled by the sacrifice of the new covenant in which the Savior Himself is the victim.

c) *Everlasting character of the kingdom.* Amos promised the people that after the return from captivity they would dwell in their land forever.[27] According to Osee Yahweh would be perpetually espoused to Israel after her amendment.[28] The coming ruler would establish a kingdom in which there would be no end of peace;[29] Yahweh "will be king over them forever."[30] In these passages the words *forever* or *always* do not mean "a long period of time;"[31] for only when the order in nature begins to totter and only when the heavens can be measured and the depths of the earth fathomed will Yahweh reject His new people.[32] By the terms of the eternal covenant Israel will have perpetual possession of Canaan,[33] Judah will always exist, and Jerusalem too.[34] Daniel explained Nabuchodonosor's statue dream by declaring that God would bring forth a kingdom which would never be destroyed.[35] Also in the vision of the Son of Man[36] the messianic kingdom embraces all nations and remains indestructible forever.[37]

d) *Joy in God.* Because the Israel of messianic times will be holy, she will be a source of pleasure to God, "He rejoices over you with gladness, in his love he shouts with joy."[38] As a bridegroom takes pleasure in his bride, Yahweh will take pleasure in Israel.[39] The redeemed too will experience the purest happiness, "Eternal joy crowns their heart, delight and exultation are their portion; sorrow and pain will flee."[40] All sadness has an end[41] as Yahweh transforms Jerusalem into jubilation.[42] God Himself will urge Sion to rejoice as He dwells in her midst.[43] He will prepare a great banquet for all peoples;[44] death will be no more, all pain will vanish,[45] and Israel's dead will rise to share the universal rejoicing.[46]

2. EARTHLY BLESSINGS. a) *Fertility of the land.* Jacob's prophetic blessing upon Judah promised wine in such abundance during the messianic era that it could be used for doing the laundry; likewise milk.[47] According to Am. 9:15 sowing and harvesting, vintage and planting would follow each other without

25. Is. 61:6; cf. 66:21.
26. Mal. 1:11.
27. Am. 9:15.
28. Os. 2:21.
29. Is. 9:6.
30. Mich. 4:7.
31. § 10:1.
32. Jer. 31:35-37; cf. 33:17-18.
33. Ez. 37:25-26.
34. Joel 4:20.
35. Dan. 2:44.
36. Dan. 7:14, 27.
37. § 52:2e.
38. Soph. 3:17.
39. Is. 62:4-5.
40. Is. 35:10.
41. Is. 60:20.
42. Is. 65:18.
43. Zach. 2:14.
44. Is. 25:6; cf. Ps. 22:27.
45. Is. 25:8.
46. Is. 26:19; § 44:3.
47. Gen. 49:11-12.

nterruption.[48] Trees would bear fresh fruit every month.[49] "The mountains drip must, the hills flow with milk, and all Judah's wadies gush with water."[50]

b) *Countless descendants.* Yahweh promised the patriarchs a countless posterity; to number them would be as impossible as to number the stars in the heavens or the sand on the seashore.[51] These promises were repeated with reference to the messianic kingdom, "The number of the sons of Israel shall some day be like the sand on the seashore which cannot be measured or numbered[52]. ... I shall increase their number, they shall not decrease."[53] The land, too narrow for its inhabitants, will ask in amazement, "Who has given these birth for me?"[54]

c) *Longevity and freedom from physical evils.* Isaias' words come easily to mind: the blind see and the deaf hear, the lame walk and the dumb receive the power to speak again.[55] There will be no sudden, premature deaths,[56] and at the age of a hundred years youthfulness will not have vanished.[57]

d) *Riches.* At the time of Solomon great treasures streamed into Jerusalem as subject nations brought tribute.[58] Later the Israelites had to pay tribute to foreign rulers, and hostile armies plundered the land. In the messianic era the riches of peoples in the east and west will again flow toward the Holy City,[59] and when enemies are conquered great booty will be gathered.[60] Jerusalem's walls will be built of sapphires, her battlements of rubies, her doors of carbuncle stones and her enclosures of jewels.[61]

3. SION, THE CENTER OF THE MESSIANIC KINGDOM. Because Israel sinned exceedingly, God finally had to abandon His sanctuary and deliver it to destruction.[62] Only when satisfaction had been made would He return to Sion[63] and lay the foundation and cornerstone of the new kingdom.[64] He would then set up His royal throne[65] and remain in His new sanctuary forever.[66] Deliverance will be granted everyone who applies to Him for aid.[67] From Jerusalem Yahweh will pronounce judgment over enemies[68] and reign over them.[69] Thither the nations will journey to learn about Yahweh, to be taught their duties,[70] to worship[71] and to celebrate the feasts.[72] In Jerusalem Yahweh will prepare for the nations a sumptuous banquet.[73]

4. MESSIANIC PEACE. Israel often groaned under the suffering which hostile invasions occasioned and reminisced sadly over the peaceful era under Solomon. Since it is sin which causes rifts between men and nations, peace between nations will mark the new kingdom of God, sin no longer having any place. At the dawn of Israelitic history Jacob's words to Judah[74] intimated that the

48. Cf. Lev. 26:5.
49. Ez. 47:12.
50. Joel 4:18; cf. Os. 2:24; 14:8; Is. 29:17; 30:23-26; 32:15, 20; 35:1-2, 6-7; Jer. 31:12; Ez. 34:26-27; 36:29-30;47:1f; Is. 51:3; 55:13; 65:10; Ps. 72:16.
51. Gen. 15:5; 22:17; 32:13.
52. Os. 2:1; 14:6-7.
53. Jer. 30:19; 3:16; 33:10-11; Ez. 36:10-11, 37-38.
54. Is.49:19-21;54:1-3; 60:22; Zach. 2:8; 8:5; 9:17; 10:8.
55. Is. 35:5-6.
56. Is. 65:20-23; Zach. 8:4.
57. Is. 65:20.
58. 3 Kgs. 5:1; 9:28; 10:10, 14-15, 21-29.
59. Is. 23:17-18; 45:14; 60: 5-17; 61:6; Agg. 2:7; Ps. 7²:10.
60. Zach. 14:14.
61. Is. 54:11-12; Tob. 13:16-17; cf. Apoc. 21:18f.
62. Ez. 8-11.
63. Ez. 43:1-9; Is. 52:8.
64. Is. 28:16.
65. Is. 24:25.
66. Ez. 37:26; Joel 4:17.
67. Joel 3:5; Jer. 31:6, 12; 3:14.
68. Is. 31:9; Abd. 16; Ez. 38-39; Joel 4:2.
69. Ps. 2:6; 110:2.
70. Is. 2:2-4; Mich. 4:1-3.
71. Is. 27:13.
72. Zach. 14:16-19; cf. Agg. 2:7.
73. Is. 25:6.
74. Gen. 49:8-12.

day of salvation would be one of peace, since an overabundance of wine and milk can exist only in peaceful periods. The great fertility of the land in Am 9:13-14 presupposes an era of peace. Osee proclaimed, "The bow, the sword, and war I shall eliminate from the land, and I shall let them live in security."[75] In the messianic age the people of God will have no enemies against whom they must defend themselves. Disarmament is prophesied in Is. 9:4; Mich. 5:9-10; Zach. 9:10. Weapons will be beaten into useful tools.[76] "Of peace there shall be no end[77]. . . . The result of righteousness will be peace, and the revenue of righteousness rest and security forever[78]. . . . No nation shall lift up the sword against another, nor shall they study any longer the tactics of war. Men shall sit, each under his fig tree, without anyone to frighten them."[79] With them Yahweh will make "a covenant of peace;"[80] no enemy shall trouble them[81] and their king shall "enjoin peace."[82]

5. TRANSFORMATION OF NATURE. Peace will reign not merely over men and nations. Ordinarily after wars which costed many lives wild animals multiplied and ravaged the countryside; accordingly such beasts were considered a scourge sent by Yahweh against His sinful people.[83] In the messianic era animals will no longer be harmful and beasts will live peaceably among themselves. In Israel's favor Yahweh will strike "a covenant on that day with the beasts of the field and with the birds of the sky and the creeping creatures of the earth[84]. . . . The wolf shall dwell with the lamb and the panther shall lie down with the kid; the calf and young lion shall *lodge* together, and a little boy shall herd them. The cow and the bear shall graze together; like an ox the lion shall eat straw; at the hole of an asp the suckling child may play—no mischief or harm will be done anywhere upon the holy mountain."[85]

The heavenly bodies too will undergo transformation in the messianic age. "The light of the moon shall be as strong as the light of the sun, and the light of the sun shall be seven times stronger."[86] Neither sun nor moon will set, there will no longer be the constant change from day to night.[87] God will fashion a new heaven and a new earth.[88]

6. MEANING OF CERTAIN PROPHECIES ON THE GLORY OF THE MESSIANIC KINGDOM. While evaluating certain difficult prophecies concerning the new kingdom of God, we may profitably keep in mind the words of St. Paul, *ex parte cognoscimus et ex parte prophetamus*.[89] Not only "at various times" but also "in various ways" God spoke through the prophets.[90]

a) *Contradictions and impossibilities.* We must never forget that the prophets loved to use metaphorical language. First of all, contradictions would certainly follow from a strictly verbal interpretation, contradictions not only in the statements of the various authors but also in the statements of the same writer.

75. Os. 2:20.
76. Is. 2:4; Mich. 4:3.
77. Is. 9:6.
78. Is. 32:17.
79. Mich. 4:3-4; Is. 2:4; Soph. 3:13; Is. 60:17-18; Zach. 3:10.
80. Ez. 34:25; 37:26.
81. Joel 4:17.
82. Zach. 9:8-10; § 51:1; cf. Agg. 2:9; Ps. 72:3-7.
83. Lev. 26:22; 4 Kgs. 17:25; Ez. 5:17; 14:15; 33:27.
84. Os. 2:20.
85. Is. 11:6-9; 35:9; 65:25.
86. Is. 30:26.
87. Is. 60:20; Zach. 14:6-7.
88. Is. 65:17; 66:22.
89. 1 Cor. 13:9.
90. Heb. 1:1.

Weapons of war according to Osee,[91] Isaias,[92] Micheas[93] and Zacharias[94] will be smashed and burnt, according to Isaias[95] and Micheas[96] they will be made into useful tools. According to Micheas[97] and Zacharias[98] the nations will be plundered, but in Isaias[99] they bring their treasures spontaneously. The water from the fountain gushing in the temple flows into the Dead Sea in Ezechiel,[100] but in Zacharias[101] it parts and some flows in the Dead Sea, some in the Mediterranean, while according to Joel[102] it simply waters the valley of Shittim. The wild animals become tame according to Isaias,[103] but according to Ezechiel[104] they are killed off. According to Isaias[105] and Zacharias[106] men will become very old, according to Isaias in another passage[107] death will be destroyed forever. In Isaias[108] Sion is the highest mountain, in Zacharias[109] it is the only mountain and all the remaining country is a depression. According to Ez. 36:25 the exiles upon their return home will rebuild and fortify their cities, according to Ez. 38:11 there will be no fortified cities in Canaan, but only open villages that can offer no resistance to Gog's attack.

Certain things which the prophets declare seem impossible. To afford the exiles a suitable road the mountains and hills will sink and the valleys rise. According to Ezechiel[110] the country will be divided into twelve equally large strips (one for each of the twelve tribes) extending from east to west regardless of mountain chains or rivers although x) there remained only certain vestiges of the northern tribes, y) the tribes did not have equal strength, z) the tribe of Simeon had coalesced with that of Judah already long before the exile. Jerusalem will be rebuilt with precious stones![111] The water flowing from the temple, after it has proceeded a little distance, becomes a mighty stream and sweetens the water of the Dead Sea.[112] The fruitfulness of the land staggers the imagination.[113] The Mount of Olives will split in two from east to west, one part moving toward the north and the other part toward the south.[114] Lions will feed on straw,[115] the moon and the sun will shine much more brightly,[116] night will be a thing of the past.[117] As you read these things you may certainly ask: did the prophets themselves seriously believe that the nature of beasts would change, carnivorous animals becoming herbivorous, that Canaan would have an entirely different terrain, that the heavenly bodies would shine far more intensely (and burn up all vegetation?), and suspend their (apparent) courses about the earth?

b) *Picture versus message.* These descriptions of the messianic era present no contradictions or utopian reveries if, instead of understanding them verbally, we properly evaluate them as picture illustrations. The prophets knew they were not giving objectively accurate descriptions of future conditions, as

91. Os. 2:20.
92. Is. 9:4.
93. Mich. 5:9-10.
94. Zach. 9:10.
95. Is. 2:4.
96. Mich. 4:3.
97. Mich. 5:7.
98. Zach. 14:14.
99. Is. 60:5-11; 66:12.
100. Ez. 47:1-12.
101. Zach. 14:8.
102. Joel 4:18.
103. Is. 11:7-9; 33:9; 65:25.
104. Ez. 34:25.
105. Is. 65:20, 23.
106. Zach. 8:4.
107. Is. 25:8.
108. Is. 2:2.
109. Zach. 14:10.
110. Ez. 48.
111. Is. 54:11-12.
112. Ez. 47:1-12.
113. § 2a.
114. Zach. 14:4.
115. Is. 11:7.
116. Is. 30:26.
117. Is. 60:20; Zach. 14:6-7.

is shown by their constant endeavor to use new pictures and their refusal to employ the details of older imagery. Take, for instance, the description of the temple fountain in Ezechiel,[118] Zacharias[119] and Joel,[120] or of Sion in Isaias[121] and Zacharias;[122] or the statement that the doctrine proceeding from Sion will enliven mankind in Isaias,[123] as against the fountain as the source of life in Ezechiel.[124] In these passages we must distinguish between the essential and the accidental, between kernel and shell. The decisive element is not the isolated dots in the picture, which in themselves and apart from the context have no meaning, as they merely serve to enliven the whole picture, but the message which the prophet seeks to convey. Now the prophets loved poetry and would have shown little interest in abstract phraseology. The differences in style in the various books prove they did not react passively to divine revelation but moulded, so to speak, their own personal forms with which they conveyed God's message. In presenting this message they acted independently of one another. One procedure was to recall historical events and in an analogical way describe future events. We may here recall how Ezechiel[125] paints the siege of Tyre. The prophet writes as if this city were not situated on an island, and as if he did not know that it could not be taken in the manner he describes; the usual siege tactics are employed only as a means to show clearly Tyre's inevitable fall. The deliverance of Israel from the bondage of Egypt and the marvels during the desert journey became types for the deliverance from exile, and this in turn a type of redemption in messianic times.[126] When heralding the exile Osee recalled the trying years Israel had to pass in the land of Pharaoh. "To Egypt they shall return," he prophesied,[127] although he knew full well that Assyria would do the enslaving. Isaias compared the destruction of the enemies of God's kingdom[128] to the liberation from the power of the Midianites.[129] The glorious days of David, when neighboring nations were subject to Israel, the rule of Solomon with its peace, riches and magnificent temple,[130] were used to picture the glory of the coming kingdom. As Yahweh preceded the people in the pillar of cloud and fire during the desert journey, so in the future He would stand at their head protecting and enlightening them.[131] God dried up the floor of the Red Sea as a passage-way for the Israelites;[132] in the future He would "dry up the tongue of the sea of Egypt" as a road for the redeemed.[133] And as the Israelites chanted a song of thanksgiving after crossing the Red Sea,[134] so too in messianic times the redeemed would sing a song of gratitude to God after their deliverance.[135] In proclaiming liberation from Babylonian servitude Isaias refers expressly to the liberation from Egyptian servitude and the passage through the Red Sea.[136] As at the Exodus from Egypt, Yahweh will accompany the Jews on leaving Babylon;[137]

118. Ez. 47:1-12.
119. Zach. 14:8
120. Joel 4:18.
121. Is. 2:2.
122. Zach. 14:10.
123. Is. 2:2-4.
124. Ez. 47:1-12.
125. Ez. 26:8-11.
126. Is. 11:15; Mich. 7:15; Is. 40:2-4; 43:19; 51:10.
127. Os. 8:13.
128. Is. 9:3.
129. Judg. 7.
130. 3 Kgs. 5:1-5; 9:26-28; 10:2, 10-29.
131. Is. 4:5-6.
132. Ez. 14.
133. Is. 11:15-16.
134. Ex. 15.
135. Is. 12.
136. Is. 43:16-18.
137. Is. 40:3, 9, 11; 42:16.

He will open fountains for them in the desert as he did for their forefathers.[138] The relationship of God to the new Israel will be determined in a "covenant," even as Yahweh made a "covenant" with Israel through Moses, and with mankind through Noe.[139] Furthermore those nations appear as hostile to the messianic kingdom who had been hostile to Israel or were still hostile to her, e.g., Edom, Moab, Ammon, Egypt, Assyria, Babylon; their weapons will be familiar ones, e.g., lances, arrows, bows, swords, shields. The background against which the judgment upon God's enemies in messianic times is painted brings to mind a) Sodom and Gomorrah's destruction through fire and brimstone,[140] b) the theophany on Sinai amidst thunder and lightning, storm and earthquake,[141] c) Israel's own judgment through sword, famine, pestilence. Because the banquets consequent upon peace-offerings were occasions of great rejoicing,[142] they served to typify the joys of messianic times.[143]

c) *Lack of perspective.* Future events were frequently manifested to the prophets by means of visions, another indication that the prophets employed pictures in telling their messages. And these pictures lacked perspective; they present events not in historical order, but place the future alongside or before the present, or intersperse present and future events without any regard for actual sequence—just as the eye discerns no depth-dimension among the stars in the firmament and judges various light rays to be equidistant, although the beam from one may be thousands of years longer on its journey than the beam from the other. Thus things which will happen at the end of time appeared immediate to the prophet. The older prophets do not distinguish clearly between the preparation for the messianic kingdom (i.e., the return from the exile) and the messianic kingdom itself; for them the inauguration of the messianic era coalesces with the fall of Babylon. Immanuel *is* a child during the invasions by Tiglath-pileser.[144] In the "Servant of Yahweh" poems the Messiah seems destined to liberate Israel from the prison-house of exile.[145] Actually the Messiah appeared centuries after the return of the Jews from Babylon; the return was a preparation for the Redeemer's appearance in the Holy Land and a type of the redemption from the servitude of sin to be accomplished by the "Servant of Yahweh." In one glance the prophet saw these two intimately connected events, viz., the liberation from Babylon and the Messiah's work of liberating mankind from the slavery of sin. Likewise the prophets telescoped the appearance of the Messiah, the inauguration of the messianic era, and its final phase at the end of the world. John the Baptist saw the Messiah putting the ax to the root and winnowing the grain with a winnowfork,[146] i.e., he bridged together the time between Christ's activity upon earth with His coming at the last judgment.

Some of the comminatory addresses of the older prophets combine long periods in one sweep. Isaias (Ch. 13-14[147]) describes the destruction of

138. Is. 41:18; 43:20; 48:21.
139. Ex. 19-24; Gen. 9:9-17.
140. Gen. 19.
141. Ex. 19.
142. Deut. 12:12.
143. Is. 23:6; Ps. 22:27; cf. Matth. 22:2f; Lk. 14:17f; 22:30.
144. Is. 7:14-15; cf. Is. 8:8.
§ 50:3.
145. Is. 42:7; 49:6, 8-9.
146. Matth. 3:10-12.
147. Cf. Is. 46-47.

Babylon; now Cyrus put an end to Babylonia as a kingdom, but Babylon as a city ceased to exist only some centuries later. The same is true of the prophecy of the downfall of Tyre.[148] Nabuchodonosor was not able to take the city, but due to the long siege it lost much of its previous importance; a thorough destruction as painted by Ezechiel was not effected by Alexander the Great, but only by the Saracens in 1291 A.D. Nabuchodonosor however became the type of all who in the future would besiege or oppress Tyre. Judgment upon individual nations were described in terms of the judgment at the end of time.[149] When the prophets give dates, they do so by symbolic numbers. Jeremias set the length of the exile at 70 years because 7 and 10 are perfect numbers.[150] Daniel too made use of number symbolism as he spoke of the 70 weeks of years.[151]

d) *Influence of time and place upon prophetic pronouncements.* A well-known passage in Kings tells of the prophet Micheas appearing before Achab and Josaphat to predict the outcome of the war they had arranged against Aram. The two kings were sitting upon thrones and the (false) prophets whom they had invited were standing about them. Then Micheas relates his vision: Yahweh too was seated upon a throne, and the whole host of heaven's angels were standing about.[152] In his inaugural vision Ezechiel saw cherubim having four faces and four wings, since he and his fellow exiles were familiar with composite Babylonian divinities. Just as the environment in which the prophets found themselves was reflected in their visions, so too various circumstances influenced their message. In times when Israel was oppressed by enemies, salvation was depicted in terms of liberation from the yoke of the Gentiles, or in terms of peace. According to Mich. 7:11 Jerusalem's walls should be rebuilt, but when the Jews had returned from captivity, they were not allowed to fortify the city. Thereupon Zacharias prophesied: Let Jerusalem be inhabited as an open territory, because walls will be an obstacle to the multitude of men and cattle that will be hers. Nevertheless the city would not lack protection: Yahweh Himself would surround them as a wall of fire.[153] When the people became downcast, because the temple which they were building would be poor due to a lack of funds and materials, Aggeus consoled them, "The future glory of this temple shall surpass that of the previous (temple)."[154] In their temple the Gentiles would acknowledge and worship Yahweh and subject themselves to Him—their temple would witness the beginning of the messianic era. Aggeus' words received unexpected fulfillment when the Son of God appeared and taught there. During the period when the house of David ruled in Jerusalem, the prophets spoke of the Messiah as a king.[155] But when the kingdom had fallen and the people lived as captives in Babylon or as refugees in distant lands and it became necessary to gather the dispersed, to lead the exiles back home, to console the oppressed, Ezechiel pictured the Messiah as a good shepherd,

148. Ez. 26-28.
149. § 45:6; 46:4.
150. Jer. 25:11; 29:10.
151. Dan. 9:24-27; § 50:4.
152. 3 Kgs. 22:10-19.
153. Zach. 2:8-9.
154. Agg. 2:9.
155. § 51:1.

a pattern for which the peasant prophet Micheas had set the precedent.[156] The "Ebed Yahweh" poems of exile days depicted the Messiah in terms of a servant patiently suffering and dying;[157] to "the Servant" the exiles could turn as to a fellow-sufferer, but also as to a prophet who, like Moses of old, would deliver them, instruct them regarding God's will and mediate a new covenant. The very people who held them in bondage would some day be their companions on the journey back to Canaan, back to their land there to act as servants and handmaids.[158] Some day the riches of the nations would become their portion.[159] These prophecies however must not be considered separately. Others may be found, frequently by the same prophet, telling how the Gentiles would enjoy equal status with Jews in the new kingdom of God. Isaias even pointed out that Israel would convert only after the Gentiles.[160] Though Jewish spirit tended toward accentuating nationalistic aspirations, these latter prophecies indicate no such tendencies on the part of orthodox prophets. The prophets were conversant with a return of the whole world to God, not merely the Jewish return from Babylon; this is proven by many passages which describe the subjection of the Gentiles to Yahweh and their incorporation into the messianic kingdom.

e) *Paradise and the messianic kingdom.* To picture the blessings of the messianic era OT writers would compare it to paradise. In paradise there was no sin, no worry, no suffering, no death, and even when the prophets do not expressly mention paradise, they parallel the coming kingdom with paradise. The wilderness becomes Eden, Sion and Canaan the garden of Eden. The fountain flowing from the temple corresponds to the river in paradise. In paradise the wild animals did not harm man, likewise in the future they will be tame. The covenant which God will make with the animals[161] recalls the covenant with the animals after the flood.[162] We may think of the cherub and the flaming sword as we read about Yahweh becoming a wall of fire for Jerusalem.[163] These figures taken by the prophets from ancient accounts were used to depict the blessings of the messianic era. Where sin and consequently death reigned (wilderness, Dead Sea), there will be life (Eden, the water of the Dead Sea becomes sweet); this will be effected by the river of grace emanating from the sanctuary. Hostility, as found among men or between men and animals or between animals, is discord in God's creation; the messianic era will be one of perfect love and peace.

f) *Earthly goods.* The produce of Canaan, wheat, wine, milk, were regarded as gifts from Yahweh, and rightly so. Most Israelites took it for granted that in the coming kingdom God would reward them most abundantly with such goods for their fidelity. This hope influenced the external form of the messianic picture. Earthly goods became symbols for the spiritual goods proper to the messianic kingdom.

156. Mich. 5:3.
157. § 52:1a.
158. Is. 14:2; 45:14; 49:22-23; 60:10-14; 61:5; 66:12.
159. Is. 23:17-18; 60:5:17; 61:6; Mich. 4:13; Agg. 2:7; Zach. 14:14; Ps. 72:8-11.
160. Is. 56:3-7; § 48:2.
161. Os. 2:20.
162. Gen. 9:10.
163. Zach. 2:9.

g) *Cult.* The center of the messianic kingdom will be Sion. From there the true faith will be heralded to mankind; there the Messiah will give Himself as a sacrifice; from there the apostles will set out on their missions. Because of Sion's significance in the history of salvation, the prophets rightly designated her as the highest mountain,[164] or as Canaan's only mountain.[165] The sanctuary of the future covenant is the temple, the levitical priesthood continues,[166] animals are brought as sacrifice by Jew[167] and Gentile,[168] the Sabbath, New Moon and other feasts are kept sacred.[169] On the other hand the ark of the covenant no longer exists,[170] the Aaronic priesthood is rejected,[171] Gentiles serve as priests,[172] a new sacrifice is promised wholly unlike current sacrifices.[173] Again we see the metaphorical character of prophetic terminology, the kernel of the message being simply: in messianic times God will be worshipped under new cult forms.[174]

h) *Obscurities.* In a prophet's message it is often difficult to decide what is kernel and what is shell, to determine exactly the range and depth of meaning. Before the exile the Israelites could not have known how the restoration would be accomplished. Even the prophets may have believed in the verbal fulfillment of certain particulars in their messages. God fulfilled certain statements in a much truer sense than expected; even the apostles for a long time held rather worldly views concerning the messianic kingdom. But since the prophets considered earthly goods as rewards restricted to such as lived holy lives, they must have regarded the love of God as absolutely primary, material blessings coming merely as a sequel. With this approach the interpretation could gradually spread that prophetic descriptions of earthly good fortune were nothing more than figurative illustrations for the spiritual blessings with which those who served God faithfully in messianic times would be laden. While fulfillment clarifies the meaning of many prophecies, obscurities still remain; and some prophecies await clarification through fulfillment. Nor may we forget that prophecies are conditional, at least to some degree, with fulfillment dependent upon the future free action of men. Would Jerusalem have become the center of the Church instead of Rome if Israel had accepted the Savior's message? Israel refused, and nations whom she despised received the inheritance which had in the first place been reserved for her; even with the Gentiles there was needed and is needed at present much hard work and self-subjection before the messianic kingdom is fully perfected. Alongside the promises of everlasting peace is the admonition, "Bless the war! arouse the fighters! beat your plow shares into swords and your vine-knives into spears! Let even the weakling say: I am a fearless fighter!"[175] Our own daily prayer is "Thy kingdom come!" God is not accepted as king by every nation,[176] and therefore particular judgments are even today being imposed upon those peoples who refuse to hear His voice; and there are nations which execute His judgments. During the

164. Is. 2:2.
165. Zach. 14:10.
166. Jer. 33:18.
167. Jer. 33:11.
168. Is. 19:21; Soph. 3:10; Is.

56:7; 60:7.
169. Is. 66:23; Zach. 14:16,
18.
170. Jer. 3:16.
171. Mal. 1:10.

172. Is. 66:21.
173. Mal. 1:11.
174. Cf. Heb. 8:5; 9:23; 10:1.
175. Joel 4:9-10.
176. Zach. 14:9.

messianic era prior to its consummation wars accordingly have a place in the divine economy of salvation. Certain prophecies dealing with the end of the world will be fulfilled only at the end of time; among these is the prophecy of everlasting peace. At Christ's second advent it will become clear what pertains to the present and what pertains to the future.

i) *Worldly hopes.* Many, perhaps most Israelites rejoiced over the seeming promises of earthly goods and did not or would not understand the fundamental supernatural, spiritual character of prophetic teaching. Hope in earthly blessings flared brightly during the centuries of Seleucid and Roman oppression. The messianic expectations of large circles were oriented toward the secular-political, while the moral-religious aspect became recessive. Most of the Jews counted upon an earthly messianic kingdom in which they would enjoy top positions, a kingdom in which they would be guaranteed every material advantage, while the Gentiles would stand at their beck and call. How prophetic metaphor was further polished to suit their purpose, is well illustrated by the following apocalyptic propaganda: the earth will bear fruit 10,000 fold; on one vine will be 1000 branches, each branch will bear 1000 clusters, each cluster 1000 berries, each berry will produce 1 kor (364 quarts) of wine.[177] Manna will fall from the sky,[178] milk will bubble forth from the earth in springs,[179] a measure of olives will give 10 baths (41 gallons) of oil.[180] A man will sire 1000 children.[181] The OT prophecies contain no basis for such speculations. Already before the exile the prophets inveighed against the popular notion of the "Day of Yahweh" being one of salvation for Israel and against the notion that patriarchal descent guaranteed divine favor.[182] For the prophets the settlement of political problems or the betterment of economic conditions was not of prime importance; of prime importance was the realization of the kingdom of God in human hearts through divine grace, the union of man with God in love and fidelity, redemption from sin, the conversion of the Gentiles, in order that all mankind could gather together to worship and serve the creator.

SECTION 3. THE MESSIAH

§ 50. THE PERSON OF THE MESSIAH

1. THE TITLE: MESSIAH. In God's eternal plans a particular person was destined to mediate a new covenant with Israel and to bring the Gentiles the knowledge of God together with the blessings of a new era. This person would not come unexpectedly—through the centuries prophets would herald Him. He would be called "The Messiah." The word itself simply means "anointed;" it is derived from *mašiah*, in Aramaic *mešiha*). By being anointed with oil persons (and also things) were dedicated to God and given special status. The high

177. Apc. Bar. I 29, 5.
178. Apc. Bar. I 29, 8.
179. Sib. III 749.
180. Hen. 11, 19.
181. Hen. 10, 17.
182. § 46:1.

priest was anointed,[1] at times also priests[2] and kings.[3] In a metaphorical sense the patriarchs and prophets were called "anointed," because they were equipped in a special manner with the spirit of God to be instruments of the divine will.[4] Isaias speaks of Cyrus the Great as Yahweh's "anointed" agent.[5] *Par excellence* the coming Redeemer may be called the "anointed," since the spirit of God rests upon Him in eminent measure, far surpassing any one else commissioned by God to work with men.[6] Upon Him God conferred the three offices of king, prophet, and priest.[7] In the OT however the Savior is called "Messiah" only in Ps. 2:2,[8] while in the NT this title is applied to Him only in John 1:42 and 4:25; otherwise the corresponding Greek word *Christos,* with or without the article, is used. The apocrypha prefer speaking of the coming *Deliverer.* In His preaching Jesus seldom made claim to the title Messiah because the Jews had surrounded it with hopes of an earthly kingdom.

2. ANCESTRY. After the first sin in paradise, the tempter heard God's sentence, "I will put enmity between you and the woman, and between your descendants and her descendants. She shall crush your head, but you shall wound her heel."[9] According to the context Eve is the woman. Though she had consented to the serpent's insinuations, in the future she would withstand his enticements. Her descendants too, viz., every person born into the world, would be hostile to the serpent and his brood, the devils. The curse upon the serpent[10] points to a deliverance; it was the first good news after the fall, the protoevangel. From his struggle with evil man carries away wounds: the serpent bites his heel seeking to injure him; but he cannot rob him of God's friendship. From the NT we know how a specific child of Eve fought the battle against the serpent. He who "was born of a woman,"[11] was first tempted by the devil in the wilderness;[12] then Satan set a "brood of vipers" against Him,[13] the Pharisees who had "the devil as father."[14] In the heart of Judas he placed the desire to betray the Master,[15] and when Jesus had delivered Himself over to His enemies the "powers of darkness" seemed to triumph.[16] Dying upon the cross He received the bite of the serpent, but by surrendering His human nature to death, He crushed His adversary's head, broke his might, and he "who triumphed on the wood (of the tree in paradise) was defeated on the wood (of the cross)."[17] Thus Gen. 3:15 is true of all men, but in an unique manner applies to Christ who, as Eve's child, delivered us from the serpent's power.

Some idea of salvation was inherent in Noe's blessing[18] and in the promises made to the patriarchs,[19] inasmuch at least as the knowledge of God would not go lost among the children of men. The first instance in which a specific son of Abraham is designated as the bearer of salvation to Israel and the Gentiles occurs in Jacob's dying blessing upon Judah, "The sceptre shall not pass from

1. Ex. 29:7; Lev. 8:12; called "anointed priest" in Lev. 4:3, 5.
2. Ex. 28:41; 30:30.
3. 1 Sam. 2:10, 35; 10:1; 12:3; 16:13, etc.
4. 3 Kgs. 19:16; Is. 61:1; Ps. 105:15.
5. Is. 45:1.
6. Is. 11:2.
7. § 51.
8. For Dan. 9:24-27, cf. § 50:4.
9. Gen. 3:15.
10. Gen. 3:15.
11. Gal. 4:4.
12. Matth. 4.
13. Cf. Matth. 3:7.
14. Jn. 8:44.
15. Lk. 22:3; Jn. 13:2, 27.
16. Lk. 22:53.
17. Preface of the Holy Cross.
18. Gen. 9:24-27.
19. Gen. 12:3; 18:18; 22:18; 26:4; 28:14; § 48:1.

Judah or the rod from between his feet, until he comes *to whom it* (the sceptre) *belongs,* and whom the nations shall obey" (G V S: "for whom the nations are waiting").[20] The ancient versions interpret the passage of the Messiah, and perhaps Ezechiel too had it in mind as he wrote: the kingdom will lie in ruins "till he comes who has a right (to it), and to him I shall give it."[21] The Targums also are slanted messianically, e.g., "till the Messiah comes, whose kingdom it is" (Onkelos). The tribe of Judah became sovereign in the person of David. Soon Nathan was promising to David, "Your house and your kingdom shall last forever before *me,* your throne shall endure forever."[22] As the context shows, these words apply to the whole Davidic dynasty; David was grateful to Yahweh because "he shows mercy to his anointed, David, and to his posterity forever."[23] According to 1 Chr. 17:14 the promise would prove true in a special sense in his successor Solomon. The psalmist develops the promise by declaring that David's throne would continue "as long as the heavens . . . as the sun before me . . . as the moon which abides everlastingly."[24] Only in Jesus, the son of David, does this prophecy find perfect fulfillment.[25] Later prophets speak of the Redeemer as a descendant, *sprout,* of David and frequently call Him "David."[26] According to Ez. 17:22 the Messiah will be born from the high cedar (the house of David); as forefather He will have the cedar's top (Joachim) that was taken to Babylon by the eagle (Nabuchodonosor).[27] The true humanity of the Messiah is also indicated in those passages which concern His birth,[28] His coming forth "from (His) mother's womb,"[29] His appearance as the "most beautiful of the children of men,"[30] and particularly His suffering and death.[31] It was common belief among the Jews that the Messiah would be a descendant of David. To the question, "What do you believe concerning the Messiah, whose son will he be?" the Pharisees unhesitatingly answered, "David's."[32] After Jesus had cured a possessed person, the crowd asked full of amazement, "Is not this the Son of David?"[33] Needy persons seeking aid addressed Him as "Son of David."[34] "Hosanna to the Son of David" resounded as He entered Jerusalem.[35] St. Matthew gives us the genealogy of Jesus from Abraham to Judah, to David, to Joachim; St. Luke continues it backward from Abraham, to Sem, to Adam. A reference to Jesus born "according to the flesh from the family of David" forms part of St. Paul's lengthy salutation to the Romans.[36]

3. THE MESSIAH: A VIRGIN'S SON. Four thousand years ago God willed to have His name honored properly in at least one family, and He intervened in a miraculous way to fashion that family. This new and privileged stock must not arise through mere natural generation; Sara was old and sterile, but in spite of these physical disabilities she would give a son to her aged husband

---

20. Gen. 49:10.
21. Ez. 21:32.
22. 2 Sam. 7:16.
23. 2 Sam. 22:50-51 (Ps. 18:50-51).
24. Ps. 89:30, 37, 38.
25. Lk. 1:32-33; Heb. 1:5.
26. Is. 9:6; Am. 9:11; Os. 3:5;

Jer. 23:5; 30:9; 33:15; Ez. 34:23-24; 37:24-25.
27. Cf. Ez. 17:3-4.
28. Is. 7:14; 9:5.
29. Ps. 22:10-11.
30. Ps. 45:3.
31. § 52:1.

32. Matth. 22:42; cf. Mk. 12:35; Lk. 20:41; Jn. 7:42.
33. Matth. 12:25.
34. Matth. 9:27; 15:22; 20:30.
35. Matth. 21:9, 15.
36. Rom. 1:3.

Abraham. "Is anything impossible for Yahweh?"[37] Centuries later when the
Messiah was about to appear upon the earth, God intervened in a similar way
in the lives of Zachary and Elizabeth.[38] But an exceedingly more stupendous
miracle would accompany the birth of Him who as the Son of God was destined
to lead the entire human race to the threshold of heaven.[39]

In the year 735 before Christ Rasin of Damascus and Phacee of Israel were
endeavoring to force Achaz of Judah to participate in a rebellion against
Assyrian domination. Isaias warned him to trust in God, and to confirm his
message offered to work any "sign" Achaz desired. The king scoffed at the
offer because he already had resolved to seek assistance from Assyria; from
Assyria he expected deliverance, not from Yahweh. In spite of his refusal God
determined to give him a sign, but this sign, given against the king's wishes,
would not be one of salvation but one of disaster for him and for the royal
house. The proffered sign was intended to confirm his faith, the sign actually
given required faith. It is introduced with the words, "Behold, the young woman
shall conceive and shall bear a son, and she shall name him Immanuel 'God with
us'."[40] (almah signifies a girl of marriageable age, one who is presumably still
a virgin.[41] Prov. 30:19, "the way of a man toward an (almah" does not contradict this interpretation. The translation given in the LXX, ἡ παρθένος, is a
wholly adequate equivalent. Nor did the Jews take offense at this rendition
until the term was used by Christians as proof for Christ's messiahship. The
article in the Hebrew singles out the Virgin as the person through whom the
prophet's message would be fulfilled.[42] Reference to the Virgin's Son as the
future deliverer is also made in Is. 8:8, where He appears as ruler over Judah,
and in Is. 9:5, where He is accredited with absolute sovereignty. Isaias' message
involves the Messiah's conception and birth, and by employing the word (almah
instead of)iššah, wife, he implies that the woman who bears the child will
remain virginal throughout the process. Furthermore, there is no mention of
a father; the mother names the child, not the father, as was customary in
kingdom times. The interpretation of this prophecy as referring to the virgin
birth, as tradition has always done, has again become common among critical
exegetes. A collective interpretation, i.e., many young women conceive and
call their babes Immanuel, is out of the question because Isaias knows only
one Immanuel. The child's mother is not the prophet's wife because He belongs
to David's family.[43] Nor can Achaz or one of his immediate successors qualify
as father because the prophecy was directed against him and his dynasty.

Before the Child would be capable of distinguishing between good and evil
(about the age of three), His food would be curd and honey.[44] According to
Is. 7:22 these items are victuals proper to a desolated land. Isaias' message
then is: a foreign power is on the point of devastating the northern kingdom
and the kingdom of Damascus.[45] We know how in 732 Tiglath-pileser herded

37. Gen. 17:15-19; 18:10-15.   41. Gen. 24:43 (cf. 24:16);   43. Is. 9:6; 11:1.
38. Lk. 1.   Ez. 2:8; Ps. 68:26; Cant.   44. Is. 7:15.
39. § 5.   1:3; 6:8; Prov. 30:19.   45. Is. 7:16.
40. Is. 7:14.   42. GK § 126r.

into captivity part of the inhabitants of the northern kingdom, laid a heavy tribute upon Achaz and made him a vassal.[46] The prophet sees the Messiah grow up in a devastated land, yet in spite of the seeming time indication, Isaias did not expect the birth of Immanuel in the immediate future. For in 9:5 he linked the birth of the Messiah with the destruction of Assyria, and the latter would take place only after the fall of the northern kingdom. Moreover the prophet stressed the fact that the Messiah would proceed "from the *root* of Jesse":[47] hence before the Messiah appeared the royal family would have lost the throne; here again the destruction of Assyria must come first.[48] The content of 7:15 becomes clear if we remember that the prophet saw in one perspective-less picture the birth of Immanuel together with more immediate events; since the Child was present before him, it could serve well as a terminus for other particulars.[49] A similar alignment of events occurring at widely separated times is found in Is. 8:8. Assyria had become hostile to Judah, and the prophet hopefully speaks of Immanuel for whose sake Yahweh will not let the people perish.—In the person of Blessed Mary, Virgin and Mother, this prophecy of Isaias was fulfilled.[50]

The prophecy of the virgin birth in Isaias may be used as the key to a difficult passage in Micheas: God will abandon Israel "till the time when she who is with child has given birth."[51] Here again there is no mention of a father, and mystery surrounds the birth. The prophet has in mind the Messiah because he is describing the deliverance from evil consequent upon the Child's birth.

Jeremias urged the exiles of the northern kingdom to return to their homeland, "How long will you resist, obstinate daughter? Yahweh is doing something new in the land: A woman courts *(tesobeb)* a man."[52] The context treats of messianic times. St. Jerome, translating *tesobeb* as "surround," saw in this passage a prophecy of the formation of the Messiah in the womb of His virginal mother, an interpretation however in which he stands alone among the Fathers. Woman, *neqebah*, and man, *geber*, are equivalent to female and male. Now the prophets loved to depict the relationship of Israel to Yahweh in terms of marriage;[53] and they also prophesied the conversion and return of the Chosen People.[54] This sheds some light upon Jer. 31:22; the new thing, the marvel which Yahweh is performing, is the conversion of Israel till then so stiff-necked. As an unfaithful wife in sorrow returns to her spouse and manifests to him her love,[55] so this nation will return to God and seek His affection. This conversion is the work of divine mercy.[56]

4. TIME AND PLACE OF BIRTH. According to Jacob's prophecy the tribe of Judah would gain a position of leadership before the Messiah's advent.[57] However the passage, "The sceptre shall not pass from Judah . . . until he comes to whom it belongs," does not imply that the Redeemer would appear while

46. 2 Chr. 28:20-21; 4 Kgs. 16:8-10.
47. Is. 11:1, 10.
48. Is. 10:33-34.
49. § 49:6c.

50. Lk. 1:26f; Matth. 1:20f.
51. Mich. 5:2.
52. Jer. 31:22.
53. § 16:4.
54. § 47:1.

55. Os. 2:18.
56. Jer. 31:18-20; Lam. 5:21; § 47:3.
57. Gen. 49:10.

Judah actually was reigning as king; nor does the word *until* indicate the loss of Judah's hegemony; it simply refers to a preparatory term[58] after which the Messiah will take possession of Judah's sovereignty—a very honorable climax. Balaam's blessing asserts that kingship would previously have been established in Israel.[59] According to Amos, "On that day (when the judgment has been completed) I shall establish the demolished house of David, wall up its breaches and re-erect its ruins; and I shall rebuild it as in the days of old,"[60] the house of David will have lost its power and prestige (the royal palace is a tent), will even have come to an end (the tent is in ruins) before the Deliverer comes. Isaias develops the same thought, "A sprig will sprout forth from the stump of Jesse, a shoot will *bud forth* from his roots."[61] When the Savior is born in David's family, that family will be of as little importance as a tree-stump, it will have no more status in the land than Jesse's family once had, and the Messiah Himself will be only a sprig or shoot, *neṣer,* at first un-recognized. According to Micheas the family of David will no longer be in power when the Messiah comes, for he places His birth in the little town of Bethlehem.[62] In Ez. 17:22 the Savior is "a tender sprig" as He appears upon the earth, and in Is. 53:2 "a shoot or a root out of hard earth," i.e., His parents and therefore He Himself live in poor circumstances. In Zach. 3:8 and 6:12 "sprout," *ṣemaḥ,* is the name given to the Messiah. Since the prophets so frequently call the Messiah sprig, shoot, root, Isaias may be referring to Him in 4:2 where he uses the term "sprout," *ṣemaḥ,* of Yahweh (usually the phrase is interpreted to mean messianic blessings). The "sprout" appears when Yahweh has executed judgment over Israel, and with His appearance the messianic era begins, sins are blotted out and all lead holy lives.[63] Because of parallelism Is. 4:2b, "the fruit of the land shall be the pride and glory of those who are saved out of Israel" would then likewise refer to the Messiah. Jesus was called a "Nazarean,"[64] probably in fulfillment of Is. 11:1 *(neṣer)*. According to Agg. 2:7-9 the second temple will be standing when the Messiah comes.[65]

At this point we may give some consideration to Daniel's prophecy of the 70 weeks.[66] Many exegetes refer the passage directly to the Messiah and try to deduce a definite date for His advent. "Seventy weeks have been allotted to your people and to your holy city to bring wickedness to a finish, to make an end to sin, to expiate evil deeds, to inaugurate eternal justice, to put the seal upon vision and prophet, and to anoint a most holy place (v. 24). Know therefore and understand: From the time when the order is given to reinhabit and reconstruct Jerusalem until (there comes) an anointed prince 70 weeks (shall pass); then during 62 weeks it shall be restored, and it shall be built (with) squares and sepulchres (?), even if the times be trying (v. 25). After the 62 weeks an anointed one shall be cut off without being given a chance; and the people of the prince who comes shall raze to the ground the city and

58. Cf. Gen. 28:15; Ps. 110:1;   61. Is. 11:1.   64. Matth. 2:23.
    112:8.   62. Mich. 5:1.   65. § 48:2; 49:6d.
59. Num. 24:7, 17-19.   63. Is. 4:3-4.   66. Dan. 9:24-27.
60. Am. 9:11.

the sanctuary, but his end shall be (after the fashion of) a flood, and war shall continue (?) its devastation unto the end (v. 26). He shall make strong alliances with many during one week, and during half a week he shall abolish bloody and unbloody sacrifices, and a hideous desecration shall defile the sanctuary (?), and (will continue) until the destruction which has been irrevocably decreed has emptied itself upon the destroyer (v. 27)."

V. 24 describes the messianic age. There will be no more sin, all guilt will be forgiven (three phrases for emphasis), justice will triumph and what the prophets had foretold ("vision—prophet") will be fulfilled, e.g., reconciliation with God, holiness of life.[67] The "most holy place" is the sanctuary of the messianic era;[68] its anointing must be understood figuratively. The interval until the inauguration of the messianic era is 70 "weeks-of-years" which is divided into three sections: 7, 62, 1.

V. 25 says that the first week extended from the prophecy of Jeremias until the Jews were allowed to return home from Babylon with the rise of an "anointed prince." The "order" is a divine command rather than a royal edict.[69] Jeremias set the duration of the exile at 70 years,[70] and promised the restoration of Jerusalem.[71] The "anointed prince" who permitted the return and the reconstruction was Cyrus.[72] The prophecy of Jeremias was fulfilled with the edict of Cyrus in the year 538.[73] According to Is. 45:13 Cyrus was predestined to rebuild the Holy City; between 587 and 538 there were 7 week-years, 49 years. In the second period, 62 weeks, the reconstruction of Jerusalem would take place under trying circumstances; the text does not say that reconstruction work would cover the whole period.

V. 26. At the beginning of the third period, 1 week, an "anointed" (without article) is put to death; he is distinguished from the "anointed prince" of v. 25. He dies innocently, either according to Theodotion's reading, "Right is denied to him," or according to the restored text, "There is no fault in him." In the year 171 the high priest Onias III was murdered at Antioch.[74] A "prince" then razes the city and the sanctuary to the ground; his must be a shameful death, but until it comes there is war and persecution. Antiochus IV comes quickly to mind; he captured Jerusalem, plundered the temple.[75] He died in the year 164, which would make this last week extend from 171 to 164.

V. 27 complements v. 26. The "prince" strikes agreements with many, i.e., the large number of apostate Jews who were willing to join him and support his efforts.[76] He put an end to sacrifices,[77] desecrated the temple by placing an altar to Zeus upon the altar of holocaust and then sacrificed pigs upon it.[78] *Šiqquṣ* frequently signifies the abomination of idolatrous worship. A profanation of the temple in this manner occurred during Dec. 168, its purification

67. § 47:3.
68. Ez. 43:12; 45:3; cf. Agg. 2:7-9; Zach. 6:12-13.
69. Cf. Dan. 9:2.
70. Jer. 25:11 (i.e., in the year 605 B.C.; cf. Jer. 25:1); Jer. 29:10 (in the year 597; cf. Jer. 29:1).
71. Jer. 30:18; 31:38 (in the year 587).
72. Called "anointed" in Is. 45:1.
73. 2 Chr. 36:22-23; Esdr. 1:1-2.
74. 2 Mach. 4:34.
75. 1 Mach. 1:21-24; 2 Mach. 5:11-21.
76. 1 Mach. 1:52; 2 Mach. 4:12.
77. 1 Mach. 1:45.
78. 1 Mach. 1:47, 54; 2 Mach. 6:4-5.

and "dedication" in Dec. 165.[79] Hence for about half a "week" no legitimate sacrifice was offered. This interpretation is supported by parallel passages, e.g., Dan. 11:31; 12:11: the daily sacrifices were abolished while the "hideous desecration" was taking place; according to Dan. 12:11 this continued for 1290 days, or roughly speaking 3½ years. The expression "hideous desecration" in 1 Mach. 1:54 points back to Dan. 9:27 and sees the passage fulfilled in the actions of Antiochus. Josephus too relates the passage to the desecration of the temple by Antiochus.[80]

The 70 week-years are not to be applied numerically but symbolically, even though the figure corresponds numerically for the first and the last period. The prophet's main concern is the last week, the other two periods merely serve as introduction and he says little regarding them. He chose the number 70 both because of its symbolical significance (i.e., completion, consummation) and to parallel Jeremias' prophecy of 70 years. What he wants to say is this: the messianic age is coming, but it is not coming as quickly as many think; 70 week-years must elapse before you may enjoy its blessings (v. 24). Nor does the prophet say that the messianic era will follow hard on the last week after the death of Antiochus; for here again there is question of simultaneous vision of events between which considerable time may elapse.[81]

Jesus referred to the "hideous desecration" when He prophesied the destruction of Jerusalem and the temple.[82] When such dreadful abominations were to be repeated, His disciples should speedily take to flight because judgment was again imminent. The outrages of the zealots, who reverenced not even the sanctuary, constituted sufficient warning for the Christians to seek security before the final Jewish uprising against Rome in the years 66-70 A.D. Wisely the Christians left Jerusalem before the city was besieged. Thereupon followed a still more horrible desecration, "the people of the prince who shall come," Titus, destroyed Jerusalem and the temple, and sacrifice ceased forever. The acts of Antiochus IV were a dress rehearsal for these events—which Jesus foretold. The "anointed" one who was put to death innocently, the high priest Onias, prefigured Christ the "anointed" One who innocently shed His blood. The "anointed prince" (cf. v. 25), who changed the fortunes of Israel by granting her freedom and decreeing the reconstruction of Jerusalem, may well be regarded as a type of the Messiah-king who redeemed mankind from the servitude of Satan and founded the new kingdom of God. An "anointed" one climaxes each of the first two periods; finally the 70 week-years upon which dawned the messianic era was climaxed by an "anointed" One who united in Himself the dignity of king and priest (Cyrus—Onias—Jesus).[83]

This typically messianic interpretation accords excellently with the message contained in v. 24, i.e., the sanctity of messianic times. The prophets do not cast their prophecies of future events into an historical sequence; neither does the typical interpretation run aground in that v. 24 proclaims messianic bless-

79. 1 Mach. 4:36-54.
80. Ant. XII 7, 6 § 322.
81. § 49:6c; 50:3.
82. Matth. 24:15.
83. Cf. Goettsberger.

ings in the literal sense, while vv. 25-27 foretell the death of Jesus and the destruction of the temple in the typical sense; nor may we demand that type and antitype (Cyrus-Onias: Jesus; Antiochus: Titus-hideous desecration) must agree in all particulars.

Daniel's numbers are interpreted mathematically by some exegetes; some likewise apply the words "an anointed one shall be cut off" to the Messiah in the literal sense, and the "hideous desecration" to the final destruction of the temple under Titus. However the death of Jesus and the destruction of the temple did not take place in the same week; and how far their computations disagree is shown by Fr. Faidl, who lists about one hundred different attempts at harmonization during ancient and medieval times; to which more have been added in recent centuries! The apostles, in any case, did not quote the 70 week-years to prove the Messiah's advent, not even St. Matthew.

It was Micheas' privilege to point out the place where the Messiah would be born, "And you, O Bethlehem Ephrathah, the smallest among the families of Judah, from out of you shall he come forth unto me who shall reign over Israel."[84] The context treats of Him whom "the one with child" would bear,[85] the sprout of David. David's father was from Ephrathah,[86] and David's home was Bethlehem.[87] "In the city of David which is called Bethlehem" was Jesus born.[88] When asked by Herod and the Magi regarding the birthplace of the expected King, the scribes quickly replied, "Bethlehem," and quoted the prophecy of Micheas.[89]

5. THE MESSIAH AS DIVINE. The Savior would not have a human father;[90] His name would be Immanuel (God with us). This should have led men to surmise that God would reveal Himself in a most extraordinary manner. Further illumination was given in the prophecy, "A child is born to us, a son is given to us, upon his shoulders rest the sovereignty, and his name shall be: Wonderful Counsellor, Strong God, Father forever, Prince of peace."[91] Yahweh was called "strong God,")el gibbor.[92] Now if the Messiah too is called "strong God,")el gibbor, it follows that Yahweh is appearing in Him. Isaias' other titles likewise have a ring of divinity in them and become more profound in the light of "Strong God." "Wonderful Counsellor": neither Moses nor Elias, Eliseus or any other prophet who by God's power performed miracles and showed men the way of God received this name. The Child in Isaias' vision is greater than all who preceded Him, for only God is full of wonders.[93] "Father forever": Yahweh is described as "inhabiting eternity," i.e., enthroned forever,[94] and "God eternal."[95] The title "Prince of peace" was accorded to none of Israel's kings. A king who slays evildoers with the mere breath of His lips[96] must not be regarded as human. Concerning the "son of man" in Dan. 7:13-14, cf. § 52:2e.

The Redeemer "has his origins from the beginning, from the days of eter-

84. Mich. 5:1.
85. Mich. 5:2.
86. 1 Sam. 17:12.
87. 1 Sam. 20:6.
88. Lk. 2:4f.
89. Matth. 2:4f.
90. Is. 7:14; Mich. 5:2.
91. Is. 9:5.
92. Is. 10:21; Deut. 10:17; Jer. 32:18; Neh. 9:32.
93. Is. 25:1; 28:29.
94. Is. 57:15.
95. Gen. 21:33.
96. Is. 11:4.

nity."[97] These words from Micheas are applied by many exegetes to the Messiah's premundane origin, to His divinity. Now since the prophet was speaking of the Savior "going forth" from Bethlehem, a little country town, he wished to point out how He was not without honor in that He was descended from a very old family. The expressions, "from the beginning . . . days of eternity," often indicate nothing more than a considerable period of time;[98] in Am. 9:11 the family of David is called "eternal."

In Ps. 2:7 the Messiah (the very word appears in v. 2) declares that Yahweh has said to Him, "You are my son, today I have begotten you." "Begotten" is here used metaphorically; of old Yahweh "begot" or "gave birth to" Israel.[99] David's descendants are Yahweh's sons by adoption.[100] But the words, "You are my son," occur nowhere in the OT in the sense of adoption. Only in Ps. 2:7 do we find the expression that God begot, or gave birth to a specific person.[101] The Messiah accordingly is the Son of God in a most unique way. Sovereignty over all nations is given to Him, and this would not apply to any of the historical kings of Israel. The word "today" is the day of the solemn proclamation of the Messiah as God's Son. According to Jewish interpretation the "anointed" One of Ps. 2:2 is the Messiah-king.[102] Ps. 2:7 is applied to Christ in Acts 13:33; Heb. 1:5; 5:5.

Ps. 110 is a prophecy as already indicated by its introduction, "Oracle of Yahweh." The king whom Yahweh commands, "Sit at my right till I have made your enemies a footstool for your feet,"[103] is not an earthly ruler, nor even an angel. He shares in Yahweh's divine power and is destined to govern the world in common with Him; and Yahweh humbles His enemies to make them acknowledge Him as highest Lord. Furthermore this king is also priest.[104] V. 3MT reads, "Your people will be fully willing on the day of your power; in holy array from the womb of the dawn yours is the dew of youth." The meaning perhaps is something like this: the Messiah must still do battle, but an innumerable host of young people are willing to join Him. The same verse in G V reads, "With you is dominion in the day of your power in the brightness of the saints, from my womb before the morning star I have begotten you." This seems to refer to the Son's eternal procession from the Father. The New Roman translation has, "before the dawn like dew I have begotten you" (beṭerem instead of mereḥem). In a mysterious manner God begot the coming ruler "before time—like the dew" falls mysteriously before the break of day. It is a picture of the supernatural Sonship of the ruler-king. Nevertheless this verse is not used in the NT in favor of the divinity of Christ, not even in its Septuagint rendition.

In Ps. 45, which pictures the union of the Messiah with Israel and mankind as a wedding (the OT frequently presents the relationship of Yahweh to Israel in terms of marriage[105]), the poet addresses the Messiah, "Your throne, O God

97. Mich. 5:1.
98. § 10:1.
99. Deut. 32:18.
100. 2 Sam. 7:14.
101. Prov. 8:24-25.
102. Strack-Billerbeck III 1926, 675f.
103. Ps. 110:1.
104. Ps. 110:4.
105. § 16:4.

(Elohim), remains for ever and ever."[106] The messianic interpretation of this psalm rests upon Jewish and Christian tradition; in Heb. 1:8, v. 7 is quoted in proof of Christ's divinity.

The messianic kingdom will continue forever.[107] Now since a kingdom without a king is simply unthinkable, and since there is but one Messiah, the Messiah-king Himself must be eternal.

How the Messiah could be both man and God remained hidden from the prophets and the psalmists, only to be revealed with the incarnation of the second person of the Blessed Trinity. But Israel was aware that a great mystery would surround the person of the Messiah and that in His person God would reveal Himself in a most extraordinary manner. Jesus was revealing His divinity to the Jews in a very intelligible way when He applied Ps. 110:1 to Himself.[108] And to the high priest's solemn question, "Are you the Christ (i.e., the Messiah), the Son of God," He clearly and solemnly replied, "You have said it."[109]

§ 51. THE MESSIAH'S MISSION

The Messiah fulfills His divinely assigned mission a) by ruling as a king, b) by teaching as a prophet, and c) by expiating sin as a priest.

1. THE MESSIAH AS KING. The patriarch Jacob was the first to foretell the Messiah's role as a ruler: to Him would belong the sceptre, Him the nations would obey.[1] In this king is fulfilled Nathan's prophecy concerning the eternal duration of the Davidic dynasty, and accordingly He is at times called "David."[2] After the exile David's family no longer reigned, but these prophecies nevertheless were confirmed. In the days to come, said Zacharias, the house of David would rule "as God, as the angel of Yahweh."[3] The Messiah's sovereignty would extend over the whole world, "The root of Jesse shall stand as an ensign for the nations, him shall the nations seek[4].... He shall rule from sea to sea and from the river to the ends of the earth. All kings shall do him homage, all nations shall serve him."[5] The messianic king "shall appoint his sons princes over all the earth."[6] Opposition however will not be wanting. Balaam prophesied, "I see him, but not near; I behold him, but not close at hand: A star shall rise out of Jacob, a sceptre shall come forth from Israel. The (coming ruler) shall crush the temples of Moab, shall dash to the earth all the sons of warmongers."[7] The introduction expressly points to a dim and distant future. The star[8] symbolized a ruler, the sceptre royal power,[9] while Moab and other nations which oppose the star are types of powers hostile to God.[10] Though kings and peoples rise up against this ruler, Yahweh, who has installed Him as king,[11] "has given him the nations as an inheritance and the ends of the

106. Ps. 45:7.
107. § 49:1c.
1. Gen. 49:10; § 50:2.
2. §50:2.
3. Zach. 12:8.
4. Is. 11:10.
5. Ps. 72:8-11; Zach. 9:10.
6. Ps. 45:17.
7. Num. 24:17.
8. The Messiah is called a "light" in Is. 42:6; 49:6;
108. Matth. 22:43-44.
109. Matth. 26:63-64.
cf. Is. 9:1.
9. Gen. 49:10; Ps. 110:2.
10. § 49:6b.
11. Ps. 2:6; 110:1.

earth as his possession,"[12] and will make him "rule in the midst of his enemies[13]. . . . smashing them with an iron sceptre."[14]

The kingship of the Messiah will bear little resemblance to earthly kingship. Even as a child,[15] sovereignty will rest upon His shoulders; as a humble "shoot" He will dwell among his fellow men.[16] As birthplace He will have little Bethlehem.[17] In no way will His rule depend upon the weapons of war, in no way will His rule be oppressive, neither will it put caprice in the place of justice. He will be the "prince of peace."[18] *Great* shall be the government, and of peace there shall be no end." He will "establish and uphold the throne through justice and righteousness thenceforth forever."[19] With Him there will be no privileges arising from birth, position, or wealth; He will be no respecter of persons. The powerful of the world or the highly esteemed will not stand nearest to Him, but rather those who are poor and despised, "With justice shall he judge the lowly and with fairness arbitrate in favor of the land's poor; the *oppressor* he shall smite with the staff of his mouth, the evildoer he shall slay with the breath of his lips."[20] Accordingly the Messiah will not come as a warrior and a conqueror, but at the head of a kingdom which is spiritual in nature. In the messianic kingdom there will be the poor, the meek and humble; there will be sinners too, weeds among the wheat.[21] The righteousness of the coming ruler is frequently stressed.[22] He has a special interest in the poor and oppressed. He will train His subjects to lead an upright moral life, "serving Yahweh, their God."[23] "In his days righteousness shall sprout up, and the fullness of peace, till the moon no longer shines.[24]

The characteristic virtues of the messianic king will be meekness and love. As a good shepherd He will be deeply attached to all His sheep, particularly those standing in greatest need of help.[25] There is a profound resemblance between the Messiah and His forefather David, who defended his sheep against lions and bears.[26] "He shall appear and pasture his flock in the strength of Yahweh, in the noble name of Yahweh, his God."[27] Zacharias bade Jerusalem rejoice at the advent of her Messiah-king, "Shout aloud with joy, Daughter Sion! Rejoice, Daughter Jerusalem! See, your king is coming to you, just is he and victorious, *humble* and riding upon an ass—indeed upon the colt of an ass . . . and he shall offer peace to the nations,"[28] and destroy all the instruments of war.[29]

From an angel's lips Mary heard the message of fulfillment, "God shall give him the throne of David his father, and he shall rule in the house of Jacob forever."[30] The Magi from the East asked for the "newborn King of the Jews."[31] When Jesus solemnly entered Jerusalem, Zacharias' words were fulfilled to the letter.[32] Before Pilate Jesus declared: "My kingdom is not of this

12. Ps. 2:8.
13. Ps. 110:2.
14. Ps. 2:9.
15. Is. 9:5.
16. Is. 11:1; Ez. 17:22; § 50:3.
17. Mich. 5:1; § 50:4.
18. Is. 9:5.
19. Is. 9:6.

20. Is. 11:4.
21. Matth. 13:20.
22. Jer. 23:5-6; 33:15-16; Ps. 45:7; cf. 2 Sam. 23:3.
23. Ps. 72:2-4, 12-14; Jer. 30:9.
24. Ps. 72:7; cf. Ps. 72:5, 17.
25. Ez. 34:23; 37:23-25.
26. 1 Sam. 17:34-36.

27. Mich. 5:3.
28. Zach. 9:9-10.
29. As far back as Gen. 49:11 the ass is the Messiah's riding beast. Cf. § 49:4.
30. Lk. 1:32.
31. Matth. 2:2.
32. Zach. 9:9; Matth. 21:2-9.

world ... I am a king. To give testimony of the truth have I been born and have come into the world."[33] But the Jews wanted a political Messiah who would break the yoke of Rome and confer world dictatorship upon them. Even the apostles entertained false notions concerning the Messiah's kingdom, believed it would bring them earthly honors.[34] Before Pilate the Jews accused Jesus of proclaiming Himself king;[35] later the soldiers mocked Him with the words, "Hail, king of the Jews!"[36] And finally the inscription, "Jesus of Nazareth, king of the Jews," was fastened on the cross above His royal head.[37]

2. THE MESSIAH AS PROPHET. "A prophet like me Yahweh, your God, will raise up from your midst, from your tribes—you must heed him .... I shall place my words in his mouth, and he will speak to them all that I shall commission him."[38] In these words Moses clearly and definitely indicated that God would raise up prophets in Israel during the centuries following his own death.[39] Prophecy however would find its consummation in the Messiah. He would teach men concerning God and God's holy will, and proclaim revelations more profound than those taught of old. Though God made a covenant with Israel through Moses, He would seal another testament, one embracing us all, through the Messiah, one destined to last until the end of time. While Moses did not lack the spirit of God,[40] the Messiah would be favored with the fullness of the spirit, "Upon him shall rest the spirit of Yahweh, the spirit of wisdom and understanding, the spirit of counsel and fortitude, the spirit of knowledge and of the fear of Yahweh."[41] God's spirit would illumine and strengthen the Messiah as He went about performing His mission of bringing salvation to the world; it would equip Him with wisdom to select the best means to attain His purpose; with understanding to apply them properly; with counsel to make the proper judgments and to give prudent advice; with fortitude to execute His decisions; with knowledge of divine secrets far surpassing all other prophets; with the fear of Yahweh spurring Him on to consummate sanctity. These gifts of grace "rest" upon Him; He does not receive them in a transitory manner merely to accomplish some specific task, but as a permanent possession.

Because the Messiah would obediently fulfill the mission imposed, He was called "Servant of Yahweh" in the second part of the Book of Isaias.[42] "Behold my servant in whom I am well pleased. I have laid my spirit upon him, he shall bring righteousness to the nations."[43] "Righteousness" consists in knowing the one true God and in performing His holy will. The "Servant's" mission is world-wide, embracing both Israel and the Gentiles. From His first appearance He will be guided by meekness and love, "He shall not break the bruised reed or extinguish the flickering wick."[44] Neither will He spare Himself, "He shall not weaken, he shall not *collapse*, until he has established righteousness upon the earth; the islands shall await his teaching."[45] God does not send Him only to Israel, for His mission is to lead all men back to their Creator, "I am making

33. Jn. 18:36-37.
34. Matth. 20:2-28; Acts 1:6.
35. Lk. 23:2.
36. Jn. 19:3.
37. Jn. 19:19.

38. Deut. 18:15, 18.
39. Cf. Deut. 34:10.
40. Num. 11:17; cf. § 20:4.
41. Is. 11:2.

42. § 52:1a.
43. Is. 42:1; cf. Is. 9:2.
44. Is. 42:3.
45. Is. 42:4.

you a covenant with the people (i.e., Israel), a light to the Gentiles, to open blind eyes, to take captives out of prison, from the house of imprisonment those who sit in darkness."[46] In Is. 49:1-6 the Servant describes His mission in the first person. God had destined Him from His mother's womb, made His mouth sharp as a sword; not only would Israel benefit from His work, for He would be a light also to the Gentiles and His activity would reach to the ends of the earth. In Is. 50:4 God fills the Servant's mouth with words to succour the weary. What Isaias says concerning himself, "The spirit of the Lord, Yahweh, is upon me, because Yahweh has anointed me. He has commissioned me to bring joyful tidings to the oppressed, to bind up the broken of heart, to announce freedom to captives, and the release (of chains) to those in bondage,"[47] is applicable in a very special sense to the Messiah.

The Jews were expecting God to send "a prophet" in messianic times. This is evident from the question certain Pharisees put to St. John the Baptist, "Are you the prophet?"[48] They were awaiting the appearance of a prophet whom they believed to be distinct from the Messiah. Some of the people regarded Jesus as this prophet, others took Him for the promised Deliverer himself.[49] Still others identified the two.[50] The Samaritans expected the Messiah to be a divinely illumined teacher;[51] since they retained only the Pentateuch as sacred, they based their hope upon Deut. 18:15, 18. On one occasion Jesus called Himself the "light of the world,"[52] perhaps because Isaias had heralded Him as "a light unto the nations."[53] On another occasion He said, "One is your teacher, the Messiah."[54] After reading Is. 61:1 in the synagogue Jesus began His sermon, "Today this Scripture has been fulfilled in your hearing."[55] The Servant of Yahweh proclaimed only such truths as God had commissioned Him, "I have not spoken on my own authority, but he who sent me, the Father, has given me commandment what I should say, and what I should declare."[56] He tendered the greatest compassion to those who were sorrowful of heart, especially to sinners, and never "broke the bruised reed." He fulfilled His mission by becoming "obedient unto death,"[57] and although He declared, "I was not sent except to the lost sheep of the house of Israel,"[58] He still spoke of "other sheep"[59] that He "must bring."[60] Into all the world He sent His apostles to proclaim the good news.[61] The disciples from Emmaus saw in Jesus "A prophet, mighty in deed and word."[62] Sts. Peter and Stephen applied Deut. 18:25 to Christ.[63] According to Heb. 1:1-2 God spoke in times past through the prophets, but lastly "in these days" through His Son. According to Jn. 1:5, 9 Jesus is "the light that shines in the darkness ... the true light that enlightens every man." Simeon greeted the Christ-Child as "a light of revelation to the Gentiles."[64]

To many prophets God revealed things of the future. Jesus however revealed

46. Is. 42:6-7.
47. Is. 61:1.
48. Jn. 1:21.
49. Jn. 7:40-41.
50. Jn. 6:14.
51. Jn. 4:25.
52. Jn. 8:12.

53. Is. 42:6; 49:6.
54. Matth. 23:10.
55. Lk. 4:16-21.
56. Jn. 12:49.
57. Phil. 2:8.
58. Matth. 15:24.

59. Jn. 10:16.
60. Cf. Jn. 17:20-23.
61. Matth. 28:19-20.
62. Lk. 24:19.
63. Acts 3:22; 7:37.
64. Lk. 2:32.

the more immediate circumstances of His own death and resurrection. And He disclosed the destiny of His church to the end of time.

God confirmed the words of His prophets through signs. Jesus proved He was sent by God through a series of miracles, proved Himself the greatest of the prophets. Already at the beginning of His mission Nicodemus acknowledged, "Rabbi, we know that you have come a teacher from God, for no one can work these signs which you work unless God is with him."[65] Jesus had in mind His activity as miracle worker as He quoted Is. 35:5, a passage which describes the blessings of the messianic era in a manner He was fulfilling to the letter.[66]

When the tribes farthest north were led into Assyrian captivity Isaias uttered a consoling prophecy, "In the past he (Yahweh) brought disgrace upon the land of Zebulon and upon the land of Naphtali, but in the future he shall make glorious the Way of the Sea, Transjordania, and Galilee of the Gentiles. The people who walk in darkness shall see a great light, upon those who live in the land of the shadow of death, a light shall rise."[67] At the time in question the land was heavily oppressed, but in messianic times great joy would be its portion. The Assyrian yoke would be broken, after which the Savior would be born. In prophetic silhouette Isaias beheld the fall of Assyria and the Messiah's birth.[68] St. Matthew saw this prophecy fulfilled when Jesus preached and worked miracles in Galilee.[69]

Later in the Book of Isaias the sacred writer notes what little success will mark the Messiah's efforts in Israel. The Servant of Yahweh laments, "To no purpose have I labored, for nothing and uselessly have I spent my strength."[70] Jesus called down "woe" upon Corozain, Bethsaida, Capharnaum, and even upon the Holy City itself, because they refused to accept His message.[71]

The Messiah would begin preaching only after a precursor had heralded His appearance and had prepared the way for Him, "See, I shall send you the prophet Elias before the great and dreadful day of Yahweh comes, that he may turn the hearts of fathers toward (their) children, and the hearts of sons toward (their) fathers, lest I come and strike the land with anathema."[72] By his preaching this "Elias" would strongly affect the hearts of old and young. It was John the Baptist who was destined to appear before the Messiah "in the spirit and power of Elias."[73] In John's preaching the evangelists hear Isaias' mysterious voices crying in the wilderness, voices which once exhorted the Jews to prepare the way for God as He led them home from exile.[74]

3. THE MESSIAH AS PRIEST. Priests are mediators between God and men; they blot out sin by offering sacrifice, and by their prayer induce God to show mercy. Yahweh solemnly declared to His anointed One, "You are a priest forever after the manner of Melchisedech."[75] Like Melchisedech the Messiah would

65. Jn. 3:2; cf. Lk. 7:16.
66. § 49:2c, 6b.
67. Is. 8:23-9:1.
68. § 49:6c; 50:3.
69. Matth. 4:14-16.
70. Is. 49:4.
71. Matth. 11:20-24; 23:37.
72. Mal. 3:23-24 (V 4:5-6).
73. Lk. 1:17; Matth. 11:14; 17:12-13.
74. Is. 4:3-4; Matth. 3:3; Mk. 1:3.
75. Ps. 110:4.

bear the double dignity of king and priest.[76] Nowhere are Melchisedech's ancestors given, a sign in St. Paul's mind that He did not owe His priestly dignity to birth.[77] God conferred the priestly office upon the Messiah in a solemn act, while the OT priests owed their status to descent from Aaron.[78] Because He is a priest *forever*, He is superior to all Aaronic priests, superior also to His forerunner Melchisedech. The latter "brought out bread and wine." These words do not imply sacrifice, but with reason we may assume that at the solemn celebration of Abram's triumph he as priest did offer sacrifice; and under the circumstances the sacrificial gifts would have been the objects present, viz., bread and wine. Ought not the Messiah offer a sacrifice similar to that of Melchisedech, yet far transcending it, even as He Himself far transcends His forerunner? It was left to history to show how Melchisedech's sacrifice typified that sacrifice which will continue to the end of time upon our altars.[79]

In his sixth chapter Zacharias tells us how he was instructed to place a crown upon the high priest Josue.[80] The import of this symbolic act would be more evident if he had crowned Zorobabel, a descendant of David from whom the "sprout" should come. Perhaps the Persian rulers would have taken offense, still the crowning of the high priest could also have aroused suspicion. Did Zacharias wish to imply that the "sprout" would be both king and priest? Since some other priest cannot sit upon the same throne with the Messiah (nor upon *His*, i.e., the Messiah's throne), v. 13 must be translated, "As priest he (the Messiah) will sit upon his throne." Here again it is stated that the "sprout" is king and priest. The words, "There shall be peaceful counsel,"[81] may be understood of the absence of conflict between the royal and priestly powers in the new kingdom of God, inasmuch as the Messiah will unite both offices in Himself. The remark may have been added because at the time there existed petty jealousies between Josue and Zorobabel—prophetic messages were never independent of the concrete mileau in which they were formulated.[82]

The expiatory sacrifices of the OT were types of the sacrifice which the Redeemer would offer in atonement for sins.[83] The Servant of Yahweh would give His life for the sins of the world.[84] The suffering Messiah of Ps. 22 looks forward to a votive offering followed by a sacrificial banquet.[85] By His sacrificial death Jesus was destined "to redeem his people from their sins."[86] In Him indeed "we have a great high priest."[87]

Lastly, every priest has the duty to pray for the people.[88] Isaias' Servant, who "made intercession for evildoers,"[89] appeared in the person of Jesus, our intercessor with the Father.[90]

§ 52. THE MESSIAH: IN SUFFERING AND IN GLORY

1. THE SUFFERING MESSIAH. a) *The "Servant of Yahweh."* The protoevangel announced both victory and wounds to the descendants of the woman

76. Gen. 14:17-20.
77. Heb. 7:3.
78. Heb. 5:4-6; 7:13-17.
79. Mal. 1:11; § 49:1b, 6g.
80. Zach. 6:11-14; § 51:1.
81. Zach. 6:13.
82. § 49:6d.
83. § 33:8.
84. Is. 53:5-12; § 51:1a.
85. Ps. 22:26-27; § 52:2b.
86. Matth. 1:21.
87. Heb. 4:14; cf. 7:27; 9:13-14, 28.
88. Joel 2:17.
89. Is. 53:12.
90. 1 Jn. 2:1; Rom. 8:34.

who would struggle against the assaults of the evil enemy.[1] Most uniquely this prophecy was destined to be fulfilled in Christ the Savior.[2] The prophets foresaw how the Messiah would appear in humble circumstances, how during His youth He would be nourished on "curd and (wild) honey,"[3] i.e., live in the midst of privations.[4] They themselves were obliged to tread thorny paths in order to fulfill their mission;[5] even if the prophet were a king—like David— suffering was his portion. Should not the greatest of the prophets, the promised shoot of David, be obliged to suffer? The sacred writers were not ignorant of how just men could suffer for others for the sake of a higher end.[6] The Israelites also learnt that satisfaction could be made vicariously, for at stated times they offered atonement sacrifices in which an animal's blood was poured out in order to obtain forgiveness of sin.[7] On the Day of Atonement the scapegoat carried the sins of the people into the wilderness.[8] Moses offered himself as a sacrifice for the sins of the people.[9] The youngest of the Maccabean brothers was willing to suffer and die in order to expiate the sins of the nation.[10] Through prayer to God any just man could intercede in behalf of others.[11] Accordingly the prophecies which told of how the coming Redeemer would blot out the sin and guilt of mankind by offering His life could have been understood by any Israelite.

Certain poems in the second section of the Book of Isaias tell of an ʿebed Yahweh, a Servant of Yahweh, who preaches to the Israelites and who brings to the Gentile world the light of the true faith.[12] He is also a Redeemer who suffers and dies for sins. In the second of these poems "He is despised by every one, abominated by the people, the slave of those in power."[13] In the third He undertakes the mission of a prophet, even though it entails the greatest sacrifices, "I did not refuse, I did not flinch. My back I gave to the smiters and my cheeks to those who drag one about by the hair. I did not hide my face from profanation and spittle."[14] This was the gratitude He would receive! How those whom He sought to save mishandled Him is further described in the fourth poem, "Many were startled at the sight of him. Disfigured—his face no longer like that of a man, or his figure like that of the children of men[15].... He was despised and forsaken by men, a man of sorrows, experienced in suffering."[16] Innocent yet condemned to death, "From misery and judgment he was taken away."[17] They even attempted to desecrate His dead body, "When he had died his grave was with the godless and evildoers, although he did no wrong and no deceit was in his mouth."[18] Personally He was without sin, yet He suffered and died to atone for our sins. "Our suffering he was carrying, and our sorrow he was taking upon himself, while we believed him to be punished and smitten and humbled by God. He was pierced because of our sins and bruised because of our misdeeds. Chastisement for our salvation

1. Gen. 3:15.
2. § 50:2.
3. Is. 7:15; § 50:3.
4. § 49:4.
5. § 2:3f; 46:4.
6. § 41:6.
7. § 33:2c.
8. § 34:5.
9. Ex. 32:32.
10. 2 Mach. 7:38.
11. § 35:5.
12. Is. 42:1-7; 41:1-9a; 50:4-9 (10-11); 52:13-53:12; § 51:2.
13. Is 49:7.
14. Is. 50:5-6.
15. Is. 52:14.
16. Is. 53:3.
17. Is. 53:8.
18. Is. 53:9.

lay upon him and through his welts we were healed. Upon him did Yahweh let fall all our guilt[19]. . . . Because of the sin of my people *he was* tortured *to death*[20]. . . . He gave his life as a guilt-offering[21]. . . . Through his knowledge (i.e., knowing the purpose of his passion) the Just One, my Servant, shall make many just, and their guilt he shall bear[22]. . . . He bore the sins of many and made intercession for evildoers."[23] Frequently the OT mentions the grave and Sheol to indicate that someone's affliction had reached its zenith.[24] The Servant of Yahweh however actually dies,[25] His self-immolation is a sacrifice consummated in death itself.

Moses, Elias, Jeremias, Job became impatient when God tried them and they even longed for death.[26] Not for a moment does the Servant of Yahweh lose His confidence in God, although He sees that His work is fruitless,[27] "The Lord, Yahweh, will aid me, therefore I shall not be put to shame. I shall make my face like flint, because I know I shall not be confounded."[28]

When Isaias was depicting the Servant of Yahweh in these terms, he did not have Israel as a nation in mind. Certainly, we find the people called "servant of Yahweh" in various Isaian texts,[29] but the people never suffered willingly or patiently; they went into exile only under compulsion; they deserved chastisement; they did not have the purpose or the capability of redeeming the Gentiles. The servant "Israel" was blind and deaf, and strove against Yahweh's will;[30] he was despondent,[31] disobedient[32] and was punished with exile for personal sins. The Servant of Yahweh was destined to "become a covenant with the people;"[33] He was commissioned to lead Jacob back to God and to gather Israel together.[34] Such a one cannot be identified with Israel as a nation. He would be the light of the Gentiles,[35] He would address the nations[36] and suffer for their sins.[37] Nor is it reasonable to understand pious men or the prophetic office by the phrase, "Servant of Yahweh," for the latter was commissioned to lead back "Israel's saved" (i.e., those who remained faithful)[38] and had the task of teaching "those who fear Yahweh."[39] Moreover the good Israelites did not suffer willingly, neither for the whole nation; nor did they die repudiated by all their fellow men.[40] Still less did the good Israelites suffer for the Gentile world and expiate their sins.[41] It follows that the prophet was speaking of an individual, as most exegetes at the present time admit, and if the servant is called "Israel" in Is. 49:3, the word in this instance is probably a gloss,[42] after the fashion of "Jacob" and "Israel" in Is. 42:1G.

A personage of exilic or postexilic times cannot qualify as the central figure in these poems. Sellin proposed Zorobabel in 1898, Joachim in 1901 and 1908, Moses in 1922, and the author of Is. 40-55 in 1930 and 1937. In 1937 he also

19. Is. 53:4-6.
20. Is. 53:8.
21. Is. 53:10.
22. Is. 53:11.
23. Is. 53:12.
24. § 44:1.
25. Is. 53.
26. § 41:7.
27. Is. 49:4.

28. Is. 50:7.
29. Is. 41:8-9; 42:19; 44:1, 2, 21; 45:4; 48:20; § 48:4.
30. Is. 42:19.
31. Is. 41:10; 44:2.
32. Is. 50:2.
33. Is. 42:6.
34. Is. 49:5-9.

35. Is. 42:4-7; 49:6.
36. Is. 49:1.
37. Is. 53:4-6, 9-12.
38. Is. 49:6.
39. Is. 50:10.
40. Is. 52:13-53:12.
41. Is. 53:11-12.
42. Occasioned by 44:23?

scribed the composition of the first three poems to the Servant Himself, the ourth to the author of Is. 56-66, who was commemorating the martyr-death f "Second Isaias." It is just as unreasonable to hold that some other prophet r sage who lived at the time these poems were composed is meant. Who, for nstance, ever exercised a mission to the Gentiles at large? whose work affected ll mankind?[43] or whose fortune changed so suddenly that kingdoms and kings tood in amazement?[44] or who lived again after he once had died?[45] There nust accordingly be question of a person living at some future date as is hown, e.g., in the fourth poem, particularly in Is. 53:10-11 (the perfects are he so-called prophetic perfects). Surely no person other than Jesus the Messiah an be named whose suffering and death has had such profound significance or humanity, who although innocent Himself became an expiatory sacrifice o appease the heavenly Father, who when cruelly slain lived and was honored y kings and nations.[46] Moreover the term "my Servant" is not peculiar to econd Isaias;[47] Isaias may not have explicitly linked his portrayal of the Messiah with earlier prophetic pictures, yet similarities are not lacking. The vord "Servant" recalls passages in Jeremias and Ezechiel; the Messiah is a umble twig, a root, or shoot,[48] a "root out of hard earth;"[49] upon Him rests od's spirit,[50] He is a light,[51] and there was plenty of precedent to present he great Deliverer as a prophet and as a patient sufferer.

Simeon looked forward to the Messiah as a man of suffering. "This Child s destined ... for a sign that shall be contradicted."[52] John the Baptist applied s. 53:7 to Jesus when he heralded Him as the "Lamb of God, who takes away he sin of the world."[53] Jesus Himself declared that those prophecies were ulfilled in Him, "The Son of Man is come to give his life as a ransom for nany."[54] On the way to Mt. Olivet He said, "I say to you that this which is vritten must yet be fulfilled in me: And he was reckoned among the wicked."[55] esus was spit upon, was struck with clenched fists.[56] His appearance must have een pitiful as Pilate cried, "Ecce Homo!"[57] He was judicially condemned.[58] Iis blood was shed for many unto the forgiveness of sins.[59] Consequently He vas an expiatory sacrifice in the fullest sense.[60] As He hung upon the cross Ie interceded for sinners.[61] His would have been given a robber's grave[62] had ot Joseph of Arimathea prevented this disgrace. To the Ethiopian minister, Philip explained Is. 53:7 as fulfilled in Jesus.[63] In Matth. 8:17, Is. 53:4 is pplied to Christ. 1 Pet. 2:22-23 considers Is. 53:9 and 53:5 fulfilled in the uffering Savior. From the very beginning the Church identified the Servant f Yahweh with Jesus. A messianic interpretation of these passages was also dvocated by a certain number of Rabbis,[64] but the Jews objected when Chris- ians proclaimed their fulfillment in the death of the crucified Savior.

3. Is. 53:12.
4. Is. 52:14-15.
5. Is. 53:10.
6. Is. 52:13, 15; 53:11.
7. Cf. Jer. 33:21, 22, 26; Ez. 34:23-24; 37:24; Zach. 3:8.
8. Is. 11:1, 10.
9. Is. 53:2.

50. Is. 11:2; 42:1.
51. Is. 9:1; 42:6.
52. Lk. 2:34.
53. Jn. 1:29, 36.
54. Matth. 20:28; cf. Lk. 18: 31-33.
55. Lk. 22:37; Is. 53:12.
56. Matth. 26:67; 27:29-30; Lk. 24:25-27; Is. 50:6.

57. Jn. 19:3; Is. 52:14.
58. Is. 53:8.
59. Matth. 26:28.
60. Is. 53:5, 10-12.
61. Lk. 23:24; Is. 53:12.
62. Is. 53:9.
63. Acts 8:30-35.
64. Strack-Billerbeck II 282, 286, 290, 291.

b) *The Sufferer in Ps. 22.* In this psalm we have the lament of a man in the throes of unbearable pain. He begins with the outcry, "My God, my God why have you forsaken me!"[65] In His death agony He finds no solace with God, and the feeling that God apparently is not listening to His appeal or has even withdrawn from Him oppresses Him the more grievously because He is no conscious of guilt. Nevertheless He soon awakens an act of confidence in God.[6] "I am a worm, no longer a man."[67] Enemies rejoice over His misfortune and scoff at His trust in God, "Trust in Yahweh! May he rescue him. May he liberate him if he is pleased with him."[68] The sufferer takes refuge in God to whom He belonged since birth,[69] although He has been brought to the point of death by enemies,[70] although all strength has vanished,[71] although He is stricken with unbearable thirst.[72] He sees how His enemies, certain of His death, divide His clothing among themselves and cast lots for His tunic.[73] No possibility of deliverance remains, yet the sufferer receives assurance that God will deliver Him from death and that His deliverance will be followed by mankind's conversion.[74]

It is an individual person, not a group or a community, who suffers in this psalm. Note that He is "despised by the people,"[75] that He distinguishes Himself from the community.[76] He speaks of His mother,[77] has bones, heart, palate tongue,[78] clothing.[79] Was there ever a man who believed it his lot to reconcile mankind with God? Was not this hope reserved to the Messiah alone? Actually our psalm reads as if it had been composed under the cross or at the tomb of the risen Savior. On the cross Jesus cried, "My God, my God, why have you forsaken me!"[80] He was mocked, He was scoffed at, "He trusted in God; let him deliver him now."[81] Another cry from the cross, "I thirst[82]. . . . in order that the Scriptures might be fulfilled."[83] His lips were moistened with vinegar an act, as noted by the evangelist, in fulfillment of the typically messianic words, "In my thirst they gave me vinegar to drink."[84] His garments were divided "that the Scripture might be fulfilled."[85] Ps. 22:17b-18a according to the Septuagint gives a further detail, "They have dug *(LXX: ὤρυξαν;* Gallican Psalter: *foderunt;* St. Jerome's Psalterium Hebraicum: *fixerunt;* "as a lion" M my hands and feet, I can number all my bones." It is remarkable that the evangelists do not point out how these words were fulfilled at the crucifixion of Jesus.[86]

c) *"The Pierced One."* Zach. 12:10 reads, "I shall pour out upon the house of David and upon the inhabitants of Jerusalem a spirit of grace and supplication, and they will look at me; him whom they pierced—for him they will mourn as one mourns over an only son, for him they will weep bitterly as one weeps for a first-born." According to the context the lament is general

65. Ps. 22:2.
66. Ps. 22:4-6.
67. Ps. 22:7.
68. Ps. 22:9.
69. Ps. 22:10-11.
70. Ps. 22:16.
71. Ps. 22:15.
72. Ps. 22:16.

73. Ps. 22:19.
74. Ps. 22:23-32.
75. Ps. 22:7.
76. Ps. 22:23.
77. Ps. 22:10-11.
78. Ps. 22:15-16.
79. Ps. 22:19.

80. Matth. 27:46 (Ps. 22:2)
81. Matth. 27:43 (Ps. 22:9)
82. Ps. 22:16.
83. Jn. 19:28-29.
84. Ps. 69:22.
85. Jn. 19:23-24 (Ps. 22:18)
86. Cf. Herkenne.

veryone takes part in it. The prophet is speaking of a man who has suffered eath, because a lamentation for the dead is raised over him. Moreover He innocent, while the people have a share in His death as is evidenced by eir sorrow. There is question here of an event proper to messianic times, nce x) God pours out His spirit upon many, y) a fountain breaks forth to eanse away sins, z) all idolatry ceases.[87] Some light is thrown upon this assage by the *'ebed Yahweh* prophecies (in which Yahweh's Servant dies nocently)[88] and by the Passion Psalm (22, in which the people are guilty of e death of the Just Man). The NT sees the passage in Zacharias fulfilled n Golgatha.[89]

d) *Prophecies typically messianic.* On one occasion during his prophetic inistry Zacharias was commissioned by God to become a shepherd. Actually is was a symbolic act in which he represented God. Soon the prophet stopped orking because the flock would not follow him; he demanded his wages, "So ey weighed out my wages, thirty pieces of silver." Upon Yahweh's command e cast the money "into the treasury of the house of Yahweh."[90] The amount f his wages showed how little Yahweh was valued in the eyes of the Jewish verlords, and, by receiving it, the prophet indicated that God was abandoning rael. In this symbolism the Evangelist saw prefigured Judas' act of betraying is Master for thirty pieces of silver and later casting the money into the mple.[91] Zach. 13:7-9 describes the judgment that would purify Jerusalem. he sword first strikes down the shepherd, "Smite the shepherd that the sheep ay be scattered." On Mount Olivet Jesus reminded His disciples of this rophecy.[92] In Wis. 2:10-20 the godless vent their hatred against "the good oor man" who claims to be a son of God. They plot against him a miserable ath, maliciously asking whether God will deliver him. The phrase, "good oor man," does not refer to a specific individual here, but rather a group of rtuous persons, for in the context the godless attack widows and orphans whom God has promised His special protection. In the OT pious persons e called "sons of God."[93] But since the author makes some allusion to Ps. 2:8-9 and since his words hold true *par excellence* of Christ, the passage may e interpreted as typically messianic. On the paschal lamb as a type, cf. § 33:8.

2. THE GLORIFIED MESSIAH. a) *The "Servant of Yahweh."* The *'ebed* ahweh poems depict the Messiah not only in His suffering, but also in His ory. He "shall be successful, he shall be lifted up, he shall be high and most :alted."[94] Triumph would be His after He had emptied the cup of suffering d death in obedience to the divine will, "He shall see posterity and live long; rough him Yahweh's plan shall prosper."[95] Slain He lives and beholds a vast ogeny; resurrection from the dead is presupposed. This is the stupendous ent which amazes kings and nations.[96] His descendants are those who accept is doctrine and are made righteous by His death.[97] They constitute "The

7. Zach. 13:1.
8. Is. 52:13-53:12.
9. Jn. 19:37; Acts 1:7.
0. Zach. 11:12-13.

91. Matth. 27:3-5, 9.
92. Matth. 26:31.
93. § 16:5.
94. Is. 52:13.

95. Is. 53:10.
96. Is. 52:15.
97. Is. 53:11.

many whom God gives to him as (his) portion,"[98] while kings and princes do Him homage.[99]

b) *The lament of the sufferer in Ps. 22* suddenly changes into a jubilant exclamation, "I will proclaim your name to my brothers, in the midst of the community I will praise you."[100] All who fear Yahweh are bidden to join Him in praising God who has answered His cry.[101] After having been delivered to a cruel death, He receives new life in a miraculous manner. He invites the good to a joyous banquet as He makes a peace-offering.[102] The joy of messianic times is the dominant thought here, and we may well sense a reference to the Eucharistic agape. As a result of this deliverance from death "all the ends of the earth shall return to Yahweh,"[103] an event which will be proclaimed to the coming ages as God's work.[104] In spreading the Gospel the apostles repeatedly spoke of Jesus' death upon the cross and of His resurrection from the tomb, and this was responsible to a great degree for their success.

c) *Ps. 16:9-11* has a joyous ring, "My flesh will dwell securely, for you will not abandon my soul in Sheol nor allow *your* Just One (GV; M plu.) to see corruption. You will let me experience the way to life, the fullness of joys in your presence, bliss in your right hand forever." The psalmist is not expecting deliverance from mortal dangers,[105] for such a theme is absent from the context; on the contrary he feels himself fortunate in God's holy fellowship as he speaks of physical death and bodily corruption. David and every other psalmist had to die, their bodies disintegrated, while their souls went and stayed in Sheol. But he who speaks these words is convinced that death will have no lasting power over him, he is certain of rising again, and of rising before the body is destroyed through the natural process of decomposition. Likewise he is certain that his soul will enjoy the beatitude of intimate union with God. The author of the psalm cannot predicate all this of himself. Only in Jesus were these judgments fulfilled, in Jesus who died and was buried, but who rose triumphant over death on the third day, whose human soul was flooded with heavenly joys. In their catechesis Sts. Peter[106] and Paul[107] used this passage as they spoke of our Savior's resurrection.

Certain passages of the OT tell of the Messiah enthroned at the right hand of God and ruling over the whole world.[108] In his Pentecostal sermon St. Peter quoted Ps. 110:1 as he spoke of Christ's ascension into heaven.[109]

d) *The "Son of Man" in Daniel.* During the first year of Baltassar's reign Daniel in a vision saw one "who resembled a son of man coming upon the clouds of heaven." To him "sovereignty and glory and kingship were given so that all peoples, nations and tongues should serve him; and his kingship is an everlasting kingship."[110] The vision was explained to the prophet as involving "the people of the saints of the Most High," who would rule over the whole world.[111] Thus the vision concerned primarily the messianic kingdom, which

98. Is. 53:12.
99. Is. 49:7.
100. Ps. 22:23.
101. Ps. 22:24-26.
102. Ps. 22:26-27.

103. Ps. 22:28-30.
104. Ps. 22:31-32.
105. Cf. § 44:1.
106. Acts 2:25-32.
107. Acts 13:34-37.

108. Ps. 2:8-9; 110:1-2; § 50; 51:1.
109. Acts 2:33-35.
110. Dan. 7:13-14.
111. Dan. 7:18, 27.

would embrace all peoples and last forever. Its citizens however would include only those numbered among "the saints of the Most High." The phrase, "who resembled a son of man," is not without symbolic content, just as the similes in the first part of the vision, e.g., like a lion, like a bear, like a panther, indicate kingdoms.[112] The "son of man" came upon the clouds of heaven because His kingdom is not an earthly one, but one established by God. These observations scarcely exhaust the meaning of the vision. Daniel is not always complete in his exegesis. For instance, in interpreting the dream of the statue shattered by a stone[113] our prophet does not comment on the statement that the stone became a mighty mountain and filled the whole earth.[114] The earthly kingdoms in Dan. 7 have their kings; from the kingdom spoken of in Dan. 7:24 ten kings arise; Dan. 8:20 explains the ram with two horns as the kings of Media and Persia; in 8:21 the he-goat is the king of Greece; in 2:38 Nabuchodonosor represents his kingdom. Therefore in 7:13-14 Daniel has his thoughts on the king of the messianic kingdom rather than upon its people. A kingdom without a king is unthinkable. The people would rule through their king, the Messiah, whom God would solemnly establish in office. Jesus called Himself "son of man," undoubtedly wishing to allude to this passage in Daniel.[115] And when He proclaimed the end of the world, He described how "the son of man" would come upon the clouds of the heavens with great power and majesty.[116] At the trial before Caiphas Jesus applied Daniel's vision of the son of man to Himself.[117] Ancient Jewish tradition saw in Daniel's son of man a personal Messiah.[118] "The people of the saints of the Most High" will share in His glory, all who in this life have faithfully served Him.[119]

§ 53. BIBLICAL AND NON-BIBLICAL MESSIANIC HOPES

1. MESSIANISM IN THE ANCIENT ORIENT. For some decades certain scholars have been insisting that the conviction of a coming Messiah arose in Israel under foreign influences. a) *Egyptian literature* contains various passages describing periods of misfortune which come to an end when an era of good fortune begins with the accession of a new king.[1] So the scholars point out similarities, e.g., a period of misfortune, war and tumults, enemies break in, lying and deceit is common, temples are desecrated, the land is fruitless, women are sterile, the Nile is low. Then come good days as the savior king defeats the foe and brings back the sacred objects; the Nile rises and overflows, everywhere there is abundance. Actually these passages are not pronouncements upon the future, but simply a picture of the past and present in the form of a prophecy. Their object was to glorify the ruling pharaoh, and therefore past dynasties are cast in gloomy colors. Note how the misfortunes are restricted to the land of Egypt; likewise the days of plenty come only to the Egyptians. Nor

112. Dan. 7:4f.
113. Dan. 2:29-45.
114. Dan. 2:35.
1. AOT 46-51.

115. Matth. 8:20; 9:6; 16:13.   7:55.
116. Matth. 24:30.   118. Hen. 46-49; 4 Esdr. 13.
117. Matth. 26:64; cf. Acts   119. Cf. Lk. 22:29-30.

are the evils a punishment for sin because the concept of a redeemer from moral evil who would appear at some future date was unknown in Egypt.

b) *In Babylonian literature* we find the gods frequently inaugurating a prosperous new era. For instance, Marduk conquers Tiamat and becomes a beneficent sovereign over gods and men. Tammuz dies and awakens to new life, personifying nature in its double aspect of death and resurrection, autumn and spring—a cycle he shares with other vegetation deities.[2] In the incantations and funeral songs good times and bad times alternate. From time immemorial the king was regarded as a savior because according to Babylonian ideology he was selected by the gods and ruled at their behest. The beginning of a reign marks the beginning of an era of blessings previous to which the people, so say the records, suffered greatly. Such a mentality existed already in the days of the Sumerian kings, later it is excellently attested by Hammurabi who at the beginning and end of his code sketches the portrait of the king through whom all good fortune comes to the people; still later the same is reflected in the records of Esarhaddon, Ashurbanipal, Merodach-Baladan, Cyrus and the rulers of the Hellenistic era. In this literature we meet flattering courtiers who praise their king as the ideal ruler. Nevertheless they do not regard their sovereign's term of office as a messianic age; it is always the acting ruler who brings "salvation," never a king of the distant future. This oriental outlook may have occasioned the promise of the child in Vergil's Fourth Eclog, with whose birth an era of peace begins. Indeed Vergil himself refers to the "Song of the Sibyll" (undoubtedly Sib III 652-660), and it would be very difficult to prove that he was unacquainted with Jewish messianic expectations. In any case the Latin poet was hoping for a golden age, not for a personal savior from moral evil, and this longing for earthly peace and worldly fortune he expressed in prophetic form. Good eras alternate with evil eras in every anthology of Babylonian "prophecies."[3] Under one monarch the nation is prosperous, under his successor enemies attack, the temple is violated, the people starve. Thereupon appears a new ruler under whom sacrifices are again offered and the land produces an abundant harvest. The exact chronological data marking the reigns of these kings are a sure sign of the absence of genuine prophecy. Babylonian literature contains nothing regarding a redeemer who will appear at some future time to blot out sin.

c) *Persian sources.* The proposition that OT eschatology was derived from Persian sources in postexilic times rests upon a preconceived literary critique and labors under all the weaknesses of such a theory. Accordingly it deserves no special consideration.

2. UNIQUE CHARACTER OF THE OT MESSIAH PICTURE. a) *Popular hopes* Promises similar to those popularized in Egypt and Babylon were sponsored in Israel by the false prophets who promised the people victory and good times but said nothing about a redeemer from sin. Their audience awaited the "Day of Yahweh"[4] as a day which would give them mastery over enemies and in

2. § 44:4.　　3. AOT 283f.　　4. Am. 5:18.

augurate a period of temporal blessings.[5] The words, "on that day," point to a divine intervention of singular importance and give evidence of popular hopes for a better future. The true prophets utilized this conviction even as they labored to modify radically the prevailing ideas.

b) *Mutual independence among the prophets.* No set formula was followed by the prophets as they spoke of the coming Redeemer. Their discourses show, although many metaphors reoccur, a rich variety in the description of the future. Note in particular that, contrary to the false prophets in Israel and the poets in Egypt and Babylon, they proclaimed against king and people an imminent judgment from which only a remnant would escape. Egyptian and Babylonian pronouncements upon a golden age were focused only upon the immediate future, while the prophecies of salvation made by Yahweh's messengers were focused upon a distant future and were fulfilled when the people no longer enjoyed political importance. It also becomes unreasonable to pin the message of the prophets onto foreign influences when once you see how they stressed the helplessness of foreign gods and proclaimed judgment upon Gentile nations. Furthermore the prophets themselves were conscious of foretelling something new.[6] Messianic expectation as such was more ancient than the prophets; the prophets did not create the hope in a Savior but only developed and furthered it. The opinion widely advanced decades ago that the desire for a Messiah was exilic and postexilic and that passages in pre-exilic prophets were later additions is now almost universally abandoned.[7]

c) *Revealed character of messianic hope.* In times of distress hopes for a better future come naturally, and any prediction about good times "just around the corner" is quickly believed. These hopes crystallize in a personal deliverer, and in the ancient Orient such a deliverer would be the king who introduced some change for the better. Thus, say the rationalists, arose the longing for the Day of Yahweh in Israel, and this movement could bolster itself upon more antique predictions of a golden era. However we may ask: how could political distress have occasioned the prophecy of Immanuel's birth of a maiden, or of Bethlehem as the place of birth? Is the exile an adequate explanation for the prophecies which describe the opposition which the Redeemer would experience, and His death? As the kingdom was weakening we find no prophecy of a Savior who would stave off the impending collapse; He was to appear only after the Davidic dynasty had wholly perished. Nor could the remembrance of the glorious era of David have produced the idea of a Messiah. Isaias' prophecy of Immanuel is directed against David's descendants,[8] and at His advent the Savior would not be esteemed, but would have to suffer and die. Moreover centuries before there was any king at all in Israel the Messiah had been heralded as such.[9] It has also been claimed that on New Year's Day Israel celebrated the feast of Yahweh's accession to the throne after the fashion in Babylon and that from this root messianic expectations gradually developed.

5. § 46:1.
6. Is. 42:9.
7. Cf. § 45:2; 48:1; 50:2; 51:1.
8. Is. 7:14.
9. Gen. 49:10; Num. 24:7, 17-18.

Now there simply is no proof that such a celebration was ever kept in Israel; rather Yahweh's kingship had neither beginning nor end, thus excluding a festivity of this kind. Nor did "the experience on Sinai" produce the desire for a Redeemer because messianic hope antedates Sinai; furthermore at the time when in a visible manner Yahweh was assisting Israel and Israel was moving forward under its greatest leader Moses, there would have been no occasion to speculate upon a Deliverer in the far distant future. Equally in sufficient to account for OT messianism is the attempt to align it with the Jewish notion that Yahweh would come to establish His dominion over the world, for the Messiah is not proposed *merely* as a world ruler.

The origin of OT messianic hope stems from faith in God. God is just and merciful. Since the fall in paradise He willed that all men might find the way back to Him. The religion which Israel received through the prophets was from the very beginning destined to be shared with all nations. Would God not find a way to make the true faith accessible to all? Would He not also send the Gentiles a prophet?[10] Consciousness of sin was preserved and strengthened in Israel through the preaching of the prophets as well as through atonement sacrifices and expiatory rites. Would mankind remain prostrate beneath this burden through all the coming ages? Certainly a special revelation was necessary to make the seed germinate, to assure men that redemption through a personal Redeemer could be awaited with confidence. Likewise the development of the messianic picture proceeded under special divine enlightenment. According to Gen. 3:15 every child of Adam could win salvation if he struggled for it; according to Gen. 9:26 salvation would come through Sem; according to Gen. 12:3 it would come through Abraham; according to Gen. 49:10 a specific descendant of Juda would be the immediate medium; 2 Sam. 7:16 mentions David and Ez. 17:22 Joachim as the Messiah's forefather.[11] Before the Messiah appeared, the dynasty of David would have lost all power; the Messiah would be born of a maiden at Bethlehem, would be king, prophet, priest, would suffer and die. No one prophet sketched a complete picture of the Redeemer, but the single strokes which the various prophets made, formed a harmonious picture despite seeming contradictory data, e.g., the Messiah stemming both from man and God; a glorious king scoffed at by His own people, persecuted and put to death; son of David and born of a maiden; king of peace and mighty warrior; dying though living forever; bringing the plenitude of blessings and demanding self-abasement; delivering from sin and smiting with the sword of His mouth.

d) *Motives inspiring messianic prophecies.* In Egypt and Babylon emphasis on the glorious days "just around the corner" was designed to divert attention from present evils and to glorify the reigning monarch. The prophets too sought to console their fellow men in trying times by speaking of the coming Redeemer but for them the really important point was to inspire obedience to God's commands, lest when the Savior came the people would be unworthy of His

10. Cf. Ez. 3:6; Jon. 1:2? 11. § 50:2.

gifts. They labored ceaselessly to move sinners to repentance, heralding the judgment which God would inflict before the Savior's advent and which the Savior Himself would hold when He came. Again and again they made it clear that salvation consists in making satisfaction for sins committed and in God's forgiveness. They foretold how the Mosaic covenant would yield to a new covenant and how God would accord to the Gentiles all His love and bestow upon them equal status with Israel in His new kingdom. When Jesus the Savior appeared the Jews ought to have realized that many of the prophecies which referred to the coming Redeemer were fulfilled in Him, and this should have induced them to acknowledge Him as the promised Messiah. Not infrequently did Jesus point out pertinent passages in the prophets, "Search the Scriptures, it is they that bear witness to me[12]. . . . If you believed Moses you would believe me also, for he wrote of me."[13] The messianic era which began with the appearance of John the Baptist had been foretold by "all the prophets and the Law until John."[14] The aged Zachary believed that with the birth of John the fulfillment of the prophecies had begun.[15] Simeon saw the Savior in the Child which Mary had put into his arms,[16] likewise Anna the prophetess.[17] Philip was convinced that in Jesus he had found him "of whom Moses in the Law and the prophets wrote,"[18] Nathaniel too.[19] To be sure, the apostles could not for a long time free themselves of the earthly expectations of their contemporaries. For a Messiah who had to suffer and die was simply incomprehensible to them,[20] and each wanted to be first in the messianic kingdom.[21] The sons of Zebedee were bold enough to ask for the chiefest places.[22] The disciples of Emmaus could not harmonize a triumphant Messiah with one who had been crucified.[23] Only after the resurrection did the apostles understand this part of the messianic mystery. In their preaching they quoted the prophecies which were fulfilled in Jesus.[24] On Scriptural grounds Apollo proved Jesus' messiahship to the Jews.[25] Later ecclesiastical writers also based solid arguments upon the messianic prophecies, which St. Justin said, are "the greatest and most convincing proofs for us."[26]

St. Stephen reproached the Jews for disbelieving the prophecies.[27] Puffed up by pride they looked askance at sinners, contemned the Gentiles and drew a picture of the coming Deliverer which did not correspond to that given by the prophets and actualized by Jesus. A Redeemer from sin, one who holds judgment over Israel, one who is poor, who demands sinlessness and self-denial, whose kingdom confers no worldly authority and foregoes all pomp, never had been natural to Israel's messianic longings. Divine judgment came upon the Chosen People already before the exile because they would not listen to the prophets, because they culled out the nonessentials in the messianic message, points which flattered their earthly leanings, and rejected the essentials which

12. Jn. 5:39.
13. Jn. 5:46.
14. Matth. 11:13.
15. Lk. 1:67f.
16. Lk. 2:26f.
17. Lk. 2:36f.
18. Jn. 1:45.

19. Jn. 1:50.
20. Matth. 16:22; 17:23; Lk. 19:34.
21. Matth. 18:1.
22. Matth. 20:20.
23. Lk. 24:21.

24. Acts 2:17f; 3:18; 8:29f; 10:43; 13:23f; 1 Pet. 1:10f.
25. Acts 18:28.
26. Ap. I 30.
27. Acts 7:52.

went counter to their worldly wishes. The prophecies which heralded everlasting blessings under the sceptre of the Messiah king were fulfilled, but in a
manner different from that imagined by the Jews in their blindness.

3. ORIENTAL COLORING IN THE MESSIAH PICTURE. a) *The possibility of
formal outside influences.* The fact that the prophecies concerning the Redeemer
originated under the influx of divine inspiration did not prevent the prophets
from utilizing colors proper to their environment as they sketched the messianic
picture, nor did it hinder them from being stimulated in their work by the
styles in vogue among Babylonian and Egyptian poets. Simply make a distinction between content and method of exposition. Now there are certain expressions in which some scholars see "mythical undercurrents." "Milk and
honey" may well have been regarded as food for the gods in the Fertile Crescent,
but the phrase as it occurs in Ex. 3:8, 17; 13:5; Num. 13:27; 16:13-14 refers
to nothing but the fertility of the land—an analogous phrase in the Ras Shamra
texts describes a well-watered land with luxuriant vegetation.[28] In Is. 7:15
however curd and (wild) honey denote the meagre produce of a land devastated
by an enemy. Is. 7:14 does not predicate a "supernatural birth" to the Messiah,
rather His wonderful birth of a maiden. The metaphors describing the land's
fertility were meant to make us think of paradise, likewise the pictures of
peace among animals.[29] Messianic peace was the object of Israel's intensest
longing because she had suffered so much through wars.[30] Divine judgment
under the figure of a storm and earthquake reflects the common Oriental concept of a theophany. The text, "He shall rule from sea to sea and from the
river (Euphrates) to the ends of the earth,"[31] need not have been coined in
Babylon; the zone of influence during Davidic-Solomonic times extended as
far as the Euphrates,[32] and the Euphrates served as the ideal boundary of
Canaan already in patriarchal times.[33] First the psalmist gazes from the western
limits (the Mediterranean) to the east, then from the eastern limits (the
Euphrates) to the west where the sea reaches to the ends of the earth. If
further similarities or verbal agreements do occur, one should not straightway
think of direct borrowing. Israelitic rulers were accorded honors after the
fashions observed in neighboring nations, and the prophets were obliged to
describe the future Son of David in a way which the people would easily understand and which would fill them with enthusiasm; into this borrowed phraseology
they poured a new and more profound meaning.

b) *The king.* It was customary in the ancient Orient to bestow special glory
upon a king who devoted himself to the oppressed and the afflicted. The ideal
Israelitic king too must practice these virtues, especially since Yahweh Himself
is just and wills that justice be accorded the poor. Surely then the Messiah,
the second David, ought to inaugurate an era of righteousness upon the earth.[34]
In Egypt and Babylon kings now and then were responsible for better times. Yet

28. R. Dussaud, Les decouver-   30. § 49:4.   33. Gen. 15:18; cf. Ex. 23:31.
    tes de Ras Shamra, Paris   31. Ps. 72:8; Zach. 9:10.   34. Is. 9:6; 11:3-5; Jer. 23:5-
    1937, 79.   32. 3 Kgs. 5:4.   6; Ps. 72:1-4; § 51:1.
29. § 49:6e.

when we read how the land will produce abundant crops when the Messiah appears, we must remember that such language is figurative and indicates spiritual values.[35] As customary throughout the Orient, wishes for a long life, an "eternal" existence, were extended to kings in Israel;[36] and the king would ask God to make his dynasty endure "forever."[37] But when Yahweh promised David an "everlasting" house,[38] the light of later prophecies forbids us to think in terms of a few decades or centuries.[39]

In Babylon the real king was the god, while the reigning ruler was his representative. The king was the god's "son," becoming such when he ascended the throne, through an adoption relationship. In Egypt the king was regarded as the god incarnate, the son of Re who had begotten him. Between Yahweh and the Chosen People there existed a father-son relationship,[40] likewise between Yahweh and every upright Israelite.[41] Since kingship came to Israel very late in her history and never attained such absolute power as in Babylon and Egypt, no movement to deify the king can be noted. In Babylon and Egypt the king was always the "god's favorite;" in Israel the king was disciplined by God and even rejected if he would not obey.[42] This consideration makes it all the more striking to find the Messiah described as God's Son, like to Him in nature and attributes.[43] Such theology could not have a natural origin in Israel, it could not have been derived from the position of Israel's king. Nor was it borrowed from polytheistic Babylon or Egypt. In the prayer of Gudea, the Sumerian king to Gatumdug, "I do not have a mother, you are my mother; I do not have a father, you are my father. Into your heart you received my seed and gave birth to me in the Unu (sanctuary),"[44] there is no assertion of a virginal birth, but simply a recognition of utter helplessness before being adopted by the goddess; consequently Gudea mentions no god as his father.[45] The Messiah's names, Wonderful-Counsellor, Mighty-God, Everlasting-Father, have parallels in Babylonian literature,[46] yet we ought not forget that in the Holy Bible they are titles inspired by God Himself.[47]

The Messiah appears as the good shepherd.[48] The title "shepherd" was highly cherished among Sumerian, Babylonian, Assyrian and Egyptian rulers.[49] The same was true in Israel: David was the shepherd of his people,[50] likewise the princes.[51] Yahweh Himself was a "good shepherd."[52] Here we simply have a widely used metaphor taken from daily life.

In Balaam's prophecy the Messiah is called "star out of Jacob,"[53] a figure immediately intelligible throughout the ancient Orient. "Sun" was a favorite title of Assyrian and Hittite kings. In the Amarna letters the Pharaoh, who represented Re, the sun-god, is addressed, "My sun."[54] In the OT light is a symbol for divinity. Yahweh is called "light of Israel."[55] In Isaias the king of

35. § 49:2a, 6f.
36. 1 Sam. 10:24; 2 Sam. 16: 16; 3 Kgs. 1:31; Ps. 21:5.
37. 3 Kgs. 2:45.
38. 2 Sam. 7:16; § 50:2.
39. § 50:5.
40. § 16:4.
41. § 16:5; 2 Sam. 7:14; Ps. 89:27-28.
42. 2 Sam. 7:14; Jer. 22:13-30.
43. § 50:5.
44. Cyl. A 3, 6-8.
45. M. Witzel, Keilinschriftl. Studien, Fulda, 1, 1918, 99, 113f.
46. Dürr 113f; Is. 9:5.
47. § 50:5.
48. § 51:1.
49. Dürr 116f.
50. 2 Sam. 5:2.
51. Jer. 2:8; 10:21; 22:22; 23:1-4; Is. 56:11.
52. § 49:1a.
53. Num. 24:17.
54. Dürr 107f.
55. Is. 10:17; Mich. 7:8.

Babylon, who sought to be like God, is described as a "shining star."[56] As the Messiah was called "shoot"[57] or "sprig of David,"[58] so the Babylonian and Assyrian kings called themselves the "royal shoot" to indicate a legitimate claim to the throne—they did not want to be considered usurpers.[59] Nevertheless Is. 11:1, 10 serves as the source for later usage of this messianic title; and may we again point out that here, as in other prophecies, the Messiah, though of royal blood, will be born only after the dynasty has been utterly humbled.[60]

c) *The Man of Sorrows.* As pagan parallels to the suffering Messiah the critics place those nature gods who die and come to life again.[61] Now with those gods such a cycle was the regular thing: they rise in order to die, they die again in order to rise. They atone for no sins through their death, neither does their resurrection affect the world's conversion. The Israelites did not need to resort to Babylonian mythology to find an instance of a dead person returning to life.[62] Certain Babylonian psalms mention the danger of death, but the reader is always sure that the poet, though perhaps speaking of his own death, is living in spite of everything, and that the expressions used are only figurative.[63] In Is. 53 the prophet (in the name of the people) speaks about the Servant of Yahweh whose death and resurrection produce unprecedented effects. In Babylon during the New Year's celebration the king was humiliated and struck, whereupon he asserted his innocence.[64] This act cannot be adjudged as a parallel to the Suffering Servant. The former was merely a ceremonial humiliation, the king actually never suffered, much less died. The Servant of Yahweh shed His blood and laid down His life, not as a king performing a rite, but in bitter fulfillment of His office as priest. The theology of vicarious suffering in atonement for the sins of others was not alien to Israelitic thought.[65] If the prophet, who was awaiting with absolute certainty the collapse of Babylonian power, actually recalled this ceremony as he depicted the Suffering Servant, it served only to set in still deeper relief the true character of the Redeemer's work.

§ 54. CONCLUSION
OLD TESTAMENT RELIGION PERFECTED IN THE NEW

Because of its elevated doctrine on God and its high ethical demands, the religion of the OT towers over all other religions of the ancient world. And this religion was destined for still greater perfection. It was the dawn preceding and heralding a glorious, radiant sunrise. The religious values contained in the OT would develop and mature in the New. "The Law was given through Moses; grace and truth came through Jesus Christ."[1] The prophecies telling of the new covenant and of the Redeemer, for instance, are a bond linking the OT

56. Is. 14:12.
57. Zach. 3:8; 6:12.
58. Jer. 23:5; 33:15.
59. Dürr 112.
1. Jn. 1:17.

60. § 50:4.
61. § 44:4.
62. § 44:1.

63. Cf. similar Biblical passages, § 44:1.
64. Dürr 125f.
65. § 52:1a.

to the NT and thereby demonstrate their mutual dependence. Upon the mount of Transfiguration Moses and Elias appeared, representing the Law and the prophets, because these had prepared the way for the Messiah; and they spoke with Jesus concerning His death which would effect mankind's salvation.[2] In a sentence that has since become classic, St. Augustine described the relationship between the two covenants, "In the Old the New is concealed, in the New the Old is revealed."[3]

The God of the old covenant remains the God of the new covenant in His justice, in His holiness, in His omnipotence, in His position relative to the universe as its creator and preserver. The fundamentals of OT law are part and parcel of the new covenant, for both rest upon the obligation of loving God and neighbor. To the question put by a doctor of the Law regarding the greatest commandment Jesus answered, "You shall love the Lord your God with your whole heart. This is the greatest and the first commandment. The second is similar to it: You shall love your neighbor as yourself. On these two commandments depend the whole Law and the prophets."[4] In the OT God demanded holiness of life;[5] in the New Jesus enjoins, "Be perfect as your father in heaven is perfect."[6] It is easy to see why our dear Lord said, "I am not come to destroy the Law and the prophets, but to fulfill."[7]

Nevertheless the advent of the Son of God, the second Adam, did involve a new beginning. Not only did He deepen the concept of God beyond that proper to the OT, not only did He reveal new truths, but He sketched a new spiritual ideal. "You have heard that it was said to them of old .... but I say to you."[8] The Christian will not pray the OT cursing psalms in the spirit in which they were written,[9] but in the spirit of Jesus. He will remember how God floods the sinner with His mercy, how he himself is also dependent upon that mercy; and he will forgive all evil inflicted upon himself.[10] Jesus brought a new wine and He does not wish to have it poured into old skins.[11] With this parable Jesus announced the freedom enjoyed by the children in His new kingdom, a freedom from the details of Mosaic Law, a freedom which St. Paul energetically championed. Jesus established the covenant proclaimed by the prophets, not through animal sacrifices as did Moses on Sinai,[12] but through His own blood on Golgotha. Sin remained under the Old, in the New it is blotted out forever.

The OT was designed to condition men's minds for Christ. The Law was a "taskmaster unto Christ," παιδαγωγὸς εἰς χριστόν,[13] inasmuch as it preserved Israel from being assimilated by her pagan environment, inasmuch as it imposed self-mastery, kept alive a consciousness of sin and fostered a yearning for salvation. As long as Jesus remained upon earth He did not seek to displace the Law[14] (He was only sent to the lost sheep of the house of Israel[15]), but

2. Matth. 17:3; Lk. 9:30-31.
3. Quaest. in Hept. II 73, MLP 34:623; cf. Sermo 160, 6, MLP 38:876.
4. Matth. 22:36-40.
5. Ex. 19:6.
6. Matth. 5:48.
7. Matth. 5:17.
8. Matth. 5:21f; 19:9.
9. Cf. Ex. 21:23-25; § 32:1g.
10. Matth. 5:38f.
11. Matth. 9:17.
12. Ex. 24.
13. Gal. 3:24.
14. Matth. 5:17.
15. Matth. 15:24.

subjected Himself willingly to it.[16] Mosaic ceremonial however could be observed only in a small nation. When the Gospel began to be preached to all peoples, this "shadow of things to come"[17] had to pass away. With Christ's death the Law was abrogated. No one insisted upon this truth more resolutely or stated it more clearly than St. Paul.[18] "Christ is the consummation of the Law unto justice for everyone who believes."[19] The "taskmaster" no longer has any right or power.

Jesus trained His disciples in Galilee far from the temple to prevent them from becoming entangled in the externals which the Pharisees and Scribes regarded as essentials. God had planted the Chosen People as a prized vine, but the vine degenerated.[20] The vineyard, Israel,[21] produced nought but sour grapes.[22] Therefore God resolved to destroy it, turn it into a wilderness.[23] The vineyard which had been nursed with tender care yielded no fruit, the keepers even sought to slay their Master's Son.[24] Israel resembled a fig tree with much fine foliage but no fruit.[25] When toward the end of His mission Jesus found no fruit upon this fig tree, He cursed it and it withered forever, withered to its very roots.[26] This was the last miracle He worked, the only miracle which was not directed toward gaining souls or alleviating human suffering. He wept over impenitent Jerusalem,[27] and prophesied ruin to the city and its temple.[28] The Jews believed it sufficient to have Abraham as father;[29] they forgot that God's choice of Abraham was an act of pure grace and that Abraham's children were obliged to fulfill the divine will even as their forefather did.[30] When Israel rejected Him on whose account she had been chosen, she spelt her own rejection; she became stale salt, "The kingdom of God will be taken away from you and will be given to a people yielding its fruits."[31]

Israel consigned her Savior to death. "The King of the Jews" died upon the cross, the King whom God "gave to the nations of the earth as (their) inheritance,"[32] the King to whom "all power has been given in heaven and upon earth."[33] Does Israel's action toward her Savior seem surprising? No. Beginning with the insurrection against Moses down to the time of Christ, Israel as a nation consistently resisted the agents of God's word. Through the centuries a good and merciful God struggled, so to speak, for the love of that people,[34] punishing them only to shower greater blessings upon them.[35] Yet despite all warnings and admonitions Israel "had a face harder than stone and refused to amend."[36] "Give up! We want to follow our own evil plans, each one of us wishes to act according to his own stubborn, evil notions."[37] God did not need Israel to realize His work. He willed to retain the imperishable religious content of the OT for His new kingdom, but first He detached

16. Matth. 17:26; Gal. 4:4.
17. Col. 2:17.
18. Acts 9:15.
19. Rom. 10:4.
20. Jer. 2:21; 8:13; Ez. 15:2.
21. Cf. § 16:4.
22. Is. 5:4.
23. Is. 5:5-6.
24. Matth. 21:33-41.
25. Lk. 13:6-9.
26. M a t t h. 21:18-20; Mk. 11:13-20.
27. Lk. 19:41.
28. Matth. 24:2, 15-22; Lk. 19:42-44.
29. Matth. 8:9.
30. Jn. 8:39; Matth. 3:9.
31. Matth. 21:43.
32. Ps. 2:8.
33. Matth. 28:18.
34. § 16:4.
35. § 46:5.
36. Jer. 5:3; Ez. 2:4-5.
37. Jer. 18:12.

His new foundation from ancient moorings lest Israel continue to impede His plan. Membership in the new kingdom of God is not dependent upon physical descent from Abraham,[38] but upon faith in Jesus and obedience to His words. We become God's children through the grace conferred upon the world through our Lord Jesus Christ.

38. Lk. 19:9.

COLLATERAL READING
FOR EACH CHAPTER

§ 1. INTRODUCTION

P. Scholz, Handbuch der Theologie des alten Bundes, Regensburg 1861.

M. Hetzenauer, Theologia biblica sive scientia historiae et religionis utriusque Testamenti catholica, I. Vet. Test., Freiburg 1908.

J. Nikel, La religion d'Israel, Paris 1912, 586-675.

N. Peters, Die Religion des AT in ihrer Einzigartigkeit unter den Religionem des alten Orients, Kempen 1913, 637-806.

F. Ceuppens, Theologia biblica, Rom I, II 1938, III 1939.

A. Kleinhans, Theologia biblica VT, Rom 1939.

P. Heinisch, De Godsdienst van Israel, Utrecht 1948.

H. Zschokke, Die Theologie der Propheten, Freiburg 1877.

..........Der dogmatisch-ethische Lehrgehalt der atl. Weisheitsbücher, Wien 1889.

J. Heln, Die biblische und die babylonische Gottesidee, Leipzig 1913.

K. Steuernagel, Atl. Theologie und Atl. Religionsgeschichte, Beih. 41 ZatW 1925, 266-273.

O. Eissfeldt, Israelitisch-jüdische Religionsgeschichte und atl. Theologie, ZatW 44, 1926, 1-12.

W. Eichrodt, Hat die atl. Theologie noch selbständige Bedeutung innerhalb der atl. Wissenschaft? ZatW 47, 1929, 83-91.

Ed. König, Die legitime Religion Israels und ihre hermeneutische Bedeutung, ZatW 49, 1931, 40-45.

L. Köhler, Atl. Theologie, ThRdsch N. F. 7, 1935, 255-276; 8, 1936, 55-69.

Joh. Lindblom, Zur Frage der Eigenart der atl. Religion, Beih. 66 ZatW 1936, 128-137.

A. Weiser, Die theologische Aufgabe der atl. Wissenschaft, Beih. 66 ZatW 1936, 207-224.

W. Eichrodt, Zur Frage der theol. Exegese des AT, ThBl 17, 1938, 73-87.

A. Wendel, Religionswissenschaftliche und theologische Auslegung des AT, Bonn 1938.

A. Dillmann, Handbuch der atl. Theologie, Leipzig 1895.

H. Schulz, Atl. Theologie[5], Göttingen 1896.

R. Smend, Lehrbuch der atl. Religionsgeschichte[2], Freiburg 1899.

B. Stade, Bibl. Theologie des AT, I, Tübingen 1905; II (von der Zeit Esras bis zum Zeitalter Christi) von A. Bertholet, Tübingen 1911.

J. Wellhausen, Israelitische und jüdische Religion, bei P. Hinneberg, Kultur der Gegenwart I 4, Leipzig, 1906.

K. Marti, Die Religion des AT unter den Religionem des vorderen Orients, Tübingen 1906.

..........Geschichte der isr. Religion[5], Strassburg 1907.

E. Kautzsch, Biblische Theologie des AT, Tübingen 1911.

K. Budde, Die altisr. Religion[3], Giessen 1912.

J. W. Rothstein, Die Religion des AT im Lichte geschichtlicher Wahrhaftigkeit, Gütersloh 1920.

G. Hölscher, Geschichte der isr. und jüd. Religion, Giessen 1922.

Ed. König, Theologie des AT[3.4], Stuttgart 1923.

..............Geschichte der atl. Religion [3.4], Gütersloh 1924.

J. Petersen, Israel, its life and culture, London-Copenhagen I-II 1926, III-IV 1940.

R. Kittel, Die Religion des Volkes Israel[2], Leipzig 1929.

A. Barton, The Religion of Israel[2], Oxford 1929.

B. D. Eerdmans, De Godsdienst van Israel, 2 Bde., Huis der Heide 1930.

W. O. E. Oesterley and Th. H. Robinson, Hebrew Religion, London 1930 (1933[4]).

J. Hänel, Die Religion der Heiligkeit, Gütersloh 1931.

C. Toussaint, Origines de la religion d'Israel, L'ancien Jahvisme, Paris 1931.

A. Loisy, La Religion d'Israel[3], Paris 1933.

E. Sellin, Atl. Theologie auf religionsgeschichtlicher Grundlage, 2 Bde., Leipzig 1933; II[2] 1936.

W. Eichrodt, Theologie des AT, 3 Bde., Leipzig 1933-1939 (I[2] 1939).

L. Köhler, Theologie des Alten Testaments, Tübingen 1936.

W. L. Wardle, The History and Religion of Israel, Oxford 1936.

A. Causse, Du groupe ethnique à la communauté religieuse, Paris, 1937.

W. Möller, H. Möllers Biblische Theologie des AT in heilsgeschichtlicher Entwicklung, Zwickau 1938.

A. Lods, La Religion d'Israel, Paris 1939.

H. Wheeler Robinson, Record and Revelation, Oxford 1938, pp. 187-348.

On the so-called Israelitic "folk-religion":

A. Jirku, Materialien zur Volksreligion Israels, Leipzig 1914.

Ed. König, Volksreligion überhaupt und speciell bei den Hebräern, ARW 17, 1914, 35-63.

..............Die sog. Volksreligion Israels eine fragwürdigste Grösse der atl. Theologie beleuchtet, 1921 (BFchrTh XXVI, 1).

Fr. X. Kortleitner, De religione populari Israelitarum, Oeniponte 1927.

K. Holzhey, Jahve der Gott Israels, sein Kampf gegen die fremden Götter von Mose bis Christus, Münster 1936 (AA XII 4).

B. Bendokat, Die prophetische Botschaft in der Auseinandersetzung mit der isr. Volksreligion, Berlin 1938.

On postbiblical Jewish religion:

E. Schürer, Geschichte des jüdischen Volkes im Zeitalter Jesu Christi[4], 3 Bde., Leipzig 1901-1909.

J. Felten, Neutest. Zeitgeschichte, 2 Bde., Regensburg 1925.

W. Bousset-H. Gressmann, Die Religion des Judentums im späthellenistischen Zeitalter[3], Tübingen 1926.

L. Couard, Die religiösen und sittlichen Anschauungen der atl. Apokryphen und Pseudepigraphen, Gütersloh 1907.

Ferd. Weber, Jüdische Theologie auf Grund des Talmud und verwandter Schriften[2], Leipzig 1897.

On ancient oriental religions:

H. Gressmann, Altorientalische Texte und Bilder zum AT[2], 2 Bde., Berlin 1926-1927.

P. Dhorme, Choix de textes religieux assyro-babyloniens, Paris 1907.

A. Jirku, Altorientalischer Kommentar zum AT, Leipzig 1923.

A. Jeremias, Handbuch der altorient. Geisteskultur[2], Leipzig 1929.

..............Das AT im Lichte des alten Orients[4], Leipzig 1930.

M. J. Lagrange, Études sur les religions sémitiques[2], Paris 1905.

M. Jastrow, Die Religion Babyloniens und Assyriens, 3 Bde., Giessen 1905-1912.

Br. Meissner, Babylonien und Assyrien, 2 Bde., Heidelberg 1920-1925.

A. Wiedemann, Das alte Ägypten, Heidelberg 1920.

A. Erman, Die Religion der Ägypter, Leipzig 1934.
G. Roeder, Urkunden zur Religion des alten Ägypten, Jena 1915.
H. Kees, Der Götterglaube im alten Ägypten, Leipzig 1941.

§ 2. DIVINE REVELATION: THE SOURCE OF OT RELIGION

On § 2:1, Pre-Mosaic Revelation:

M. J. Lagrange, Études sur les religions sémitiques, Paris 1905.
F. X. Kortleitner, De polytheismi origine quae sit doctrina sacrarum litterarum patrumque ecclesiae, Oeniponte 1911.
A. Lemonnyer, La révélation primitive, Paris 1914.
W. Schmidt, Die Uroffenbarung als Anfang der Offenbarungen Gottes, bei Esser-Mausbach, Religion, Christentum, Kirche I², Kempten 1913, 481-636.
............Der Ursprung der Gottesidee, VI, Endsynthese der Religionen der Urvölker Amerikas, Asiens, Australiens, Afrikas, Münster 1935.
O. Menghin, Weltgeschichte der Steinzeit, Wien 1931.
O. Clemen, Urgeschichtliche Religion, Bonn 1932.
W. Mooch, Urreligion—Sie ältesten Menschheitszeugnisse der Gottesoffenbarung, Warendorf 1935.
K. L. Bellon, Inleiding tot de natuurlijke Godsdienstwetenschap, Nymegen-Utrecht 1943.
W. F. Albright, From the Stone Age to Christianity, Baltimore 1940 (1946²).
............Archaeology and the Religion of Israel, Baltimore 1942.
F. X. Kortleitner, Religio a patriarchis Israelitarum exercitata, Oeniponte 1936.
E. Dhorme, La Religion des Hebreux nomades, Bruxelles 1937.
P. Heinisch, Die stammesgeschichtliche Deutung der Patriarchenerzählungen, Stc 10, 1934, 269-296, 447-464.
............Probleme der biblischen Urgeschichte, Luzern 1947.

On § 2:2, Moses:

P. Karge, Geschichte des Bundesgedankens im AT, Münster 1910 (AA II 1-4).
H. Gressmann, Mose und seine Zeit, Göttingen 1913.
A. Mallon, Les Hébreux en Egypte, Rom 1921 (Orientalia 3).
E. Sellin, Mose und seine Bedeutung für die isr.-jüd. Religionsgeschichte, Leipzig 1922.
A. Šanda, Moses und der Pentateuch, Münster 1924 (AA IX).
M. H. A. Halévy, Moïse dans l'histoire et dans la legende, Paris 1927.
P. Volz, Mose und sein Werk², Tübingen 1932.
F. X. Kortleitner, Formae cultus Mosaici cum ceteris religionibus orientis antiqui comparatae, Oeniponte 1933.
W. Stoderl, Das Gesetz Israels nach Inhalt und Ursprung, Prag 1933.
A. Alt, Die Ursprünge des isr. Rechts, Leipzig 1934.
M. Noth, Die Gesetze im Pentateuch, ihre Voraussetzungen und ihr Sinn, Halle 1940.
H. Cazelles, Études sur la Code de l'Alliance, Paris 1946.
............L'auteur du Code de l'Alliance (Exod. 20:22-23:19), Vivre et penser 3, 1945, 173-191.
P. Heinish, Das Buch Exodus, Bonn 1934.
............Das Buch Leviticus, Bonn 1935.
............Das Buch Numeri, Bonn 1936.

On § 2:3, The Prophets:

H. Zschokke, Theologie der Propheten des AT, Freiburg 1877.
Fr. Nötscher, Die Gerechtigkeit Gottes bei den vorexilischen Propheten, Münster 1915 (AA VI 1).

G. Ch. Aalders, De Propheten des Ouden Verbonds, Kampen 1918.
D. Buzy, Les symboles de l'AT, Paris 1923.
E. Tobac, Les prophètes d'Israel, 3 Bde., Malines 1919-1921.
H. W. Herzberg, Prophet und Gott, Gütersloh 1923 (BFchrTh 28, 3).
N. Peters, Osee und die Geschichte, Paderborn 1924.
M. A. van den Oudenrijn, Nebu)ah, De prophetiae charismate in populo Israelitici libri quattuor Rom, 1926.
L. Dürr, Wollen und Wirken der atl. Propheten, 1926.
A. Eberharter, Die vorexilischen Propheten und die Politik ihrer Zeit, Münster 1927 (BZF XII 6).
............Die soziale und politische Wirksamkeit des atl. Prophetentums, Salzburg 1924.
H. Junker, Prophet und Seher in Israel, Trier 1928.
E. Fascher, ΠΡΟΦΗΤΗΣ, Eine sprach-und religionsgeschichtliche Untersuchung, Giessen 1927.
J. Ziegler, Die Liebe Gottes bei den Propheten, Münster 1930 (AA XI 3).
H. L. Newton, Notes on the Covenant—A study in the theology of the Prophets, Cleveland 1934.
A. van den Born, De symolische handelingen der OT profeten, Utrecht-Nymegen.
A. Heschel, Die Prophetis, Krakau 1936.
A. C. Welch, Prophet and Priest in Old Israel, London 1936.
J. Hoschander, The Priests and Prophets, New York 1938.
B. Bendokat, Die prophetische Botschaft in der Auseinandersetzung mit der isr. Volksreligion, Berlin 1938.
F. Siegman, The False Prophets of the OT, Washington 1939.
G. Contenau, La Divination chez les Assyriens et les Babyloniens, Paris 1940.
A. Halder, Association of Cult Prophets among the ancient Semites, Uppsala 1945.

§ 3. OFFICIALS AND SPIRITUAL LIFE IN ISRAEL

A. van Hoonacker, Le sacerdoce Levitique dans la loi et dans l'histoire, London 1899.
E. F. Morison, The Relation of Priest and Prophet in the History of Israel before the Exile, JthSt 11, 1910, 3, 211-245.
J. Gabriel, Untersuchungen über das atl. Hohepriestertum, Wien 1933.
J. Berich, Die priesterliche Tora, Giessen 1936 (Beih. 66 ZatW 1936, 63-88).
A. C. Welch, Prophet and Priest in Old Israel, London 1936.
Schrenk, Theol. Wörterbuch zum NT III 1938, 259-262, 268-270.
J. Hoschander, The Priests and Prophets, New York, 1938.
A. M. A. van den Oudenrijn, Priester en profeten hij Isaias (28, 7-13), Stc 14, 1938, 299-311.
Th. Böhl, Priester und Prophet, NthSt 22, 1939, 298-313.
H. Gressmann, Die neugefundene Lehre des Amen-em-ope und die vorexilische Spruchdichtung Israels, ZatW 42, 1924, 272-296.
P. Humbert, Recherches sur les sources égyptiennes de la litterature sapientiale d'Israel, Neuchâtel 1929.
L. Dürr, Das Erziehungswesen im Alten Testament und im antiken Orient, Leipzig 1932 (Mitt. der vorderas.-aegypt. Gesellschaft 36, 2).
J. Fichtner, Die altorientalische Weisheit in ihrer isr.-jüd. Ausprägung, Giessen 1933 (Beih. 62 ZatW).
A. Druppel, Le conflit entre la Sagesse profane et la Sagesse religieuse, Bb 17, 1936, 45-70, 107-128.

H. Duesberg, Les scribes inspirés—Introduction aux Livres sapientiaux de la Bible, 2 Bd., Brugge-Paris 1938-1939.
H. Kaupel, Die Stellung des Königs im atl. Kult, ThGl 18, 1926, 106-116.
..............Die Beziehungen des atl. Königtums zum Kult, Hamburg 1930.
F. Gypkens, König und Kult im AT, Emstetten 1940 (Diss. Bonn 1939)
R. Labat, Le caractère religieux de la royauté assyro-babylonienne, Paris 1939.

§ 4. BELIEF IN GOD'S EXISTENCE

W. Reiss, Gott nicht kennen, ZatW 58, 1940-1941, 70-98.
V. Zapletal, Der Totemismus und die Religion Israels, FreiburgSchw 1901.
J. Nikel, Der Ursprung des atl. Gottesglaubens[4], Münster 1912 (BZF I 1).
A. Alt, Der Gott der Väter, Stuttgart 1929 (BWAuNT 48).
W. Schmidt, Handbuch der kulturhistorischen Ethnologie, Münster 1937.
K. I. Bellon, Inleiding tot de natuurlijke Godswetenschap, Nymegen-Utrecht 1943.

§ 5. THE NAMES OF GOD

J. Hehn, Die biblische und die babylonische Gottesidee, Leipzig 1913, 150-271.
M. Noth, Die israelitischen Personennamen im Rahmen der gemein-semit. Namengebung, Stuttgart 1928 (BWAuNT III 10).
W. W. Graf Baudissin, Kyrios als Gottesname und seine Stelle in der Religionsgeschichte, 4 Bde., Giessen 1929.
H. Bauer, Die Gottheiten von Ras Schamra, ZatW 51, 1933, 81-101; 53, 1935, 54-59.
O. Grether, Name und Wort Gottes im AT, Giessen 1934 (Beih. 64 ZatW).
F. X. Kortleitner, Religio a patriarchis Israelitarum exercitata, Oeniponte 1936, 48-62.
H. W. Obbink, De magische beteekenis van den naam inzonderheid in het Oude Egypte, Amsterdam 1925.
O. Eissfeldt, Jahwe-Name und Zauberwesen, Zeitschr. f. Missionskunde und Religionsw. 42, 1927, 161-186.
W. Schulz, Der Namenglaube bei den Babyloniern, Anthropos 26, 1931, 895-928.
L. Sp. Chafer, Biblical Theism—The Names of Deity, Bs 96, 1939, 138-163; 264-284; 390-411.
W. Baumgartner, Ras Schamra und das AT, ThRdsch 13, 1941, 85-102; 157-183.
R. de Langhe, Les Textes de Ras Shamra-Ugarit et leurs rapports avec le milieu biblique de l'AT, 2 Bd., Gemblouz-Paris 1945.
  On the divine name "Yahweh":
W. W. Graf Baudissin, Studien zur semit. Religionsgeschichte I, Leipzig 1876 (reprinted 1911) 179-254.
J. Theis, Friedrich Delitzsch und seine "Grosse Täuschung" oder Jaho und Jahwe, Trier 1921, 49-65.
S. Landersdorfer, BZ 10, 1912, 24-35.
G. Breitschaft, BZ 10, 1912, 238-241.
H. Grimme, BZ 17, 1925, 29-42.
G. R. Driver, ZatW 46, 1928, 7-25.
J. Hänel, NkZ 40, 1929, 608-641.
L. Cerfaux, RSphth 20, 1931, 27-51.
K. G. Kuhn, Orient. Stud. für E. Littmann, Leiden 1935, 25-42.
A. Vaccari, Bb 17, 1936, 1-10.
A. Schleiff, ZdmG 90, 1936, 679-702.
Quell im Theol. Wörterbuch zum NT III, 1938, 1056-1080.
A. Vincent, La religion des Judéo-Araméens d'Elephantine, Paris 1937, 25-143.
J. Schmidt, Der Ewigkeitsbegriff im AT, Münster 1940, 36-48 (AA XIII 5).

R. de Langhe, Un Dieu Yahweh à Ras Shamra, EphThLov 19, 1942, 91-101.
Moore, AmJTh 12, 1908, 34-52; AmJsemL 25, 1908-1909, 312-318; 28, 1911-1912, 56-62.
Neubauer, OrLz 20, 1917, 73-77.
Kleinhans, Bb 6, 1925, 94f.
Eissfeldt, ZatW 53, 1935, 59-76.
A. L. Williams, ZatW 54, 1936, 262-269.
B. Alfrink, Oudtestamentische Studien, V, Leiden 1948, 43-62.
   On the divine name "El":
M. J. Lagrange, Rb 12, 1903, 362-386.
P. Kleinert, Beih. 33 ZatW 1918, 261-284.
O. Procksch, NkZ 45, 1924, 20-37.
W. W. Graf Baudissin, Beih. 41 ZatW, Giessen 1925, 1-11.
   On the divine name "Shaddai":
F. Zorell, Bb 8, 1927, 215-219.
W. F. Albright, JbL 54, 1935, 173-204.
   On the divine name "Melekh":
A. v. Gall, βασιλεία τοῦ θεοῦ, Heidelberg 1926.
O. Eissfeldt, ZatW 46, 1928, 81-105.
M. Buber, Das Kommende, I, Königtum Gottes[2], Berlin 1936.
H. W. Wolff, ZatW 54, 1936, 168-202.

§ 7. UNICITY OF GOD: MONOTHEISM

F. X. Kortleitner, De polytheismi origine quae sit doctrina sacrarum litterarum patrumque ecclesiae, Oeniponte 1911.
J. Hehn, Die biblische und die babylonische Gottesidee, 1913.
K. Holzhey, Jahve, der Gott Israels, Münster 1936 (AA XII 4).
Br. Balscheit, Alter und Aufkommen des Monotheismus in der isr. Religion, Giessen 1938 (Beih. 69 ZatW).
F. X. Kugler, Im Bannkreis Babels, Münster 1910.
E. Herzfeld, Die Religion der Achämeniden, RHR 113, 1936, 21-41.
J. de Grott, De Godsdienst van Ras Shamra (Oegarit), bei G. van der Leeuw: De Godsdiensten der wereld, Amsterdam 1940, I 261-272.
R. de Langhe, Les Textes de Ras Shamra-Ugarit et leurs rapports avec le milieu biblique de l'AT, 2 Bd., Gembloux-Paris 1945.
H. Junker, Giza I-VI, Berichte über die von der Akad. der Wiss. in Wien mit Dr. W. Pelizaeus vorgenommenen Grabungen auf dem Friedhof des Alten Reiches bei den Pyramiden von Giza, Wien 1923-1943 (cf. A. de Buck, Bibl. Or. 1, 1944, 23f).
H. Junker, Der sehende und blinde Gott, 1942 (J. Janssen JEOL 9, 1944, 31).
H. Kees, Der Götterglaube im alten Ägypten, Leipzig 1941, 172, 366-377.

§ 8. GOD'S IMMATERIALITY

Fr. Nötscher, Das Angesicht Gottes schauen, 1924.
H. Middendorf, Gott sieht, Freiburg 1935.
B. Stein, Der Begriff Kebod Jahweh und seine Bedeutung für die atl. Gotteserkenntnis, Emstetten Westf. 1939.
H. Hempel, Die Grenzen des Anthropomorphismus Jahwes im AT, ZatW 57, 1939, 75-85.

§ 10. THE ETERNITY AND CHANGELESSNESS OF GOD.

H. Lasse, col. 197-209 Theol. Wörterbuch zum NT, I, 1933.
Joh. Schmidt, Der Ewigkeitsbegriff im AT, Münster 1940 (AA XIII 5).

§ 11. GOD'S HOLINESS

M. Schumpp, Das Heilige in der Bibel, ThGl 22, 1930, 331-343.
J. Hänel, Die Religion der Heiligkeit, Gütersloh 1931.
F. X. Kortleitner, Quid sanctitas in VT valeat, Oeniponte 1939 (Comm. bibl. 14).
L. O. Procksch, col. 92 Theol. Wörterbuch für NT, I, 1933.

§ 13. GOD'S IMMENSITY AND OMNIPRESENCE

G. Westphal, Jahwes, Wohnstätten nach den Anschauungen der alten Hebräer,
    Giessen 1908 (Beih. 15 ZatW).

§ 15. GOD'S JUSTNESS

Fr. Nötscher, Die Gerechtigkeit Gottes bei den vorexilischen Propheten, Münster,
    1915 (AA VI 1).
Th. Paffrath, Gott, Herr und Vater, Paderborn 1930, 144-257 (Kath. Lebens-
    werte 13).
Fr. Küchler, Der Gedanke des Eifers Jahwes im AT, ZatW 28, 1908, 42-52.
A. Schulz, Festschr. G. v. Hertling, München 1913, 93-100.
R. Press, ZatW 51, 1933, 121-140, 227-255.

§ 16. GOD'S LOVE AND MERCY

J. Ziegler, Die Liebe Gottes bei den Propheten, Münster 1930 (AA XI 3).
Th. Paffrath, Gott, Herr und Vater, Paderborn 1930, 273-577 (Kath. Lebens-
    werte 13).
N. Glueck, Das Wort ḥesed im atl. Sprachgebrauch, 1927 (Beih. 47 ZatW).
W. F. Lofthouse, Ḥen and Ḥeseḏ in the OT, ZatW 51, 1933, 29-38.
M. J. Lagrange, La paternité de Dieu dans l'AT, RB 5, 1908, 481-499.
R. Gyllenberg, Gott, der Vater im AT und in der Predigt Jesu, Studia Orientalia
    I, Helsingfors 1925, 51-60.
W. Thomas, The Root)āgēb "love" in Hebrew, ZatW 57, 1939, 57-64.
Andr. ab Aloe, Dei amor erga homines in VT, VD 22, 1942, 233-239.
G. Behler, Divini amoris suprema revelatio in antiquo foedere data (Os 11),
    Ang 20, 1943, 102-116.

§ 17. EXPRESSIONS EXPLAINED AS CONTAINING INDICATIONS OF THE BLESSED TRINITY

M. A. van den Oudenrijn, Gen. 1:26 und Grundsätzliches zur trinitarischen
    Auslegung, Divus Thomas (Freiburg) 15, 1937, 145-156.

§ 18. "MAL'AKH-YAHWEH"

M. J. Lagrange, L'ange de Jahvé, Rb 12, 1903, 212-225.
P. Heinisch, Personifikationen und Hypostasen im AT und im alten Orient,
    Münster 1919, 24-27 (BZF IX, 10-12).

J. Rybinski, Der Mal'akh Jahwe, Paderborn 1930.
F. Stier, Gott und sein Engel im AT, Münster 1934 (AA XII 2).
A. Lods, L'ange de Jahvé et l'âme extérieure, Beih. 27 ZatW 1914, 263-278.
A. Škrinjar, Angelus Testamenti (Mal. 3:1), VD 14, 1934, 40-48.
B. Stein, Der Engel des Auszugs, Bb 19, 1938, 286-307.
W. Heidt, Angelology of the Old Testament, Washington 1949.

§ 19. WISDOM

P. Heinisch, Die griechische Philosophie im Buche der Weisheit, Münster 1908 (AA I 4).
..........Das Buch der Weisheit, Münster 1912, XXXVII—XLI, 149-158.
E. Krebs, Der Logos als Heiland im ersten Jahrhundert, 1910 (Freib. theol. Stud. 2).
W. Schencke, Die Chokma in der jüd. Hypostasen-spekulation, Kristiania 1913.
A. Hudal, Die religiösen und sittlichen Ideen des Spruchbuches, Rom 1914, 96-162.
J. Lebreton, Les origines du dogme de la Trinité[5], Paris 1919, 110-119.
J. Göttsberger, Die göttliche Weisheit als Persönlichkeit im AT, Münster 1919 (BZF IX 1, 2).
P. Heinisch, Personifikationen und Hypostasen im AT und im alten Orient, Münster 1921 (BZF IX, 10-12).
..........Die persönliche Weisheit des AT in religionsgeschichtlicher Beleuchtung, Münster 1923 (BZF XI 1, 2).
P. Schütt, Revelatio SS. Trinitatis in VT praeparata, VD 6, 1926, 359-367.
P. van Imschoot, La sagesse dans l'AT est-elle une hypostase? Coll. Gand. 21, 1934, 3-10.
..........Sagesse et esprit dans l'AT, RB 47, 1938, 23-49.
H. Windisch, Die göttliche Weisheit der Juden und die paulin. Christologie, Neutest. Stud. f. G. Heinrici, Leipzig 1914, 220-234.

§ 20. THE "SPIRIT" OF YAHWEH

R. Volz, Der Geist Gottes und die verwandten Erscheinungen im AT, Freiburg 1910.
J. Lebreton, Les origines du dogme de la Trinité[5], Paris 1919, 100-110.
J. Hehn, Zum Problem des Geistes im alten Orient und im AT, ZatW 43, 1925, 210-225.
P. van Imschoot, L'action de l'esprit de Jahvé dans l'AT, RSphth 23, 1934, 553-587.
..........L'esprit de Jahvé, source de vie dans l'AT, Rb 44, 1935, 481-501.
..........L'esprit de Jahvé et l'alliance nouvelle dans l'AT, EphThLov 13, 1936, 201-220.
..........Sagesse et esprit dans l'AT, Rb 47, 1938, 25-49.
..........L'esprit de Jahvé principe de vie morale dans l'AT, EphThLov 16, 1939, 457-467.
C. Armerding, The Holy Spirit in the OT, Bs 92, 1935, 277-291, 433-441.
H. Koch, Der Gottesgeist und der Messias, Bb 27, 1946, 241-268, 376-403.
P. Volz, Der heilige Geist in den Gathas des Sarathuschtra, Eucharisterion, Göttingen 1923, 323-345 (FRLAuNT 19, 1).

§ 21. THE WORD OF GOD—THE NAME OF GOD

E. Krebs, Der Logos als Heiland im ersten Jahrhundert, 1910 (Freib. theol. Stud. 2).

J. Szeruda, Das Wort Jahves, Diss. Basel 1921.

P. Heinisch, Das "Wort" im AT und im alten Orient, Münster 1922 (BZF X 7, 8).

J. Hempel, Die israelit. Anschauungen von Segen und Fluch im Lichte altor. Parallelen, ZdmG 79, 1925, 20-110.

O. Grether, Name and Wort Gottes im AT, Giessen 1934 (Beih. 64 ZatW).

L. Dürr, Die Wertumg des göttlichen Wortes im AT und im antiken Orient, Leipzig 1938 (Mitt. der vorderas. -äg. Ges. 42, 1).

V. Hamp, Der Begriff "Wort" in den aram. Bibelübersetzungen, München, 1938. Procksch, col. 89-100 Theol. Wörterbuch zum NT IV, 1939.

A. Moret, Le Verbe créateur et révélateur en Egypte, RHR 59, 1909, 278-298.

H. Masing, The Word of Yahweh, Acta Comment. Univ. Tartuensis 1938, B 4, 1-4, 1-59.

H. Odeberg, Fragen über Metatron, Schekina und Memra, Bulletin de la Societé Royale des Lettres de Lund, 1941-1942.

§ 22. THE ANGELS

J. Nikel, Die Lehre des AT über die Cherubim und Seraphim, 1890.

L. Dürr, Ezechiels Vision von der Erscheinung Gottes (Ezechiel 1 und 10) im Lichte der vorderasiat. Altertumskunde, Münster 1917.

P. Dhorme et L. H. Vincent, Les Chérubins, Rb 35, 1926, 328-358, 481-495.

G. H. Dix, The seven Archangels and the seven Spirits, JthSt 28, 1927, 233-250.

M. Schumpp, Das Buch Tobias, Münster 1933, LXXVIII-LXXXI, 229-231 (Exeg. Handb. z. AT).

F. B. König, Die Amesha Spentas des Avesta und die Erzengel im AT, Diss. Melk 1935.

E. Langton, The Ministries of the Angelic Powers according to the OT and Later Jewish Literature, London 1936.

N. Johannsson, Parakletoi—Vorstellungen von Fürsprechenn für die Menschen vor Gott in der atl. Religion, im Spätjudentum und Urchristentum, Lund 1940.

   On postbiblical Jewish angelology:

L. Hackspill, L'angélologie juive à l'époque néotest., Rb 11, 1902, 527-550.

L. Couard, Die religiösen und sittlichen Anschauungen der atl. Apokryphen und Pseudepigraphen, Gütersloh 1907, 52-62.

J. B. Frey, L'angélologie juive autemps de J.-Chr., RSphth 5, 1911, 75-110.

W. Bousset-Gressmann, Die Religion des Judentums[3], Tübingen 1926, 320-331, 499 f.

M. J. Lagrange, Le Judaïsme, Paris 1931, 117, 259, 265, 428.

Ferd. Weber, Jüdische Theologie[2], Leipzig 1897, 166-177.

W. Heidt, Angelology of the Old Testament, Washington 1949.

§ 23. DEMONOLOGY

H. Duhm, Die bösen Geister im AT, Tübingen 1904.

A. Jirku, Die Dämonen und ihre Abwehr im AT, Leipzig 1912.

H. Kaupel, Die Dämonen im AT, Augsburg 1930.

............"Sirenen" in der Septuaginta, BZ 23, 1935, 158-165.

T. Canaan, Dämonenglaube im Lande der Bibel, Leipzig 1929.

S. Landersdorfer, Studien zum biblischen Versöhnungstag, Münster 1924 (AA
X 1).
..............BZ 18, 1929, 294-300.
P. Heinisch, Die Trauergebräuche bei den Israeliten, Münster 1931 (BZF XIII
7, 8).
J. Schur, Versöhnnungstag und Sündenbock, Helsingfors 1934 (Soc. Scient.
Fennica, Comm. Hum. Litt. 6, 3).
A. Brock-Utne, "Der Feind"—Die atl. Satansgestalt im Lichte der sozialen
Verhältnisse des nahen Orients, Klio 28, 1935, 219-227.
A. Lods, Les origines de la figure de Satan, ses fonctions à la cour céleste,
Melanges Syriens à M. R. Dussaud, Paris 1939, II 649-660.
　　On late Jewish demonology:
L. Couard, Die religiösen und sittlichen Anschauungen der atl. Apokryphen und
Pseudepigraphen, Gütersloh 1907, 62-72.
W. Bousset-Gressmann, Die Religion des Judentums³, Tübingen 1926, 251-254,
331-342, 514-517.
M. J. Lagrange, Le Judaïsme, Paris 1931, 111, 403.
Ferd. Weber, Jüdische Theologie², Leipzig 1897, 251-259.
　　On Mesopotamian demonology:
C. R. Thompson, The Devils and Evil Spirits of Babylonia, London 1903.
R. L. Tallquist, Die assyr. Beschwörungsserie Maqlū, Leipzig 1894.
G. Meior, Die assyr. Beschwörungssammlung Maqlū, 1937.
H. Zimmern, Die Beschwörungsserie Šurpu, Beiträge zur Kenntnis der babyl.
Religion, Leipzig 1896.
L. W. King, Babylonian Magic and Sorcery, London 1896.
M. Jastrow, Die Religion Babyloniens und Assyriens, I, 1905, 273-392.
Br. Meissner, Babylonien und Assyrien, Heidelberg 1925, II, 198-241.
O. Weber, Dämonenbeschwörung bei den Babyloniern und Assyrern, Leipzig
1906 (AO VII 4).
Grundmann, Das böse Prinzip im Parsismus, Theol. Wörterbuch zum NT III,
1938, 476f.
　　On Egyptian demonology:
A. Wiedemann, Magie und Zauberei im alten Ägypten, Leipzig 1905 (AO VI 4).
Ad. Erman, Die Religion der Ägypter, 1934, 295-313.

§ 24. THE CREATION OF THE WORLD

N. Peters, Glauben und Wissen im ersten biblischen Schöpfungsbericht, Pader-
born, 1907.
Al. Kirchner, Die babyl. Kosmogonie und der biblische Schöpfungsbericht,
Münster 1911 (AA III 1).
Al. Schmitt, Bibel und Naturwissenschaft³, 1912 (BZF III 7).
Al. Konrad, Das Weltbild in der Bibel, Graz-Wien, 1917.
Aem. Schoepfer, Bibel und Wissenschaft², Innsbruck 1932, 139-201.
H. Junker, Die biblische Urgeschichte, Trier 1932.
F. Ceuppens, De historia primaeva (Gen. 1-11), Rom 1934.
A. Deimel, Enuma eliš und Hexaemeron, Rom 1934.
F. X. Kortleitner, Sacrae litterae doceantne creationem universi ex nihilo,
Oeniponte 1935 (Com. bibl. 9).
R. Labat, Le poème babylonien de la Création, Paris 1935.
F. M. Th. Böhl, Het babylonische Lied van der wereldschepping en de wereldorde,
De eerste zang, JEOL 9, 1944, 145-153.
H. A. Brongers, De Scheppingstradities hij de profeten, Amsterdam 1945.

P. Heinisch, Probleme der biblischen Urgeschichte, Luzern 1947.
Fr. Böhl, bārā⁾ als Terminus der Weltschöpfung im atl. Sprachgebrauch, BWAT 13, 1913, 42-60.
G. v. Rad, Das theol. Problem des atl. Schöpfungsglaubens, Beih. 66 ZatW 1936, 138-147.
A. Bea, Ras Šamra und das AT, Bb 19, 1938, 435-453.
W. Baumgartner, Ras Schamra und das AT, ThRdsch 13, 1941, 162-165.
J. Coppens, Les Parallèles du Psautier avec les Textes de Ras-Schamra-Ougarit, Louvain 1946 (Bulletin voor Geschiedenis en Exegese van het OT 18).

§ 25. THE CONSERVATION AND GOVERNMENT OF THE WORLD

W. Staerk, Vorsehung und Vergeltung—Zur Frage nach der sittlichen Weltordnung, Berlin, 1931.
W. Eichrodt, Vorsehungsglaube und Theodizee im AT, Festschrift O. Procksch, Leipzig 1934, 45-70.

§ 26. THE CREATION AND NATURE OF MAN

V. Zapletal, Alttestamentliches, Freiburg Schw. 1903, 1-15 (Das Ebenbild Gottes im Menschen, Gen. 1:26f.).
Al. Schmitt, Der Ursprung des Menschen, Freiburg 1911.
..........Katholizismus und Entwicklungsgedanke, Paderborn 1923 (Kath. Lebenswerte 9).
J. Nikel, Der geschichtliche Charakter von Gen. 1-3, Weid. Stud. III 1909.
J. Goettsberger, Adam und Eva³, Münster 1912 (BZF III, 11).
A. Struker, Die Gottebenbildlichkeit des Menschen in der altchristl. Literatur der ersten zwei Jahrhunderte, Münster 1913.
J. Schwab, Der Begriff der nefeš in den heiligen Schriften des AT, Diss. München 1913.
M. Lichtenstein, Das Wort nepheš in der Bibel, Berlin 1920.
J. Hehn, Zum Terminus "Bild Gottes," Festschr Ed. Sachau, 1915, 36-52.
..........Zum Problem des Geistes im alten Orient und im AT, ZatW 43, 1925, 210-224.
L. Dürr, nepheš = akk. napištu = Gurgel, Kehle, ibid. 262-269.
F. Rüsche, Blut, Leben und Seele—Ihr Verhältnis nach Auffassung der griech. und hellen. Antike, der Bibel und der alten alexandr. Theologen, Paderborn 1930 (Stud. z. Gesch. und Kultur des Altertums 5. Ergänzungsband).
J. H. Becker, Het begrib Nefesj in het OT, Amsterdam 1942.
J. Kreiten, Theologie und Naturwissenschaft über dem Ursprung des ersten Menschenleibes, Diss. Bonn 1930.
E. C. Messenger, Evolution and Theology—The problem of man's origin, London 1931.
A. Dondeyne, Scripturae de natura hominis doctrina, Coll. Brug. 31, 1931, 142-147, 226-231, 269-272, 292-296; 32, 1932, 10-15.
..........De communi generis humani origine, Coll. Brug. 32, 1932, 126-131, 199-203.
..........De evolutionismo sub respectu theologico, ibid. 234-238, 270-278.
J. Hempel, Gott, Mensch und Tier im AT—Mit besonderer Berücksichtigung von Gen. 1-3, ZsystTh 9, 1931, 211-249.
H. Junker, Der Mensch im AT: Das Bild vom Menschen, Festschrift Fr. Tillmann, Düsseldorf 1934, 3-13.
P. van Imschoot, L'esprit de Jahvé, source de vie dans l'AT, Rb 44, 1935, 481-501.
J. Frazer, Études d'anthropologie biblique, RHPhr 15, 1935, 28-69.

R. Schütz, Les idées eschatologiques du livre de la Sagesse, Paris-Strassburg 1935, 1-62.
P. M. Périer, L'origine de l'homme, Rap 62 (1936 1), 446-460, 513-528, 641-651; 63 (1936 2), 28-52.
..........Le Transformisme—L'origine de l'homme et le dogme catholique, Paris, 1938.
..........Le Transformisme mecaniste, Rap 65 (1937 2), 300-317, 398-410, 579-587.
A. Mignon, Pour et contre le Transformisme; Darwin-Vialleton, Paris 1937.
F. Rüschkamp, Der Mensch als Glied der Schöpfung, StZ 135, 1939, 367-385.
Arnold Gehlen, Der Mensch, seine Natur und seine Stellung in der Welt, Berlin 1940.
W. Schölgen, Die Abstammungslehre im Lichte der philosophischen Anthropologie, ThGl 33, 1941, 121-129.
O. Kuhn, Die Deszendenztheorie—Eine kritische Übersicht, ZkTh 67, 1943, 45-74.
F. Ceuppens, Le Polygénisme et la Bible, Ang 24, 1947, 20-32.
P. Heinisch, Probleme der biblischen Urgeschichte, Luzern 1947.

§ 27. THE FIRST COUPLE

J. Feldmann, Paradies und Sündenfall, Münster 1913 (AA 4).
W. Goossens, L'immortalite corporelle dans les recits de Gen. 2:4b-3, EphThLov 12, 1935, 722-742.
W. Moock, Die Einheit des Menschengeschlechts, Z. kath. Religionsunt. 12, 1935, 227-239; 13, 1936, 1-10, 95-103.
S. Landersdorfer, Der Sündenfall, ThGl 17, 1925, 38-60.
K. Fruhstorfer, Die Paradiesessünde, Linz 1929.
P. Mayrhofer, Der Fall des Menschen, ThGl 28, 1936, 133-162.
F. Mijula, Zur Frage des Sündenfalls, ThGl 28, 1936, 724-730.
B. Brodmann, Quid doceat S. Scriptura utriusque Testamenti de indole historica narrationis de paradiso et lapsu Gen. 2-3, Ant 12, 1937, 125-164, 213-236, 327-356.
M. A. P. van Oudenrijn, De zonde in den tuin, Roermond-Masseik 1939.
J. Coppens, De zonde in den tuin, EphThLov 18, 1941, 75-85.
..........De Kannis van Goed en Kwaad in het Paradijsverhaal, Antwerpen-Utrecht 1944.

§ 28. DUTIES TOWARD GOD

L. Dürr, Religion und Frömmigkeit der atl. Propheten, Düsseldorf 1926.
R. Storr, Das Frömmigkeitsideal bei den Propheten, Münster 1926 (BZF XII 3, 4).
..........Die Frömmigkeit im AT, 1928.
R. Sander, Furcht und Liebe im paläst. Judentum, Stuttgart 1935 (BWAuNT IV 16).
J. Hempel, Gott und Mensch im AT, Studie zur Geschichte der Frömmigkeit[2], Stuttgart 1936 (BWAuNT III 2).

§ 29. DUTIES TOWARD FELLOWMEN

E. Merz, Die Blutrache bei den Israeliten, Stuttgart 1916 (BWAT 20).
J. Weismann, Talion und öffentliche Strafe im mos. Recht, Leipzig 1913 (Festschrift Ad. Wach).

M. Löhr, Das Asylwesen im AT, Halle 1930.

F. Walter, Die Propheten in ihrem sozialen Beruf und das Wirtschaftsleben ihrer Zeit, Freiburg 1900.

J. Hejck, Das atl. Zinsverbot im Lichte der ethnologischen Jurisprudenz, Freiburg 1907 (BSt XII⁴).

J. Nikel, Das AT und die ᾽ chstenliebe, Münster 1913 (BZF VI 11, 12).

A. Eberharter, Die soziaᵌᵉ und politische Wirksamkeit des atl. Prophetentums, Salzburg 1924.

N. Peters, Die soziale Fürsorge im AT, Paderborn 1936.

W. Lauterbach, Der Arbeiter in Recht und Rechtpraxis des AT und des alten Orients, Diss. Heidelberg 1937.

§ 30. DUTIES TOWARD SELF

A. Rahlfs, ʿānī und ʿānāw in den Psalmen, Göttingen 1892.

P. Jedzink, Die Arbeitspflicht im AT, Braunsberg 1920.

A. Causse, Les "pauvres" d'Israel (Prophètes, Psalmistes, Messianistes), Strassburg-Paris 1922.

H. Bruppacher, Die Beurteilung der Armut im AT, Zürich 1924.

H. Birkeland, ʿānī und ʿānāw in den Psalmen, Oslo 1933.

P. A. Munch, Das Problem des Reichtums in den Psalmen 37, 49, 73, ZatW 55, 1937, 36-46.

A. Kuschke, Arm und reich im AT mit besonderer Berücksichtigung der nachexilischen Zeit, ZatW 57, 1939, 31-57.

§ 31. FAMILY DUTIES

A. Eberharter, Das Ehe und Familienrecht der Hebräer, Münster 1914 (AA V 1, 2).

J. Döller, Das Weib im AT, Münster 1920 (BZF IX 7-9).

L. Dürr, Die Wertung des Lebens im AT und im antiken Orient, Münster 1926.

P. Heinisch, Wesen und Zustandekommen der isr. Ehe, Stc 12, 1936, 118-139.

............Das Sklavenrecht in Israel und im alten Orient, Stc 11, 1935, 201-218, 276-290.

Th. W. Crul, Het huwelijk bij de ethnologische oervolken, Diss. Utrecht-Leiden 1942.

§ 32. CRITIQUE OF OT MORALITY

J. Döller, Der Bann im AT und im späteren Judentum, ZkTh 37, 1913, 1-24.

A. Fernandez, El ḥerem biblico, Bb 5, 1924, 3-25.

H. Bückers, Kollektiv-und Individualvergeltung im AT, ThGl 25, 1933, 273-286.

P. Cruveilhier, Le code de Hammourabi, RClfr 69, 1912, 275-308.

............Le code de Hammourabi et la législation civile des Hébreux, ibid. 641-673.

A. F. Puukko, Die altassyr. und hethit. Gesetze und das AT, Stud. orient. I in hon. Tallquist, Helsingfors 1925, 125-166.

E. Ring, Israels Rechtsleben im Licht der neuentdeckten assyr. und hethit. Rechtsurkunden, Stockholm-Leipzig 1926.

P. Cruveilhier, Recueil des lois assyr., Muséon 38, 1925, 189-242; 39, 1926, 325-344; 40, 1927, 1-30; 41, 1928, 1-48; 42, 1929, 1-32, 129-156.

K. Fuchs, Die atl. Arbeitergesetzgebung im Vergleich zum Codex Hammurapi, zum altassyr. und hethit. Recht, Diss. Heidelberg 1934.

Charles F. Jean, Le Milieu biblique avant Jesus-Christ, III—Les idees reli-
gieuses et morales, Paris 1936.
W. Lauterbach, Der Arbeiter im Recht und Rechtpraxis des AT und des alten
Orients, Diss. Heidelberg 1936.
H. Junker, Das theologische Problem der Fluchpsalmen, Pb 1940, 65-74.
A. Miller, Fluchpsalmen und israelitisches Recht, Ant 20, 1943, 92-101.

§ 33. SACRIFICES AND OFFERINGS

M. J. Lagrange, Études sur les religions sémitiques[2], Paris 1905, 247-274.
J. Herrmann, Die Idee der Sühne im AT, Leipzig 1905.
O. Schmitz, Die Opferanschauung des späteren Judentums, Tübingen 1910.
R. Dussaud, Les origines cananéennes du sacrifice israélite, Paris 1921.
A. Médebielle, L'expiation dans l'A et le NT, Rom 1923 (Scripta Pont. Inst.
Bibl.).
..........De sacrificii israelitici origine et natura, VD 6, 1926, 214-219, 238-244,
266-273.
N. Peters, Osee und die Geschichte, 1924.
G. B. Gray, Sacrifice in the OT, Oxford 1925.
H. Kaupel, Gibt es opferfeindliche Stellen im AT? ThGl 17, 1925, 172-178.
A. Wendel, Das Opfer in der altisr. Religion, Leipzig 1927.
A. Lods, Éléments anciens et éléments modernes dans le rituel du sacrifice
israélite, RHPhr 8, 1928, 399-441.
D. Schötz, Schuld-und Sündopfer im AT, Breslau 1930 (Bresl. Stud. z. hist.
Theol. 18).
F. X. Kortleitner, Formae cultus Mosaici cum ceteris religionibus orientis antiqui
comparatae, Oeniponte 1933.
K. H. Miskotte, Het wezen der Joodsche religie, Amsterdam 1933.
F. Blome, Die Opfermaterie in Babylonien und Israel I, Rom 1934 (S. Script.
Antiqu. Orient. illustrata 4).
P. Volz, Die radikale Ablehnung der Kultreligion durch die atl. Propheten,
ZsystTh 14, 1937, 63-85.
W. O. E. Oesterley, Sacrifices in Ancient Israel, London 1937.
A. Matzinger, Die Substitionstheorie und das atl. Opfer, Bb 21, 1940, 159-187,
247-272.
V. Schönbächler, Die Stellung der Psalmen zum atl. Opferkult, Freiburg Schw.
1941.
A. Bertholet, Der Sinn des kultischen Opfers, Berlin 1942.
C. Lattey, The Prophets and Sacrifice, JthSt 42, 1941, 155-165.
J. E. Coleran, The Prophets and Sacrifice, ThSt 5, 1944, 411-438.
E. Mader, Die Menschenopfer der alten Hebräer und der benachbarten Völker,
Freiburg 1909 (BSt XIV 5, 6).
H. Vincent, Canaan[2], Paris 1914, 188-201.
F. X. Kortleitner, Cananaeorum auctoritas num ad religionem Israelitarum
aliquid pertinuerit 1932, Oeniponte 1932.
F. Böhl, Die Menschenopfer bei den alten Sumerern, ZA 39, 1929, 83-98.
Fr. Blome, Die Opfermaterie, 362-414.
O. Eissfeldt, Molk als Opferbegriff im Punischen und Hebräischen und das
Ende des Gottes Moloch, 1935.
A. Bea, Kinderopfer für Moloch oder für Jahve? Bb 18, 1937, 95-107.
N. Schneider, "Melchom, das Scheusal der Ammoniter," Bb 18, 1937, 337-343;
19, 1938, 204.

N. Schlögl, Das Wort molek in Inschriften und Bibel, WZKM 45, 1938, 203-211.
A. Jirku, Gab es im AT einem Gott Molek (Melek)? ARW 35, 1938, 93-114 (gegen Eissfeldt).
O. Eissfeldt, Erstlinge und Zehnten im AT, Stuttgart 1917 (BWAT 22).

§ 34. FEASTS

J. Hehn, Siebenzahl und Sabbath, Leipzig 1907.
............Der israelitische Sabbath, Münster 1912 (BZF II 12).
............Zur Sabbatfrage, BZ 14, 1917, 198-213.
............Zur Bedeutung der Siebenzahl, Beih. 41 ZatW 1925, 128-136.
B. D. Eerdmans, Der Sabbath, Beih. 41 ZatW 1925, 79-83.
A. Prešeren, Die Beziehungen der Sonntagsfeier zum dritten Gebot des Dekalogs, ZkTh 37, 1913, 563-603, 709-759.
Strack-Billerbeck IV 1, 1928, 41-76.
G. Beer, Pesachim, Giessen 1912 (Die Mischna II 3).
J. Pedersen, Passahfest und Passahlegende, ZatW 52, 1934, 161-175.
B. D. Eerdmans, Alttest. Studien IV 1912, 73-82.
F. X. Kugler, Von Moses bis Paulus, 1922, 70, 125-133.
S. Landersdorfer, Studien zum biblischen Versöhnungstag, Münster 1924 (AA X 1).
............Keilinschriftl. Parallelen zum bibl. Sündenbock (Lev. 16) BZ 19, 1931, 20-28.
Joh. Friedrich, Aus dem hethit. Schrifttum, Leipzig 1925, 9-13 (AO XXV 2).
M. Löhr, Das Ritual von Lev. 16, Halle 1925 (Schriften der Königsberger gelehrten Ges., Geistesw. Kl. 2, 1).
D. Schötz, Schuld- und Sündopfer im AT, Breslau 1930, 21-27 (Bresl. Stud. z. hist. Theol. 18).
J. Schur, Versöhnungstag und Sündenbock, Helsingfors 1934 (Soc. Scient. Fennica, Comm. Hum. Litt. 6, 3).
H. Speyer, Der Festag bei den Propheten, Breslau 1934, Wiss. Beil. 9-61.

§ 35. PRAYER

J. Döller, Das Gebet im AT in religionsgeschichtl. Beleuchtung, Wien 1914.
A. Greiff, Das Gebet im AT, Münster 1915 (AA V 3).
P. Heinisch, Das "Wort" im AT und im alten Orient, Münster 1922 (BZF X 7, 8).
J. Hempel, Gebet und Frömmigkeit im AT, Göttingen 1922.
............Die isr. Anschauungen von Segen und Fluch im Lichte der altor. Parallelen, ZdmG 79, 1925, 20-110.
............Gott und Mensch im AT², Stuttgart 1936 (BWAuNT III 2).
L. Dürr, Religion und Frömmigkeit der atl. Propheten, Düsseldorf 1926.
R. Storr, Die Frömmigkeit im AT, 1928.
J. Begrich, Die Vertrauensäusserungen im isr. Klagelied des Einzelnen und in seinen babyl. Gegenstück, ZatW 46, 1928, 221-260.
A. Wendel, Das freie Laiengebet im vorexil. Israel, Leipzig 1931.
J. Herrmann, Theol. Wörterbuch zum NT II, 1935, 782-799.
P. A. H. de Boer, De Voorbede in het Oude Testament, Leiden 1943 (Oudtest. Stud. III).

§ 36. VOWS

A. Wendel, Das israelitisch-jüdische Gelübde, Berlin, 1931.

§ 37. FASTING

A. W. Groenman, Het vasten bij Israel, Leiden 1906.
A. Neuwirth, Das Verhältnis der jüd. Fasten zu denen der alten Heiden, Berlin 1910.
K. Fruhstorfer, Fastenvorschriften und Fastenlehren der Heiligen Schrift des Alten Bundes, ThprQS 69, 1916, 59-72.
M. S. Freiberger, Das Fasten im alten Israel, Zagreb 1927 (Diss. Würzburg).
Strack-Billerbeck, IV, 1928, 77-114.
P. R. Arbesmann, Das Fasten bei den Griechen und Römern, Giessen 1929 (Religionsgeschichtl. Versuche und Vorarb. XXI 1).

§ 38. SIN

J. Köberle, Sünde und Gnade im religiösen Leben des Volkes Israel bis auf Christus, München 1905.
W. Staerk, Sünde und Gnade nach der Vorstellung des älteren Judentums, Tübingen 1905.
F. Bennewitz, Die Sünde im alten Israel, 1907.
L. K. H. Bleeker, De zonde der gezindheid in het OT, Groningen 1907.
A. Eberharter, Sünde und Busse im AT, Münster 1924 (BZF XI 10-12).
R. Storr, Die Frömmigkeit im AT, 1928, 232-245.
J. B. Frey, L'état original et la chute de l'homme d'après les conceptions juives au temps de J.-C., RSphth 5, 1911, 507-545.
Quell, Theol. Wörterbuch zum NT 1, 1933, 267-288.
A. Verrièle, Les textes bibliques sur le péché original et leur interprétation theologique, Rap 63 (1936, 2), 385-402, 513-532, 656-680; 64 1937, 1), 8-25.
J. Slaby, Sünde und Sündenstrage sowie deren Nachlass im alten Babylonien und Assyrien, BZ 8, 1910, 236-247, 339-350.
A. van Selms, De babyl. Termini voor Zonde, Wageningen 1933.
K. Prümm, Der christliche Glaube und die altheidnische Welt II, 1935, 218-248 (über das Sünden und Schuldbewusstsein der Antike).

§ 39. THE SEQUEL TO SIN

J. Laroche, La rétribution sous l'ancienne alliance, Montauban 1905.
Fr. Nötscher, Die Gerechtigkeit Gottes bei den vorexil. Propheten, Münster 1915 (AA VI 1).
A. Schulz, Der sinn des Todes im AT, 1919.
G. Quell, Die Auffassung des Todes in Israel, Leipzig 1925.
H. Bückers, Kollektiv und Individualvergeltung im AT, ThGl 25, 1933, 273-286.

§ 40. THE RETURN TO GOD

J. Herrmann, Die Idee der Sühne im AT, 1905.
A. Médebielle, L'expiation dans l'A et le NT I, Rom 1923 (Script. Pont. Inst. Bibl.).
A. Eberharter, Sünde und Busse im AT, Münster 1924 (BZF XI 10-12).
F. Schollmeyer, Biblische und babylonische Sühne, ThGl 20, 1928, 608-617.
E. K. Dietrich, Die Umkehr (Bekehrung und Busse) im AT und im Judentum, Stuttgart 1936.

Herrmann, Sühne und Sühneformen im AT, Theol. Wörterbuch zum NT III, 1938, 302-311.
J. J. Stamm, Erlösen und Vergeben im AT, Bern 1940.
Sven Herner, Sühne und Vergebung in Israel, Lund 1942.

§ 41. SUFFERING

N. Peters, Die Leidensfrage im AT, Münster 1923 (BZF XI 3-5).
E. Balla, Das Problem des Leidens in der Geschichte der isr.-jüd. Religion, Göttingen, FRLAuNT N.F. 19, 1, 1923, 214-260.
H. Schmidt, Gott und das Leid im AT, Giessen 1926.
L. B. Paton, The Problem of Suffering in the Pre-exilic Prophets, JbL 46, 1927, 111-131.
F. Dijkema, Het problem van het lijden in het latere Jodendom, NthT 18, 1929, 39-53.
W. Wichmann, Die Leidenstheologie — Eine Form der Leidensdeutung im Spätjudentum, Stuttgart 1930 (BWAuNT IV 2).
W. Staerk, Vorsehung und Vergeltung, 1931.
W. Eichrodt, Vorsehungsglaube und Theodizee im AT, Festschrift O. Procksch, Leipzig 1934, 45-70.
J. Jelito, Zum babyl. und bibl. Leidensproblem, Collectanea Theol. 18, 1937, 201-217.
Oepke, Krankheit und Heilung im AT, Theol. Wörterbuch zum NT III, 1938, 200-202.
A. Charne, Job et le problème des rétributions dans l'AT, Coll. Nam. 33, 1939, 251-271.
J. Paulus, Le thème du juste souffrant dans la pensée grecque et hébraique, RHR 121, 1940, 18-68.
J. J. Stamm, Das Leiden des Unschuldigen in Babylon und Israel, Zürich 1946.

§ 42. SHEOL

Fr. Schwally, Das Leben nach dem Tode nach den Vorstellungen des alten Israel, Giessen 1892.
Joh. Frey, Tod, Seelenglaube und Seelenkult im alten Israel, Leipzig 1898.
J. Royer, Die Eschatologie des Buches Job, Freiburg 1901 (BSt VI 5).
H. Weiss, Quid de immortalitate animarum Hebraei et gentes Hebraeis finitimae antiquiore tempore senserint, 1902, 1904 (Index lect. Braunsberg).
A. Lods, La croyance à la vie future et le culte des morts dans l'antiquité israélite, Paris 1906.
............Le culte des ancêtres dans l'antiquité hebraïque, Paris 1906.
P. Dhorme, Le séjour des morte chez les Babyloniens et les Hébreux, Rb 4, 1907, 59-78.
M. Flunk, Die Eschatologie Altisraels I, Innsbruck 1908.
P. Torge, Seelenglaube und Unsterblichkeitshoffnung im AT, Leipzig 1909.
R. H. Charles, A Critical History of the Doctrine of a Future Life in Israel, in Judaism and in Christianity, London 1913.
J. Schwab, Der Begriff der nefeš in den hl. Schriften des AT, Diss. München 1913, 48-55.
A. Bertholet, Die isr. Vorstellungen vom Zustand nach dem Tode[2], Tübingen 1914.
J. Scheftelowitz, Der Seelen und Unsterblichkeitsglaube im AT, ARW 19, 1919, 210-232.

A. Vaccari, De immortalitate animae in VT, VD 1, 1921, 258-269, 304-310.
P. Heinisch, Die Trauergebräuche bei den Israeliten, Münster 1931 (BZF XIII 7, 8).
..........Die Totenklage im AT, Münster 1931 (BZF XIII 9, 10).
A. Miller, Aufbau und Grundproblem des Predigers, Miscl. Bibl. II, Rom 1934, 104-122.
A. de Bondt, Wat leert het OT aangaande het leven na dit leven? Kampen 1938.
A. Parrot, Le "refrigerium" de l'au-delà, Paris 1937.
J. Schmidt, Der Ewigkeitsbegriff im AT, Münster 1940 (AA XIII 5).
E. Dhorme, L'idée de l'au-de là dans la religion hébraique, RHR 123, 1941, 113-142.
J. H. Becker, Het begrip Nefesj in het OT, Amsterdam 1942.
J. Leipoldt, Der Tod bei Griechen und Juden, Leipzig 1942.
B. Alfrink, L'expression ne)esaph)el-(ammaw, Oudtest. Stud. 5, Leiden 1948, 118-131.
..........L'expression šakhab (im)abotam, Oudtest. Stud. 2, Leiden 1943, 106-118.
J. Schildenberger, Alttestamentliche Jenseitsvorstellungen und Irrtumslosigkeit der inspirierten Schriftsteller, Bb 25, 1944, 335-345.
E. F. Sutcliffe, The OT and the Future Life, London 1946.
M. J. Lagrange Études sur les religions sémitiques, Paris 1905, 314-341.
E. Ebeling, Tod und Leben nach den Vorstellungen der Babylonier, Berlin 1931.
H. Kees, Totenglaube und Jenseitsvorstellungen der alten Ägypter, Leipzig 1926.

§ 43. RETRIBUTION IN THE NEXT LIFE

M. J. Lagrange, Le Livre de la Sagesse, sa doctrine des fins dernières, Rb 4, 1907, 85-104.
..........Le Messianisme chez les Juifs (150 av. J.-C. à 200 ap. J.-O.), Paris 1909.
..........Le Judaïsme avant Jésus-Christ, Paris 1931.
A. Schulz, Der Sinn des Todes im AT, Braunsberg 1919.
G. Quell, Die Auffassung des Todes in Israel, Leipzig 1925.
L. Dürr, Die Wertung des Lebens im AT und im antiken Orient, Münster 1926.
J. B. Frey, La vie de l'au-delà dans les conceptions juives au temps de Jésus-Christ, Bb 13, 1932, 129-168.
P. Volz, Die Eschatologie der jüd. Gemeinde im ntl. Zeitalter, Tübingen 1934.
R. Schütz, Les idées eschatologiques du livre de la Sagesse, Paris-Strassburg 1935.
H. Bückers, Die Unsterblichkeitslehre des Weisheitsbuches, Münster 1938 (AA XIII 4).

§ 44. RESURRECTION

P. Heinisch, Das jüngste Gericht im Buche der Weisheit, ThGl 2, 1910, 89-106.
W. W. Graf Baudissin, Adonis und Esmun—Eine Untersuchung zur Geschichte des Glaubens an Auferstehungsgötter und an Heilgötter, Leipzig 1911.
W. Weber, Der Auferstehungsglaube im eschatologischen Buche der Weisheit Salomos, ZwTh 54, 1912, 205-239.
Fr. Nötscher, Altorient. und alttest. Auferstehungsglauben, Würzburg 1926.
R. H. Charles, The Resurrection of Man and other Sermons, Edinburgh 1929.
W. Baumgartner, Der Auferstehungsglaube im alten Orient, Z. f. Missionskunde und Religionsw. 48, 1933, 193-214.
     On Job 19:25-27.
J. M. Vidal, L'idée de résurrection dans Job, RClfr 57, 1909, 295-309, 677-697.

A. Hudal, Die Auslegung von Job 19:25-27 in der kath. Exegese, Kath 17, 1916, 331-345.

............Textkrit. und exeg. Bemerkungen zu Job 19:25-27, BZ 14, 1917, 214-235.

A. Beel, In Job 19:25-27, Coll. Brug. 34, 1934, 3-8.

On related problems:

E. Stave, Über den Einfluss des Parsismus auf das Judentum, Haarlem 1898.

N. Söderblom, La vie future d'après le Mazdéisme, Paris 1901 (Annales du musée Guimet IX).

E. Boeklen, Die Verwandtschaft der jüd.-christ. mit der parsischen Eschatologie, Göttingen 1902.

A. Causse, Der Ursprung der jüd. Lehre von der Auferstehung, Cahors 1908.

E. Albert, Die isr.-jüd. Auferstehungshoffnung in ihren Beziehungen zum Parsismus, Diss. Königsberg 1910.

A. Bertholet, Zur Frage des Verhältnisses von parsischem und jüdischem Auferstehungsglauben, Festschrift F. C. Andreas 1916, 51-62.

E. Sellin, Die atl. Hoffnung auf Auferstehung und ewiges Leben, NkZ 30, 1919, 232-256.

J. Scheftelowitz, Die altpers. Religion und das Judentum, Giessen 1920, 194-216.

§ 45. JUDGMENT UPON THE GENTILES

P. Dornstetter, Das endzeitliche Gottesreich nach der Prophetie, Würzburg 1896.

W. Cossmann, Die Entwicklung des Gerichtsgedankens bei den atl. Propheten, Giessen 1915 (Beih. 29 ZatW).

N. Messel, Die Einheitlichkeit der jüd. Eschatologie, Giessen 1915 (Beih. 30 ZatW).

L. Dennefeld, Les problèmes du livre de Joël, Paris 1926.

H. Gressmann, Der Messias, Göttingen 1929, 97-148 (FRLAuNT 43).

B. Rigaux, L'Antéchrist et l'opposition au royaume messianique dans l'A et le NT, Gembloux-Paris 1932 (Diss. Löwen).

P. Volz, Die Eschatologie der jüd. Gemeinde im ntl. Zeitalter[2], Tübingen 1934.

H. Schmökel, Jahwe und die Fremdvölker, Breslau 1934 (Bresl. Stud. zur Theol. und Religionsgesch. 1).

v. Rad, "Der Tag" im AT, Theol. Wörterbuch zum NT 11, 1935, 946-949.

§ 46. JUDGMENT UPON ISRAEL

J. Köberle, Sünde und Gnade im religiösen Leben des Volkes Israel, München 1905, 129-145, 212-250.

W. Cossmann, Die Entwicklung des Gerichtsgedankens bei den atl. Propheten, Giessen 1915 (Beih. 29 ZatW).

H. Gressmann, Der Messias, Göttingen 1929, 67-93 (FRLAuNT 43).

R. de Vaux, Le "Reste" d'Israël d'après les prophètes, Rb 42, 1933, 526-539.

H. Schmökel, Jahwe und die Fremdvölker, Breslau 1934, 69-80.

v. Rad, "Der Tag" im AT, Theol. Wörterbuch zum NT II, 1935, 946-949.

W. Vollborn, Innerzeitliche oder endzeitliche Gerichtserwartung? Ein Betrag zu Amos und Jesaja, Diss. Greifswald 1938.

§ 47. THE RESTORATION OF ISRAEL

P. Dornstetter, Das endzeitliche Gottesreich nach der Prophetie, Würzburg 1896.

M. Lagrange, Le règne de Dieu dans l'AT, Rb 5, 1908, 36-61.

............Le Messianisme chez les Juifs, Paris 1909.

E. L. Dietrich, šūb šebūth—Die endzeitliche Wiederherstellung bei den Propheten, Giessen 1927 (Beih. 40 ZatW).

A. Vaccari, De regno Dei in VT, VD 7, 1927, 327-331.

H. Gressmann, Der Messias, Göttingen 1929, 149-284 (FRLAuNT 43).

E. Baumann, šūb šebūth, ZatW 47, 1929, 17-44; cf. N. Schlögl. WZKM 38, 1930, 68-75.

M. Hoepers, Der neue Bund bei den Propheten, Freiburg 1933 (Freib. theol. Stud. 39).

M. Buber, Das Kommende, I. Königtum Gottes[2], Berlin 1936.

E. K. Dietrich, Die Umkehr (Bekehrung und Busse) im AT und im Judentum, Stuttgart 1936.

H. Junker, Die messianische Verkündigung des Buches Isaias, Pb 48, 1938. 189-193; 49, 1938, 5-11, 240-251, 279-285, 338-346; 50, 1940, 5-11.

§ 48. THE CONVERSION OF THE GENTILES

E. Schürer, Geschichte des jüd. Volkes, III[4], 1909, 150-188, 545-629.

P. Heinisch, Die Idee der Heidenbekehrung bei den vorexil. Propheten, Z. f. Missionswissenschaft 4, 1914, 81-106.

..........Die Idee der Heidenbekehrung im AT, Münster 1916 (BZF VIII, 1, 2).

..........Griechentum und Judentum im letzten Jahrh. v. Chr.[4], Münster 1921 (BZF I 12).

A. Causse, Israël et la vision de l'humanite, Strassburg-Paris 1924.

M. Meinertz, Jesus und die Heidenmission[2], Münster 1925 (Ntl. Abh. I 1, 2).

. Felten, Neutest. Zeitgeschichte, Regensburg 1925, I 504-531.

H. Gressmann, Der Messias, Göttingen 1929, 193-200 (FRLAuNT 43).

. Ziegler, Die Liebe Gottes bei den Propheten, Münster 1930, 100-110 (AA XI 3).

H. Schmökel, Jahwe und die Fremdvölker, Breslau 1934, 93-123.

F. X. Kortleitner, Religio VT habitu et nationali et universali eminuit, Oeniponte 1937 (Com. bibl. 12).

H. H. Rowley, Israel's Mission to the World, London 1939.

§ 49. THE GLORY OF THE MESSIANIC KINGDOM

J. J. Lagrange, Le règne de Dieu dans l'AT, Rb 5, 1908, 36-61.

..........Le règne de Dieu dans le Judaïsme, Rb 5, 1908, 350-366.

..........Le Messianisme chez les Juifs, Paris 1901, 116-121, 148-157.

. Nikel, Der Friedensgedanke im AT (Rede), Breslau 1914.

N. Peters, Weltfriede und Propheten, Paderborn 1917.

..........Sache und Bild in den messianischen Weissagungen, ThQ 112, 1931, 451-489.

I. A. van den Oudenrijn, Nebū)āh—De prophetiae charismate in populo Israelitico, Rom 1926, 223-237.

F. Schlagenhaufen, Der geistige Charakter der jüd. "Reichs"-Erwartung, ZkTh 51, 1927, 370-395, 473-531.

d. Tobac-J. Coppens, Les Prophètes d'Israël, Malines 1932, 59-88.

G. C. Alders, Het Herstel van Israel volgens het OT—De chiliastische Uitlegging getoetst, Kampen 1934.

. Volz, Die Eschatologie der jüd. Gemeinde im ntl. Zeitalter[2], 1934.

. Mariani, De sacrificio a Malachia praedicto (Mal. 1:11), Ant 9, 1934, 193-242, 361-382, 451-474.

. van Imschoot, Le règne de Dieu dans l'AT, Coll. Gand. 23, 1936, 254-258; 24, 1937, 3-9.

............L'esprit de Jahvé et l'alliance nouvelle dans l'AT, EphThLov 13, 1936, 201-220.

J. Schmidt, Der Ewigkeitsbegriff im AT, Münster 1940, 148-174 (AA XIII 5).

J. Schildenberger, Weissagung und Erfullung, Bb 24, 1943, 107-124, 205-230.

§ 50. THE PERSON OF THE MESSIAH

A. Schulte, Die messianischen Weissagungen des AT, Paderborn 1906.

M. J. Lagrange, La paternité de Dieu dans l'AT, Rb 5, 1908, 481-499.

............Le Messianisme chez les Juifs, Paris 1909.

A. Lémann, Historie complète de l'idée messianique chez le peuple d'Israel, Lyon 1909.

J. Döller, Die Messiaserwartung im AT, Münster 1911 (BZF IV 6, 7).

G. Hoberg, Katechismus der mess. Weissagungen, Freiburg 1915.

P. Heinisch, Die Weissagungen des AT von dem kommenden Erlöser[2], Paderborn 1925 (Atl. Predigten 6, 7).

Ed. König, Die messianischen Weissagungen des AT, Stuttgart 1925.

C. Cordonnier, Les voix qui montent, Paris 1926.

O. Procksch, Der Menschensohn als Gottessohn, Christentum und Wissenschaft 3, 1927, 425-443, 473-481.

L. Dennefeld, Le Messianisme, Paris 1929; Dict. de Theol. Cath. 10, 1404-1568.

H. Gressmann, Der Messias, Göttingen 1929 (FRLAuNT 43).

A. Jeremias, Die biblische Erlösererwartung, Berlin 1931.

W. Vischer, Das Christuszeugnis des AT, I Das Gesetz, München 1934.

T. V. Gerster, Jesus in ore prophetarum, Turin-Rom 1934.

F. Ceuppens, De prophetiis messianicis in AT, Rom 1935.

A. Vaccari, De Messia "Filio Dei" in VT, VD 15, 1935, 48-55, 77-86.

H. W. Wolff, Herrschaft Jahves und Messiasgestalt im AT, ZatW 54, 1936, 168-202.

H. Junker, Die messianische Verkündigung des Buches Isaias, Pb 48, 1938, 189-193; 49, 1939, 5-11, 240-251, 279-285, 338-346; 50, 1940, 5-11.

M. Colacci, Il Semen Abraham alla luce del Vecchio e del Nuovo Testamento, Bb 21, 1940, 1-27.

A. Edelkoort, De Christusverwachting in het OT, Wageningen 1941.

J. Brierre-Narbonne, Les prophéties messianiques de l'AT dans la littérature juive en accord avec le NT, Paris 1933.

............Exégèse Talmudique des prophéties messianiques, Paris 1934.

............Exégèse Midrašique des prophéties messianiques, Paris 1935.

............Exégèse targumique des proph. mess., Paris 1936.

............Exégèse apocryphe des proph. mess., Paris 1937.

On Is. 4:2:

T. Búda, Şemah Jahweh, Bb 20, 1939, 10-28.

On Is. 7:14:

A. Schulz, BZ 23, 1935, 229-241.

F. Ogara, VD 17, 1937, 3-9.

A. Vaccari, VD 17, 45-49, 75-81.

J. Coleran, VD 17, 303-312.

A. Feuillet, RchScr 30, 1940, 129-151.

F. Ceuppens, Ang 23, 1946, 53-59.

On Is. 9:1f:

F. Ogara, VD 16, 1936, 353-360; 17, 1937, 3-9.

On Jer. 31:22:
G. E. Closen, VD 16, 1936, 295-304.
On Dan. 9:24-27:
Fr. Faidl, Die Exegese der siebzig Wochen Daniels, Graz 1883.
P. Szczygiel, ThGl 15, 1923, 268-283.
M. J. Lagrange, Rb 39, 1930, 179-198.
St. Szydelski, Collectanea Theol. 19, 1938, 59-114.
G. E. Closen, VD 18, 1938, 47-56, 115-125.
A. Vaccari, VD 19, 1939, 146-147, 284-286.
On Matth. 2:23 (Is. 11:1):
U. Holzmeister, VD 17, 1937, 21-26.

§ 51. THE MESSIAH'S MISSION

K. Schlütz, Isaias 11:2 (die sieben Gaben des hl. Geistes) in den ersten vier
christl. Jahrhunderten, Münster 1932 (AA XI 4).
On Mal. 3:1:
A. Škrinjar, VD 14, 1934, 40-48.
On Mal. 3:23-24:
A. Škrinjar, VD 14, 1934, 361-367.

§ 52. THE MESSIAH: IN SUFFERING AND IN GLORY

F. Feldmann, Der Knecht Gottes in Isaias Kap. 40-55, Freiburg 1907.
..........Die Weissagungen über den Gottesknecht im Buche Isaias[3], Münster
1913 (BZF II 10).
I. Fischer, Isaias 40-55 und die Perikopen vom Gottesknecht, Münster 1916
(AA VI 4, 5).
..........Wer ist der Ebed? Münster 1922 (AA VIII 5).
S. Mowinckel, Der Knecht Jahwähs, Giessen 1921.
R. Kittel, Geschichte des Volkes Israel III, Gotha 1927, 222-257.
H. Gressmann, Der Messias, Göttingen 1929, 285-340 (FRLAuNT 43).
. Schelhaas, De Lijdende Knecht des Heeren (Het Ebed-Jahwe-Problem),
Groningen 1933.
O. Eissfeldt, Der Gottesknecht bei Deuterojesaja, Halle 1933.
P. Alexius, De Passione Servi Yahweh, VD 14, 1934, 342-352.
. S. van der Ploeg, Les chants du serviteur de Jahvé dans la seconde partie
du livre d'Isaïe (Chap. 40-55), Paris 1936.
E. Sellin, Die Lösung des deuterojesajanischen Gottesknechträtsels, ZatW 55,
1937, 177-217.
O. Procksch, Jesus und der Gottesknecht, Abh. der Herder-Gesellschaft zu Riga,
1938, 3, 146-165.
. Begrich, Studien zu Deuterojesaja, Stuttgart 1938 (BWAuNT IV 25).

§ 53. BIBLICAL AND NON-BIBLICAL MESSIANIC HOPES

. Sellin, Der alttest. Prophetismus, Leipzig 1912, 103-193.
W. Eichrodt, Die Hoffnung des ewigen Friedens im alten Israel, Gütersloh 1920
(BFchrTh XXV 3).
. Mowinckel, Psalmenstudien II, Kristiania 1922.
Ed. Norden, Die Geburt des Kindes, Leipzig 1924.
R. Kittel, Die hellenistische Mysterienreligion und das AT, Giessen 1924 (BWAT
N. F. 7).
.. Dürr, Ursprung und Ausbau der israelitisch-jüdischen Heilandserwartung,
Berlin 1925.

A. Pohl, De ortu et evolutione spei messianicae, VD 6, 1926, 284-287.
A. von Gall, βασιλεία τοῦ θεοῦ, Heidelberg 1926 (Religionswiss. Bibl. 7).
A. Jeremias, Die ausserbiblische Erlösererwartung, Leipzig 1927.
H. Gressmann, Der Messias, Göttingen 1929, 1-64, 415-445 (FRLAuNT 43).
L. Desnoyer, Historie du peuple hébreu, III, Paris 1930, 296-328.
W. Staerk, Soter—Die biblische Erlösererwartung als religionsgeschichtliches Problem, I, 1933 (BFchrTh II 31).
..........Die Erlösererwartung in den östlichen Religionen (Soter II), Stuttgart 1938.
K. Prümm, Der christliche Glaube und die altheidnische Welt, I, 1935, 255-281 (heidn. Mythen über jungfräuliche Empfängnis und Geburt).
F. Taeschner, W. Förster, H. Schaeder, F. Schmidtke, Orientalische Stimmen zum Erlösungsgedanken, Leipzig 1936.
M. Buber, Das Kommende, I. Königtum Gottes², Berlin 1936.

ABBREVIATIONS

M	—Masoretic text.		HL	—Hittite Law.
G	—Septuagint.		JbL	—Journal of Biblical Literature.
Sam	—Samaritan Pentateuch.		JthSt	—Journal of Theological Studies.
Aq	—Translation of Aquila.		Kath	—Der Katholik.
Sym	—Translation of Symmachus.		Meissner	—Br. Meissner, Babylonien und Assyrien, I. II 1920-25.
Th	—Translation of Theodotion.		ML	—Mosaic Law.
Targ	—Aramaic versions (Targums).		NkZ	—Neue kirchliche Zeitschrift.
Onq	—Onqelos.		NthT	—Nieuw theologisch Tijdschrift.
It	—Old Latin translation.		OrLz	—Orientalistische Literaturzeitung.
V	—Vulgate.		Rap	—Revue apologétique.
AA	—Alttestamentliche Abhandlungen.		Rb	—Revue biblique.
AL	—Assyrian Law.		RClfr	—Revue du Clergé français.
AmJsemL	—The American Journal of Semitic Languages and Literatures.		RHPhr	—Revue d'histoire et de philosophie religieuses.
AmJTh	—The American Journal of Theology.		RHR	—Revue d'histoire des religions.
AO	—Der Alte Orient.		Roeder	—G. Roeder, Urkunden zur Religion des alten Ägypten, 1915.
AOK	—Anton J i r k u, Altorientalischer Kommentar zum Alten Testament, 1923.		RSphth	—Revue des Sciences philosophiques et théologiques.
AOTB	—H. Gressmann, Altorientalische Texte und Bilder zum AT², I, II 1926-27.		SL	—Sumerian Law.
			Strack-Billerbeck	—Strack und Billerbeck, Kommentar zum Neuen Testament aus Talmud und Midrasch, 4 Bde., 1922-28.
ARW	—Archiv für Religionswissenschaft.			
Bb	—Biblica.		Stc	—Studia catholica.
BFchrTh	—Beiträge zur Förderung christlicher Theologie.		StZ	—Stimmen der Zeit.
Bs	—Bibliotheca sacra.		ThBl	—Theologische Blätter.
BSt	—Biblische Studien.		ThGl	—Theologie und Glaube.
BWAT	—Beiträge zur Wissenschaft vom Alten Testament.		ThprQ	—Theologisch-praktische Quartalschrift.
BWAuNT	—Beiträge zur Wissenschaft vom Alten und Neuen Testament.		ThQ	—Tübinger theologische Quartalschrift.
BZ	—Biblische Zeitschrift.		VD	—Verbum Domini.
BZF	—Biblische Zeitfragen.		WZKM	—Wiener Zeitschrift für Kunde des Morgenlandes.
CH	—Code of Hammurabi.		ZA	—Zeitschrift für Assyriologie.
Coll. Brug.	—Collationes Brugenses.		ZatW	—Zeitschrift für alttestamentliche Wissenschaft.
Coll. Gand	—Collationes Gandavenses.			
EphThLov	—Ephemerides Theologicae Lovanienses.		ZdmG	—Zeitschrift für Deutschen Morgenländischen Gesellschaft.
Erman	—Ad. Erman, Die Religion der Ägypter, 1934.		ZkTh	—Zeitschrift für katholische Theologie.
FRLAuNT	—Forschungen zur Religion und Literatur des Alten und Neuen Testaments.		ZsystTh	—Zeitschrift f ü r systematische Theologie.
GK	—Gesenius - Kautzsch, Hebräische Grammatik²⁸, 1909.		ZwTh	—Zeitschrift für wissenschaftliche Theologie.